D1134599

Reformed Historical Theology

Edited by
Herman J. Selderhuis

in Co-operation with
Emidio Campi, Irene Dingel, Benyamin F. Intan,
Elsie Anne McKee, Richard A. Muller, and Risto Saarinen

Volume 68

Robert C. Sturdy

Freedom from Fatalism

Samuel Rutherford's (1600–1661) Doctrine
of Divine Providence

Vandenhoeck & Ruprecht

With 9 figures

Bibliographic information published by the Deutsche Nationalbibliothek:
The Deutsche Nationalbibliothek lists this publication in the Deutsche Nationalbibliografie;
detailed bibliographic data available online: https://dnb.de.

© 2021 by Vandenhoeck & Ruprecht, Theaterstraße 13, 37073 Göttingen, Germany, an imprint of the
Brill-Group
(Koninklijke Brill NV, Leiden, The Netherlands; Brill USA Inc., Boston MA, USA; Brill Asia Pte Ltd,
Singapore; Brill Deutschland GmbH, Paderborn, Germany; Brill Österreich GmbH, Vienna, Austria)
Koninklijke Brill NV incorporates the imprints Brill, Brill Nijhoff, Brill Hotei, Brill Schöningh,
Brill Fink, Brill mentis, Vandenhoeck & Ruprecht, Böhlau, Verlag Antike and V&R unipress.

All rights reserved. No part of this work may be reproduced or utilized in any form or by any means,
electronic or mechanical, including photocopying, recording, or any information storage and
retrieval system, without prior written permission from the publisher.

Typesetting: le-tex publishing services, Leipzig
Cover design: SchwabScantechnik, Göttingen
Printed and bound: Hubert & Co. BuchPartner, Göttingen
Printed in the EU

Vandenhoeck & Ruprecht Verlage | www.vandenhoeck-ruprecht-verlage.com

ISSN 2198–8226
ISBN 978–3–525–56863–7

Abstract

The legacy of Samuel Rutherford (1600–1661) endures chiefly through his devotional letters. His scholastic theology on the other hand has been criticized as overly deterministic and even fatalistic, a charge common to Reformed Orthodox theologians of the era. Recent scholarship on Reformed Scholasticism has provided the opportunity to reevaluate such claims. This project applies the new scholarship on Reformed Orthodoxy to Rutherford's doctrine of divine providence. The doctrine of divine providence touches upon many of the disputed points in the older scholarship, including the relationship between divine sovereignty and creaturely freedom, necessity and contingency, predetermination, and the problem of evil. Rutherford describes God's providence as a work of God's being, knowledge, will, and power. Therefore, following an introduction to his life and work, this project dedicates a chapter each to God's being, knowledge, will, and power. Utilizing all three of his Latin works of scholastic theology (*Exercitationes Apologeticae pro Divina Gratia* 1636, *Disputatio Scholastica de Divina Providentia* 1649, *Examen Arminianismi* 1668), special attention is paid throughout to place Rutherford within the larger scholastic context of his medieval forbears as well as his early modern contemporaries. In these first five chapters, the reader will note Rutherford's emphasis on an absolutely independent Creator and an absolutely dependent creation. Counterintuitively, the absolutely free and independent Creator does not utilize his sovereignty to dominate his subordinate creatures, rather he uses his own freedom to guarantee the freedom of his creatures. This will become clear in the final two chapters of this project, which deal with the scholastic definition of providence and the relationship between providence and human freedom, respectively. This analysis of Rutherford's understanding of God's sovereignty and free will challenges the older scholarship while making useful contributions to the ongoing, lively conversation concerning the same.

Contents

Figures

Preface

"We do not slander the dead." Prof. Dr. Antonie Vos spoke these words bluntly over breakfast early during my course of studies at the Evangelische Theologische Faculteit. His words, spoken with typical exuberance, one finger pointed to the sky, left an impression upon me and upon this work. Samuel Rutherford has been described as one of the leading Reformed scholastics of his era. He has been renowned as a pious man of letters, a superb preacher of the Gospel, and also characterized as a man that helped introduce a fearful form of theological fatalism into Scottish piety. The last of these characterizations is at the greatest risk of running afoul of Dr. Vos's admonition. As the reader will learn, it is simply a misrepresentation of Rutherford and his rich and robust understanding of human freedom under God's providence.

Despite being regarded as "the leading theologian of Scotland's Second Reformation," modern scholarship has not been entirely kind to Rutherford.[1] Beginning in 1981, James B. Torrance initiated what would become a series of highly critical evaluations of Scottish theology during the period of Reformed Orthodoxy.[2] Following Torrance, and clearly taking advantage of R.T. Kendall's work *Calvin and English Calvinism,* Charles Bell carried out a similar line of critique in his *Calvin and Scottish Theology.*[3] Thomas F. Torrance contributed as well, noting that Rutherford's rigid, forensic, "necessary" theology led to a form of predestination and limited atonement that was a departure from the more evangelical Gospel of Calvin and Knox.[4] More recently David Fergusson described Rutherford as a man whose theological convictions were the kind that do "violence...to the Christian message."[5]

The past several decades have witnessed renewed attention devoted to Reformed Scholasticism that present an opportunity to reassess the older scholarship, in particular, the work of Richard Muller as well as the work of the Research Group John Duns Scotus and The Research Group Classic-Reformed Theology. Several recent

---

1 Guy Richard, *The Supremacy of God in the Theology of Samuel Rutherford*, Studies in Christian History and Thought (Milton Keynes: Paternoster, 2008), 1.

2 James B. Torrance, "Covenant or Contract?": A Study of Theological Background of Worship in Seventeenth-Century Scotland," *Scottish Journal of Theology* 34, no. 3 (1981): 225–43.

3 Charles Bell, *Calvin and Scottish Theology: the Doctrine of Assurance* (The Handsel Press: Edinburgh, 1985).

4 Thomas F. Torrance, *Scottish Theology: From John Knox to John Mcleod Campbell* (Edinburgh: T&T Clark, 1996), 107.

5 David A. S. Fergusson, "Predestination: A Scottish Perspective," *Scottish Journal of Theology* 46, no. 4 (1993), 466.

studies have benefitted from the insights of these contributions and applied them to Rutherford. John Coffey's superb intellectual biography of Rutherford, *Politics, Religion, and the British Revolutions: The mind of Samuel Rutherford* (Cambridge: Cambridge University Press, 1997) is one such work. Guy Richard's careful study of Rutherford, *The Supremacy of God in the Theology of Samuel Rutherford* (Eugene, Or: Wipf and Stock, 2008) is another.

Simon Burton and Aza Goudriaan essays can also be added to these works. Both appeared in *Reformed Orthodoxy in Scotland: Essays on Scottish Theology 1560-1775*.[6] This work aims to contribute to the existing literature by examining Rutherford's theology of divine providence. Attention given to Rutherford's scholastic method, medieval background, and context in early modern thought, will address an identified gap.

I have found Rutherford to be richly rewarding and also a source of fairly sizable frustration. His letters and other devotional works are moving and poetic. The reader of such will find easy rewards. His works of scholastic theology on the other hand, require a bit more effort. This is not merely because they are written in Latin or use scholastic terms and distinctions neglected for hundreds of years. It is also because Rutherford's organizational structure and thought are not as tidy as many of his English and European counterparts. Rutherford's organization is not always obvious, and his main point is often buried under pages of citations and quotes from his "adversaries." Nevertheless, his obsessive dedication to citing sources, both friend and foe, rewards readers by inserting them in a truly catholic, international, and ecumenical conversation. One goal of this project has been to place the reader, who may lack proficiency in Latin or understanding of scholastic method, into this rich and complex conversation, where theological giants of old speak one to another across time, with Rutherford acting as host and moderator.

It is fair to say that my previous theological education gave me little preparation to enter such a conversation. As such, I owe a particular debt of gratitude to the two research groups named above. This debt has not only been absorbed through reading their work, but through many personal conversations where difficult concepts were patiently conveyed over, and over, and over (!) again. Scholars such as the late Willem J. van Asselt, Antonie Vos, Andreas J. Beck, Dolf te Velde, Philip J. Fisk, among others, are not only filled with knowledge of the history and complexity of Reformed Scholasticism, but they are also filled with the traditional Christian

---

6 Simon J. G Burton, "Samuel Rutherford's Euthyphro Dilemma: A Reformed Perspective on the Scholastic Natural Law Tradition," in *Reformed Orthodoxy in Scotland: Essays on Scottish Theology 1560-1775*, ed. Aaron Clay Denlinger (London: Bloomsbury Academic, 2014), 123–140; Aza Goudriaan, "Samuel Rutherford on the Divine Origin of Possibility," in *Reformed Orthodoxy in Scotland: Essays on Scottish Theology 1560-1775*, ed. Aaron Clay Denlinger (London: Bloomsbury Academic, 2014), 141–156.

virtues of kindness, patience, and encouragement. It is the later of their gifts that have made the daunting task of studying such complex work a joy rather than a burden. Studying such work in the midst of a community such as ETF only added to the joy of the overall project. Though appreciative of each of the above, none deserves my personal thanks more than Prof. Dr. Andreas J. Beck, from whose attention to detail, knowledge, encouragement, and Christian commitment I have benefited and learned a great deal.

Not all debts are academic in nature. I have benefitted from several wonderful relationships with churches that I have ministered in, chief among these being Trinity Church in Myrtle Beach, S.C. and St. Alban's Anglican Chapel at The Citadel. There have been many days spent locked away with books, where I felt I was letting a congregation down. However, these two churches were never anything but fully supportive. In addition to these, St. Thomas's Church in Mount Pleasant, S.C., provided much needed support towards the end of this project.

At the beginning of this project, my children David and Genevieve thought what Daddy was doing was "cool." That time has passed! They have been a tremendous source of encouragement throughout, and it appears that they are ready to have a bit more of me present in the house. I'm sure my wife is ready for this project to be concluded as well. Her support, interest, and attention have benefited me more than anyone else. I'm especially grateful for her and owe her many thanks for helping bear the burden of this dissertation in ways too many to count.

It is my hope that the labors of many that have made this project possible will help the reader gain a better understanding of the Sovereign God who in his sovereignty, graciously guarantees the freedom of his creatures. This is Rutherford's doctrine of divine providence. It is both intellectually stimulating, spiritually challenging, and worthy of investigation.

ETF Leuven, Belgium
Rev. Robert C. Sturdy, July 2020

Introduction

In the Southwest corner of Scotland, along the sea bay known as the Solway Firth is a tiny rural settlement known as Anwoth in a parish of the same name. The parish is approximately 6.5 miles long and 2.5 miles wide, comprising some 10,500 acres.[1] There is little left of old Anwoth. However, if one takes a footpath from Gatehouse of Fleet to Creetown, it is possible to take a slight detour and come upon a fifty foot white granite obelisk, a monument erected to Samuel Rutherford, Anwoth's most famous minister. Following on further, after a bit of wood, is the "old-ivy smothered Kirk of Anwoth" where Rutherford preached twice every Sunday. Heaps of stone here and there and the largely intact church walls are all that remain of the little parish church. The ruins are described as "picturesque" and "eerie."[2]

In many ways the old Kirk at Anwoth is symbolic of the legacy of its first parish minister. Though his letters have seen over one hundred editions, his scholastic treatises are just as neglected as the old Kirk. Those who have ventured off the beaten path to explore Rutherford's neglected writings have not always been kind. Modern interpreters of Rutherford have identified him as exemplary of "High Calvinism" or "Legalistic Calvinism" that represents a radical departure from what they perceived as the more grace filled, heartfelt "Evangelical Calvinism" of John Knox (1514–1572), Robert Leighton (1611–1684), and the Marrow Men. What replaced "Evangelical Calvinism," according to this reading of Scottish Reformed Scholasticism, was a cold, rationalized, scholastic theology that was logically deduced from the cornerstone of double-predestination. Rutherford's theology of God's sovereignty and human liberty has been described as rigidly logical, determinist, and indistinguishable from philosophical necessity or pagan fatalism.

This study aims to reassess Rutherford's work through an investigation of his doctrine of divine providence, which this research project aims to outline in detail. Therefore, the main research question states: "What is Samuel Rutherford's doctrine of divine providence, and given its scholastic nature, how should it be properly understood against the background of medieval scholasticism and in the context of early modern thought?" In many ways, Rutherford's doctrine of divine providence is the perfect place to re-examine the readings outlined above. The doctrine of

---

1 Samuel Lewis, "Anwoth," in *A Topographical Dictionary of Scotland, Comprising the Several Counties, Islands, Cities, Burgh and Market Towns, Parishes, and Principle Villages, with Historical and Statistical Descriptions Embellished with a Large Map of Scotland and Engravings of the Seals and Arms of the Different Burghs and Universities* (London: Lewis and Co., 1846), 54.

2 Mountford John Byrde Baddeley, "The Lowlands," in *Scotland*, eds. M. J. B. Baddeley and C. S. Ward (London: Dulau and Co., 1901), 25.

divine providence is where the doctrines of God's sovereignty and decrees meet human liberty. For some recent interpreters of Rutherford, the intersection of these doctrines is explicitly threatening. God's providence approaches human liberty as an enemy to overthrow the freedom of the will, which is helpless to resist the arbitrary and fatal progress of God's will and power. However, in his own words, Rutherford described this mysterious encounter as a "friendly union," without threat or hindrance to the fundamental liberty of the human will. This study offers a comprehensive outline of how such a "friendly union" is possible, beginning with the foundational level of God's being, knowledge, will, and power before concluding with a detailed account of God's providence and human liberty.

1. Perspectives on Rutherford

As Coffey notes, Rutherford's posthumous reputation rests almost entirely upon his famous pastoral letters. His letters have seen over eighty editions in English and over fifteen editions in Dutch. They have also appeared in French, German, and Gaelic.[3] A contemporary of Rutherford, the English nonconformist minister Richard Baxter (1615–1691), described Rutherford's collection of pastoral letters as second only to the Bible.[4] The Church of England priest and leader within the Methodist movement, Charles Wesley (1703–1791), commended the letters for the "vein of piety, trust in God and holy zeal which runs through them."[5] The English Baptist Charles Spurgeon (1834–1892) declared the letters to be the "nearest thing to inspiration which can be found in all the writings of mere men."[6] The letters are marked with a style Alexander Whyte, moderator of the General Assembly to the Free Church of Scotland, described as "seraphic."[7]

---

3 John Coffey, *Politics, Religion and the British Revolutions: The Mind of Samuel Rutherford*, Cambridge Studies in Early Modern History (Cambridge: Cambridge University Press, 1997), 6.

4 Robert Woodrow, *Analecta: Or Materials For a History of Remarkable Provinces; Mostly Relating to Scotch Ministers and Christians*, vol. 3 (Edinburgh: Maitland Club, 1842), 89.

5 Wesley published a selection of letters from Samuel Rutherford. See: Robert McWard, IX, ed., *Joshua Redivivus: Or, Three Hundred and Fifty-Two Religious Letters, by the late Eminently Pious Mr. Samuel Rutherford, Professor of Divinity, at St. Andrews* (Glasgow: John Bryce, 1765). The letters presented by Wesley can be found in: John Wesley, "Extracts from the Letters of Mr. Samuel Rutherford," in *Christian Library: Consisting of Extracts from and Abridgements of the Choicest Pieces of Practical Divinity Which Have Been Published in the English Tongue* (Bristol: Felix Farley, 1753).

6 Spurgeon, quoted in: Alexander Whyte, "Samuel Rutherford and Some of His Correspondents," in *Lectures Delivered in St. George's Free Church Edinburgh* (Edinburgh and London: Oliphant Anderson and Ferrier, 1894), 12.

7 Whyte, "Samuel Rutherford and Some of His Correspondents," 78.

Coffey describes Rutherford's letters as a "puzzling phenomenon" made more puzzling by the fact that Rutherford's reputation during his own lifetime did not rest upon his letters or devotional works at all.[8] Rather, the high regard with which he was held at home and his distinguished reputation abroad was due almost entirely to his works of scholastic theology, two of which were published on the continental mainland rather than in Britain. These works earned him the respect of such luminaries as the Dutch Reformed theologian Gisbertus Voetius (1589–1676). Furthermore, his insights were responsible for him being invited to take the appointment of Chair of Divinity and Hebrew at the University of Harderwyck and a similar invitation was extended from the University of Utrecht. However, Rutherford declined both. Nevertheless, the invitations are a testimony to the international respect commanded by Rutherford for his works of scholastic theology.[9]

Though his reputation at home and abroad depended heavily upon his Latin treatises, the importance of his work was intentionally diminished by biographers within one generation of Rutherford's death. Thomas Murray, Rutherford's first biographer described his Latin works of scholastic theology as being "marked, we confess, with scholastic jargon, to a degree which renders it at the present day extremely forbidding, or altogether useless." He continued by wondering whether "such a composition should ever have been regarded as suited to the capacities, or favorable to the improvement, of theological students."[10] Shortly thereafter Andrew Thomson described Rutherford's Latin treatises as suffering from "minute subdivisions and verbal distinctions, as well as by the undo obtrusion of logical forms."[11] Even Andrew Bonar writing in the nineteenth century, whose work is more hagiography than biography, described Rutherford's theological writing as "uninteresting and dry."[12]

In the secondary literature it is easy to gather an aversion to, lack of patience with, and even unwillingness to understand the methodology present in Rutherford's Latin works of scholastic theology.[13] Such anti-scholasticism is no doubt the reason

---

8 John Coffey, "Letters by Samuel Rutherford (1600–1661)," in *The Devoted Life: An Invitation to the Puritan Classics*, ed. Kelly M. Kapic and Randall C. Gleason (Downers Grove: InterVarsity Press, 2004), 97.

9 Thomas Murray, *The Life of Samuel Rutherford, One of the Ministers of St. Andrew's, and Principal of the College of St. Mary's With an Appendix* (Edinburgh: William Oliphant, 1828), 257–62.

10 Murray, *The Life of Samuel Rutherford*, 169–170.

11 Andrew Thomson, *Samuel Rutherford* (London: Hodder and Stoughton, 1884), 112.

12 Andrew Bonar, "Sketch of Samuel Rutherford," in *Letters of Samuel Rutherford With a Sketch of his Life and Biographical Notices of His Correspondents* (Edinburgh and London: Oliphant Anderson and Ferrier, 1891), 12.

13 For other examples see James Walker, *The Theology and Theologians of Scotland: Chiefly of the Seventeenth and Eighteenth Centuries* (Edinburgh: T&T Clark, 1888), 9–10; John Macleod, *Scottish Theology in Relation to Church History Since The Reformation*, 3rd ed. (Edinburgh: Banner of Truth

for the significant gap identified by Richard regarding Rutherford's scholastic theology.[14] However, anti-scholasticism has been responsible for more than a gap in the literature insofar as it concerns Rutherford. In the last century studies pertaining to Scottish theology have viewed scholasticism as a "bad thing" that invaded Scottish theology from the continent.[15] In Hugh Trevor-Roper's colorful description, Scottish scholasticism was "refreshed mainly by the stale waters of Calvinist bigotry fed to it through the narrow conduits of Utrecht and Sedan and Geneva."[16] Such observations have fed into a larger narrative that seventeenth century Scottish Reformed scholasticism was nothing more than an intellectual backwater poisoned by continental Reformed theology. This is a historical claim that rests upon the thesis that an alternative form of Calvinism emerged around the Synod of Dordt (1618–1619). This alternative form was harshly predestinarian and replaced the more heartfelt "evangelical Calvinism" of John Calvin and John Knox.[17]

This predisposition against scholasticism, matched with the historical thesis of discontinuity between evangelical Calvinists and federal Calvinists has led to some unbalanced portraits of Rutherford. In his study *Calvin and Scottish Theology*, Charles Bell credits Rutherford and other Scottish scholastic theologians as ushering in a golden age of Scottish teaching and preaching. Yet at the same time he argues that such men "expounded their teaching in such a way as to produce very deleterious results."[18] Clearly relying upon the thesis developed by R. T. Kendall in his study *Calvin and English Calvinism*, Bell argues that "the writings of Samuel Rutherford represent a further step in the development of Scottish theology away from that of John Calvin."[19] Bell portrayed Rutherford as captive to the theological, political, and social thought of his day. He also noted Rutherford's tendency to trust more in syllogistic deduction than the biblical witness. Not only did Bell clearly

---

Trust, 1974); P.G. Ryken, "Scottish Reformed Scholasticism," in *Protestant Scholasticism: Essays in Reassessment*, ed. Carl R. Trueman and R. Scott Clark, Studies in Christian History and Thought (Eugene, OR: Wipf & Stock, 2005), 197.

14 Guy Richard, *The Supremacy of God in the Theology of Samuel Rutherford* (Eugene, OR: Wipf and Stock, 2008), 6.

15 Ryken, "Scottish Reformed Scholasticism," 197.

16 Hugh Trevor-Roper, "The Scottish Enlightenment," in *Studies on Voltaire and the Eighteenth Century*, ed. Theodore Besterman (Geneva: Institut et Musee Voltaire, 1967), 1643.

17 See Alasdair Heron, "Foreword," in *Evangelical Calvinism*, ed. Myk Habets and Bobby Grow (Eugene: Pickwick Publications, 2012), xiii; Jason Goroncy, "Tha mi a' toirt fainear dur gearan: J. McLeod Campbell and P.T. Forsyth on the Extent of Christ's Vicarious Ministry," in *Evangelical Calvinism: Essays Resourcing the Continuing Reformation of the Church*, eds. Myk Habets and Bobby Grow (Eugene, OR: Pickwick Publications, 2012), 253–54.

18 Charles Bell, *Calvin and Scottish Theology: The Doctrine of Assurance* (Handsel Press, 1985), 71.

19 Bell, 83–84. See also Robert Tillman Kendall, *Calvin and English Calvinism to 1649*, Studies in Christian History and Thought (Eugene, OR: Wipf and Stock, 2011).

assert a discontinuity thesis, but he also argued that Rutherford's commitment to the tools of scholastic theology predetermined certain theological outcomes that were antithetical to scripture.[20]

J. B. Torrance also advanced the thesis that a gap had emerged between the evangelical humanism of Calvin and the logically rigid, legalistic scholasticism of the seventeenth century Scottish divines. J. B. Torrance largely blamed this upon federal theology as well as the incorporation of the contractual nature of the Scottish concept of "banding" into their covenant theology.[21] Unlike Bell, he had little to say regarding scholasticism. Rather, he argued that the Scottish concept of "banding" was a legal relationship based upon mutual conditions rather than unconditional love. Such a contract was therefore inherently legalistic.[22] Torrance argued that this legalistic concept was read into the biblical language of covenant. Built upon this misreading, the Scots constructed their own version of federal theology which Torrance described as a "theology of politics which could be readily grasped by the man in the street in a land struggling for freedom."[23] Rutherford is implicated in this thesis by name.[24] Though Torrance does not see the problems inherent in scholasticism that Bell identified, he nevertheless argued that Rutherford and others were bound to the logic of federal Calvinism, which obscured their ability to rightly read the biblical witness.[25]

T. F. Torrance, J. B. Torrance's brother, accepted much of the above though he broadened the conclusions.[26] T. F. Torrance described the general character of Rutherford's thought as a "logicalized form of Calvinism in which he quarried medieval and post-medieval argumentation used to 'great effect' against Arminians and Antinomians."[27] Elsewhere in the same book, he described it as a "scholastic brand of Calvinism."[28] The chief effect of this logicalized form of Calvinism was that the doctrines of God's grace were put forward in a necessitarian way.[29] The double decree of salvation and reprobation were interpreted in "necessary, causal, and forensic terms" resulting in "rigidly logically and determinist lines of thought." This system of logic was so strong that it could even force Rutherford to conclusions

---

20 Bell, *Calvin and Scottish Theology*, 70; 84.

21 J. B. Torrance, "Covenant or Contract?: A Study of Theological Background of Worship in Seventeenth-Century Scotland," *Scottish Journal of Theology* 34, no. 03 (1981): 253–4.

22 J.B. Torrance, "Covenant or Contract?," 228.

23 J.B. Torrance, 228.

24 J.B. Torrance, 226, 229, 236.

25 J.B. Torrance, 240.

26 Thomas F. Torrance, *Scottish Theology: From John Knox to John McLeod Campbell* (Edinburgh: T&T Clark, 1996).

27 T.F. Torrance, *Scottish Theology*, 93.

28 T.F. Torrance, 96.

29 T. F. Torrance, 97.

that he would not have come to otherwise.[30] Despite the above, Torrance concluded his study on an optimistic note suggesting "Rutherford's faithfulness to the Gospel message could be stronger than his logic." In other words, Christ clothed with the Gospel rescued Rutherford from his captivity to scholastic reasoning![31]

David Fergusson neatly ties together many of the previously mentioned themes in his "Predestination: A Scottish Perspective." As with Bell and the Torrance brothers, Fergusson also accepts the thesis of radical discontinuity between Calvin and the "High Calvinists" of seventeenth century Scotland. If the Scottish theology of predestination is marked by "harshness, legalism, and a fatalistic attitude towards life" it is not because of Calvin and Knox during the Reformation, but rather the "High Calvinists" of which Rutherford is exemplary.[32] Fergusson argues that God's double decree of predestination and reprobation dominated the theological system Rutherford inherited.[33] Rutherford's views on predestination had a series of disastrous theological and pastoral consequences.[34] His theology, logically deduced from the cornerstone of double-predestination, resulted in something akin to pagan fatalism which has no room for a genuine "sense of freedom that accompanies much human activity."[35]

There have been exceptions to these trends. Rutherford has been the subject of several academic dissertations.[36] Of these, William Campbell's thesis is the most historically detailed, though it has been surpassed by Coffey's work, covered below. David Strickland's thesis offers a careful reading of Rutherford's popular works of piety written in English. Strickland addresses issues of the freedom of the will as it relates to God's sovereignty, albeit the discussion is short, and the intricate

---

30 T.F. Torrance, 105.

31 T.F. Torrance, 107.

32 David A. S. Fergusson, "Predestination: A Scottish Perspective," *Scottish Journal of Theology* 46, no. 4 (1993): 457 and 466.

33 Fergusson, "Predestination," 464.

34 Fergusson, 466.

35 Fergusson, 466, 475, and 476. More recently Fergusson has moderated some of his conclusions in light of reappraisals in Reformed Scholasticism. See: David Fergusson, "Divine Providence," in *The Oxford Handbook of Theology and Modern European Thought*, ed. Nicholas Adams, George Pattison, and Graham Ward (Oxford: Oxford University Press, 2013), 655.

36 C.N. Button, "Scottish mysticism in the seventeenth century, with special reference to Samuel Rutherford" (PhD diss., University of Edinburgh, 1927); O.K. Webb Jr., "The Political Thought of Samuel Rutherford" (PhD diss., Duke University, 1964); David Strickland, "Union With Christ in The Theology of Samuel Rutherford" (PhD diss., University of Edinburgh, 1972); J.P. Burgess, "The Problem of Scripture and Political Affairs as Reflected in the Puritan Revolution: Samuel Rutherford, Thomas Goodwin, John Goodwin and Gerrard Winstantley" (PhD diss., University of Chicago, 1986); J.L. Marshall, "Natural Law and The Covenant: The Place of Natural Law in the Covenantal Framework of Samuel Rutherford's *Lex Rex*" (PhD diss., Westminster Theological Seminary, 1995).

scholastic distinctions Rutherford relies upon are absent.[37] Nevertheless, he comes nearer to Rutherford's position than those outlined above. One of the most useful contributions of Strickland's thesis is an appendix of Rutherford's patristic, medieval, and early modern sources. While the author cautions that his list is incomplete, it is nevertheless impressively comprehensive.[38]

2. Reassessments of Rutherford in Recent Literature

The first major reassessment of Rutherford in recent literature is John Coffey's superb intellectual biography *Politics, Religion and the British Revolutions: The Mind of Samuel Rutherford*.[39] Coffey's portrait of Rutherford avoids the hagiographical tendencies of some of the earlier biographers while also steering clear of the problems posed by more recent contributions. He is sympathetic to his subject, taking great pains to introduce the reader to Rutherford the scholar, pastor, theologian, political theorist, ecclesiastical statesman, and national prophet.[40] Coffey's treatment merits adding Rutherford the humanist and mystic to this list.[41]

Coffey's aim and achievement are much broader than this study, which more narrowly focuses on Rutherford's theology. Coffey's contribution in this narrower regard is important. Departing from Bell, the Torrance brothers, and Fergusson, Coffey argues that claims of discontinuity between the Reformers and the seventeenth century Reformed are exaggerated.[42] Applying Richard Muller's scholarship on Reformed Orthodoxy, Coffey gains the critical insight that "scholasticism was a rigorous methodology that did not yield any particular set of doctrines, and it was employed by Calvin and Arminius as well as by the Reformed Orthodox."[43] Coffey argues that the case of Rutherford tends to confirm Muller's argument.[44]

---

37 Strickland, "Union with Christ in the Theology of Samuel Rutherford," 81–7, and also Ch. 4.

38 Strickland, 210–255.

39 Coffey, *Politics, Religion and the British Revolutions*.

40 These are the chapter headings of Coffey's study. See Coffey, *Politics, Religion and the British Revolutions*, ix.

41 Coffey, 62–70; 82–97.

42 Coffey, 116.

43 Coffey, 118. Concerning Muller's scholarship regarding the "Calvin vs. the Calvinists" thesis, see especially: Richard A. Muller, *God, Creation, and Providence in the Thought of Jacob Arminius: Sources and Directions of Scholastic Protestantism in the Era of Early Orthodoxy* (Grand Rapids, MI.: Baker Book House, 1991); R. Muller, *Post-Reformation Reformed Dogmatics Vol I: Prolegomena to Theology*, 2nd ed. (Grand Rapids: Baker Academic, 2003); Richard A. Muller, *After Calvin: Studies in the Development of a Theological Tradition*, Oxford Studies in Historical Theology (Oxford: Oxford University Press, 2003).

44 Coffey, *Politics, Religion and The British Revolutions*, 118.

Following Muller, Coffey's neutral view of scholasticism permits him to engage Rutherford without the presuppositions of earlier scholars. Coffey does not assume that Rutherford's scholasticism represents a betrayal of the Reformation legacy of Calvin. Neither does he assume that it necessarily leads to theological fatalism. He rightly notes that that when the controversy raged between the "Antinomian" Marrow men and their more legalistic opponents in the eighteenth century, both appealed to Rutherford to support their cause. This is because a high view of grace as well as a high view of personal responsibility and freedom may be found in Rutherford's writings. Coffey argues that "the problem here is that historians fail to acknowledge that the orthodox believed in both predetermination and human agency."[45] The complex relationship between the two is outlined with painstaking detail in Rutherford's Latin works of scholastic theology. These works, entirely ignored by Bell, the Torrances, and Fergusson, are provisionally treated in Coffey's work. Coffey's summary treatment of this issue is admirable, especially considering it is but a small feature of a larger whole.[46]

Three academic dissertations followed Coffey's work.[47] All three benefit from the new scholarship on Reformed scholasticism. San-Deog Kim's thesis uses Rutherford's catechism, *The Soume of Christian Religion,* as an organizational tool to analyze Rutherford's scholastic theology. This decision is understandable in one sense, as *The Soume* offers a systematic presentation of Rutherford's theology. It is problematic in another sense, in that while *The Soume* inevitably employs certain scholastic distinctions, it is by no means a work of scholastic theology.[48] A strength of Kim's thesis is an admirable engagement with Rutherford's contemporary sources, including Arminian and Jesuit theologians as well as an attempt to trace medieval influences. The thesis is at its best when Kim offers a close reading of Rutherford's English works.[49] Unfortunately, his engagement with Rutherford's Latin works of scholastic theology is minimal, and his exegesis of distinctions in these works can be unreliable.[50] Sang Hyuck Ahn's work is a detailed and comprehensive reading of

---

45 Coffey, 39.

46 Coffey, 117–38.

47 San-Deog Kim, "Time and Eternity: A Study in Samuel Rutherford's Theology, with Reference to His Use of Scholastic Method," (PhD diss., University of Aberdeen, 2002); Richard, *The Supremacy of God in the Theology of Samuel Rutherford* (Eugene, OR: Wipf and Stock, 2008); Sang Hyuck Ahn, "Covenant in Conflict: The Controversy Over the Church Covenant Between Samuel Rutherford and Thomas Hooker," (PhD diss., Calvin Theological Seminary, 2011).

48 For Kim's justification of using *The Soume,* see Kim, "Time and Eternity," 20.

49 See especially Kim, ch. 5.

50 See for example his discussion on the *potentia absoluta et ordinata* distinction, which he equates to distinctions concerning the divine will. Though the distinctions concerning God's will and power relate, it is not clear that Kim understands them to be separate. Another critical distinction between natural and free causes also seems to have been misunderstood, thus confusing some of Kim's good

Rutherford's ecclesiology in relation to his covenant theology, and critically engages some of the previous scholarship on Rutherford.[51] The third, Guy M. Richard's study, stands out as the only to be published as well as the first book length treatment of one of Rutherford's Latin works of scholastic theology.

As Coffey had done earlier, Richard also benefits from the new scholarship on Reformed scholasticism, which he applies to the *Examen Arminianismi*, a work of scholastic theology published shortly after Rutherford's death. Seeing the neutral, primarily methodological character of scholasticism leads Richard to a nuanced and balanced portrait of Rutherford. This is particularly evident in a shorter study of Rutherford's supralapsarianism, where Richard effectively argues for a softening of the interpretation of Rutherford's position. Richard rightly notes that the previous scholarship greatly overestimated the importance placed upon the decrees by Rutherford, arguing that "Rutherford has no dogmatic preoccupation with supralapsarianism or with the decrees in general." Richard even goes so far as to argue that Rutherford's supralapsarianism is often framed in infralapsarian terms.[52] The overall effect is to moderate Rutherford's supralapsarianism, which had been described as stern and harsh in much of the secondary literature.[53]

Though Richard's study is focused on a Latin work of scholastic theology, the wider world of scholastic theology, both in its continental expressions contemporary to Rutherford as well as in relation to medieval forerunners, remains largely unexamined. As Simon J. G. Burton has noted, "Richard's interpretation of Rutherford's scholasticism, while acknowledging an important Scotist dimension, still remains for the most part at the level of general scholastic paradigms."[54] In some places, Richard exhibits a lack of patience with scholasticism that was typical of the earlier scholarship on Rutherford. He describes Rutherford's other works of scholastic theology as burdened with a "prolix style" and a "nit-picking nature" of argumentation which was influenced by "Aristotelian categories of logic."[55] He continues, "the value of such writings in teaching theology is rightly to be questioned."[56] This lack of patience with scholasticism sometimes leads Richard to superimpose the thought of modern theologians and commentators onto Rutherford's theology

---

remarks concerning Rutherford's understanding of the freedom of the will. See Kim, "Time and Eternity," 98–100, 239–40.

51 See for example his engagement with Bell, Ahn "Covenant in Conflict," 100.

52 Guy M. Richard, "Samuel Rutherford's Supralapsarianism Revealed: A Key to the Lapsarian Position of the Westminster Confession of Faith?" *Scottish Journal of Theology* 59 (2006), 27.

53 Richard, "Samuel Rutherford's Supralapsarianism Revealed," 35.

54 Simon J.G. Burton, "Samuel Rutherford's Euthyphro Dilemma: A Reformed Perspective on the Scholastic Natural Law Tradition," in *Reformed Orthodoxy in Scotland: Essays on Scottish Theology 1560–1775*, ed. Aaron Clay Denlinger (London: Bloomsbury Academic, 2014), 123–24.

55 Richard, *The Supremacy of God*, 5.

56 Richard, 5.

rather than exploring what Rutherford might be saying in his own context.[57] On other occasions, this aversion to scholasticism leads Richard to pass over significant debates in seventeenth century scholasticism, which he characterizes as minor disagreements. According to Richard, Rutherford only engages in these because of his overwhelming intolerance.[58] Unfortunately, this means that Richard occasionally misrepresents or overlooks significant features of Rutherford's theology.

In addition to the above, Richard also maintains a feature of the earlier scholarship that saw manifestations of theological fatalism in Rutherford's system. Richard attempts a detailed discussion on the relationship between God's permission and sin, as well as grace and free will. However, the latter is weakened by an overreliance on Calvin to interpret Rutherford's position as well as a reluctance to comprehensively evaluate scholastic distinctions.[59] Though Richard describes Rutherford as a "compatibilist," he is left wondering whether "there is anything that separates his [Rutherford's] understanding from fatalism." Richard is non-committal on this question.[60]

Recent essays, most notably by Aza Goudriaan and Simon Burton, have done a better job bringing Rutherford's scholasticism and historical context more clearly into focus.[61] Both place Rutherford within the scholastic context of his own day, while tracing influences from medieval predecessors. Burton's essay, "Samuel Rutherford's Euthyphro Dilemma," adds nuance to Rutherford's "voluntarism" while Goudriaan's essay, "Samuel Rutherford on the Divine Origin of Possibility," emphasizes God's radical independence, a key theme that will be developed in this study. Both Burton and Goudriaan note the special influence that the fourteenth century Archbishop of Canterbury, Thomas Bradwardine (1300–1349), had upon

---

57 A particularly egregious example is as follows: "If we are to use the Barth-Brunner debate as a grid through which to read Rutherford's own understanding of natural theology, we will find that Rutherford sides with Brunner in viewing natural theology much more positively than Barth." For other examples, see Richard, *The Supremacy of God*, 79, 94, and 139.

58 Richard, *The Supremacy of God in the Theology of Samuel Rutherford*, 82.

59 Richard, 105–12; 168–77.

60 Richard, 109.

61 Simon Burton, "Samuel Rutherford's Euthyphro Dilemma: A Reformed Perspective on the Scholastic Natural Law Tradition," in *Reformed Orthodoxy in Scotland: Essays on Scottish Theology 1560-1775*, ed. Aaron Clay Denlinger (London: Bloomsbury Academic, 2014); Burton, Simon, "Disputing Providence in Seventeenth-Century Scottish Universities: The Conflict between Samuel Rutherford and the Aberdeen Doctors and its Repercussions," in *History of the Universities*, vol XXIX/2, ed. Alexander Broadie (Oxford: Oxford University Press, 2017); Burton, Simon, "The Scholastic and Conciliar Roots of Samuel Rutherford's Political Philosophy: The Influence of Jean Gerson, Jacques Almain, and John Mair" in *Scottish Philosophy in the Seventeenth Century*, ed. Alexander Broadie, A History of Scottish Philosophy (Oxford: Oxford University Press, 2020); Aza Goudriaan, "Samuel Rutherford on the Divine Origin of Possibility," in *Reformed Orthodoxy in Scotland: Essays on Scottish Theology 1560-1775*, ed. Aaron Clay Denlinger (London: Bloomsbury, 2014).

Rutherford. Burton sees a Scotist influence in Bradwardine, later adopted by Rutherford, that introduced a new systematic and structural context into Christian theology.[62]

3. New Research on Reformed Scholasticism and Freedom of the Will

Burton's observation represents a development in Rutherford scholarship. The new systematic and structural context identified by Burton is the concept of synchronic contingency. The concept of synchronic contingency recently gained importance in the study of Reformed scholasticism. As was seen in the earlier scholarship on Rutherford, there has been a tendency to read the Reformed scholastics in a determinist and necessitarian way. Recent scholarship, most notably that of Willem J. van Asselt, J. Martin Bac, Dolf T. te Velde, and Andreas J. Beck have strongly challenged this characterization of the Reformed Orthodox.[63] Partly indebted to a conceptual framework advanced by Antonie Vos, this team of scholars has argued that Reformed scholasticism was neither a form of determinism nor even compatibilism. Rather, the Reformed Orthodox put forward a theory of "dependent freedom," which offers a robust account of God's sovereignty and a sophisticated rendering of human liberty. This team of scholars argue that this synthesis rests upon an approach by the Reformed Orthodox that borrowed heavily from medieval theories of synchronic contingency, which is said to provide a structural alternative to reality.[64] These scholars argue that this structural alternative to reality offers a real

---

62 Burton, "Samuel Rutherford's Euthyphro Dilemma," 134–5.

63 Willem J. van Asselt, J. Martin Bac, and Dolf T. te Velde, eds, *Reformed Thought on Freedom: The Concept of Free Choice in Early Modern Reformed Theology,* Texts and Studies in Reformation and Post-Reformation Thought (Grand Rapids, MI: Baker, 2010); J. Martin Bac, *Perfect Will Theology: Divine Agency in Reformed Scholasticism as against Suárez, Episcopius, Descartes, and Spinoza,* Brill Series in Church History 42 (Leiden: Brill, 2010); Andreas J. Beck, "Gisbertus Voetius (1589–1676): Basic Features of His Doctrine of God," in *Reformation and Scholasticism: An Ecumenical Enterprise,* eds. Willem J. van Asselt and Eef Dekker, Texts & Studies in Reformation & Post-Reformation Thought (Grand Rapids, MI: Baker Academic, 2001); Beck, *Gisbertus Voetius (1589–1676) Sein Theologieverständnis und seine Gotteslehre.* Forschungen zur Kirchen- und Dogmengeschichte 92. (Göttingen: Vandenhoeck & Ruprecht, 2007); Beck, "The Will as Master of Its Own Act: A Disputation Rediscovered of Gisbertus Voetius (1589–1676) on Freedom of the Will," in *Reformed Thought on Freedom: The Concept of Free Choice in Early Modern Reformed Theology,* eds. Willem J. van Asselt, J. Martin Bac and Dolf T. te Velde, Texts and Studies in Reformation and Post-Reformation Thought. (Grand Rapids, MI: Baker Academic 2010), 145–170.

64 Antonie Vos et al, *John Duns Scotus: Contingency and Freedom,* The New Synthese Historical Library 42 (Dordrecht: Kluwer Academic Publisher, 1994); Antonie Vos, "Knowledge, Certainty and Contingency," in *John Duns Scotus (1265/6–1308): Renewal of Philosophy,* ed. Egbert P. Boss, Elementa 72 (Amsterdam: Rodopi, 1998); Antonie Vos, "Ab Uno Disce Omnes," *Bijdragen* 60 (1999). Vos's

account of freedom of choice. Contrasted with a diachronic understanding of contingency, a synchronic understanding of contingency holds that in any given state of affairs a true alternative remains a possibility. When applied to God's sovereignty and human freedom, synchronic contingency means that while God's decree of a human action makes what is decreed an actual reality, it leaves other actions as possibilities.[65]

This new scholarship on Reformed scholasticism and freedom of will has initiated a lively debate.[66] Paul Helm has energetically critiqued the authors of *Reformed Thought on Freedom*. In these critiques, Helm reasserts the compatibilist nature of the Reformed tradition while also arguing against the historical claim that the Reformed Orthodox accepted synchronic contingency from the Medieval scholastics.[67] Helm claims that in ruling out determinism as well as compatibilism, the authors of *Reformed Thought on Freedom* are essentially left with a libertarian account of the freedom of the will, even though the authors of the book reject this characterization of their work.[68] Adding intrigue to the overall debate, Oliver Crisp has recently argued for a libertarian reading of the Reformed tradition.[69]

Richard Muller contributed to this discussion with his *Divine Will and Human Choice*.[70] Muller challenged Vos's historical thesis that synchronic contingency was an epistemological breakthrough achieved by Scotus.[71] Nevertheless, Muller appears to be in broad agreement with the authors of *Reformed Thought on Freedom* with certain caveats. "The views of contingency and freedom," writes Muller, "including the assumption of alternativity in the definition of freedom, were in the main line of early Reformed theological and philosophical development."[72]

---

scholarship is largely in line with Knuuttila. See: Simo Knuuttila, "Time and Modality in Scholasticism," in *Reforging the Great Chain of Being: Studies in the History of Modal Theories*, ed. Simo Knuuttila (Dordrecht: D. Reidel Publishing Company, 1981).

65 van Asselt, Bac, and te Velde, *Reformed Thought on Freedom*, 41.

66 For an excellent overview of the current state of the debate, see Richard A. Muller, *Divine Will and Human Choice: Freedom, Contingency, and Necessity in Early Modern Reformed Thought* (Grand Rapids, MI: Baker Academic, 2017), 19–45.

67 Paul Helm, "Synchronic Contingency in Reformed Scholasticism: A Note of Caution," *Nederlands Theologisch Tijdschrift* 57, no. 3 (2003): 207–22; "Reformed Thought on Freedom: Some Further Thoughts," *Journal of Reformed Theology* 4 (2010): 185–207; "Structural Indifference," *Journal of Reformed Theology* 5 (2011): 184–205; "Jonathan Edwards and the Parting of Ways?" *Jonathan Edwards Studies* 4, no. 1 (2014): 42–60.

68 Paul Helm, "Review of Perfect Will Theology," *Themelios* 36, no. 2 (2011): 322.

69 Oliver Crisp, *Deviant Calvinism: Broadening Reformed Theology* (Minneapolis, MN: Fortress Press, 2014).

70 Richard A. Muller, Divine Will and Human Choice: Freedom, Contingency, and Necessity in Early Modern Reformed Thought (Grand Rapids, MI: Baker Academic, 2017).

71 Muller, 83–177.

72 Muller, 311.

Muller sees Rutherford's theology as consistent with this view of contingency and freedom, though he disagrees with Burton on the issue of Scotist influences upon Rutherford.[73]

4. Significance of this Study

Though Burton and Goudriaan's essays make Rutherford's scholasticism a matter of primary interest, there has yet to be a book length treatment with the same focus. This research project aims to fill a gap in the existing literature. This project will also directly address the overwhelming characterization of Rutherford as a theological fatalist, a characterization that has held even in Richard's more recent monograph. A focus on Rutherford's doctrine of God's providence directly implicates the doctrines of God's sovereignty and power and how these interact with human liberty, thus providing a useful theological locus to explore such characterizations. This endeavor will be aided by the lively debate concerning Reformed Orthodoxy and human liberty outlined immediately above. Aside from Burton's essay, which introduced Rutherford as a subject in this recent debate on freedom of the will, Rutherford makes appearances in Muller's work as well as in Beck's contribution to *Reformed Thought on Freedom*.[74] This study, which takes a broad look at Rutherford's doctrine of divine providence by beginning at the foundational level of God's being, will make important contributions to this current dialogue.

5. Methodological Considerations

This study aims to answer the question: "What is Samuel Rutherford's doctrine of divine providence and given its scholastic nature, how should it be properly understood against the background of medieval scholasticism and in the context of early modern thought?" The question reveals several methodological considerations, partially guided by the "Cambridge school" of intellectual history and exhibited in the study of Reformed Orthodoxy by Richard Muller as well as the so-called

---

73 Muller, 271–72; 286.

74 Muller, 271–72; Andreas Beck, "The Will as Master of Its Own Act: A Disputation Rediscovered of Gisbertus Voetius (1589–1676) on Freedom of the Will," in *Reformed Thought on Freedom: The Concept of Free Choice in Early Modern Reformed Theology*, eds. Willem J. van Asselt, J. Martin Bac, and Dolf T. te Velde, Texts and Studies in Reformation and Post-Reformation Thought (Grand Rapids, MI: Baker Academic, 2010), 149–51.

"new" school on Reformed orthodoxy.[75] In the application of the above, this study is particularly indebted to the example of Andreas J. Beck in his study on Gisbertus Voetius.[76]

It is assumed that Samuel Rutherford's doctrine of divine providence cannot be properly understood outside of Rutherford's own historical context, as well as within the theological and intellectual tradition of which he was a recipient. Therefore, this study begins with a brief overview of Rutherford's person and work. This overview is meant to assist the reader who has not encountered Coffey's work, while concurrently devoting special attention to Rutherford's education, in particular his training in scholastic method. The sections devoted to Rutherford's training in scholasticism offer new insights into his education and prepares the reader to encounter the scholastic method of argumentation in later chapters.

Rutherford received training in scholastic method while attending the University of Edinburgh. The scholastic method employed a specific method of discourse and a specialized vocabulary that was characteristic of the European academic tradition, transmitting a form of disputation and argumentation that stretched from the thirteenth to the eighteenth century.[77] In the examination of Rutherford's writings, great effort has been made to place certain terms within their broader scholastic context, as well as to understand how Rutherford may have used these terms in ways that depart from assumed meanings. Whenever possible, Rutherford's own definition of the term has been used. His copious citation of sources is useful for connecting Rutherford to medieval sources, as well as placing him in the context of the sixteenth and seventeenth century international academic dialogue. In this study, Rutherford's citations are often referenced and interpreted. In instances where Rutherford's words are not sufficient for understanding the concept, positive citations of other theologians employed by Rutherford are used to better understand the idea. Finally, theological dictionaries and handbooks, contemporary to Rutherford, have been utilized.

An understanding the *quaestio* method is important for this study. This method presents (1) a question, (2) a list of arguments against one's own position, (3) a list of arguments from the tradition in favor of one's own position, before offering a

---

75 Quentin Skinner, "Meaning and Understanding in the History of Ideas," in *Visions of Politics* (Cambridge: Cambridge University Press, 2002); Muller, *After Calvin: Studies in the Development of a Theological Tradition*; Willem J. van Asselt and Eef Dekker, "Introduction," in *Reformation and Scholasticism: An Ecumenical Enterprise*, ed. Willem J. van Asselt and Eef Dekker, Text and Studies in Reformation and Post-Reformation Thought (Grand Rapids, MI: Baker Academic, 2001), 1–30.

76 Beck, *Gisbertus Voetius*, 19–25.

77 Beck, *Gisbertus Voetius*, 19.

(4) rebuttal of the aforementioned objections and a conclusion.[78] This method of analysis is essential because Rutherford, in accordance with the *quaestio* method, often begins to answer a question not with his own opinion, but with the opinion of his adversaries. This study seeks to follow Rutherford by introducing the persons and viewpoints of polemical opponents before presenting Rutherford's own opinions and resolutions to the question. This approach further situates Rutherford in his broader scholastic context, as well as demonstrates that far from being extremely intolerant, Rutherford was well acquainted with opposing viewpoints and could employ a Jesuit or Arminian to further establish his point.[79] Rutherford's extensive use of sources, both for and against his position, also demonstrates his commitment to an ecumenical, catholic conversation of the most debated topics of his own day.[80]

In examining Rutherford's style of argumentation, it should not be assumed that use of a particular authority in one instance implies that Rutherford follows that authority in another instance. For example, simply because Rutherford may cite Aristotle positively in one instance, it is not assumed that Rutherford is therefore "Aristotelean." Furthermore, it has not been taken for granted that a citation of Thomas implies that Rutherford is part of an "intellectualist" tradition. Nor has it been taken for granted that a citation of Scotus implies he is part of a "voluntarist" or "nominalist" tradition. The terms are useful for describing broad contours of certain medieval and early modern currents of thought, nevertheless they are problematic when applied to specific actors who may incorporate tendencies that could be ascribed to both "intellectualism" as well as "voluntarism."[81] Rather than placing Rutherford in one school or another, an attempt has been made in this study to recognize the complexity of his thought, and as much as possible to place him on a spectrum within these two schools.

Finally, though Rutherford dedicated an entire Latin work of scholastic theology to the doctrine of divine providence (*Disputatio Scholastica de Divina Providentia*), this study will not be limited to that work. Rutherford's understanding of divine

---

78 Pieter L. Rouwendal, "The Method of the Schools: Medieval Scholasticism," in *Introduction to Reformed Scholasticism*, eds. Willem J. van Asselt, T. Theo J. Pleizier, Pieter L. Rouwendal, trans. by Albert Gootjes, Reformed Historical-Theological Studies (Grand Rapids, MI: Reformation Heritage Books, 2011), 62.

79 The characterization of Rutherford as extremely intolerant comes from: Richard, *The Supremacy of God*, 82.

80 van Asselt and Rouwendal have identified this as a feature of scholasticism. See Willem J. van Asselt and Pieter L. Rouwendal, "Introduction: What Is Reformed Scholasticism?," in *Introduction to Reformed Scholasticism*, eds. Joel R. Beeke and Jay T. Collier, Reformed Historical-Theological Studies (Grand Rapids, MI: Reformation Heritage Books, 2011), 1–3.

81 Tobias Hoffmann, "Intellectualism and Voluntarism," in *The Cambridge History of Medieval Philosophy*, eds. Robert Pasnau and Christina Van Dyke (Cambridge: Cambridge University Press, 2017), 414–27.

providence relies upon his understanding of the doctrine of God, which includes investigations into God's being, knowledge, will, and power. Though these topics are discussed in his work on divine providence, some are only discussed tangentially. In some instances, Rutherford explicitly expects his reader to be familiar with his treatment of topics in his other works. This study will rely extensively upon all three of Rutherford's Latin works of scholastic theology (*Exercitationes Apologeticae pro Divina Gratia* 1636, *Disputatio Scholastica de Divina Providentia* 1649, *Examen Arminianismi* 1668) and to a lesser extent his English works. Where possible, Rutherford's distinctive poetic flourish from his letters has been applied in order to better convey an idea, as well as to keep the reader of Rutherford's scholastic theology better connected to Rutherford's more mystical, humanist, and heartfelt expressions of Christianity.

6. Organization

This study consists of a total of seven chapters and a conclusion. The first chapter provides an overview of Rutherford's life, published works, and controversies. This chapter also introduces certain features of Rutherford's formation, such as the scholastic method, which will aid the reader in better understanding his style of argumentation.

Chapter 2 begins an examination of Rutherford's doctrine of God with a focus on God's being. This is followed by a further analysis of the doctrine of God in later chapters, with a focus on God's knowledge (Chapter 3), God's will (Chapter 4), and God's power (Chapter 5). Chapter 2 outlines the human knowledge of God (section 2.1); the divine essence, unity, and omnipresence (section 2.2); and the Holy Trinity (section 2.3). Rutherford lived in a time when the doctrine of God faced serious controversy. The new distinction of the *scientia media* raised significant problems in relation to composition and the divine intellect, which certain Remonstrants aggressively advanced to offer a full critique of the doctrine of divine simplicity. This study shows that Rutherford's response to these developments was to insist on a radically independent deity, which is reinforced particularly in his discussions on an essentialist reading of the divine name and his treatment of omnipresence. Rutherford's radically independent God is a precursor to his understanding of a radically dependent creation.

Chapter 3 is a focused analysis of Rutherford's doctrine of God's knowledge, which paves the way for further discussions regarding God's knowledge in relation to God's will (Chapter 4) and God's power (Chapter 5). Chapter 3 begins with an introduction to structure and terms (section 3.1); before moving on to an examination of the classic distinction of God's necessary and free knowledge (section 3.2). From there, God's knowledge of truth concerning future contingent events is presented (section 3.3). At this juncture the implications for God's providence will take a clearer shape as the highly sophisticated and nuanced discussions of the sixteenth and seventeenth century pertaining to God's certain knowledge of future events is outlined. Finally, the constitutive nature of God's knowledge is outlined (section 3.4). The ongoing theme of God's radical independence is seen in this chapter, as Rutherford disputes that God's knowledge is not dependent upon any created being.

Chapter 4 offers an analysis of Rutherford's doctrine of God's will. Since it has been argued by some that the divine decrees implied composition in God's being, this chapter begins with Rutherford's assertion of the divine simplicity by looking at God's being and God's will (section 4.1). This is followed by an analysis of classic scholastic distinctions within the divine will such as the *voluntas signi et beneplaciti* as well as the *voluntas antecedens et consequens* (section 4.2). The third section of this chapter surveys Rutherford's understanding of God's will and the moral law (section 4.3). The final section examines God's will and the free expression of punitive justice (section 4.4). As with Chapters 2 and 3, the reader will notice a theme of Rutherford's opponents presenting the independence of created beings. However, Rutherford counters this with a critique of creaturely independence and a reassertion of God's radical independence.

Chapter 5 surveys Rutherford's doctrine of God's power. As with previous chapters, this chapter begins with a survey of certain terms, in this case with an examination of Omnipotency (section 5.1.1) and Sovereignty (section 5.1.2). Students of medieval and early modern scholasticism will recognize a close parallel to the medieval power distinction of God's absolute and ordained power in these two terms. This power distinction played an important role in undermining deterministic outcomes by providing a coherent explanation for the contingency of the world. The chapter continues by examining the relation between God's power and several modalities of being such as the necessary, the impossible, the possible, and the actual (section 5.2). The chapter concludes with an examination of several "modes" of dominion by which God exercises sovereignty over possible and actual worlds. Not only is God's absolute independence again emphasized, but here one will see clearly that God's independence and dominion are not used to impose his will upon an unwilling creation, thus depriving the created being of its freedom. Rather, God's independence and dominion ensure the freedom of created being.

Having laid the foundations for an investigation of God's providence through an in-depth examination of Rutherford's doctrine of God, Chapter 6 begins with a focus on creation. The chapter begins with the doctrine of creation because providence is presented by Rutherford as the ongoing care of creation (section 6.1). From here, Rutherford's full scholastic definition of God's providence is given (section 6.2). Following this, certain problems associated with God's providence, such as the problem of evil and sin (section 6.3); the divine permission (section 6.4); and the specter of theological fatalism (section 6.5) are examined. Again, certain tendencies of Rutherford's polemical opponents seek a means by which created entities can achieve some manner of independence. These are identified as well as Rutherford's strategies to refute them.

Chapter 7 is dedicated to Rutherford's doctrine of providence, *concursus*, and human freedom. The chapter begins, as Rutherford did, with a survey and critique of Jesuit and Arminian *concursus* (section 7.1). Following from there, Rutherford's own doctrine of the general *concursus* as well as physical predetermination is presented (section 7.2). Next, Rutherford's understanding of the role of the human will and the contribution of its own determination is analyzed (section 7.3). Having presented Rutherford's understanding of the human will and its determination, the reader will be prepared to understand Rutherford's concept of God's will and the human will acting jointly and freely in a friendly union (section 7.4). This chapter covers the most controversial element of Rutherford's doctrine of divine providence—the relationship between God's sovereign determination and the determination of the created will.

The cumulative effect of the study is to present a stark contrast between two approaches to the doctrine of divine providence, each of which begin at the foundational level of God's being. Both approaches seek to secure human freedom in light of God's sovereignty, but they go about it in radically different ways. One approach, favored by Arminian and Jesuit theologians, is to posit a measure of creaturely independence that God's providence is somehow subject to. However, as will be shown, this had the unintended effect of making God's providence eternally subjected to independent entities, thus opening the door to theological fatalism. Rutherford's approach seeks to safeguard the absolute independence of God, ensuring God is entirely free from fatal necessity. God's freedom from fatal necessity allows him to safeguard the dependent, yet nevertheless genuine freedom of his creatures. Rutherford described the relationship between God's independent freedom and the creature's dependent freedom as a "friendly union." Rutherford's approach defies easy categorization and does not fit neatly within the traditional categories of determinism, compatibilism, or libertarianism.

1. Samuel Rutherford: An Introduction to His Life, Education, Major Controversies, and Writings

What tongue or Pen or Skill of Men
Can Famous Rutherford Commend?
His Learning justly raised his Fame,
True Godliness Adorned HIS Name.
He did converse with things Above
Acquainted with Emmanuels Love
Most orthodox He was and sound
And Many Errors Did confound.
For Zion's king and Zion's cause
And Scotland's covenantal LAWS
Most constantly he Did contend
Until His Time Was At An End.
Then He Won to the Full Fruition
Of That which He Had seen in vision.[1]

The following is an introduction to Samuel Rutherford, his life, education, major controversies, and writings. Rather than a comprehensive overview, this chapter will provide enough information to situate Rutherford in his historical, ecclesial, and theological context in order to better orient the reader to engage Rutherford's scholasticism in the subsequent chapters.[2] Furthermore, by adding Rutherford's own commentary on events taken principally from his letters, the reader will gain

---

1 This inscription was taken from a photo of Samuel Rutherford's tombstone in the churchyard at St. Andrews Cathedral in St Andrews, Fife, Scotland. The photo was taken by the author in the Summer of 2018.

2 For those interested in biographical literature as it relates to Rutherford, Coffey's intellectual biography of Rutherford is comprehensive and truly excellent. See John Coffey, *Politics, Religion and the British Revolutions*. Of the older literature, Murray's is thorough and balanced. See Murray, *The Life of Samuel Rutherford*. Other lengthy treatments, which can at times be marred by hagiographical tendencies are Bonar, "Sketch of Samuel Rutherford."; Thomson, *Samuel Rutherford*; and Whyte, "Samuel Rutherford and Some of His Correspondents." See also: George Norman Macleod Craven, *Samuel Rutherford, Saint and Statesman* (S.l.: The Evangelical library, 1961); and Kingsley G. Rendell, *Samuel Rutherford: A New Biography of the Man & His Ministry* (Fearn: Christian Focus, 2003). For short, article length introductions to Rutherford see "Samuel Rutherford" in *Biographia Scoticana or a Brief Historical Account of the Lives, Characters, and Memorable Transactions of the Most Eminent Scots Worthies, Noblemen, Gentlemen, Ministers, and Others* (Glasgow: Khull, Blackie, & Co. and by A. Fullerton & Co. Edinburgh, 1824), 181–89; Macleod, *Scottish Theology in Relation to Church History Since The*

an appreciation of Rutherford's sense of God's providence in his life and in the grand historical events of which he was a participant. This will provide a different portrait of providence than the scholastic treatment of the doctrine found in later chapters, which is largely abstracted from practical application.

1.1 Birth and Education (1600–1621)

1.1.1 Birth and Early Life

Rutherford was born sometime around the turn of the seventeenth century. The Westminster biographer James Reid has claimed Rutherford was born in the parish of Tongland, near Kirkcudbright, in the south of Scotland. Attached to the story of Rutherford's birth in Kirkcudbright is also a story of divine rescue, whereby Rutherford fell headlong into a well and was saved by an angel. After the angelic intervention, Rutherford's father dedicated him to divine service.[3] However, the truth is far less interesting. It appears as if Reid was misled by the fact that there was another Rutherford in Tongland, Samuel's brother George. George Rutherford received charge of a parish in Tongland by the General Assembly of 1639 and acquired lands of modest significance, which he bequeathed to his daughters Marion, Martha, and Barbara. This is the basis for Reid's claim that Rutherford was born to respectable parents, having confused George for Rutherford's father.[4] In addition to this, G. Rutherford had a son whom he named Samuel. It was George's son Samuel who fell into the well at Argrennan. Unlike the hagiographical myth of our subject's brush with death at the bottom of the well, there was no divine rescue for George's young son. Nevertheless, this is the most likely basis for one of the more famous stories surrounding Rutherford.[5]

It is believed that Rutherford was born in the parish of Nisbet in the county of Roxborough.[6] This would seem to be confirmed by Rutherford himself, who in a letter to Mr. John Scott the minister at Oxnam, wished him ministerial success in

---

Reformation, 3rd ed., 68–78; T. F. Torrance, *Scottish Theology* (Edinburgh: T&T Clark, 1996.), 93–111; and M. Charles Bell, *Calvin and Scottish Theology: The Doctrine of Assurance*, 70–91.

3 James Reid, *Memoirs of the Lives and Writings of Those Eminent Divines, Who Convened The Famous Assembly at Westminster in the Seventeenth Century* (High Street: Stephen and Andrew Young, 1811), 1:345; Bonar, "Sketch of Samuel Rutherford," 2.

4 Reid, *Memoirs of the Lives and Writings of Those Eminent Divines*, 1:345.

5 *Minute Book kept by the War Committee of the Covenanters in the Stewartry of Kirkcudbright, in the Years 1640 and 1641* (Kirkcudbright: J. Nicholson, 1855), 229.

6 Murray, *The Life of Samuel Rutherford*, 2; Thomson, *Samuel Rutherford*, 10; Coffey, *Politics, Religion and the British Revolutions*, 30.

that place to "which I owe my first breathing."[7] Oxnam is the neighboring parish to Crailing.[8] Though Reid concludes that Rutherford was born to respectable parents from the faulty premise that George Rutherford was Samuel's father, there is still reason to believe that Rutherford's father was a man of means. Rutherford had two brothers, George and James. It is known that George and Samuel were provided with a generous education as Samuel would go on to study at the University of Edinburgh and George became a schoolmaster at Kirkcudbright before he took the parish at Tongland.[9] It is likely that George and Samuel, if not also James received primary education at the grammar school in Jedburg.[10] As such educational pursuits demanded some means, it would be reasonable to conclude that the Rutherford family at Nisbet was part of a growing, ascendant class of landowners that had been increasing steadily since the Reformation.[11]

1.1.2 Education

The aspiration among Protestant nations that all Christians should be able to read the Scriptures for themselves meant there was an emphasis upon education and literacy for the entire populace. As R.A. Houston notes, this desire was nearly universal amongst religious reformers, but in Scotland the church was able to "recruit the aid of the state in implementing legislation to realize this aim." Houston notes that acts were passed in the Scottish parliament in 1616, 1633, 1646, 1696, and 1803 to facilitate universal literacy.[12] Some have argued Scotland's early adoption of a national education program centralized in the hands of the state gave Scotland a distinct advantage in literacy as well as educational standards.[13] However, the picture is not so clear at the time of Rutherford's schooling. The effectiveness of

---

7 Samuel Rutherford, *Joshua Redivivus: Or, Three Hundred and Fifty-Two Religious Letters*, ed. Robert McWard, IX (Glasgow: John Bryce, 1765), 490–91.

8 Coffey, *Politics, Religion and the British Revolutions*, 30.

9 Murray, *The Life of Samuel Rutherford*, 3.

10 Murray, *The Life of Samuel Rutherford*, 4.

11 This is substantiated by Woodrow, who claimed that Rutherford was the son of a modestly wealthy landowner. See: Woodrow, *Analecta*, 3:88.

12 R. A. Houston, *Scottish Literacy and the Scottish Identity: Illiteracy and Society in Scotland and Northern England 1600–1800*, Cambridge Studies in Population, Economy and Society in Past Time 4 (Cambridge: Cambridge University Press, 1985), 5. See also R. A. Houston, "Literacy Campaigns in Scotland, 1560–1803," in *National Literacy Campaigns: Historical and Comparative Perspectives*, ed. Robert F. Arnove and Harvey J. Graff (New York: Plenum Press, 1987), 53.

13 See Peter Harrison, *The Bible, Protestantism, and The Rise of Natural Science* (Cambridge: Cambridge University Press, 1998), 118; also David Stevenson, *The Scottish Revolution 1637–1644: The Triumph of the Covenanters* (Edinburgh: John Donald Publishers, 2003), 42.

these national programs probably remained more at the level of aspiration than achievement in the early 1600s.[14]

Rutherford's proximity to Jedburg gave him a distinct educational advantage. Though the Scottish Parliament had determined that there would be a teacher in each of its 900 parishes, the reality was that such local village schools remained elementary schools in the best cases. In the Burghs however, an influx of apprentices meant the Burgh schools could offer more advanced training. As a result, the Burgh schools became grammar schools where young students could acquire Latin, a necessary skill if they aimed to advance to a university level education. Houston notes the emerging Scottish rural middle class sent their children to the grammar schools in the towns.[15] This helps determine Rutherford's socio-economic status, as it is probable he made the four-mile walk from Nisbet to attend the grammar school at Jedburg.[16] Coffey, citing Murray, notes that in 1669 the master of the school at Jedburg was made rector of the High School of Edinburgh. From this, Coffey concludes that the grammar school at Jedburg may have had "a long tradition of academic excellence and links with Edinburgh."[17]

1.1.3 University Education

Murray records that Rutherford began his studies at the University of Edinburgh in 1617.[18] According to Murray, at the time Rutherford entered the University, "division of labor was nearly unknown, and had been very slowly introduced."[19] What this meant was that one college master would take one group of students through the entire course of studies. Therefore, four college masters were required if the University was to have a full complement of students. At the time of Rutherford's matriculation, the four college masters were: William King, James Fairly, James Reid, and Andrew Young.[20] In addition to these was the well-respected principal, Henry Charteris.[21]

The summer before Rutherford's matriculation was a significant time for the University. After a fourteen year absence, King James I (1566–1625) had returned

---

14 R.A. Houston, *Scotland: A Very Short Introduction* (Oxford: Oxford University Press, 2008), 61.

15 Houston, *Scottish Literacy and the Scottish Identity*, 51.

16 Thomson, *Samuel Rutherford*, 11.

17 Coffey, *Politics, Religion and the British Revolutions*, 31; Murray, *The Life of Samuel Rutherford*, 5.

18 Murray, *The Life of Samuel Rutherford*, 5.

19 Murray, *The Life of Samuel Rutherford*, 7.

20 T. Craufurd, *History of the University of Edinburgh: From 1580–1646* (Edinburgh: A. Neill & Co., 1808), 79–88.

21 Dalzel, *History of the University of Edinburgh From Its Foundation*, 2:65; Craufurd, *History of the University of Edinburgh*, 82.

to his native Scotland. Of the many matters the King took in, one was a public disputation hosted by the King at Stirling Castle that included the faculty at the University of Edinburgh. A record of the disputation survives in *The Muses Welcome to the High and Mightie Prince*, printed a year after the King's visit in 1618.[22] Each disputation was given a short, witty introduction followed by a presentation of the theses to be disputed. Patrick Sands, "sometime regent" disputed upon whether the lower magistrates (*magistratibus inferioribus*) should have hereditary titles. Andrew Young disputed upon a matter of physics and causality with reference to Book VIII of Aristotle's *Physics* and Book XII of the *Metaphysics*. James Reid disputed upon the metaphysical thesis of the source and fount of being.[23] Finally, William King disputed upon the relationship between the will's freedom of indifference in relation to immoral acts such as rage and violence. The heavy use of Aristotle by all four disputants is indicated by the King's concluding remarks that "these men were as well acquainted with the meaning of Aristotle as he was himself when alive."[24] Of these, Andrew Young was singled out as particularly distinguished in Aristotle.[25]

The significance of these disputations for our present subject concerns Young, who having advanced the *magistrands* on June 29, 1617 began a new rotation with the *bajan* class of 1617. Young would be Rutherford's professor when he entered the University in the fall of 1617. At the time, the University students were grouped into four distinct classes, these being the *bajan*, *semi-bajan*, *bachelor*, and *magistrand*.[26] Murray described the purpose of the curriculum at the University during Rutherford's time there as follows:

> The principal object of education, in these days, seems to have been to form expert disputants, and subtle dialecticians; and hence, in this University, not only were several hours a day set apart for disputations, but the students of the different classes, from the month of January till July annually, had daily conferences for this purpose—each class successively proposing a thesis, while the regents presided in rotation.[27]

---

22 *Τα των μουσων εισοδια: The Muses Welcome to the High and Mightie Prince James By the Grace of God King of Great Britain France and Ireland, Defender of the Faith &c. At his Majesties happy Returne to his olde and natiue Kingdome of Scotland, after 14 yeeres absence, IN ANNO 1617*, (Edinburgh, 1618).

23 Craufurd, *History of the University of Edinburgh*, 83.

24 Dalzel, *History of the University of Edinburgh From Its Foundation*, 2:66.

25 The King quipped "Mr. Young is Very Old in Aristotle." See Dalzel, *History of the University of Edinburgh From Its Foundation*, 2:68.

26 The student classifications of *bajan*, *semi-bajan*, *bachelor*, and *magistrand* correspond to the number of years that the student has been studying at university. This begins with the *bajan* class, who are first-year students. This system of classification is still in use at the University of Aberdeen and the University of St Andrews.

27 Murray, *The Life of Samuel Rutherford*, 10.

The above is a typical description of how students were prepared according to the method of the schools. Typically, students participated in a *lectio*, or reading of a lecture, a *meditatio*, or reflection upon the lecture by a student, and then the *quaestio*, where questions were posed regarding the reading. Apart from the *lectio, meditatio, quaestio* pattern, disputations were also organized around controversial issues or topics of broader interest. The professor was responsible for organizing the disputation, which included assigning the question for the disputation and then organizing theses related to the topic. [28]

Rutherford's *bajan* year began in October with the reading of Latin and Greek.[29] By November, his abilities were tested through a series of public demonstrations where students were prescribed a text in Scots called "The Public Theme" at 9:00 a.m. in the morning.[30] Students were expected to provide a written translation of the text into Latin and turn it in to the Regent by noon of the same day. Later in the day the students read their Latin translations after which the written copy would be examined by the Principal and Regents.[31] If the student was found to be deficient in Latin, he would be sent home to sharpen his skills. This was not necessary for Rutherford. The grammar school at Jedburg served him well. The rest of Rutherford's *bajan* year was spent improving his language skills, studying Greek from the New Testament and Homer, and improving his Latin with Cicero among others. According to the custom of humanist reforms, dialectic and rhetoric were practiced with concrete examples from Cicero and Demosthenes.[32]

In his *semi-bajan* year Rutherford began his study of Aristotle under the expert instruction of Young. The latter half of the year was spent in the *Organan*, studying *De Interpretatione, Priora Analytica, Topica* and *De Sophisticis Elenchis*. Porphyry's commentary upon *De Interpretatione* was also employed. In his *bachelor* year he read *Posteriora Analytica* and *Ethica Nicomachea*. He also began a study of Hebrew grammar. In his *magistrand* year, Rutherford read more Aristotle which included *De Caelo, De Generatione et Corruptione, Meterologica,* and *De Anima*.[33]

On the evening before graduation, the *magistrand* class gathered with their tutor, Andrew Young, to subscribe to the Confession of Faith. This was followed by a moral exhortation from the Principal. Graduation was normally appointed for a Monday, wherein a public disputation was begun in front of the Privy Councillors,

---

28 Rouwendal, "The Method of the Schools," 59.

29 Dalzel, *History of the University of Edinburgh From Its Foundation*, 2:46.

30 Dalzel, 2:46.

31 Craufurd, *History of the University of Edinburgh*, 57–8.

32 Coffey, *Politics, Religion and the British Revolutions*, 63.

33 Dalzel, *History of the University of Edinburgh From Its Foundation*, 2:47–8; Craufurd, *History of the University of Edinburgh*, 58–9; Robert S. Rait, "Andrew Melville and the Revolt Against Aristotle in Scotland," *The English Historical Review* 14, no. 54 (1899): 254.

the Lords of the Exchequer, the Lords of Session, Advocates, and Clerks to the Signet, the Lord Provost, Magistrates, Town-Council, Patrons of the College, and other esteemed guests. The disputation began at six in the morning and was to be concluded by sundown.[34]

1.1.4 University of Edinburgh: Curriculum Analysis

Rutherford was a beneficiary of educational reforms brought to the Scottish universities by Andrew Melville (1545–1622), a Scottish scholar, theologian, and reformer.[35] A sense of the reforms is gained by looking at the pre-Melvillian curriculum. According to the diary and autobiography of James Melville (1556–1614), the pre-reform curriculum consisted of rhetoric and the *Organon* in the *bajan* year. This was followed by further reading in the *Organon* and the *De Sophisticis Elenchis* in *the semi-bajan* year. In the *bachelor* year Aristotle's *Ethics*, the *Physics* and *De Generatione et Corruptione* were studied. In the *magistrand* year students studied *De Caelo, Meteorologica,* and also *Metaphysica*. There was only a rudimentary introduction to Greek and no training in Hebrew. In 1574, Andrew Melville, newly returned from the continent, began to set about with his reforms at Glasgow. According to James Melville, in his own words, the curriculum reform appeared as follows:

> He teached tham the Greik grammer, the Dialectice of Ramus, the Rhetoric of Taleus, with the practise thairof in Greik and Latin authors, namlie, Homer, Hesiod, Phocilides, Theognides, Pythagoras, Isocrates, Pindarus, Virgill, Horace, Theocritus, &c. From that

---

34 Dalzel, *History of the University of Edinburgh From Its Foundation*, 2:49.

35 Melville's place in the Scottish Reformation is a matter of dispute. Thomas McCrie, a biographer of John Knox believed him to be the rightful successor to the first-generation Scottish Reformer John Knox. See Thomas McCrie, *The Life of Andrew Melville Containing Illustrations of the Ecclesiastical and Literary History of Scotland, During the Latter Part of the Sixteenth Century and Beginning of the Seventeenth Century With an Appendix Consisting of Original Papers* (Edinburgh: William Blackwood, 1819). He is followed by J. Bass Mullinger, *A History of the University of Cambridge* (London: Longmans, Green, and Co., 1888); Macleod, *Scottish Theology in Relation to Church History*, 3rd ed., 41–48; G.D. Henderson, *Religious Life in Seventeenth-Century Scotland* (Cambridge: Cambridge University Press, 1937), 39–42; and Torrance, *Scottish Theology*, 60–79. Walker gives Melville's place in the ongoing Scottish Reformation faint praise, noting his "contributions were small." See: Walker, *The Theology and Theologians of Scotland*, 2. More recently MacDonald and Kirk have challenged Melville's power and influence, arguing McCrie's hagiographical tendencies carried over into scholarship that naively took in McCrie's portrait of Melville. See: Alan R. MacDonald, *The Jacobean Kirk, 1567–1625: Sovereignty, Polity, and Liturgy* (Aldershot: Ashgate, 1998); J. Kirk, *The Development of the Melvillian Movement in Late Sixteenth Century Scotland* (University of Edinburgh, 1975). For a summary of these developments see Ernest R. Holloway III, *Andrew Melville and Humanism in Renaissance Scotland 1545–1662,* Studies in the History of Christian Traditions 154 (Leiden: Brill, 2011), 1–34.

he enterit to the Mathematiks, and teatched the Elements of Euclid, the Arithmetic and Geometrie of Ramus, the Geographie of Dyonisius, the Tables of Hunter, the Astrologie of Aratus. From that to the Morall Philosophie; he teatched the Ethiks of Aristotle, the Offices of Cicero, Aristotle de Virtutibus, Cicero's Paradoxes and Tusculanes, Aristot. Polyb. And certean of Platoes Dialoges. From that to the Naturall Philosophie; he teatched the buiks of the Physics, De Ortu, De Coelo, &c., also of Plato and Fernelius. With this he joined the Historie, with the twa lights thairof, Chronologie and Chirographie, out of Sleidan, Menarthes, and Melancthon. And all this by and attoure his awin ordinar profession, the holie tonges and Theologie; he teachit the Hebrew grammar, first shortlie, and syne mor accuratlie; thairefter the Caldaic and Syriac dialects, with the practice thairof in the Psalmes and warks of Solomon, David, Ezra, and Epistle to the Galates. He past throw the hail comoun places of Theologie verie exactlie and accuratlie; also throw all the Auld and New Testament. And all this in the space of sax yeirs; during the quhilk he teatchit everie day, customablie, twyse, Sabothe and uther day, with an ordinar conference with sic as war present efter denner and supper.[36]

There are several important aspects to note about the curriculum reform. The first to note is the introduction of humanist learning. There was a renewed emphasis in languages. No longer was Latin merely assumed, but it appeared as part of the trials in the *bajan* year, a system that carried on through to Rutherford's fall in 1617. Greek and Hebrew were added to the language curriculum. An introduction to Syriac and Chaldaic were also woven into the curriculum. As can be seen from the above, emphasis on Greek provided students not simply with access to the New Testament but also to Homer, Hesiod, Pseudo-Phocylides, Pythagoras, and Aristotle. It would now be an expectation to read Aristotle in his own words in the original Greek. Latin was no longer preserved for philosophy and theology, but the classic works of Virgil and Cicero were also read in Latin. Melville's emphasis upon dialectic, rhetoric, grammar, and moral philosophy were each hallmarks of the new humanist learning.[37]

In addition to the humanism that Melville systematically introduced into the Scottish University curriculum, attention can also be drawn to Ramism. Melville had personal acquaintance with Peter Ramus (1515–1572), having attended his lectures at the University of Paris. Ramist influences may be seen first and foremost in the stated curriculum. One notes the presence of Ramus's *Dialectic* as well as Taleus's *Rhetoric*. In addition to these manuals, the principles of rhetoric were to be

---

36 Robert S. Rait, "Andrew Melville and the Revolt Against Aristotle in Scotland," *The English Historical Review* 14, no. 54 (1899): 254.
37 Paul Oskar Kristeller, *Renaissance Thought and its Sources* (New York: Columbia University Press, 1979), 22.

demonstrated in the *bajan* year by the reading of Cicero, Demosthenes, Homer, and Aristophanes. A similar pattern may be discerned in the *semi-bajan* year, with the art of rhetoric being more fully treated in Aristotle and Cicero's *de Oratore* with applications sought in Demosthenes, Sophocles, and Pindar.[38] Lisa Jardine has demonstrated the links between humanism and Ramism arguing that the latter was a natural development from the former. She argues that there was a shift in the way humanists approached dialectics, with increased emphasis on probability and the art of persuasion rather than syllogistic deduction. This was especially important as the arts curriculum was broadened towards those subjects (civics, ethics, politics, etc.) in which opinion and the art of persuasion had typically held sway. As education was offered to a literate laity, not just technically literate clerics and teachers, a method of simplifying dialectics was needed. Peter Ramus was instrumental in the process of simplification.[39]

The Melvillian reforms were taken to the University of Edinburgh through Melville's pupil, Robert Rollock (1555–1599). Through Rollock, Rutherford would receive another aspect of the Ramism that Melville brought back from Paris. Ramus sought to simplify the presentation of his material through dichotomous charts that were meant to present the entire system visually to the student.[40] Stephen J. Reid described Rollock's theological writings as "some of the most explicitly Ramist organization of any Scottish text of the period."[41] He also argues that evidence relating to teaching at the University of Edinburgh during this period suggests Rollock used his position to ensure Ramist texts were incorporated into the curriculum.[42]

Reid argued that the chief benefit of Ramism to Melville was that it offered Melville the opportunity to "expedite the practical process of education in a university that had almost completely decayed since the Reformation."[43] Walter J. Ong

---

38 Winifred Bryan Horner, *Nineteenth Century Scottish Rhetoric: The American Connection* (Carbondale and Edwardsville: Southern Illinois University Press, 1993), 65.

39 Lisa Jardine, "Humanism and the Teaching of Logic," in *The Cambridge History of Later Medieval Philosophy* (Cambridge: Cambridge University Press, 1992), 797–807; see also P. A. Duhamel, "The Logic and Rhetoric of Peter Ramus," *Modern Philology* 46, no. 3 (1949): 168.

40 This is a method Rollock seems to have taken to heart, as is evidenced by the structure and presentation of his *Tractatus de vocatione efficaci*. See Robert Rollock, *Tractatus De Vocatione Efficaci, Quae Inter Locos Theologiae Communissimos Recensetur, deque locis specialioribus, qui sub vocatione comprehenduntur* (Christopher Corvinus, 1600).

41 Stephen J. Reid, *Humanism and Calvinism: Andrew Melville and the Universities of Scotland, 1560–1625*, St. Andrews Studies in Reformation History (Surrey: Ashgate, 2011), 207.

42 Reid, *Humanism and Calvinism*, 210.

43 Stephen J. Reid, "Andrew Melville and Scottish Ramism," in *Ramus, Pedagogy, and the Liberal Arts: Ramism in Britain and the Wider World*, eds. Stephen J. Reid and Emma Annette Wilson (Surrey: Ashgate, 2011), 27.

has argued that this was the secret to the commercial success of the Ramist text-books.[44] In an era where the need for such textbooks was increasing, the simplified introductions to the material paired with the Ramean charts, blended accessibility with a sophisticated visualization of the material.[45] Thus the Ramist textbooks were perfect for Melville, who needed elementary introductions to difficult subjects for his unprepared pupils. This understanding of the role of Ramism in the Scottish universities is strengthened when one considers when the Ramean textbooks were employed during the course of studies. The Ramist textbooks appear early in the *bajan* and *semi-bajan* years and should be seen as preparatory to the more difficult works of Aristotle that appear in the *bachelor* and *magistrand* years. The Ramist texts were still being used during Rutherford's time at the University of Edinburgh. In fact, according to Murray, these texts were used until the middle of the seventeenth century in the Scottish Universities.[46] It is likely that Rutherford himself was at one point responsible for teaching such texts. After his graduation he was elected to the new position of Professor of Humanity at the University of Edinburgh. In this role he would have been responsible for teaching Ramus's *Dialectic* and Taleus's *Rhetoric*.[47] Despite this, it is difficult to find much trace of Ramist influences in Rutherford's practical or theological writings. When it came time for Rutherford to produce his own theological textbooks, he eschewed the Ramean charts in favor of the scholastic disputation. Even in his popular works written in English, the *quaestio* method of the scholastic disputation is not far beneath the surface, neither are scholastic terms and distinctions. In this regard, Rutherford should be seen as part of a broader movement of seventeenth century British scholarship that drifted away from Ramism, returning to the tried and true roots of medieval scholasticism as a pedagogical methodology.[48] This drift away from Ramism, even during Rollock's lifetime, has been noted by Reid.[49]

Some interpreters of the period have viewed the dual presence of humanism and Ramism as an indication that Melville and the Scottish Universities opposed scholasticism and "Aristoteleanism."[50] This supposed diametrical opposition of

---

44 Walter J. Ong, *Ramus, Method, and the Decay of Dialogue: From the Art of Discourse to the Art of Reason* (Chicago: The University of Chicago Press, 2004), 10.

45 Walter J. Ong, "Ramist Method and the Commercial Mind," *Studies in the Renaissance* 8 (1961): 155–72.

46 Murray, *The Life of Samuel Rutherford*, 9.

47 Murray, *The Life of Samuel Rutherford*, 17.

48 Mordechai Feingold, "English Ramism: A Reinterpretation," in *The Influence of Petrus Ramus: Studies in Sixteenth and Seventeenth Century Philosophy and Sciences*, eds. Wolfgang Rother, Mordechai Feingold, and Joseph S. Freedman, Schwabe philosophica 1 (Basel: Schwabe, 2001), 136.

49 Reid, *Humanism and Calvinism*, 210–15.

50 For example, Murray notes that the "Ramean philosophy prevailed" during Rutherford's time at the University of Edinburgh and "displaced the Aristotelian philosophy." See Murray, *The Life of Samuel*

humanism and Ramism to the classic Medieval scholastic curriculum carries over into modern scholarship.[51] However, the reality of the relationship, as Rutherford's return to scholastic method demonstrates, is far more complex than this simple portrait of diametrical opposites would suggest.[52] Rather than seeing scholasticism and humanism as separate movements, scholars such as Kristeller and van Asselt have argued that the two movements (humanism and scholasticism) developed alongside one another at roughly the same time.[53] These two movements were not opposed to one another as much as they addressed different subject matter. The *studia humanitatis*, notes Kristeller, was not such a new "philosophical tendency or system, but rather a cultural and educational program which emphasized and developed an important but limited area of studies."[54] These studies included morals, rhetoric, and literature but excluded "by definition such fields as logic, natural philosophy and metaphysics."[55] Thus, the humanist fields of grammar, rhetoric, poetry, and moral philosophy developed alongside the scholastic fields of logic and natural philosophy, with the humanist interest in language and *ad fontes* greatly enhancing scholastic curriculum.[56] Recently, Giovanni Gellera has applied a similar argument specifically to the Scottish universities, noting the enduring presence of Aristotle as well as the scholastic method, which he argues represents "an innovation of the best humanist scholarship of the time."[57]

Muller and van Asselt apply these insights to challenge the thesis that the Reformation was anti-scholastic in nature. Acknowledging anti-scholastic and anti-Aristotelian polemical statements made by the Reformers, Muller notes that the divide between scholasticism and the humanist Reformers was "not nearly as pronounced" as the more polemical statements would lead one to believe.[58] Medieval

---

Rutherford, 8. Craufurd and Dalzel draw similar conclusions. See: Craufurd, *History of the University of Edinburgh,* 45; Dalzel, *History of the University of Edinburgh From Its Foundation,* 2:31.

51 For example, see William C. Kneale and Martha Kneale, *The Development of Logic* (New York: Oxford University Press, 2008), 300; and also Alister McGrath, *Reformation Thought: An Introduction,* 3rd ed. (Oxford: Blackwell, 2001), 61.

52 See Kristeller, *Renaissance Thought and Its Sources*; Muller, *Post-Reformation Reformed Dogmatics,* Vol. 1; and William J. van Asselt, "Open Hand and Fist: Humanism and Scholasticism in the Reformation," in *Introduction to Reformed Scholasticism,* ed. T. J. Rouwendal Pleizier, P. L. Rouwendal, and Maarteen Wisse, Reformed Historical-Theological Studies (Grand Rapids, MI: Reformation Heritage Books, 2011), 73–85.

53 Kristeller, *Renaissance Thought and its Sources,* 46 and 55; van Asselt, "Open Hand and Fist," 79.

54 Kristeller, 22.

55 Kristeller, 23.

56 Kristeller, 101.

57 Giovanni Gellera, "Philosophy and Theology After John Mair," in *The History of Scottish Theology,* vol. 1, *Celtic Origins to Reformed Orthodoxy,* ed. David Fergusson and Mark W. Elliot, (Oxford: Oxford University Press, 2019), 113.

58 Richard Muller, *Post-Reformation Reformed Dogmatics,* 1:363.

and Renaissance scholasticism was primarily a method not a philosophy. It was a relatively uniform method of exposition, with a clear structure, patterns of reasoning, well organized topics and subtopics, and extensive citation of texts that served as revered authorities. This method was used to argue "a variety of theological and philosophical conclusions, and not a particular theology or philosophy."[59] The medieval method was enhanced, not displaced by humanism, as theologians acquired technical mastery in the ancient languages and their preference for rhetorical over demonstrative argumentation.[60] Despite their negative caricatures of many medieval scholastic theologians, recent scholarship has convincingly argued that both Luther and Calvin continued to use scholastic methods of argumentation as well a number of important scholastic distinctions.[61] Philip Melanchthon (1497–1560) continued to find scholastic theology and the distinctions of Aristotle useful in both the philosophy as well as the theology curriculum at Wittenberg. Peter Martyr Vermigli (1499–1562) continued to rely upon scholastic exposition, distinctions, and Aristotelean argumentation.[62] Van Asselt has identified scholastic methodological tendencies in Calvin's commentaries as well as scholastic distinctions in his theological writings. He concludes that there was a dual development of a "scholastic line" and "humanist line" from the outset of the Reformation, which ran parallel and was mutually beneficial to one another.[63]

This parallel development of humanism and scholasticism described by van Asselt makes more sense of the Melvillian reforms at the Scottish universities than a supposed antagonism between the two movements. After all, one can see the new emphasis on languages as well as rhetoric, but these new emphases exist alongside the more traditionally scholastic curriculum on logic, physics, and metaphysics. The notion that humanism and Ramism aligned to assault the time worn scholastic curriculum of the medieval period must be rejected. Rather, what could be said is that the humanist curriculum introduced new subjects and methods, which rather than competing with the scholastic curriculum helped sharpen and enhance it.

---

59 Muller, 1:35.

60 Muller, 1:36.

61 See D.V.N. Bagchi, "Sic et Non: Luther and Scholasticism," In *Protestant Scholasticism: Essays in Reassessment,* ed. Carl R. Trueman and R. Scott Clark, Studies in Christian History and Thought (Eugene, Or: Wipf and Stock, 2005), 1–15; David C. Steinmetz, "The Scholastic Calvin," in *Protestant Scholasticism: Essays in Reassessment,* 16–30; Cornelis Augustijn, "Wittenberga contra Scholasticos," in *Reformation and Scholasticism: An Ecumenical Enterprise,* eds. Willem J. van Asselt and Eef Dekker, Text & Studies in Reformation & Post-Reformation Thought (Grand Rapids: Baker Academic, 2001), 65–77; Richard Muller, "Scholasticism in Calvin: A Question of Relation and Disjunction," in *The Unaccommodated Calvin: Studies in the Foundation of a Theological Tradition,* Oxford Studies in Historical Theology (Oxford: Oxford University Press, 2000), 39–61.

62 Muller, 1:364–66.

63 van Asselt, "'Open Hand and Fist': Humanism and Scholasticism in the Reformation," 54.

Rutherford was a beneficiary of a nearly half century of reform that brought the best of Renaissance humanism to bear upon the robust Reformed scholasticism of seventeenth century Scottish higher education.

1.1.5 The Curriculum's Influence on Rutherford

The curriculum had its influence upon Rutherford in a variety of observable ways. The first is his competency in Latin, Greek, and Hebrew. In his *Disputatio Scholastica de Divina Providentia* for example, when he undertook the typically scholastic discipline of defining the term *providentia Dei*, he began first with the Latin term, moving then to the Greek before concluding with the Hebrew. These are printed in Greek and Hebrew typeset and Rutherford exerted himself to gain a sense of the word in each of the three languages he has surveyed.[64] Occasionally Old Testament paraphrases in Chaldean and Syriac are also commented upon. New Testament texts are presented in Greek and Latin. Aristotle is presented in the original Greek, as are patristic sources when applicable.[65]

Rutherford exhibits familiarity with a wide variety of classical authors. Of these, Aristotle is the most frequently quoted. Rutherford's use of Aristotle ᵗᵉ to do with his scholastic training than his humanism, however Rutherfo__ 'of Aristotle in the original Greek is a mark of humanist influences upon the tra. ing at the University of Edinburgh. Rutherford's appropriation of Aristotle is mostly positive, occasionally defending the philosopher from what he considers to be an improper interpretation.[66] Nevertheless, Rutherford distanced himself from Aristotle when the philosopher contradicts Reformed and catholic orthodoxy. Though Rutherford borrowed the language and even concepts from Aristotle, it is important to realize that in many cases he uses it in a way that is a conscious departure from the manner that Aristotle used.[67] Besides Aristotle, one can find the occasional positive reference to Plato. Coffey has noted that Rutherford readily employed the theological language of Neo-Platonism.[68] However, it is important to note that Rutherford's use of Plato is generally negative. This could be because

---

64 Samuel Rutherford, *Disputatio Scholastica de Divina Providentia* (Edinburgh: Georgii Andersoni, 1649), 1–2.

65 Samuel Rutherford, *Exercitationes Apologeticae pro Divina Gratia* (Amsterdam: Henricum Laurentii, 1636), 1; Rutherford, *Disputatio Scholastica*, 104.

66 See: Samuel Rutherford, *A Free Disputation Against Pretended Liberty of Conscience*, 349.

67 For example, see Rutherford's rejection of the "eternal world of Aristotle" in Samuel Rutherford, *The Tryal and Triumph of Faith: or, An Exposition of the History of Christ's Dispossessing of the Daughter of the Woman of Canaan* (London: John Field, 1645), 296.

68 Coffey, *Politics, Religion and the British Revolutions*, 73. See also chapter 5.2.2 of this study for a positive reference to Neo-Platonism in Rutherford's understanding of God's power in relation to the property of impossibility.

Rutherford's adversaries often resourced their own arguments with specific appeals to Plato or what could be described as Platonic lines of thought.[69]

Other classical authors used by Rutherford include Cicero, Tacitus, Plutarch, Xenophon, Sallust, Herodotus, Seneca, and Homer. In regard to these sources, Tacitus, Plutarch, Xenophon, Sallust, Herodotus and Homer are used to supply historical examples. Cicero and Seneca's relationship to Rutherford's writing is more complex. Cicero generally receives negative treatment for his refutation of the Stoics. Following Augustine, Rutherford argued that Cicero's attempt to reign in the excess of the Stoics went too far and destroyed any meaningful understanding of God's providence.[70] This defense of the Stoics found in the *Disputatio*, along with certain positive references found in Rutherford's *Letters* and other writings, has led Coffey to argue for a Stoic trait in Rutherford.[71]

Humanist appropriations of classical references must be analyzed with caution. Reference is no clear indication that ideas were absorbed uncritically. For example, the humanist scholar, pedagogue, and philosopher Justus Lipsius (1547–1606) stood at the forefront of the neo-stoic revival of the late sixteenth century. Nevertheless, A.A. Long has noted that "Lipsius's works were a disaster for the interpretation of Stoicism as a systematic philosophy," principally because "he [Lipsius] accepts Christianity as the criterion by which to assess the meaning and propriety of Stoicism."[72] In his *De constantia* (1583), Lipsius identified critical differences between Stoicism and Christianity in regards to fate and providence.[73] Rutherford followed Lipsius in this, citing him directly and with much admiration.[74] Rutherford's "Stoicism" is therefore a good test case for the numerous classical sources he was exposed to and employed as a result of the humanist curriculum at Edinburgh. The use of Aristotle, Plato, or Seneca is no clear indicator of the presence of such "isms" as "Aristotelianism," "Platonism," or "Stoicism" in Rutherford's theology. Rather,

---

69 See for example John Maxwell, *Sacro-Sancta Regum Majestas: Or the Sacred and Royal Prerogative of Christian Kings* (London: Thomas Dring, 1680), 105–7; and Rutherford's critique in Samuel Rutherford, *Lex Rex: The Law and the Prince* (London: John Field, 1644), 61–2. The Arminian in Laud's circle, Thomas Jackson, also frequently appealed to Plato. See Thomas Jackson, *The Works of Thomas Jackson, D. D., Sometime President of Corpus Christi College, Oxford and Dean of Peterborough.* Vol V, *A Treatise on the Divine Essence and Attributes* (Oxford: Oxford University Press, 1844), 341–7.

70 Rutherford, *Disputatio Scholastica*, 99–118.

71 Coffey, *Politics, Religion and the British Revolutions*, 72. See chapter 6.5.2 of this study for Rutherford's critique of Stoicism as it relates to the doctrine of divine providence.

72 A. A. Long, "Stoicism in the Philosophical Tradition: Spinoza, Lipsius, Butler," in *The Cambridge Companion to the Stoics*, ed. Brad Inwood, Cambridge Companions to Philosophy (Cambridge: Cambridge University Press, 2003), 379–80.

73 Justus Lipsius, *De constantia* (Antwerp: Christophorum Plantinum, 1583), 63–67.

74 Rutherford, *Disputatio Scholastica*, 101.

one must be sensitive to how Rutherford appropriated such terms, concepts, and thoughts and how they may have been "Christianized" to suit his own arguments.

The robust scholasticism of the University of Edinburgh remained an explicit feature of Rutherford's writings throughout his life. Rutherford's scholasticism may be seen in such works as his *Exercitationes Apologeticae pro Divina Gratia* (1636), *Disputatio Scholastica de Divina Providentia* (1649), and his *Examen Arminianismi* (1668). There is a general commitment to the *quaestio* method, which consists of the following four elements:

1. A statement of the question (*status quaestionis*).
2. A list of arguments from the tradition against one's own view (*objectiones*).
3. A list of arguments from the tradition in favor of one's own view, in the process of which the author expounded his own view.
4. A refutation of the aforementioned objections (*fontes solutionem*).[75]

In the *Exercitationes Apologeticae pro Divina Gratia* Rutherford presented the *status quaestionis* as a thesis. The *objectiones* are not presented from tradition, but rather from Jesuit and Arminian adversaries. Rutherford answered these objections from tradition, citing revered authorities such as Augustine (354–430), Bonaventure (1221–1274), Peter Lombard (1096–1160), Thomas Aquinas (1225–1274), and John Calvin (1509–1564). The *Examen Arminianismi* represents a slightly different presentation of the scholastic method. Rather than exercises prepared as theses with objections and counter-objections, the *Examen* is structured according to a series of either/or (*an/vel*) questions led by a *Quaeritur* (*It is asked*). The question is answered by an Arminian polemical opponent, most often Conrad Vorstius (1569–1622). Rutherford responds with Scripture and tradition, just as he had done in the *Exercitationes*.

Rutherford's *Disputatio Scholastica de Divina Providentia* is one of his longest and most complex works, written during his regency at St Andrews and first delivered as a series of lectures to his students. As the title suggests, the methodology is scholastic. Also, the specific form of this scholastic presentation takes the form of a sub-genre of scholastic method, this being the disputation. Alex J. Novikoff marks the first half of the thirteenth century as the critical moment where scholastic disputation emerged and began to take concrete form.[76] Within time, the disputation took on a recognizable structure. The moderator would present the question, supply necessary authorities, respond to objections, and then finally offer a solution.[77] Joshua Rodda

---

75 Rouwendal, "The Method of the Schools," 62.
76 Alex J. Novikoff, *The Medieval Culture of Disputation, Pedagogy, Practice and Performance* (Philadelphia: University of Philadelphia Press, 2013), 133.
77 Novikoff, *The Medieval Culture of Disputation*, 137.

notes that over time scholastic disputations evolved and adapted to account for local and personal customs, yet maintained a blend of "shared fundamental structures."[78] Rutherford's *Disputatio Scholastica de Divina Providentia* appears to be a *disputatio privata*, presented only to those graduates training in theology, though upon its publication it was of course available to all. How this disputation was presented to the students is difficult to determine. Murray notes that William Tullidelph, a student of Rutherford's, recorded the substance of the lectures in handwritten notes. There is some indication that the classroom may have been livelier than the written record, providing time for dispute and exploration of practical implications.[79] As for the published work itself, Rutherford plays the role of master, *opponens,* and *respondens* himself. Predictably, he is always declared the winner of the disputation.

Apart from organization, another important feature of scholasticism was the methodical arrangement of *auctoritates*, certain revered authorities who were marshaled to lend the weight of age and tradition to an argument. Rutherford's obsessive citations, particularly in his works of scholastic theology, offer valuable insight into the catholic tradition from which he drew. Augustine (354–430) looms large in much of Rutherford's writings. This Augustinianism is mediated in the medieval period through Anselm (1033–1109), Thomas Aquinas (1225–1274), John Duns Scotus (1266–1308), Thomas Bradwardine (1300–1349), and William Ockham (1285–1347), among others. Of these, Thomas Bradwardine, the *Doctor profundus*, comes across as one of Rutherford's most respected and frequently cited medieval sources.[80]

Rutherford also shows familiarity with his theologian peers. He is not averse to drawing upon Roman Catholics, such as Domingo Báñez (1528–1604) and Diego Álvarez (1550–1632), who share with him a reverence for the Augustinian tradition. Rutherford however, preferred Reformed Scholastics such as Paul Baynes (1573–1617), William Twisse (1578–1646), Franciscus Gomarus (1563–1641), and Gisbertus Voetsius (1589–1676).[81] Rutherford also drew from the Augustinian heritage of the Reformation. From the Reformation, Luther is a frequently quoted source, whom he employs against his adversaries in antinomian controversies.[82] In his scholastic disputations regarding God's foreknowledge, will, and election, he

---

78 Joshua Rodda, *Public Religious Disputation in England, 1558–1626,* St. Andrews Studies in Reformation History (Surrey: Ashgate, 2014), 38.

79 Murray, *The Life of Samuel Rutherford,* 169.

80 Bradwardine is singled out amongst Rutherford's sources as the "great man" (*viri Magni*). See the "Epistola Theologiae Candidatis" in: Rutherford, *Disputatio Scholastica.*

81 See the "Epistola Theologiae Candidatis" in: Rutherford, *Disputatio Scholastica.*

82 See especially: Samuel Rutherford, *A Survey of the Spiritual Antichrist* (London: Andrew Crooke, 1648).

leans upon Calvin and Beza.[83] Nevertheless, Rutherford shows a preference for his medieval sources.

1.2 Theological Training, Ministry, and Confinement (1621–1638)

1.2.1 Professor of Humanity

Rutherford graduated Master of Arts in 1621. There is no clear indication he aspired to the ordained ministry. Two years after his graduation he participated in trials to select the newly created Chair of Humanity for the University of Edinburgh. Four scholars appeared to compete for the position. Rutherford was the youngest. The position was initially intended for training in law. Though it seems one of the candidates performed better, the judges' knowledge of Rutherford, his "virtuous disposition," and "eminent abilities of mind" won them over. Rutherford was awarded the position.[84] Unfortunately, he held his professorship for less than two years. Craufurd simply states that "having given some scandal in his marriage," Rutherford was "forced to dimit his charge."[85] There exists two views regarding the scandal. The first is that of John Adamson, who related the charge against Rutherford that he had "fallen in fornication."[86] The scandal of sex outside of the bounds of marriage in the strict, Presbyterian community of seventeenth century Edinburgh would be more than enough grounds for dismissal and potentially worse. The second view held by Murray and many of Rutherford's admirers, is that some indiscretion short of fornication took place. To save the University's reputation from an investigation, which would have been prolonged and public, Rutherford resigned. Whereas other biographers of Rutherford simply dismiss the charges of fornication outright, Murray takes some pains to establish his case. He notes that Rutherford's enemies, of which were many by the end of his life, never brought up this embarrassing moment in their polemics. Also, the University granted Rutherford "an honest gratification at his demission." Shortly after his demission, he was admitted to theological training and ordained into the ministry. Many years later, the same presbytery of Edinburgh that would have known of his demission elected to have him serve as a minister in the city.[87]

---

83 For a representative sample, see Chapter 29 in: Rutherford, *Disputatio Scholastica*, 478–523.
84 Murray, *The Life of Samuel Rutherford*, 16–7.
85 Craufurd, *History of the University of Edinburgh*, 104.
86 Extracts from *The Records of the Burgh of Edinburgh, 1604–1626*, ed. M. Wood (Edinburgh, 1931), 296.
87 Murray, *The Life of Samuel Rutherford*, 19–20.

Coffey has evaluated Murray's defense and found it wanting. He notes that the committee appointed to investigate the scandal appointed a successor to Rutherford, suggesting a scandal did occur. He also notes that Adamson, who leveled the charge of fornication against Rutherford, actually sat on commissions with him in the 1640s. It is hard to imagine that Rutherford would be willing to serve on a commission with a man who had deliberately and falsely accused him of fornication. Third, contra Murray, Rutherford's enemies did use this incident against him late in his life, describing him as "louse in hes zouthe (youth)." Next, Rutherford did have a child with Eupham Hamilton. If he had married her nine months previously, it is hard to conceive of how such a charge as fornication would have stuck. Finally, Coffey notes that Rutherford makes frequent mention of the sins of his youth, which Coffey takes to refer to the Edinburgh scandal.[88] The weight of the evidence seems to rest with Adamson and Coffey.

1.2.2 Theological Training

Whatever the great scandal was, the immediate implication was that Rutherford walked away from his academic career, at least for a time. While away from the University, he married Eupham Hamilton, a woman about whom very little is known. He was married to her for a mere five years, after which she succumbed to a tormenting illness that lasted the span of thirteen months. As to the number of children that this marriage produced, we can only be certain of one. Nevertheless, this child and any others predeceased their mother.[89]

Shortly after stepping down from the Chair of Humanity, Rutherford began his study of theology under Andrew Ramsay (1574–1659). There is frustratingly little known about the course of theology in which Rutherford participated under Ramsay. Rollock's *Tractatus de Vocatione Efficaci*, Robert Boyd's massive and comprehensive *In Epistolam Pauli Apostoli ad Ephesios*, and Rutherford's *Examen Arminianismi* as well as his *Disputatio Scholastica* provide a window into the theological education of seventeenth century Scotland. Ramsay left behind only an exhortation, *A Warning to Come out of Babylon*, to a Jesuit who converted to the Reformed Church of Scotland. Though short, Ramsay's exhortation presents many of the major theological interests and points of controversy common in seventeenth century Scotland.[90]

---

88 Coffey, *Politics, Religion and the British Revolutions*, 38.

89 Coffey, 40.

90 Andrew Ramsay, *A Warning to Come Out of Babylon, in a Sermon Preached by Master Andrew Ramsay, Minister at Edinburgh; at the Receiving of Thomas Abernathie, Sometime Jesuite, into the Society of the Truly Reformed Church of Scotland* (Edinburgh: George Anderson, 1638).

G.D. Henderson has commented and convincingly argued that the Synod of Dort was a measuring stick for the standard of orthodoxy in seventeenth century Scotland.[91] Though Ramsay never mentions the Synod explicitly, the opening paragraphs of *A Warning* nod to the major doctrinal disputes of Dort, arguing for the corruption of the soul under the power of sin, the case for divine and unconditional election, the atonement made for the elect, the irresistible work of the Spirit in sealing the soul for the day of redemption, as well as the perseverance of the elect. Ramsay's reference to the elect in every age was part of the important apologetic task demonstrating that the Reformed Church of Scotland was not an innovative body, but rather stood in line with the catholic church throughout the ages.[92]

One of the more interesting, and unexpected features of *A Warning* is Ramsay's identification of saints through the ages. Prosper of Aquitaine (390–455), Hilary of Poitiers (310–367), and Augustine of Hippo (354–430) are identified as saints who defended the orthodox doctrines of God's true church. Cyprian (200–258), Jerome (345–420), and Gregory Bishop of Rome (540–604), are acknowledged as heroes who stood against the threat of idolatry. Rabanus Marus (780–856), Ratramnus (800–868), John Scotus Eriugena (815–877), Berenger of Tours (999–1088), and John Duns Scotus (1266–1308) are all listed as saints who held to orthodox doctrine. Aside from demonstrating the self-conscious Catholic nature of seventeenth century Scottish Reformed theology, this list also gives us a snapshot of patristic and medieval authorities from Rutherford's own professor in theology. Moving beyond the patristic and medieval period, Ramsay mentions John Wycliffe (1320–1384), Jan Hus (1369–1415), Lorenzo Valla (1407–1457), Desiderius Erasmus (1466–1536), and Beatus Rhenanus (1485–1547). Interestingly, the sole Protestant Reformer in Ramsay's list is Martin Luther (1483–1546), a man who loomed large in Rutherford's own writings.[93]

According to Ramsay, one of the key indicators of divine election in ages past was sincere and dogged opposition to idolatry. The matrix of ideas that compose the Scottish covenanting tradition, particularly those that identified the people and monarch's responsibility to drive out idolatry, are implicitly seen in Ramsay's *A Warning*. They would be explicit in Rutherford's graduation, upon which he would have been required to "take the Covenant" himself pledging to drive far from Scotland all idolatries. The tradition of "banding" and covenanting had a clear impact upon Rutherford's theology. He used the specific practice of national

---

91 Henderson, *Religious Life in Seventeenth-Century Scotland.* See especially Chapter 4, 77–99.

92 For more on this apologetic task, as well as the Scots perception that the Covenanter movement had older catholic roots, see: S. A. Burrel, "The Apocalyptic Vision of the Early Covenanters," *The Scottish Historical Review* 43, no. 135 (1964): 1–24.

93 See especially: Rutherford, *A Survey of the Spiritual Antichrist,* 129–161.

covenanting as a theological framework, as political philosophy, as a means of accountability in theological and ecclesiological disputes, as well as a mechanism of personal piety.[94] When Rutherford took the Covenant, he was not simply pledging to maintain a system of church government or to defend points of Reformed orthodoxy. Rather, he was taking a solemn oath before God, replete with blessings and curses of biblical proportions.[95]

1.2.3 Ministry at Anwoth

At the completion of his theological training Rutherford had to be licensed for ministry. According to Henderson, the licensing was conducted by the presbyteries and could last several months. The prospective ministers were given exercises in Hebrew and Greek. They were also queried in theology, which consisted of being given a text in Latin from the patristic or medieval period on a common point of doctrine. They were expected to comment on the text and provide critical analysis, contrasting and comparing the text to other theologians and linking it to their contemporary context. Even for ministers, skill in scholastic disputation was therefore not taken for granted. Finally, the candidate was asked to prepare a popular sermon.[96]

Rutherford's ministry at Anwoth lasted from 1627 until 1636. Murray records that before Rutherford arrived, the congregation at Anwoth had a pastoral visit once every other week, when a sermon was preached in the morning and people were (presumably) visited and catechized in the afternoon.[97] Though the congregation had not enjoyed consistent ministry, Anwoth had benefited from William Daglesh, who had upheld the soteriological interests of the Reformed tradition, Presbyterian polity, as well as the robust spirituality that typified the "godly" party.[98]

---

94 For examples see: Samuel Rutherford, *The Due Right of Presbyteries or, A Peaceable Plea, for the Government of the Church of Scotland* (London: E. Griffin for Richard Whittaker and Andrew Crook, 1644), 60, 96–7, 101, 109, 110, 189–90; Samuel Rutherford, *The Covenant of Life Opened: Or a Treatise of the Covenant of Grace* (Edinburgh: Robert Brown, 1655), 118–19; Rutherford, *Lex Rex: The Law and the Prince*, 148, 151, 179–80, 192, 215, 231–32, 250, 336, 379, 399–400, 427.

95 For more on the Scottish covenanting tradition, see Daniel J. Elazar, *Covenant and Commonwealth: From Christian Separation Through the Protestant Reformation*, vol. 2 (New Brunswick and London: Transaction Publishers, 1996); R. L. Greaves, "John Knox and the Covenant Tradition," *Journal of Ecclesiastical History* 24, no. 1 (1973): 23–32. Knox records the first "bands," or Covenants in John Knox, *The Historie of the Reformation of the Church of Scotland; Containing Five Books: Together with Some Treatises Conducing to the History*, vol. 1 (London: John Raworth for George Thomason and Octavian Pullen, 1644), 110; 150.

96 Henderson, *Religious Life in Seventeenth-Century Scotland*, 124–25.

97 Murray, *The Life of Samuel Rutherford*, 38.

98 Murray, *The Life of Samuel Rutherford*, 39.

The surrounding area of Kirkcudbright, only seven miles from Anwoth, shared similar commitments. John Welsh, the son-in-law of John Knox had been the minister there and instilled the Reformed faith and Presbyterian polity deeply into the lives of the people in the surrounding area, leaving behind a legacy of Reformed and "godly" pastors with whom Rutherford would seek companionship, plan to strengthen the church, and plot against the rising tide of prelacy.[99]

Rutherford was reported to have risen at three in the morning, spending the early part of the day in prayer and study and the later in visitations. Visitations could have been to strengthen and encourage the sick and suffering or to catechize families. During Rutherford's time at Anwoth, like many other "godly" pastors in seventeenth century Britain, he wrote a catechism. This catechism would most likely have been the one used on his visitations. It provides valuable insights into his organization of the major headings of doctrine as well as how he accommodated the complex doctrines of the schools, making them accessible for the local parish.[100]

Rutherford was also responsible for preaching. This happened twice on the Sabbath, though at times due to illness Rutherford was restricted to only once per Sabbath. Woodrow has described Rutherford as "one of the most moving and affectionate preachers of his time."[101] It is hard not to feel Rutherford's personal wonder at the subjects upon which he preached and it is easy to imagine that his wonder would be infectious. Rutherford reports of spontaneous outbreaks of ecstasy, crying, laughing, and praise during his worship meetings. He believed such displays of emotions could be works of the Spirit and even argued such displays were inviting to God.[102] Similar activity was not uncommon in eighteenth century North American revivalism. Rutherford's revivalism, if it can be called that, was not confined to Anwoth. A significant part of his ministry was devoted to organizing communion fairs and festivals. Leigh Eric Schmidt has argued that the Scottish communion fairs, of which Rutherford both planned and preached, were precursors to the American revivals of the Great Awakening.[103]

Rutherford also lent his strength to the difficult and highly political task of advancing Reformed theology and Presbyterian polity in Scotland. He entered the ministry in turbulent times when Presbyterian power began to recede due to James's preference for prelacy. James consolidated his preference through passage

---

99 Thomson, *Samuel Rutherford*, 22.
100 See: Samuel Rutherford, "Ane Catachisme: Conteining the Soume of Christian Religion," in *Catechisms of the Second Reformation*, ed. Alexander F. Mitchell (London: James Nisbet & Co, 1886).
101 Quoted from: Thomson, *Samuel Rutherford*, 23.
102 Rutherford, *A Survey of the Spiritual Antichrist*, 304–5.
103 For an example of Rutherford organizing for a communion festival see his letter to Marion Mc-Naught in: Rutherford, *Joshua Redivivus*, 434–5. See also: Leigh Eric Schmidt, *Holy Fairs: Scotland and the Making of American Revivalism*, 2nd ed. (Grand Rapids, MI: W. B. Eerdmans Pub, 2001).

of The Five Articles, which were first proposed to a general assembly following his visit to Scotland in 1617. They were not passed until an assembly held at Perth in 1618. These were later ratified by parliament in 1621. The Articles permitted private baptisms and private communion, which Rutherford would forcefully oppose later in life.[104] However, these same Articles also enshrined episcopal confirmation, observance of the holy days of Christ's life, and kneeling at communion. Kneeling at communion would have been especially pernicious to the Scots who celebrated communion at tables. For the Scots, kneeling during communion smacked of Roman idolatry, which many of the Scottish ministers had already pledged to drive far from the land. Because James was able to have such acts passed without a revolution is generally viewed as a testimony to his political skill. This skill, however, was not passed down to his son Charles, who pursued James's reforms in Scotland with equal parts clumsiness and ruthlessness.[105]

The tensions are brought out clearly in Rutherford's letters while at Anwoth. As early as 1630, Rutherford can be seen warning his patrons against the "masks of Antichristian ceremonies," that no doubt referred to the Laudian reforms that Charles I imposed upon the Scottish Kirk.[106] Elsewhere he speaks of a "wearied Lord Jesus," seeking lodging in Scotland, but finding none because the "irreverent Bishops" have come in with the "din and noise of ceremonies, holy-days, and other Romish corruptions."[107] The sense of the impending crisis for Rutherford and the Scottish "godly" comes across most clearly in a letter to Lady Kenmure dated June 26, 1630. He wrote:

> We are in great fears of a great and fearful trial to come upon the kirk of God; for these, who would build their houses and nests upon the ashes of mourning Jerusalem, have drawn our king upon hard and dangerous confusions, against such are termed Puritans, for the rooting of them out. Our prelates (Lord take the keys of his house from these bastard porters) assure us, that for such as will not conform, there is nothing but imprisonment and deprivation. The spouse of Jesus will ever be in the fire; but I trust in my God, she shall not consume, because of the good-will of him who dwelleth in the bush, for he dwelleth

---

104 John Lightfoot, *The Whole Words of the Rev. John Lightfoot D.D*, ed. J. R. Pitman (London: J.F. Dove, 1824), 297.

105 For more information regarding the Articles of Perth see: Julian Goodare, "The Scottish Parliament of 1621," *The Historical Journal* 38, no. 1 (1995): 29–51; Laura A.M. Stewart, "The Political Repercussions of the Five Articles of Perth: A Reassessment of James VI and I's Religious Policies in Scotland," *The Sixteenth Century Journal* 38, no. 4 (2007): 1013–36; John D. Ford, "The Lawful Bonds of Scottish Society: The Five Articles of Perth, the Negative Confession and the National Covenant," *The Historical Journal* 37, no. 1 (1994): 45–64.

106 Rutherford, *Joshua Redivivus*, 325.

107 Rutherford, 328.

in it with good will. All sorts of crying sins without controulment abound in our land; the glory of the Lord is departing from Israel, and the Lord is looking back over his shoulder, to see if any will say, Lord tarry, and no man requesteth him to stay.[108]

Rutherford not only feared for the Kirk, but by this time it is clear that he feared for his own life. In the same letter he tells Lady Kenmure that he had been summoned before the High Commission Court. These courts, first instituted by James in 1610, were noticeably different under James's son Charles. Whereas James had a sense of how to use the high courts, often exercising remarkable restraint in cases of insubordination, Charles had neither his father's political savvy nor patience.[109] Worse was Charles's Archbishop, William Laud (1573–1645), whose persecutions contributed to tens of thousands of "godly" fleeing to the New World.[110] Fortunately for Rutherford, a great storm arose on the day he was meant to appear before the commission, preventing the Bishops from making safe passage to the trial. As if he was not under enough pressure, he laments at the end of the letter, that his wife, whom we met earlier, "[has] departed this life." He added solemnly, "the Lord hath done it, blessed be his name."[111]

Though Charles ascended to the throne in 1625 he would not visit Scotland until 1633. As if this delayed visit was not enough to injure Scottish pride, Charles determined that his coronation as King of Scots in 1633 would be a communion service done according to the English Book of Common Prayer. Austin Woolrych notes that the service, being unfamiliar to the Scots, would have struck them as "half way to the Mass."[112] Charles had also determined to call a parliament during

---

108 Rutherford, 328.

109 James's patience and political skill is on its greatest display with the Melville brothers. See: Stephen King, "Your Best and Maist Faithfull Subjects": Andrew and James Melville as James VI and I's "loyal opposition," *Renaissance and Reformation / Renaissance et Reforme* 24, no. 3 (2000)): 17–30. Despite the undeniably difficult situation in which Charles was placed, he is nevertheless widely recognized as lacking the political skill of his father. Hugh Trevor-Roper, *Archbishop Laud 1573–1645*, 2nd ed. (London: Macmillan and Co, Limited, 1962); Austin Woolrych, *Britain in Revolution 1625–1660* (Oxford: Oxford University Press, 2002); and Peter Donald, *An Uncounselled King: Charles I and the Scottish Troubles 1637–1641*, Cambridge Studies in Early Modern British History (Cambridge: Cambridge University Press, 2004).

110 Woolrych, *Britain in Revolution*, 80–1.

111 Rutherford, *Joshua Redivivus*, 328–29.

112 Charles's marriage to Henrietta Maria of France required a number of political concessions relaxing laws regarding Roman Catholics, which would only have fueled rumors of a reestablishment of Roman Catholicism. See Robert E. Shimp, "A Catholic Marriage for an Anglican Prince," *Historical Magazine of the Protestant Episcopal Church* 50, no. 1 (1981): 3–18. See also Woolrych, *Britain in Revolution 1625–1660*, 126–28.

his stay in Scotland. Rutherford had low expectations for the stalwartness of the Scottish representatives, writing again to Lady Kenmure:

> I am afraid now (as many others are) that at the sitting down of our parliament, our Lord Jesus his spouse shall be roughly handled: and it must be so, since false and declining Scotland, whom our Lord took off the dunghill of hell, and made a fair bride to himself; hath broken her faith to her sweet Husband, and hath put on the forehead of a whore; and therefore he saith, he will remove.[113]

Rutherford's crude description of the state of the church no doubt reflected his feelings that Scotland had breached that most sacred pledge that existed in the Kirk at that time, the National Covenant. Rutherford's concerns for the parliament were not entirely unwarranted. Charles's "Coronation Parliament" of 1633 succeeded in its primary aim of passing the highly controversial "revocation." The revocation was the right of a new king to revoke any grants of royal property that were made in his name before he came of age.[114] Charles expanded the purview of the revocation, insisting that all land granted for the past sixty years, all the way back to 1540, that had been annexed without parliamentary consent, should be returned to the king.[115] The primary targets in the revocation were those lands that once belonged to the Roman Church, which had been sold to the crown or the Lords after the Reformation. As Walter Makey points out, the lands re-acquired by the revocation were "earmarked for the endowment of bishoprics."[116] Charles was taking land from Presbyterian landowners and gifting it to strengthen the hands of the much-hated prelates. To make matters worse, the same Coronation Parliament that oversaw a massive transfer of wealth and land to the bishops also re-confirmed the Articles of Perth, affirmed Charles's right to regulate clerical dress, and insisted that the members of the Court of Session take communion kneeling after the manner of the English service book once a year at the King's chapel in Holyrood.[117]

By 1634 rumors were circulating that Charles was having the Scottish Bishops prepare a service book that would bring the Kirk into conformity with the Church of England. It was this year that Rutherford ran afoul of the High Commission for the second time. "Send me word," he wrote to his trusted friend Marion Macknaught, "if you obtain any thing at my Lord's hands, anent the giving up of our names to the high commission." He continued:

---

113 Rutherford, *Joshua Redivivus*, 341.

114 Woolrych, *Britain in Revolution*, 86.

115 Woolrych, 87.

116 Walter Makey, *The Church of the Covenant 1637–1651: Revolution and Social Change in Scotland* (Edinburgh: John Donald Publishers LTD, 1979), 14.

117 Woolrych, *Britain in Revolution*, 91.

I hear daily what hath been spoken of myself most unjust and falsly; and no marvel, the dragon with the swing of his tail, hath made the third part of the stars to fall from heaven, and the fallen would have many to fall with them.[118]

The papers that most likely fell into the king's hands was Rutherford's treatise defending conventicles, although it must not be ruled out that some of his correspondence, unflattering to both King and bishops, may have been responsible. Either way, providence moved slowly for Rutherford. It was not until 1636 that he was called before the Court of High Commission in Edinburgh and there was deprived of his ministry and sentenced to house arrest in Aberdeen.[119]

1.2.4 Prisoner in Aberdeen

Rutherford was ultimately undone by the endeavors of Thomas Sydserf (1581–1663), the Bishop of Galloway. Sydserf, following the lead of the other Scottish bishops, had set up his own Court of High Commission in his diocese.[120] Allan Iain Macinnes notes that a distinguishing feature of the bishops under Charles and Laud was that they were willing to provoke confrontation over ecclesial conformity.[121] Ecclesial conformity was not the only reason Rutherford was hauled before the High Commission in Edinburgh. A certain book he had written "against the Arminians" as well as preaching against the Articles of Perth also caused alarm at the Court of High Commission.[122] According to Rutherford it was the *Exercitationes Apologeticae pro Divina Gratia*, published in Amsterdam in 1636, that brought him before the High Commission:

> It hath pleased our sweet Lord Jesus to let loose the malice of these interdicted lords in his house, to deprive me of my ministry at Anwoth, and to confine me eightscore miles from thence to Aberdeen: and also (which was not done to any before) to inhibit me to speak at all in Jesus his name, within his kingdom, under pain of rebellion. The cause that ripened their hatred was my book against the Arminians, whereof they accused me those three days I appeared before them.[123]

---

118 Rutherford, *Joshua Redivivus*, 462.
119 Coffey, *Politics, Religion and the British Revolutions*, 43.
120 Murray, *The Life of Samuel Rutherford*, 86.
121 Allan Iain Macinnes, *Charles I and the Making of the Covenanting Movement 1625–1641* (Edinburgh: John Donald Publishers, 2003), 155.
122 Rutherford, *Joshua Redivivus*, 1.
123 Rutherford, 1.

Makey has argued that Rutherford was politically naïve, often failing to apprehend the ramifications of his imagery and polemics.[124] Though it may be true, in the case of the *Exercitationes Apologeticae pro Divina Gratia*, it seems as if Rutherford was intentionally provoking a confrontation with the ecclesial powers. Henderson records that the Doctors at Aberdeen, who had a reputation for Arminianism as well as an enthusiasm for Laudian reforms held *exercitationes*, or exercises on disputed points of doctrine.[125] The *exercitationes*, being organized by the doctors at Aberdeen, were most likely one-sided affairs.[126] Rutherford wished to enter into the fray, which he did through his published work. In addition to the probable offense of the title, Rutherford also attacked Thomas Jackson (1579–1640) by name, a prominent theologian in Laud's circle as well as the Scottish theologian John Cameron (1579–1625), whom the Aberdeen doctors held in great esteem.[127] Furthermore, Rutherford's sustained arguments against the *scientia media* and its proponents would have provoked the doctors at Aberdeen. Burton has shown the doctors at Aberdeen relied upon Jesuits such as Pedro Fonseca, Luis de Molina, and Francisco Suárez, not only to resource non-controversial doctrines such as the Holy Trinity, but also more controversial matters relating to God's providence and free will.[128] It would have been hard for the Aberdeen doctors not to view Rutherford's *Exercitationes* as an intentional provocation.

Rutherford was under more serious accusations than skirmishing with the favorite theologians of the Aberdeen doctors. He also fell under the charge of treason. "Now for myself," he wrote to John Stewart, "I was three days before the high commission, and accused of treason preached against our king: a minister being witness, went well nigh to swear it."[129] It is easy to see how in preaching or a heated private conversation he may have let his words get away from him. "Kings earthly are well favoured little clay gods," he wrote to Lord Lindsay. They are "time's idols." But a

---

124 Makey, *The Church of the Covenant 1637–1651*, 19.

125 Henderson, *Religious Life in Seventeenth-Century Scotland*, 125.

126 For more on the Aberdeen Doctors, see Aaron Clay Denlinger, "The Aberdeen Doctors and Henry Scougal," in *The History of Scottish Theology*, vol. 1., *Celtic Origins to Reformed Orthodoxy*, ed. David Fergusson and Mark W. Elliott (Oxford: Oxford University Press 2019); Burton, "Disputing Providence."

127 For modern scholarship on Thomas Jackson see Sarah Hutton, "Thomas Jackson, Oxford Platonist, and William Twisse, Aristotelian," *Journal of the History of Ideas* 39, no. 4 (1978): 635–52; Anne Jacobson Schutte, "An Early Stuart Critique of Machiavelli as Historiographer: Thomas Jackson and the "Discourse," *Albion: A Quarterly Journal Concerned with British Studies* 15, no. 1 (1938): 1–18. For a brief biographical sketch of Cameron see Gaston Bonet Maury, "John Cameron: A Scottish Protestant Theologian in France (1579–1625)," *The Scottish Historical Review* 7, no. 28 (1910): 325–45.

128 Burton, "Disputing Providence," 127–129.

129 Rutherford, *Joshua Redivivus*, 87 and 479.

time was coming, he continued, when "At the day of Christ, truth shall be truth and not treason."[130]

In 1636 Rutherford was caught up in a purge of non-conforming churchmen and banished to Aberdeen. Early in his imprisonment Rutherford began to appeal to the nobility to join him in resistance. In March of 1636, Rutherford wrote to Lord Lowdon, "I would the zeal of God were in the nobles to do their part for Christ."[131] Rutherford explicitly ruled out any kind of armed resistance. Rather his purpose seems to have been to prepare Lowdon for imprisonment or banishment for the sake of non-conformity.[132] To Lord Lindsay he wrote: "It is now time my worthy and noble Lord, for you who are the little nurse-fathers (under our sovereign prince) to put on courage for the Lord Jesus."[133] He also encouraged Lord Lindsay to "engage your estate and nobility for this noble King Jesus."[134] To the Earl of Cassilis he demanded "set your shoulder under the Lord's glory, now falling to the ground, and to back Christ now, when so many think it wisdom to let him fend for himself."[135] Such exhortations provide a more balanced portrait to Rutherford's understanding of God's providential governing of the affairs of Scotland. The government of all things is "upon Christ's shoulders," but for Rutherford such confidence did not lead to the stoic withdrawal from public affairs or resigned conformity popular amongst certain noble persons.[136] As can be seen from the above exhortations, God's sovereignty did not excuse human responsibility or the free exercise of effort in obedience to the covenant.[137]

Rutherford's efforts appear to have paid off. On July 23, 1637 the new service book was set to be unveiled at St. Giles by the Bishop and the Dean of the Cathedral. Nobles and the City Fathers were also required to attend. It was hoped that their presence would communicate that both the civil and the ecclesiastical authorities would enforce the new service book. Makey, citing Guthrie, argues that David Dickson and Hugh Henderson, fellow ministers and correspondents of Rutherford's,

---

130 Rutherford, 65.

131 Rutherford, 34.

132 "I dare not speak to others what God hath done to the soul of this poor, afflicted, exiled prisoner: his comfort is more than I ever knew before." Rutherford, 34.

133 Rutherford, 65.

134 Rutherford, 66.

135 Rutherford, 74.

136 Rutherford, 419.

137 For more on the neo-stoicism popular amongst some of the Scottish nobility, see John Robertson, *The Case for the Enlightenment: Scotland and Naples 1680–1760*, Ideas in Context (Cambridge: Cambridge University Press, 2005), 121.

came to Edinburgh in April of 1637 to organize resistance to the new service book.[138] A crowd turned out to riot at the unveiling of the service book. The dean was pelted with stools, bibles, and rocks. The crowd outside of St. Giles battered at the door and flung stones through the newly renovated windows. The bishop was attacked by the angry mob, but nevertheless escaped with his life.[139]

The non-conformists organized into groups to petition the King to suspend the service book. The petitions circulated through the presbyteries. These groups eventually coalesced into an identifiable political entity called the "Supplicants," who held elections in November of 1637 for a committee to await the reply of the King to the petitions.[140] Out of these elections eventually arose a provisional government, which in February of 1638 proposed again the National Covenant. The revolutionary nature of the National Covenant has been debated, but the theological critique of kingly rule certainly held the seeds of revolution. Though the document called for the preservation of "true religion and the King's majesty," in reality the covenant regarded true religion as necessary and the King's majesty as merely contingent.[141] The covenant effectively put an end to the personal rule of Charles. As Charles's power in Scotland waned, and the influence of the bishops crumbled, Rutherford was released from Aberdeen. He had returned to Anwoth by 1638.[142]

1.3 University Career and Westminster Assembly (1639–1646)

1.3.1 Professor at the University of St Andrews

One of the tasks of the assembly that gathered following the Covenanter Revolution was to "translate" clergy. In Rutherford's case this meant that the Assembly decided he was too important a figure to remain in the small country parish of Anwoth. After all, Rutherford had helped organize massive political resistance to the King and bishops through his letters as well as published a major theological treatise that was warmly received in continental Reformed circles. Though his parish at Anwoth

---

138 To Henderson, Rutherford spoke of laying a "causeway to the temple with the carcases of bastard and idol shepherds," and in March of 1636 Rutherford was clearly advising Dickson on theological as well as political matters. See: Rutherford, *Joshua Redivivus*, 18.

139 Stevenson, *The Scottish Revolution*, 61.

140 Macinnes, "Charles I and the Making of the Covenanting Movement," 166.

141 Macinnes, 136.

142 Murray, *The Life of Samuel Rutherford*, 127–30.

lodged a thoughtful protest, and Rutherford himself put up a spirited defense, both he and his congregation were forced to bend to the will of the Assembly.[143]

Though the Assembly knew he was too important to remain at Anwoth, it was not entirely clear where he should be sent. His alma mater, the University of Edinburgh, made an attempt to bring him back as a professor on February 27, 1639.[144] However, St Andrews University pointed out that the Chair of Divinity was not open in Edinburgh, and though Rutherford's ministerial gifting was well recognized, if he were at St Andrews his academic gifting would "in a few yiers…make many able minsters." He was accordingly appointed to St Andrews by the 1639 Assembly and took his post in October of the same year.[145]

Robert Woodrow reports that Rutherford "would not take a Professour's place without having some pastoral charge." As a result of this, he forged an arrangement with the town and University to serve under Robert Blair (1593–1666), a minister in the city of St Andrews of whom Rutherford showed enormous respect.[146] St Andrews was the seat of the primate of Scotland as well as a center of resistance to the National Covenant. Rutherford's appointment was not merely for the sake of future ministerial candidates but also a shrewd move by the Assembly to place a man committed to the Covenanter cause at the center of resistance.[147]

Rutherford set to work quickly. It was during this period that he began the lectures that would become the *Disputatio Scholastica de Divina Providentia*. He also continued to participate in the Covenanter cause, participating in the *bellum episcopi* (Bishop's war) as a chaplain.[148] The English troops were routed on August 28, 1640 at the Battle of Newburn. Six days before the battle of Newburn Rutherford preached "A Charge to the Prophet."[149] The sermon is a delicate balance of trusting God's providential governance while exhorting the troops to allow their wills to be guided by the grace of God.[150] The battle that followed days later confirmed the assertions of the National Covenant, a subject of Rutherford's sermon, in blood.[151] Charles's personal rule would never again be what he had conceived it to be. The

---

143 For the congregation's letter of protest see Murray, *The Life of Samuel Rutherford*, 151–3. For Rutherford's own protests, see Rutherford, *Joshua Redivivus*, 339.

144 Murray, *The Life of Samuel Rutherford*, 157.

145 Murray, 158.

146 Woodrow, *Analecta*, 3:89.

147 Murray, *The Life of Samuel Rutherford*, 169.

148 For an excellent overview see: Mark Charles Fissel, *The Bishop's Wars: Charles I's Campaigns against Scotland 1638–1640* (Cambridge: Cambridge University Press, 1994).

149 Samuel Rutherford, *Quaint Sermons of Samuel Rutherford Hitherto Unpublished* (London: Hodder and Stoughton, 1885), 43–65.

150 Rutherford, 58.

151 Rutherford argued that God's anger burned against his own people because they had transgressed the covenant. See Rutherford, *Quaint Sermons of Samuel Rutherford*, 45.

Scottish victory at Newburn also ensured that the crown and parliament would have to reckon the Scottish Kirk and state as major players in future matters of British politics.[152]

Several months before the battle of Newburn, Rutherford married again. His wife's name was Jean McMath, and with her he would have three children over the span of the next three years.[153] Outside of his family responsibilities Rutherford became embroiled in ecclesial controversies within the Kirk. The debates, held at the General Assembly at Aberdeen in 1640, revolved around the practice of private prayer meetings called "conventicles." These private prayer meetings proved useful before the Covenanter's Revolution, when Covenanting ministers had been driven to work outside of the establishment. Now that the Covenanters were the establishment, the conventicles appeared a threat. The matter was put before the assembly in 1640 and was opposed by Rutherford. His efforts fell short. The Assembly passed a law forbidding all persons who were not ministers from expounding upon the scriptures and that private worship should be confined to family members.[154]

The other ecclesial controversy in which Rutherford became embroiled was the matter of independency, which at the time was called "Brownism." The term refers to Robert Browne (c. 1550–1633), a Protestant Congregationalist who believed that genuine reformation could not exist in an ecclesial body with a national profession. Rather, genuine reformation began with the regenerate individual, who withdrew from society to form a truly spiritual, regenerate community of saints.[155] Rutherford himself was identified with the Brownists by his nemesis Bishop Sydserf, presumably for his demand that the church be purely reformed according to the scriptures.[156]

Rutherford responded to the Brownists in his book *A Peaceable and Temporate Plea for Paul's Presbyterie in Scotland*.[157] Those familiar with Rutherford's more acidic forms of polemic will be surprised at the moderate, friendly tone of this particular work. Throughout the book he spoke persuasively to his "friends," and fellow lovers of truth and godliness who "possibly liketh not well of Presbyteriall government."[158] Rutherford maintained his warm tone throughout, and at times appears to make certain concessions in regards to conventicles and freedom in

---

152 Stevenson, *The Scottish Revolution*, Chapter 6, 183–213.

153 Murray, *The Life of Samuel Rutherford*, 374.

154 Murray, 182.

155 Robert Harrison, *The Brownists in Norwich and Norfolk about 1580* (New York, NY: The MacMillan Co, 1920), 3.

156 See D. G. Mullan, *Scottish Puritanism 1590–1638* (Oxford: Oxford University Press, 2000), 130.

157 Samuel Rutherford, *The Divine Right of Church Government and Excommunication: Or a Peaceable Dispute for the Perfection of the Holy Scripture in Point of Ceremonies and Church Government* (London: John Field for Christopher Meredith, 1646).

158 See "To the Christian Reader" in Rutherford, *The Divine Right of Church Government and Excommunication*, B-B4r.

corporate worship that Coffey has described as a nod to independency.[159] Though he believed them to be in error, he nevertheless expressed that God would forgive them for such errors.[160] Elsewhere, lamenting the divisions tearing apart the church in Scotland, Rutherford expressed his gratitude for the Brownists and independents who he believed came closest to his own party as being "walkers with God."[161]

1.3.2 The Solemn League

While Rutherford and the Scots were busying themselves consolidating their victory, the Long Parliament, an outcome of the Treaty of Ripon, had devolved into a tangled mess. By August of 1642, Parliament and Charles had reached an impasse. On the 22nd of the same month, the King raised his standard at Nottingham effectively signaling the beginning of the English Civil War. Things did not start well for Charles, but by the summer of 1643 he had the upper hand over the parliamentary forces. Parliament appealed to the Scottish Lairds, who agreed overwhelmingly to support the Parliamentary forces upon the condition that they signed a treaty called the *Solemn League and Covenant*.[162]

This is the immediate backdrop to the Westminster Assembly. The English Parliament's Assembly had been called earlier in 1643 to produce a "confession of faith, form of church-government, directory of worship" and a directory for "catechizing." By virtue of the *Solemn League and Covenant*, Scottish delegates were invited to become full members of the Assembly, however they declined. Robert Letham has argued that too much attention had been paid to the Scottish delegates at Westminster, noting that they were "not members at all."[163] However, membership is not necessarily equivalent to influence. As Chad B. Van Dixhoorn has noted, the Scots were quick to realize that "they would have an influence disproportionate to their number if they remained a separate entity at the Assembly." The Scots, Rutherford included, had other plans to exercise influence upon Westminster.[164]

---

159 Coffey, *Politics, Religion and the British Revolutions*, 201–2. See also Rutherford, *The Divine Right of Church Government and Excommunication*, 325–26.

160 Rutherford, *Joshua Redivivus*, 431.

161 Rutherford, 483.

162 Woolrych, *Britain in Revolution 1625–1660*, 234.

163 Robert Letham, *The Westminster Assembly: Reading its Theology in Historical Context* (Phillipsburg: P&R Publishing, 2009), 41, 48.

164 Chad B. van Dixhoorn, "Unity and Disunity at the Westminster Assembly (1643–1649): A Commemorative Essay," *The Journal of Presbyterian History* 79, no. 2 (2001): 103–17.

1.3.3 The Westminster Assembly

The Scots selected five ministers to attend the Assembly. These were Samuel Rutherford, Alexander Henderson (1583–1646), Robert Douglas (1594–1674), Robert Baillie (1599–1662) and George Gillespie (1613–1648). They were to be accompanied by John Kennedy the Earl of Cassilis (1601–1668), Lord John Maitland (1616–1682), and Archibald Johnstone of Warristone (1611–1663). Baillie records that virtually none selected wished to attend, but only Douglas and Kennedy failed to appear.[165] A large part of their strategy depended upon pamphlets and book length publications against their theological opponents. In the fall of 1643, Rutherford was not only arguing furiously in the Assembly against independency, he was also laboring privately to produce a book against the independents. Baillie recorded on January 1, 1644 that "Rutherford's other large book against the Independents is on the press, and will do good."[166] The book was *The Due Right of Presbyteries* published in London in 1644.[167] The work is heavily scholastic in nature, subjecting New England Congregationalism to a friendly, yet at times overwhelming, critique. The work is over 700 pages and enlists the aid of dozens upon dozens of authorities ranging from patristic, medieval, reformation, to post-Reformation Reformed as well as Roman Catholic. Baillie not only eagerly anticipated this book, but also planned for Rutherford to prepare for battle in the Assembly upon its publication.[168]

In 1644 Rutherford published his *Lex Rex*.[169] He had labored on a work of political theory since at least 1643, though the occasion for refining and ultimately publishing the work was the provocation of John Maxwell's royalist treatise, *Sacro-Sancta Regum Majestas; or, The Sacred and Royal Prerogative of Christians Kings*, which appeared in print in 1644.[170] From its intellectual context, *Lex Rex* is often described as a work of natural law political theory, however its extensive use of biblical revelation as well as resources from patristic and medieval theology mean that its designation as a work of natural law political theory is better qualified by the word "Christian."[171] Thus, *Lex Rex* is not only the work of a political theorist,

---

165 Robert Baillie, *The Letters and Journals of Robert Baillie, A.M. Principal of the University of Glasgow. M.DC.XXXVII.—M.DC.LXII. Edited from the Author's Manuscripts*, ed. David Lang (Edinburgh: Robert Ogle, 1842), 55.

166 Baillie, 124.

167 Rutherford, *The Due Right of Presbyteries or, A Peaceable Plea, for the Government of the Church of Scotland* (London: E. Griffin for Richard Whittaker and Andrew Crook, 1644).

168 Baillie, *The Letters and Journals of Robert Baillie*, 161.

169 Rutherford, *Lex Rex: The Law and the Prince*.

170 Maxwell, *Sacro-Sancta Regum Majestas*; see also Coffey, *Politics, Religion and the British Revolutions*, 148.

171 See Coffey's helpful remarks in Coffey, *Politics, Religion and the British Revolutions*, 146–57; and J. F. Maclear, "Samuel Rutherford: The Law and the King," in *Calvinism and the Political Order: Essay*

but also, if not especially, the work of a Reformed theologian. The nature of the *Lex Rex*, as well as its extensive use of medieval distinctions common to scholasticism, reveal it to be the work of a theologian trained and committed to the methodology of the schools. Finally, as many commentators have noted, there are numerous distinctively Scottish features of the *Lex Rex*, such as its deep reflection on the typically Scottish theme of covenanting, its reliance upon scholastic argumentation, as well as its backwards glance to Scottish history and sources.[172]

Outside of Westminster, matters were slowly deteriorating between Parliament and the Assembly. Disagreements arose as to who had the final say in matters of excommunication. The Presbyterian majority at the Assembly desired that the power of excommunication remain in control of the presbytery. Parliament argued that the power of excommunication ought to remain in the hands of the government. Rutherford contributed to this debate for the Presbyterians with *The Divine Right of Church Government and Excommunication* published in London in 1646. Once again, Rutherford produced a dazzling demonstration of his learning, as well as his serious commitment to scholastic methodology.[173]

1.4   Final Years (1647–1661)

1.4.1 Resolutioners and Remonstrants

The General Assembly of Scotland recommended Rutherford become the Principal of New College in August of 1647. He remained in London during the fall to finish work on both the Long and Short Westminster Catechisms. He was released from the Westminster Assembly on November 9, 1647. The Prolocutor, by order of the Assembly, and in the name of the Assembly, expressed its thanks to Rutherford personally.[174] Despite the accolades, a storm was brewing. Cromwell's ascension

---

Prepared for the Woodrow Wilson Lectureship of the National Presbyterian Center Washington, D.C, ed. George L. Hunt (Philadelphia: The Westminster Press, 1965), 65–87.

172 See especially John D. Ford, "*Lex, rex iusto posita*: Samuel Rutherford on the Origins of Government," in *Scots and Britons: Scottish Political Thought and the Union of 1603*, ed. Robert A. Mason (Cambridge: Cambridge University Press, 1994), 262–290.

173 Samuel Rutherford, *The Divine Right of Church Government and Excommunication: Or a Peaceable Dispute for the Perfection of the Holy Scripture in Point of Ceremonies and Church Government in which the Removal of the Service Book is Justifi'd* (London: John Field for Christopher Meredith, 1646).

174 *Minutes of the Sessions of the Westminster Assembly of Divines*, eds. Rev. Alex F. Mitchell and Rev. John Struthers (Edinburgh: William Blackwood and Sons, 1874), 487–8.

gave independency the advantage, which the Scots viewed as a threat to the Solemn League and Covenant.[175]

Rutherford's concern over the ascendancy of the independents is reflected in his publications during this period. In 1647 he published *Christ Dying and Drawing Sinners to Himself* in London.[176] Though mostly pastoral in nature, it is not without polemical jabs at Arminians, Antinomians, and Libertines. In 1648 he published *A Survey of the Spiritual Antichrist*. This was an attack upon the Antinomians and the Familists, who Rutherford had come to believe were exercising an enormous influence upon Cromwell's New Model Army.[177] In 1649 he published his *Free Disputation Against Pretended Liberty of Conscience*. In *A Free Disputation* Rutherford returned again to matters of the covenant:

> A word to the wise of forcing within, and of the Covenant, endeavouring of uniformity, not the Prelaticall in Ceremonies and canonicall obedience, which *Familists* impute to the Covenant, but Scripturall uniformity in the same faith and forme of wholesome words, and externall worship and ordering of it, which is not indifferent, as *Libertines* and *Familists,* who in this are breathing in *England,* (but we intended good to men, not to sects) endeavouring of nearest uniformity in the three kingdoms, which we did sweare is contrary to actuall tolerating of all sects and Religions, but the Sectaries endeavor the later, and have compassed it, *ergo,* the Sectaries are gone contrary to their Oath and Covenant.[178]

Rutherford believed true Christianity was not only about passionate love for God, but it was also about faithful obedience to the commands of God. These commands included the proper ordering of the church, which he and many others had covenanted to discover from scripture for the uniformity and reformation of religion in the three kingdoms. Rutherford believed that independency and toleration were a casting aside of this common goal, which was sealed by covenant. Cast aside the covenant and one might as well cast aside the presence and power of Christ. Or at least, so thought Rutherford.[179]

---

175 The Scots had outlined their concerns in a letter to English Divines at Westminster. See *A Declaration and Brotherly Exhortation of the General Assembly of the Church of Scotland, Met at Edinburgh August 20, 1647. To Their Brethren of England* (Edinburgh: Evan Tyler, 1647).

176 Samuel Rutherford, *Christ Dying and Drawing Sinners to Himselfe or a Survey of our Saviour in His Soule Suffering, His Lovelyness in His Death, and the Efficacie Thereof* (London: J.D. for Andrew Crooke, 1647).

177 Rutherford, *A Survey of the Spiritual Antichrist,* (London: J.D. for Andrew Crooke 1648).

178 Samuel Rutherford, *A Free Disputation Against Pretended Liberty of Conscience* (London: Andrew Crook, 1649), 231.

179 Rutherford, *Joshua Redivivus,* 517–8.

While Rutherford was grappling with issues of independency and toleration, The King's predicament worsened and eventually led to a split within the Covenanter party. On one side, the more radical Covenanters insisted that they would not throw their support behind Charles unless he signed the Covenant without reservation. By August of 1647 however, some saw the situation as quite desperate and were prepared to relax Charles's subscription to the covenant and support him anyway. In December of 1647, three Scottish commissioners signed a secret pact with Charles, which came to be known as the "Engagement." In the pact, the commissioners pledged their support to Charles. In exchange, Charles pledged to approve the *Solemn League and Covenant* in Parliament and impose Presbyterian government in the three kingdoms for the span of three years, after which he would call for a new assembly at Westminster to settle the matter of church governance.[180]

The Engagement was ratified by Parliament but drew a swift denunciation from the General Assembly of the Kirk. A series of petitions were organized against the Engagement, one being drafted by Rutherford himself. The Covenanters were effectively split into two parties, those who supported the Engagement and those who opposed it. The split placed Rutherford at odds with his one-time divinity professor Andrew Ramsay, this being only one of many unhappy divisions that resulted from the Engagement.[181]

The Engagers marched south from Scotland and were met by Cromwell at Preston in August of 1648. They were handily routed. When news of the Engagers' defeat at Preston reached Scotland, several thousand rose up and marched on Edinburgh in the name of the Kirk in what came to be known as the Whiggamore Raid. With the majority of noblemen discredited due to their association with the Engagement, the political stage was left to the radical covenanters.[182] Shortly thereafter, Charles was brought to the scaffold for treason. He died January 30, 1649. Charles's death had a chilling effect on the political prospects of the Engagers. This worked out quite well for Rutherford and his band of radical Covenanters, who had opposed the Engagement loudly and publicly for many months leading up to Hamilton's disastrous march south.[183]

---

180 For an overview of the Engagers see Robert Ashton, *Counter-Revolution: The Second Civil War and Its Origins, 1646–8* (New Haven: Yale University Press, 1994), 300–38.

181 Coffey, *Politics, Religion and the British Revolutions*, 54–5.

182 David Scott, *Politics and War in the Three Stuart Kingdoms, 1637–49*, British History in Perspective (New York: Palgrave Macmillan, 2004), 280.

183 The victory for the Radical Covenanters was short lived. Charles I's execution only served to reveal deep seated resentments and disagreements over what fidelity to the Covenant meant in politically compromised times. Charles I's execution, though providing temporary advantage to the radical Covenanters, may have ultimately spelt their doom. See Laura A.M. Stewart, *Rethinking the Scottish Revolution: Covenanted Scotland, 1637–1651* (Oxford: Oxford University Press, 2016), 256–300.

The Covenanter victory was solidified by an act excluding all Engagers from holding political office. From a position of relative strength, the Covenanters sought to bargain with Charles II, insisting a stronger pledge to the Covenant than his father had given. This was obtained on February 5, 1649 when the Covenanter party proclaimed Charles II the lawful successor to his father. The conditions of his accession to the throne were that Charles must take both covenants, agree to establish Presbyterianism in both realms, and dismiss the Engagers at court. Much like his father however, Charles II halfheartedly agreed to the covenant.[184]

The proclamation of Charles II as his father's successor provoked a strong response from Cromwell, who once again marched north with his army to confront another king. As the military position of Charles weakened, so did the Covenanter's resolve towards their oaths. Following a massive defeat by Cromwell's forces in September of 1650, certain parties within the Kirk began to argue that the battle would have been won if the army had been strengthened by the presence of Engagers and Royalists. Rutherford took a different reading of the providential hand of the Lord. It was not an army weakened by the absence of Engagers and Royalists. Rather, it was God's punishment upon a "mixed" army, which included the godly as well as "Malignants"—royalists and Engagers that spoiled the purity of the Army of the Lord. "I hope ye will mix with none of them," he wrote. If a victory were to be had, it would not be an army composed of the mixed company of "Sectaries and Malignants," but an "army of the Lord's carving."[185]

These disagreements fostered bitter and ugly disputes in the Kirk. Those who supported the weakening of the covenant by including Engagers and Royalists were called the Resolutioners, due to the two public resolutions intended to undo restrictions on the above.[186] On the other side of the divide were the Remonstrants, who on October 17, 1650 published *The Humble Remonstrance of the Gentlemen, Commanders and Ministers, attending the Forces in the West.* The Remonstrants complained of Charles's admission to the Covenant without solid evidence of a true profession, the admission of royalists and Engagers into the Scottish armies, the unjust plans to invade England and force monarchy on an independent nation, and general "backsliding from the covenant."[187]

The Resolutioners sought to silence the opposition of the Remonstrants at an Assembly held at St Andrews in July of 1651. Rutherford personally wrote against this

184 Ronald Hutton, *Charles the Second, King of England, Scotland, and Ireland* (Oxford: Oxford University Press, 1999), 37.

185 Rutherford, *Joshua Redivivus*, 411–2.

186 I. B. Cowan, "The Covenanters: A Revision Article," *The Scottish Historical Review* 47, no. 143 (1968), 42.

187 James King Hewison, *The Covenanters: A History of the Church in Scotland From the Reformation to the Revolution* (Glasgow: John Smith and Son, 1913), 2:22.

assembly, declaring it unconstitutional. Only twenty-one other ministers signed the protest.[188] Within a few short months from this divisive assembly, the Resolutioners were soundly defeated at the Battle of Worcester in September of 1651. The anti-royalist leanings of the Remonstrants found favor with Cromwell, who governed Scotland for the remainder of the decade until the restoration. The Remonstrants quickly sought to nullify any and all assemblies of a "mixed" composition, that is, those assemblies where Engagers and Resolutioners participated. Though the Covenanters were now split between the Resolutioners and Remonstrants, a further split within the Remonstrant party was to occur. Some of the Remonstrants were open to compromise with Cromwell in regard to Presbyterianism, independency, and toleration. Rutherford and an ever-shrinking number of ultra-conservative covenanters flatly refused such compromises. By the late 1650s, these divisions had caused Rutherford to become deeply alienated from many of his closest friends and colleagues.[189]

1.4.2 Rector of the University of St Andrews

However, all was not spent in controversy. In 1651 Rutherford was made Rector of the University of St Andrews, a post that could only be held by a principal of one of the university's colleges.[190] It was also during this time that he published his massive *Disputatio Scholastica de Divina Providentia*. That same year he was invited to become the Chair of Divinity at Utrecht not once but twice, declining both times. He declined a similar offer at Harderwyck in 1648.[191] Baillie records that the invitations were stirred up by Gisbertus Voetius, whom he believed to have looked with favor upon Rutherford's Latin treatises "against the Jesuits and Arminians."[192]

In 1655 he published *The Covenant of Life Opened*, a sprawling practical treatise meant to apply "Covenant-promises" to the operations of the Spirit and troubled consciences.[193] Nevertheless, even this work could not escape the polemics and divisions of the Kirk. Rutherford notes that he had recently been called a "Protester," "Schismatick," and a "Separatist" for his refusal to seek union with the Resolutioners or compromise even within his own Remonstrant party.[194] Such accusations were not helped by his highly polemical treatise *A Survey of the 'The Survey of that Sum*

---

188 Hewison, 2:35.

189 Coffey, *Politics, Religion and the British Revolutions*, 56–7.

190 Rutherford, *Disputatio Scholastica*, 247.

191 Murray, *The Life of Samuel Rutherford*, 257–62.

192 Baillie's *Letters*, 3:82.

193 Rutherford, *The Covenant of Life Opened*, (Edinburgh: Robert Brown, 1655).

194 See the "Notice to the Christian Reader" in: Rutherford, *The Covenant of Life Opened*.

of Church Discipline' wherein Rutherford accused the Resolutioners of being worse persecutors of the church than the bishops.[195] Even Rutherford's former colleagues at Westminster felt he had gone too far with such accusations.[196]

1.4.3 Death

By 1660 Rutherford was mostly isolated. His colleagues at the university were all Resolutioners. What little protection was afforded to him by Cromwell's toleration ended on the 14th of May, 1660 when Charles II was proclaimed king (for the second time) in Edinburgh. Rutherford received harsh treatment from the king. His book, *Lex Rex*, was proclaimed treasonous and burnt by the hangman. Rutherford was deprived of his position at the university, as well as of his stipend, and confined to his house. He was summoned to appear before parliament for charges of treason, but serious illness prevented him.[197] On March 8, 1661, he issued his last will and testimony. "I shall shine," he said to his friends shortly before his death. "I shall shine, I shall see him as he is, I shall see him reign." "Let my Lord's name be exalted," he said. "And if he will, let my name be grinded to pieces, that he may be all in all. If he should slay me ten thousand times ten thousand, I'll trust." Rutherford died on March 29, 1661.[198]

---

195 Samuel Rutherford, *A Survey of the 'Survey of that Summe of Church Discipline'* (London: Andrew Crook, 1658).

196 See Coffey, *Politics, Religion and the British Revolutions*, 59.

197 This final period of Rutherford's life is covered in Murray, *The Life of Samuel Rutherford*, 304–23.

198 Murray, *The Life of Samuel Rutherford*, 318–9.

2. The Doctrine of God's Being

> There is another way of praising God, formal, when we are either formally blessing God, and speaking his praises. And this I take to be twofold, 1. When we directly and formally direct praises and thanksgiving to God.... 2. When we speak good of God, and declare his glorious nature and attributes, extolling him before men to excite men to conceive highly of him.[1]

Having situated Rutherford and his works in their historical context, we are now prepared to look more specifically at his theology. The following four chapters provide an overview of Rutherford's doctrine of God with chapters devoted to God's being (Chapter 2), knowledge (Chapter 3), will (Chapter 4), and power (Chapter 5). Each are necessary precursors to understanding Rutherford's doctrine of divine providence. The current chapter begins with a focus on human knowledge of God (2.1) followed by a section on God's being, with special attention paid to the divine simplicity (2.2.1). From there the divine nameability and the problem of predication will be explored. Following this will be a brief survey of certain regulative attributes, the brevity warranted by Rutherford's scant treatment of the attributes elsewhere in his work (2.2.3–4). This chapter will conclude with remarks concerning the Trinity and the relation of the three persons to the divine attributes (2.3). Implications for the doctrine of divine providence will be identified throughout.

2.1 The Knowledge of God

2.1.1 Scripture as the Means to the Knowledge of God

Rutherford understood the task of acquiring knowledge of God, including in his essential nature, as a task worthy in and of itself (*per se*) and for its own sake (*propter se*). This approach into the investigation of God's nature was not without controversy in the seventeenth century. Critiques from contemporary polemical opponents, such as the Remonstrant Simon Episcopius (1583–1643), suggested that explorations into the divine essence and nature were grounded in philosophical speculation rather than the revealed truth of scripture. Such speculation was even

---

1 Rutherford, *Joshua Redivivus*, 178.

understood to be counterproductive to a life pleasing to God.[2] Contrary to such critiques, Rutherford argued that this task was not undertaken in spite of scripture, but rather because it is clearly commanded by God in scripture.[3]

The role of scripture and its relation to the knowledge of God is laid out principally in two works: Rutherford's *Ane Catechisme* and his *Examen Arminianismi*.[4] His comments in the *Ane Catechisme* regarding this topic are straightforward and practical.

> Quastion. Quhat is the way to lif aeternall?
>
> *Answere.* To know God and him quhom he hes sent, Jesus Christ—Joh.xvii.3.
>
> Q. Quherein standeth this knowledge?
>
> A. In faith and good works, that ar the fruits of faith.—Tit. i.16; 1 Tim i.5; Psalm xxxvii.3.
>
> Q. Quher may wes learne the doctreyne of faith?
>
> A. In Godis wisdome (1 Cor ii.6) in the Old and New Testament, conteining all things to mak us wise to salvatione.—2 Tim iii.15.[5]

There are a few points of interest in the above. To begin, knowing God is given primary place of importance in relation to eternal life. It is both the means to eternal life, as well as the goal of eternal life. Knowledge of God is acquired through scripture. This is not to discount other important avenues of gaining knowledge of God. Natural reason has certain powers of discovery in relation to God, albeit these are limited.[6] The importance of a practical knowledge of God acquired through the

---

2 Rutherford references a critique from the Dutch Remonstrant Simon Episcopius (1583–1643). See: *Confessio, sive Declaratio, Sententiae Pastorum, qui in Foederato Belgio Remonstrantes vocantur, Super praecipuis articulis Religionis Christianae* (Harderwijk: Theodorum Danielis, 1622). Elsewhere Episcopius, said to be the primary author of the *Confessio*, offers a more measured, yet nevertheless similar critique in Simon Episcopius, *Apologia Pro Confessione Declaratione Sententiae eorum, Qui in Foederato Belgio vocantur Remonstrantes, super praecipuis Articulis Religionis Christianae. Contra Censuram Quatuor Professorum Leidensium.* (1630), 40.

3 Rutherford's response to Episcopius is rendered as a "sed contra." The scholastic pattern followed by Rutherford in the *Examen* is typical. The question is asked (*Quaeritur*), followed by an opinion from a polemical opponent. The question is resolved to the contrary of the polemical opponent. Hence the "sed contra." "Sed contra. I. Ipsa cognitio, *per se*, & *propter se*, mandatur. I Chron 28.9. *Tu quoque,* Solomon, *fili, cognosce Deum Patris tui, & cole eum integro corde. Eph 4.23. Et renovemini spiritu mentis.* Ergo, ipsa mens ad imaginem Dei renovari debet." Samuel Rutherford, *Examen Arminianismi,* ed. Matthia Netheno (Utrecht: Antoninii Smitegelt, 1668), 139.

4 Rutherford, "Ane Catechisme: Conteining the Soume of Christian Religion," 161–2; Rutherford, *Examen Arminianismi,* 1–141.

5 Rutherford, *Examen Arminianismi,* 161.

6 "Tam perfectam Legis & Evangelii doctrinam, nulla creata sapientia invenire potuit. Et licet doctrina Legis sit aliquo modo creaturae rationali naturalis, uti ipsa anima rationalis; eam tamen primitus

experience of faith and obedience is alluded to in the second question in the cate-chism listed above.[7] Furthermore, Rutherford's own account of mystical encounters with the risen Lord while exiled in Aberdeen should discourage the notion that knowledge of God is only acquired in scripture.[8] Despite these other aids, scripture is nevertheless both the primary place to acquire knowledge of God as well as the rule by which these other aids must be judged.[9]

2.1.2 Scripture and Doctrinal Controversy

Rutherford lived in an era when the doctrine of God was subject to intense contro-versy. The Remonstrant Simon Episcopius, mentioned above, questioned whether pursuing knowledge of God according to his essence and attributes was even a legitimate endeavor. Beyond this, the investigations into the divine knowledge by Jesuits such as Luis de Molina (1535–1600), Pedro de Fonseca (1528–1599), Fran-cisco Suárez (1548–1617), and the Dutch Protestant theologian Jacobus Arminius (1560–1609), posited that the divine foreknowledge of future contingent events lay outside the divine will. As will be seen in later chapters, these developments had far reaching effects upon the doctrine of God's being and certain divine at-tributes.[10] Apart from these, the German-Dutch Remonstrant theologian Conrad Vorstius (1569–1622) introduced certain heterodox ideas on divine simplicity, in-finity, immensity, and eternity. Closer to home, the English non-trinitarian John Biddle (1615–1662) initiated similar attacks upon the traditional doctrine of God,

---

invenire, est opus infinitae sapientiae, non minus quam creatio animae rationali est infinitae sapien-tiae & omnipotentiae." Rutherford, *Examen Arminianismi*, 83.

7 Episcopius and Rutherford may be closer here than either would care to admit. Neither the Re-monstrants in general, nor Episcopius specifically, said that knowledge of God, even in his essential nature, was speculative or unprofitable. Rather, they argued that such knowledge was made perfect in this life through obedience to God's commands: "Adeo ut ea sola notitia Dei salutaris dici mereatur, quae cum praxi pietatis est conjuncta." Episcopius, *Confessio* Chapter 2.2, 9. See also the practical application of God's attributes listed in the *Confessio*, 2.5, 2.6, 2.7, and 2.8. Also see Episcopius's com-ment in the *Apologia*: "Nam cognitionem hic non subordinat cultui, sed coordinat, sive consociat, quia cognitionem & cultui vult esse duos fines medios, sive conditiones praerequisitas, ad vitam beatam consequendam, & rationem addit; *Interdum* enim in Scripturis *una sub altera reciproce ordinatur, cognitio veritatis sub pietate.*" Episcopius, *Apologia pro confessione*, 40.

8 See for example his letter to Lady Culross, where he recounts a visit with the risen Lord while a prisoner in exile. Rutherford, *Joshua Redivivus*, 71–73.

9 Rutherford's nuanced approach, while nevertheless relying upon the primacy of scripture as the ultimate grounds for acquiring knowledge of God, is consistent with other Reformed Orthodox. In relation to the doctrine of God specifically, see Richard A. Muller, *Post-Reformation Reformed Dogmatics*. Vol 3, *The Divine Essence and Attributes* (Grand Rapids: Baker Academic, 2003), 95–101.

10 See this study Ch. 3.3.

especially upon the doctrine of God's omnipresence.[11] The polemical challenges to the orthodox Christian doctrine of God in the seventeenth century necessitated a defense of God's nature and attributes.[12]

Before wading into the controversies directly, Rutherford first took the time to establish how he intended to resolve such controversies. He addressed the matter in his *Examen Arminianismi*, where he asked: "Whether scripture, or the Holy Spirit speaking in Scripture, is the judge of controversies?"[13] Behind the question are statements on scripture from Simon Episcopius's *Apologia Pro Confessione Sive Declaratione Sententiae Eorum*. These are briefly surveyed below.[14]

Episcopius was wary of attributing scripture with the ability to bind the conscience, especially when the binding judgement was issued by the church. Such thinking, argued Episcopius, is more closely aligned with Roman Catholicism than the religion of the Reformation and gives atheists and profane people occasion to insult the religion of the Reformation.[15] His position was to deny that the scriptures could render a binding judgment. In matters of controversy the law (*lex*) must be distinguished from the judge (*judex*). If scripture is law, so the argument goes in the *Apologia*, then it cannot be a judge. "Scripture therefore is no more rightly said to be the judge of controversy… than the law is the judge of lawsuits."[16] The law and the judge are distinct, and it is necessary that they are distinct in matters of controversy.[17]

---

11 Carl R. Trueman, *John Owen: Reformed, Catholic, Renaissance Man*, Great Theologians (Burlington, VT: Ashgate, 2007), 40.

12 For an overview of the challenges facing Orthodox doctrines of God in the seventeenth century, see: Muller, *The Divine Essence and Attributes*, 119–29.

13 "Quaeritur. An Scriptura, vel Spiritus Sanctus in Scripturis loquens, sit Judex Controversiarum? Vel, an Deus nobis in Verbo suo, nullam normam coactive obligantem conscientias, reliquerit: sed tantum normam directive judicantem?" Rutherford, *Examen Arminianismi*, 1.

14 The relevant section comes from "Chapter I: De S. Scripturae Auctoritate, Perfectione, & Perspicuitate," in: Episcopius, *Apologia pro confessione*, 23–38.

15 "Tantum hoc voluerunt: Totum illud, quod Ecclesiae suae reliquit Deus, & in verbo suo nobis patefecit, non esse nisi normam dirigentem, sive directive, non a coactive judicantem, id est, cujus totum ac proprium quarto modo officium est dirigere judicium in cognitione veritatis & officii nostri. Nuspiam in verbo Dei aliud quid Ecclesiae relictum aut traditum esse. Hoc a opposito voluerunt tum Pontificiis, qui praeter normam dirigentem, judicium etiam Ecclesiae coactivum, id est quod cum potestate & autoritate irrefragabili fertur, nobis in verbo Dei relictum ac datum esse afferunt: Tum iis qui Scripturam judicem controversiarum perperam vocant, &, sic loquendo Pontificiis, allisque seu atheis seu profanis occasionem dant sugillandi Religionem Reformatam, quasi ea dicat, quae per se sunt absurda." Episcopius, *Apologia pro confessione*, 30.

16 "Scriptura enim non magis recte dici potest judex controversarium, si proprie loqui velis, quam Lex judex est litium." Episcopius, *Apologia pro confessione*, 30.

17 "Lex & Judex distincta sunt, & distincta sint necesse est, ubi de Legis sensu contraversia aut lis incidit." Episcopius, *Apologia pro confessione*, 30.

If scripture is law then the individual's conscience is judge. Episcopius argued that scripture expressly sets forth doctrine in a clear and perspicuous way enabling the individual to render a reliable judgment.[18] Greatly assisting this project of judgment are the tools of human reason as well as human conscience. After all, if human reason and judgment are not useful in the interpretation of scripture, why then does Jesus appeal to the crowds saying, "Listen and understand" (Matt. 15:10)? Or why does John teach to "test the spirits to see if they are from God" (1 John 4:1)? If right reason (*recta ratio*) is not useful, then why does the scripture appeal so frequently to human reason and human understanding?[19] And yet, according to the *Apologia*, there are matters of doctrine that exceed human reason and wisdom, and upon which sincere Christians may disagree. Therefore, fundamental articles of the faith must be few, and freedom of profession must be maintained in matters not strictly and necessarily related to salvation.[20]

Rutherford rejected Episcopius's fundamental distinction between *lex* and *judex* as inapplicable to the scriptures. Scripture is certainly law, in the sense that it can be appealed to in order to establish doctrine. Christ himself does as much by saying, "You search the Scriptures because you think that in them you have eternal life; and it is they that bear witness about me" (John 5:39). "If you do not believe the writings, how will you believe my words?" (John 5:47).[21] But scripture is not merely law. Scripture is also the standard of judgment (*norma judicandi*) because God himself speaks through the scriptures as the Judge (*judex*) by the person of the Holy Spirit.[22] This authoritative, binding speech act in matters of

---

18 Rutherford summarizes the position as follows: "Quia Scriptura est perfecta & perspicua, ideo illa tantum Fundamentalia sunt, quae sunt ῥητῶς & expressis verbis in Scripturis, aut per consequentiam tam necessariam & omnibus obviam, quam est haec, currit, ergo movetur." Rutherford, *Examen Arminianismi*, 5. See also: Episcopius, *Apologia pro confessione*, 33.

19 An interesting feature of Episcopius's argument is that the truth of scripture is not rejected because it is not understood. Rather, the truth of scripture is rejected precisely because humans have understood it perfectly and judged it worthy of rejection. "Confirmatur hoc ex eo, quod idem Christus dicatur *scandalum Iudais*: Scandalum autem esse non poterat, nisi intelligerent quid doctrina Christi contineret." Episcopius, *Apologia pro confessione*, 37.

20 Rutherford summarizes the position as follows: "Sed hic Remonstrantes, nullam licitam esse confessionem fidei, in quam jurandum est, nisi quae meris Scripturae verbis exprimit tantum creditu necessaria ad salutem: non quae exprimit diversas de Religione sententias, circa dogmata non praecise creditu necessaria." Rutherford, *Examen Arminianismi*, 9.

21 "Sed nos, Scripturas, ad coactivas decisiones controversiarum, sufficientes esse docemus. I. Quia Christus ad Scripturas provocat, Joan 5.39. Scrutemini Scripturas; in iis enim vos creditis habere vitam aeternam; nam ipse sunt quae de me testantur. Sic Joan 5.47. Si non creditis Scriptis Mosaicis, quomodo meis verbis credetis?" Rutherford, *Examen Arminianismi*, 2.

22 "Quia si Scriptura esset mera Lex, & nihil ultra, Judex & Lex necessario distinguerentur: Sed quia Scriptura est norma judicandi, & simul adjunctum habens Spiritum Sanctum, qui hominibus, quibus Evangelium non est tectum, litem decidat & obstrepentes convincat; ideo non necesse est, ut hic

controversy proceeds from God and the Holy Spirit and is mediated through the ministry of the church. Brushing aside Episcopius's pointed comparisons of the Reformed Assemblies to Roman Catholicism, Rutherford insisted that if the church cannot receive judgements from God through the scriptures, then all will be left to their own private doubts and conjectures.[23] Rutherford's comments reflect the practical considerations of post-Reformation Orthodoxy to speak authoritatively on matters of dispute, including those matters pertaining to divine providence. Rutherford's interest in justifying the judgements of the church no doubt had in mind the Synod of Dort, the various assemblies of the Scottish Covenanters, as well as the divines assembled at Westminster. Regarding the present subject, Rutherford is laying the groundwork for which he will address controversies pertaining to God's being, essence, and attributes, all of which directly relate to his doctrine of divine providence.

2.1.3 De Cognitione Dei: The Study of God in the Scriptures

Chapter 2 of the *Examen* is dedicated exclusively to the doctrine of God. The first section of the chapter is titled *"De Cognitione Dei,"* which can be translated as "Concerning the Study of God."[24] The controversy here, already indicated above, was whether the study of God in his essence and attributes was a legitimate and scripturally warranted pursuit.[25] Rutherford argued that the pursuit of such knowledge was commanded in scripture.[26] He understood the same knowledge to be a gift from God which was part of the renewal of the image of God in human beings and the pursuit of which was pleasing to him.[27] Ignorance of God is the cause of all other sins, therefore it is a Christian's duty to pursue knowledge of God.[28] Those

---

Lex & Judex distinguantur, uti distinguuntur Lex humana & Judex terrenus." Rutherford, Examen Arminianismi, 3.

23 "Absurdum est Ecclesiae secundum Scripturas judicantis judicium, non esse normam controversiarum, quia hoc est negare *Deum & Spiritum Sanctum* loquentem e Scripturis, quas *Ecclesia* proponit ut Ministra; quia si non ut Ministerialis Judex potest decidere fidei controversias, tum omnes dubitantes relinqueret." Rutherford, *Examen Arminianismi*, 3.

24 The chapter is likely a response to Episcopius's chapter heading in his *Apologia*, which is "De cognitione essentiae seu Naturae divinae." See: Episcopius, *Apologia pro confessione*, 38.

25 "Quaeritur, An non praecipiatur cognitio vera & recta de Deo, & conformitas mentis cum Deo?" Rutherford, *Examen Arminianismi*, 138.

26 "Ipsa cognitio, per se, & propter se, mandatur. I Chron. 28.9. Tu quoque, Solomon, fili, cognosce Deum Patris tui, & cole eum integro corde. Eph. 4. 23. Et renovemini spiritu mentis. Ergo, ipsa mens ad imaginem Dei renovari debet." Rutherford, *Examen Arminianismi*, 139.

27 "Quia cognitio in mente est pars imaginis Dei Col. 3.10." Rutherford, *Examen Arminianismi*, 139.

28 "Quia ignorantia Dei est causa omnium aliorum peccatorum, & temporalis atque aeterni hominum exitii." Rutherford, *Examen Arminianismi*, 140.

who believe they can be saved through obedience, while having a false conception of God according to his nature, attributes, and operations as they are revealed in Scripture are guilty of heresy.[29]

Rutherford believed Scripture to be the source for the knowledge of God. Furthermore, Rutherford believed that scripture was the answer to resolving the controversies pertaining to the doctrine of God that raged throughout the sixteenth and seventeenth centuries. He argued that God had commanded an investigation into his essence and nature not only to resolve controversies, but also to attain to true faith and worship. Though investigations into the divine essence and nature were characterized by some Arminians as unscriptural, overly-philosophical and even pagan, it has been demonstrated that Rutherford believed his endeavor to be thoroughly rooted in scripture.

2.2 The Divine Essence, Unity, and Omnipresence

2.2.1 The Divine Simplicity and the Divine Name

Having grounded his inquiry in Scripture, Rutherford began his discourse on the divine essence with the divine simplicity, a doctrine he rooted in the divine name. This section begins with two assertions. The first assertion, "Truly to us, God is one," is reminiscent of the Hebrew liturgical prayer, the *Shema Yisrael* (Deut 6:4).[30] The second assertion states that where there is perfect unity, it is necessary that there must be perfect simplicity.[31] In the *Examen*, much like Thomas Aquinas had done in the *Summa Theologiae*, Rutherford gave the divine simplicity place of priority within the discussion pertaining to God's essential unity.[32] Thus, the divine simplicity sets the tone for all that follows.[33]

---

29 "Quia Socinianum est, & haereticum, putare, nos salvari posse per observantiam praeceptorum Dei, etsi perperam mente concipiamus Deum: & Deum, ejusque Naturam & Attributa & Operationes, quatenus in Scripturis revelantur, ignoremus." Rutherford, *Examen Arminianismi*, 140.

30 "Nobis vero, unus tantum Deus est." Rutherford, *Examen Arminianismi*, 141.

31 Rutherford, 141.

32 Thomas addresses the divine simplicity immediately following his treatment of God's existence. See Aquinas, *Summa Theologiae*, I, q. 23, a. 1–8. For the centrality of the doctrine of divine simplicity for Thomas, see Robert M. Burns, "The Divine Simplicity in St. Thomas," *Religious Studies* 25, no. 3 (1989): 271–93. See also: J.E. Dolezal, *God Without Parts: Divine Simplicity and the Metaphysics of God's Absoluteness* (Eugene, OR.: Wipf and Stock, 2011), especially Chapter 5, 125–163.

33 This does not mean that this sets the pattern for similar discussions elsewhere in Rutherford's writing. For example, in both the "Ane Catachisme" as well as *Christ Dying and Drawing Sinners to Himself,* Rutherford takes an approach more consistent with that of John Duns Scotus, relying upon the divine infinitude of each attribute to establish God's essential unity. See Rutherford, "Ane Catachisme:

"It is asked," wrote Rutherford, "whether God in his nature is most simple, being free from all composition, from act and potency, from subject and accidents, and from all increase and difference?" Two citations, one from Episcopius's *Apologia* and one from Vorstius's *Tractatus Theologicus De Deo*, provide a foil to Rutherford's position. In the *Apologia*, Episcopius argued that the doctrine of divine simplicity was entirely philosophical and metaphysical. Not even "one jot" of it is to be found in scripture.[34]

For Episcopius, the scriptural witness posed seemingly insurmountable problems to this supposedly metaphysical doctrine of divine simplicity. The doctrine of divine simplicity, as the *Quaeritur* above suggests, implies that God is free from composite parts. Episcopius takes this to mean that there is no distinction to be made between God's essence, will, and works. If no such distinction can be made, then there is no explanation for how God can use his will to cease an action. Episcopius makes the problem clearer through a practical, scriptural example from Ezek. 18.24:

> But when a righteous person turns away from his righteousness and does injustice and does the same abominations that the wicked person does, shall he live? None of the righteous deeds that he has done shall be remembered; for the treachery of which he is guilty and the sin he has committed, for them he shall die.

At present, the righteous person is an object of God's love. However, the righteous person is potentially an object of God's hatred if he turns from his righteousness. The problem posed by the above asks how it is possible for a God whose simple essence demands immutability, could love a person at one point and cease loving him at another. Divine simplicity poses major problems for the free exercise of divine providence because it suggests that divine freedom would be inhibited from changing affections (i.e. love and hate).[35] Episcopius took these to be an insurmountable problem to the traditional doctrine of divine simplicity.[36] Vorstius

---

Conteining The Soume of Christian Religion." 162; Rutherford, *Christ Dying and Drawing Sinners to Himselfe*, 291–92. For the importance of infinitude to Scotus's doctrine of God see: Richard Cross, *Duns Scotus*, Great Medieval Thinkers (New York, NY: Oxford University Press, 1999), 26; James E. Dolezal, *God Without Parts: Divine Simplicity and the Metaphysics of God's Absoluteness* (Eugene, OR: Wipf and Stock, 2011), 7.

34 "Addit Censor, nihil etiam de *simplici natura* Dei docent: Quid mirum? De ea ne jota quidem in Scriptura est. Deinde disputatio ista tota metaphysica est; de ipso termino simplicitatis nondum convenit inter Philosophos." Episcopius, *Apologia pro confessione*, 41.

35 The doctrine of divine simplicity posing problems for the divine freedom was a standard line of attack from Arminian theologians toward the Reformed scholastics. For example see Jackson, *A Treatise on the Divine Essence and Attributes*, 344.

36 "An simplicitati Dei repugnet, si volitiones actiones Dei liberae ab essentia Dei dicantur distinctae; quia inexplicabile videtur, quomodo, si distinctio nulla sit, volitio Dei libera non sit, sed semper

offered similar objections on both fronts in the *Notae Disputationem III*, which can be found in the *Tractatus Theologicus de Deo.*[37]

Rutherford responded with a reassertion of the traditional doctrine of divine simplicity, noting that God is absolutely perfect and immutable, without parts, components, or composition since such implies imperfection. His scriptural support for the doctrine of divine simplicity is derived from an essentialist reading of the divine name, taken from Exod. 3:14 and Amos 9:6.[38] Whereas the *Apologia* noted that there is "not one jot" of the doctrine of divine simplicity in scripture, Rutherford roots the doctrine of divine simplicity in the divine name *Jehovah.*[39] His brief discussion of the divine name precedes his more detailed remarks on the divine simplicity, thus rooting the discussion within the witness of scripture. For Rutherford, the doctrine of divine simplicity and those things logically deduced from the doctrine are a fundamental truth about God that is revealed in scripture through the divine name. This approach was common amongst the Reformed Orthodox. Muller notes:

> The Reformed motive in developing a doctrine of the divine names is fundamentally exegetical and does not at all relate to a theory of attributes as mere terms or concepts grounded not in the thing but in our perception only. Rather the Reformed interest in the divine names, whether among the Reformers themselves or among the later orthodox, relates to a fundamental Biblicism and to the assumption that the names offer a primary way of approach to the identity of God.[40]

---

eadem prorsus maneat, nec desinere unquam possit: Item, cum de Deo expresse dicatur, quod justum quem amat, a justitia sua deficientem odio habeat & aversetur, quomodo amori iste & odium subsequens amorem, respectu ejusdem subjecti, sit ipsa Dei essentia, quae eadem semper manet, & quae sunt ejus commatis alia." Episcopius, *Apologia pro confessione*, 41.

37 Conradus Vorstius, Tractatus theologicus de deo, sive natura & attributis dei, omnia fere ad hanc materiam pertinentia (saltem de quibus utiliter & religiose disputari potest) decem disputationibus, antehac in illustri schola steinfurtensi, diverso tempore, publice habitis, breviter & methodice comprehendens. (Steinfurt: Theophilus Caesar, 1606), 206–7.

38 "Nos contra. I. Deus est absolute perfectus & immutabilis. Nullae ergo, sunt in Deo partes componentes; nulla mixtura; nulla compositio: quia partes sunt toto imperfectiores. Qui est essentia *Jehova*, I. essentia simpliciter, prima, perfecta, ex se esse habens, absoluta, independens; Is est Simplicissimus, Sed prius, de Deo, est verum. *Exod. 3.14. Ero qui ero, misit me. Genes 15.7. Ego sum Jehovah. Amoz. 9.6.* Jehovah est nomen ejus." Rutherford, *Examen Arminianismi*, 141.

39 "Qui est essentia Jehovah, i.e. essentia simpliciter, prima, perfecta, ex se esse habens, absoluta, & independens; is est Simplicissimus, Sed prius, de deo est verum Exod 3.14. Ero, qui ero, misit me. Genes 15.7. Ego Sum Jehovah. Amoz 9.6. Jehovah est nomen ejus." Rutherford, Examen Arminianismi, 141.

40 Muller, *Post-Reformation Reformed Dogmatics*, 3:246.

In the *Examen*, Rutherford passed over the divine name with few remarks. His brief discussion took for granted that the divine name of *Jehovah* implies essential simplicity and those attributes logically derived from the doctrine.[41] Rutherford offered a fuller treatment to the subject of the divine name in his *Disquisitiones Metaphysicae*, a short metaphysical treatise appended to the end of his *Disputatio Scholastica de Divina Providentia.*[42]

The context of Rutherford's discussion of the divine name in the *Disputatio* falls under a metaphysical investigation (*disquisitiones metaphysicae*) of whether being precedes non-being in the metaphysical order.[43] Important to Rutherford's overall argument is the demonstrative science of Aristotle, mediated through the patristic and medieval Christian tradition. In the *Posterior Analytics* Aristotle argued for the necessity of "principles of demonstration" in order to prevent infinite regress in the construction of syllogisms. Unlike conclusions, which depend upon preceding terms, "principles of demonstration" are independent and known simply in and of themselves prior to any argumentation.[44] The principle of demonstration *par excellence* was the law of non-contradiction, which Aristotle had argued was the first and strongest principle of demonstration.[45]

As Aza Goudriaan has shown, Rutherford noted that the law of non-contradiction cannot be rock bottom because it relies upon a prior principle, namely that "the same is the same."[46] What Rutherford did next is quite interesting. With an appeal to the divine name, Rutherford asserted that the principle "the same is the same" has its origin first in God who is "I am who I am."[47] Thus, the "rock bottom" principle of demonstration is not the law of non-contradiction, but rather the simple truth

---

41 This is entirely consistent with other Reformed Orthodox exegesis of the divine name "Jehovah." See Muller, *The Divine Essence and Attributes*, 246–51.

42 Rutherford, *Disputatio Scholastica*, 531–620.

43 "An Ens sit prius simpliciter non ente." Rutherford, *Disputatio Scholastica*, 531.

44 For an excellent overview see: John Longeway, "Medieval Theories of Demonstration," in *The Stanford Encyclopedia of Philosophy* (online). See also: Eileen Serene, "Demonstrative Science," in *The Cambridge History of Later Medieval Philosophy*, ed. Norman Kretzmann, Anthony Kenny, and Jan Pinborg, 496–517 (Cambridge: Cambridge University Press, 1982).

45 See: Aristotle's *Metaphysics*, Book 4, Chapter 4. See also Terrence Irwin, *Aristotle's First Principles* (Oxford: Oxford University Press, 1990), 3–4; "Aristotle's Logic," *The Stanford Encyclopedia of Philosophy* accessed March 23rd, 2017, https://plato.stanford.edu/archives/spr2017/entries/aristotle-_logic.

46 In what follows, I rely upon Aza Goudriaan, "Samuel Rutherford on the Divine Origin of Possibility," in *Reformed Orthodoxy in Scotland: Essays on Scottish Theology 1560–1775*, ed. Aaron Clay Denlinger (London: Bloomsbury, 2014), 142–143.

47 "Quia vero simplex est prius complex: principium hoc est. (*Idem est idem.*) Sed quia nihil docet praedictio identica, haec supposito est simplicissima forte verius, quam principium. Itaque principium adhuc prius est. (*Deus est,*) (*Deus intelligit,*) (*Deus vult,*) *&c.* Id autem (*Idem simul esse & non esse est impossibile*) veritatem obtineat necesse est, in eo qui est primus idem, cui suavissimum nomen & plus quam nomen, אֶהְיֶה אֲשֶׁר אֶהְיֶה." Rutherford, *Disputatio Scholastica*, 531.

of the divine name, which when given an essentialist reading as Rutherford did, implied that the rock bottom principle is actually God's being. For Rutherford, such conclusions warrant a strong doctrine of the divine simplicity.[48]

Rutherford's essentialist reading of the divine name would hardly assuage Episcopius's fears of sophistical investigations into the divine nature. Nevertheless, Rutherford believed his logic was scripturally warranted, his conclusions being derived from the significance of the divine name. This allowed him to reassert traditional aspects of the divine simplicity, such as the absence of increase, composition, and potency in God, in the face of new controversies.[49] Furthermore, the ontological necessity of God's simplicity in the metaphysical order leads to a variety of conclusions relevant to the doctrine of divine providence. Rutherford's exegesis of the divine name, along with the questions following, establish God's being as the first principle of all things, to include: being and non-being, possibility and impossibility, as well as necessity and contingency.[50] The affairs governed by God's providence are rooted in God's being and understood within the context of an essentialist reading of the divine name and God's most simple nature.[51] How Rutherford navigated concerns raised by Episcopius in light of the divine simplicity are further outlined below.

2.2.2 Distinction of Attributes

The doctrine of divine simplicity has implications for God's attributes and how these are to be distinguished from God's essence and existence as well as from one another. Given Rutherford's denial of composition, the doctrine of divine simplicity poses challenges to how one is to understand the attributes predicated of God. The act of predication is the act of affirming or attributing a quality to a subject.[52] Attribution as applied to God would be the uniting of God as subject to a predicate such as the

---

48 See: Aza Goudriaan, "Samuel Rutherford on the Divine Origin of Possibility," 143.

49 "In quo non sunt multiplicatio, dissolubilitas, in eo est simplicitas summa. At in Deo haec non sunt. 3. Omnis Compositio, aliquid potentiae & perfectibilitatis admixtum habet. Nihil est quod Deum perficiat." Rutherford, *Examen Arminianismi*, 141.

50 "An Deus causa dominans sit entium & non-entium." Scripture proofs supplied are Deut 10.14; Psa 89.12; Psa 115.16; Psa 24.1; Psa 15.5; Rom 11.26; and Prov 16.4. See Rutherford, *Disputatio Scholastica*, 532–3; "An Deus sit Origo & Causa impossibilium & possibilium." Scripture proof supplied is Deut 32.39. See: Rutherford, *Disputatio Scholastica*, 538.

51 Further discussion on the implications for Rutherford's essentialist reading of the divine name are covered in this study: Ch. 5.2.

52 Muller defines predication as "the activity or operation by means of which something is affirmed of or attributed to a subject." Richard A. Muller, "Praedicatio," in *Dictionary of Latin and Greek Theological Terms: Drawn Principally from Protestant Scholastic Theology*, 2nd ed. (Grand Rapids, MI: Baker Academic, 2017), 277.

attribute of simple, immense, infinite, or the like. This is done in order to form a simple premise such as "God is love," or "God is omniscient."[53] Attribution assumes a relationship between subject and predicate while at the same time maintaining a formal difference.[54] According to Rutherford, the relationship between subject and predicate cannot be understood in the same way that such a relationship pertains to creatures. For instance, when one says white is in milk or righteousness is in man, the attribute can be distinguished from the creature. Contrarily, attributes describing God are identical with him. "They (the attributes) are God himself," and are proposed to our understanding in a different way than if they belonged to a creature.[55]

Thus far, Rutherford had affirmed that the attributes are identical with God. He proceeds to argue that the attributes may nevertheless be distinguished from God's essence as well as from one another. In a dense paragraph, Rutherford outlines the manner in which these two theological priorities are maintained:

> The distinction of attributes and essence is after this manner: it is neither formal (*formalis*) as diverse entities and essences are distinguished: nor is it modal (*modalis*), as being and the existence of being are distinguished: nor is it potential, as parts and the whole: but it is a distinction of reason (*rationis*), and even reasoned (*ratiocinatae*); as we distinguish Socrates in regards to subject and attribute, thus by intellect he understands, not by will, etc. even still they differ from the imperfection and inadequacy of our conception.[56]

The above excerpt from the *Examen* is laden with logical distinctions common to scholasticism. Absent from the above is the *real distinction (distinctio realis)*. A real distinction is used to distinguish between two independent things or substances, such as a tree and a bird.[57] In terms of the doctrine of God real distinctions are non-

---

53 These simple statements serve as bedrock principles of demonstration outlined above.

54 Muller, *The Divine Essence and Attributes*, 197–8.

55 "Attributa, Relationes, & Modi subsistendi, non sunt in Deo ad modum forme Deum qualificantis, actuantis, aut informantis; uti *album* est in *lacte, justitia* in *homine*. Sed sunt ipse Deus, alio atque alio modo consideratus, & Intellectui nostro objectus: uti homo manens in eodem situ, nullo modo mutatus est, huic dexter, alteri sinister." Rutherford, *Examen Arminianismi*, 142.

56 "Et distinctio *Attributorum* & *Essentia*, a modis est: nec est *formalis*, quomodo distinguuntur diversae entitates & essentiae: nec *modalis*, uti ens & existentia entis distinguuntur: nec *potentialis*, uti partes & totum: Sed est distinctio *Rationis*, & quidem *ratiocinatae*, uti *Socratem* in *subjectum & attributum*, distinguimus; sic *Intellectu* intelligit, non *voluntate*, &c. adeoq; etiam formalitate imperfectorum & inadequatorum conceptuum nostrorum differunt." Rutherford, *Examen Arminianismi*, 142.

57 Muller, "Distinctio," in *Dictionary of Latin and Greek Theological Terms: Drawn Principally from Protestant Scholastic Theology*. 2nd ed. (Grand Rapids, MI: Baker Academic, 2017), 95.

essential differences reserved for the persons of the Trinity.[58] "If relations were not really distinguished from each other," wrote Thomas, "there would be no real trinity in God, but only a conceptual (*rationis*) trinity, which is the error of Sabellius."[59] Whereas real distinctions are necessary for an account of relationships within the Holy Trinity, real distinctions within the divine essence jeopardize the essential unity upon which the doctrine of the Trinity depends. Thus, real distinctions are not applicable to the divine essence and attributes, but only to the relationships of the Trinity. That is why this critical distinction is absent from Rutherford's description above.[60]

The *formal distinction* (*distinctio formalis*) is another manner of accounting for distinctions within the divine essence while maintaining the divine simplicity. Whereas in the above, *distinctio realis* means a real distinction between separate things, in the *distinctio formalis* the distinction is between two things that are necessarily related. Thus, there is a formal distinction between object *a* and object *b* if the nature of *a* entails both object *b* as well as the relation between the two.[61] Rutherford denied that such a distinction could be applied to God in his essence and attributes. This distinguishes him from the position of John Duns Scotus (1266–1308), a medieval theologian whom Rutherford is typically content to follow. Scotus argued that there is a formal extramental distinction between God and his attributes that is (a) necessary and (b) does not threaten the essential unity of the divinity. This is true because the distinction demands that God's nature entails both his attributes and their relationship with the divine essence. Whether Rutherford understood Scotus's position and rejected it, or misunderstood Scotus is difficult to discern. Nevertheless, the point is denied. Rutherford does not apply the formal distinction to God in his essence and attributes.[62]

---

58 "Distinctio realis non essentialis est distinctio aliquorum, quorum unum negatur de alio, id est uno non est aliud, sed aliquod singular & simpliciter unum est utrumque, sic distinguuntur personae in divinis & relations oppositae, ut generatio active, & spiratio passive, & relationes disperatae quae non conveniunt eidem supposito, nam pater non est filius, nec paternitas est filiatio, & tamen una singularis & simplicissima divina essentia est pater & filius, paternitas, & filiatio." Joannes Altenstaig, "Distinctio," in *Theologicum complectens vocabulorum* (Antwerp: Petri Belleri, 1576), 88.

59 "Si ergo relationes non distinguuntur ab invicem realiter, non erit in divinis Trinitas realis, sed rationis tantum, quod est Sabellianis erroris." Thomas Aquinas, *Summa Theologiae*, trans. O. P. Fr. Laurence Shapcote, ed. John Mortensen and Enrique Alarcon (Lander: The Aquinas Institute for the Study of Sacred Doctrine, 2012), I, q. 28, a.3, 303–304.

60 Rutherford's own doctrine of the Trinity is outlined in Chapter 2.3 of: Rutherford, *Examen Arminianismi*, 147–62. See also this study, Ch. 2.3.

61 Antonie Vos, *The Philosophy of John Duns Scotus* (Edinburgh: Edinburgh University Press, 2006), 256.

62 See fn. 56 above

The second distinction denied by Rutherford is the *modal distinction* (*distinctio modalis*). Peter King notes that Duns Scotus introduced the *distinctio modalis* in his *Ordinatio*.[63] If the *distinctio realis* is a hard distinction and the *distinctio formalis* is a softer distinction, the *distinctio modalis* would move further into the territory of soft distinctions. Intensity is one way to understand the *modal distinction*. Take for example the color red. The color red can come in a range of shades or intensities without altering the formal or essential property.[64] Rutherford uses the metaphysical example of being (*ens*) and the stronger mode of existent being (*existentia entis*) as an example.[65] Thus the divine attributes are not different intensities or "shades" of the divine essence, nor do they represent more intense modes of being. Though Rutherford denies *modal distinctions* in terms of divine essence and attributes, he does employ *modal distinctions* in the *Disquisitiones Metaphysicae* to discuss various modalities of being.[66]

The third distinction denied by Rutherford is the *potential* (*potentialis*). The *potential* distinction is drawn from Aristotle's *Metaphysics Z* where he introduced two key distinctions. The first distinction is between matter and form. The matter of a substance is the stuff it is made of. The form is the way that the matter is put together. Matter plus form constitutes the whole. The second key distinction, closely related to the above, is between potentiality and actuality. Consider a wood table. The matter is wood. The form is that of a table. There was a point in the creation of the table however, when the matter (wood) was only potentially a table. Only when power was applied to the matter was the potential actualized and the matter took the form of a table.[67] Rutherford denies that there are such potential distinctions between the divine essence and attributes as between "parts and the whole" (*partes & totum*). What this means in terms of the divine essence is that the essence is not the matter that takes on the form of the attributes. Neither at any point in time is the divine essence potentially good, loving, merciful, etc. Rather, each is fully actualized.[68]

The fourth and final distinction offered by Rutherford, being the one he accepted, is the distinction of reason reasoned (*distinctio rationis rationatae*), which was

---

63 Peter King, "Scotus on Metaphysics" in *The Cambridge Companion to Duns Scotus*, ed. Thomas Williams, Cambridge Companions to Philosophy (Cambridge: Cambridge University Press, 2003), 25.

64 Peter King, "Scotus on Metaphysics," 25.

65 "Nec modalis, uti ens & existentia entis distinguuntur." Rutherford, *Examen Arminianismi*, 142.

66 Rutherford, *Disputatio Scholastica*, 532.

67 For an overview see Cohen. S. Marc, "Aristotle's Metaphysics," in *The Stanford Encyclopedia of Philosophy*, ed. Edward N. Zalta (Winter 2016: Metaphysics Research Lab, Stanford University, 2016). https://plato.stanford.edu/archives/win2016/entries/aristotle-metaphysics/.

68 Rutherford, *Examen Arminianismi*, 142.

employed by Thomas Aquinas. This is a distinction with an extramental foundation in the object, which is why it is sometimes qualified as a distinction of reason reasoned which has its foundation in the thing (*distinctio rationis ratiocinatae quae habet fundamentum in re*).[69] It is important to contrast this *distinctio rationis rationatae* with the *distinctio rationis rationans*. Whereas the *distinctio rationis rationatae* is an extramental concept founded in the thing, the *distinctio rationis rationans* is purely conceptual with no foundation outside of the mind.[70] The *distinction of reason reasoned* pertains to a conceptual difference in the diversity of effects produced by God's power. However, what is presented to the human knower as a multiplicity of effects is only an inadequate understanding of what is truly the divine simplicity.[71]

In summary, Rutherford's understanding of the distinction between essence and attributes, as well as distinctions amongst the attributes themselves, is consistent with the traditional understanding of such distinctions. In rejecting the formal distinction in favor of the distinction of reason reasoned, Rutherford exhibited a Thomistic reading of the distinction between essence and attribute, though as will be seen below, Rutherford reinterpreted these distinctions along different lines.[72] Finally, in the above Rutherford navigated the thorny problem of maintaining God's essential simplicity while at the same time making distinctions among attributes identified in scripture. In doing so, Rutherford was able to maintain a doctrine that is scriptural, traditional, and sufficient to support the metaphysical considerations identified above that pertain to God's providence.

2.2.3 The Problem of Relative Names and the Divine Simplicity

Rutherford introduced the problem of relative names and attributes with a discussion on whether a "new entity" (*novus entitas*) might be added to God in time as he exercises divine providence, thus creating a relation between God and his creatures. In raising this issue, Rutherford moves the discussion of the divine essence and attributes into what some Reformed Orthodox termed "absolute" and "relative"

---

69 Muller, *Post Reformation Reformed Dogmatics*, 3:287. See also Beck, *Gisbertus Voetius*, 243–245.

70 Muller, 3:287.

71 "Sed est distinctio *Rationis*, & quidem *ratiocinatae;* uti *Socratem* in *subjectum* & *attributum*, distinguimus; sic *intellectu* intelligit, non *Voluntate*, &c. adeoq; etiam formalitate imperfectorum & inadequatorum conceptuum nostrorum differunt." Rutherford, *Examen Arminianismi*, 142. See: Dolezal, *God Without Parts*, 135.

72 See the discussion below regarding relative names, where Rutherford explicitly follows Thomas but uses the Scotist theologian (Rutherford's description) Theodore Smising to give a particular emphasis to Thomas's distinction. See also Beck's interesting discussion regarding Voetius's Scotistic accent to the Thomist *distinctio rationis rationatae*. Beck, *Gisbertus Voetius*, 236–245.

attributes. "Absolute" attributes are considered in and of themselves, without reference to anything else towards which their power could be applied. Other attributes were understood in relation to created things towards which God's power could be applied in the act of creation and the exercise of his providential care. These were described as "relative" since they were understood to be in relation to things other than God. Though the concerns pertaining to the divine simplicity are closely related between absolute and relative attributes, the relative attributes pose a unique set of problems discussed below.[73]

Rutherford's discussion on relative attributes was focused on the "new entities" that are created by virtue of a relation between God and his creation. These new entities are descriptive names whose foundation is the relationship that exists between the two. For example, the name "Creator" is significant of a relationship that begins to exist between God and his creatures at the moment of creation. Other names such as Pastor, Father, Redeemer, Protector, Savior, and Lord are also significant of relations that exist between God and his creatures. In the instance that such creatures are destroyed or their relationship with God changes, the names that were attributed to God by virtue of his relation to them could be withdrawn.[74]

An important aspect of this discussion is to carefully define the nature of the relation that exists between God and creation that warrants the relational name. In the *Categories* and *Metaphysics*, Aristotle introduced the logic and language of relation (*relatio*), which was later incorporated into the discussion of God's relative names and attributes. Central to the Aristotelean framework that helped shape the medieval discussion was the understanding that relations are items that relate substances. It was concluded that these items are accidents. Furthermore, no substance was considered a relation.[75]

The medieval heritage that Rutherford inherited from his scholastic training at Edinburgh held that relations exist on a spectrum.[76] On one end of the spectrum, the relation between two entities can be purely conceptual with no basis in extramental reality. This was called a relation of reason (*relatio rationis tantum*). On the other end of the spectrum, the relation between the two entities exists in reality and it exists independently of mental concepts. This relation was called a real relation

---

73 For an overview of relative names in Reformed Orthodoxy, see: Muller, *The Divine Essence and Attributes*, 217–9.

74 "Aliquid Deo adderetur reale, & fieret in eo accessio nove entitatis realis, quando in tempore sit Creator, Pastor, Pater, Redemptor, Protector, Salvator, Dominus: & si Creaturas annihilaret, uti potest, novae entitates Deo adimerentur." Rutherford, *Examen Arminianismi*, 142.

75 Jeffrey Brower, "Medieval Theories of Relations," in *The Stanford Encyclopedia of Philosophy*, ed. Edward N. Zalta (Winter 2018: Metaphysics Research Lab, Stanford University, 2018). URL = <https://plato.stanford.edu/archives/win2015/entries/relations-medieval/>.

76 For an overview of these concepts see Brower, "Medieval Theories of Relations."

(*relatio realis*). Relations can also exist in the middle of the spectrum, being logical for one entity while actual for the other.[77] The above can be demonstrated as follows: (1) stands for a relation of reason, (2) stands for a real relation, and (3) stands for the middle position on the spectrum.

(1) purely conceptual for *a* and *b* with no basis in reality
(2) real for *a* while being real for *b* at the same time
(3) conceptual for *a* but real for *b*.

The relation between God and creation is clearly not merely conceptual; therefore, the first explanation is insufficient. There is an actual creation that enjoys extramental reality, thus the relation is more than conceptual. However, this does not mean that the second explanation is the answer. Rutherford argues that if the relation is real for both God and the creature at the same time, then created entities would be coeval and coeternal with God. Thus, God would not be the only eternal being. This implies a necessary rather than contingent creation, which raises the specter of a fatal universe. The same problem, addressed from a different angle, argues that if God's relation to his creatures is real, when this relation changes so too does God. The divine immutability would therefore be jeopardized.[78]

Following Thomas Aquinas, Rutherford charted a middle road. Thomas argued in favor of the third option above. There is a relation of reason that exists between God and creation. But there existed a real relation between creation and God. Thomas wrote:

> Since therefore God is outside the whole order of creation, and all creatures are ordered to Him, and not conversely, it is manifest that creatures are really related to God Himself; whereas in God there is no real relation to creatures, but a relation only in idea, inasmuch as creatures are referred to Him. Thus there is nothing to prevent these names which import relation to the creature from being predicated of God temporally, not by reason

---

77 "Veruntamen sciendum est quod, cum relatio requirat duo extrema, tripliciter se habere potest ad hoc quod sit res naturae et rationis." Aquinas, *Summa Theologiae*, I, q. 13, a7, 133.

78 "Si aliquid superadderetur reale Essentiae Dei, per Decreta, Creationem, Redemptionem, Relationes Personales; illud vel esset creatum, vel increatum. Si creatum: Decreta Dei saltem erunt entitates creatae, coaevae, & coeternae Deo; & Deus non erit simmpliciter aeternus; & novae creationes accedent Deo, & recedent, quae vera esset mutatio. Si vero est increatum; tum aliquod increatum est temporale (nam esse Creatorem, Redemptorem, Pastorem, in tempore Deo accedunt) quod implicat contradictionem." Rutherford, *Examen Arminianismi*, 142.

of any change in Him, but by reason of the change of the creature; as a column is on the right of an animal, without change in itself, but by change in the animal.[79]

Rutherford follows Thomas on this point, employing a nearly identical example to illustrate the concept. Rather than an animal appearing to the right or left of an unmoved and unchanged column, Rutherford uses the example of things appearing to the right and left of a person remaining unmoved and unchanged in the same place.[80]

Rutherford took his discussion slightly further than Thomas, citing the Franciscan theologian Theodore Smising (ca. 1580–1626). Rutherford's reference to Smising is interesting because Smising's discussion on the relative names follows certain "Scholastic Nominalists" who argued that there existed a real relation not only between the creature and God, but also between God and the creature. Smising noted that these were "gravely censured," however he went on to note that there was nothing worthy of censure if what the "Nominalists" said was understood properly. Smising cited *Durandus of Saint-Pourçain* (1275–1332), William Ockham (1285–1347), and Gabriel Biel (1420–1495), among others as those who held that the relative names and attributes were "real relations." The severe censure, at least as far as Smising is concerned, is the implication that a real relation between God and creation implies an essential, and thus necessary relation between God and the creature. However, Smising argued that this was not the opinion of the "Nominalists."[81]

Ockham is Smising's most relied upon theologian in this section. In order to properly understand Ockham's use of the term "real relation," one must first un-

---

79 "Cum igitur Deus sit extra totum ordinem creaturae, et omnes creaturae ordinentur ad ipsum, et non e converso, manifestum est quod creaturae realiter referuntur ad ipsum Deum; sed in Deo non est aliqua realis relatio eius ad creaturas, sed secundum rationem tantum, inquantum creaturae referuntur ad ipsum. Et sic nihil prohibet huiusmodi nomina importantia relationem ad creaturam, praedicari de Deo ex tempore, non propter aliquam mutationem ipsius, sed propter creaturae mutationem; sicut columna sit dextera animali, nulla mutatione circa ipsam existente, sed animali translato." I have followed the translation in Thomas Aquinas, *Summa Theologiae*, trans. O. P. Fr. Laurence Shapcote, ed. John Mortensen and Enrique Alarcon (Lander: The Aquinas Institute for the Study of Sacred Doctrine, 2012), I, q. 13. A 7, 134.

80 "Sed sunt ipse Deus, alio atque alio modo consideratus, & Intellectui nostro objectus: uti homo manens in eodem situ, nullo modo mutatus est, huic dexter, alteri sinister." Rutherford, *Examen Arminianismi*, 142.

81 "Fuerunt ergo ex Scholasaticis Nominales, asserentes Deum ratione temporalis actionis, ex tempore ad creaturam referri relatione reali Creatoris Domini, &c. Ita *Occam I. dist. 30. Quaest. 5. Gabriel eadem distinc. & question. Gregorius d. 28. Quaest. 3. Durandus d. 30. Quaestion. 3. Marsil. I. quaest. 32. A. I. Soncinas 5. Met. Quest. 25. Ad. 4.* Quam sententiam aliqui graviter censurarunt: sed nullam meretur censuram, prout a Nominalibus explicatur." Theodore Smising, *Disputationum theologicarum de Deo Uno et Trinio* (Antwerp: Gulielmum Lesteenium, 1627), 92.

derstand his division of first and second intentions. The language of intentions was introduced to the Latin West through the writings of the Islamic philosophers Al-farabi (872–950) and Avicenna (980–1037). "Intention" (*intentio*), translated from the Greek νόημα was understood as a concept or thought that had to be understood in its relation to things outside of the soul (first intention) or in its relation to words (second intention). This basic construct underwent considerable development over the course of the medieval period. Ockham's use of the terms is what is of interest.[82]

As Gordon Leff has observed, Ockham held that relations of the first intention refer to those terms that can stand in a personal supposition, such as "mover" and "moved" or "father" and "son."[83] Such terms are linked together by abstract terms such as "movement" and "paternity." These abstract terms are those that Ockham classified as relations of the second intention. Unlike "father" and "son," which can stand in personal supposition, the term "paternity" cannot. For example, the terms "father" and "son" can stand in the simple sentence "Man is a father," or "Man is a son." Ockham noticed that the same is not true for the abstract term "paternity." The sentence "Man is paternity," is nonsensical. Thus, the distinction between first and second relations is that first intentions refer to absolute terms that signify real substances. Relations of the second intention however, "stand for nothing as such, independently or distinct from absolute things, but signifies the relation between "mover" and "moved" as terms of "first intention."[84]

Ockham argued that relations of the second intention are indeed "real relations," not in the sense taken by Thomas and Duns Scotus, but rather in the sense that two absolute terms can be really related and signified by a relative, abstract, and mental concept. Leff explains:

(The mind) can form an absolute concept, say that Socrates and Plato is white; and from that it can make these terms into a relation by stating that Socrates and Plato are similar in virtue of each being white. Thus it arrives at a real relation by means of a relative concept like 'similar'; it is that latter which only exists in the mind.[85]

In the above, Socrates is an absolute with personal supposition. The same is true for Plato, as for the color white. A relation can be drawn between Socrates and Plato

---

82 For an overview of these developments see Christian Knudson, "Intentions and Impositions," in *The Cambridge History of Later Medieval Philosophy*, eds. Norman Kretzmann, Anthony Kenny, and Jan Pinborg (Cambridge: Cambridge University Press, 1982), 479–95.

83 In what follows, I rely heavily upon Gordon Leff, *William of Ockham: The Metamorphosis of Scholastic Discourse* (Manchester: Manchester University Press, 1975), 213–237.

84 Leff, *William of Ockham,* 219.

85 Leff, 225.

based upon their whiteness that the mind calls "similar" Socrates and Plato are *really related*, independently of the mind. However, the term "similar," is a purely mental construct not existing outside of the mind. The same logic applies to God and creation. God can be understood as active in relation to a passive creature, which is produced by God and dependent upon him. Both exist independently of the mind as does their relationship, which is real because it is extramental. However, the relation of second intention (creation) is a purely mental construct connoting the relation between these two absolute realities.[86]

Smising followed the basic construct of Ockham's real relations, comparing God's relation to the created world as of the measure (*mensurae*) and thing measured (*mensurati*) or of cause (*causae*) and caused (*causati*). There is an association (*concomitantia*) and coexistence (*coexistentia*) between the two that is independent of the mind and thus real. Nevertheless, the term we use to relate the two is of the second intention, thus purely mental though "real" in the Ockhamist sense. God as primary subject remains immutable and utterly simple, since the "real relation" speaks of the conjunction between the two absolutes and not specifically about God.[87]

Rutherford explicitly followed Smising's use of "real relations" outlined above. He maintained that certain "real relations" come about in time, but the relation speaks specifically about the thing that joins two terms (i.e. God and the created world) and not about the subjects themselves. Thus, the relational names and attributes are not really added to God's essence during the act of creation or the exercise of divine providence. The relational names and attributes can come about in time and be taken away without affecting God's essence whatsoever. The divine simplicity, immutability, and impassability are maintained in the face of temporally successive relations. Furthermore, via Smising and the "Scholastic Nominalists," Rutherford adopted a position where God's relation to created entities can be taken beyond a mere relation of reason, underscoring both God's independence as well as the radical dependence of the created world.

---

86 Leff, 463–4.

87 "Ipsi enim sentient relationem (praeter relationis personarum in divinis) non esse aliquod ens medium inter absoluta, sed solum esse concomitantiam seu coexistentiam entium absolutorum eiusdem aut diversae naturae, aut inter se dependentiam habentium in ratione mensurae & mensurati, vel causae & causati...quia talis entium concomitantia non est quid confictum per intellectum, sed realiter existent talia entia, ideo dixerunt eam concomitantiam esse relationem realem." Smising, *Disputationes Theologicae*, Tract II, Disp III, 92.

2.2.4 Omnipresence

Following his discussion on the problem of relative names, Rutherford proceeded to ponder "whether God is omnipresent, not only according to his power and work but also according to his essence."[88] The question is asked in response to a section concerning God's infinitude, immensity, and omnipresence in Episcopius's *Apologia.*[89]

Episcopius's objection to the orthodox articulation of the divine omnipresence is twofold. The first is similar to objections he posed in regard to the divine simplicity. While scripture does express that God is omnipresent, scripture does not express the mode of God's presence. Therefore, Episcopius argued that it is overly speculative to insist that God is present according to his essence. Furthermore, it is overly speculative to insist that God is present outside of heaven and earth, even in "imaginary" spaces.[90] Episcopius's second objection concerns God being present in his essential nature and trinity of persons not only to filth, idols, devils, and hell, but even in such things. For Episcopius the thought is enough to cause one to slide into atheism.[91]

Having stated Episcopius's objections to his own position, Rutherford argued that God is present everywhere according to his essence.[92] The scripture proofs for this doctrine are stated as Psalm 139:8; Jer. 23:23–24; Isa. 66:1; 1 Kings 8:27; Acts 17:27; and Eph. 4:6. Beyond these scripture proofs, Rutherford offered additional arguments pertaining to the orthodox doctrine of God's essential omnipresence. These are briefly reviewed below.[93]

---

88 "Quaeritur, An Deus non tantum Potentia & operatione, sed etiam secundum Essentia suam, sit omnipraesens?" Rutherford, *Examen Arminianismi,* 143.

89 "De cognitione essentiae seu Naturae divinae." Episcopius, *Apologia pro Confessione,* 38–47.

90 "Nec enim uspiam in Scripturis legitur Deum *secundum essentiam* suam ubique esse, nedum Deum secundum essentiam suam esse extra caelum & terram in spatiis omnibus, etiam imaginariis. Remonstrantes cum Scriptura & ad Scripturae formulam, divinam omnipraesentiam agnoverunt, modum praesentiae, utpote sibi incomprehensibilem, & in Scriptura non expressum, desinere non fuerunt ausi, rati sufficere, si intra Scriptruae locutionem starent, & ab intricatis Scholarum litibus, de hoc praesentiae modo in totum abstinerent, aut professione ignorantiae sese subducerent." Episcopius, *Apologia pro confessione,* 43.

91 "Et bone Deus! Quis atopicam & atomicam istam essentiae divinae & personarum trium divinarum praesentiam, non dico tantum in caelo & terra, in cloacis, in Idolis foedissimis, in diabolis, in inferno ipso, sed extra caelum & terram in spatiis etiam imaginariis, quae non constat uspiam esse, & quae fingi necesse est, & ficta quid sint, intelligi non potest, sic comprehendit, ut non haereat, non stupeat, non tremat, non horreat? Quis ista, cum dicit intelligit? Ab istis sane facilis prolapsus est in Atheismum." Episcopius, *Apologia pro confessione,* 43.

92 "Nos Dei essentiam, ubisque praesentem esse docemus." Rutherford, *Examen Arminianismi,* 144.

93 Rutherford, *Examen Arminianismi,* 143–146.

Rutherford's first argument concerning the divine presence pertains to location. If the divine essence is not everywhere, then it must be somewhere in a determinate location. If so, where is this location? If the divine essence is in a determinate location, then the divine essence is able to be somewhere that it was not before. This implies a change in location and thus introduces mutability into the divine essence.[94]

His other arguments pertain directly to the doctrine of divine providence. Both Rutherford and his polemical opponents presupposed the presence of God's work and power as a necessary prerequisite for the exercise of creaturely work and power. In the scholastic discourse of the day the continuing support of creaturely activity by God's divine providence was termed *concursus divinus*.[95] Rutherford argued that it was absurd to maintain the presence of God's work and power in creaturely activity, but not his essence, as if any being could exert power apart from its essential presence.[96] Rutherford has established that if God's power is present, so is his essence and vice versa. If God's presence is absent, then so too is his power. According to Rutherford, such has troubling implications for the more devotional aspects of God's providence. If God is not present with the elect, then God cannot work in the elect.[97] Neither could God work amongst the demons or the wicked unless he is present among them. The absence of God's providential *concursus* from demons and the wicked is a disturbing thought. If such wicked creatures are not under the divine *concursus* then they are outside of the dominion of God's providence, and thus beyond God's control.[98]

Rutherford also argued that God's presence extended to the abstract and difficult notion of "imaginary spaces" (*spatia imaginaria*), a point denied in the Remonstrant *Apologia*. At its simplest, imaginary spaces are nothing more than spaces outside of creation (*extra caelum & terram*). Beyond this simple notion, imaginary spaces can refer to the "somewhere" God was before the creation of the world. When

---

94 "Si essentia non est ubisque, est in aliquo certo & determinato loco; & est ita hic, ut non sit alibi. Quaero de loco, in quo essentia Dei non est: Vel potest illic esse, vel non potest illic esse. Si potest illic esse, tum potest Dei Essentia incipere de novo esse in loco, ubi antea non fuerit. At haec est vera loci mutatio." Rutherford, *Examen Arminianismi*, 144.

95 Rutherford's doctrine of divine concursus is covered in this study, ch. 7.1–7.2.

96 For a similar point in Thomas, see Aquinas, *Summa theologiae*. I, q, 8, a. 1.

97 "Quia Deus non operaretur in Electis, si in iis non esset: nec cognosceret renes & cogitationes, si ejus cogitatio & operatio essent, ubi ipse esse non potest; & *essentia a potentia* divelleretur." Rutherford, *Examen Arminianismi*, 145.

98 "Si Deus coinquinatur per praesentiam cum rebus vilissimis, etiam per operationem nefariis & vilissimis actibus, coinquinaretur: Unde non concurret sic ad actus entitativos Diabolorum, Muscarum, &c." Rutherford, *Examen Arminianismi*, 145–6.

used in this manner, imaginary spaces function as a means of conveying God's transcendence. "Heaven, and even the highest heaven" cannot contain God (1 Kings 8:27). Imaginary space can thus function as that transcendent space filled by God's essence outside of all creation. Imaginary spaces can also function as possible worlds, which potentially exist by virtue of God's omnipotence. In the *Disputatio* Rutherford argued that an infinite number of worlds, beings, acts, and moments exist within the "huge bosom of God's omnipotence." Of these infinite potential worlds known to God, only those chosen by his will and brought to pass by his power will see actual existence.[99] From the context in the *Examen,* it is clear that the potential space of these possible worlds spoken of in the *Disputatio* corresponds to imaginary spaces spoken of in the *Examen.*[100]

The seemingly obscure point about God's presence in imaginary spaces, when linked with possible worlds, has far reaching implications for the doctrine of divine providence. If imaginary spaces are taken as possible worlds as the context suggests, then such spaces are not independent of God's presence and power. As will be shown in Chapter 3 of this dissertation, creaturely independence in possible future events was a key feature of both the Jesuit and Arminian accounting of the *scientia media,* and thus also of human freedom. However, as will also be shown in the following chapters, if such spaces were understood as independent of God's will and power, their fundamental contingency was greatly undermined. The specter of fatal necessity was not far behind. Contrary to this position, Rutherford argued that such possible worlds signified by these imaginary spaces never achieve actuality unless God's will and power are applied. By insisting that such imaginary spaces are not independent of God's presence and power, as Rutherford does, the contingency of the created order is preserved, since the actualization of such spaces is not determined by the necessity of nature, or some other fatal necessity, but freely following a determination of God's will.[101]

Richard has characterized the above remarks concerning God's omnipresence as a "relatively minor disagreement" that reveals Rutherford's "profound attitude of intolerance." He argues that other seventeenth century polemical treatises "do not make an issue of omnipresence," and that the "Arminians explicitly acknowledge that God is omnipresent." Therefore, Richard concludes that Rutherford's remarks

---

99 "Cum infinita sint possibilia, quae nunquam futura sunt, in gremio quasi vastissimae omnipotentiae nempe plures mundi, plures soles, lunae infinitae, ascribendum Deo dominanti in illa quae potest, si vult producere, quod fieri, hunc mundum non alios millenos mundos, hunc, non tres alios, vel quator *soles* vel *lunas,* has, quae de facto creatae sunt, decreverit creaturas." Rutherford, *Disputatio Scholastica,* 533.

100 "Quia non posset Deus, infinitos mundos, extra hec spatia imaginaria conderere: quia necesse esset, inciperet esse, ubi antea non esset." Rutherford, *Examen Arminianismi,* 145.

101 For more on the implications of God's presence and power for possible worlds, see Chapter 5.2.

are entirely unjustified, stating, "There appears to be no reason for Rutherford's tirade except his intolerance and zeal for the divine glory."[102] Richard's interpretation could be improved by more closely considering the historical and scholastic context. Other seventeenth century treatises did mention God's omnipresence as a point of disagreement, including the point made about imaginary spaces.[103] Furthermore, as was shown above, Episcopius explicitly denied God's essential presence not just in imaginary spaces, but in many created spaces as well. Far from being a matter of mere intolerance, Rutherford's argument pertains to a significant doctrinal debate with high stakes in regard to God's simplicity as well as the doctrine of divine providence.

2.2.5 The Free Exercise of Attributes

The final section of Rutherford's discussion on God's essence and attributes concerns whether or not God freely expresses these attributes, particularly the attribute of goodness. The question comes from the *Apologia D. Jacobi Arminii.*[104] The controversy came about during a disputation where it was asked whether "necessity and liberty can be so far reconciled to each other, that a person may be said to necessarily or freely produce one and the same effect."[105] Arminius denied that necessity and liberty could be so reconciled. To disprove his position an argument was brought forward that God is both necessarily and freely good. This declaration offended Arminius so greatly that he argued that it was not far from blasphemy.[106] He went on to argue that God is by natural necessity and according to his very essence good. God is goodness itself and therefore he is not freely good.[107] Liberty

---

102 Richard, *The Supremacy of God in the Theology of Samuel Rutherford*, 82.

103 God's essential omnipresence, contra-Richard, was a point of serious doctrinal controversy between the Reformed Orthodox and the Remonstrants. See Muller, *The Divine Essence and Attributes* 338–42; also Beck, *Gisbertus Voetius*, 253–60.

104 Jacobus Arminius, "Apologia D. Jacobi Arminii adversus Articulos XXXI," in *Opera Theologica* (Leiden: Godefridum Basson, 1629).

105 "Disputatum est an *necessitas & liberate* eosque inter se conciliari possint, ut aliquis dici possit *necessario* aut *libere unum undemque effectum produce.*" Arminius, "Apologia D. Jacobi Arminii," 166.

106 "Ut hanc meam sententiam infringerent, attulerunt *instantiam*, seu *exemplum*, in quo *necessitas & libertas* concurrerent, nempe Deum, qui *necessario & libere bonus est.* Quod ipsum *dictum* ita vehementer mihi displicuit, ut dicerem non procul abesse a blasphemia." Arminius, "Apologia D. Jacobi Arminii," 166.

107 "Qui naturali necessitate & secundum ipsam essentiam & naturam suam totam bonum est, imp ipsum bonum, summum bonum, primum bonum…Deus autem est naturalis necessitate, secundum naturam totam & essentiam bonum, ipsum summum, primmum bonum, a quo per quem in quo omne bonum, &C. Ergo Deus non est libere bonus." Arminius, "Apologia D. Jacobi Arminii," 166–7.

and contingency pertain to the divine will, not the divine essence, thus again God is not freely but necessarily good.[108]

Rutherford agreed that God was essentially and necessarily good. However, he drew a distinction between God's goodness *ad intra* and the expression of God's goodness *ad extra*.[109] Whereas God is necessarily good *ad intra*, the expression of his goodness *ad extra* is free. The usefulness of this distinction is that it permits God to remain essentially good, whether or not there is a creation towards which he may providentially express his goodness to. The point is also made in *The Covenant of Life Opened*, where Rutherford wrote:

> Common sense will say no more followeth, but goodnesse and bounty intrinsecall are essentiall to God, and these attributes are essentiall to him, and were from eternity in him, and are his good and bountifull nature.[110]

Because God is essentially and necessarily good, even if he never extended his goodness *ad extra* through an act of creation or providence, he would still remain essentially and necessarily good. "Though not either man, Angel, or any thing else had been created, to which he doth actually extend his goodnesse; *Ergo*, this actual extension of goodnesse is not essentiall to God."[111] Likewise, it pertains to God's goodness to create the world, to give faith to Peter, and to communicate being and goodness to creatures. Nevertheless, if God never created the world, gave faith to Peter, or communicated being and goodness to creatures, God would still be essentially and necessarily good. Because God is essentially and necessarily good whether he expresses this goodness *ad extra* or not, any expression of God's goodness *ad extra* must therefore be contingent and free. Rutherford's insistence on the free expression of God's attributes not only ensured God's freedom and ultimate independence, but it also ensured the contingency of the created world.[112]

Rutherford was able to apply the above in quite moving ways. In *The Covenant of Life Opened* he wrote:

---

108 "Libertas est affectus voluntatis divina non essentiae, non intellectus, non potentia: ideoque non natura divina in sua totalitate consideratae…Bonitas vero est affectus totius natura divina, essentia, vita, intellectus, voluntatis, potentia, &C. Ergo non est libere bonus, hoc est, non est bonum per modum libertatis, sed naturalis necessitates." Arminius, "Apologia D. Jacobi Arminii," 167.

109 "Nos dicimus, nostros hoc non loqui, de Bonitate Dei *ad intra*, qua Deus est essentialiter bonus." Rutherford, *Examen Arminianismi*, 146.

110 Rutherford, *The Covenant of Life Opened*, 21.

111 Rutherford, *The Covenant of Life Opened*, 21.

112 "Sed de Bonitate Dei *ad extra*, qua libere suam bonitatem creaturis comunicat. Quia ita bonus est Deus, creando mundum, dando fidem *Petro*, & entitatem & bonitatem creaturis communicando, ut potuerit esse hoc modo non bonus, si non creasset mundum, nec dedisset Fidem *Petro*, & creaturas annihilaret." Rutherford, *Examen Arminianismi*, 146.

> Now the Lord does not love himself of free grace for he every way, for the infinite excellency of His Nature is love-worthy, and there is no intervening of freedom, or free grace, or sovereignty in the Lords loving of himself and his own essential glory.[113]

Much like God's goodness, God is love necessarily. Furthermore, as is shown above, the exercise of God's love towards himself is necessary. God therefore loves his own essence and nature, but also, within the Godhead the Persons of Trinity essentially and necessarily love one another. In a separate work, *Christ Dying and Drawing Sinners to Himselfe,* he wrote:

> The love of the *Father* to the Sonne, as his *consubstantial Son,* and so farre as it's essentially included in his love to *Jesus Christ Mediator,* is not a love founded on grace and free-mercy, which might never have been in *God*; because essentially, the *Father* must love his Sonne *Christ,* as his Sonne.[114]

The same is not true for God's love *ad extra.* Whereas the Father's love for the Son and vice versa is of the nature of necessity, God's Trinitarian love for the world is of the nature of liberty, contingency, and therefore choice. "God out of free love sent his Son into the world, *John 3:16.*"[115] "The love wherewith the Father loveth us for his Son, Christ, is founded on *free grace and mercy.*"[116] For Rutherford, the glory of God's love *ad extra* is not bound up in its necessary nature but rather in its free and contingent nature. It is God's free, unnecessary expression of love in the gift of his Son upon the cross that reveals the depths and riches of the divine love and thus the divine glory. It is also the theme that finds Rutherford at his poetic best. "What then could have made him (Christ) stir his foot from heaven…except free, strong and vehement love, that was a bottomless river unpatient of banks?"[117] "There was a sad and bloudy war between divine justice and sinners: *Love, Love* pressed *Christ* to war."[118] The marvel of this, at least for Rutherford, lay in the fact that God did not have to take on the work of redemption, but out of divine love he wanted to. The doctrine of the contingent expression of God's attributes *ad extra* is not purely about preserving the divine freedom. It has practical use as well. It serves to warm the soul and elicit love from the heart for the purposes of the worship of God.[119]

---

113 Rutherford, *The Covenant of Life Opened,* 29.

114 Rutherford, *Christ Dying and Drawing Sinners to Himselfe,* 74.

115 Rutherford, *The Covenant of Life Opened,* 231.

116 Rutherford, *Christ Dying and Drawing Sinners to Himselfe,* 75.

117 Rutherford, 13.

118 Rutherford, 14.

119 See "Preface to the Reader" in Rutherford, *Christ Dying and Drawing Sinners to Himselfe,* A2.

2.3 The Holy Trinity

2.3.1 Trinity and Simplicity

Having treated first the knowledge of God, then proceeding to the divine essence and unity, Rutherford continues with the doctrine of the Holy Trinity. The progression has a tight internal logic, with the first (*de cognitione Dei*) establishing whether knowledge of God can be attained. The second heading seeks to establish "what" God is. Having established the "what," Rutherford now turns to the "who." This question is answered by the doctrine of the Trinity.

Rutherford's only dedicated treatment of the doctrine of the Trinity comes from the *Examen* and it is disappointingly short. This is not to suggest that Rutherford was disinterested in the doctrine or did not understand its central place in the Christian faith and life. Rather, it means that the subject matter of Rutherford's writings are often dictated by the political and polemical challenges at his doorstep. Thus, his three major Latin treatises, the *Exercitationes pro Divina Gratia, Disputatio Scholastica de Divina Providentia*, and his *Examen Arminianismi* were all written before 1650. As was seen in the previous chapter, the great challenges facing Rutherford and the Scottish Kirk were coming from Charles I and the Laudian Bishops, who had largely embraced Arminianism. The marriage of the political and polemical challenges focused Rutherford on the central theological problem of his opponents, this being the *scientia media*. As will be seen, Rutherford does identify problems in statements concerning the Trinity from certain Arminian theologians. These opinions, however, were never adopted by the Laudian bishops. The brevity with which Rutherford handles this important doctrine has more to do with the general level of agreement amongst the various parties that Rutherford is concerned with addressing than it does his lack of interest in the doctrine itself.

"It is asked," wrote Rutherford, "whether there are three essences in God or whether there is only one?"[120] The question is prompted by remarks concerning God's essence and Triunity made by Vorstius as well as the German Socinian Valentinus Smalcius (1572–1622). Vorstius's remarks hinged upon a wide reading of the term "essence," which he took to be interchangeable with "being" (*ens*), and "thing" (*res*).[121] Vorstius maintained that scripture testifies that there is indeed one God, but he also maintained that this one God is clearly presented in scripture as three distinct beings or entities. With his broad reading of the term essence, Vorstius concluded that while there is one God, the Trinity of persons implies this one God

---

120 "Quaeritur, An tres Essentia sint in Deo? An una tantum?" Rutherford, *Examen Arminianismi*, 147.
121 Conrad Vorstius, *Apologetica exegesis sive plenior declaratio*. (Lugdunum Batavorum: Joannis Patij, 1611), 3.

exists in three distinct essences.[122] The point made from Smalcius is similar. "Where there are two," he wrote, "it is necessary that there are two essences."[123]

Vorstius and Smalcius's comments should be seen as part of a broader trend that has been seen also in Episcopius, which looks suspiciously to the doctrine of divine simplicity. Divine simplicity and a plurality of persons are thought to be mutually exclusive, in much the same way that the divine simplicity was thought to be contradictory to the divine attributes and the divine decrees. Rutherford's response was a simple reassertion of essential unity within the divinity. His insistence upon one simple divine essence is based on the scripture proofs Deut. 6:4, 32:39 and I Cor. 8:6.[124]

Beyond this simple reassertion of the divine unity, Rutherford offered two additional arguments. If there are three distinct divine essences, then there are three distinct divine natures, and thus three distinct gods. Arminius was unfairly implicated in this critique by virtue of arguments made concerning his Christology, which could be described as subordinationist.[125] Richard rightly notes that Rutherford unfairly exaggerated the position of Arminius. However, he is wrong to characterize Rutherford's overall concerns as exaggerated and excessive. Richard only focuses on Arminius, ignoring Rutherford's first two references of Vorstius and Smalcius, each being overtly tri-theistic.[126] Arminius's comments, no matter how innocent, received heightened scrutiny after the increasingly heterodox opinions of the Re-

---

122 "Et sane S. literae non obscure hoc sensu singulis personis suam quandam peculiarem essentiam, respective sumtam, sive entitatem aliquam propriam attribuunt: cum verbi gratia ajunt, *tres esse qui in caelo testantur, Patrem, Sermonem, & Spiritum S.* denique *Filium a Patre genitum esse, & Spiritum S. ab eodem procedere, &c.* Ubi enim tres sunt, vere inter se distincti, & quibus singulis propriae quaedam actiones competunt, ibi certe 3. distincta entia sunt, eoque 3. Distinctae essentiae, sive entitates: sicut ipsa conjugatorum ratio evincit." Vorstius, *Apologetica responsio ad ea omnia*, 2.

123 "Ubi enim duo sunt, ibi duae ut sint essentiae necesse est." Valentino Smalcio, *Responsio ad Librum* (Racovia: Sternacianis, 1613), 39.

124 "Nos contra, cum Orthodoxis, uniam tantum Essentiam in Trinitate, statuimus. I. Quia unus est tantum Deus, Essentia unica & numero, & praeter eum non est alius Deus. Deut 6.4 & 32.39. I Cor 8.6." Rutherford, *Examen Arminianismi*, 147.

125 "Caeterum justificandae isti phrasi & sententiae dicunt, quum *Filium* dicitur esse *a se Deus*, tunc hoc *sensu* accipiendum esse, quod *essentia* quam *Filium habet a seipsa sit*, hoc est, *a nullo Filium* enim considerandum esse qua Deus est & qua Filium: qua Deus, esse *a seipso, qua Filium*, esse *a Patre*." Arminius, "Apologia D. Jacobi Arminii," 165.

126 There is a distinction to be made between the work of Arminius and the later Remonstrants such as Episcopius and Vorstius. The later exhibit a far greater departure from orthodox theology than Arminius did. In this section of the *Examen*, most of Rutherford's comments are directed towards the later Remonstrants and some Socinians such as Valentinus Smalcius. Missing the context of Rutherford's remarks can cause Richard to minimize the significance of the discussion. See Richard, *The Supremacy of God in the Theology of Samuel Rutherford*, 87.

monstrants who followed him.[127] It would have been easy to draw associations between Vorstius and Arminius, as Rutherford did, especially in light of the fact that Vorstius accepted a call to Leiden to fill Arminius's chair after his death.[128] In ignoring this historical and scholastic context, Richard minimizes what was in reality a serious and overt threat to orthodox teaching on the nature of God and the Holy Trinity.[129]

Rutherford identifies this threat when he notes that if there was a multiplication of divine essences, as Vorstius and Smalcius argue, then there would be a multiplication of divine attributes. If there are three distinct essences, there would be three distinct attributes of infinity as well as three distinct attributes of omnipotence. More problematic is the notion that there would be three distinct intellects and three distinct wills rather than three persons sharing one essence and one essential will and intellect.[130] The implications for God's providence are made clear when the words "intellect" and "will" are read in their scholastic context. The distinctions pertaining to God's intellect apply to God's knowledge of all possibility. They also apply to God's knowledge of those possibilities he has freely willed to actualize. The distinctions pertaining to God's will apply to what God could will, what God has willed, and the will he has revealed as an appropriate standard for his creatures.[131] The importance of the point here is that God's knowledge and will belong to the one essence of God, and are not distinct powers present in three distinct beings. Vorstius's heterodox, tri-theistic theology suggests that there might be three distinct personal intellects comprehending three distinct sets of possibilities open to God. The same applies to God's will.[132]

The above poses several difficulties pertaining to the doctrine of divine providence. In his *Ane Catechisme*, Rutherford asks:

---

127 See: Jan Rohls, "Calvinism, Arminianism, and Socinianism in the Netherlands Until the Synod of Dordt," in *Socinianism and Arminianism: Antitrinitarians, Calvinists, and Cultural Exchange in Seventeenth-Century Europe*, eds. Martin Mulsow and Jan Rohls, Brill's Studies in Intellectual History 134 (Leiden: Brill, 2005), 3–48.

128 See: Frederick Shriver, "Orthodoxy and Diplomacy: James I and the Vorstius Affair," *The English Historical Review* 85, no. 336 (1970): 449–74.

129 For general comments on Vorstius's tri-theistic theology, see: Muller, *The Divine Essence and Attributes*, 282–3.

130 "At si hic sunt tres distinctae Essentia, hic sunt tria Infinita, tres Omnipotentes, tres Intellectus, tres Voluntates; non tres, habentes eandem Infinitatem, eandem Omnipotentiam, & eundem Intellectum & Voluntatem." Rutherford, *Examen Arminianismi*, 148.

131 These distinctions are covered in Chapters 3 (God's Knowledge) and 4 (God's Will) of this study.

132 "At vero licet Personae, non sint nudi modi subsistendi, sed connotent substantiam; non connotant tamen tres substantias, & singulae singulam substantiam; sed omnes, unam numero substantiam." Rutherford, *Examen Arminianismi*, 148.

Q. Quhat learne yee of this that there are three persons heir?

A. That our salvatione is sure, because thre witnesses in heaven hes said that our life is empaunded in Christ's hand. —1 John v.11.[133]

The prospect of three distinct intellects and three distinct wills raises the prospect that the three persons may understand and will distinctly, rather than jointly. If such is the case, then the certainty of God's promises pertaining to salvation, as well as any other promises that must be providentially brought about in time, are no longer certain.[134]

There is another problem regarding the above. This is the epistemological problem concerning the revelation of God in the incarnation of the Son. In a sermon delivered at Anwoth in 1630, Rutherford preached:

> We see the printing iron leaves behind it every way, the printing of itself; so the Lord from eternity brought forth another like Himself, the Second Person of the Trinity, stamped with the same glorious God-head, with all the essential properties that are in the Father…The brightness of God's glory is a great word, a rare and great mystery. The glancing brightness coming from the sun, is not another sun; nor is the glancing brightness of a precious stone, another stone. And so it is here with Him. Because, all that is in God is God, and there is nothing in Him but what is in His nature; therefore the riches and beams of infinite glory, and that substantial glancing glory, and beauty in God is God, and the very nature of God, and the same God with the Father.[135]

The epistemological problem is made plain in Rutherford's moving text. The Second Person of the Trinity reveals both the Father, as well as the nature of God, because the Second Person is God. To borrow the language from above, the problem posed by the tri-theistic theology of Vorstius is that the Second Person would be "another sun" and "another stone" than God the Father. If this were true, the Second Person's revelation of the divinity would begin and end with his own person, since he would be his own distinct being and distinct essence.[136]

---

133 Rutherford, *Ane Catachisme*, 162.

134 Though the divine persons have distinct actions, their shared intellect and will are applied to singular, shared ends. For an example, see Rutherford, *Ane Catachisme*, 164.

135 Samuel Rutherford, *Fourteen Communion Sermons*, ed. Andrew A. Bonar, 2nd ed. (Glasgow: Charles Glass & Co, 1878), 34–5.

136 This is nearly made explicit in Vorstius. See Nota ad Disputationem III, in Vorstius, *Tractatus Theologicus De Deo, Sive Natura & Attributis Dei, Omnia Fere Ad hanc Materiam pertinentia (saltem de quibus utiliter & religiose disputari potest) decem Disputationibus, antehac in Illustri Schola Steinfurtensi, diverso tempore, publice habitis, breviter & methodice comprehendens*, 208–9.

2.3.2 The Aseity of the Second Person of the Trinity

Closely related to the above discussions concerning the divine simplicity and the Holy Trinity are controversies pertaining to the *per se* divinity of the divine persons, specifically that of the Second Person of the Trinity. Rutherford asks whether the Son is αυτοθεος (God in and of himself).[137] The problem is introduced by Jacobus Arminius's subordinationist Christology, briefly alluded to above. However, Rutherford did not identify the problem ultimately with Arminius. Citing the Dutch Protestant Theologian Lucas Trelcatius (1542–1602), Rutherford argues that subordinationist Christology was the first step on the path to tri-theism. Others, such as Vorstius, had walked through the door opened by Arminius to posit triplicity in God.[138]

Rutherford argued that the Second Person of the Trinity was essentially and truly God. Rather than being motivated by a speculative, philosophical concern to maintain the doctrine of divine simplicity, Rutherford argued that scripture demands this position. He cites John 1:1–3, Rom. 9:5, Col. 1:15, and 1 John 5:20 as scripture proofs.[139] In regard to subordinationist Christology, Rutherford argued that there is a difference between the essence that communicates and the essence that is communicated. Whether or not those who hold to a subordinationist Christology intend to introduce two essences into the Godhead is irrelevant. The subordinationist Christology in and of itself implies at least two essences and therefore at least two Gods.[140] The specter of two Gods, one deriving essential divinity from the other, also introduces the problem that the communication of the divine essence from the Father to the Son occurred in time. Rutherford attributed this problem to the Dutch non-Trinitarian John Geisteranus (1586–1622).[141]

Distinctions are made within the Trinity, but these distinctions are not made according to essence. The distinctions are made according to Persons (i.e. Father,

---

137 "Quaeritur, An *Filius sit* αυτοθεος & ex se, & a se Deus?" Rutherford, *Examen Arminianismi*, 149.

138 "Et D. Telecatium juniorem carpit, quod Filium, qua Deum αυτοθεος vocet; quia sic Pater, nomine solum tenus, a Filio differret, (quod asseruit Sabellius) & in Tritheismum incideremus: Quia sic tres dii essent, qui simul collateraliter, divinam essentiam haberent." Rutherford, *Examen Arminianismi*, 149.

139 "Nos contra, Christum esse essentialiter & vere Deum. *Isa 9.6. Vocabitur, Deus fortis. Joan. 1.1,2,3. Sermo erat Deus. Rom 9.5. Coloss. 1.15. 1 Joan. 5.20*, Ergo, est Deus a seipso; & divinam naturam, qua Deus, a nullo habet." Rutherford, *Examen Arminianismi*, 149.

140 "Si *Filius*, non tantum qua *Filius*, sed & qua Deus habet Essentiam communicatam *a Patre* (quia Essentia communicata, est distincta ab Essentia communicante) erunt hic duae Essentiae, communicans & communicata: Et idem dicendum de *Spiritu Sancto*; & sic tres Essentia, & tres Deitates, & tres Dii; & *Arminius*, non *Trelcatius*, est *Tritheita*." Rutherford, *Examen Arminianismi*, 149.

141 "Impius Joan Geisteranus, in sua confessione, in tempore, Filium, Deitatem a patre, accepisse, ait." Rutherford, *Examen Arminianismi*, 149.

Son, and Holy Spirit). Such distinctions are real, rather than conceptual. Distinctions may also be made according to actions, including those involved in the exercise of divine providence. In his *Tryal and Triumph of Faith*, Rutherford wrote:

> *The Designation* was an act of Divine and voluntary Dispensation, according to which the *second Person of the Trinity, the Son of God, not the Father, not the Holy Ghost,* was designed and set apart to take on him our nature, place and the office of Mediator to redeeme us, in his owne Person.[142]

In the above, that act of "Divine and voluntary Dispensation" should be ascribed to an act of God according to his singular essence. The Divine Persons are distinguished within this act according to the manner in which it is actualized. Only the second person of the Trinity, in an act of divine providence, is incarnate.[143] Drawing distinctions between Persons of the Trinity became a matter of greater importance later in Rutherford's career, with the ascendancy of the independents, who tolerated antinomian and non-Trinitarians, such as John Saltmarsh (d. 1647). Saltmarsh was on the other end of the extreme from Vorstius, arguing that there were no true distinctions between the Persons of the Trinity, but that they were rather simply different manifestations of an essential divinity.[144] Nevertheless, it was Vorstius's attack on the aseity of the Second Person of the Trinity, implying composition and mutability in the divinity, that posed a greater threat not only to the divine simplicity but also doctrines pertaining to divine providence.

2.4 Summary

It has been shown that Rutherford's doctrine of the divine nature and essence, while heavily resourced by Scholastic reasoning and distinctions was intended to be grounded in Scripture. Rutherford held that Scripture was the primary source from which knowledge of God could be acquired. Furthermore, Rutherford argued that it is a scriptural imperative to gain knowledge of God, not only according to saving faith and the practical acts of Christian life, but also according to the more theoretical interests of God's essential nature.

Rutherford lived in a time when the doctrine of God faced significant controversy. The *scientia media,* a new distinction pertaining to the divine knowledge introduced

---

142 Rutherford, *The Tryal and Triumph of Faith,* 91.

143 The same point is made in the *Examen:* "nullo diverso respectu, Essentia divina est incarnata in *Filio,* & non incarnata in *Patre;* In *Filio, personaliter* est incarnata: In *Patre,* absolute sumpta, non est incarnata." Rutherford, *Examen Arminianismi,* 150.

144 See Rutherford's comments in: Rutherford, *A Survey of the Spiritual Antichrist,* 276–7.

by Jesuits such as Luis de Molina (1535–1600), Pedro de Fonseca (1528–1599), and later promoted by Francisco Suárez (1548–1617), as well as the Dutch Protestant theologian Jacobus Arminius (1560–1609), introduced the specter of composition into the divine intellect. These fears were realized when Remonstrants such as Simon Episcopius (1583–1643) and Conrad Vorstius (1569–1622) began to aggressively critique the doctrine of divine simplicity. The attacks by Episcopius and Vorstius, among others, had far reaching consequences not only on the doctrine of divine simplicity, but also on attributes such as infinitude, omnipresence, and even the doctrine of the Trinity.

Rutherford's reassertion of the doctrine of divine simplicity is hardly novel. There are, nevertheless, several interesting features. Rutherford's essentialist reading of the divine name *YHWH* was employed by him to establish God's being as a rock bottom principle of demonstration. The same also established God's being as the only absolutely independent and necessary being. Being and non-being, possibility and impossibility, as well as necessity and contingency, are all properties that are dependent upon God for their meaning. Rutherford's essentialist reading of the divine name means there is nothing outside of God that is truly independent of him.

The above point is reinforced by Rutherford's discussion of God's omnipresence. Whereas Episcopius sought to carve out spaces independent of God's presence, Rutherford denied that there was any space independent of God's essential presence. Implications for God's providence are manifold, but two were identified above as especially important. The first is that God's essential presence in all things is necessary for the divine *concursus* as well as for the providential governance of the created order. The second is that God's essential presence in all things, including imaginary spaces, is a necessary prerequisite for creation. As shown above, the context in the *Examen* makes clear that Rutherford's use of "imaginary spaces" corresponds to his use of as yet uncreated possible worlds. If God's presence does not precede such possible worlds, then he cannot create them. Therefore, the actualization of such possible worlds is radically dependent upon his essential omnipresence.

Finally, Rutherford's doctrine of the Trinity safeguards properties threatened by the attacks upon the divine simplicity. His insistence on a Trinity of persons existing in one simple, divine essence is an insistence that God is without composition. As was seen above, this rules out multiple intellects and wills within God, which rules out divine indecision or disagreement. Rutherford's discussion on the aseity of the Second Person of the Trinity also rules out that the Son is dependent upon the Father for his divinity. Thus, the radical independence of God is maintained for each person of the Trinity. As we proceed to examine Rutherford's doctrine of the divine intellect, will, and providence, God's radical independence will be seen as a major doctrinal theme. This doctrinal theme, having its basis in the divine nature and essence, is not only important for asserting catholic creedal orthodoxy, but it will also be shown as the most significant bulwark against the threat of a fatal universe.

3.   God's Knowledge

Shall any teach the Almighty knowledge? If he pursue dry stubble, who dare say, what dost thou? Do not wonder, to see the Judge of the world weave in one web…he can make one web of contraries.[1]

Having treated God's essence and nature, the following chapters continue with a focus on the doctrine of God, treating God's knowledge, will, and power. Just as the survey of Rutherford's doctrine of God was meant to assist the reader in better understanding his conception of divine providence, so too is this chapter meant to further fill out the contours of this discussion. Beneath the broad term of the *scientia dei* lie multiple distinctions. For Rutherford and others of the Reformed Orthodox, these served to distinguish God's essential and necessary knowledge from his contingent and free knowledge. As has been mentioned previously, in the sixteenth century a new distinction was introduced into the scholastic discussion on the *scientia dei*, this being the "middle knowledge" (*scientia media*). The bulk of Rutherford's writings on the divine knowledge are dedicated towards interacting with this new doctrine. The following chapter offers a comprehensive overview of Rutherford's understanding of the divine knowledge. The chapter begins with a brief survey of the structure and terms associated with the doctrine (3.1) followed by a discussion of Rutherford's understanding of God's necessary and free knowledge (3.2). After this, God's knowledge of truth concerning future contingent events will be examined from the perspective of two different distinctions (3.3). The chapter concludes with the constitutive nature of God's knowledge (3.4). In each section, consequences for the doctrine of God's providence will be highlighted.

3.1   Introduction to Structure and Terms

Rutherford addressed the *scientia dei* in each of his three Latin works of scholastic theology. The clearest presentation of the structure of his doctrine is found in the *Examen*, where he follows a well-worn established pattern treating God's essence and nature, before addressing his knowledge, will, and works.[2] Besides the *Examen*,

---

1 Rutherford, *Joshua Redivivus*, 355.

2 Rutherford's doctrine of God is presented in Chapter 2 of the *Examen*. As was seen in the previous chapter, he begins with human knowledge of God (*De cognitione dei*) in Chapter 2.1, before proceeding to God's essence, unity and omnipresence (*De deo secundum essentiam, ejusque unitate, omnipraesentia*

the closest Rutherford comes to this pattern is in the *Disputatio*, though God's will is treated before God's knowledge and works.[3] The *Exercitationes* has many fascinating comments on God's knowledge, though the structure of the comments is dictated by polemics rather than the precedence set by Rutherford's scholastic forbears.[4]

In the *Examen*, Rutherford provided a clear and useful statement pertaining to God's necessary and free knowledge. He wrote:

> Knowledge is twofold (I will not say anything of God's reflexive knowledge, which is clearly natural, by which he knows himself): some is of vision, or intuitive, or determinate, by which God knows all being outside of himself, which are now, were, or will be in the future, or are not. The other is of simple intelligence, by which God knows possible things (*possibilia*), and is called natural, indeterminate, and abstractive.[5]

As can be seen, Rutherford divided God's knowledge into two broad categories that pertain to God's necessary and free knowledge. He employed a variety of distinctions pertaining to God's necessary knowledge (*scientia necessaria*). These are his knowledge of simple intelligence (*scientia simplicis intelligentiae*), which he also terms his natural knowledge (*scientia naturalis*). Such knowledge is also indeterminate (*indeterminata*) and abstractive (*abstractiva*). The distinctions used by Rutherford to discuss God's free knowledge (*scientia libera*) are God's knowledge of vision (*scientia visionis*), intuition (*intuitiva*), or determinate knowledge (*determinata*). This broad division of God's knowledge into necessary and free is analogous to other divisions within the Reformed Orthodox tradition that group

---

essentiali) in Chapter 2.2. From here he treats the Holy Trinity (*De Trinitate*) in Chapter 2.3. After this he addresses God's knowledge (*De Scientia Dei*) in Chapter 2.4 and God's will (*De Voluntas Dei*) in Chapter 2.5. See: Rutherford, *Examen Arminianismi*, 138.

3 There is no formal presentation of the doctrine of God's being in the *Disputatio*. Rather, the work begins with a scholastic definition of God's providence (*Quid sit providentia dei*) in Chapter 1. Rutherford defines providence as a work of God's knowledge, will, and power. The following chapters therefore treat God's will (Chapter 2), knowledge (Chapter 3), and power (Chapter 4) in relation to God's providence. Rutherford, *Disputatio Scholastica*, Chapters 1–3.

4 A chapter of interest to the present discussion is *Exercitatio* I. Cap. 5, "Suáreziis, Fonseca, & Arminiano-rum de nova Dei Scientia, quam conditionatam, seu mediam vocant, rationes examini subjiciuntur." See: Rutherford, *Exercitationes Apologeticae*, 158–200.

5 "Scientia est duplex (ut nihil dicam de Scientia *reflexa* plane naturali, qua Deus novit seipsum) alia *Visionis*, seu *intuitiva*, seu *determinata*, qua Deus omnia entia extra se, quae sunt, fuerunt, aut futura sunt, vel non sunt, novit. Alia *Simplicis Intelligentiae*, qua possibilia novit; & vocatur *naturalis*, *indeterminata*, *abstractiva*." Rutherford, *Examen Arminianismi*, 163.

similar terms under these two broad headings. These distinctions are covered in greater detail below.[6]

3.2 God's Necessary and Free Knowledge

3.2.1 Scientia Reflexa

God knows himself through a knowledge that refers back to him as a primary subject and, as such, can be described as reflexive knowledge (*scientia reflexa*). In the *Examen*, Rutherford has little to say in regard to the *scientia reflexa* other than to say it is entirely natural and it is the knowledge by which God knows himself.[7] It can be inferred from the *Disputatio* that God both knows himself and loves what he knows about himself. He knows his attributes and loves his attributes. Positively citing the Italian Roman Catholic Cardinal Thomas Cajetan (1469–1534), Rutherford noted that God knows and necessarily loves his omnipotence and the possibilities open to God by virtue of his omnipotence.[8] God does not love the possibilities in and of themselves, but rather as they exist in him. This last point, which directly relates to the doctrine of divine providence, underscores the reflexive nature of the possibilities themselves as well as God's knowledge of them.[9] Furthermore, that God knows and loves the possibilities as they are in him, rather than as they are in themselves, reinforces a point emphasized in the previous chapter concerning God's simplicity. Because God knows the possibilities as they exist in him, the prospect of composition in God is ruled out, since he is not acquiring knowledge of possibilities that exist independently of his power. Beyond God's knowledge of and love of his essence and attributes, there is personal knowledge and love that exist between the members of the Trinity, and this love is intellectually informed. The Father knows the Son and loves what he knows about the Son and vice versa. The same is of course true of the Spirit.[10]

---

6 For a general survey of these distinctions as they are represented in Reformed Scholasticism, see Muller, *The Divine Essence and Attributes*, 406–7; Beck, *Gisbertus Voetius*, 265–277.

7 "Ut nihil dicam de Scientia *reflexa*, plane naturali, qua Deus novit seipsum." Rutherford, *Examen Arminianismi*, 163.

8 See Thomas Cajetan, *Summa sacrae theologiae in tres partes divisa, et quattuor distincta tomis, d. Thoma Aquinate angelico doctore authore* (Bergamo: Comini Venturae, 1590), I, q. 34, a. 3.

9 "Deus amando omnipotentiam suam necessario coadamat possibilia, infinita ad intra, sed recte *Suárez* dicat, *Deum non posse esse omnipotentem, quin creaturae sint possibiles,* non temere affirmarem, nisi sermo sit de possibilibus ad intra: Recte forte *Cajetanus* ait (quem immerito refutat *Suárez*) *Deum necessario amare creaturas possibiles, ut sin in ipso Deo, non ut sin in seipsis.*" Rutherford, *Disputatio Scholastica*, 560.

10 See for example, Rutherford, *Joshua Redivivus*, 227.

3.2.2 *Scientia Naturalis / Simplicis Intelligentiae*

In addition to God's knowledge of himself, God also has natural or necessary knowledge of every possibility open to God through his omnipotence. Rutherford expressed God's knowledge of possibility through two distinctions: these being his natural knowledge (*scientia naturalis*) and his knowledge of simple intelligence (*scientia simplicis intelligentiae*). Of these two distinctions used to express this concept, Rutherford preferred to use the term *scientia simplicis intelligentiae* rather than *scientia naturalis*.[11] Much like God's reflexive knowledge, the knowledge of simple intelligence is natural and necessary, preceding any act of the divine will. The knowledge of simple intelligence differs from God's reflexive knowledge not by way of necessity, but rather by way of object. Whereas the object of God's reflexive knowledge is himself, the object of God's knowledge of simple intelligence is all possible states of affairs. *Quaestio VII* of the *Disquisitiones Metaphysicae* asks, "By what kind of knowledge and will does God comprehend possible objects (*possibilia*)?"[12] It is by his knowledge of simple intelligence (*scientia simplicis intelligentiae*). By this knowledge God knows those things that he is "able to make in this or that order of things."[13]

Rutherford's definition can be misleading to modern ears. One may think that the intention is merely to describe God's knowledge of possible creatures such as animate or inanimate objects. Rutherford certainly intended as much. However, included in the things God is "able to make" are also possible states of affairs such as the popular example of David at Keilah. In 1 Samuel chapter twenty-three David learns that if he remains at Keilah, Saul will besiege the city. By virtue of his knowledge of simple intelligence, God first knows this merely as a possibility. Thus, God knows that if David remains at Keilah, it is possible Saul will besiege the city.

---

11 In the *Examen*, Rutherford holds the terms *scientia simplicis intelligentiae* and *scientia naturalis* as roughly equivalent. See Rutherford, *Examen Arminianismi*, 163. In the *Exercitationes*, one finds the use of the term *scientia simplicis intelligentiae* to describe God's knowledge of possible states of affairs. Shortly thereafter, Rutherford will use the term *scientia naturalis* to describe the same concept. See Rutherford, *Exercitationes Apologeticae pro divina gratia*, 158 and 196. In the *Disputatio*, Rutherford uses the term *scientia simplicis intelligentiae* exclusively. Rutherford, *Disputatio Scholastica*, 559.

12 "Quali scientia & voluntate complectitur Deus possibilia?" Rutherford, *Disputatio Scholastica*, 559.

13 "Scit Deus quid creatura in hoc vel illo rerum ordine possit facere, scientia simplicis intelligentiae, in speculo Omnipotentiae." Rutherford, *Disputatio Scholastica*, 559. Freddoso makes the useful point that "God's natural knowledge includes a comprehensive grasp of all the active and passive causal powers creatures might have and exercise, since such causal powers are ultimately rooted in their natures." Though he is commenting on Molina, Freddoso's remarks seem universally applicable in sixteenth and seventeeth-century thought on God's natural knowledge. This would not be a disputed observation. Alfred J. Freddoso, "Introduction," in *On Divine Foreknowledge: Part IV of the Concordia* (Ithaca, New York: Cornell University Press, 1988), 12.

Because this state of affairs is initially known only as a possibility, Rutherford also believed that God knows the alternate possibility of David remaining at Keilah. In this alternate scenario, it is possible that Saul will not besiege the city.[14]

There are two things that are worth noting at this point. First, though Rutherford provided no definition for "possible" here, it could be inferred from his definition of the *scientia simplicis intelligentiae* (knowledge of what God is able to make) that something is possible because God is able to make it so. Thus, possibility as well as God's knowledge of what is possible is inextricably linked to and dependent upon God's power. The second feature, which reinforces the first, is that the *scientia simplicis intelligentiae* is an intellectual reflection of God's omnipotence. God's knowledge of the possibilities open to him is a mirror image of his own omnipotence, giving Rutherford's use of this traditionally Thomist term a nominalist accent.[15]

Rutherford's careful definition of the *scientia simplicis intelligentiae* as God's knowledge *in speculo omnipotentiae* was an intentional contrast to the position taken by Jesuit theologians Francisco de Oviedo (1602–1651) and Martinez de Ripalda (1594–1648).[16] Whereas Rutherford argued that something is possible because God is able to make it, Oviedo and Ripalda inverted the sequence. Oviedo understood God's omnipotence as "relative to the possibility of the effect produced by his power."[17] Martinez de Ripalda took a similar position arguing "created things truly have existence from another, yet they do not have internal logical consistency (*intrinsecam non repugnantiam*) from another."[18] Thus for Oviedo and Ripalda, God is able to make something because it is possible, not that something is possible because God is able to make it. God's power is therefore relative to the logical consistency of the possible object. This means God's knowledge of what he is able to make is not a reflexive knowledge of his own omnipotence, but rather knowledge of an entity with its own logical consistency independent of God. Rutherford described the position bluntly as "absurd."[19]

Oviedo and Ripalda's argument rested on the belief that logical possibility founded upon the law of non-contradiction was a principle independent from God

---

14 Rutherford, *Disputatio Scholastica*, 138–43. God's knowledge of *every* alternate possibility was a contested point in the sixteenth and seventeenth centuries. Certain Jesuits and Arminians argued that God *did not know* every alternate possibility according to his *scientia media*. See Chapter 5.3.2 of this study.

15 See Chapter 3 of this study, fn. 13.

16 This is covered in Goudriaan, "Samuel Rutherford on the Divine Origin of Possibility.", 147–149.

17 "Licet Oviedo dicat Omnipotentiam dici absolute potentem a possibilitate effectus." Rutherford, *Disputatio Scholastica*, 539.

18 "Tum quia res creatae, licet vere habeant existentiam ab alio, tamen non habent ab alio intrinsecam non repugnantiam existendi, sed a se ipsis sunt non repugnantes existere ab alio." Juan Martinez de Ripalda, *De ente supernaturali* (Lyon: Horatii Boissat & Georgii Remeus, 1663), 335.

19 "Quod est absurdum." Rutherford, *Disputatio Scholastica*, 539.

and prior to any act of God's will. As was shown in the previous chapter however, Rutherford's essentialist reading of the divine name established God's being as prior to the law of non-contradiction. Therefore, God's knowledge of the logical consistency of a possible being, contra Oviedo and Ripalda, is a derivative of God's own knowledge of his omnipotence. The disagreement between Rutherford and the aforementioned Jesuits is illustrative of two trajectories identified in the previous chapter. One trajectory, represented by Jesuits, Arminians, and Remonstrants, is a trajectory towards increasing creaturely independence. This begins early in the theological system, at the foundational level. On the other hand, as was just seen, Rutherford's trajectory was to establish radical creaturely dependence upon God. God's knowledge of simple intelligence (*scientia simplicis intelligentiae*), by which he knows all possible states of affairs, is therefore not merely knowledge of the logical consistency of possible beings but also knowledge derived from God's self-knowledge (*scientia reflexa*) of his own being and power. Herein lies the key to understanding the importance of this issue for Rutherford. By tying the *scientia simplicis intelligentiae* so tightly to God's knowledge of his own power, and thus the *scientia reflexa*, Rutherford has argued that God's knowledge of the realm of possibility is not dependent upon anything outside of God. God's knowledge underscores the point.[20]

3.2.3 Scientia Libera / Visionis

Whereas God's natural or necessary knowledge is of what God could do, God's free knowledge (*scientia libera*) or knowledge of vision (*scientia visionis*) is knowledge of what God has willed to do. Just as before, Rutherford was careful to note that God's knowledge of such things is not knowledge of the things in and of themselves. Rather God's knowledge of such things is seen primarily in the light of God's decree. Once again, God's knowledge is self-referential and absolutely independent.[21]

Typically, God's necessary (*scientia necessaria*) or natural knowledge (*scientia naturalis*) is paired with God's free knowledge (*scientia libera*). The distinction between these two terms draws attention to the decisive role that the divine will plays in distinguishing between these two forms of knowledge. As was shown above,

---

20 Richard writes that Rutherford's two categories of God's knowledge describe "the divine knowledge of all things outside of God, without respect to God's knowledge of himself." However, as was shown above, this is clearly not what Rutherford intends. The divine knowledge of all things outside of God is always reflective of God's own self-knowledge. See: Richard, *The Supremacy of God in the Theology of Samuel Rutherford*, 90.

21 "Sed quod Deus sit finem consequuturus perhaec, non illa media, & hae causae sint hos non illos effectus producturae, non videt nisi scientia libera; ideoque in praestrati decreti sui lumine." Rutherford, *Disputatio Scholastica*, 559.

God's natural knowledge is pre-volitional, thus necessary. God's post-volitional knowledge is contingent upon the divine will and thus free, hence the term *scientia libera*. The common counterpart to God's knowledge of simple intelligence (*scientia simplicis intelligentiae*) is his knowledge of vision (*scientia visionis*). Whereas the aforementioned distinction between God's necessary and free knowledge emphasizes the decisive role of the divine will, the distinction between God's knowledge of simple intelligence and knowledge of vision emphasizes the divine intellect and infinite vision. As Muller notes concerning the *scientia visionis*, it is identical in scope with the *scientia libera* (i.e. the actual world), but with an intellectualist implication. Muller describes the object of this knowledge as "the realm of all that God 'sees' or comprehends as belonging to the realm of divinely willed existence."[22] What can be confusing about Rutherford's use of these two pairs of terms is that, unlike other Reformed Orthodox who have separate treatments of the *scientia naturalis/libera* and *scientia simplicis intelligentiae/visionis* dichotomies, Rutherford often conflated the terms failing to identify any real distinction between them. Adding to the confusion, at times he will pair the terms in ways not traditionally done by either his predecessors or contemporaries. Therefore care must be taken to determine precisely what is intended when Rutherford employs these terms.[23]

Rutherford's earliest work of scholastic theology, the *Exercitationes Apologeticae*, employed both *scientia libera* as well as *scientia visionis* to describe God's knowledge of those things that absolutely will be or are now. Thus, the object of the *scientia libera* is the actual world, both as it is now and as it will be in the future. Between God's natural knowledge of things that could be, and God's free knowledge of things that are, the Jesuits argued that there was a middle knowledge (*scientia media*) of possible events that would be under certain conditions. The object of God's middle knowledge were those states of affairs that were described as "conditionally future" (*conditionaliter futurum*). One classic example of a conditional future event was David at Keilah. In the biblical account from 1 Sam. Ch. 23, David is told by Abiathar the Priest that if he remains in Keilah, the residents will hand him over to his nemesis King Saul. Thus God knows, based upon the condition of David remaining in Keilah, that the residents will hand him over.[24]

Rutherford shared the opinion with some Reformed theologians that the *scientia media* was unnecessary in light of God's knowledge of simple intelligence and vision. David's unfortunate fate based on the condition of his remaining at Keilah could just as easily be expressed as a possibility, and thus would be an object of God's knowledge of simple intelligence. While Rutherford sympathized with this

---

22 Muller, *The Divine Essence and Attributes*, 407.
23 See for example: Rutherford, *Exercitationes Apologeticae*, 158 and 196.
24 For Rutherford's summary see: Rutherford, *Exercitationes Apologeticae*, Exercitatio 1, Cap. 5., 158–200.

critique of the *scientia media*, he argued that this is not the reason that the *scientia media* is redundant, noting that the object of the *scientia media* is not possibility but rather a determinate future event under certain conditions. That David will be handed over to Saul if he remains at Keilah is not an expression of possibility, but rather an expression of what will absolutely be under certain conditions.[25] Therefore, according to Rutherford, the proper object of the *scientia media* was a determinately future event under certain conditions. Such properly belonged to the *scientia libera*, whereby God freely determines the conditions that bring about certain events.[26]

In the *Examen,* Rutherford largely avoided the term *scientia libera* showing preference for the intellectualist term *scientia visionis* to describe God's knowledge of those things that are now, were, or will be in the future, as well as those things that never will be.[27] The distinction has its origins in the *Summa Theologiae* (I, q. 14, a 9).[28] Rutherford's use of the term demonstrates important continuity with Thomas as well as important departures. Rutherford stated the object of God's knowledge of vision in terms nearly identical to Thomas. Nevertheless, he departed from Thomas in regard to the means by which this knowledge is acquired. The emphasis for Thomas, as the term indicates, is on God's eternal vision. Thomas wrote:

> God's understanding, which is his being, is measured by eternity; and since it exists without succession comprehending all time, the present gaze of God (*intuitus dei*) extends over all time, and to all things that exist in any time, as to subjects present to him.[29]

---

25 "Ergo, talis Resipiscentia est tantum quid possibile & extra limites statumve entium mere possibilium nunquam est egressa: & scientia simplicis intelligentiae scitur tale objectum, talisque Resipiscentia. 2. At vero Resipiscentia haec vestita Dei aeterno decreto, cujus est futuritionem vel absolutam vel conditionatam dare, tali conditione, nempe si Tyrii viderint miracula, est vere futurum & aliquid plus & ultra id quod est mere possibile, quia quod *Salvator* noster ait futurum, si talis conditio ponatur: id certissime & indeclinabiliter est futurum, si talis conditio ponatur: At Christus cujus nec scientia, nec praedictio salli potest, ait, Tyrios acturos Paenitentiam & Respicientiam, si viderint signa. Ergo talis Respiscentia sub reduplicatione talis conditionis est futurum quid, & non est mere possibile." Rutherford, *Disputatio Scholastica*, 14.

26 "Ergo inter scientiam naturalem, qua Deus possibilia cognoscit, & liberam; qua quæ absolute futura sunt & existunt, datur media scientia. Resp. Sententia libera Deus cognoscit futura conditionata, ideoque media hæc est vana, quia ex sola Dei voluntate necessario connectuntur interse Tyriorum resipiscentia & visio signorum." Rutherford, *Exercitationes Apologeticae pro divina gratia,* 190.

27 See this study, 3.2.3.

28 Beck, *Gisbertus Voetius,* 268–71.

29 "Quia, cum intelligere Dei, quod est eius esse, aeternitate mensuretur, quae sine successione existens totum tempus comprehendit, praesens intuitus Dei fertur in totum tempus, et in omnia quae sunt in quocumque tempore, sicut in subiecta sibi praesentialiter." I have followed the translation in *Summa*

Rutherford's appropriation followed Thomas's language of vision, but Rutherford employed it in a noticeably different way. Rather than beholding the objects themselves through God's infinite vision, Rutherford argued that God sees the objects in the light of his decree. Returning again to the example of the repentance of the Tyreans, Rutherford noted that God infallibly sees the future in his own decree by which God determines that the conversion of the Tyreans is joined to the condition of them beholding the sign.[30]

In the *Disputatio* Rutherford returned to the language of the *scientia libera*, but he maintained the language of vision and decree that he cultivated in the *Examen*. God sees the ends and the means, causes and effects of actual events through the *scientia libera*, which is illumined by the light of God's decree.[31] Scholars have noted that the intellectualist terms such as the *scientia simplicis intelligentiae/visionis* used by seventeenth century Reformed Orthodox are often interpreted in ways more consistent with models that emphasize the divine will. As can be seen from the above, Rutherford employed intellectualist terms. Nevertheless, for Rutherford, God's vision of actual and future events is seen only in the light of the decree. Thus, even in the midst of intellectualist metaphors, an emphasis upon the divine will is never far removed from the structure of the theology.[32]

3.3 God's Knowledge of Truth Concerning Future Contingent Events

The distinctions outlined above address God's knowledge of possibility and actuality. The series of distinctions that follow are conceptually closely related to the distinctions outlined above in that they follow the pattern of God's necessary knowledge of possibility and God's free knowledge of the actual world. Whereas the distinctions outlined above broadly address the nature of possibility and actuality, the distinctions that follow more narrowly address God's knowledge of the truth-value of conditional propositions concerning future contingent events.

Theologiae, trans. O.P. Fr. Laurence Shapcote, ed John Mortensen and Enrique Alarcon (Lander: The Aquinas Institute for the Study of Sacred Doctrine, 2012), I, q. 14, a 9, 159.

30 "Haec videt infallibiliter futura, in Decreto suo concatenante conversionem Tyriorum, & visionem miraculorum." Rutherford, *Examen Arminianismi*, 166.

31 "Sed quod Deus sit finem consequuturus per haec, non illa media, & hae causae sint hos non illos effectus producturae, non videt nisi scientia libera; idque in praestrati decreti sui lumine." Rutherford, *Disputatio Scholastica*, 559.

32 This serves as a confirmation of similar points made in Vos, "Ab Uno Disce Omnes." See also Beck's discussion on Voetius's use of the *scientia simplicis intelligentiae et visionis* distinction in Beck, *Gisbertus Voetius*, 270; and also Muller, *The Divine Essence and Attributes*, 408.

3.3.1 *Scientia Indeterminata et Determinata*

This distinction, as was seen above, was part of Rutherford's broad division of God's natural and free knowledge, where the *scientia indeterminata* belongs to God's natural knowledge and the *scientia determinata* belongs to God's free knowledge.[33] The object of this knowledge is the truth-value of a proposition concerning merely possible as well as future contingent events.[34] An example of such a proposition would be: *if the Tyreans see the sign, they will repent.* The example of the Tyreans' hypothetical repentance comes from Matthew chapter 11 and Luke chapter 10. Jesus denounced the cities where he performed his signs because they did not repent. "If the mighty works done in you had been done in Tyre and Sidon," said Jesus, "they would have repented long ago in sackcloth and ashes" (Matthew 11:21). Rather than taking this as a merely rhetorical point, scholastic theologians understood Jesus to be making a definitive claim regarding the repentance of the Tyreans. Both the Reformed as well as the proponents of the *scientia media* believed that the truth-value of the proposition regarding the Tyreans could be determined and therefore known as true or false. Where they differed was how they accounted for the determined truth-value of this proposition. Their arguments, along with preliminary remarks on the nature of propositions, are outlined below.[35]

According to one influential philosophical manual used by Rutherford, the *Collegium Complutense Philosophicum*, propositions were defined as a declarative sentence indicative of something true or false.[36] If the proposition could be affirmed, its contradictory could be denied and vice versa. The principle of bivalence suggested that between a pair of contradictory propositions there is only one truth

---

33 See fn. 5 above.

34 There is a distinction to be made between the merely possible and a contingent future event. The merely possible will never be, though it could have been. A contingent future event will be, though it could not have been. It was generally agreed amongst scholastic theologians that God had certain knowledge of propositions concerning both. For more, see this study: Chapter 5.2.4.

35 Rutherford offers brief remarks on other propositions such as the *promissory* (*Si servieris Petro, dabo tibi mercedem*) and *illative* (*si est homo, Ergo est animal*) conjunctions. But, as he saw the point of controversy to primarily lay in the realm of conditional and disparate conditional conjunctions, the following remarks will remain narrowly focused on these two sets of propositions. For Rutherford's brief remarks on these two sets of propositions see: Rutherford, *Disputatio Scholastica*, 15. For extended commentary on the nature of these propositions as well as others familiar to Rutherford see: E. J. Ashworth, *Language and Logic in the Post-Medieval Period*, Syntheses Historical Library 12 (Dordrecht: D. Reidel Publishing Company, 1974), 147–70.

36 "Propositio solet definiri sic: *Est oratio verum, vel falsum significans.*" Antonio de la Madre Dio, *Collegium Complutense Philosophicum* (Frankfurt: Erasmi Kempfferi, 1629), 19. Rutherford relies upon Antonio de la Madre Dio elsewhere in the *Disputatio*. See: Rutherford, *Disputatio Scholastica*, 101.

value that can be assigned to each. Thus, one part of the pair could be known as true and its contradictory as false.[37]

Propositions could be broadly divided under two categories: the *simple* and the *composite*.[38] A *simple* proposition is a sentence where subject and predicate correspond to one another, such as *a human is an animal*.[39] The *composite* or *hypothetical* proposition is a proposition where two independent clauses are joined by some kind of propositional connective.[40] Composite propositions could be conjunctive, disjunctive, or conditional.[41] Of these, the conditional was the one that demanded the most attention in the period.[42]

Being a composite proposition, the conditional proposition was composed of two parts, the antecedent and the consequent. These were united by a propositional connective that allowed the consequent to be logically inferred from the antecedent,

---

37 There is considerable debate as to what this means for the Jesuit account of the determinate truth-value of a proposition. E.J Ashworth has noted that some of the period "who linked true conditionals with valid consequences also made the traditional claim that all true conditionals were necessary and all false ones impossible." She goes on to note that "Conditional propositions, being propositions, were said to be true or false, which suggests only two possibilities; but their truth depended upon their necessity, and this introduces three possibilities, necessity, impossibility, and contingency. They paired truth with necessity, and falsity with impossibility, forgetting about contingency." Ashworth, *Language and Logic in the Post-Medieval Period*, 149–150. Alfred J. Freddoso and William Lane Craig have argued that Molina did not understand bivalence in such a way that the truth of a future conditional proposition depended upon necessity. Rather, they argue that Molina understood the truth-value of propositions concerning future contingent events could be known and thus "determined" by God, however "determined" does not mean causally necessary but rather causally contingent. God knows a future conditional proposition as true and *could have known* its contradictory as true. See Fredosso's note in Molina, *Concordia*, ed. and trans. Alfred J. Freddoso (Ithaca and London: Cornell University Press 1988), 168, fn. 13; and also William Lane Craig, *The Problem of Divine Foreknowledge from Aristotle to Suárez* (Brill: Leiden, 1988), ch. 7. Richard Gaskin has argued against this interpretation. See: Richard Gaskin, "Molina on Divine Foreknowledge and the Principle of Bivalence," *Journal of the History of Philosophy 32*, no. 4 (October 1994): 551–571. See also this study Ch. 5.3.2.
38 "Prima est, qua dividitur proposito in simplicem, & compositam; seu categoricam, & hypotheticam." Antonio de la Madre Dio, *Collegium Complutense Philosophicum*, 19.
39 "Ad primam ergo divisionem deueniendo: propositio simplex sue categorica est, quae constate subiecto, & praedicato, tanquam partibus principalibus, & copula tanquam unione, ut homo est animal." Antonio de la Madre Dio, Collegium Complutense Philosophicum, 19.
40 E.J. Ashworth, "Propositional Logic in the Sixteenth and Early Seventeenth Centuries," *Notre Dame Journal of Formal Logic 9*, no. 2 (April 1968), 180–182.
41 Propositional connectives for the copulative could be *et, ac,* and *nec.* Connectives for disjunctive propositions are listed as *vel, aut, sive.* Connectives for the conditional, or hypothetical, are simply listed as *si,* or something similar. See Antonio de la Madre Dio, *Collegium Complutense Philosophicum,* 21.
42 Ashworth, "Propositional Logic," 181.

such as *if Peter argues, he speaks,* or *because it is fire, it is hot.*[43] In conditional propositions, the truth-value of the proposition doesn't depend upon the truth of the antecedent or the consequent. Rather, the determinate truth-value of the proposition depends solely upon whether or not the consequent can be logically inferred from the antecedent. If such can be done, the proposition has determinate truth-value and can be affirmed.[44]

Conditional propositions could be formed in such a way that a sentence concerning a future, contingent event could be said to be either true or false, such as *if Peter is tempted, he will sin.* When constructed this way, conditional propositions were an important element in accounting for God's knowledge of future contingent events, especially for Jesuits and Arminians who relied upon the *scientia media* to reconcile God's certain knowledge of future contingents with free will.[45] For the proponents of the *scientia media*, the conditional proposition represented a future contingent event in such a way that the truth concerning it could be affirmed or denied. The same also provided the means for explaining why the proposition could be affirmed or denied, thus rendering a comprehensive explanation for how God knows truth concerning future contingent events.[46]

In keeping with the general rules concerning such propositions, the Jesuits argued that the determinate truth value of conditional propositions can be known based upon whether the consequent could be inferred from the antecedent.[47] Rutherford

---

43 "Propositio conditionalis est illa, cuius partes principales uniuntur media particula, si, aut alia consimili: v.g. Si Petrus disputat, loquitur; si equus est rationalis, est risibilis; aliae huiusmodi. In quibus: quia simul etiam sunt argumentationes, ut supra in praeambulis vidimus; ideo una oratio, seu propositio categorica unitur alteri per modum cuiusdam consecutionis; atque ita prima appellatur antecedens; secunda vero, consequens." Antonio de la Madre Dio, Collegium Complutense Philosophicum, 21.

44 An example from the *Collegium Complutense Philosophicum* serves as a good illustration of the point. *Si equus est rationalis, est risibilis.* Horses are not rational and do not laugh, thus the propositions *equus est rationalis* and *equus est risibilis* are false. However, a horse that laughs rather than neighs would be rational by necessity. Thus the proposition, though the parts are false, is true when related by a propositional connective. See: Antonio de la Madre Dio, *Collegium Complutense Philosophicum*, 21. The more common example from the period of two false clauses that are nevertheless true when joined in a compound proposition was *si asinus volat, habet pennas.* Ashworth, "Propositional Logic," 181.

45 "Operosae sunt de actibus Dei immanantibus, puta scientia & voluntatis disputationes: *Jesuitae, Arminiani,* aliique id genus unicam litium moderatricem & arbitram statuunt *scientiam mediam* quae immutabilitatem divini decreti conciliat cum actibus liberae voluntatis." Rutherford, *Disputatio Scholastica,* 12.

46 What follows is a summary of Rutherford's understanding of the Jesuit position taken largely from: Rutherford, *Disputatio Scholastica,* 12–28.

47 The Jesuits, with whom Rutherford interacts, all devote extended sections to discussing the rules concerning conditional conjunctions. For example see Roderico de Arriaga, *Cursus Philosophicus*

noted that there were different accounts of why the antecedent and consequent were connected and how God came to such knowledge of this connection.[48] For example, Leonardus Lessius (1554–1623) defended a psychological account of God's knowledge of conditional propositions reminiscent of Molina. In this accounting, God knows what Peter would do in such and such circumstances.[49] Suárez took a different approach, whereby the object of God's perfect and infinite intuition was the actual truth-value of the proposition.[50] The unifying factor, no matter the account, was the emphasis upon the logical connection between the two parts.[51]

Rutherford was aware that for the Jesuits, there is more to the matter than merely the logical bond between the antecedent and consequent. He noted that the terms on their own are not sufficient to gain knowledge of the truth-value of the proposition. The terms imply that a number of conditions and circumstances must be added to them to strengthen the logical inference. Rutherford summarized the Jesuit position as follows:

> The knowledge of future contingents is not in God unless they are determined with all circumstances and conditions. For this is not determinately true (*If Peter petitions alms from John, then he will receive*), but rather that is determinately true and therefore

---

(Antwerp: Plantiniana Balthasaris Moreti, 1632), Disputatio XIV, Sectio VI "Utrum propositiones de futuro contingenti conditionato sint verae vel falsae;" P. Petro de Arrubal, *Commentariorum ac disputationum in primam partem Diui Thomae* (Madrid: Thomam Iuntam, 1619). "An scientia contingentium conditionatorum sit in Deo ante actualem determinationem voluntatis," Disput. XLV. Chap I; *De Scientia Dei, Q. XIV Art XIII dub XIII*, 176.

48 For an overview of the *ratio cognoscendi* of the determinate truth-value of conditional propositions, see Bac, *Perfect Will Theology*, 77–84. Suárez's account of God's knowledge of the determinate truth-value of conditional propositions will be dealt with in greater detail in Ch. 3.3.2 of this study.

49 Rutherford, *Disputatio Scholastica*, 16; Leonardus Lessius, *De gratia efficaci decretis divinis: Libertate arbitrii et praescientia dei conditionata. Disputatio apologetica* (Barcelona: Sebastiani Matheuad & Laurentij Deu, 1610), Chapter 19, fig. 2, 214–215.

50 *Intuition* is a technical term, the significance of which will be covered in greater detail in the following section. For an overview of Suárez's position see: J. Martin Bac, *Perfect Will Theology: Divine Agency in Reformed Scholasticism as Against Suárez, Episcopius, Descartes, and Spinoza*, ed. Wim Janse, Brill Series in Church History 42 (Leiden: Brill, 2010), 143–148. See also: Suárez, "Tractatus de gratia dei seu de deo salvatore, justificare, et liberi arbitrii adjutore per gratiam suam," in *Prolegomena II*, Chapter 7; fig. 24 and 94.

51 For examples of the importance of the use of logical connections in the determinate truth-value of conditional propositions, Rutherford cites the following: Leonardus Lessius, *De gratia efficaci decretis divinis: Libertate arbitrii et praescientia dei conditionata. Disputatio apologetica* (Barcelona: Sebastiani Matheuad & Laurentij Deu, 1610), 214; Petro de Arrubal, *Commentariorum*, 290; Didaci Ruiz, *Commentarii ac disputationes de scientia de ideis, de veritate ac de vita dei: Ad primam partem Sancti Thomae, a questione 14 usque ad 18* (Paris: Sebatiani Cramoisy, 1629), 568–70.

knowable by God before the divine decree (*if Peter petitions alms from John, manner and time richly and liberally obliging with the remaining circumstances, then he will receive*).[52]

Rutherford used the Jesuit Peter Arrubal (1559–1608) to illustrate his point. Arrubal argued that the proposition *if Peter petitions alms from John, then he will receive* could not be known as determinately true, presumably because the consequent is not a strict implicative of the antecedent. One could still say that the consequent is probable given the antecedent, but Arrubal's denial of the determinate truth-value of the proposition indicates that he is looking for something stronger than mere probability. What lends the proposition strength are circumstances and conditions, such as time, place, and mood that are implied in the terms.[53] These circumstances and conditions, implied in the terms, are sufficient for the consequent to be logically inferred from the antecedent, thus the truth-value of the conditional proposition concerning a future contingent event can be determined.[54]

Though the truth-value of the proposition is determined pre-volitionally, the Jesuits were clear that God is free to will or not will such a world where all the required circumstances attain actuality. Thus, the future event remains contingent upon the divine will. Rutherford cited an example of how God's pre-volitional knowledge of the determinate truth-value of a conditional proposition engages with God's contingent will from the Jesuit Hieronymus Fasolus (1566–1639). Fasolus relied upon the simple example of God's conditional stopping of the sun to illustrate this sequence of events.[55] According to God's conditional knowledge, God pre-volitionally knows that if he stops the sun over the earth then the earth will heat. God's absolute will (*voluntas absoluta*) is open to either the possibility of (a) stopping the sun or (b) not stopping the sun. In the eventuality that God chooses (a) by his conditional will (*voluntas conditionalis*) the consequence is that the earth will

---

52 "Non est in Deo scientia futurorum contingentium nisi quando determinata sunt cum omnibus circumstantiis & conditionibus. Nam non est haec determinate vera (*si Petrus petet eleemosynam ab Ioanne, eam accipiet*) sed hac est determinate vera ideoque scibilis ante Dei decretum (*si Petrus petat eleemosynam ab Ioanne divite & liberalis debito modo & tempore cum reliquis circumstantiis debitis, eam accipiet*)." Rutherford, *Disputatio Scholastica*, 17.

53 "*Si Petrus pauper eleemosyna peteret a Paulo, tali loco & tempore, ea impetraret*: licet enim ea conditio petendi eleemosynam, non sit necessario connexa cum consequenti, id est, cum illius impetratione, ex se tamen talis est, ut possit ad illum effectum conducere." Arrubal, *Commentariorum ac disputationum*, 290.

54 Rutherford cites the following from Arrubal: "Ille enim circumstantiae talis temporis, & loci ponuntur in propositione ad comprehendendas omnes conditiones, ex quibus significatur futurum consequens." Arrubal, *Commentariorum ac disputationum*, 291.

55 This could be based upon the Biblical account of God stopping the sun after Joshua's prayer during a battle between the Israelites and the Amorites (Joshua 10). Fasolus gives no indication either way.

heat.[56] To use a familiar example, God pre-volitionally knows that under certain circumstances if Peter is tempted, he will sin. By God's absolute will, the possibility of enacting such a world where this certain set of circumstances leads to Peter's sin is open to God. He may or may not enact it. Under the condition that God chooses to enact such a world, the connection between Peter's temptation and sin will obtain. Just as it is right to infer that the earth would heat if the sun were stopped, it is also right to infer that if Peter were tempted in such a way, in a certain place, at a certain time, he would sin.[57]

Though right to infer that if the sun were stopped, it would necessarily heat the earth, Rutherford did not believe that it was right to infer that if Peter was tempted in such and such a way, he would consequently sin. Rutherford didn't believe that the logical bond between the antecedent and consequent in future conditional propositions was, in and of itself, strong enough to warrant the kind of certain and infallible knowledge required of God's providence.[58] This is because Rutherford believed such propositions to have an indeterminate truth-value, being neither true nor false in and of themselves.

Rutherford demonstrated this point by reviewing a series of propositions from the *Collegii Salmanticensis*, such as the illative, promissory, and conditional.[59] Examples of each are as follows:

---

56 "Sicut in materia necessaria, ad sciendum, v.g. quod si sol non volveretur, vehementius, calefaceret terram; non oportet ponere quod Deus prius actu velit, solem vehementius calefacere, si non moveretur; & deinde in posteriori signo hoc ipsum certo cognoscat: sed satis est, voluntatem Dei ponere in ipsa conditione inclusam, ut obiectum cognitionis; ita ut tantum cognoscat Deus, quod si vellet, non movere solem, & praebere totum coagendi concursum, quem sol in quiete naturaliter postulat, vellet etiam, solem vehementius terram calefacere." Hieronymus Fasolus, *In primam partem summae D. Thomae commentariorum tomus secundus: cum tribus indicisum locupletissimis.* (Lyon: Andreae, Jacobi, & Matthaei, 1629), 184.

57 Fasolus's example, though vivid, undermines the freedom of the will in the contingent cause. The sun after all is not a free cause. It is not free to heat or not heat. Under the condition that the sun was stopped, it would heat the earth necessarily. However, it is by no means clear that under the condition of Peter's temptation, he would certainly sin. And yet, God's certain knowledge of this future contingent event requires that the bond between the two terms be strong enough to draw a good inference.

58 "Sed ad rem, probo hanc scientiam mediam evertere, non salvare providentiam Dei. I. Non stat certitudo divinae scientiae cum hac scientia. Ergo per hanc scientiam evertitur providentia." Rutherford, *Disputatio Scholastica*, 16.

59 "Fratres discalceati Collegii Salmatincensis, observant juxta regulas Soci conjunctionem (si) trisariam sumi: 1. illative, ut *si est homo, ergo est animal*: 2. *Promissive*, Ut (*si servieris Petro dabo tibi mercedem:*) 3. *Conditionate*, Ut, Si *Tyrii viderint signa, resipiscent*) sed ego hic duo observo. I. Addi posse quartam acceptionem, quando (Si) notat meram coexistentiam sine ulla extremorum connexione. (Ut *si Pap legerit, Turca ridebit*) & tales propositiones Disparatas, doctrinae gratia, appellamus." Rutherford, *Disputatio Scholastica*, 15.

Illative: If it is a man, it is an animal.
Promissory: If you serve Peter, I will give you money.
Conditional: It is a rational animal, if it is a man.

Each of the above propositions can be affirmed because the consequent is strictly implied by the antecedent.[60] Following the *Collegii Salmanticensis,* Rutherford noted that the Jesuits deny that the truth-value of *disparate propositions* can be determined, because unlike the propositions reviewed above, the disparate proposition is a proposition where there is no reasonable, causal connection between the two extreme terms.[61] Examples of such disparate propositions are as follows:

If Paul sleeps in Rome, Peter writes in Spain.
If the stick is at an angle, it is raining.

Rutherford argued that if the Jesuits rejected God's knowledge of disparate propositions because they lacked the means to make a good inference, they should also reject God's knowledge of future conditional propositions for the same reason. Whereas the conditional proposition *It is a rational animal, if it is a man,* is necessarily true, the consequent being a strict implication of the antecedent, the future conditional proposition *if Tyre sees the sign, they will repent,* is not true. Repenting is not a strict implication of seeing the sign, as Chorazin and Bethsaida's refusal to do so proves (Matt. 11:21). Rutherford did not call the proposition regarding the repentance of the Tyreans false. Rather he simply noted that in and of itself, there is nothing about the proposition that gives it the nature of truth. Therefore, apart from the divine decree, it cannot be known as determinately true any more than the disparate proposition can.[62] The consequence of the above, according

---

60 The above examples are taken directly from the source cited by Rutherford. Collegii Salmanticensis, *Cursus Theologicus et Moralis* (Lyon: Joannis Antonii Huguetan, & Soc, 1679), 438. In each of the above, Rutherford believed that the consequent was a strict implication of the antecedent, with the exception of the *promissory.* If a human makes the promise, the proposition is bad. However, if God makes the promise, the proposition is good and can be known as true. "Ut (*si servieris Petro, Ergo dabo tibi mercedem*) si promissio sit humana, consequentia est mala & non necessaria; Quia omnis homo fallax est & potest datam fidem violare: si est promissio divina, est omnino fortissime & necessario illativa & bona." Rutherford, *Disputatio Scholastica,* 16.

61 "Propositiones disparate ut (*Si Papa legerit, Turca ridebit*) (*Si baculus est in angulo, jam pluit*) non sciuntur a Deo infallibiliter, antecedenter ad Decretum." Rutherford, *Disputatio Scholastica,* 16.

62 Nam citra Dei Decretum, nulla est veritas determinata in talibus, nam in se non sunt verae, non enim sunt necessario verae, ut notum, quia extrema cohaerent plane per accidens, nec sunt contingenter verae, nisi possibiliter, quia nulla est causa a parte rei connectens extrema inter se, cum nullum adhuc ponatur Dei Decretum." Rutherford, *Disputatio Scholastica,* 16.

to Rutherford, is that the Jesuits had failed to render an account of God's certain knowledge of future contingent events.[63]

Rutherford's solution was to argue, contra the Jesuits, that future conditional propositions were known by God as indeterminate, being neither true nor false. He wrote:

> The first operation of the divine intellect, being ultimately simple and without division or composition apprehends such propositions as neither true nor false and therefore without any affirmation or denial.[64]

Such propositions gained determinate truth-value, not based upon the logical connection between the two extreme parts, but rather upon God's divine decree. Rutherford wrote:

> Whenever Holy Scripture makes use of consequences of this kind, often the consequence is not simply by reason of the connection of the terms, but from the free constitution and predetermination of God. Therefore this consequence would have been clearly ridiculous and absurd: The Tyreans see the sign, *therefore they repent* if *per impossibile* we assume there is no decree, nor any strength in God's providence which joins these extreme [terms] among one another, for out of itself, and out of the nature of the thing, there is no way that the repentance of the Tyreans and the seeing of the sign indeclinably cohere among one another.[65]

Rutherford reasserted that in and of itself there is no logical connection between the two terms of a conditional proposition that would allow the truth-value of a

---

63 "Non stat certitudo divinae scientiae cum hac scientia." Rutherford, *Disputatio Scholastica,* 16.

64 "Uti in simplice & prima operatione intellectus, quae compositione & divisione careat, nihil veritatis, nihil falsitatis est, quia omnis veritas est in affirmatione & negatione, *prout ita res sese habet vel non habet,* in objectiva connexione rerum quae subjecti & attributi locum tenent." Rutherford, *Disputatio Scholastica,* 541. There is a similar remark in the *Exercitationes* that is polemically focused upon Suárez's notion of intuition. Nevertheless, the point is very much the same. "De ente vere futuro, neutra pars ante Dei Decretum, est vel vera, vel falsa proprie, quia extrema propositionis nempe (*Petrus*) (constitutio in tali-ordine) & (peccatum) sunt non entia, ideoque non vera, non scibilia, ac proinde eorum connexio est non ens & non verum, sed indifferens ad veritatem & falsitatem." Rutherford, *Exercitationes Apologeticae,* 191.

65 "Quoties ergo sacra Scriptura hujusmodi consequentiis utitur, toties valet consequentia non ex connexione terminorum simpliciter, sed ex libera constitutione & predeterminatione Dei: Haec enim consequentia plane ridicula & vana foret. (*Tyrii videbunt signa, Ergo Tyrii resipiscent*) Si per impossibile ponamus nullum esse decretum, nullamve in Deo providentiam quae connectat inter se haec extrema, nam ex se, & ex rei natura, nullo modo indeclinabiliter inter se cohaerent, Tyriorum resipiscentia & signorum visio." Rutherford, *Disputatio Scholastica,* 22.

proposition to be infallibly determined. Such propositions are either indeterminate or absurd. The propositions can be determined to be true or false when God wills to join the two extreme terms of the proposition. Whereas in the Jesuit account, the implied condition in the terms was circumstances such as time and place, the implied condition in Rutherford's account was God's will. God post-volitionally determines the truth-value of a proposition. In light of his own free decree, God is able to determine whether or not such a proposition is true or false.

Rutherford's account is clearly suggestive of the theory of neutral propositions, commonly associated with John Duns Scotus (c. 1266–1308). Beck has described the theory as a model of the "structural interaction between God's knowledge and will."[66] The theory plays out in a series of three "structural moments" whereby God (a) apprehends a pair of contingent propositions as neutral, (b) determines a truth-value to one of a pair of propositions by the divine will and (c) gains post-volitional knowledge of the determinate truth-value of the proposition by the divine intellect.[67] In the case of Rutherford's most often used example, the repentance of the Tyreans, it looks like the following:

Structural Moment I (Indeterminate Knowledge): The object of God's knowledge is a pair of contradictory conditional propositions that God knows as neither true nor false.
– If the Tyreans see the sign, they will repent.
– If the Tyreans see the sign, they will not repent.

Structural Moment II (Determination by the divine will): God assigns determinate truth-value to one part of the pair of contradictory conditional propositions.
– If the Tyreans see the sign, they will repent (True).

Structural Moment III (Determinate Knowledge): God gains free knowledge of the determinate truth-value of the proposition in light of his free decision.[68]

Rutherford's solution resonates within the Reformed Orthodoxy of the seventeenth century and is ultimately rooted in the medieval catholic theology that emphasizes the determinative role of the divine will. Beck has noted that Scotus's theory of

---

66 Beck, "Divine Psychology' and Modalities," 123.
67 Beck, 130–1.
68 Beck, *Gisbertus Voetius*, 398.

neutral propositions played a key role in the "question of how God's definite fore-knowledge of future contingencies (*futura contingentia*) can be compatible with their contingency."[69] He has also shown that this solution was employed by the Dutch Reformed scholastic Gisbertus Voetius.[70]

According to Rutherford, the determination of the divine will permits God to determine whether a future conditional proposition is true or false.[71] The certitude of God's knowledge concerning future contingent events is thus resolved, but is this achieved at the expense of human liberty? According to Rutherford's understanding of the *scientia media*, God knows a future conditional proposition to be either true or false. The affirmation of the proposition leads to the denial of its contradictory and vice versa. For example, if God determines that *if Peter is tempted, he will sin* is true, then he also knows *if Peter is tempted, he will not sin* is false. While it is possible that Peter could be tempted and not sin, it is not entirely clear if God knows of such a possibility via his *scientia media*.[72] If God does not know via his *scientia media* of the possibility where Peter could be tempted and not sin, is Peter's freedom diminished in the moment of his temptation? By beginning with God's indeterminate knowledge of such future contingent events, God knows both the possibility of Peter sinning and not sinning during his temptation, thus avoiding the particular problem with the *scientia media* highlighted above.[73]

3.3.2 Scientia Abstractiva et Intuitiva

Just as with the *scientia indeterminata et determinata* distinction, this distinction was also seen earlier as part of Rutherford's broad division of God's natural and free knowledge. Here the *scientia abstractiva* belongs to God's natural knowledge and the *scientia intuitiva* belongs to God's free knowledge.[74] Beyond the *Examen*, Rutherford's most extensive comments regarding this type of knowledge appear in his *Exercitationes*. His comments are written in response to the Spanish Jesuit

---

69 Beck, *Gisbertus Voetius*, 271–72.

70 Beck, *Gisbertus Voetius*, 312; Beck, "The Will as Master of It's Own Act," 162–63.

71 There is a distinction to be made between how "determination" relates to the mind and the will. When Rutherford says God "determines" something with the will, it is synonymous with "choose." However, when God "determines" a proposition to be true, it should be read as God "understands" the proposition to be true.

72 See Alfred J. Freddoso, "Introduction," in *On Divine Foreknowledge: Part IV of the Concordia*, 1–81, (Ithaca, New York: Cornell University Press, 1988), 48–49.

73 For more on this point, see this study Ch. 5.3.2.

74 See fn. 5 above.

Francisco Suárez (1548–1617).[75] Rutherford offered a series of critiques to Suárez's understanding of intuition and abstraction as it applied to the determinate truth-value of a proposition.[76]

Before wading into Rutherford's critiques of Suárez's account of God's abstractive and intuitive knowledge, an introduction to the scholastic background as well as a brief presentation of Suárez's doctrine will be useful. The distinction between intuitive and abstractive knowledge is often associated with John Duns Scotus.[77] The distinctions as conceived by Scotus were not initially formed as pertaining to God's knowledge, but rather creaturely knowledge of God as it relates to both angelic and human knowledge *in patria* as well as *in via*.[78] In book two, distinction three of the *Lectura*, Scotus sought to answer the question of whether or not angels could have distinct knowledge of the divine essence naturally or *in patria* apart from the beatific vision. Scotus answered in the affirmative, arguing not only that angels could have knowledge of God's essence apart from the beatific vision, but also that they could even have perfect knowledge of God's essence short of the beatific vision. This does not mean that Scotus believed angels naturally have beatific knowledge of God, but rather they naturally have a non-intuitive complete and explicit comprehension of all the necessary features of God's nature. This type of non-intuitive comprehension was called "abstractive" by Scotus because the object of knowledge was "abstracted" from the actual presence of the angelic knower.[79]

Abstractive knowledge was contrasted with intuitive knowledge. Unlike abstractive knowledge, intuitive knowledge was dependent upon the actual presence of

---

75 Rutherford primarily engages Suárez, *Opera Omnia*, vol. 7., *Tractatus de Gratia Dei: Seu de Deo Salvatore, Justificare, et Liberi Arbitrii Adjutore Per Gratiam Suam* (Paris: Ludovicum Vives, Bibliopolam Editorem, 1857).

76 Rutherford, *Exercitationes Apologeticae*, Exercitatione 1, Caput 5, 158–200.

77 See: Armand Maurer, *Being and Knowing: Studies in Thomas Aquinas and Later Mediaeval Philosophers*, Papers in Mediaeval Studies 10, (Toronto: Pontifical Institute of Mediaeval Studies, 1990), 312. Vos notes that Scotus's theory shaped the discussion on intuitive cognition for the next 500 years. See: Vos, *The Philosophy of John Duns Scotus*, 322–23. For Henry of Ghent's contribution to the terms as they developed see: Stephen D. Dumont, "Theology as Science and Duns Scotus's Distinction between Intuitive and Abstractive Cognition," *Speculum* 64, no. 3 (1989): 579–99.

78 For an overview of Scotus's concepts of intuitive and abstractive cognition see Marilyn McCord Adams and Allan B Wolter, "Memory and Intuition: A Focal Debate in Fourteenth Century Cognitive Psychology," Franciscan Studies 53, no. 1 (1993); Dumont, "Theology as Science and Duns Scotus's Distinction between Intuitive and Abstractive Cognition."; James B South, "Scotus and the Knowledge of the Singular Revisited," History of Philosophy Quarterly 19, no. 2 (2002); R.A. te Velde, "Intuïtieve kennis en contingentie bij duns scotus," Tijdschrift voor Filosofie 47, no. 2 (1985): 125–47.

79 For an overview of this complicated argument, see: Dumont, "Theology as Science," 581–4. Wolter and Adams argue that Scotus did admit some *ante-mortem* intuitive cognition of singulars though these are imperfect as opposed to the perfect intuitive cognitions of the beatific vision. See: Adams and Wolter, "Memory and Intuition," 177–8.

the knowable object. Stephen Dumont notes that Scotus initially referred to this type of knowledge as *visio*, however when revising the *Lectura* for publications as the *Ordinatio*, *cognitio intuitiva* replaced many of the earlier occurrences of *visio*.[80] The link between the conceptual apparatus of vision and intuition expresses the importance of presence for this type of knowledge. The same may be said of the coupling of *existentia* (step forth/appear) and *praesentia* (present/at hand) to describe the necessary elements of intuitive knowledge. Because of the emphasis on presence, intuitive knowledge of God can only be had *in patria*, the heavenly country, by means of the beatific vision.[81]

What is at stake in the discussions of abstractive and intuitive knowledge? Scotus found these distinctions useful, even necessary for validating claims about contingent propositions. The mind has access through abstractive knowledge to the unchanging essence of an object. For example the abstract notion of "a dog" lacks the contingent, existential and variable knowledge of said dog sitting on a mat by a rocking chair at 5:30 p.m. on April 26, 1981. This knowledge must be confirmed by the external sensation of vision or intuition. It is at this point that the truly important breakthrough occurs. Through abstractive knowledge it is possible to imagine the same dog standing (rather than sitting) on a mat by a rocking chair at 5:30 p.m. on April 26, 1981 even if such a thing were never to occur. The causal link between imagination, or *phantasms,* and intuitive cognition is severed. As James South notes:

> The imagination is able to form phantasms that have no direct causal connection with external objects, whether because the external object is not currently present, or because the external object does not exist.[82]

Scotus's distinction between abstractive and intuitive knowledge provides a means by which one could acquire certain knowledge of contingents. Since abstractive knowledge understands the existence of an object as non-necessary, any knowledge gained by intuition verifies the contingent truth of the object's existence. For Rutherford, when applied to God's cognition, such distinctions fit neatly within the *scientia necessaria/libera* dichotomy.[83] God's abstractive knowledge is understood as pre-volitional and necessary. God's intuitive knowledge is post-volitional and contingent.[84]

---

80 Dumont, "Theology as Science," 581.

81 Vos, *The Philosophy of John Duns Scotus*, 324.

82 South, "Scotus and the Knowledge of the Singular Revisited," 137.

83 See this study, 3.2.3.

84 When functioning in this manner, abstractive and intuitive knowledge only pertains to *knowledge of* creatures. The intuitive knowledge of God gained at the beatific vision pertains to the necessary

Scotus's distinction underwent significant challenges and revisions. The most relevant to Rutherford were those of Francisco Suárez, who rather than maintaining the distinction between abstractive and intuitive knowledge significantly weakened the distinction, collapsing them within God's knowledge. Much like the Jesuits examined in the previous section, Suárez grounded God's certain knowledge of future contingents upon the logical foundation of the determinate truth-value of the conditional proposition.[85] Suárez argued that God obtained such knowledge intuitively. Though he used the language of intuition, and even retained the intuitive/abstractive dichotomy, he radically redefined the terms. Suárez understood abstractive knowledge in much the same way as his predecessors: in that abstractive knowledge is knowledge that abstracts from existence and is thus equivalent to God's knowledge of simple understanding. It is therefore necessary and pre-volitional knowledge. At times Suárez also closely ties intuition with temporal existence exhibiting a more traditional understanding of intuition, which is contingent and post-volitional. At the same time however, Suárez has a way of speaking about intuition that has less to do with temporal existence and more to do with presence. This is Suárez's more radical move. Suárez argued that the beings known by God's abstractive knowledge had within themselves (*in se*) their own proper being, grounded in their possibility. God sees these beings in their possibility, pre-volitionally, as objects of his knowledge. As Timothy Cronin has pointed out, "since these beings as such are not made nor are they what they are by reason of the divine will, the divine will in their regards has no free act."[86] Such beings, Cronin summarizes, are not actual in that they do not yet exist *in actua*. Neither are they merely possible. Rather, Suárez argued such beings were real and present to God as objects of his intuition.[87]

It is important to carefully define both what is meant by "real" as well as what is meant by "present." The easiest way to understand both is to return to the earlier example of the disjunctive conditional proposition concerning Peter's temptation:

(a) If Peter is tempted, he will sin.
(b) If Peter is tempted, he will not sin.

---

truths of God's being. The same may be said of the abstractive knowledge of God's being available to angels and imperfectly available to humans. Such knowledge is of necessary theological truths. See Dumont, "Theology as Science." For the important role of sensory experience verifying contingent truth see: Vos, "Knowledge, Certainty and Contingency," 83–87; South, "Scotus and the Knowledge of the Singular Revisited," 137–41.

85 Bac, *Perfect Will Theology*, Chapter 3, especially 72 and 96.

86 See Timothy J. Cronin, *Objective Being in Descartes and in Suárez*, Analecta Gregoriana 154 (Rome: Gregorian University Press, 1966), 46.

87 Cronin, *Objective Being in Descartes and in Suárez*, 47–50.

Suárez argued that the object of God's intuitive knowledge was one part of the conditional proposition, namely the part that will obtain truth in time. As was seen in the above, the truth of the proposition is dependent neither upon Peter's temptation nor his sin. Rather, the proposition is true because there is a logical connection between Peter's temptation and his sin that makes one of the above statements true and the other false. Though neither Peter, his temptation, nor his sin yet exist, the connection is nevertheless true and real. This is how Suárez understood the "real" being of the possible object of Peter's temptation and its resultant consequences.[88]

Because there is real connection between the antecedent and consequent in such propositions, God sees the truth of them as eternally present (*intueri res ut praesentes aeternitati*) as objects of the divine intellect.[89] Though the objects are abstracted from their existence, God nevertheless sees the objects in their "reality," and thus comes to certain knowledge of future contingent events such as Peter's temptation and ensuing sin. It is important to note that such objects have no real existence outside of the divine intellect. Suárez is not positing beings eternally coexistent with God. Rather, the knowable object is somehow eternally present as an object of intuition to the divine intellect.[90] Through intuition, God is able to know with certainty future contingent events, not in their causes since these are indifferent, but he is able to see the effect flowing from the cause.[91] Simply put, he is able to foresee what will be done.[92]

Rutherford believed that such an accounting of God's intuitive knowledge imposed a fatal necessity upon God. If God knows through divine intuition the

---

88 Cronin, 49–50.

89 "Deum per scientiam visionis intueri res ut praesentes aeternitati, quod etiam de praesentia secundum realem coexistentiam dicti moderni Thomistae volunt intelligi; ergo coexistentia illa in aeternitate supponitur ex parte rerum ad scientiam visionis Dei; ergo non facit illam, nec est causa illius, sed supponit illam et ratione illius omnes intuetur." See Suárez, *Tractatus de Gratia Dei*, 123.

90 "Haec autem praesentia secunda veram sententiam, non est per realem coexistentiam, quam res futura, antequam in suo tempore sit, habeat in aeternitate; repugnat enim esse coexistentem alteri rem, quae in se nondum existit, ut in dicto libro latius dictum est, sed est illa praesentia obiectiva respectu intuitus aeterni divini intellectus." Francisco Suárez, *De Divina Gratia* (Mainz: Hermanni Mylii Birckmanni, 1620), 57.

91 "*Sicut absolutis* (inquit *Suárez*) *de causa existente vel praesente in intuitu Dei, ut existens vere affirmatur in eadem mente Dei tale effectum esse libere dimanaturum ab illa, non quia in virtute causae hoc videat Deus, sed quia intuitu suo videt causam illam, tamen si liberam, tanquam influentem in illum effectum, ita in his conditionatis de causa ex hypothesi conceptu, ut praesenti sub tali existentia possibilis potest vere affirmari & cognosci in menti Dei, hunc determinatum effectum esse dimanaturum ab illa causa libera ex eadem hypothesi, non quia in virtute causa talis effectus determinate cognoscitur, sed quia vere in se & actu secundo esset ad actum illum determinanda.*" Suárez quoted in Rutherford, *Exercitationes Apologeticae*, 193. Rutherford refers to Suárez, *De Divina Gratia*, 53.

92 Bac, *Perfect Will Theology*, 84.

outcome of future contingent events antecedent to his free decree, then he is not free to direct such events in any other way than how he knew them pre-volitionally. Therefore, according to Rutherford, God is subjected to fatal necessity.[93] Furthermore, Rutherford argued that if God sees the effect, rather than in the contingent cause, then God no longer knows contingency as contingency but as necessity. The same charge he notes, was levelled at the Reformed by their "adversaries."[94]

Contra Suárez, Rutherford argued that "it is not necessary that one [part of a pair of contradictory conditional propositions] is determinately true antecedent to the cause connecting to each extreme [term]."[95] This represents a critical denial by Rutherford of Suárez's position, since the logical connection between the two parts of the proposition was how Suárez accounted for the determinate truth of the proposition being "really" present before the divine knower. However, in denying the logical connection between the two extreme terms, Rutherford was not only denying the determinate truth-value of a proposition antecedent to the divine decree, but he was also denying that the truth of such propositions could be really present as objects of the divine intuition antecedent to the divine decree.[96]

As was seen earlier, such propositions can be known as determinately true if the antecedent and consequent are joined by God's decree. God's free decision, being a truly contingent cause, creates a real bond between the two terms, thus making it a knowable object according to God's *scientia libera*. According to Rutherford, if such objects are not determined by God, then they are determined by fatal necessity or the blind causes of fortune.[97] The propositions are either determinately true by some fatal necessity or they are freely true being determined by God. For Rutherford, there was no middle ground on this issue.[98]

---

93 "Si objectum hujusce scientiae praecedit liberum dei decretum, tum omnia contingentia antevertunt Dei libertatem, nec poterit misereri quorum vult, Christum revelare, quibus vult, neque aliter disponere contingentia, quam sese disposuerunt antecedenter ad Dei decretum & Deus fatali necessitate omnia velle cogetur." Rutherford, *Exercitationes Apologeticae*, 186.

94 "Sed tum dico Deum non videre effectum contingentem qua contingentem, sed qua necessarium, quod nobis vitio dant adversarii: & sic Deus non cognoscit contingentia qua contingentia." Rutherford, *Exercitationes Apologeticae*, 194.

95 "At non est necesse ut una sit determinate vera antecedenter ad causam connectentem inter se extrema." Rutherford, *Exercitationes Apologeticae*, 191.

96 "De ente vere futuro, neutra pars ante Dei decretum, est vel vera, vel falsa proprie, quia extrema propositionis nempe (*Petrus*) (constitutio in tali ordine) & (peccatum) sunt non entia, ideoque non vera, non scibilia, ac proinde eorum connexio est non ens & non verum, sed indifferens ad veritatem & falsitatem." Rutherford, *Exercitationes Apologeticae*, 191.

97 "At si sit determinatum, manet quaestio unde est illa determinatio? non aliunde quam vel a fortuna, vel a constellatione, quod non est dicendum, vel a Dei voluntate, quod necessario est admittendum." Rutherford, *Exercitationes Apologeticae*, 196.

98 "Semper Jesuita petit principium: nam unde est quod talis habitudo sit objectiva praesentia intuitui divino & scientiae subjecta. Hæc enim praesentia vel est ab ipso effecta contingente, quod est

3.4 Scientia Practica et Speculativa

The discussion so far has centered on God's knowledge of possibilities via his omnipotence as well as those possibilities he has willed to actualize. These possibilities correspond to concrete potential or actual beings such as Peter's temptation and sin (or its contrary). This has been shown in both the *scientia indeterminata/determinata* and *scientia abstractiva/intuitiva* dichotomies. These distinctions do not address how God produces concrete forms of potential beings that could be instantiated in reality. The distinction of the *scientia practica* and *scientia speculativa* serves to address this particular aspect of God's knowledge.[99]

"By his practical knowledge," wrote Rutherford, "God forms the ideas of possible and future beings."[100] There are three component parts to this definition. The first is the doctrine of divine ideas. The second is the possibility or potentiality of the idea. The third is the idea concretely actualized in the created world. Rutherford addressed the doctrine of the divine ideas within the question as to "whether something is impossible if it is not originally impossible for God." His answer to the question, that impossibility as it exists in the created world is ultimately dependent upon God, was largely derived from his doctrine of the divine ideas.[101]

The importance of the divine ideas is that they are representable in the created order. The ideas are the pattern or exemplar of creatable being. Thus, as Beck notes concerning Voetius, "they are grounded in God's imitability" and function something like the mental images of an artist. He is able to depict what he sees in his mind.[102] For Rutherford, God's imitability begins with the divine simplicity. Just as God is simple, the divine ideas are originally simple.[103] By "simple," Rutherford meant that the divine idea is conceived as a simple operation, without composition

---

absurdum, vel a Dei voluntate in qua Deus habitudinem hanc praesentem videt, vel in alia aliqua causa, quam dare non possunt." Rutherford, *Exercitationes Apologeticae*, 196.

99 The primary section of Rutherford's writings pertaining to God's practical and speculative knowledge, as well as to the doctrine of the divine ideas, comes from his *Disquisitiones Metaphysicae* Q IIII-VII in *Disputatio Scholastica,* 538–561; see also *Exercitationes Apologeticae*, 538–62.

100 "Practica sua scientia format Deus possibilium & futurorum ideas." Rutherford, *Disputatio Scholastica,* 560.

101 "An aliquid sit impossibile, nisi quod a Deo orginaliter sit impossibile." Rutherford, *Disputatio Scholastica,* 540.

102 Beck, *Gisbertus Voetius*, 322–26.

103 "Quia omne ens simplex est creabile, potestque ex idea simplicissima essentiae divinae, qua in infinitum est representabilis in creaturis possibilibus ad extra produci & simplex ens ex simplice Dei essentia per Omnipotentium extrahibile est, quia nihil repugnans, dissonum nihil est in eo qui est primus idem, prima & simplicissima unitas, quin quodlibet ens creare possit." Rutherford, *Disputatio Scholastica,* 541.

or division, or without any attribution, affirmation, or denial.[104] Rutherford made an explicit appeal to Aristotle's *De Interpretatione*, wherein Aristotle made the distinction between simple expressions of which nothing may be affirmed or denied, and simple statements that affirm or deny something about the subject.[105]

Rutherford's use of the term simplicity pertained to the first order of simple expressions. The first operation of the divine intellect strictly concerns the simple *vox*, or word, such as human, and this is so without any attribution, affirmation, or denial. It is important to further clarify what without attribution means. Rutherford used the language of abstraction and intuition that was previously outlined to distinguish between substantial attributes and accidental attributes. For example, if one considers a human intuitively, that is created in time, this human would have a name, a birthplace, and an ethnic identity. However, if one considers a human abstractly, stripped from the contingent properties of creation, then one is left with the simple statement that a human is a rational animal. This is the simple *vox* that is the first operation of the divine intellect and it relates only to the substantial properties of the being for which the idea is the archetype.[106]

As Rutherford expanded the consideration of the divine ideas from one possibility open to God's omnipotence (i.e. "human") to all possibilities open to God's omnipotence, including not only other beings in their simple and substantive essences but also beings instantiated in time with contingent attributes, he was also beginning to construct an accounting for the constitution of difference, impossibility, and incompossibility at the ontological level. God is the creator and is therefore the creator of difference among species. The one who creates species is also the one who establishes the differences between species.[107]

---

104 "Uti in simplice & prima operatione intellectus, quae compositione & divisione careat, nihil veritatis, nihil falsitatis est, quia omnis veritas est in affirmatione & negatione, *prout ita res sese habet vel non habet*, in objectiva connexione rerum quae subjecti & attributi locum tenent." Rutherford, *Disputatio Scholastica*, 541.

105 *De Intrepretatione*, 16a1–17a35. The edition referenced here is Aristotle, "De Interpretatione," in *The Complete Works of Aristotle*, ed. Jonathan Barnes (Princeton: Princeton University Press, 1984), 25–27.

106 "Sed necessario veras & earum veritates a tempore abstrahere, & semper veras hoc sensu largior, quod quidditativo conceptu subjecti includatur conceptus attributi, propter identificationem attributi cum subjecto, qui enim concipit hominem, concipit animal, homo in potentia includit animal objective in potentia, & homo in actu, animal in actu....At quando concipitur homo, concipitur animal rationale, & si tu ponis hominem ab aeterno, necesse est ponas animal rationale ab aeterno, qui essentia & essentiam non possunt non semper identificari & tamen essentiatum est creatum in tempore sicut & essentia, & simul concreata est identitas inter essentiam & essentiatum, quando creatur res constans essentia." Rutherford, *Disputatio Scholastica*, 558.

107 "Qui Deus *Creator* in saecula celebrandus creando differentias speciei constitutivas *v.g.* hirci & cervi simul differentias divisivas constituit: eadem enim differentia specifica, est & speciei constitutiva & divisiva generis, ut *Porphyrius* ait. Qui enim creat ens, creat unum, creat diversum, creat repugnans.

Impossibility, as constructed above, is a derivative effect of the incompossibility of diverse beings. For example, God's practical knowledge produces the divine idea of the goat as well as the stag and thus constitutes the difference between the species. Rutherford argues that these two diverse natures cannot be combined into one creature such as the legendary *hircocervus*, or "goat-stag," because such a creature would be goat and not a goat simultaneously, and thus run afoul of the principle of non-contradiction (*Idem est idem & Idem simul esse & non esse est impossibile*).[108] As was shown earlier, the principle of non-contradiction is not an independent truth, but rather a truth revealed by the divine name and dependent upon the divine being. "There is nothing in God that involves the same to be and not be and is contradictory to the practical ideas of possible being." Thus, impossibility is not a matter of something outside of God that he is not able to do, but rather it is a property that arises out of the incompossibility of the divine ideas *ad intra*, the realization of which contradict the rock bottom principle of the divine simplicity.[109]

The preceding paragraph presents a very interesting argument against the Jesuit theory of determinate knowledge. Rutherford considered the "atheist hypothesis," raised by certain Jesuits, as to whether possibility and impossibility would be in the nature of things without a first cause.[110] It may be remembered that Suárez argued that conditional propositions had an eternal real presence before the divine intuition, antecedent to the divine will. Similarly, there are other propositions such as (*possible is possible*) or (*impossible is impossible*) that some Jesuits argued were antecedent to God's will as well as logically independent of God's being and God's power. If such propositions are considered valid without a first cause, then they are not dependent upon nor must they conform to a first cause, including God in his simplicity. For Rutherford, the modal properties of possibility and impossibility are derived from God's being and power. Hence the simplicity of God is ultimately the explanation for a logically coherent universe as we experience it. If one removes God's being and power as the foundation of these modal properties, then there no longer remains an explanation for a logically coherent universe. Without this explanation there is no reason that an infinite number of propositions and "Platonic

---

Qui producit frigidum, producit quid congregativum heterogeneorum, & eodem actu producit quid repugnans calido." Rutherford, *Disputatio Scholastica*, 540.

108 "Deus ergo creando essentias hirci & cervi possibiles vel actuales, creat eodem actu incompossibilitates inter naturam hirci & cervi. Itaque in *Creatorem*, qui hircum specie & natura distinctum a cervo creavit, originaliter reducitur hoc (*Impossibile vel incompossibile est idem animal esse & hircum & cervum*) quia cum specie & incompossibiliter diversae sunt naturae, idem esset simul hircus & non hircus." Rutherford, *Disputatio Scholastica*, 540.

109 "At nihil est in Deo quod involvit idem esse & non esse in Deo, & est repugnans ideae practicae entis possibilis." Rutherford, *Disputatio Scholastica*, 543.

110 "An ex hypothesi quod prima causa non esset, an propterea possibile vel impossibile foret in rerum natura." Rutherford, *Disputatio Scholastica*, 545.

forms," have not emanated from eternity into created time. The same can be said for such impossible creatures as the *Chimera*. For Rutherford, a created world whose archetype is found in the divine ideas, formed by God's practical knowledge, and consistent with the divine simplicity, is the only explanation for an ordered and logically coherent universe.[111]

There is more at stake in God's practical knowledge than accounting for a logically coherent world. Within God's practical knowledge is also an account of the world as it is, rather than the world as it could have been. Rutherford was clear that God's practical knowledge fashions the ideas that compose an infinite number of possible worlds. Out of this treasury of possibility, God elects this world to be actualized. Thus for Rutherford, God's practical knowledge forms the ideas that compose worlds that are purely possible as well as the particular world that God wills to actualize. Nevertheless, Rutherford's use of the term was not only consistent with his contemporaries, but also consistent with a certain theological instinct to emphasize the pivotal role of the divine will. As Beck notes, such denies any notion of a Platonic theory of necessary emanation. Rather the emphasis is on the radical dependency and contingency of creation upon the will of God.[112]

God's practical knowledge was paired with God's speculative knowledge (*scientia speculativa*). Rutherford has much less to say in this regard, but what little he does say further consolidates his previous points. God's speculative knowledge relies upon the metaphor of sight much like God's knowledge of vision (*scientia visionis*) and intuition (*scientia intuitiva*). If God's practical knowledge is knowledge that forms the ideas of possible creatures, it is clear God cannot have practical knowledge of himself because of his eternal being. Thus, God has purely *speculative* knowledge of himself. In regard to creatable being God has both practical as well as speculative knowledge. Still, Rutherford argued that God does not have purely speculative knowledge of merely possible or actual being. Rather than propositions enjoying a real presence before the divine intuition, Rutherford argued that "nothing intelligible precedes the intellect of God nor offers itself to the intellect of God as an object that by nature precedes him."[113] Whereas the created intellect is dependent upon objects outside of itself to cause intellection, the "infinite intellect either makes

---

111 "Infinitum numerum & thesaurum *Platonicum* animarum, formarum, essentiarum, apud Deum ab aeterno fuisse, & Chimericas, nescio, quas, rerum existentias creatas in tempore." Rutherford, *Disputatio Scholastica*, 559.

112 Beck, *Gisbertus Voetius*, 326.

113 "Nihil intelligibile proprie praevenit intellectum Dei, neque offert sese intellectui Dei, tanquam objectum ipso natura prius. I. Quia intellectus creatis imperfectio est venari ab objecto extra se causam suae intellectionis, 2. Intellectus infinitus vel facit vel permissive vult fieri: finitus vero factum praesupponit objectum suum. Nulla ergo est in Deo scientia pure speculativa sejuncta ab omni praxi." Rutherford, *Disputatio Scholastica*, 560.

or permissively wills it [the object of intellection] to be." Thus, there is no purely speculative knowledge of God that is excluded from praxis. The significance of this last statement was to further contradict the Jesuit instincts regarding God's intuition/vision of possible beings independent of the divine being or antecedent to the divine will. Rutherford's emphasis throughout has been that all beings (whether possible or actual) and propositions are ultimately dependent upon God and remain under his dominion.[114]

3.5 Summary

The foundation upon which Rutherford's entire doctrine of the knowledge of God was built was the distinction between various expressions of God's necessary and free knowledge. By his necessary knowledge he knows both himself, as well as all possible states of affairs. Rutherford ties God's knowledge of possible states of affairs to God's knowledge of his own being and power, thus revealing an emphasis upon the created order's radical dependence upon God that Rutherford stresses throughout.

When discussing God's necessary and free knowledge, Rutherford often preferred the intellectualist terms of *scientia simplicis intelligentiae* and *scientia visionis*. However, as was shown, this should not lead the interpreter to assume that Rutherford maintained these distinctions without modifying their substance. Rather, Rutherford, like many of his Reformed Scholastic contemporaries, reinterpreted intellectualist distinctions along more voluntaristic lines, emphasizing the role of the divine will in actualizing possibilities open to God's omnipotence. This is seen most clearly in Rutherford's definition of the *scientia visionis*, whereby God knows the actual world not as an object of his vision, but rather "in light of his decree." However, since God's being and power precede all possibility and God's will precedes all actuality, God only knows possibility and actuality as radically dependent upon himself.

Rutherford further emphasized this radical dependence of the possible and actual world upon God as he engages the distinctions of God's indeterminate and determinate knowledge. Rutherford's Jesuit contemporaries argued that God had pre-volitional determinate knowledge of the truth-value of conditional propositions. The truth-value of conditional propositions was consequently obtained independently of God's power and will. Not only did such an accounting for God's determinate knowledge threaten to blur the distinction between necessary and contingent truth, but according to Rutherford it also subjected both God and the

---

114 Rutherford, *Disputatio Scholastica*, 560.

actual world to fatal necessity. Therefore, Rutherford utilized the theory of neutral propositions to argue that God first knew the truth-value of conditional propositions as indeterminate. Post-volitionally, God assigns a truth-value to one part of a pair of propositions and thereupon gains determinate knowledge of the truth-value of the proposition. God, no longer subject to fatal necessity, post-volitionally knows a world of radical contingency freely created by him.

Similar concerns are highlighted as he addresses the distinctions of God's abstractive and intuitive knowledge. The classic understanding of the terms as employed by Scotus emphasized the necessity of presence for intuition. Intuition became a means for verifying knowledge of contingent truths whereas abstraction was used to discuss knowledge of possible truths. Rutherford's Jesuit contemporaries collapsed the abstractive/intuitive distinction, arguing that the truth-value of one part of a pair of conditional propositions enjoyed a real presence as an object of God's eternal intuition. Again, the Jesuits revealed a theological instinct to grant independency to possible beings. Rutherford argued that such an accounting of God's knowledge in this fashion subjected both God and man to fatal necessity. Rutherford denied that such propositions had real presence, arguing that such propositions were not real since there was no first cause to join the two extreme terms. God only knew such propositions intuitively after the terms were joined by the divine decree. In maintaining the traditional understanding of the distinction, Rutherford maintained both the freedom of God as well as the contingency of the actual world. Such is achieved by negating the Jesuit instincts for the independence of possible worlds and insisting upon its radical dependence.

Finally, through the distinctions of God's speculative and practical knowledge, Rutherford argued that even the modal property of impossibility was ultimately derived from and is dependent upon God. By virtue of his practical knowledge, God forms the ideas of possible and future beings. However, these ideas must conform to the divine simplicity. Complex ideas that mingle the simple essences of beings, for example the goat-stag, are ultimately impossible. Impossibility is therefore not a property independent of God, but again radically dependent. This is used by Rutherford to deny that propositions as basic as *possible is possible* and *impossible is impossible* could enjoy an existence independent from God.

In light of the above, it is worth noting two things. First, Rutherford's doctrine of God's knowledge emphasizes the dependence of both the possible and actual world throughout. This is a theological instinct of Rutherford's that is never far removed from the main arguments. God's independence is a means by which Rutherford preserved the contingent nature of the created world. Furthermore, it is clear that in Rutherford's mind if other beings or propositions are independent of God's being, power, or will, both God and the created world are then logically subjected to fatal necessity. The second thing worth noting is that God's pre-volitional knowledge of possibility and the impossibility that arise from the incompossibility of the practical ideas of the divine intellect, are ultimately reflective of the divine being and power. As much emphasis as Rutherford placed upon the divine will, God's knowledge of himself was the basis of his knowledge of possibility. The foundation of God's knowledge of his own omnipotence creates the "treasury of omnipotence" from which his will elects the actual world.

4. God's Will

All God's justice toward man and angels floweth from an act of absolute, sovereign free-will of God, who is our Former and Potter, and we are but clay.[1]

In keeping with the typical organizational structures of the doctrine of God in Reformed Scholasticism, the treatment of the divine will follows the treatment of the divine knowledge. This structure is explicit in the *Examen*.[2] The sequence is present, although inverted in the *Disputatio*.[3] Just as with the divine knowledge, the divine will is exposited using several important distinctions. As was shown in the previous chapter, God's free knowledge of the actual world follows the divine will and is entirely dependent upon it. Therefore, as the discussion moves towards the divine will, it also comes closer to the doctrine of divine providence. The following chapter begins with an exploration of God's will and God's being, with an emphasis on the regulative role of the divine simplicity in relation to the divine will. From here, certain classic scholastic distinctions such as the *voluntas signi et beneplaciti* and the *voluntas antecedens et consequens* will be outlined. Following these distinctions, two controversies pertaining to God's will are explored. The first relates to God's will and sin punishing justice. The second looks to God's will and the moral law. Both have far reaching implications for Rutherford's doctrine of divine providence.

4.1 God's Will and God's Being

As Richard has noted in his study, the doctrine of divine simplicity looms large in Rutherford's exposition of the divine will.[4] Rutherford identified several important features to the regulative role of the divine simplicity in regard to the divine will.

---

1 Rutherford, *Joshua Redivivus*, 105.

2 The second and third headings of the first chapter of the *Examen* deal with God's essence and the Trinity, followed by the fourth heading *De scientia Dei* and then the fifth and final heading of the first chapter, *De voluntas Dei*.

3 As was mentioned in the previous chapters, the systematic structures of the doctrine of God are implied in the *Disputatio* rather than explicit. Nevertheless, the structure is inverted. After dealing with the scholastic definition of providence in Chapter 1, Rutherford addresses God's will in Chapter 2 and then proceeds to offer a polemical account of God's knowledge in Chapter 3. Thus in the *Disputatio*, a brief discussion of God's will precedes a discussion on God's knowledge. Following Chapter 3, Rutherford returns to an extended treatment on the divine will.

4 See Richard, *The Supremacy of God in the Theology of Samuel Rutherford*, 95. Rutherford's emphasis on the divine simplicity in his exposition of the doctrine of the divine will is common amongst the

The first is an insistence upon the notion that the divine will and associate actions such as the divine decree are not separate from the divine essence and therefore are not accidents of the divine substance.[5] Such declarations were important due to the Remonstrant critique of the Reformed position, which challenged the Reformed equation of the divine will with the divine essence. Rutherford engages specifically with Conrad Vorstius (1569–1622) in this matter.[6]

Vorstius argued that the divine decree ought to be considered separate from the divine essence, the former being accidental and the latter being substantial.[7] His critique rested upon five pillars which have been summarized by the Reformed Orthodox theologian Gisbertus Voetius (1589–1676).[8] Rutherford followed Voetius closely in his own discussion.[9] Voetius's summary of Vorstius's five pillars is as follows:

1. The decrees are many but God is one.
2. The decrees are free, but God is a simple being and absolutely necessary.
3. The efficient cause of the decrees is God himself, and they follow after him.
4. God is eternal, but the decrees are not.
5. The decrees are mutable, conditional, and dependent, but God is immutable, absolute and independent.[10]

Reformed Orthodox. See also: Muller, *The Divine Essence and Attributes*, 450–5; Beck, *Gisbertus Voetius*, 329–34.

5 The question is posed as follows: "Quaeritur, An decreta & liberae volitiones, & actiones in Deo, sint quid diversum a Dei Essentia; & falsum sit illud Theologorum nostrorum, quicquid est in Deo, est Deus; item, an in Deo ulla sint accidentia?" It is answered in the negative for both: "Nos negamus." Rutherford, *Examen Arminianismi*, 169–70.

6 Rutherford primarily engages with Chapter 10 of Conrad Vorstius, *Apologetica exegesis sive plenior declaratio* (Lugdunum Batavorum: Joannis Patij, 1611).

7 The chapter title indicates that Vorstius will address "Whether or not one may attribute accidents to God." "An & quatenus Accidentia Deo tribui possint, realiter ab ipso diversa. Ubi de descrimine essentiae & voluntatis in Deo," Vorstius, *Apologetica exegesis*, 40–44. For a helpful overview of Vorstius's position see Stephen Hampton, *Anti-Arminians: The Anglican Reformed Tradition from Charles II to George I* (Oxford: Oxford University Press, 2008), 204–6.

8 For Voetius's engagement with Vorstius see: Beck, *Gisbertus Voetius*, 346–51.

9 Compare Rutherford's comments in Rutherford, *Examen Arminianismi*, 169–70 with Gisbertus Voetius, *Selectarum disputationum theologicarum, prima pars* (Utrecht: Joannem a Waesberge, 1648), 139–41.

10 "*Prima*, quia decreta sunt multa, Deus est unus. *Secunda* quia decreta sunt libera, Deus est ens simpliciter & summe necessarium. *Tertia*, quia decreta habent causam efficientem Deum, & sunt illo posteriora. *Quarta*, quia Deus est ab aeterno, decreta minime. *Quinta*, quia decreta sunt mutabilia, conditionata, dependentia: Deus autem est essentia immutabilis, absoluta, independens." Voetius, *Selectarum disputationum theologicarum, prima pars*, 239.

Rutherford countered Vorstius with a typically orthodox insistence that the will of God is not an extrinsic denomination, but a vital action of God.[11] The extrinsic denomination (*denominatio extrinseca*) is contrasted with the intrinsic denomination (*denominatio intrinseca*). Brower traces the distinction to the twelfth century work attributed to Gilbert of Poitiers (1076–1154), *Liber sex principiorum*, wherein the author distinguished between the first four Aristotelean categories as intrinsic (substance, quantity, quality, and relation) and the final six (place, time, position, state/condition, doing, affection) as extrinsic.[12] God's will falls into the former category, being intrinsic, therefore it is essential to his being and indispensable to his active life.[13] Rutherford stated that God has this mode or manner of acting completely within his own being. Though the act of God's willing has effects *ad extra*, the end proposed (i.e. God's glory) is self-contained within God's own life. In Rutherford's words, "God's will is only God willing through himself" and not through the "power of the will conditioned by a distinct act" as it is in humans.[14] Because the will of God is entirely self-referential, and done in an eternal logical moment, nothing new is added to God by his freely willed relation to creation.[15]

What is God's relationship then to those things he has willed *ad extra*? God's will has a relation of reason (*relatio rationis*) to creatable being *ad extra*.[16] Again, Rutherford appears to have been following Voetius closely. Voetius's longer, more precise comments help illumine Rutherford's thinking on the matter. Voetius described

---

11 "Quia volitiones Dei, licet non sint extrinsecae denominationes, sed vitales actiones Dei; tamen duo includent. 1. Essentiam Dei, tali modo sese habentem. 2. *Relationem rationis* ad res extra Dei voluntatem." Rutherford, *Examen Arminianismi*, 170.

12 Jeffrey Brower, "Medieval Theories of Relations," in *The Stanford Encyclopedia of Philosophy* (online), fn. 35.

13 See Ch. 4, 88, fn. 11.

14 "& sic volitio Dei, est tantum Deus volens per se, & per Essentiam suam, & non per potentiam volitinam ab actu distinctam; prout est in nobis." Rutherford, *Examen Arminianismi*, 170.

15 The point is explicitly made by Voetius: "Deus immediate per essentiam intelligit, vult, & decernit, & ad creaturas libere terminatur, estque ipsius intellectio simul intellectio, amor, & decretum; nec in se producit novas actiones intellectus & voluntatis, quae sint accidentia a substantia ejus distincta." Voetius, *Selectarum disputationum theologicarum, prima pars*, 140–1. Rutherford does not make the point explicitly here in the *Examen*, though it is clearly assumed. Elsewhere Rutherford writes: "Deus non est in potentia ad ullam rem; sed ab aeterno, ipsius Voluntas determinata fuit ad omne volibile, & nolibile, hic es res extra Deum, aliter se habere potuerint. Nam nullum est volibile, nullum nolibile, quin ab aeterno, id vel voluerit, vel noluerit Deus. Nec incipit, de novo aliquid volle, aud do novo nolle." Rutherford, *Examen Arminianismi*, 178.

16 "Relationem rationis ad res extra Dei voluntatem." Rutherford, *Examen Arminianismi*, 170. This relation is different than that discussed in ch. 2.2.3 of this study. There the discussion pertained to the divine names that signified such a relation, rather than the relation itself.

three logical, as opposed to temporal, moments seen in the divine decree.[17] These moments are distinct from the structural moments considered in the previous chapter, nevertheless they do correspond exactly and serve much the same purpose here. The three logical moments are:

> First Logical Moment: God comprehends all the possibilities open to him, which are able to be made according to the ideas of the divine mind through a vital act of God's essential nature.
>
> Second Logical Moment: God's will terminates on the actual essence of those creatures he wills to create and govern. God's will also negatively terminates on those possible creatures he has chosen not to create.
>
> Third Logical Moment: A relation of reason is established between those creatures God has chosen to create in time and govern by providence.[18]

Of the three features, both Rutherford and Voetius placed special emphasis on the significance of the third—being the establishment of a relation of reason.[19] As was shown in chapter 2, Rutherford's qualified use of the relation of reason did not mean that the relation was purely conceptual, with no basis in reality. Rather, Rutherford emphasized that the relation of reason was a contingent relation, denying any necessary aspects to its reality.[20] Beck has shown that Voetius understood the

---

17 "Decretum Dei potest a nobis concipi secundum tria momenta seu instantia rationis, aut naturae, non vero temporis seu durationis, quia decretum est Deo coaeternum, In primo concipimus essentiam divinam per modum actus vitalis significatam, quatenus libere terminatur ad creaturas producendas aut gubernandas, sine ulla sui mutatione, vel reali additione: quia Deus immediate per essentiam intelligit, vult & decernit, & ad creaturas libere terminatur, estque ipsius intellectio simul intellectio, amor, & decretum; nec in se producit novas actiones intellectus & voluntatis, quae sin accidentia a substantia ejus distincta." Voetius, *Selectarum disputationum*, 240–42; for more on Voetius's treatment of the divine willing and the three structural moments see: Beck, *Gisbertus Voetius*, 344–51; Beck has linked these three structural moments to John Duns Scotus's "theory of neutral propositions." For more on this theory, see Beck, "'Divine Psychology' and Modalities", 129–136.

18 "In decreto Dei tria spectanda sunt. I. Essentia Dei per modum actus vitalis significata, quatenus necessario terminatur ad ipsam divinam bonitatem amandam, & ad omne possibile seu a Deo producibile, secundum ideas in mente divina. 2. Terminatio illius essentiae actuosae ad creaturas producendas & sic regendas; aut non producendas & sic regendas: illam melioris doctrinae causa dicemus positivum, istam negativam. 3. Relatio rationis, quae resultat ex illa terminatione." Voetius, *Selectarum disputationum*, 240.

19 "Tertius fons solutionum est." Voetius, *Selectarum disputationum theologicarum, prima pars*, 140. Rutherford does not deal directly with the three logical moments that are understood to compose the single act of the divine decree, nevertheless he does specifically single out the third structural moment, lending it special significance.

20 See this study, Ch. 2.2.3.

relation in a similar way.[21] In Voetius's construction, the relation between *God and his creatures* is based upon God's free decree, which being logical rather than temporal is coeternal with God. The relation between *creatures and God* is based upon their future existence in reality. In this eternal moment the relation between God and his creatures has no basis in actuality, existing only in the divine mind.[22] As Beck has noted, this does not mean that God's relationship with creatures is "unreal." If God's relationship with creatures was "real," from eternity, this would imply a necessary relationship with creation. The relation of reason implies that the relation was accidental. Furthermore, as was seen in chapter 2, Rutherford's qualified use of the relation of reason allowed a real association between Creator and creature in such a way that nothing was implied about the subjects.[23]

This careful construction achieves two critical things. First, as Beck notes, because the above takes place in a logical moment outside of time, there is no hint of temporal change or "accidentality" introduced into God's essential nature. The relation between God and his creatures being merely a relation of reason further underscores this point.[24] Second, what is outlined above is the structure of a coeternal, free decision God makes on behalf of a future creation. This makes God, as Stephen Duby has noted, "eternally decisive."[25] That the decision is coeternal prevents temporal change or "accidentality" from being introduced into God's essential nature, thus preserving the divine simplicity. Because it is a free decision it introduces contingency into the future created order since the future created order freely determined by God could have been otherwise.

4.2 Distinctions Within God's Will

The main distinctions within God's will addressed by Rutherford fall broadly under two pairs. The first is the *voluntas beneplaciti* and the *voluntas signi*, or the will of God's good pleasure and the will of the sign. The second of these is the *voluntas antecedens* and *voluntas consequens*, or the antecedent and consequent will. Related to both pairs is a matrix of ideas fleshed out in a series of further distinctions derived from the governing concepts. This section will define these distinctions, as well as

---

21 Beck, *Gisbertus Voetius*, 258–259.

22 "In tertio ergo instanti concipimus decretum quatenus hinc resultat respectus rationis, qui ex parte Dei fundatur in ipso decreto jam libere terminato; & ex parte creaturae in ipsa futuritione seu existentia illius." Voetius, *Selectarum disputationum*, 241.

23 See this study, Ch. 2.2.3.

24 Beck, *Gisbertus Voetius*, 347–8.

25 Steven J. Duby, *Divine Simplicity: A Dogmatic Account*, T&T Clark Studies in Systematic Theology (London: Bloomsbury Publishing, 2015), 197.

their derivatives, in order to provide a framework for Rutherford's conception of the divine will especially in regard to its relationship to the work of divine providence.

4.2.1 Voluntas Beneplaciti et Signi

"Our doctrine of divine providence concerning sin is not able to be made clear and plain unless we set forward these distinctions of the divine will."[26] The distinction Rutherford referenced here is the *voluntas beneplaciti et voluntas signi*, or the will of God's good pleasure (*voluntas beneplaciti*) and the will of the sign (*voluntas signi*).[27] Rutherford addressed the distinction in each of his three major Latin works as well as many of his English works. Each distinction is dealt with in turn in the following section.[28]

The will of good pleasure, or the *voluntas beneplaciti*, is also called the will of decision. Elsewhere, Rutherford called the *voluntas beneplaciti* God's discerning will, the will of counsel, and the will of purpose.[29] Being God's will of purpose and decision, Rutherford explicitly equates the *voluntas beneplaciti* with the divine decree.[30] While the divine decree certainly has soteriological implications, the scope of the decree and the *voluntas beneplaciti* is much broader.[31] As Rutherford states in his catechism, "In his [God's] free and absolute decree appoynted all things in the world and bringeth all to passe in his own time."[32] In regards to actual existence, Rutherford makes the same point in the *Disputatio* though he broadens it, noting that the object of the *voluntas beneplaciti* is "being that has certain existence or non-existence in the actual nature of things." Consequently, the object of the *voluntas*

---

26 "Non potest nostra doctrina de Dei providentia circa peccatum omnibus plana & obvia fieri, nisi nonnihil de natura voluntatis divinae & hisce distinctionibus praemittamus." Rutherford, *Disputatio Scholastica*, 3.

27 For a general overview of this distinction see Muller, *The Divine Essence and Attributes*, 457–9; Beck, *Gisbertus Voetius*, 331–34. For a summary overview of Rutherford's exposition of this distinction see: Richard, *The Supremacy of God in the Theology of Samuel Rutherford*, 103–14..

28 See: Exercitatio 2, Chapter 1 in Rutherford, *Exercitationes Apologeticae*, 200–20; Chapter 2 in Rutherford, *Disputatio Scholastica*, 3–12; and Chapter 1, titulus v, in Rutherford, *Examen Arminianismi*, 169–237.

29 Rutherford, *The Covenant of Life Opened*, 342.

30 Rutherford, *Examen Arminianismi*, 181.The link is also explicitly made in Rutherford's English work: Rutherford, *Christ Dying and Drawing Sinners to Himselfe*, 126.

31 References for the soteriological implications of the divine decree in Rutherford are myriad. For a concise explanation his catechism is sufficient. "*Q. Quhat decrees hes God concerning mankynd?/ A.* Two, the decrees of electione and reprobatione." See: Rutherford, "Ane Catachisme: Conteining the Soume of Christian Religion," 164.

32 Rutherford, "Ane Catachisme," 163.

beneplaciti is not only actual beings and states of affairs, but also those possibilities known to God that he wills not to actualize.[33]

The point above serves to underscore God's freedom in creation as well as the radical contingency of the actual world. "God is free to create humans, for out of the affluence of his goodness, he creates all. Therefore, he is able not to have created."[34] The world is as it is because God has freely determined it to be this way. Just as freely however, he could have determined otherwise. The primary cause of what has been, is now, and will be is the free decision of God in accordance with his good pleasure. That which is not, remains so by the same free decision. The riddle of all that is, as well as all that is not, is ultimately resolved in the mystery of the *voluntas beneplaciti*. God does not reveal all the purposes and plans of his will, thereupon leaving a great deal of his will mysterious. For this reason, the *voluntas beneplaciti* is also called God's hidden or secret will (*voluntas occulta*).[35]

A further distinction may be made in regard to the *voluntas beneplaciti*. This distinction addresses the manner in which the will of God (*voluntas beneplaciti*) is fulfilled. God's will (*voluntas beneplaciti*) is either effective (*efficiens*) or permissive (*permissiva/permittens*). God's will (*voluntas beneplaciti*) can be said to be effective (*efficiens*) in one of two ways. First, God's will is said to be effective when he decrees to make something through his own, immediate power. An example of this would be the creation of the world *ex nihilo*. God's will can also be said to be effective when he determines to effect his will through a rational creature. An example of this is the conversion of Peter to faith in Christ upon the hearing of the Gospel. Though this happens in time, it was willed from eternity and carried out efficiently by God.[36]

The *voluntas beneplaciti* can also be fulfilled in an indirect way through permission (*permittens/permissiva*). Properly speaking, divine permission concerns sin.[37] The theological function of permission, at least as far as it concerns Rutherford, is to (a) provide a means by which God can will to permit sin while (b) denying

---

33 "Objectum voluntatis beneplaciti est ens eveniens in rerum natura quod actualem existentiam vel non existentiam certo habiturum est, sive bonum sive malum, sive consonum *voluntati signi* seu approbanti, sive dissonum & contrarium, modo consideratur sub ratione eventus in rerum natura, vel, modo eveniat." Rutherford, *Disputatio Scholastica*, 4.

34 "Liberum est Deo creare hominem, nam ex libera affluentia bonitatis suae, omnia condidit. Ergo poterat non creasse." Rutherford, *Disputatio Scholastica*, 565.

35 Rutherford, *Disputatio Scholastica*, 3.

36 "Voluntas rursus beneplaciti alia est efficiens, qua ipse Deus vel per immediatam suam omnipotentiam aliquid facere decrevit, qua ipse Deus vel per immediatam suam omnipotentiam…vel per creaturas rationales aliquid efficere decrevit, sic, quod *Petrus* audiret Evangelium & ad fidem Christi converteretur, fuit ab aeterno volitum." Rutherford, *Disputatio Scholastica*, 4.

37 "Permissio proprie circa peccatum versatur." Rutherford, *Disputatio Scholastica*, 67.

God's direct efficiency and authorship of sin.[38] The key difference between God's effective will and his permissive will is that the effective will is direct and efficient. The permissive will is indirect and inefficient, in that God lends no power bending the will towards an evil outcome.[39]

The *voluntas beneplaciti* is paired with the *voluntas signi* or the "will of the sign." Unlike the *voluntas beneplaciti,* which Rutherford described as hidden and mysterious, the *voluntas signi* is said to be revealed. The object of God's revealed will is humankind's duties and obligations to its Creator, thus the *voluntas signi* is also called God's approving (*approbans*) and commanding (*approbativa*) will.[40] The object of the *voluntas signi* also includes God's promises as well as threatenings, and commands.[41]

In the *Exercitationes* Rutherford said that the *voluntas signi* may be considered in two ways.[42] The first way is in regard to actual reality decreed by God from eternity. In this way, the lines between the *voluntas signi* and *voluntas beneplaciti* are not easily recognizable. For example, through his *voluntas signi* God wills that the hearts of the elect *must be* made new. In addition, via his *voluntas signi* God promises that the hearts of the elect *will be* made new (Ezek. 36.26–27). Though such commands and promises are both made and fulfilled in time, God has nevertheless willed from eternity via his *voluntas beneplaciti* that the hearts of the elect will be made new in reality. In this example, God's revealed will (*voluntas signi*) makes known and contributes to fulfilling God's hidden will (*voluntas beneplaciti*).[43]

In the second way, the *voluntas signi* is more clearly distinguished from the *voluntas beneplaciti*.[44] Here the good and holy things of God's commands are revealed to the creature via the *voluntas signi*, but the actual act of obedience to

---

38 "Alia rursus est voluntas beneplaciti, quae permittens, sive permissiva nuncupatur, qua Deus decrevit ut peccatum a creatura rationali patraretur, se permittente, minime vero se efficiente aut Authore." Rutherford, *Disputatio Scholastica,* 4.

39 A fuller treatment of the divine permission is offered in Chapters 6 and 7 of this study.

40 "Voluntas Dei alia est beneplaciti…alia signi, quae approbans vel approbativa vel revelata dicitur." Rutherford, *Disputatio Scholastica,* 3.

41 See: Rutherford, *Disputatio Scholastica,* 4.

42 "Voluntas signi, seu illa, quae alio nomine est revelata & approbans seu praecipiens, consideratur bisariam." Rutherford, *Exercitationes Apologeticae,* 201.

43 "Ut objectum ipsius est a Deo decretum ab aeterno ut actu existeret: nam uti Deus voluntate signi imperat electis ut sibi faciant cor novum, ita hoc in iis operari ab aeterno decrevit, & in tempore promittit *Ezechiel.* 36. vers. 26, 27. sic voluntas revelata quoad objectum cum voluntate occulta seu decernente, seu efficiente coincidit, neque de eo hic proprie disputatio admodum est intricata." Rutherford, *Exercitationes Apologeticae,* 201.

44 "Contradistinguitur haec voluntas signi a voluntate beneplaciti, hoc modo: Deus revelat creaturae rem bonam & sanctam, quae ipsam ad obedientiam obliget, sive obedientia illa actu existat, sive non." Rutherford, *Exercitationes Apologeticae,* 201.

God's commands is not effectually willed via his *voluntas beneplaciti*. Here again the importance of properly identifying the object of the two wills is critical for distinguishing one from the other. Returning to the above example, the renewal of the heart (Ezek. 36.26–27) is considered a good thing regardless of whether or not such an act occurs in reality. Indeed, Rutherford will argue that whether or not such an event occurs in reality is accidental to God's revealed will (*voluntas signi*). The object of God's revealed will is not what will actually happen, but what is approved, commanded, or forbidden by God. Whether a particular heart will actually be renewed or not is properly the object of God's *voluntas beneplaciti*.[45]

Controversy surrounded this distinction of the *voluntas beneplaciti et signi* because of the second understanding of the *voluntas signi* outlined immediately above. If God could publish the command (*voluntas signi*) that sinners are to repent, or hearts are to be renewed, but he did not actually intend for such commands to be fulfilled (*voluntas beneplaciti*), in what way can it be said that the *voluntas signi* is actually a representation of God's will? Some resolved this tension by arguing that the *voluntas signi* is only improperly God's will by means of metaphor. This position is reviewed below.[46]

Rutherford traced the metaphorical assignation of the *voluntas signi* to the medieval heritage of Thomas Aquinas (1225–1274) and Durandus of Saint-Pourçain (1275–1332). The same is maintained in the early modern period by the Jesuits Gregory of Valencia (1550–1603) and Francisco Suárez (1548–161) as well as some Arminians. These theologians identified by Rutherford bring us back to a problem addressed in an earlier chapter, namely the problem of divine predication. Rutherford drew attention to Thomas's *Summa* I, q. 19. a. 12., as worthy of special notice.[47]

---

45 "Nam hoc diligenter notandum, actualem obedientiam vel non obedientiam, ut a Deo volitam vel nolitam, esse accidentale plane quid voluntati signi: sive enim actu fiat, sive non, quod Deus in verbo revelat, salvatur essentia voluntatis signi, ideoque res revelata qua volita, hoc est, approbata est objectum voluntatis signi: & eadem res quatenus existit actu vel non existit in natura, est objectum voluntatis beneplaciti." Rutherford, *Exercitationes Apologeticae*, 201.

46 "Hinc est quod *Aquinas, Valentia, Durandus, & Suárez* velint voluntatem Dei hic divisam, improprie esse voluntatem & divisionem esse homonymi in homonymata, eo quod voluntas signi sit improprie voluntas." Rutherford, *Exercitationes Apologeticae*, 201.

47 Both Durandus as well as the Jesuits of the early modern period mentioned by Rutherford rely on this critical section of Thomas's *Summa*. For relevant sections of each see: Durandi Portiano, *In sententias theologicas Petri Lombardi commentariorum* (Venice: Gulielmum Rovillium, 1563), Lib I, disp 48, q iii.; Francisco Suárez, *"Disputationes in Primam Partem Divi Thomae, De Deo uno & trino,"* (Mainz: Balthasari Lippij, 1608). Lib III De Attributis Dei positiuis, c. VIII, 148– 149; Gregory de Valencia, *Commentariorum Theologicorum Tomi IIII* (Leiden: Horatii Cardon, 1609), Lib I, dips I, q xix, punct iii, 332–5.

In the *Summa Theologiae*, Thomas made the argument that some things are said of God properly and some metaphorically.[48] Those which are said of God metaphorically are done so because of a likeness in effect (*similitudinem effectus*). For example, an angry man may punish someone and thus punishment becomes an expression of anger. Divine punishment is therefore called an expression of divine anger, since there is a likeness in the effect (i.e. punishment).[49] Thomas is careful to note that the same equivalence that is drawn between the will of an angry man and punishment cannot properly be drawn between God and divine punishment. "But this is the difference between will and wrath," wrote Thomas, "because wrath is never properly said to be in God, since wrath is principally understood to include passion." Because of the doctrine of divine simplicity, passion may not be admitted into the Godhead because it implies change. Though punishment is an expression of the divine will since God wills to punish evil, it is only metaphorically an expression of divine wrath in the sense outlined above.[50]

It might be assumed that one would be on safer ground drawing an equivalence between the divine commands and the divine will, but this is not necessarily true. For creatures, commands are a reliable expression of the will. Thomas and Durandus argued that the same cannot be said for God. For God, commands could merely be an expression that God desires obedience. But commands are not a reliable expression of God's actual intentions.[51] Rutherford summarized a similar passage from Durandus where he noted, "A command is not directly and always a sign that the one commanding wants the thing commanded to be, but only that he wants to obligate the subject." Therefore, in both the first instance (divine wrath) as well as the second (divine commands), they argued that neither are properly said to be God's will.[52]

---

48 "Ad secundum dicendum quod, sicut Deus potest significari metaphorice velle id quod non vult voluntate proprie accepta, ita potest metaphorice significari velle id quod proprie vult." Aquinas, *Summa Theologiae*, I, q. 19, a. 12, 226.

49 "Cum autem aliquae passiones humanae in divinam praedicationem metaphorice assumuntur, hoc sit secundum similitudinem effectus: unde illud quod est signum talis passionis in nobis, in Deo nomine illius passionis metaphorice significatur. Sicut, apud nos, irati punire consueverunt, unde ipsa punitio est signum irae." Aquinas, *Summa theologiae*, I, q. 19, a. 12, 226.

50 "Sed hoc distat inter voluntatem et iram, quia ira de Deo nunquam proprie dicitur, cum in suo principali intellectu includat passionem." I have followed the translation in Thomas Aquinas, *Summa Theologiae*, trans. O. P. Fr. Laurence Shapcote, ed. John Mortensen and Enrique Alarcon (Lander: The Aquinas Institute for the Study of Sacred Doctrine, 2012), I, q. 19, a. 11, 224.

51 "Sicut, cum aliquis praecipit aliquid, signum est quod velit illud fieri: unde praeceptum divinum quandoque metaphorice voluntas Dei dicitur, secundum illud Mt. 6.10: fiat voluntas tua, sicut in caelo et in terra." Aquinas, *Summa theologiae*, I, q. 19, a. 11, 224.

52 "Praeceptum enim (inquit) non est directe & semper signum quod praecipiens velit rem praeceptam fieri, sed solum quod velit subditum obligare." Rutherford, *Exercitationes Apologeticae Pro Divina Gratia*, 201–2. The relevant section from Durandus reads as follows: "Quia enim in nobis ille qui

There was another solution to the difficulty posed by the *beneplaciti et signi* distinction. This was to blur the difference between the two terms. In the *Examen* Rutherford identified this broadly as the Arminian position. "It is asked," wrote Rutherford, "whether the distinction of the will of good pleasure and of the sign as conveyed by the Arminians may be admitted. I respond, no."[53] The reason given by Rutherford is that the Arminians, specifically Jacobus Arminius in his *Disputationes publicae* (Disp 4, Thes. 58), argue that God wills the same thing in both the *voluntas beneplaciti* as well as the *voluntas signi*. The distinction is not a matter of a difference in will or even the objects of the will, but rather that God's will is hidden in the *voluntas beneplaciti* and revealed in the *voluntas signi*.[54] Rutherford's summary is a good representation of Arminius's early position where he described the *voluntas beneplaciti* as that which God wills to do or impede (*facere vel impedire*) and the *voluntas signi* as that which God wills to make known to rational creatures. The *voluntas signi*, according to Arminius's early position, is nothing more than the partially revealed *voluntas beneplaciti*.[55]

Arminius would later abandon the distinction altogether, noting in his *Articuli nonnulli* that "the will of God is rightly and usefully distinguished according to antecedent and consequent [will]."[56] He went on to say that the distinction of the will of God according to good pleasure (*beneplaciti*) and sign (*signi*) "is not able to bear rigid examination."[57] Arminius's later position was known to Rutherford,

---

praecipit vel consulit aliquid fieri, videtur illud velle. Similiter qui prohibit aliquid fieri, videtur velle illud non fieri. Qui autem aliquid facit, vult illud fieri. Qui vero permittit aliquid fieri cum possit impedire, videtur illud velle. Ideo in Deo idem ponitur, scilicet quod praeceptum, consilium, prohibitio, operatio, et permissio sunt vel dicitur voluntas divina, propter dictam similitudinem, vel magis proportionem." See Durandus of Saint-Pourçain, *In sententias theologicas Petri Lombardi commentariorum libri quatuor* (Leiden: Gulielmum Rovillium, 1563), Book I, Dispt 48, q 3.

53 "Quaeritur, An admittenda sit distinctio Voluntatis *Beneplaciti* & *Signi*, prout eam tradunt *Arminiani*? Res. No." Rutherford, *Examen Arminianismi*, 181.

54 "Quia illis, Voluntate Beneplaciti, Deus eadem illa vult fieri, quae fieri vult Voluntate Signi; & volunt, eandem esse Voluntatem Beneplaciti, sed occultam, quae est Voluntas Signi, sed nobis revelata." Rutherford, *Examen Arminianismi*, 181.

55 "Inde distinguitur voluntas Dei in illam, qua vult facere vel impedire aliquid, quae beneplaciti dicitur vel potius placiti; & in illam, qua vult fieri vel non fieri aliquid a creaturis intellectu, praeditis, & voluntas Signi dicitur; haec revelata est; illa partim revelata est, partim occulta est." Jacobus Arminius, *Opera Theologica* (Lugduni Batavorum, Apud Godfridum Basson, 1629). *Disp* 4. *Thes.* 58, 226. Arminius mentioned this distinction in his *Disputationes publica* (1603), however later in life he omitted the distinction writing that the "distinction of the will of God into that of good pleasure and that of the sign cannot bear a rigid examination." See: Keith D. Stanglin and Thomas H. McCall, *Jacobus Arminius: Theologian of Grace* (Oxford: Oxford University Press, 2012), 72.

56 "Voluntas Dei & recte, & utiliter in Antecedem, & consequentem distinguitur." Jacobus Arminius, "Articuli nonnulli perpendendi," in *Opera theologica* (Leiden: Goderfridum Basson, 1629), 949.

57 "Distinctio voluntatis Dei in beneplaciti & signi rigidum examen ferre non potest." Arminius, 949.

who acknowledged that some Arminians and even Jesuits charged the Reformed with positing the *voluntas beneplaciti* and *signi* as two contradictory wills within God.[58] The critique is easy to understand. If God wills that the sinner might repent and be saved via his *voluntas signi*, but via his *voluntas beneplaciti* wills that only some may repent and be saved, is this not evidence of a contradiction? For some it represented something worse than a contradiction. To these it represented a bad trick on behalf of God who says one thing (*voluntas signi*) and yet intends another (*voluntas beneplaciti*).[59]

Rutherford rejected both the metaphorical reading of the *voluntas signi* used by Thomas and the early modern Jesuits as well as the modified reading of the *voluntas signi* by Arminius. He argued that the *voluntas signi* represents God's genuine approval and even love for the good, as well as hatred for the bad. This is emphasized in another term for the *voluntas signi*, which is God's will of simple complacency. Complacency is not to be taken in the modern sense of the word signifying uninformed self-satisfaction or demonstrating a lack of concern. Rather Rutherford meant for it to mean a basic agreeableness and even love (*simplex amatio rei*) of a thing by God.[60]

Complacency taken in this way, as Rutherford meant for it to be taken, helps the interpreter come to a better understanding of the *voluntas signi* and its object. Whereas the object of the *voluntas beneplaciti* is possible and actual being, the object of the *voluntas signi* is good and evil, or what is commanded or forbidden. Thus, in the *Disputatio* Rutherford notes that the object of the *voluntas signi* is what is morally good and honest as well as that which is unjust and evil. Critically, Rutherford notes that the nature of God's "complacency" towards such acts and

58 "Hae duae voluntates beneplaciti & signi non sunt contrariae vel contradictoriae, ut nobis impingunt Jesuitae & Arminiani." Rutherford, *Disputatio Scholastica*, 4.

59 Rutherford cites Schaafman's *De Praedestinatione*. See Rutherford, *Exercitationes Apologeticae pro divina gratia*, 220. I have been unable to locate Schaafman's treatise. The reader may be interested in Johannn Piscator's (1545–1625) lengthy rebuttal of Schaafman which includes extensive quotes from Schaafman's treatise. See Johanne Piscatore, "ad Disputationem de Praedestinatione contra Schaafmannum," in *Thesium theologicarum in illustri schola nassovica, partim Herbornae, partim sigenae disputatarum: praeside Johanne Piscatore* (Herborn: Christophori Corvini, 1607).

60 "Voluntas signi est actus divinae complacentiae de re non facienda, sed simplex amatio rei, sive fiat sive non." Rutherford, *Exercitationes Apologeticae pro divina gratia*, 201. Rutherford's exposition of the *voluntas signi* on this point is not unique. Muller notes that for the Reformed Orthodox, "The *voluntas signi*, therefore, is not a "mere sign" but one that corresponds with something that is truly in God." See: Muller, *The Divine Essence and Attributes*, 458.

beings remains the same regardless of whether or not they come to be in the nature of things.[61]

This introduces an interesting aspect to the *voluntas beneplaciti et signi* distinction. The distinction is yet another means whereby the contours of necessity and contingency can be further outlined. God reveals, via his *voluntas signi*, many good things that he wills and approves. Nevertheless, following Twisse, Rutherford notes that just because he wills and approves of a good thing, does not mean that such a thing must necessarily come to pass.[62] Out of a vast treasury of things God loves and approves, he freely chooses some good things to actualize via his *voluntas beneplaciti*.[63]

There are a handful of things at stake in this careful exposition of the *voluntas beneplaciti et signi* distinction. The first, and arguably the most important to Rutherford, was to maintain God's independence and freedom over anything that would impose necessity upon God in the actual world. Rutherford argued that there were many good and holy possibilities that will never be actualized; thus God could not be obligated to actualize all of them. God, being free from necessity of this sort, was free to actualize his chosen world via his will of good pleasure (*voluntas beneplaciti*). But this does not make his *voluntas signi* a bad trick (as per Schaafman) or a contradiction (as per Arminius). Rather, God does genuinely love the good and hate the bad as expressed in his *voluntas signi*. Rutherford's point is that God's love of the good does not impose necessity upon him to actualize every good. Again, the contingency of the created order, and God's absolute freedom and independence is maintained.

---

61 "At vero objectum voluntatis Dei signi vel approbantis, est illud quod est moraliter bonum & honestum, improbantis vero, quod est iniquum & malum: sive eveniat in rerum natura, sive non." Rutherford, *Disputatio Scholastica*, 5.

62 Rutherford illustrates the point through a false syllogism. "Deus approbat obedientiam existentem, vel non existentem. Ergo ab aeterno decrevit ut existeret obedientia: Non sequitur." Rutherford, *Disputatio Scholastica*, 9.

63 "Nam ex voluntate signi, non est proprie, quod res volita existat vel non existat, Deus enim multa sic vult, ut obedientiam reproborum, quæ actu existere non vult; hoc tamen non est praetereundum, quod voluntas signi respectu sui objecti est propriissime voluntas. Nam quod Deus præcipit, vult & approbat ut rem bonam & sanctam; quod vetat, improbat ut malum: & ab æterno decrevit ut illa res sit bona etiam voluntate beneplaciti & decernente, ideoque objectum omne voluntatis signi, est volitum voluntate beneplaciti, at non continuo objectum omnis voluntatis beneplaciti est à Deo decretum & volitum voluntate signi, sed id tantum quod verbo revelatur, ut justum aut injustum; & hoc sensu voluntas signi & in præceptionem & prohibitionem, & in rem præceptam & prohibitam terminatur & transit." Rutherford, *Exercitationes Apologeticae pro Divina Gratia*, 202. The relevant section that Rutherford cites can be found in William Twisse, *Vindiciae gratiae, potestatis, ac providentiae dei: Hoc est, ad examen libelli perkinsiani, de praedestinationis modo & ordine, institutum a iacobo arminino, responsio scholastica, iii libris absoluta* (Editio Secundua, Amsterdam: Guilielmum Blaen, 1632), Liber I, Pars Prima, Sectio XII, 140.

4.2.2 *Voluntas Antecedens et Consequens*

"It is asked," Rutherford wrote in the *Examen,* "whether there is in God an antecedent and consequent will?" He answered in the affirmative, though he did so within the conceptual framework of his own Reformed convictions. Just as in the above, the distinction of the *voluntas antecedens et consequens* arose to reflect the complex portrayal of God's will in the scriptures. The distinction attempts to grapple with the problem of God's general will for all people and his specific will for some people. The crux of the matter relates to salvation. The scriptures state that God generally wills that "all people be saved" (1 Tim. 2:4). At the same time however, the scriptures speak of "vessels of wrath prepared for destruction" (Rom. 9:22) as well as others predestined for glory (Romans 8:30). How then is God's general will for the salvation of all to be reconciled with his specific will of salvation for some and punishment for others? These are the complex and pastorally significant issues at stake in this distinction.[64]

The distinction was primarily championed and employed by Arminian and Jesuit theologians. In the British Isles this distinction was preferred over the *voluntas beneplaciti et signi* distinction by the Laudian theologian Thomas Jackson (1579–1640). Rutherford led with this distinction, rather than that of the *voluntas beneplaciti et signi* in his *Examen Arminianismi,* almost certainly because it was the favored distinction of the Arminians.[65]

Rutherford admitted the distinction in a twofold sense. He wrote:

(1) If the antecedent will (*voluntas antecedens*) concerns the end, proposed by God, and the consequent will (*consequens*) concerns the means to the end, we embrace this distinction.
(2) If the antecedent will is only complacency of the thing pleasing in itself, that coincides with the *voluntas signi* by approving (*approbante*), and by obliging us to our duty: And the consequent will coincides with the *voluntas beneplaciti*; then we embrace this distinction.[66]

---

64 For a general overview of this distinction see Muller, *The Divine Essence and Attributes,* 465–9; Beck, *Gisbertus Voetius,* 333–34. For a specific treatment of Rutherford's exposition of this distinction see: Richard, *The Supremacy of God in the Theology of Samuel Rutherford,* 112–3.

65 This is not to say that the Reformed abandoned the distinction. Muller notes that Maccovius, Cocceius, Heidanus, Owen, Turretin, Rijssen, and as will be seen Rutherford, all admitted the distinction. Nevertheless, the distinction had to be carefully defined to avoid the implications posed by the Arminian understanding of the distinction. See: Muller, *The Divine Essence and Attributes,* 465.

66 "Sed I. Si Voluntas *antecedens* esset de fine, a Deo, proposito, *consequens* de mediis ad finem; agnosceremus distinctionem. 2. Si *antecedens* Voluntas esset tantum complacentia rei per se gratae, ut coincidit cum *voluntate* signi *approbante,* & obligante nos ad officium nostrum: Et Voluntas

Interpretation (2) is easily understood. Here the antecedent and consequent wills are virtually identical to the *voluntas beneplaciti et signi* distinction outlined above. Nothing further will be said regarding this interpretation. Concerning interpretation (1), Rutherford links the antecedent will to the end proposed by God. Thankfully Rutherford's extended comments in the *Exercitationes* illumine his meaning here in the *Examen.*[67] He wrote:

> But truly, as Scotus says, God wills antecedently, that what he not wills in himself and immediately, but that what he wills in the antecedent causes, from which (as Durandus says) effects follow, though not necessarily; so that God antecedently wills that all people be saved, insofar as he gives to everyone the natural capacity for salvation, and does not deny sufficient means, and God consequently wills not in the causes but in himself, that believers be saved.[68]

From the above, a clearer picture emerges of interpretation (1) of the antecedent and consequent will. The end proposed by God in his antecedent will is humanity's natural capacity for salvation. This interpretation is strengthened by Durandus's own words, cited by Rutherford, where Durandus explicitly linked the natural capacity for salvation with the end antecedently proposed by God.[69]

As Rutherford noted in the above, just because humans are made for salvation does not necessarily mean that they will be saved. The effect of salvation and blessedness "may follow, though not necessarily." He also noted that God's antecedent will is neither willed in himself nor immediately and thus is not understood to be an effectual will. As effects need not necessarily follow, an explanation is required as to why they do follow. Within the parameters of this distinction, having antecedently willed that humans be capable of salvation, God consequently and effectually wills

---

consequens, cum Voluntate beneplaciti; sic amplecteremur distinctionem." Rutherford, *Examen Arminianismi,* 171.

67 Richard understands interpretation (1) to "be useful to differentiate between the end and the means to the end." Later in his comments, Richard discusses a third interpretation of the distinction found in the Exercitationes, but in reality what Richard cites as a "third option" is just an elaboration on the first interpretation, which fills out the meaning of the language of means and ends. See Richard, The Supremacy of God in the Theology of Samuel Rutherford, 112.

68 "At vero *Scotus* ait Deum id velle antecedenter quod non in se & immediate, sed quod vult in antecedente causa, ex qua (inquit *Durandus*) effectus sequitur, quamvis non necessario; ut Deus antecedenter vult omnes salvari, quatenus dedit omnibus naturam salutis capacem, & media sufficientia non negavit, & Deus id vult consequenter quod non in causa sua, sed in se vult, ut credentes salvari." Rutherford, *Exercitationes Apologeticae,* 362.

69 Durandus, *In sententias theologicas Petri Lombardi commentariorum,* Lib I. Dist. XLVI. Q. II.

"not in the causes but in himself" that some humans (i.e. believers) are saved from the mass of humanity capable of salvation.[70]

Rutherford contrasted his own understanding of the *antecedens et consequens* distinction (in both senses) with the Jesuit and the Arminian respectively. Rutherford understood the two groups to have a functionally equivalent use of the terms, where God's antecedent will is the will most aligned with God's natural disposition. By this will, under the weight of a natural inclination, God wills good and salvation to all of his rational creatures.[71] This will, however, is without efficacy.[72] Therefore, God has no power to bring about the salvation he antecedently wills to his creatures. If a creature is obedient, God consequently and necessarily wills that creature's salvation. If the creature is disobedient, God consequently and necessarily wills that creature's damnation.[73]

Rutherford offered a series of objections to this understanding both in the *Examen* and the *Exercitationes*, however his most noteworthy comments in relation to this distinction and God's providence come from the *Disputatio* as he engaged the Laudian theologian Thomas Jackson, who held an interesting interpretation of God's antecedent and consequent will.[74] On the basic definitions of God's antecedent and consequent will, Jackson was fairly representative of the Arminian position. God wills, antecedent to any human action, to approve of and reward "whatsoever is good in itself, and good withal for a reasonable creature to make a choice of."[75] If however, the human sins, God consequently wills that the sinner must suffer.[76] The novelty of Jackson's treatment of this distinction did not come from the definitions, but rather

---

70 This is in keeping with Rutherford's own understanding of God's effectual will outlined above, which requires that God's effectual will be willed in and through himself. Rutherford explicitly relies upon John Duns Scotus, whose own remarks make clear that only God's consequent will is to be understood to be his effectual will. See: Joannes Duns Scotus, *Quaestiones in Lib I. Sententiarum* (Leiden: Lavrentii Durand, 1639), 1384.

71 "Jesuitae recentiores praesertim, Gab. Vasquez & Francisc. Suárez. & Arminiani docent voluntatem antecedentem esse naturalem in Deo affectum, 3 qua naturae impetu vult bonum & salutem creaturarum intelligentium quatenus sunt creaturæ, & nihil adhuc merito aut demerito egerunt: at quatenus obedientes sunt vel inobedientes, consequenter vult quosdam damnari." Rutherford, *Exercitationes Apologeticae*, 363–4.

72 "At Arminianis, Voluntas antecedens, est Deo desiderium naturale expers efficacia, quo naturaliter desiderat obedientiam & salutem omnium mortalium; eam tamen minime efficit." Rutherford, *Examen Arminianismi*, 171.

73 "Consequens est, qua vult Deus quorundam obedientiam & salutem; si, nempe, vocatione dignos, se praestiterint: sin minus, iis negat media externa, & salutem." Rutherford, *Examen Arminianismi*, 171.

74 The relevant section comes from Chapters 11–12, in Rutherford, *Disputatio Scholastica de Divina Providentia*.

75 Jackson, *A Treatise on the Divine Essence and Attributes*, 333.

76 Jackson, 333.

from his unique application of the language of fate to the *antecedens et consequens* distinction which helped him develop the language of "degrees of necessity." God's consequent will to punish sinners enacted a minor degree of necessity, however over a lifetime of sin this developed into a major, even fatal degree of necessity leading to damnation.[77]

Jackson's understanding of the degrees of necessity within God's consequent will is based upon the Platonic notion of strong and weak fates (*fata minora* and *fata majora*). In this "heathenish division" Jackson notes there was nevertheless "a true glimpse of a Christian truth."[78] An illustration is employed to make Jackson's point.

> Many games at both, which at the beginning, or until the middle of time spent in them, are very fair, and more than ten to one, after some few oversights or ill dice, become desperate and irrecoverable by any skill that can be used: so events properly fatal become at length unpreventable, irresistible; but such they were not from the beginning of time, or from their infancy or first attempt on whom they fall.[79]

For Jackson, one's eternal destiny is not determined in an instant but over the course of a lifetime. Prior to any human action, God has willed to reward the just and punish the unjust. Following an unjust action, God's consequent will is likened to a "weak fate" or "weak necessity" which narrows the probability of a heavenly reward. A lifetime of unjust actions will harden weak necessity into a strong necessity until eternal punishment becomes "truly fatal and altogether unavoidable."[80]

Rutherford's most important critique of the above was that Jackson's account of God's reflexive and necessary justice, rather than offering the dynamic portrait of God's grace and providence in the Bible, is more akin to a "sleepy Epicurean providence." He wrote:

> If truly every man is antecedently able to freely and absolutely change, namely to simply hear or never to hear, to believe or not, to pray or not, to persevere or fall away, then none of these is from the decree of God. Ah! What kind of passive, sleepy, Epicurean providence![81]

---

77 Jackson, 341.

78 Jackson, 341.

79 Jackson, 360.

80 Jackson, 360.

81 Si vero homo omnes varietates antecedentium libere & absolute potest, nempe, audire simpliciter, nunquam audire, credere, vel non, orare, resipiscere, vel non, perseverare, vel deficere, nihil ex hisce decretum a Deo. Vah qualis, quam supina, somnolenta, Epicurea providentia?" Rutherford, *Disputatio Scholastica*, 122.

Such an account not only rendered God distant, but it also rendered God's grace and providence mechanical. For Jackson, God's providence does not arise from his freedom, but rather is bound by necessity to respond to human activity. As humans sin, weak necessity becomes strong necessity and God's decree of reprobation hardens. Human activity imposes itself in a necessary and fatal way upon the decree, and thus upon God himself.

In an earlier section dealing with the *voluntas beneplaciti et signi* distinction, it was pointed out that God is under no necessary obligation to actualize every good. In this distinction, it can be seen that God is under no necessary obligation to punish every evil. The point is not inconsequential. Because God is not obligated to punish every evil, he is free to extend grace even to sinners. Furthermore, humans themselves are freed from the *fata majora* posited by Jackson. More so, from Rutherford's perspective, this also frees God from the fatal necessity that Jackson's arguments inevitably burdened him with.[82]

4.3 God's Will and the Free Nature of Sin Punishing Justice

God's freedom to punish or not punish evil, as seen in Rutherford's exposition of the *voluntas antecedens et consequens* distinction, involved him in a hotly contested seventeenth century debate concerning the relationship between God's will and sin punishing justice. The point at issue is whether punitive justice, also called sin punishing justice or vindicatory justice, is expressed *ad extra* by the necessity of God's nature or is a free expression of the divine will. Rutherford's position on this question roots him firmly within the voluntarist tradition of the church, associating him with contemporaries such as William Twisse (578–1646) and Gisbertus Voetius (1589–1676), while linking him with the Reformation tradition of John Calvin (1509–1564) and the medieval tradition of John Duns Scotus (1266–1308), Jean Gerson (1363–1429), and Thomas Bradwardine (1300–1349).[83]

---

82 "Sequitur ex hoc, Dei decreta non esse rerum causas, sed contra res extra Deum esse causas quae dant stabilitatem, firmitatem & immutabilitatem decretis Dei Deum facit pendulum, quasi nec posset nec auderet complete, peremptorie & irresistibiliter decernere captivitatem, donec videret poculum iniquitatum *Iudaorum* impletum, paratuique esset pari passu incedere decernendo, quo *Iudai* pergunt peccando, neque compleri decretum Dei nec adolescere in decretum firmissimum & immutabile, quod *Jacksono* est *majus fatum*, nisi temporum successu, valeant ergo & facessant Aeterna Dei decreta: nec decretum integrari & consummari donec res decretae actu existerint in tempore." Rutherford, *Disputatio Scholastica*, 130.

83 For examples see William Twisse, *Vindiciae gratiae, potestatis, ac providentiae dei: hoc est, ad examen libellil perkinsiani, de praedestinationis modo & ordine, institutum a iacobo arminino, responsio scholastica, III libris absoluta* (Amsterdam: Guilielmum Blaen, 1632). Lib I, Pars Tertia, Digressio I,

Rutherford's stance on this issue, alongside Twisse, placed him at odds with some Jesuits and Arminians. Adding a new wrinkle, however, is that Rutherford's position in this controversy placed him at odds with those within Reformed Orthodoxy who held a more intellectualist approach to the question of God's sin punishing justice. Of note among these is the English non-conformist John Owen (1616–1683), who while Dean of Christ Church Cathedral and Vice-Chancellor of Oxford University publicly engaged Rutherford on this issue in his *Dissertation on Divine Justice.*[84]

In *The Covenant of Life Opened*, Rutherford wrote: "It is not written in the heart of man by nature that God should promise life eternal to man, upon condition of obedience."[85] In this opening argument Rutherford sought to dissolve any necessary connection between obedience and reward on one hand, or sin and punishment on the other. Though humans may sense a certain "quietnesse of conscience" as a result of obedience or unease as a result of sin, in neither case, he argued, can it be logically inferred that there is an "intrinsecall connexion, *ex natura rei*, between our obedience and a reward to be given of God" or an unsettled conscience after sin to deduce that God must necessarily punish the sinner. Rutherford argued both are an example of a bad inference.[86]

How is this a bad inference? The contingency of the present world provides the key. "For a natural conscience may, and does know," he wrote, "that God doth freely create the world, and that he might not have created it."[87] God does not create the world by a natural, necessary obligation. Thus, he does not communicate good to the world by a natural necessary obligation. Though his goodness is an essential attribute, the providential communication of this attribute *ad extra* is a free matter of the will, not a necessary obligation to God's nature and being. "Ergo, this actual extension of goodnesse is not essential to God, so neither is the actuall punishing of sin essential to God but free."[88] If the expression of God's goodness in creation was not free, then neither is his sin punishing justice. And if neither is free, then God was bound to create this world and do good to it. Likewise, God would be necessarily obligated to punish sin. And if this is true, according to Rutherford,

---

Sect. 4, 313–14; Thomas Bradwardine, *De causa Dei, contra pelagium, et de virtute causarum, ad suos mertonenses* (London: Joannem Billium, 1618). Lib I, Cap 39, 343.

84 The relevant sections in Owen can be found in Chapter 17 in: John Owen, "A Dissertation on Divine Justice," in *The Works of John Owen*, Vol 10, ed. William H. Goold (Edinburgh: Johnstone & Hunter, 1850–53), 607–18. Owen's remarks are treated in Carl Trueman, *The Claims of Truth: John Owen's Trinitarian Theology* (Carlisle: Paternoster Press, 1989), 105–11. Owen's engagement with Rutherford is treated in: Richard, *The Supremacy of God in the Theology of Samuel Rutherford*, 133–8.

85 Rutherford, *The Covenant of Life Opened*, 20.

86 Rutherford, 20–21.

87 Rutherford, 21.

88 Rutherford, 21.

then both God and his creatures are bound to a necessary, fatalistic reality that could not have been otherwise than what it is.[89]

The contingent nature of the present reality places the expression of God's sin punishing justice under a hypothetical necessity from the very beginning. The question is not therefore, is the expression of sin punishing justice necessary? Clearly it is not. Rather, the question is, under the condition that God wills to create rational creatures with the moral capacity to sin, is God obligated by his nature to punish sin? For Rutherford the answer was a clear no. His supporting reasons for this denial are found in a succession of arguments from the *Disputatio*.[90]

Rutherford's first argument was based upon the substitutionary work of Christ. "God, according to his punitive justice," wrote Rutherford, "surrendered to death his own innocent Son, the Lord Jesus Christ." He noted however, "that he was able to not sentence him to death."[91] Christ himself was innocent (Isa. 53.9; John 8.46; Heb. 7.26; and John 5.30), thus God was under no necessary obligation to punish his own innocent Son.[92] Nevertheless, though he was innocent, Christ was counted as a sinner and punished. How does one account for this, seeing that Christ had neither moral nor physical sin, thus God was not obligated to punish him? The answer, according to Rutherford, is that Christ was found to be a sinner legally, in that he was found to be a sinner by a free act of divine legislation. Christ was not handed over to death as a matter of necessity, but rather of the divine will.[93]

In his *Dissertation on Divine Justice*, Owen critiqued this point, arguing that Christ was handed over to death by a necessary obligation. "God could not have been God—that is just and true,—if he had not devoted to death his Son, when thus appointed our mediator."[94] Owen's peculiar language, that "God could not have been God," is consistent with Rutherford's own language in the *Disputatio*,

---

89 Rutherford, 22.

90 Rutherford, *Disputatio Scholastica*, 312–56.

91 "Deus ex justitia punitiva Filium suum innocentem *Dom. J. Christum* in aeternum adorandum morti dedit, & potuit non addixisse morti." Rutherford, *Disputatio Scholastica*, 345.

92 "Sic libera Dei aestimatione *CHRISTUS qui violentiam non fecit, & in cujus ore non fuit dolus,* Esa 53.9. Joan 8.46. Heb 7.26. John 5.30. qui nunquam peccavit, fuit peccator, & punitus fuit ac si esset peccator." Rutherford, *Disputatio Scholastica*, 346.

93 "Nam vere Christus & intrinsece innocuus erat, nam intrinsece peccator non erat; nulla enim physica, nulla moralis macula peccati inerat Christo qua intrinsece peccator esset, sicut fidei jussor non est intrinsece & formaliter debitor; neque enim alienum contraxit neque profuse decoxit, est tamen debitor, sed non intrinsece, non formaliter, non per inhaerentiam physicam, sed legaliter." Rutherford, *Disputatio Scholastica*, 345–46.

94 Owen, "A Dissertation on Divine Justice," 609.

and is meant to make a simple point in regards to God's necessary attributes.[95] God is, for example, necessarily omnipotent. If there were such an inconceivable scenario where he was no longer omnipotent, then he would no longer be God. God necessarily loves himself. If there were such an inconceivable scenario where he no longer loved himself, then he would no longer be God. Owen argued that once God had appointed Christ to be the mediator, Christ was from that point onward necessarily obligated to be punished on behalf of sinners.[96] Owen believed he was making a point against Rutherford, but Rutherford actually made the same point. Rutherford argued that having been appointed mediator by divine decree, Christ was under a hypothetical (not actual) necessity to be punished for sin.[97] Subsequent to the decree, Rutherford agreed that God would not be God if Christ failed to make atonement, since this would contradict God's immutability. Owen actually conceded the same point, though he avoids the distinction of hypothetical necessity in favor of the terms absolute and conditional necessity. Despite the difference in terminology, Owen's preferred distinction corresponded neatly with Rutherford's own categories.[98]

Rutherford's second assertion pertained to the exercise of mercy *ad extra*. "God freely has mercy on whom he will," wrote Rutherford, "because he is obligated to no one, nor is he obliged to anything, nevertheless mercy is essential to God." What Rutherford established here is the simple point that an essential attribute *ad intra* is under no necessary obligation to be expressed *ad extra*. Mercy is an essential attribute of God, but it is not necessarily expressed to each and every person. Rather, God "has mercy on whom he will." The expression of mercy *ad extra* therefore, is a matter contingent upon the divine will. In a similar way, argued Rutherford, justice is an essential attribute of God, but its expression *ad extra* is a matter also contingent upon the divine will.[99] Owen appears to have misread Rutherford's argument on this point, falsely claiming that Rutherford believed mercy to be an

---

95 "Nulla enim necessitate naturae Deus Filium morti addixit, quia sic Deus non fuisset Deus, si Filium morti non addixisset, quod absurdum, nam ex gratuito amore morti Filium tradidit." Rutherford, *Disputatio Scholastica*, 345.

96 Owen, "A Dissertation on Divine Justice," 609.

97 "Et confirmatur, quoniam imputatio peccati Christo nullam naturalem, sed mere hypotheticam necessitatem ferendi supplicum, aut poenas alieni peccati luendi imponere potest; at nos facile damus, ex hypothesi quod Dei decreto Christus fidei jussor pro nobis semel factus sit eum non posse non plecti a Deo sed tamen libere, uti Deus mundum condidit, ex mera libertate, tamen necessario etiam, ratione immutabilitatis, postquam Deus semel mundum creare decrevit." Rutherford, *Disputatio Scholastica*, 346.

98 Owen, "A Dissertation on Divine Justice," 615.

99 "Sicut Deus libere miseretur quorum vult, quia nemini obligatur, aut quicquam debet, attamen misericordia est Deo essentialis, ita nec Deus debet peccatori necessitate naturae poenam." Rutherford, *Disputatio Scholastica*, 347.

essential attribute but that justice exists in God freely.[100] Rutherford argued that both justice and mercy exist in God necessarily, but that their expression *ad extra* was free. As before, it is not entirely clear whether or not Owen would disagree with this point.[101]

Rutherford's third argument asked how those who insist upon the punishment of sin as a necessary consequence of the divine nature (*ex necessitate Divinae naturae*) can account for the different measures by which God punishes sin. For example, God prescribes capital punishment for adultery in Lev. 20:10, but there is only a fourfold restitution required as renumeration for theft.[102] This argument is very closely related to another that Rutherford makes, which states that God "suffers no relaxation, moderation, or postponement of that which he does by necessity of nature."[103] If God punishes sin by necessity of nature, then there could be no difference between the punishment of adultery and theft, since both would be punished necessarily without relaxation or moderation. Rutherford anticipated a response to this line of reasoning in his *Covenant of Life Opened*, where he writes:

> Which is as good as to say, the fire must, by necessity of nature burn, the Sun cast light; But the fire hath free will to burn when it pleaseth, and at this time, and not at this time, and the Sun must shine, by necessity of nature, but it is free to shine at ten hours of the day, and not at twelve, and it may shine as bright as the Sun, or as dimme as the Moon. Or God the Father loves himself, but is free to him to love himself today and not tomorrow, and to love himself so much or not so much.[104]

Rutherford's account of his adversaries' position, as well as what follows from it, is no doubt exaggerated and perhaps unfair. Nevertheless, he has established the point that even those who insist that sin-punishing justice follows necessarily from the divine nature, still resort to the divine will to explain God's moderated expression

---

100 Owen, "A Dissertation on Divine Justice," 613.

101 In the *Disputatio,* it has already been shown that Rutherford argued that justice was an essential attribute of God. The same may be seen elsewhere, as in: Rutherford, *The Covenant of Life Opened,* 21.

102 "Qui docent peccatum mereri poenam ex necessitate Divinae naturae citra interventionem liberi Dei decreti, ii simul docent Deum non posse homini prohibere peccatum, quin necesse sit prohibeat sub poena aeternae mortis; quasi vero, cum Deus adulterium, furtum prohibeat in foro humano, ea prohibeat cum moderamine poenae, nempe quod finitum non morte sed quadrupli restitutione plectatur, non possit ea prohibere nulla poenae sanctione, & cum ea plecti jubeat ab hominibus, quia peccata sunt, cur non possit pari ratione in foro suo interno & moderati & omnem suspendere poenam & eadem tamen delicta prohibere." Rutherford, *Disputatio Scholastica,* 347.

103 "Quicquid etiam Deus ex necessitate naturae facit, id nullam patitur dispensationem, moderationem, aut dilationem." Rutherford, *Disputatio Scholastica,* 348.

104 Rutherford, *The Covenant of Life Opened,* 27.

of justice. And if so, then it is not truly necessary, in the classic scholastic use of the term, but rather a qualified necessity contingent upon the divine will. Owen himself is forced to concede this ground, admitting that neither the timing nor the degree of punishment is necessary, but only that sin must be punished. How the sin is punished, according to Owen, is a matter of the divine will. Though Owen at times approaches Rutherford's arguments with more than a degree of sarcasm, the voluntarist ground he concedes to Rutherford in the course of his interaction is a testimony to the overall strength of Rutherford's arguments.[105]

Rutherford offered a subpoint to the preceding argument when he speculated whether it would have been possible for God to merely make a promise of reward conditional upon obedience without any threatening of punishment at all. He contended that there was no contradiction or conflict with God's essential justice if in fact he had done so.[106] He grounded this possibility in the notion seen in the previous chapter that God is able, by his will, to join the two extreme terms of a conditional proposition. Consider the proposition: If Adam eats from the Tree of Knowledge, he will be punished. Rutherford argued that there was no pre-volitional, necessary connection between Adam's eating from the Tree of Knowledge and punishment. Therefore, God could not necessarily be bound to punish the sin of eating. Rather, because God freely joins the extreme connections of a proposition to make them true, Adam's punishment is constituted upon the divine will rather than upon the divine nature. God's freedom in this regard is an important aspect in safeguarding God's freedom from the fate that would oblige him to necessarily punish sin apart from any free decision of the divine will.[107]

---

105 See: Owen, "A Dissertation on Divine Justice," 613–5. Trueman has written extensively on Owen's "intellectualist" shift in the *Dissertation on Divine Justice*. See for example Trueman, *The Claims of Truth: John Owen's Trinitarian Theology*, 105–10 and 42–6. In light of the above observations, it is worth asking just how much of a shift this actually represents. To be sure, Owen moves away from the "voluntaristic" approach in his *Death of Death in the Death of Christ* towards a more "intellectualist" position in his *Dissertation on Divine Justice*, but as can be observed above, Owen retains a significant place for the divine will in his intellectualist approach to vindicatory justice. If Rutherford should be seen as a moderate "voluntarist," as was argued above, Owen's interaction with Rutherford reveals him to be more of a moderate "intellectualist."

106 "At vero Deus desineret esse Deus justus si vetasset *Adamum* vesci arboris scientia, addita nulla poena, sed promissione, fore ut, si abstineat, gratia confirmante in praemium obedientiae donetur. At quaenam in tali lege contradictio?" Rutherford, *Disputatio Scholastica*, 347–48.

107 Rutherford, *The Covenant of Life Opened*, 21–4.

4.4   God's Will and the Moral Law

Rutherford's doctrine of the will thus far has depicted a God who is absolutely free, independent, and unburdened. Furthermore, his emphasis upon the primacy of the divine will clearly places him within that pedigree of medieval scholasticism broadly described as voluntarism. But what does it mean to describe Rutherford as a voluntarist?[108] Does it mean, as Richard has recently argued, that according to Rutherford the divine will is a rule or law unto itself?[109] Or are there necessary limits and obligations laid upon the divine will? What sources does Rutherford enlist to shape his understanding of such issues and where does this situate him in the important scholastic debates over the primacy of God's intellect and God's will?[110]

A useful place to begin to explore these questions is in Chapter twenty-two of the *Disputatio*, which asks "Whether the free good pleasure of God is the first rule of all good morality in creatures?"[111] As Burton has pointed out, the chapter represents Rutherford's own *Euthyphro* Dilemma.[112] Is something loved by God because it is good? Or is something good because God loves it? Broadly speaking, theologians from the intellectualist tradition argued that the good was inherently so, thus God loved the good because it was good. On the other hand, theologians from the voluntarist tradition argued that the good was established by an act of the divine will. Both the intellectualist and voluntarist positions exist on a spectrum

---

108 The labels of "intellectualism" and "voluntarism" are useful for describing the broad contours of certain medieval and early modern currents of thought. Nevertheless they are problematic when applied to specific actors, since individual thinkers may incorporate certain tendencies that would be ascribed to both labels. For an overview of the development of the tradition, as well as some of the problems associated with the terms, see: Hoffmann, "Intellectualism and Voluntarism," 414–27.

109 Richard, *The Supremacy of God in the Theology of Samuel Rutherford*, 99.

110 The debates that surround the "intellectualist" and "voluntarist" schools evolved throughout the medieval period on into the early-modern era. These debates concerned a variety of issues, but often had direct implications for the doctrine of providence and the freedom of the will. For an overview of the development in the medieval tradition see J.B. Korolec, "Free Will and Free Choice," in *The Cambridge History of Later Medieval Philosophy*, ed. Norman Kretzmann, Anthony Kenny, and Jan Pinborg (Cambridge: Cambridge University Press, 1992), 629–641. For interesting comments on the development of the tradition as it impacted the doctrine of providence see also Antonino Poppi, "Fate, fortune, providence, and human freedom," in *The Cambridge History of Renaissance Philosophy*, ed. Charles B. Schmitt et al. (Cambridge: Cambridge University Press, 1988), 641–667.

111 "An liberum Dei Beneplacitum sit prima regula omnis bonitatis moralis in creaturis." Rutherford, *Disputatio Scholastica*, 312.

112 Burton, "Samuel Rutherford's Euthyphro Dilemma: A Reformed Perspective on the Scholastic Natural Law Tradition," in *Reformed Orthodoxy in Scotland: Essays on Scottish Theology 1560–1775*, edited by Aaron Clay Denlinger (London: Bloomsbury Academic, 2014), 122–140. For Voetius's approach to the Euthyphro dilemma, see Beck, *Gisbertus Voetius*, 364–369.

and require nuanced readings. Rutherford is no exception to this rule. To say that Rutherford is a voluntarist does not imply that he believes all good is established by the divine will, rather as will be shown, Rutherford's voluntarism is moderated by a host of complex considerations.[113]

4.4.1 The Moral Law and God's Being

"The adversaries teach sin is opposed to God's nature."[114] Rutherford's adversaries on this topic were the Remonstrant Conrad Vorstius (1569–1622), the Jesuit Gabriel Vasquez (1549/51–1604), and the Scottish Reformed theologian John Cameron (1579–1625). These men argued that the moral status of sin is determined pre-volitionally, antecedent to God's will. Sin is sin essentially and necessarily because it is opposed to God's being. Rutherford engaged them individually and, in doing so, his own position becomes clearer.[115]

Rutherford's engagement with the "adversaries" began with the Remonstrant Conrad Vorstius. Vorstius's remarks are taken from his *Amica Duplicatio*, a treatise written in response to the German Reformed Theologian Johannes Piscator in a long running dialogue between the two.[116] In the relevant section of the *Amica Duplicatio*, Vorstius critiqued the argument that God's dominion was established

---

113 There has been a rigorous debate concerning "voluntarist" and "intellectualist" influences in the Reformed tradition. Some have argued that the Reformed tradition is decidedly "voluntarist" with medieval associations most closely tied to John Duns Scotus. See for example the introduction in: Willem J. van Asselt, J. Martin Bac, and Dolf T. te Velde, eds. *Reformed Thought on Freedom: The Concept of Free Choice in Early Modern Reformed Theology*, Texts and Studies in Reformation and Post-Reformation Thought (Grand Rapids, MI: Baker, 2010); and also J. Martin. Bac, *Perfect Will Theology: Divine Agency in Reformed Scholasticism as against Suárez, Episcopius, Descartes, and Spinoza*, ed. Wim Janse, Brill Series in Church History 42 (Leiden: Brill, 2010). More recently, Muller has challenged this reading arguing that the Reformed Orthodox were more "eclectic" in their sources, and in some instances arguing for an "intellectualist" reading tied more closely to Thomas Aquinas. See: Muller, *Divine Will and Human Choice*, 317–22. Regarding this specific issue, it will be argued that while Rutherford is not an extreme "voluntarist," he is nevertheless well within the "voluntarist" tradition. Though his position is self-reflectively following in the footsteps of Bradwardine, there are marked similarities to that of John Duns Scotus and even some specific references. See for example Rutherford, *Disputatio Scholastica*, 325.

114 "At dicunt adversarii peccatum opponi Dei naturae." Rutherford, *Disputatio Scholastica*, 313.

115 The works engaged by Rutherford are: Conradus Vorstius, *Amica duplicatio ad Johannis Piscatoris, theologi herbonensis, apologeticam responsionem & notas eiusdem amicae collationi oppositas* (Gouda: Andream Burier, 1617); John Cameron, *Praelectionum, in selectiora quaedam N. Test. loca, Salmurij habitarum* (Saumur: Girardum & Dan Lerpinerium, 1628).

116 See: Andreas Mühling, "Arminius und die Herborner Theologen: Am Beispiel von Johannes Piscator," in *Arminius, Arminianism, and Europe*, ed. Th. Marius van Leeuwen, Keith D. Stanglin, and Marijke Tolsma, Brill's Series in Church History 39 (Leiden: Brill, 2009), 115–34.

by God's will and power, in that he is able to save or damn whosoever he pleases.[117] Vorstius held that such an arbitrary understanding of eternal destinies made God's dominion that of a tyrant.[118] Thus he argued that God's dominion was not so much a matter of the will, but rather a matter of God's nature aligning with specific acts of beneficence towards creatures. Vorstius argued that God could not create a creature with the specific intention of that creature's destruction, for such would go against God's nature of beneficence.[119] The moral status of such an act is established pre-volitionally, according to God's nature.[120]

Rutherford offered a fascinating critique to Vorstius's position. "God is able," he wrote, "to exercise absolute dominion in many possible worlds, in many Angels, which according to his own dominion he is able to create or not to create, and nevertheless God conveys no beneficence to many possible worlds."[121] Rather than seeing God's dominion established by a communication of good to creatures as per Vorstius, Rutherford argued that God's dominion is established by his freedom to communicate or not to communicate actual being to potential being. His argument emphasized the contingency of the actual world and the unrealized potential of non-existent worlds. The actual world is not necessary but could have been otherwise, thus God could have communicated the goodness of reality to many possible worlds but has not.[122] For Rutherford, this was enough to prove that God's nature does

---

117 The relevant section comes from Vorstius, *Amica duplicatio,* 334–86.

118 "Jus Dei & dominium niti aliquo beneficio quod in creaturas ipse contulit, aut aliquo maleficio creatura & eatenus tantum Deum misereri quorum vult, & quos vult, indurare, aliqui fore tyrannicum." Rutherford, *Disputatio Scholastica,* 313; Vorstius, *Amica duplicatio,* 343.

119 "Male negat Vorstius Deum exercere posse aut exercere Dominium suum, nisi in ea in quae beneficium contulit, ac proinde (inquit) non potest Deus pro suo dominio homines ad interitum creare, aut antequam creentur, destinare." Rutherford, *Disputatio Scholastica,* 313; Vorstius, *Amica duplicatio,* 340–1.

120 Arminius held a similar position, that God was necessarily bound by his nature to communicate goodness to his creatures. See Arminius, "Opera Theologica." *Disputationes Privata XXIV, ix,* 365. See also Muller's comments in: Muller, *God, Creation, and Providence in the Thought of Jacob Arminius,* 230–2.

121 "Nam Deus Absolutum dominium potest exercere in plures mundos possibiles, in plures Angelos, quos pro suo dominio potest creare vel non creare, & tamen nullum beneficium Deus contulit in plures mundos possibiles." Rutherford, *Disputatio Scholastica,* 313.

122 Caution should be applied to interpreting the term "possible worlds." Recent scholarship in Reformed Orthodoxy has seen the roots of modern possible world semantics in Scotus's so-called theory of "synchronic contingency." The same scholars have argued that modern possible worlds semantics are a useful tool in analyzing the modal logic inherent in certain strands of medieval scholasticism and modern Reformed scholasticism. See for example: Vos et al, *John Duns Scotus: Contingency and Freedom,* 30–2; van Asselt, Bac, and te Velde, *Reformed Thought on Freedom: The Concept of Free Choice in Early Modern Reformed Theology,* 42; and Bac, *Perfect Will Theology,* 409–17. Muller has argued that such application of modern possible worlds semantics is useful, nevertheless important differences between modern possible world semantics and the medieval

not necessitate a communication of goodness to creatures. God is free to do so, therefore his dominion is established upon the free exercise of choice, rather than as a necessary consequence of an antecedent condition.[123]

Rutherford engaged a more radical position in the Jesuit Gabriel Vasquez (1549/51–1604), who argued that the moral status of an act was established independent and antecedent to any act of God's will or intellectual judgement.[124] The foundation of Vasquez's argument was based upon Thomas's intellectualist approach to the moral law, though Vasquez went beyond Thomas in significant ways. Thomas grounded his understanding of the natural law in the teleological principle that all beings have within themselves inclinations that direct and oblige them towards their proper end.[125] Whereas Thomas held that rational creatures ultimately participate in the divine reason, thus tightly linking the natural law to the divine mind, Vasquez argued that the natural law preceded any judgement not only of the divine will, but also of the divine reason. Thus, the natural law had its own *per se* rule, apart from any divine act.[126] "Our immorality is inconsistent with natural reason by its own rule," wrote Vasquez. The moral status of such acts as hatred of God (*odium dei*) and lying are established by natural reason and not from the will of God. If such were not the case, argued Vasquez, such acts could be good if they were not forbidden by God from eternity. Since such acts are self-evidently immoral, the idea that they could be good based upon the will of God is an absurd proposition.[127]

---

and early modern use of possible worlds exist. The critical difference is that the medieval and early modern use is not merely a matter of semantics, but "the issue being broached ontologically by these understandings is the resident possibility or potency in *this actual world* for things to have been, or indeed, to be otherwise." See: Muller, *Divine Will and Human Choice*, 50.

123 Rutherford uses possible worlds not merely to demonstrate how the actual world could have been other than what it is, but he often uses the contingency of the actual world to reveal truths about God's nature, will, and power. In this regard, Muller may be overlooking the ontological importance of some of the arguments the authors of *Reformed Thought on Freedom*.

124 See discussion in Jill Kraye, "Introduction," in *Moral Philosophy on the Threshold of Modernity*, ed. Jill Kraye and Risto Saarinen, New Synthese Historical Library 57 (Dordrect: Springer, 2005), 41–2; Terence Irwin, *The Development of Ethics: A Historical and Critical Study*, Vol 2, *From Suárez to Rousseau* (Oxford: Oxford University Press, 2007), 2:13–16; and Benjamin Hill and Henrik Lagerlund, *The Philosophy of Francisco Suárez* (Oxford: Oxford University Press, 2012), 188–90.

125 D. E. Luscombe, "Natural morality and natural law," in *The Cambridge History of Later Medieval Philosophy*, eds. Norman Kretzmann, Anthony Kenny, and Jan Pinborg (Cambridge: Cambridge University Press, 1992), 709–13.

126 Hill and Lagerlund, *The Philosophy of Francisco Suárez*, 188–9.

127 "Nostra malitia moralis est disconvenientia a natura rationali, tanquam a regula sua, sicut calor aquae ab aqua. Ergo ex se, & non ex voluntate Dei, odium Dei & perjurium sunt disconvenientia naturae rationali, alioqui etiam sequeretur odium Dei & perjurium potuisse esse bona, si Deus nempe, ab aeterno ea non vetuisset." Vasquez as quoted in: Rutherford, *Disputatio Scholastica*, 316.

Rutherford's response conceded certain elements to Vasquez. Hatred of God, antecedent to the divine will or judgment of the intellect is always immoral. However, hatred of God is not a general concept but must be instantiated in a specific act of being.[128] Rutherford illustrated this point in two steps. The first is to argue the privative nature of sin. "Sin is surely ἀνομία, and is taken privatively."[129] To modern eyes this first step may seem inconsequential, but it was a vital move in Rutherford's overall argument. Keeping broadly within the catholic tradition, he refused to define sin positively. It is neither an essential power of the soul nor is it being with its own power to act.[130] Sin is not defined by what it is, but rather by what it is not. Sin is a failure of the acts and inclinations of the soul to render obedience to God. Just as before, obedience is not a general concept, but rather one instantiated in specific acts.[131]

Rutherford held that certain acts, antecedent to the divine decree, were morally indifferent. These he determined to be simple acts.[132] An example of a simple act would be eating. Eating in and of itself is neither good nor bad and thus not capable of establishing obedience to or hatred of God. However, once divine legislation is added to the act, it becomes a complex act. At this point the act gains moral worth.[133] Once the positive law regarding eating from the Tree of Knowledge is imposed, then the simple act of eating becomes a complex act with moral worth. The point at stake is aptly illustrated from Rutherford's *The Covenant of Life Opened*:

> The Question is, whether (laying aside respect of Gods unchangeablenesse and truth) there be such a connexion internall, between eating and dying, or between eating forbidden of God, and punishment, as God cannot be equally and essentially just, nor can he be God, except he punish forbiden eating.[134]

---

128 "Non sequitur, quia odium Dei est in se, & sine omni actu divinae voluntatis malum, quod certe ego verum esse concedo. Ergo actus entitativus in illo odio Dei est in se malus: quia certe est indifferens in se, licet ut vestitus detestatione Dei sit in se malus." Rutherford, *Disputatio Scholastica*, 316.

129 "Peccatum certe ἀνομία est, & privative, aliquid tollit." Rutherford, *Disputatio Scholastica*, 312.

130 "Non autem tollit essentiales potentias animae, nec actus entitativos potentiarum." Rutherford, *Disputatio Scholastica*, 312.

131 "Sed peccatum privative tollit rectitudinem illam obedientialem inclinationibus animae & actibus inesse debitam." Rutherford, *Disputatio Scholastica*, 312.

132 "Nam nullum actus humanus simplex est essentialiter bonus vel malus; sed ex se indifferens." Rutherford, *Disputatio Scholastica*, 323.

133 "Quia antecedenter ad Dei decretum & mandatum omnes actus physici sunt inidfferentes. Vana ergo est ante Dei decretum & mandatum illa distinctio, qua quidam actus dicuntur boni, quidam mali, quidam adiaphori: quia omnes sunt adiaphori ante decretum." Rutherford, *Disputatio Scholastica*, 323.

134 Rutherford, *The Covenant of Life Opened*, 33.

Rutherford argued the answer was no. There is no essential connection between God's justice, his punishment, and the moral status of eating from the forbidden Tree of Knowledge. In the same passage he notes that "the Lord would have been no lesse essentially just, had he commanded *Adam* to eat of the Tree of Knowledge."[135] The same argument is replicated in the *Disputatio*.[136] The point is, the moral status of eating from the tree is an arbitrary matter, established freely by the forbidding will of God. Therefore, it is a matter of God's choice rather than a matter of God's nature. "It must follow," he argued, "that God hates not all sin, by necessity of nature; And that he hates such eating only conditionally, if he forbid it, be he from his meer free will did forbid it."[137]

Thus, while conceding ground to Vasquez that hatred of God is always immoral, how hatred of God is expressed in specific acts is dependent upon God's will rather than upon natural reason. The point is further underscored by the famous example of God's command to Abraham to kill his only son. Such a command is opposed to natural reason as well as the revealed will of God in the decalogue. Nevertheless, in this instance obedience and love to God require that Abraham must act against his own natural reason and submit to God's command in the moment. Hence, the limits of natural reason are exposed. Natural reason fails to apprehend the immorality of eating from the tree but is dependent upon the revealed will of God. At the same time, natural reason can cut against the grain of obedience to God, as evident in the disturbing example of Abraham and Isaac. Natural reason, contra Vasquez, is not a *regula regulans* but rather a *regula regulata*, a rule that is ruled by the divine will and legislation.[138]

---

135 Rutherford, 33.

136 The argument from the *Disputatio* appears to be based upon a reading of Proverbs 3.14, that links the tree spoken of in Proverbs to the Tree of Life in Genesis 2. Rutherford argued that eating from the Tree of Knowledge was forbidden in Genesis 2.9 and Genesis 2.17. However, he also argues that David encouraged his son Solomon to feast on this same tree in the Book of Proverbs. He argues that if God could forbid something in Genesis and command it in Proverbs, then there could be nothing in the act itself contrary to God's nature. Rutherford's argument stems from the fact that the expression עֵץ הַחַיִּים (Tree of Life) is found only in Genesis 2.9, 2.17 and in the Book of Proverbs, where wisdom is metaphorically depicted as a "tree of life." For the linguistic similarities between the two texts see Ralph Marcus, "The Tree of Life in Proverbs," *Journal of Biblical Literature* 62, no. 2 (1943): 117–20. For Rutherford's argument relying upon the positive command to eat from the metaphorical Tree of Knowledge in Proverbs see: Rutherford, *Disputatio Scholastica*, 313.

137 Rutherford, *The Covenant of Life Opened*, 33.

138 "Dicunt alii *disconvenientiam malitia, non saltem omnem, esse contrariam naturae rationali,* tanquam sua regulae regulanti & primae & adequatae; nam ratio non est actuum nostrorum regula regulans & adequata, sed est regula regulata a Dei libera voluntate; imo naturae rationali *Abrahami* disconveniens & contraria erat mactatio filii *Isaaci,* jure tamen Deus *Abrahamum* filium suum mactare jussit, & ea mactatio contraria naturae rationali *Abrahami,* hoc ipso bona & honesta fuit, quod Deus eam imperaverit, & rursus mala quod eam etiam idem Deus prohibuerit. Quod argu-

Rutherford's final engagement with what could be broadly categorized as an intellectualist approach to the problem of the divine will and the natural law is the Scottish Reformed theologian John Cameron (1579–1625).[139] As Burton has noted, Rutherford's engagement with Cameron derives from the latter's remarks on Matt. 16:20 found in his *Praelectiones*.[140] In the passage, Jesus commands his disciples "to tell no one that he was the Christ." This seems to conflict with the mandate to preach the Gospel. Cameron's solution to this apparent contradiction is to seek for a way to distinguish between commands that are good in and of themselves, which must be obeyed irrespective of the divine command and those merely indifferent.[141] In this case, the prohibition to preach the Gospel is not good in and of itself, but only by virtue of the divine command. Unlike the prohibition to preach the Gospel, there are some moral goods that have a certain concord or resonance with the divine essence, the chief among those being the divine image. The image of God is essentially good, holy, just and loved by God necessarily and thus pre-volitionally. God was under no obligation to create a being made in his own image, however, having done so, he does necessarily love that creature because it bears his own image.[142]

---

mento est actum mactandi filium non ex convenientia, aut disconvenientia cum natura rationali *Abrahami*, sed ex libera Dei voluntate eum jubente aut vetante esse bonum vel malum moraliter, & idem dicendum de actu entitativo in odio Dei & perjurio, quos actus manens in linea pure physica potest Deus vel imperare vel vetare, quia nullus actus est essentialiter malus: haec esset enim gravis, in Deum omnis entitatis positivae Authoorem, injuria." Rutherford, *Disputatio Scholastica*, 316.

139 There are several older studies of Cameron. For a serviceable overview of his life, training, and ministry see Maury, "John Cameron: A Scottish Protestant Theologian in France (1579–1625)." Also: John Macleod, *Scottish Theology in Relation to Church History Since the Reformation*, 3rd ed. (Edinburgh: Banner of Truth Trust, 1974), 60–3. Cameron was treated as part of the "Calvin vs. the Calvinists" thesis. See: Brian G. Armstrong, *Calvinism and the Amyraut Heresy; Protestant Scholasticism and Humanism in Seventeenth-century France* (Madison: University of Wisconsin Press, 1969). T.F. Torrance has interpreted Cameron in light of this thesis, classifying him as part of the "Older Scottish Tradition," which Torrance read as more aligned with the Biblical humanism of Calvin. See Torrance, *Scottish Theology*, 64–66. More recently, Muller has argued for a much closer alignment of Cameron with Reformed Orthodoxy as well as Reformed Scholasticism. See: Richard Muller, "Divine Covenants, Absolute and Conditional: John Cameron and the Early Orthodox Development of Reformed Covenant Theology," *Mid-America Journal of Theology*, no. 17 (2006): 11–56.

140 Burton, "Samuel Rutherford's *Euthyphro Dilemma*," 124–5. The relevant section from the Cameron's *Praelectiones* can be found in: Cameron, *Praelectionum*, 139–153.

141 "Rerum enim quae praecipiuntur vel prohibentur alia sunt *in se bona, vel male*, alia vero sunt ἀδιάφορα." Cameron, *Praelectionum, in selectiora quaedam N. Test. loca, Salmurij habitarum*, 140. See: Burton's comments in: Burton, "Samuel Rutherford's *Euthyphro Dilemma*," 124–6.

142 "Illa sunt in se bonae in quibus refulget imago Dei qua iustus, bonus & sanctus est, ad quam imaginem in Christo recreati sumus, & quae (teste Apostolo Coloss. 3.10) consistit in iustitia, pietate & sanctitate." John Cameron, *Praelectionum, in selectiora quaedam N. Test. loca, Salmurij*

Things which are good in and of themselves are those which most closely relate to the divine image. Those things which are bad in and of themselves are those which are opposed to the divine image.[143] Cameron drew attention to the first table of the Law as especially exhibiting the image of God. Those commands in the second table also exhibit the image of God, though some more so than others. For example, murder is considered a more severe offense against the image of God than adultery. Proximity to the image of God appears to be the key to understanding the moral heft of the command.[144] In contrast to these commands, which Cameron argues that God is obligated to by necessity, other commands are contingent upon the divine will and thus adiaphora. The command in question from Matt. 16:20 forbidding the disciples from telling others he is the Christ is adiaphora, contingent upon the command of Christ to a specific people at a specific time but does not obligate all people at all times like the prohibition of murder.[145]

Rutherford responded to Cameron with a scriptural example that exposed problems in Cameron's logic. The example is the sacrifice of Isaac. Rutherford argued that if God loves his image antecedent to the divine decree, then he would be incapable of commanding Abraham to sacrifice the same image. The command to destroy the image of God in Isaac would be akin to God commanding someone to hate him, which Rutherford held God cannot do.[146] In light of this scriptural dilemma, another solution must be found.

4.4.2 God's Will as *Prima Regula*

An alternative solution to those provided above is one that places greater stress upon the divine will, a position often described as voluntarist. Our first encounter

---

habitarum (Saumur: Girardum & Dan Lerpinerium, 1628), 140. Rutherford's summary reads as follows: "Deum non velle res quia sunt bonae, & consonantiam habent cum essentiali Dei puritate & justitia, sed res esse bonas & imaginem Dei referre, quando ita Deus ex libero suo beneplacito decreverit." Rutherford, *Disputatio Scholastica*, 318.

143 "Res in se malae sunt quae pugnant cum illa Dei imagine." Cameron, *Praelectionum*, 140.

144 "Mandata primae tabulae seuerius praecipiuntur quam mandata secunde, quia in illis magis refulget imago Dei. Et in secunda Tabula seuerius parricidium quam adulterium prohibetur, quod illud magis quam istud pugner cum imagine Dei. Atque hoc pacto variant Dei de rebus in se bonis vel malis mandata, maiorisque sunt vel minoris authoritatis, prout in se magis vel minus referunt Dei imaginem; vel ab ea magis vel minus abhorrent." Cameron, *Praelectionum*, 141.

145 "At res adiaphoras potest vel precipere, vel non praecipere, vetare vel non vetare, prout ipsi videtur id conducere ad finem sibi propositum." Cameron, *Praelectionum*, 141.

146 "Ergo ex *Cameronis* sententia tam repugnaret Deum jubere ut *Abrahamus* mactet filium quam ut ipse Deus sese odio haberet, & illud mandatum, Abrahame, immola mihi filium tuum Isaacum erat impium & divinae naturae repugnans, & Dei naturali & immutabili propensioni contrarium." Rutherford, *Disputatio Scholastica*, 319.

with a more voluntarist solution comes through an anonymous *manuscriptor*, an apologist for John Cameron who gave Cameron's thesis a distinctively voluntarist interpretation. The *manuscriptor* argued that God's decree freely established the nature of both *per se* goods as well as those that are *adiaphora*, or morally indifferent. Having freely decreed something to be a *per se* good, the *manuscriptor* argued that this constituted it as essentially good and holy. Consequent to this free act of the divine will, God is necessarily bound to love what he has freely constituted as good. The same logic is applied to *adiaphora*.[147] What is interesting about the *mansucriptor's* position is that he argues that God establishes the essential nature of goods by an act of the will. Thus the *manuscriptor* is able to retain, to some degree, Cameron's *per se* goods but with a noted voluntarist twist. Furthermore, as Burton notes, the *manuscriptor* argued that this voluntarist reading of the argument was Cameron's true intention.[148]

Rutherford took time to demonstrate that the *manuscriptor* had badly misunderstood Cameron.[149] But for the present purposes this is not as important as outlining the *manuscriptor's* own voluntarist approach to the problem. As was demonstrated earlier, the *manuscriptor* argued that the good nature of an act was established by the will of God. This was applied even to the worship of God, which the *manuscriptor* argued was good in and of itself and by virtue of an internal principle, but both the *per se* goods as well as the internal principle were constituted by God. Thus the worship of God is good because God has determined it to be so. However, as Rutherford pointed out, if the essential goods of a being are freely established by the divine decree, then God could just as easily have decreed that the worship of God is immoral, which would contradict his own natural love for himself. Worse, if the decree freely establishes the *per se* goods of a being, then God could have freely decreed that he is not God. *Macte Patrone Cameronis!* was Rutherford's sarcastic reply to the *manuscriptor's* logic.[150]

---

147 "Addit Manuscriptor. Colere Deum in se & in principio interno & forma propria bonum est, quia Deus decrevit ut natura τῷ colere Deum sit in se bona, Idolatria est in se mala, non in extrinseca ratione praecepti, sed in principio ejus interno, A Dei libero decreto est ut natura idolatriae in se mala sit. Ceremonia Mosis sunt adiaphora quia non habent rationem boni aut mali moralis in sua natura ex Dei decreto, sed tantum sunt bonae vel malae extrinsecus ratione praecepti: prima non potest Deus prohibere, secunda non potest imperare puta odium sui, quae sunt tertii generis, potest Deus imperare vel vetare." Rutherford, *Disputatio Scholastica*, 322.

148 Burton, "Samuel Rutherford's *Euthyphro Dilemma*," 126–127.

149 "Nam Camero vult ea que Deum referunt ut ens, esse bona, quia Deus eorum bonitatem decrevit, sed vult ea quae referunt Deum ut est Sanctus & Justus, seu quae referunt Dei imaginem, esse in se & sua natura citra omnem divinae voluntatis actum, bona & Sancta." Rutherford, *Disputatio Scholastica*, 318. See also: Cameron, *Praelectionum*, 140–1.

150 "Respondeo I. Nemo, qui Philosophiam aut Theologiam vel a limine salutarit, diceret Deum colere, esse in sua forma essentiali bonum, quia Deus decrevit ut natura τῷ colere Deum sit in se bona;

Rutherford clearly wished to temper some of the implications of the *manuscriptor's* reasoning, which he did with the assistance of the medieval theologian, Thomas Bradwardine (1300–1349). Bradwardine provided Rutherford with a framework built around three categories of moral determination that enabled him to maintain pride of place to the divine will while tempering more extreme expressions of voluntarism with aspects of God's being that necessarily influenced and restrained the divine will. The first category acknowledged certain necessary determinations in relation to God's being, the second category applied those determinations contingent upon the divine will, and the third and final determination was a complex category he simply termed mixed.[151]

In regards to the first category, Rutherford argued that some things are good according to reason antecedent to the divine decree. Such goods are essentially good such as the eternality of God.[152] Two important points are established here. First, Rutherford denied that God's own *per se* goods are contingent upon the divine will. This was no doubt in response to the *manuscriptor's* logic, which Rutherford believed would lead to the erroneous assertion that God's own *per se* goods were established by the divine will. The second thing was that this category of goods exercises influence upon the divine will. Expressions of God's will *ad extra* are not purely expressions of the divine will, as if the will could be disconnected somehow from God's attributes and essence. Rather, God's will is informed and influenced by necessary aspects of his own being.[153]

Unlike the first category, the second category of moral goods is determined by and dependent upon God's will.[154] This category of goods was covered earlier in the overview of Rutherford's engagement with Vazquez. Nevertheless there are a few more things that may be said. Following the Spanish jurist Fernando Vazquez de Menchaca (1512–1569), Rutherford argued that when God constituted rational

---

quasi vero Deus libere decerneret ut quod est essentialiter bonum sit bonum, nempe, libere decrevit Deus ut Deus sit bonum, homo sit animal rationale, at quod Deus libere decernit esse, potest decernere non esse. Potest ergo Deus decernere ut essentia & essentiatum inter se non cohaerant, ut homo non sit animal, ut Deus non sit bonus, ut sic homo non sit homo, Deus non sit Deus. Macte Patrone Cameronis." Rutherford, *Disputatio Scholastica*, 322.

151 Rutherford drew from Bradwardine's *De causa Dei*, Book 1, Chapter 21. See: Thomas Bradwardine, *De causa Dei, contra pelagium, et de virtute causarum, ad suos Mertonenses* (London: Joannem Billium, 1618), 228–34. For Bradwardine, see Jean-François Genest, *Prédétermination et Liberté créée à Oxford au XIVe Siècle: Buckingham contre Bradwardine*, with an edition of Thomas Buckingham *Determinatio de contingentia futurorum*, Etudes de Philosphie Medievale, 70 (Paris: J. Vrin, 1992).

152 "Et recte manus ille vir Bradwardinus. Quadam (inquit) sunt rationalibilia (& sic moraliter honesta) priora Dei volunte, ut Deum esse Aeternum, &c." Rutherford, *Disputatio Scholastica*, 315.

153 "Et horum ratio bene potest movere Dei voluntatem." Rutherford, *Disputatio Scholastica*, 315.

154 "Alia posteriora & dependentia ab ea causative & nullum horum determinat Dei voluntatem." Rutherford, *Disputatio Scholastica*, 315.

creatures, he also created the common principles of the natural law which are "insculpted" on the human heart.[155] Critically, these common principles regarded as natural law by rational creatures could have been other than what they are.[156] Thus Rutherford argued that God could have established a race of people where cannibalism was permitted or on the other hand he could have established a race of vegetarians. The interest here is not in the peculiar nature of these observations, but rather in Rutherford's recourse to alternative possible worlds. Just as in the earlier discussion regarding Vorstius, the contingency of the present founded on God's free decision is an assumed fact upon which Rutherford's theological and ethical positions are built.[157]

Rutherford's colorful remarks in regards to a race of cannibals offer a clear indication as to his position on the vexed theological question of whether God could dispense with elements of the decalogue. The answer is clearly yes. However, there are important constraints placed upon this affirmation.[158] Whereas Vazquez de

---

155 Rutherford is drawing from: Fernando Vasquez de Menchaca, *Illustrium controversiarum* (Frankfurt: Joannis Baptistae Schonwetteri, 1668), Book I, Chapter 29, 123–128. The citation is found in: Rutherford, *Disputatio Scholastica*, 327. For more on Menchacha, see: Annabel S. Brett, *Liberty, Right, and Nature: Individual Rights in Later Scholastic Thought*, Ideas in Context 44 (Cambridge: Cambridge University Press, 1997), 165–205. See also Burton's discussion in: Burton, "Samuel Rutherford's *Euthyphro Dilemma*," 131–2.

156 "Et potuit Deus aliud animal rationale natura, specie que & essentiae perfectione distinctum ab homine creare, & creasse cordi ipsius jus naturale insculptum diversum, (ut non dicam contrarium) & longe aliud quam illud quod concreatum est cum homine qui nunc creatut animal rationale, & dedisse poterat alia & diversa decalogi mandata aeque bona & justa, atqui sunt illa decalogi mandata quae nunc tradita sunt homini." Rutherford, *Disputatio Scholastica*, 328.

157 "Ita potuit Deus homines alios vel alia animalia rationalia essentia & natura hoc homine perfectiora quae etiam se invicem devorare poterant, absque omni in legem Dei, quae nunc est, reatu aut transgressionis nota, & potuit Deus hominibus in prima Creatione legem indidisse qua interdicerentur occisione brutorum animantium, ita ut brutis non magis qum hominibus absque horrendo, in legem natura peccato vitam adimere licitum foret, uti jam credunt Pythagorici Philosphi non esse licitum bestias occidere, aut occisi vesci magis quam hommicidium committere possumus." Rutherford, *Disputatio Scholastica*, 328.

158 Whether God could dispense with some or all of the Ten Commandments is a question answered on a spectrum that mirrors that of the intellectualist and voluntarist positions. Some of the theologians on this spectrum have been outlined by Beck, *Gisbertus Voetius*, 371–2. These are listed below. Existing on the extreme edges of the voluntarist tradition is William of Ockham, Jean Gerson (1363–1429), Piere d'Ailly (1351–1420) and Jacques Almain (d. 1515). These held that God could dispense with all the commandments in the Decalogue. Rutherford cites both Ockham and Gerson positively, however on this point he distances himself from this extreme position in regards to the moral law. See Rutherford, *Disputatio Scholastica*, 324; 327. Some theologians, such as John Duns Scotus, Durandus de Sancto Porciano (1275–1334) and John Major (1467/9–1550) held that God could dispense with some elements of the decalogue, specifically the commandments of the second table. From within the intellectualist tradition, theologians such as Thomas Aquinas (1225–1274),

Menchaca, taking a more Ockhamist line, argued that God could have constituted a race of rational creatures where hatred of God was morally good, Rutherford argued against Menchaca that there is no possible world where hatred of God would be reasonable and morally upright.[159] As Burton notes, there are necessary obligations that limit and constrain God's freedom in regards to matters of the moral law that are contingent upon the divine will. The joining of necessary obligations and contingently willed laws brings us to a third and final category of moral obligations that Rutherford, following Bradwardine, termed mixed.[160]

The category described as mixed is composed of some pre-volitional obligations, as well as some post-volitional obligations. For example, Rutherford took it for granted that the subjection of the creature to the Creator, and the Lordship of God over all created things is a pre-volitional necessary truth. However, at the same time, it is not necessary that God create. Therefore, there are post-volitional, contingent elements to the subjection of the creature to the Creator. This means there are both pre-volitional and post-volitional considerations, making the reasons for the moral obligation mixed.[161]

This third and final category leads Rutherford, who in this instance follows the Dutch Reformed Scholastic Gisbertus Voetius, to make an interesting observation in regards to the divine will and the moral law. The divine will cannot be the first rule of moral uprightness in creatures, because all rational creatures are bound to obey right reason, and right reason dictates that all creatures are necessarily subject to their Creator and thus obligated to obedience.[162] First and foremost this

---

William of Auxerre (d. 1213), Richard Middleton (1249–1308) and Pedro de la Palu (d. 1342) held that all the commandments in the decalogue were indispensable.

159 "In hoc vero mihi cum Vasquio non convenit quod putet cum Occamo potuisse Deum sui odium complexe & formaliter imperare, suique amorem verare. At vero quoniam odium Dei sic sumptum peccatum est: repugnant santissimae Dei naturae mandare peccatum, imo repugnat Deum imperare posse esum arboris vetitae, si semel vetita sit arbor. Sic si semel hic actus sit odium Dei, est jam essentialiter peccatum. Si ergo Deus imperaret odium sui, simul vellet & approbaret odium sui, quia ex te, imperat & simul non vellet, non approbaret, quoniam ex rei veritate odium Dei est peccatum, Sic hoc sit adulterium, si homicidium, non potest Deus id mandare." Rutherford, *Disputatio Scholastica*, 328.

160 Burton notes that Rutherford's critique of Menchaca places him "well short" of Menchaca's "extreme moral voluntarism." See: Burton, "Samuel Rutherford's *Euthyphro Dilemma*," 132.

161 "Alia denique sunt rationabilia mixta ex utrisque, ut creaturam subjici Creatoris, Deum esse Dominium hujus rei. Haec sunt rationabilia conditionaliter, ut si creatura existat, necesse est subjiciantur Creatori." Rutherford, *Disputatio Scholastica*, 315.

162 "At dices Dei beneplacitum ergo non erit prima regula omnis rectitudinis moralis in creaturis, quoniam ut recte dicit claris, & doctiss. Vir Gisber. Voetius. Dependentia creaturae rationalis, qua scil. rationalis est, & in genere moris ac in ordine ad rectam rationem tam necessaria est, ut oppositum ejus repugnantiam dicat in terminis ac contradictionem implicet: — sic omnis creatura rationalis DEO subjici debet rationabiliter, & obligatur ipsi ad obedientiam." Rutherford, *Disputatio*

is an argument from God's ontological priority. Beyond this however, there are other aspects of God's nature such as his perfection, supreme power, and essential worthiness, that also oblige rational creatures to obedience.[163] Thus Rutherford argued "we do not teach that the free will of God is the rule of all moral rectitude in creatures without any restriction." The divine nature places some restrictions upon the divine will in regards to the moral law.[164]

With these observations, Rutherford was able to maintain a significant role for natural reason in regards to the moral law, avoiding the extreme position of some voluntarists.[165] Rutherford has a vested interest in not only distancing himself from this extreme position, but also distancing others such as Twisse, Ockham and Bradwardine from this extreme position.[166] At the same time that he moved farther from the extreme edges of voluntarism, his high view of the central role of the divine will prevented him from falling into certain difficulties outlined above within the intellectualist tradition, such as God being subjected to the fatal necessity of an independent natural law. Here again Rutherford is shown safeguarding God's independence while once again underscoring the absolute dependence of all else, including the natural law, upon God's being and will.

4.5   Summary

Rutherford's familiar use of traditional distinctions concerning God's will hardly makes his contribution unique. Nevertheless, there is an emphasis placed within the exegesis of these catholic distinctions that lend a particular flavor to Rutherford's treatment of the doctrine as well as further outline the contour of his doctrine of divine providence. This emphasis is upon the divine freedom and independence.

Scholastica, 329. Rutherford cites Voetius, *Selectarum Disputationum Theologicarum, prima pars,* 364–65.

163 "I. Quia Dei primitas, independentia, perfectio, suprema potestas, & similia divina attributa hoc requirunt, & tale jus fundant. 2. Quia necessario & immutabiliter in Deo est adorabilitas, quippe reciprocum Dei attributum, nec data quocunque creatura rationali per liberum Dei decretum, oppositum decerni potest, sine implicatione contradictionis." Rutherford quoting Voetius in: Rutherford, *Disputatio Scholastica*, 329. Voetius, *Selectarum disputationum*, 364–65.

164 "Nos discimus liberum Dei voluntatem esse regulam omnis rectitudinis moralis circa omnem restrictionem." Rutherford, *Disputatio Scholastica*, 329.

165 Burton, "Samuel Rutherford's *Euthyphro Dilemma*," 134.

166 "Sed a nemine dictum putem, nec a me, nec a Clairs. Domino *Twisso*, nec ab *Occamo*, nec a *Bradwardino* tam laxe a citra omnem distinctionem, Dei beneplacitum & liberum decretum esse primam regulam omnis rectitudinis moralis sine exceptione, sive ea sit creata & in simplice actu creaturae, sive increata & in Deo, imo ego contrarium docui." Rutherford, *Disputatio Scholastica*, 329.

This is not merely a nod to the divine sovereignty, but as will be shown in upcoming chapters, is used as a critical piece in Rutherford's accounting of human liberty.

Rutherford's treatment of the divine will began with the insistence that, while distinctions may be drawn between the divine will and the divine being, the regulative nature of the divine simplicity means such distinctions do not imply complexity. This was important to emphasize due to the challenges posed by Remonstrant theologians such as Conrad Vorstius, who argued that the divine will, expressed through the divine decrees, was an accidental property of the divine being. Against this, Rutherford argued that God's will is an intrinsic, essential property of God's own self. When God wills, he wills in and through himself. His will is not "conditioned by a distinct act" of another willing agent. Thus God's will is not subject to events and actions outside of himself, rather such things are subject to God. This not only serves to underscore the divine sovereignty, but also the divine freedom from necessity and in particular the necessity of fate and fortune.

God's freedom from necessity is further consolidated in the distinctions of the *voluntas beneplaciti et signi* as well as the *voluntas antecedens et consequens*. Everything that is and will be is the object of God's *voluntas beneplaciti*, or his will of good pleasure. All that is good, worthy, upright, and genuinely loved by God is the object of the *voluntas signi*, or the will of the sign. Not everything that God loves and approves of via the *voluntas signi* will be actualized via the *voluntas beneplaciti*. God is not subject even to the necessity to actualize every good. The same emphasis is seen in Rutherford's treatment of the *voluntas antecedens et consequens*. The Arminians posited a moral interpretation of this distinction, arguing that God antecedently wills a moral law and consequently rewards or punishes based upon the keeping of this law. The Laudian theologian Thomas Jackson employed the language of strong and weak fates to illustrate how this will is accomplished. God antecedently wills to reward the just and punish the unjust. Following a sinful act, God consequently wills to punish the unjust. But Jackson said this punishment was a weak fate, which narrowed the probability of heavenly reward. A lifetime of sin turns the weak fate into a strong fate, which became "truly fatal and altogether unavoidable." Rutherford's treatment of the *antecedens et consequens* distinction made the *voluntas antecedens* functionally equivalent to the *voluntas signi*, and the *voluntas consequens* functionally equivalent to the *voluntas beneplaciti*. Such an interpretation frees God from the necessity of Jackson's strong and weak fates.

Rutherford's emphasis upon the divine will clearly places him within that theological tradition broadly termed voluntarist. This holds true not only in his understanding of the aforementioned distinctions, but also in matters more closely related to divine providence, such as the expression of punitive justice towards sinners. Rutherford argued for a free expression of sin punishing justice towards sinners. The contingency of the present world again serves as a useful device for establishing the decisive role of God's will in establishing the actual world, as well as a useful device for maintaining God's freedom from fatalism.

Though Rutherford falls within the voluntarist tradition, extreme care must be taken in understanding how this label applies to him. The final section demonstrated that there are elements within the intellectualist approach to certain theological problems, such as the relationship between God's will and morality, that Rutherford appreciated and incorporated into his own system. The incorporation of such elements helped temper his own voluntarism, which he studiously attempted to distinguish from more extreme versions in his own day. In doing so, he follows the lead of the medieval scholastics, particularly that of Thomas Bradwardine, who provided him with a means by which he could maintain the primacy of the divine will and thus the divine freedom, while safeguarding against the specter of a purely arbitrary God.

5. God's Power

> Every creature is under the awe of Omnipotence, and dare not without (as it were) a written and signed Ordinance and Statute of the Almighty, exercise their naturall operations: As the Lord sendeth an awful mandate to the Sea, and *God* saith, Do not ebbe and flow; and the sea is dried up at his rebuke.[1]

God's providence is an external act connoting immanent acts of intellect and will. In addition to being an immanent act of these vital faculties, Rutherford also noted that providence is an act of God's power.[2] If God's knowledge pertains to what God can and post-volitionally will effect through his providential care and God's will determines those acts of being to be brought about by God's providence, then it is God's power that brings such acts into existence that were known and willed by God.

Unlike aspects of God's being and life addressed in previous chapters, there is no dedicated treatment of God's power in any of Rutherford's written works. Nevertheless, there is opportunity to explore Rutherford's doctrine of God's power as he addresses certain metaphysical questions in his *Disquisitiones Metaphysicae,* as well as questions concerning God's will in his *Exercitationes Apologeticae pro Divina Gratia.*[3] In addition to these, there is a full sermon dedicated to God's omnipotence in Rutherford's *The Tryal and Triumph of Faith*, a collection of sermons published in 1649.[4]

The following explores features of God's power pertinent to the overall purpose of examining Rutherford's doctrine of divine providence. This chapter begins with a definition of God's power as well as distinctions within derived from various writings of Rutherford. This will be followed by Rutherford's metaphysical explorations into the origin of created being as well as the grounds for modal properties such as possible and impossible as they relate to God's power. This chapter concludes

---

1 Rutherford, *The Tryal and Triumph of Faith: Or an Exposition of the History of Christs Dispossessing of the Daughter of the Woman of Canaan* (London: John Field, 1645), 307.

2 "Quia providentia formaliter non est consilium, sed quaedam continuata rerum Creatio & externa Administratio connotans actus immanentes scientiae & consilii: non est autem actus solius intellectus, sed & voluntatis & potentiae, & prout restringitur ad sanctos Dei Filios complectitur singularem Dei, erga suos favorem." Rutherford, *Disputatio Scholastica*, 2.

3 Of particular interest to this chapter are Q.2 – Q.4. in the *Disquisitiones Metaphysicae*. See Rutherford, *Disputatio Scholastica*, 532–45; also Ex. 1. Chapter 4 and Ex. 2. Chapter 3 in Rutherford, *Exercitationes Apologeticae*, 87–157, 332–61.

4 Rutherford, *The Tryal and Triumph of Faith*, 306–20.

with a discussion on dominion—a concept closely related to God's power in the scholastic literature of the sixteenth and seventeenth centuries. This section will also introduce certain problems that Rutherford believed were introduced into God's dominion by the *scientia media*.

5.1   Definition and Distinctions

As with earlier examinations of God's being, knowledge, and will, Rutherford's discussions concerning God's power rely upon careful terms and distinctions. These distinctions pertaining to God's power match neatly with distinctions encountered in previous chapters that draw sharp lines between necessity and contingency. As will be seen, when applied to God's power, these lines are drawn between all the possibilities that are naturally open to God by virtue of his power, and those actualized possibilities that follow the determinations of the will.

5.1.1 Omnipotency

Rutherford's preferred English term for God's power is omnipotency. The word is derived from the Latin compound *omnipotens,* which is constructed by combining *omnis* and *potens*. When used as an adjective, *omnis* may be translated as "all." When used as a noun, the same may be translated as "everything" or in some instances "every person." *Potens* is the present active participle of *possum*, which can be translated as "able to." When *possum* is rendered as *potens*, it can mean simply "powerful," but can also be translated as "capable." In the form of the noun *potentia,* it can mean "power," "capacity," or "possibility."[5] These two words have different emphases in the scholastic literature. Power implies efficiency to bring about an effect. Capability implies that the agent is able to bring about the effect. The capability implied by omnipotency is natural to God, which means it belongs to God whether he chooses to exercise it or not.[6]

As omnipotency is an attribute of God, one might conclude from the above that omnipotency simply means that God is able to or has power to do anything and everything. But the matter is not so simple. When pushed to the extreme, the notion that God is able to do anything and everything could imply that God is able to create a world where there is no God, or where the creature is not dependent upon God

---

5 Beck, *Gisbertus Voetius*, 381.

6 There is a further distinction to be made between active potency (*potentia operativa*) and passive potency (*potentia passiva*). The former is power to act upon or effect something, the latter is power to be acted upon. When speaking of God's power, his omnipotency is an active potency. See "Potentia" in: Muller, *Dictionary of Latin and Greek Theological Terms*, 270.

for its being.[7] Rutherford believed that such things were simply impossible. Here, possibility is taken to be the non-repugnance of terms. Because God is eternally existent, a world where there is no God is a contradiction and, thus, impossible. Such a world is not able to be made.[8]

Rutherford, explicitly following medieval scholastics, such as Henry of Ghent, Scotus, and Bradwardine, was careful in how he discussed impossible things in their relation to God's power and ability. Rather than saying that something is impossible and therefore God is not able to do it, Rutherford and his scholastic predecessors sought to emphasize the sovereignty and independence of God by saying that God is not able to do something, therefore it is impossible. This subtle difference prevented an impossibility from imposing itself upon God or restricting his power.[9]

Omnipotency therefore concerns those things that God is able to do. God can do anything that can be done. There are two separate, yet related emphases concerning those things that God is able to do. One emphasis is placed upon God's ability to actualize every possibility. The other emphasis is placed upon God's power to produce any effect. The former tends to be more philosophical and is dealt with as a metaphysical investigation by Rutherford. The latter is more theological and closely associated with the nominalist school of theology and its famous *potentia absoluta et ordinata* distinction.[10]

---

7 Rutherford deals with each of these in Questio IIII and V of his *Disquisitiones Metaphysicae*. See: Rutherford, *Disputatio Scholastica*, 544–57. For an overview of similar thorny philosophical considerations, see Anthony Kenny, *The God of the Philosophers* (Oxford: Oxford University Press, 1986), Part 3, 89–117.

8 Rutherford, *The Tryal and Triumph of* Faith, 307. Rutherford is in line with other Reformed scholastics of his era in founding possibility on the non-repugnance of terms. See Beck's comments on Voetius in Beck, *Gisbertus Voetius*, 382–3. For more on the concept of logical possibility, see: Steven P. Marrone, "Duns Scotus on Metaphysical Potency and Possibility," *Franciscan Studies* 56 (1998): 265–89; Antoine Vos, "Ab uno disce omnes," *Bijdragen* 60, (1999): 173–204.

9 "Henricus a Gandavo, Scotus, Bradwardina recte putant dicendum, quod non est verum dicere & aliquo impossibilis simpliciter, quod Deus non potest haec facere, quia illud non potest fieri: sed potius hoc non potest fieri, quia Deus non potest facere, licet contrarium tueantur Jesuitae, praesertim Fonseca. At vero impossibile ideo est impossibile, quia est non ens contradictionem involvens, & repugnans enti, & imprimis primo enti cui repugnat, nam si ideo est impossibile, quia est incompossibile cuna ente creato, multo magis quia repugnat enti primo, & ideae practicae in intellectu divino, juxta quod formatur eus cui contradicit." Rutherford, *Disputatio Scholastica*, 543. For references, see Henry of Ghent, *Quodlibeta tomus primus* (Venice: Jacobum de Franciscis, 1613), 8. Q. 3.; John Duns Scotus, *Quaestiones in lib i. sententiarum* (Lyon: Lavrentii Durand, 1639). Dist. 43; Bradwardine, *De causa Dei, contra pelagium, et de virtute causarum, ad suos Mertonenses*, Lib.I. Q. 13. For some helpful analytical comments regarding these issues, see: Vos, "Ab uno disce omnes," 195–6.

10 These two emphases are identified in Johann Altenstaig's (1480–1524) theological dictionary as two "modes" or "ways" of discussing God's omnipotence. "*Omnipotens* accipitur dupliciter (ut

Rutherford addressed the first emphasis, God's ability to actualize every possibility, by insisting that all possibility is preceded by and ontologically dependent upon God's being and power. In his *Disquisitiones Metaphysicae*, Rutherford wrote:

> God obtains his rule in possible things (*possibilia*) in this way, because he is omnipotent, and therefore because of omnipotency, all possible things are possible, not because they are possible in and of themselves and intrinsecally so, therefore God is omnipotent.[11]

The significance of the above is better understood if one remembers that *potens* can also be translated as "possibility." Potential beings and acts are not possible intrinsically, but rather they are possible because God is all-possible. Possibility is intrinsic to God, but it is extrinsic to possible beings and acts.[12] Just as the child's being is carried about in the womb of the mother, Rutherford argued that God carries about all possibility within himself, "as though in the womb of his vast omnipotence." Within God's vast omnipotence is a treasury of possibilities that could be actualized such as alternative worlds, suns, moons, and the like. Included in this vast treasury are also acts and events that could be future events, but which never will be.[13]

Rutherford's understanding of possibility being an extrinsic denomination of beings and acts is important for his overall interest in avoiding necessitarian outcomes. If possibility were an inherent property to potential beings, then God's power would be limited to work within these possibilities.[14] Like a person assembling

---

notat Gabriel dist. Xlij. Quaest. Unica, artic. i. libr. i.) Uno modo, quia est agens quod potest in omne possibile mediate vel immediate. Alio modo accipitur proprie theologice pro illo qui potest in omnem effectum immediate & in quodcunque possibile, quod non est ex se necessarium, nec includit contradictionem: ita inquam, immediate, quod sine omni operatione, cuiuscunque alterius causae agentis potest in quemlibet effectum." Joanne Altenstaig, "Omnipotens," in *Theologicum complectens vocabulorum descriptiones, diffinitiones & intereipretationes* (Antwerp: Petri Belleri, 1576), 218.

11 "In possibilia autem dominatum Deus hoc obtinet, quod sit Omnipotens, & ideo quia Omnipotens, omnia possibilia sunt possibilia, non autem quia sunt possibilia in se & intrinsece, ideo Deus est Omnipotens." Rutherford, *Disputatio Scholastica*, 532.

12 "Ergo possibile dicitur possibile per denominationem extrinsecam, quia possibile est quid potens fieri, per potentiam extra possibile in solo Deo omnipotente." Rutherford, *Disputatio Scholastica*, 534.

13 "Cum infinita sint possibilia, quae nunquam futura sunt, in gremio quasi vastissimae omnipotentiae nempe plures mundi, plures soles, lunae infinitae, ascribendum Deo dominanti in illa quae potest, si vult producere, quod fieri, hunc mundum non alios millenos mundos, hunc, non tres alios, vel quatuor *soles* vel *lunas*, has quae de facto creatae sunt, decreverit creaturas;" Rutherford, *Disputatio Scholastica*, 533.

14 Rutherford identified this tendency in certain Jesuit theologians such as Franciscus de Oviedo, who argued that God's omnipotence is his absolute power relative to the effect. "Nam Deus esset actu primo & absolute Omnipotens, & si ad extra nihil esset possibile, & actu primo Creator & absolute,

furniture at home, who can only work within the parts and instructions provided, God could only assemble the created order in a certain number of limited ways.[15] The necessitarian consequences are obvious. Since God's power is not limited nor conditioned by the inherent possibilities of potential beings, he is free to apply his power to actualize an infinite number of created realities. The world is as it is, but it could have been otherwise. The explanation for this actual reality, and not some other, is solely rooted in the free decision of God followed by a free application of his power.[16]

In regards to the second emphasis, God's power to produce any physical effect, Rutherford argued that God's power is able to immediately produce any effect without the natural causal concurrence of the secondary cause.[17] In the scholastic literature of the day, this viewpoint is associated with Scotus.[18] Contemporary historians have maintained this association.[19] God's omnipotence means that he can bring about any physical effect immediately, either by suspending the natural operations of the secondary cause to produce a supernatural effect or by bypassing cooperation with the secondary cause altogether. For Rutherford, this was expressed in his understanding of God's absolute power and authority over all created being, and explicitly entailed God's extraordinary power to act in a way apart from the established order of things. Thus, God's power can act directly to make iron float, allow Peter to walk on water, or have stones become children of Abraham.[20]

God's ability to immediately produce any effects, either supervening the natural order or temporarily setting aside its laws, has strong associations with the medieval concept of God's absolute power (*potentia absoluta*). Muller notes that God's *potentia absoluta* "emphasizes the transcendence and omnipotence of God

---

etsi nihil creasset, neque esset Creator relative ad creaturas. Licet *Oviedo*, dicat Omnipotentiam dici *absolute potentem a possibilitate effectus*. Quod est absurdum." Rutherford, *Disputatio Scholastica*, 539. For the Oviedo reference, see: Francisco Oviedo, *Cursus philosophicus* (Leiden: Phillippie Borde, Lavrentii Arnaud, Petri Borde, & Guilielmi Barbier, 1663), Cont. X, Sec. 2, Punct. 5.

15 In a reference to Bradwardine, Rutherford notes the importance of placing priority on God's power rather than the inherent possibility of created being he writes: "unde recte Bradwardina, quia ergo Deus prius potuit facere mundum, antequam fieret, ideo est mundus non quia potuit mundus prius esse." Rutherford, *Disputatio Scholastica*, 533. See also Bradwardine, *De causa Dei, contra pelagium, et de virtute causarum, ad suos Mertonenses*, Lib I, Cap 4.

16 "Ideoque non sunt tres mundi, sed unus, non quia duo mundi sunt possibiles ex se & ex sua intrinseca natura, non enim per se & ex se ab infinito ente deficiunt, sed quia primum ens per se non dedit esse effectivum duobus mundis." Rutherford, *Disputatio Scholastica*, 535.

17 Samuel Rutherford, *Influences of the Life of Grace* (London: Andrew Cook, 1659), 33.

18 See: Altenstaig, "Omnipotens," 218.

19 See: Francis Oakley, "The Absolute and Ordained Power of God in Sixteenth and Seventeenth Century Theology," *Journal of the History of Ideas* 59, no. 3 (1998): 437–61; and also Cross, *Duns Scotus*, 27 and 56–7.

20 Rutherford, *The Tryal and Triumph of Faith*, 308; Rutherford, *Influences of the Life of Grace*, 33.

by setting God even above and beyond the laws he has ordained for the operation of his universe." He continues that the *potentia absoluta* can be used as the "basis of the miraculous and is sometimes associated with the extraordinary power of God (*potentia extraordinaria*), in contrast with the ordinary or usual exercise of divine power (*potentia ordinaria*)."[21] When taken in this sense, God's power can be understood as God's absolute power to work above the ordinary laws of the universe. Rutherford makes this point when he writes in his *Tryal and Triumph of Faith*, "There is a power obedientiall, in creatures to be instruments that can be elevated above, and contrary to their nature..."[22]

Rutherford's description of the "power obedientiall" of potential and actual creatures was an important feature of his overall concept of omnipotence. Obediential potency (*Potentia obedientialis*) was a common notion in early-modern scholasticism, being frequently employed especially by Jesuit theologians to describe the human's intrinsic capacity and desire, with divine aid, to render to God the obedience he is owed.[23] Rutherford's use here is a departure from this understanding. Rather than emphasizing the rational creature's intellectual assent and desire to render obedience to God, Rutherford's use broadened the concept to emphasize a power intrinsic to all created being, both rational and non-rational alike. God's sovereign speech act and the creature's response serves to underscore God's sovereignty over all created being, as well as created being's radical dependence upon God. In provocative and poetic language, Rutherford wrote in his *Tryal and Triumph of Faith* that "God can speak to *Mother-nothing*, as if *Nothing* had ears and reason, and could hear, Rom. 4:17."[24] God's omnipotence, expressed in a sovereign creative speech act, can exercise absolute power over the creature causing it to infinitely exceed its created boundaries. "This obedientiall power is not any created in the creature different from their being," wrote Rutherford, "for God may use any creature to finite effects of omnipotence and so there should be infinite created qualities in every finite creature."[25]

In the more philosophical language of the *Disquisitiones Metaphysicae*, God's sovereign speech act effects pure non-being. "Only by speaking, the authority and

---

21 "Potentia absoluta" in: Muller, *Dictionary of Latin and Greek Theological Terms*, 271.

22 Rutherford, *The Tryal and Triumph of Faith*, 307–8.

23 "Aptitudo rerum creatarum, ut pro arbitrio agentis superioris, eiusque auxilio ipsis indebito, munus impleant, quod nativa virtute et concursu sibi debito implere non possent." Ripalda, Juan Martinez de. *De ente supernaturali,* 236; Francisco Soares, *Cursus Philosophicus in Quatuor Tomos Distributus* (Coimbra: Pauli Craesbeeck, 1651), 195. See also James T. Bretzke, "Potentia Obedientialis," in *Consecrated Phrases: A Latin Theological Dictionary,* 2nd ed., (Collegeville, Minn: The Liturgical Press, 2003).

24 Rutherford, 306.

25 Rutherford, 306–7.

command of Omnipotence stretched out into pure non-being. "*And he said,* to who I ask did he say? To pure non-being, *let there be light, and light was made, Genes 1.3.*"[26] This application of God's absolute power infinitely exceeds the capacity of pure non-being and has the power to bring forth something from nothing.[27]

God's omnipotence, expressed through his absolute power to work in ways above and beyond the established order of nature or God's own historical acts is an important aspect in Rutherford's overall account of God's freedom and the contingency of the created order. God's absolute power is not restricted by the natural order, nor is God's absolute power restricted by human expectations of God based on God's own historical dealings with human beings in salvation history. God's power can supersede the natural order and Rutherford believed that God's absolute power could have been applied to effect salvation and pardon through means other than the blood redemption of Christ. "But God," wrote Rutherford, "if we speak of absolute power, without respect to his free decree, could have pardoned sin without a ransom, and gifted all mankind and fallen angels in heaven, without any satisfaction of either the sinner, or his surety." God "neither punishes sin, nor tenders heaven" by the necessity of nature. Rather, he does so freely. God's ability to apply power to achieve different effects than what are currently known and experienced in the actual world testify to the absolute liberty from which God brought about this created reality.[28]

The emphasis in Rutherford's use of omnipotence was upon what God is able to do. The next distinction, concerning God's sovereignty, focuses more narrowly, though not exclusively, on how God has chosen to exercise his power. Whereas God's omnipotency is necessary and precedes any act of the will, God's sovereignty emphasizes the executive role of God's power as it brings about what God has willed.

5.1.2 Sovereignty

In his *Influences on the Life of Grace*, Rutherford wrote, "To know what Soveraignty is. Let us see what it is not." Sovereignty is not omnipotency. Omnipotency looks to "what the Lord *can doe.*" Sovereignty has a different emphasis. Rutherford's dense definition of sovereignty is worth quoting in full:

---

26 "Solus ille loquendo, imperium & mandatum Omnipotentiae extendit in pure non entia. *Et dixit*, cui, quaeso, dixit? Pure non entia, *esto lux, & facta est lux*, Gen 2.32." Rutherford, *Disputatio Scholastica*, 533.

27 "Verbo & nutu Omnipotentiae vocat non entia. Ita verbum אָמַר est vocare. Ecce tale dominium quo non entia obedieant Deo vocanti. 2 Cor 4.6. Deus, qui dixit, ὁ θεὸς ὁ εἰπών, ut e tenebris lux splendesceret, &c." Rutherford, *Disputatio Scholastica*, 533.

28 Rutherford, *Christ Dying and Drawing Sinners to Himselfe*, 8.

Omnipotency and Soveraignty thus differ; Omnipotency looks simply to effects physically, what the Lord can doe: he can of stones make sons to Abraham; he can create millions of Worlds; his Soveraignty is not only his holy Nature what he can doe and so supposeth his Omnipotency, but also what he doth freely, or doth not freely, and doth by no natural necessity, and so it includes his holy supreme Liberty, and also what the Lord may doe, as it were Jure he may doe all things, and (as Elihu saith) gives not an account of his matters to any, Job 33. 13., by his holy soveraign Will as above all Laws that bind the rational Creatures, he does as he pleaseth, and what he pleaseth.[29]

Omnipotency belongs to God by natural necessity. Sovereignty on the other hand pertains to what God does freely under no natural necessity. Sovereignty is the execution of God's power following a determination of the divine will. Encompassed in this concept is not only the positive execution of God's power to actualize a determination of the divine will, but also the negative aspect of withholding power. Thus sovereignty is both "what he doth freely" as well as what God "doth not freely." This distinction closely parallels certain distinctions concerning God's knowledge covered in chapter three, such as God's natural and free knowledge.[30]

In his own study of Rutherford, Richard has noted that Rutherford's distinction between omnipotence and sovereignty parallels the power distinction of God's absolute and ordained power (*potentia absoluta et ordinata*).[31] Though rough equivalents of this distinction had existed for quite some time, the distinction took on new prominence after the Condemnation of 1277, where Edward Grant notes it was a useful theological tool to combat the "often deterministic" philosophical and scientific explanatory principles of the Greco-Arabic physics and natural philosophy. The distinction undermines deterministic outcomes by providing a coherent explanation for the contingency of the world.[32] As Heiko Oberman argues, "The contingent character of our world can be explained by the innumerable possibilities which God could have chosen to actualize his purposes, in addition to the one he actually did choose."[33]

Rutherford used the dialectics of God's power to achieve similar outcomes to those mentioned above, namely to underscore the contingency of the created order thus providing a bulwark against fatalistic accounts of reality. According to

---

29 Rutherford, *Influences of the Life of Grace*, 33.

30 See Chapter 3.2.

31 Richard, *The Supremacy of God in the Theology of Samuel Rutherford*, 98.

32 Edward Grant, "The effect of the condemnation of 1277," in *The Cambridge History of Later Medieval Philosophy*, ed. Norman Kretzmann, Anthony Kenny, and Jan Pinborg (Cambridge: Cambridge University Press, 1982), 537.

33 Heiko A. Oberman, "Some Notes on the Theology of Nominalism: With Attention to Its Relation to the Renaissance," *The Harvard Theological Review* 53, no. 1 (1960), 65.

Rutherford, the only sufficient explanation for how merely possible beings transition from a state of potentiality into a state of actuality is a determination of the divine will.[34] When speaking of God's power, it is his sovereignty, not his omnipotence that is the explanation for why the actual world exists. God's sovereignty, which is both a free and absolute determination of the divine will, underscores the fundamental contingency of the created world precisely because in his sovereignty, God could have applied his power to actualize a different set of possibilities. Furthermore, God's free and sovereign determination to actualize this world and not some other, does not make this actual world less contingent than it would have been otherwise. Neither does it diminish the contingent nature of unactualized possibilities. The contingency of these is safeguarded by God's omnipotence, which guarantees their possibility and contingency whether they are actualized or not.[35]

5.2 God's Power and the Modalities of Being

God's power as it relates to various modalities of being is closely related to the discussion above concerning the contingency of the actual world. These conversations compose the bulk of Rutherford's sustained arguments in his *Disquisitiones Metaphysicae*, Q. I-VIII. What follows is a summary of *Questio* I-VIII, with a special focus on the issues identified immediately above.

5.2.1 God's Power and Necessity

There are two modal notions that are not objects of God's power. These are necessary states of affairs and impossible states of affairs. Beginning with the necessary, God's being, his essence, attributes, and life are all necessary antecedents to any possible created order. There can be no created being, unless there is first a necessary being. The argument was introduced in the first *Questio*, where Rutherford asked whether being precedes non-being.[36] The question was answered within the

---

34 "Ergo necessario dicendum Dei voluntatem ut libere decernente esse causam hujus transitus e statu possibilitatis ad statu futuritionis. Quartus rerum status est status actuationis, quo res e statu futuritionis transeat ad statum actuationis & hujus transitus causa est voluntas omnipotentia armata; in Deo." Rutherford, *Exercitationes Apologeticae pro divina gratia*, 59.

35 "Possibile itaque est quod potest esse vel non esse, hoc est cui non repugnat esse: at vero possibile contingens est quod de facto & actu potest esse vel non esse, non simpliciter sed antecedente futuritione, ideoque quamvis possibilitates superent numero actualitates, at vero futurorum contingentium & effectorum contingentium actu & de facto, planè & idem est numerus, nec illa vel unitate hæc excedunt." Rutherford, *Exercitationes Apologeticae*, 89.

36 "An Ens sit prius simpliciter non ente." Rutherford, *Disputatio Scholastica*, 532.

framework of the demonstrative science of Aristotle, covered earlier in chapter 2.2.1 of this study.[37] As was discussed, Aristotle posited knowable, anterior premises or principles of demonstration, that did not depend upon preceding terms, but rather were independent and known simply in and of themselves without any prior argumentation.[38] According to Aristotle, the law of non-contradiction was the first and strongest principle of demonstration.[39]

However, as Rutherford noted, the law of non-contradiction cannot be foundational. As a complex proposition (*idem simul esse & non esse est impossibile*), it depends upon a prior, simple proposition (*idem est idem*) for its composition. Rutherford argued that since the nature of this simple proposition is identical predication, it is not able to teach anything conclusive. Therefore, it cannot serve as a principle of demonstration. Rutherford concluded that this simple proposition must be a supposition rather than a principle. Here "supposition" simply means that *idem est idem* is significant of something more substantial, which can serve as a principle, this being God himself, "who is first the same, whose sweetest name, and more than a name is I am who I am." Rutherford's essentialist reading of the divine name establishes God as necessarily antecedent to all logical propositions and possible states of affairs.[40]

God's being is therefore a necessary antecedent to any complex, created being. Rutherford continued his argument for the precedence of being in the second *Questio,* where he asked "Whether God is the ruling cause in being and non-being."[41] He noted that non-being and the denial of being presuppose being and affirmation. One must conceptually hold the concept of "being" in the mind before one can deny it. The word "being" must first be produced before the prefix "non" is added to create the complex notion of "non-being." For Rutherford, the negation of being composed by the addition of the prefix "non" implies a recession from being

---

37 See Ch. 2.2.1.

38 For an excellent overview see: John Longeway, "Medieval Theories of Demonstration," in *The Stanford Encyclopedia of Philosophy* (Spring 2009 Edition), edt. by Edward N. Zalta, https://plato.stanford.edu/archives/spr2009/entries/demonstration-medieval. See also Eileen Serene, "Demonstrative Science," in *The Cambridge History of Later Medieval Philosophy*, ed. Norman Kretzmann, Anthony Kenny, and Jan Pinborg (Cambridge: Cambridge University Press, 1982), 496–518.

39 Aristotle's *Metaphysics*, Book 4, Chapter 4. See also: Irwin, *Aristotle's First Principles* (Oxford: Oxford University Press, 1990); Smith, "Aristotle's Logic," *The Stanford Encyclopedia of Philosophy*, edt. by Edward N. Zalta, https://plato.stanford.edu/archives/sum2019/entries/aristotle-logic.

40 "Quia vero simplex est prius complex: principium hoc est. (*Idem est idem.*) Sed quia nihil docet praedictio identica, haec supposito est simplicissima forte verius, quam principium. Itaque principium adhuc prius est. (*Deus est,*) (*Deus intelligit,*) (*Deus vult,*) &c. Id autem (*Idem simul esse & non esse est impossibile)* veritatem obtineat necesse est, in eo qui est primus idem, cui suavissimum nomen & plus quam nomen, אֶהְיֶה אֲשֶׁר אֶהְיֶה." Rutherford, *Disputatio Scholastica*, 531.

41 "An Deus causa dominans sit entium & non entium." Rutherford, *Disputatio Scholastica*, 532.

rather than an outright absence. Non-being is removal and separation from being, as darkness is a removal and separation from light or blindness is the removal and separation from sight.[42] The point here is that God is a necessary antecedent to any created being. In addition to this, God is a necessary antecedent to a state of affairs where there are no created beings. God is a necessary antecedent to both something, as well as nothing.[43]

What this means in relation to God's providence, is that in every conceivable created order made possible by God's omnipotence, the existence of God is necessary. As has been seen, God could have chosen not to create a world at all. He also could have chosen to create a world with different moral and even natural laws. He could have created a world with different historical realities, such as a world where Christ did not die to ransom sinners.[44] A proposition that is true in the actual world (i.e. *if Peter is tempted he will sin*), may not be true in a different, unactualized possible world. But in every possible world, certain principles pertaining to God's being, essence, attributes, and life, are necessarily true.[45] Because such are necessarily true, they are not objects of God's will and thus cannot be objects of God's power.[46]

5.2.2 Impossibility

Propositions such as God is (*Deus est*) are necessary and thus true in any possible state of affairs. God is not (*Deus non est*), on the other hand, is an impossible proposition not true in any possible state of affairs. From these basic considerations, one could extrapolate that the necessary and the impossible both complement

---

42 "Non necesse est probemus Ens non ente, affirmativum negativo prius esse, quia non ens & negatio presupponit ens & affirmationem, non contra. 2. Non ens est elongatio & distantia ab ente simpliciter, & terminus simpliciter a quo est prior, eo quod ab ipso recedit: & laesio, seu entis quasi privatio, est posterior ente simpliciter, ut tenebrae luce, caecitas visu: at non ens est laesio entis, & ab ente elongatio." Rutherford, *Disputatio Scholastica*, 532.

43 The argument follows Thomas's identification of God as a pure act. Rutherford adopts this description, noting that a God who is fully actualized cannot at the same time "not be" without involving the proposition in a contradiction. "Primus actus infinitus quem non esse involvit contradictionem (quam pulcherrimo & superexcellentissimo enti entium tribuere nefas est)." Rutherford, *Disputatio Scholastica*, 532. See also: Thomas Aquinas, *Summa Contra Gentiles Book Three: Providence Part II* (Notre Dame: University of Notre Dame, 2001), Chapter 100, 79–81.

44 See Chapter 4.4.2.

45 This is also true in modern modal logic. See: Kenneth Konyndyk, *Introductory Modal Logic* (Notre Dame: University of Notre Dame Press, 1986), 16.

46 Examples of such necessary first principles given by Rutherford are "God is" (*Deus est*), "God understands" (*Deus intelligit*), and "God wills" (*Deus vult*). Given that these first principles are constructed by equating an essentialist reading of the divine name with *idem est idem*, it is reasonable to conclude that other propositions concerning God's attributes and life (i.e. God is omnipotent, God is omnipresent, etc.) are equally necessary. See: Rutherford, *Disputatio Scholastica*, 532.

and mutually exclude one another.[47] There are similarities between the necessary and the impossible. Neither are subject to God's will, thus neither are objects to the willed expression of his sovereign power. There are also subtle differences. Necessary truths, such as God's existence, belong to God as aspects of his very being. Impossibility on the other hand, is a concept that does not properly belong to God but rather depends upon him set within a participatory framework. In *Questio III* of his *Disquisitiones Metaphysicae*, Rutherford asked "whether God is the origin and cause of the impossible and the possible."[48] By this question, he was not intending to investigate whether or not God could cause something that is contradictory to be true. Rather, he was seeking to investigate whether possibility and impossibility were originally and participatively from God.[49]

The question was answered in the affirmative. The principle, it is impossible for the same thing to be and not be at the same time (*idem simul esse & non esse, impossibile est*), is a truth that first obtains in God. This truth also obtains in creatures, but not intrinsically so. Rather, it obtains through participation.[50] Participation is a philosophical term associated with Platonic realism.[51] Coffey has made note of certain Platonist tendencies in Rutherford.[52] Rutherford's own rare appeal to the Neoplatonist Philosopher Porphyry (234–305) makes such Platonism explicit, at least in this section of the *Disputatio*.[53] Briefly, Platonic realism maintains that universals exist outside of the human mind as ideal forms. These forms are instantiated in reality as particulars. The particulars share a likeness to the universal forms. This is called participation, from the Latin *participatio*, which can be translated as "participation" or "sharing."

The Neoplatonic doctrine of divine participation was employed by Christian theologians from the Patristic on through the Medieval period and has often been

---

47 Bac, *Perfect Will Theology*, 319.

48 "Questio III. An Deus sit Origo & Causa impossibilium & possibilium." Rutherford, *Disputatio Scholastica*, 538.

49 "Non est quaestio, an Deus causa sit, quod idem simul posset esse & non esse, vel quod contradictoria sint simul vera, Deus enim talia efficere non potest. Sed an possibilia & impossibilia sint participative & originaliter a primo ente, ut ab efficiente." Rutherford, *Disputatio Scholastica*, 538.

50 "Quia hoc principium (*idem simul esse & non esse, impossible est*) prius veritatem obtinet in Deo primo ente, pulcherrimo fonte, causa causalissima, puro & purissimo vero, quam in entibus per participationem, in rivulis, in effectibus, aut in vero per participationem." Rutherford, *Disputatio Scholastica*, 539.

51 For a helpful overview, see Anthony Kenny, *A New History of Western Philosophy* (Oxford: Clarendon Press, 2012), 44–50.

52 Coffey, *Politics, Religion and the British Revolutions*, 73.

53 Rutherford, *Disputatio Scholastica*, 540. See also A. C. Lloyd, "The Later NeoPlatonists," in *The Cambridge History of later Greek and Early Medieval Philosophy* (Cambridge: Cambridge University Press, 1980), 272–330.

associated by modern scholars with Thomist and Orthodox theologians.[54] It has largely been assumed that the Reformed tradition was an inhospitable tradition to the doctrine of divine participation.[55] Rutherford's appeal to Porphyry and his explicit use of participation demonstrates that Rutherford found the doctrine of divine participation both orthodox and useful in certain circumstances. The appeal to Porphyry comes as an answer to *Questio IIII*, which asks "whether something is impossible if it is not originally impossible by God?" The question was denied.[56]

Rutherford argued that the forms of possible beings are representations of the divine ideas, which are the pattern and exemplars of created being.[57] Participation, or a creature's share in God's likeness, begins with the divine simplicity. Just as God is simple, the divine ideas are originally simple.[58] The divine idea is conceived as a simple operation; without composition or division; or without any attribution, affirmation, or denial.[59] Rutherford made an explicit appeal to Aristotle's *de Inter-*

---

54 Recently, this conversation has been driven by the *Nouvelle théologie* on the one hand, and more recently by a team of scholars out of Cambridge that have come to be identified as "Radical Orthodoxy." For representative examples concerning the *Nouvelle théologie*, see H. de Lubac, *Augustinianism and Modern Theology*, trans. Lancelot Capel Sheppard, Milestones in Catholic Theology (Chestnut Ridge, NY: Crossroad Publishing Company, 2000); Yves Congar, *Tradition and Traditions: The Biblical, Historical, and Theological Evidence for Catholic Teaching on Tradition* (New York: Macmillan, 1967). For representative examples from Radical Orthodoxy, see: John Milbank, *Theology and Social Theory: Beyond Secular Reason* (Oxford: Blackwell, 1990); *Radical Orthodoxy*, ed. John Milbank, Catherine Pickstock, and Graham Ward (London: Routledge, 1999).

55 For examples see John Milbank, "Alternative Protestantism: Radical Orthodoxy and the Reformed Tradition," in *Radical Orthodoxy and the Reformed Tradition*, ed. James K. A. Smith and James H. Olthuis (Grand Rapids, MI: Baker Academic, 2005), 25–41; Michael S. Horton, "Participation and Covenant," in *Radical Orthodoxy and the Reformed Tradition*, ed. James K. A. Smith and James H. Olthuis (Grand Rapids, MI: Baker Academic, 2005), 107–30. Milbank takes a generally negative view of participation in the Reformed tradition. Horton argues that a covenant framework is a better representation of the Reformed tradition than the "ontological union" set forth through divine participation.

56 Rutherford begins by acknowledging the difficulty of the question. "An altera quaestionis pars longe difficilior est, nempe, *An aliquid sit impossibile, nisi quod a Deo originaliter sit impossibile*. Et respondetur nihil esse impossibile tale." Rutherford, *Disputatio Scholastica*, 540.

57 See: Ch. 3.4.

58 "Quia omne ens simplex est creabile, potestque ex idea simplicissimae essentiae divinae, qua in infinitum est representabilis in creaturis possibilibus ad extra produci & simplex ens ex simplice Dei essentia per Omnipotentiam extrahibile est, quia nihil repugnans, dissonum nihil est in eo qui est primus idem, prima & simplicissimae unitas, quin quodlibet ens creare possit." Rutherford, *Disputatio Scholastica*, 541.

59 "Uti in simplice & prima operatione intellectus, quae compositione & divisione careat, nihil veritatis, nihil falsitatis est, quia omnis veritas est in affirmatione & negatione, *prout ita res sese habet vel non habet*, in objectiva connexione rerum quae subjecti & attributi locum tenent." Rutherford, *Disputatio Scholastica*, 541.

pretatione, wherein Aristotle made the distinction between simple expressions of which nothing may be affirmed or denied, and simple statements that affirm or deny something about the subject.[60]

As was shown in an earlier chapter, the first operation of the divine intellect strictly concerns the simple *vox*, or word, abstracted from the contingent properties of creation.[61] The simple *vox* is arrived at by considering entities abstractly, stripped from the contingent properties of creation. On the other hand, to consider an entity intuitively is to consider its creation in time, with distinctive accidental properties. What concerns Rutherford is the first operation of the divine intellect, which is abstractive, uncreated, and generic, rather than intuitive, created, and specific.[62]

Difference between entities, as well as impossibility and incompossibility are established here at the ontological level. Appealing to Porphyry, Rutherford noted that God is therefore the creator of difference among species. The one who creates species is also the one who establishes the differences between species, since the one who creates cold is also the one who establishes what is opposite to cold.[63] At this point we are better prepared to relate Rutherford's doctrine of the divine ideas to the *Quaestio*, "whether something is impossible if it is not originally impossible for God." Impossibility, as constructed above, is a derivative effect of the incompossibility of diverse beings. For example, God's practical knowledge produces the divine idea of cold, and as a result also produces the divine idea of its opposite. Rutherford argued that these two diverse natures cannot be combined into one creature because such a creature would be cold (a) and not cold (−a) simultaneously, and thus run afoul of the principle of non-contradiction (*Idem est idem & Idem simul esse & non*

---

60 *De intrepretatione*, 16a1–17a35. The edition referenced here is Aristotle, "De Interpretatione," in *The Complete Works of Aristotle*, ed. Jonathan Barnes (Princeton, NJ: Princeton University Press, 1984), 25–28.

61 See Ch. 3.4.

62 "Sed necessario veras & earum veritates a tempore abstrahere, & semper veras hoc sensu largior, quod quidditativo conceptu subjecti includatur conceptus attributi, propter indentificationem attributi cum subjecto, qui enim concipit hominem, concipit animal, homo in potentia includit animal objective in potentia, & homo in actu, animal in actu, quod agnovit adversarius *Hurtado Jesuita*. At quando concipitur homo, concipitur animal rationale, & si tu ponis hominem ab aeterno, necesse est ponas animal rationale ab eterno, qui essentia & essentiam non possunt non semper identifica & tamen essentiatum est creatum in tempore sicut & essentia, & simul concreata est identitas inter essentiam & essentiatum, quando creatur res constans essentia." Rutherford, *Disputatio Scholastica*, 558.

63 "Qui Deus *Creator* in saecula celebrandus creando differentias speciei constitutivas *v.g.* hirci & cervi simul differentias divisivas constituit: eadem enim differentia specifica, est & speciei constitutiva & divisiva generis, ut *Porphyrius* ait. Qui enim creat ens, creat unum, creat diversum, creat repugnans. Qui producit frigidum, producit quid congregativum heterogeneorum, & eodem actu producit quid repugnans calido." Rutherford, *Disputatio Scholastica*, 540.

esse est impossibile).[64] Created being's inability to be and not be at the same time shares a likeness, and thus participates in God's own being in whom the principle of non-contradiction first obtains. Just as necessary states of affairs are not objects of God's power, neither are impossible states of affairs.

5.2.3 Possibility and Contingency

Moving beyond the necessary and the impossible are the properties of the possible and the contingent. Recently, some scholars of Reformed Orthodoxy have analyzed the use of these terms by the Reformed scholastics with the analytical aid of modal logic.[65] These studies have yielded interesting results, providing useful tools to examine modal concepts employed by the scholastics more exactly. Though useful, caution must be exercised to define the terms as the Reformed Scholastics would have.[66]

One area in need of care is the definition of the term possible. A proposition is possible according to the modern understanding of modal logic as long as it is not necessary that the proposition be false.[67] This would allow for certain propositions that Rutherford considered necessary (i.e. *Deus est*) to also be possible.[68] Rutherford would surely agree that the proposition *Deus est* is possible in the sense that it is free from logical contradiction and not necessarily false. But the framework more readily available to Rutherford would have been the Aristotelean framework of act and potency.[69] God being pure act is what establishes the truth of the proposition (*Deus est*). Because he is eternally and perfectly actualized, applying the modal terms of both "necessary" and "possible" would most likely have made little sense to Rutherford. In any event, truths about God's essence, being, and existence, being

---

64 "Deus ergo creando essentias hirci & cervi possibiles vel actuales, creat eodem actu incompossibil-itates inter naturam hirci & cervi. Itaque in *Creatorem,* qui hircum specie & natura distinctum a cervo creavit, originaliter reducitur hoc (*Impossibile vel incompossibile est idem animal esse & hircum & cervum*) quia cum specie & incompossibiliter diversae sunt naturae, idem esset simul hircus & non hircus." Rutherford, *Disputatio Scholastica*, 540.

65 See for example Vos et al, *John Duns Scotus*, 30–32; van Asselt, Bac, and te Velde, *Reformed Thought on Freedom*, 42; Bac, *Perfect Will Theology*, 409–17.

66 See Muller's note of caution in: Muller, *Divine Will and Human Choice*, 50.

67 Konyndyk, *Introductory Modal Logic*, 16–17.

68 Bac applies modal logic to make this very point. He writes: "Recalling the modal definitions in terms of repugnancy, the necessary (self-contradiction being denied) is definitely possible as well (not self-contradiction being affirmed)." See Bac, *Perfect Will Theology*, 318–9.

69 "Possibility, contingency, and necessity are grounded, not in the Leibnizian notion of possible worlds, but in the Aristotelean theory of act and potency." See, Edward Feser, *Scholastic Metaphysics: A Contemporary Introduction* (Piscataway: Transaction Books, 2014), 141.

necessary truths, are considered to be a separate category from the possible by Rutherford.[70]

Possibility, defined by Rutherford, is some thing or a state of affairs that is free from contradiction and is able to be or not be (*potest esse vel non esse*).[71] The possible states of affairs made possible by God's omnipotence is vast and innumerable. Each possible state of affairs is also contingently future, where the futurition of the state of affairs is contingent upon a free determination of the divine will and an influx of God's power. Sometimes Rutherford's use of possibility and contingency is nearly synonymous.[72] Though in the above a subtle distinction can be noted. The emphasis with the modal term possible is on the possible being's freedom from internal contradiction and subsequent ability to be or not be. The emphasis with the term contingent is upon a possible being's futurition and actualization, as well as the means by which this process is affected.[73] Possible states of affairs could be or not be. Contingent states of affairs are or will be, but need not have been. Both the possible and the contingent, being grounded in God's omnipotence, are antecedent to the divine will, thus their possibility and contingency are both maximally necessary.[74]

5.2.4 Futurition and Actuality

Mere possibilities, grounded in God's power, are non-being (*non-ens*) and non-future (*non futurum*). Contra certain Jesuits who argued for the real and eternal existence of certain beings such as propositions, Rutherford denied that the merely

---

70 This is not to imply that the conclusions drawn by studies that have relied on the tools of modal logic are wrong. Rather, it is simply to point out that there is not an exact correlation between the terms employed by the Reformed scholastics and modern analytical philosophy.

71 "Possibile itaque est quod potest esse vel non esse, hoc est qui non repugnat esse: at vero possibile contingens est quod defacto actu potest esse vel non esse, non simpliciter sed antecedente futuritione, ideoque quamvis possibilitates aperent numero actualitates, at vero futurorum contingentium & effectorum contingentium actu & de facto, par plane & idem est numerus, nec illa vel unitate haec excedunt." Rutherford, *Exercitationes Apologeticae*, 89.

72 Rutherford's synonymous use of these terms was not unique. See "Possibile" in: Muller, *Dictionary of Latin and Greek Theological Terms*, 269.

73 See fn. 72, above.

74 "Secundus status est vastissimus nempe status possibilitatis, quo omnia futura contingentia, & omnia tum necessaria tum contingentia, quae sunt nunquam futura, habent esse, hoc est non repugnantiam ut sint, in habitudine nempe ad Dei omnipotentiam, & dato quod nunquam fuisset in Deo decretum producendi ulla entia extra se, omnia quae jam sunt possibilia in eo casu possibilia forent: possibilia enim sunt antecedenter ad Dei voluntatem, hoc modo contingentia omnia sunt antecedenter ad Dei volitiones, & in signo rationis aliquid prius natura est possibile, quam futurum & futurum aliquid super addit possibili, sicut species aliquid superaddit generi, hoc sensu contingentia, simpliciter possunt esse vel non esse, & omnia etiam maxime necessaria possunt esse vel non esse." Rutherford, *Exercitationes Apologeticae*, 88.

possible had real being.[75] *Non-ens* and *non-futurum* can be understood in one of two ways. In one sense, they can be understood negatively as simply impossible. In another sense, these terms can be understood privatively, as capable of futurition yet without an efficient cause to bring this state of being about.[76] An important aspect of the merely possible is that it is both capable of futurition and non-futurition and is completely indifferent to either state of affairs.[77] Rutherford's insistence that such *non-entia* are indifferent to futurition excluded certain theories of the Jesuits and Arminians that argued under certain circumstances *x* will be determinately true. The same also excluded theories that argued that under certain circumstances *x* will probably take place. That the future existence of a merely possible *non-ens* is entirely indifferent means there are no hidden forces weighting the scales one way or another. Because the future existence of a merely possible *non-ens* is indifferent, a causal explanation is required for how a mere possibility enters a state of futurition.[78] The status of possible changes to determinately future by God's decree.[79]

The indifferent nature of a future event is represented below in two propositions concerning Peter's temptation and possible sin.

(a) If Peter is tempted, he will sin. (*possibile, non-ens, non-futurum*)
(b) If Peter is tempted, he will not sin. (*possibile, non-ens, non-futurum*)

Prior to the action of the divine will, Rutherford noted that both propositions are possible. Being merely possible, they are both *non-ens* as well as *non-futurum*. Consequent to an action of the divine will, one part of the pair becomes determinately future.

(a) If Peter is tempted, he will sin. (*non-ens, possibile & futurum*)
(b) If Peter is tempted, he will not sin. (*non-ens, possibile & non-futurum*)

---

75 This position, as well as Rutherford's rebuttal, was covered in Chapter 3.3.2 of this study.

76 "Duplex est *non-ens* & *non-futurum*. Aliud est pure negativum & non ens & simpliciter impossibile, quod est negative non futurum, & aliud est non-ens tale & non-ens privative negans ens vel creatum vel increatum. Haec duo non entia sic distinguuntur quod prius sit pure negativum, posterius privativum." Rutherford, *Disputatio Scholastica*, 547.

77 "Prius non ens est capax futuritionis & non futuritionis & indifferens ut sit futurum vel non futurum per Dei decretum, & capax entitatis positivae vel privativae." Rutherford, *Disputatio Scholastica*, 547.

78 "Sicut itaque res sunt possibiles in habitudine ad aliquam causam, (aliqui essent impossibiles, & haec causa est omnipotentia) ita etiam res possibiles e statu possibilitatis, ad statum futuritionis evehuntur, & remotius a non ente elongantur per aliquam causam." Rutherford, *Exercitationes Apologeticae*, 88.

79 "Tertius vero status rerum est status futuritionis quo res possibiles acipiunt (esse) futurum a Dei decreto, possibile: itaque est terminus a quo, futurum, terminus ad quem, & futuritio motus intermedius, quo res possibilis transit a statu possibilitatis ad statum futuritionis." Rutherford, *Exercitationes Apologeticae*, 88.

Proposition (a) remains a non-being. The possibility is not established as a being until it has been actualized in time in real creation by God's power. Proposition (a) remains possible. Though it will be actualized in time, it is actualized freely, not by necessity. It is able to be or not be. Finally, proposition (a) is designated as a future being, meaning that it will be actualized in creation at some point by an influx of God's power. It is worth pointing out that even though proposition (b) is *non-futurum*, this designation has not deprived it of its status as possible. The significance of this is that though proposition (b) will not be a future event, it could have been.

Finally, the state of futurition passes into a state of actualization, where for example, proposition (a) no longer *will be*, but *is,* and eventually *has been.* The cause of this is God's will, effectualized by God's power.[80] The relation between the modalities covered above can be represented below as follows:

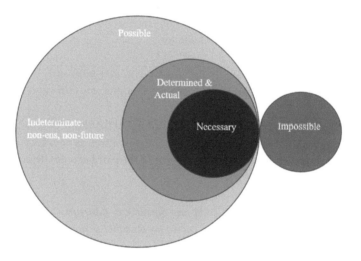

Fig. 1   God's Power in Relation to Necessary, Impossible, Possible, and Actual Worlds According to Rutherford

In the above, the necessary and the impossible are depicted as complementary, yet mutually exclusive sets. The necessary represents those propositions such as *God is* (*Deus est*) that pre-exist and make possible any logically possible state of affairs. The large circle labelled possible represents the innumerable state of affairs able to be actualized by virtue of God's omnipotence. Because this space is both *non-ens*

---

80 "Quartus rerum status est status actuationis, quo res e statu furutitionis transeat ad statum actuationis & hujus transitus causa est voluntas omnipotentia armata; in Deo." Rutherford, *Exercitationes Apologeticae*, 89.

and *non-futurum*, it contains pairs of contradictory conditional propositions such (a) and (b) outlined above. The smaller space represents those states of affairs, such as proposition (a) that God has determined to actualize at some point in the future. The same space also represents those states of affairs that God has actualized. The two spaces are exactly equal in scope. Rutherford was clear that what God has determined to a state of futurition is exactly commensurate to that which is actualized. Numerically, futurition and actualization represent the same number of beings, the only difference being the stage of succession.[81]

5.3   God's Power and God's Dominion

Muller notes that in Reformed Orthodoxy, God's power is closely connected to the doctrine of God's dominion.[82] God's power (*potentia*) is what God is able to do. God's dominion (*potestas*) is what God has authority to do.[83] There was considerable disagreement between Rutherford and his adversaries concerning both. In this final section of the chapter, the nature of some of these disputes will be outlined. A clear portrait of Rutherford's own doctrine of dominion will emerge with the benefit of a contrasting picture provided by certain polemical opponents.[84]

5.3.1 Dominion

The subject of the fourth chapter of the *Disputatio* is the relation between middle knowledge and God's dominion. The title of the chapter, "Middle Knowledge Overthrows God's Dominion," leaves no doubt as to where Rutherford stood on the issue.[85] From Rutherford's negative polemic, a positive definition of what he believed dominion is can be constructed. Regarding the relation between middle knowledge and God's dominion, Rutherford wrote that for the sake of safeguarding their conception of the independence of the human will, "this middle knowledge overthrows God's dominion in all being (*omnia entia*), what God is able to effect in

---

81 "Observo, esse futurum, quod est, a Dei voluntate commensurandum esse exactissime ab esse praesente, quod illud futurum in tempore habet & accipit, ita ut esse futurum & esse praesens, sint unum & idem esse & tantum different durationis ordine." Rutherford, *Exercitationes Apologeticae*, 89.

82 See Muller, *The Divine Essence and Attributes*, 517–24.

83 See "potentia" and "potestas" in: Muller, *Dictionary of Latin and Greek Theological Terms*, 270, 272.

84 The following is primarily taken from Chapter 4 of the *Disputatio*. Rutherford, *Disputatio Scholastica*, 28–49. For an overview of the relation between God's power and God's dominion, see Muller, *The Divine Essence and Attributes*, 517–23.

85 "Scientiam mediam Dei dominium evertere." Rutherford, *Disputatio Scholastica*, 28.

order that they may be in the nature of things, or may not be, according to his own independent will."[86]

Several positive features can be pulled from this bit of negative polemic. First, the object of God's dominion is "all being." Being (*ens*) could be understood in a variety of ways in seventeenth century scholasticism.[87] Broadly speaking, being is first understood as that which is logically possible. From here, a being might exist only in the intellect or it could have a real, extra-mental existence in creation. When taken in this later way, a being could be a living creature or an inanimate object. A being could also be a state of affairs represented by a hypothetical proposition, as long as the extreme terms of the proposition are not logically contradictory. Beings that are only and ever will be objects of the intellect could also be described as mere possibilities. Their being, which as has been seen above, was understood by Rutherford as non-being (*non-ens*), can also be understood privately as the absence of being, as darkness is the absence of light. Rutherford's denial that a being other than God could be a real being antecedent to God's will and power is a reminder of the radical contingency of the nature of created being since there is no being other than God that has independent existence.[88]

The object of God's dominion is such beings. God exercises his dominion by his power, which is able to effect being by granting it power to enjoy actual existence in the created order or by withholding the same power so that it will never exist in the actual world. The controversy regarding the above is that Rutherford believed that God had power and authority to grant being to a state of affairs that implicated the operations of the human free will. Rutherford's Jesuit and Arminian polemical opponents denied the point. Thus, Rutherford argued that such had overturned God's dominion by denying his power and authority to grant or deny being to operations of the human free will.[89]

---

86 "Haec scientia media evertit Dei dominium in omnia entis, quae Deus efficere potest, ut sint in rerum natura, vel non sint, pro suo independenti arbitrio." Rutherford, *Disputatio Scholastica*, 28.

87 See for example: Joannes Altenstaig, "Ens," in *Theologicum complectens vocabulorum* (Antwerp: Petri Belleri, 1576), 98.

88 Rutherford's preferred term to an unactualized possibility is a "mere possibility" or *non-ens*. This is most likely to distinguish his own position from those Jesuits who argued certain propositions antecedent to the divine decree were "real being" (*ens reale*). See: Chapter 3.3.2 of this study, 80–84. Regarding Reformed approaches to metaphysics, Bac has commented that this is a demonstration that a "contingency model" systematically affected Reformed thinking on a variety of subjects. See Bac, *Perfect Will Theology*, 27.

89 "Is non habet Dominium in omnia entia, qui non habet Dominium in actus liberos, nec potest causari ut actus liberi sint, vel non sint, prout ipsi libitum fuerit, sed stante scientia media, & doctrina Arminiana de gratiae operatione resistibili, & efficacia gratiae a libero arbitrio pendente, & libertate, ab omni Dei praedeterminatione soluta, non potest Deus causari ut sint actus liberi in rerum natura,

Rutherford used a variety of scripture to support his position.[90] Of note are those scriptures that Rutherford used while providing his own commentary alongside. Commenting on Eph. 3:20, Rutherford concluded that since God's power exceeded the free requests and intentions of the saints, God's dominion must include the free acts of the will. Then, commenting on Rom. 11:13, Rutherford argued that since God's power could procure the free conversion of the Jews, then God's dominion must include the free acts of the will.[91]

5.3.2 Dominion and the *Scientia Media*

The Jesuit and Arminians sought to maintain a dimension of God's dominion while also granting a high measure of independence to the human free will. The means by which this was attained, as has been seen in previous chapters, was through a complex interplay of God's knowledge, will, and power. Returning to the example used above, God knows that under a certain set of circumstances (if Peter is tempted) he will sin. Summarizing his perspective on the Jesuit and Arminian position, Rutherford argued that the truth of this proposition was prior by nature (*prius natura*) to God's middle knowledge.[92] Prior by nature (*prius natura*), or sometimes priority of nature (*prioritas naturae*), was a term derived from Aristotle and employed by scholastic theologians to designate something prior in causality.[93] The proposition being prior by nature means that the truth of the proposition precedes any causal contribution of the divine will or the divine power. Such truths were objects of God's intuition, known by his middle knowledge.[94]

---

potius quam non sint, aut contra. Ergo stante scientia media & doctrina Arminiana, &c. non habet Deus Dominium in actus liberos." Rutherford, *Disputatio Scholastica*, 28.

90 Rutherford uses the following scripture: Eph 3:20; Jud 5:24; Rom 11:23, 14:4; John 4:4, 10:29; 1 Pet 1:5. Rutherford, *Disputatio Scholastica*, 29.

91 "Ephes 3.20. Cum exuperantia Deus potest omnia facere, supra ea quae petimus (Fidem ergo, liberosque perseverantiae actus quos indies sancti Deum orant, potest praestare) aut cogitamus, pro illa vi agenti in nobis…Rom 11.23. Potens est Deus eos rursus inferere, adeoque procurare liberam Judeorum conversionem." Rutherford, *Disputatio Scholastica*, 23.

92 "Ergo futuritionem habent prius natura, quam Deus eam cognoscat intuitu scientiae mediae. Ergo multo magis futuritionem habet, quam Deus decernat tales actus libere fore." Rutherford, *Disputatio Scholastica*, 30.

93 This should not be confused with the Scotist first and second instance of nature, which was also employed to discuss God's knowledge of future contingent events. For the general use of *prius natura* during sixteenth and seventeenth-century scholasticism, see: Altenstaig, "Prior," in *Theologicum complectens*, 262. Altenstaig distinguishes between seven different uses. The two most applicable to the above are of nature and causality.

94 Rutherford's characterization of the Jesuit and Arminian position, employing terms such as divine intuition and prior by nature in his description most likely means that he is using Suárez as the representative position. See: Ch. 3.3.2 of this study. Also, for Suárez's use of the term *prius natura*

Rutherford argued that if such is the case, then God no longer has any providential control over future contingent events such as the hypothetical repentance of the Tyreans upon seeing the miracles of Christ, the patience of Job following his travails, or the conversion of Peter when called. However, the Jesuits and Arminians argued that this was not so. They aimed to maintain God's dominion and providential control, while at the same time also safeguarding the independence of the human free will by conceiving of possible worlds with tightly ordered states of affairs. Returning again to Peter's temptation, God's middle knowledge is knowledge of what Peter would do under a certain set of circumstances. For example, there is a Possible World A, where the circumstances given in Peter's denial of Christ (Matt 26:69–75) (i.e. the location, the servant girl's questions, and Peter's fear) exist. This set of circumstances is part of a tightly ordered possible world where God knows it is true that if Peter is tempted, he will sin. God also knows, via his middle knowledge, of another Possible World B, where this set of circumstances does not exist. Perhaps Peter is never in the courtyard. Or if he is, perhaps he is never questioned by the servant girl. Thus, he is not afraid and never sins.[95] These two possible worlds can be represented as follows:

---

see Gracia's comments in: Jorge J. E. Gracia, "English-Latin Index," in *Suárez On Individuation. Metaphysical Disputation V: Individual Unity and Its Principle* (Milwaukee, WI: Marquette University Press, 1982), 251.

95 The Jesuit Hieronymus Fasolus demonstrates the importance of the circumstances to different outcomes, as well as God's power to change circumstances in the following: "Quia si Deus praescit, quod Petrus, si poneretur in tali occasione, tempore, cum aliis omnibus circumstantiis extrinsecis, & intrinsecis, negaret Christum; potest quidem simpliciter facere ut non neget, nimirum auferendo aliquam circumstantiam praevisam, v.g. timorem mortis, vel addendo aliam, v.g. maius lumen in intellectu, maiorem inclinationem in voluntate ad bonum confessionis Christi; tamen si nihil prorsus velit addere circumstantiis praevisis, & ex illis demere, est intelligibile, & manifestam contradictionem implicas, ut si sub talibus conditionibus praescit futuram negationem, possit vel ut sub iisdem omnino conditionibus non sit futura negationem, possit velle ut sub iisdem omnino conditionibus non sit futura negatio: neque enim Dei voluntas potest facere ut non sit verum quod verum esse praescit eius intellectus." Hieronymus Fasolus, *In primam partem summae d. thomae commentariorum tomus secundus* (Lyon: Andreae, Jacobi, & Matthaei Prost, 1629), 181.

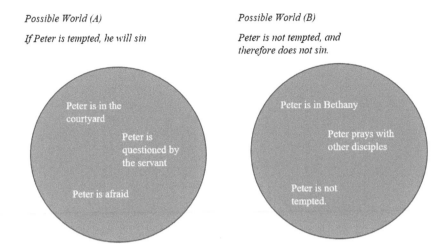

Possible World (A)

If Peter is tempted, he will sin

Peter is in the courtyard

Peter is questioned by the servant

Peter is afraid

Possible World (B)

Peter is not tempted, and therefore does not sin.

Peter is in Bethany

Peter prays with other disciples

Peter is not tempted.

Fig. 2   Possible Worlds with Ordered States of Affairs

God's providence and dominion are established, according to the Jesuits and Arminians, in that God can elect Possible World A and actualize it with an influx of his power. Peter's freedom is preserved in that God has foreseen what Peter's innate free will would choose given the order of things in Possible World A.

There is a third possible world that can be introduced. This can be called Possible World C. Possible World C shares all the same circumstances as Possible World A. Peter is in the courtyard during Christ's trial. Peter is also questioned by the servant girl. Perhaps, Peter is even fearful for his life. However, in Possible World C, Peter does not deny Christ.[96]

---

96 Rutherford makes this point in a variety of ways, but his summary is as follows: "Ergo reviviscit argumentum idem in eum ordinem, an in eum Deus habeat Dominium, quod non habeat sic demonstro. Quia Deus non potest non praesci re futuritionem illius ordinis qui de facto futurus est. Nam non potest non praescire omne futurum, nullum enim scibile (at hic ordo est juxta adversarios scibilis) effugere potest infinitam Dei cognitionem, & non potest praescire alios mundos possibiles at futuros, quia revera nunquam sunt futuri, ligatur itaque hic Dei scientia, at sic multo magis ligatur voluntas Dei, & perbit omne liberum Dei Dominium." Rutherford, *Disputatio Scholastica*, 31.

Possible World (C)

If Peter is tempted, he will not sin

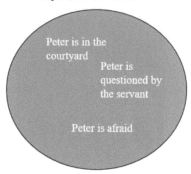

Fig. 3 An Example of a Possible World Not Known to God According to the Theory of Middle
Knowledge

The Jesuits argued that Possible World A and Possible World B are known to
God by virtue of his middle knowledge. These two possible worlds are prior in
nature both to God's middle knowledge as well as will, being antecedent to any
causal contribution of God. By virtue of this condition, they are known by God
as objects of his intuition. But God does not know Possible World C according to
his middle knowledge because there is no possible world where in this given set of
circumstances, Peter does not sin. God can therefore exercise his providence and
dominion in Possible Worlds A and B, but he can neither will Possible World C nor
apply his power to actualize it.[97]

The three worlds as they relate to God's dominion and providence can be sym-
bolized as follows:

97 Possible World C is still possible, in that it is logically possible for Peter to be tempted and not
sin. Therefore, the Jesuits would argue that such a world is known by God's natural knowledge.
Nevertheless, according to the above, God has not foreseen a world where, all circumstances being
requisite, Peter does not sin when tempted. Therefore, Possible World C is logically possible, but in
the Jesuit and Arminian scheme it can never be future.

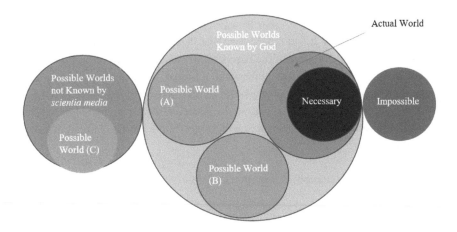

Fig. 4 God's Power in Relation to Necessary, Impossible, Possible, and Actual Worlds According to the Theory of Middle Knowledge

There are similarities and differences to the model depicting Rutherford's position above. Just as before, there are necessary states of affairs (i.e. *Deus est*). Also, there is a complementary yet mutually exclusive disc symbolizing impossible states of affairs. Whereas the disc in Rutherford's model simply said "possible," indicating a vast array of indeterminate propositions, here the possible is filled with tightly ordered states of affairs where circumstances produce specific outcomes. The worlds can be actualized by a determination of the divine will and an influx of God's power. Thus the actual world could be either Possible World A or B. Possible World C never could be, since there is no possible world where such circumstances produce such an outcome. Thus it is possible, but not an object of God's intuition and thus not known to him as a possibly future world.[98]

God's inability to actualize Possible World C is critical to Rutherford's main attack against the above. God is free to actualize Possible World A, where Peter is tempted and sins. He is free to actualize Possible World B, where Peter is not tempted and does not sin. But he is not free to actualize a world where Peter is tempted and does not sin. The causal relationship between Peter's temptation and his sin is a relationship that is antecedent to God's will. Therefore, God does not have dominion over the circumstances and their causal relationship to their

---

98 In his own remarks on Molina, Fredosso writes: "For instance, if He knows prevolitionally in CS (w) that Adam will sin if placed in *H*, then he cannot arrange things in such a way that Adam will be in *H* and yet not sin. For no world that includes this absolute future contingent is a member of the galaxy for CS (w). See Freddoso, "Introduction", 49.

effects.[99] Given that God is not free to actualize a world where Peter is tempted and does not sin, the question may be asked whether Peter is free in the moment of his own temptation. It is not necessary that Peter sin in such a way. God could actualize a world where none of the requisite circumstances for Peter's sin are met. Nevertheless, it could be argued that when tempted, Peter does sin by necessity since there is no possible world that could be actualized where he is tempted and does not sin. In Rutherford's estimation, the Jesuit and Arminian gambit to salvage God's dominion while preserving free will, subjects both God and the human will to fatal necessity.[100]

5.3.3 Modes of Dominion: Delegation or Subordination

Rutherford outlined two main approaches to the doctrine of God's dominion. One he associated with the Jesuits, and the other he referred to as his own position. The first is delegation or transfer, by which God delegates his dominion in the free acts of the will to human agents. The second approach is subordination, by which two powers, one superior and one subordinate, act jointly in such a way that the dominion of neither is threatened. These two approaches are outlined below.

The first position outlined by Rutherford is delegation or transfer of power. He relied upon the Spanish Jesuit Diego Ruiz de Montoya (1562–1632) to explain. At the time of writing, Ruiz was not in conflict with Rutherford but rather with the Spanish Dominican Domingo *Báñez*. Báñez argued that an aspect of God's dominion was the act of physical predetermination, by which the secondary cause of the created

---

99 "Ad *Fasolum* redeo. Neque, secundum tutores scientiae mediae potest Deus efficere ut Petrus non negaret Christum, si in tali occasione poneretur, auferendo circumstantias, quia illae circumstantiae, nempe, ingressus Petri in aulam, Ancillae exploratio, & Petri timor, sunt res mere contingentes ex arbitrio liberrimo Petri & Ancillae pendentes; ideoque futuritionem ab aeterno habuerunt antecedenter ad scientiam mediam, & sic antecedenter ad Dei liberum decretum, at impossibile est Deum in id dominari, & id efficere ut sit in natura, vel non sit, prout libere vult, quod futurum erat antecedenter ad liberam ipsius voluntatem; nam impossibile est me habere hodie dominium in actus meos liberos hesternos." Rutherford, *Disputatio Scholastica*, 32–33.

100 It might be argued that Peter is not under strict necessity, but hypothetical necessity, where the necessity is not absolute but contingent on a prior condition. In the case of Peter's sin, it is true that Peter is under a hypothetical necessity to sin based upon the prior condition that God actualizes a world where Peter is tempted and the requisite circumstances are met. However, what Rutherford is pointing out is *in any possible world where such circumstances are met Peter will sin.* Thus the proposition *if Peter is tempted (in such and such a way) he will sin* is true in any possible world. In this case, the necessity is no longer hypothetical but absolute. For more on hypothetical necessity, see "ex hypothesi" in: Muller, *Dictionary of Latin and Greek Theological Terms*, 112. For a definition of necessity in Reformed scholasticism see: van Asselt, Bac, and te Velde, *Reformed Thought on Freedom*, 33; For a definition of necessity in modern analytical philosophy see: Konyndyk, *Introductory Modal Logic*, 16.

will could not will an object unless God had first physically predetermined the will towards that act.[101] Ruiz understood Báñez's theory of physical predetermination as establishing theological fatalism, but that is not Ruiz's critique here.[102]

Rather, Ruiz's critique of Báñez's position was that, if God's dominion is truly absolute and independent, then he should be able to transfer his dominion in certain acts to other persons. By way of example, a landowner might be said to have dominion over all the land that he owns. Part of his dominion is that he has both power and authority to transfer his dominion to an heir or a friend. Ruiz's argued that if God cannot transfer his dominion in created acts of the will, then he does not truly have dominion over such acts.[103]

Rutherford had a few responses to the above. If one were to argue that God does not have dominion over the free acts of the will because it is not lawful for God to have dominion over the free acts of the will, then God cannot grant this dominion to created persons because it is not his to grant.[104] If however, one was to argue

---

101 Rutherford has used one of Ruiz's critiques of Báñez for this section of the Disputatio. "Did. Ruiz sibi sic objicit, & respondet. Definitur dominium propria cujusque facultas utendi re in omnes usus lege permissos, Quoniam igitur Deus est verus Dominus omnium causarum secundarum, utitur illis, quando, & quomodo vult, hoc autem non potest facere nisi Physice praedeterminet voluntatem ad suos actus." Ruiz quoted in: Rutherford, *Disputatio Scholastica*, 35. For the Ruiz quote, see: Ruiz, *Commentarii ac disputationes*, Disp. 49. Sect. 2.

102 For a more in-depth look at physical predetermination, Jesuit critiques of the same and Rutherford's own defense, the reader is referred to Ch. 7.2., of this study.

103 "Respondeo, ideo habet absolutum & independens dominium, quia potest dominium aliud se-cundarium in voluntatem creatam transferre, quod ligaretur praedeterminatione Physica, & ideo ligaretur plenitude dominii Dei, si non posset hoc transferre, non enim est perfectus fundi Domi-nus qui non possit dominium ejus & usum alteri persone concedere." Ruiz quoted in Rutherford, *Disputatio Scholastica*, 36. For the Ruiz quote, see Ruiz, *Commentarii Ac Disputationes De Scientia De Ideis, De Veritate Ac De Vita Dei: Ad primam partem Sancti Thomae*, Q 14 usque ad 18, Disp. 49. Sect. 2.

104 "Nam dominari in actum liberum, is dicitur primario & independenter, independentia liberi dominii in actus, penes quem est, ut potius sit velle, vel eligere, quam nolle & repudiare, At tale dominium, ex adversariis convenit creatae voluntati, non Deo, nisi cum aperta contradictione. Deus ergo non potest creaturae rationali dominium concedere, quod ipse non habet, imo quod ipsum habere involit contradictionem." Rutherford, *Disputatio Scholastica*, 36. An example of the position being critiqued by Rutherford can be found in Jacobus Arminius in "De Dominio Dei in creaturas, & praecipue in Hominem" in his "Articuli nonnulli perpendendi." Arminius defined dominion as a "communication of good to creatures" and stated its exercise must be "lawful and proper." There are a variety of limits placed on what is lawful and proper, but the most interesting statement comes at Thesis VI. "Deum de suo facere posse quicquid vult at non velle neque posse velle de suo facere quicquid secundum infinitam potentiam & absolutam de suo facere posset," Arminius, "De Dominio Dei," 953. Another example used by Rutherford in this section of the *Disputatio* comes from the Jesuit Theophile Raynaud (1583–1663), who argued that God did not properly have dominion to impede sin. See: Theophile Raynaud, *Theologica Naturalis, Sive Entis Increati Et Creati* (Leiden: Horatius Boisat & Georgii Remeus, 1665), Dist I. q. 3. Art. I. fig. 52.

as Ruiz does, that God has transferred his dominion in the free acts of the will to created persons, then God no longer has dominion in those contingent events that depend upon the free decisions of human wills. If God does not have dominion over such events, then Christians are deprived of a significant source of their hope, faith, consolation, and gratitude since they pray to God trusting he has both authority and power to effect a good outcome. However, if what Ruiz is saying is true, then God does not have dominion to effect a good outcome, thus the faith, hope, and prayers of Christians are in vain.[105]

Rutherford's own approach to the doctrine of God's dominion could be described as subordination. The concept is introduced through an objection from Ruiz. Citing commonly accepted juridical knowledge, Ruiz argued that dominion is properly understood as the right to administer one's own corporeal affairs. He raised the example of a wife seeking to distribute her property to heirs. He noted that the wife is not able to distribute her own property to heirs without the permission of her guardian or her husband, thus she cannot properly be said to have dominion over her own affairs. Rather than having dominion over her own affairs, she is in subjection or servitude to her husband. Ruiz argued that the doctrine of physical predetermination was like the example above. The human will may wish to administer its own affairs in a certain way, but cannot do so without God's permission. Thus, the human will does not have true dominion over its own affairs.[106]

Rutherford argued that this scenario could be turned back upon the Jesuits. If Ruiz was willing to concede that it is lawful and right for a guardian to have this kind of dominion over a woman's affairs, how much more lawful and proper would it be for God himself to have the same kind of dominion over his own creatures?[107] Rutherford was careful to point out that God's dominion does not function in the

---

105 "Nullum firmum spei, fiduciae, consolationis, patientiae, aut gratitudinis in Deum argumentum peti posset ex hisce locis, nisi penes Deum effect Dominium efficax actus liberi, ita ut possit, non obstante omni vi aut innata potentiae creatae voluntatis, procurare vel existentiam vel non existentiam omnium actuum liberorum." Rutherford, *Disputatio Scholastica*, 29.

106 "Si voluntas physice praedeterminetur a Deo, tum voluntas libera non habet dominium sui actus, nam (juridici dicunt) dominium est jus perfecte disponendi de re corporali nisi lege prohibeatur. Nemo diceret eum habere dominium pecuniae, cui talis esse relatio ad pecuniam, ut ex intrinseca sua quidditate postularet semper, non alio modo disponere de pecuniis, nisi quod, & sicut dominus ejus praescripserit, sic haeredum & uxor res suas in dominio non habent, quia absque tutoris & mariti consensu disponere non possunt res suas." Ruiz quoted in Rutherford, *Disputatio Scholastica*, 41.

107 "Hoc argumentum in adversarium retorqueri potest. Nam si voluntas creata tale habeat dominium, ut possit disponere de actu vel non actu, sicut is qui tutori non subest, potest res suas absque tutoris consensu disponere, negari non potest, quin Deo actus dominium longe majus & potentius conveniat, quam ipsi voluntati liberae, atqui Deo tale dominium in actus liberos non convenit, secundum dogmata adversariorum." Rutherford, *Disputatio Scholastica*, 41–2.

same way as the dominion of the guardian over the wife. Rather than servitude, where one power binds and restrains a lesser power, Rutherford suggested the paradigm of subordinate powers.[108]

Rutherford constructed his paradigm of superior and subordinate powers with an appeal to Bradwardine's *De Causa Dei*, Lib 2, Cap. 28., where he noted Bradwardine rightly said that "the will has dominion in its own acts, but this does not exclude superior power."[109] Bradwardine's own quote was taken from Thomas Aquinas's *Quaestiones Disputatae De Potentia Dei*, Q III, A. VII, an important text for the doctrine of physical premotion, which would not be fully articulated until the 16th century by Spanish Dominicans in their struggle with Molinism. In this section of Thomas's *De Potentia*, he asks "Whether God works in the operations of nature?" In keeping with the quaestio method, the question was answered in the negative so that objections to Thomas's own position could be treated first.[110]

The question was denied on various grounds. For the purposes of this discussion, focus is given to Thomas's remarks concerning the will and its dominion. Quoting from the apocryphal Book of Ecclesiasticus, Thomas noted that "God made man and left him in the hand of his own counsel. But he would not have left him, if he always operated in man's will." Furthermore, Thomas asserted that "the will is master of its own act. But this would not be the case if it were unable to act without God operating in it, for our will is not master of the divine operation."[111] It would seem that if God works in the operations of the will, then the acts of the will are no longer its own but rather God's. The negative implications for the freedom of the will are obvious, as Thomas made plain.[112]

---

108 This is not the only place Rutherford employs the language of subordinate powers. In his *Exercitationes*, the language of subordinate powers is used explicitly in his account of the freedom of the created will. Rutherford, *Exercitationes Apologeticae*, 500.

109 "Recte *Bradward. Voluntas* (inquit) *habet dominium sui actus, sed per hoc non excluditur superior potestas.*" Rutherford, *Disputatio Scholastica*, 41.

110 "Septimo quaeritur utrum Deus operetur in operatione naturae. Et videtur quod non." See: Thomas Aquinas, *Quaestiones Disputatae De Potentia Dei*, trans. The English Dominican Fathers (Westminster, Maryland: The Newman Press, 1952), Q. III, A. VII.

111 "Praeterea, Eccli. XI, 14, dicitur, quod Deus fecit hominem, et reliquit eum in manu consilii sui. Non autem reliquisset, si semper in voluntate operaretur. Ergo non operatur in voluntate operante. Praeterea, voluntas est domina sui actus. Hoc autem non esset, si agere non posset nisi Deo in ipsa operante; cum voluntas nostra non sit domina divinae operationis. Ergo Deus non operatur in voluntate nostra operante." Thomas Aquinas, *Quaestiones Disputatae De Potentia Dei*, Q. III, A. VII.

112 "Praeterea, liberum est quod causa sui est, ut dicitur in I Metaph. Quod ergo non potest agere nisi causa in ipso agente non est liberum in agendo. Sed voluntas nostra est libera in agendo. Ergo potest agere, nulla alia causa in ipsa operante: et sic idem quod prius." Thomas Aquinas, *Quaestiones Disputatae De Potentia Dei*, Q. III, A. VII.

However, according to Thomas, these objections were not true. Rather than depriving the fundamental freedom of the will, God's operations in human nature actually establish it. "God is not said to have left man in the hand of his counsel," said Thomas, "as though he did not operate in the will: but because he gave man's will dominion over its own act." Here, "dominion" means that the will is not necessarily determined to one act but has freedom to do the opposite. The human will is able to exercise dominion over its own act because God, who has dominion over all his creatures, has gifted such freedom to rational beings.[113] In this scheme, God's gift of dominion to the rational creature is necessarily prior to the exercise of this gift by the creature, which acts as a secondary cause. Hence the emphasis seems to be on causal, rather than temporal priority.[114]

As noted, Bradwardine's use of superior and subordinate powers to describe the relationship between God's sovereignty and human liberty is explicitly indebted to Thomas.[115] With Thomas, Bradwardine insisted that no creature can move unless it is first moved by a primary cause. God's causal activity as a prime mover is necessary for any activity of a creaturely, secondary cause in the actual world.[116] As Leff

---

113 "Ad duodecimum dicendum, quod Deus non dicitur hominem dereliquisse in manu consilii sui, quin in voluntate operetur; sed quia voluntati hominis dedit dominium sui actus, ut non esset obligata ad alteram partem contradictionis: quod quidem dominium naturae non dedit, cum per suam formam sit determinata ad unum." Thomas Aquinas, *Quaestiones Disputatae De Potentia Dei*, trans. The English Dominican Fathers (Westminster, Maryland: The Newman Press, 1952), Q. III, A. VII.

114 Scholars have noted the causal, rather than temporal priority of God as first cause in the doctrine of divine premotion. Though these scholars are discussing the sixteenth-century doctrine of premotion developed by Spanish Dominicans in the *controversy de auxiliis, the point nevertheless appears relevant in analyzing this section of Thomas's De Potentia. For remarks concerning the causal priority of God in the sixteenth-century doctrine of premotion, see: Thomas Osborne, "Thomist Premotion and Contemporary Philosophy of Religion," Nova et Vetera, 4, no. 3 (2006): 607–632; Davis S. Oderberg, "Divine Premotion," International Journal of Philosophy of Religion, 79, no. 3 (2016): 207–222.*

115 "Unde & sanctus Thomas in libro suo de potentia Dei, quaestione 20. Qua quaeritur, Utrum Deus operetur in omni operatione naturae, arguit isto modo; Voluntas est Domina sui actus: hoc autem non esset, si agere non posset, nisi Deo in ipsa operante, cum voluntas nostra non sit domina divinae operationis: ergo Deus non operatur in voluntate nostra operante. Et respondet hoc modo; Dicendum, quod voluntas dicitur habere dominium sui acts, non per exclusionem causae primae, sed causa prima non ita agit in voluntate, ut eam de necessitate ad unum determinet, sicut determinat naturam, & ideo determinatio actus relinquitur in potestare rationis & voluntatis." Bradwardine, *De Causa Dei, Lib 2. Cap. XXVIII, 569.

116 "Prima, Quod nihil potest quicquam movere sine Deo idem per se & proprie comovente. Secunda, Quod nihil potest quicquam movere ine Deo immediate idem movente. Tertia, quod nihil potest quicquam movere sine Deo idem movente immediatius alio motore quocunque. Quarta, Quod nulla propositio tribuens quodcunque creatum cuicunque causae secundae, est immediata simpliciter." Bradwardine, *De Causa Dei, Lib I, Cap. 4, 174.* For commentary see Gordon Leff, *Bradwardine and the Pelagians,* Cambridge Studies in Medieval Life & Thought New Series (Cambridge: Cambridge

noted, this is set within an explicitly participatory framework, where Bradwardine borrowed from Scripture, Patristic, and Neo-platonic sources alike.[117] An example of the relation between primary and secondary causes is that of the divine ideas. The ideas, originating in God's intellect, form the basis for creation. These same ideas, instantiated in creation, present themselves to the intellect and thus the intellect is set in motion as it apprehends the objects. The intellect, unable to exercise its powers without external stimuli, depends upon God as a prior cause.[118]

So far, Bradwardine was content to follow Thomas. Nevertheless, Bradwardine makes two significant departures from Thomas, both of which can plainly be traced to Scotus. The first significant departure regards God's knowledge of future contingent events. Whereas God knows himself necessarily, through his own essence, God knows the created world contingently by virtue of his will.[119] Explicitly following Scotus, Bradwardine argued that if God knew future contingent events based upon his knowledge of what a human would will, then God's knowledge would be dependent upon a created entity. Furthermore, God's will would be determined to one part by the will of the creature. Denying that God is either dependent upon or determined by created entities, Bradwardine insisted that God knows future contingent events because he freely willed them.[120] The implications of Bradwardine's position

---

University Press, 1957), 48–51; H.A. Oberman, *Archbishop Thomas Bradwardine: A Fourteenth Century Augustinian* (Drukkerij En Uitgever-Maatschappij v/h Kemink 7 Zoon N.V.: Utrecht, 1957), 77.

117 Leff, 49–50.

118 "Ecce quod Deus est virtus motiva quasi artifex; & ars ipsa, & intellectus est organum motum ab eo, quod & testantur multae Autoritates Philosophicae & Theologicae allegatae capitulo 4. Primi." Bradwardine, *De Causa Dei*, Lib 2. Cap. XX, 541.

119 "Ostenso igitur quod Deus scit omnia scibilia scientia incomplexa, non per scita posteriora, sed per suam claram essentiam, sibi omnia distinctissime praesentem, nunnc restat consequenter ostendere quomodo Deus scit omnia scibilia complexa: Pro quo est primo sciendum, quod scibilia complexa & vera sunt duplicia: quaedam enim naturaliter praecedunt voluntatem divinam, & quaedam eam naturaliter subsequuntur. Praecedit eam naturaliter Deum esse, Deum esse aeternum, Deum esse omnipotentem, & similia: Non enim quia Deus vult sic esse, ideo sic est, sed potius e contrario. Sequuntur autem eam mundem esse, quamlibet creaturam esse & universaliter omnia illa vera complexa, quorum veritas causatur & pendet ab ipsa. Illa igitur ver complexa quae voluntatem divinam praecedunt, scit Deus per suam solam essentiam, sicut alia vera incomplexa, sicut potest cognosci ex proxim huius scriptis: Illa vero quae voluntatem eius sequuntur, non scit Deus per illa complexa, neque per aliquid aliud voluntate eius semota, sed per suam voluntatem, vel per suam substantiam cum sua voluntate, ita quod ad scientiam eius complexam est sua voluntas necessario prius naturaliter requisita." Bradwardine, *De Causa Dei*, Lib I. Cap. XVIII, 221; Leff, 37.

120 "Item haec ultima ratio, & conclusio principalis pater per Iohannem Scotum super 2. Sentent. Distinct. 37. Quaest. 2. Redarguentem opinantes quod voluntas creata sit causa totalis sui velle sine Deo coagente, per hoc, quod si sic esset, Deus non esset naturaliter praescius futurorum, quia non habet scientiam de futuris contingentibus, nisi quia certitudinaliter novit determinationem voluntatis suae respectu eorum; quae voluntas est immutabilis, & impotentialis. Sed si voluntas

disturb Leff, who described God's control over his creatures as "far-reaching" and "intense."[121]

Because the language of superior and subordinate powers is unfolded within a system that lays heavy emphasis upon the divine will, Leff argued that Bradwardine's position is determinist to the point where the activity of the human will is reduced to nothing more than a formality following God's irrepressible decrees.[122] But Bradwardine's second departure from Thomas safeguarded the integrity of the human will from the worst implications of Leff's interpretation.[123] Perhaps sensitive to the specter of fatal theological determinism in a heavily voluntaristic system, Bradwardine appealed to Scotus's important passage from the *Ordinatio* 2.37.2, to safeguard the freedom of the will as a subordinate power.

As Frank explains, the basic idea set forth in the *Ordinatio* 2.37.2 is that two causes concur in the causation of a single effect. Neither cause is sufficient, in and of itself. Rather, both must act together.[124] Causes may be accidentally ordered or essentially ordered. Accidentally ordered causes exercise powers of the same sort, whereas essentially ordered causes exercise powers of a different sort. An example of an accidentally ordered cause used by Scotus is that of two mules pulling a cart. The two mules exercise power of the same sort, though their union as a team pulling the cart represents an accidental difference in quantity.[125] An essentially ordered cause, on the other hand, is the union of two causal powers that each contribute powers of a different nature. Taking another example used by Scotus, the union of man and woman as co-causes to produce a child represents two generative powers each with unique contributions.[126] This is the sort of causal union that represents the co-causes of God and the human will. One more important clarification may be made. Scotus held that in essentially ordered causes, one may be prior and the other posterior, with the prior being more superior and more perfect because it gives more. Though the superior cause is more perfect and even can be said to contribute the lion's share of the causal load, it nevertheless remains insufficient to bring about the total causal effect.[127]

---

creata sit causa totalis sui velle, & ipsa se habet contingenter ad illud velle, ergo quantumcunque ponatur voluntas divina determinat ad unam partem eorum quae dependent a voluntate creata, ipsa potest aliter velle, & ita non sequitur certitudo ex cognitione determinationis voluntatis divinae." Bradwardine, *De Causa Dei*, Lib I. Cap. XVIII, 223.

121 Leff, 38.

122 Leff, 98.

123 For a critique of Leff's position along different lines, see Oberman, 77–94.

124 William Frank, "Duns Scotus on Autonomous Freedom and Divine Co-Causality," *Medieval Philosophy and Theology* 2 (1992), 152.

125 Frank, "Duns Scotus on Autonomous Freedom and Divine Co-Causality," 152–3.

126 Frank, 153–6.

127 Frank, 154.

Because Leff detected a participatory framework in Bradwardine, he described the relationship between superior and subordinate powers as "divine participation." Leff's commitment to participation as an interpretive framework drove a great deal of his deterministic critique of Bradwardine. But as Oberman noted, "participation" is not the language Bradwardine himself used to describe the relationship between these two powers.[128] Rather, after several explicit nods to Scotus, Bradwardine described the causal contributions of the divine and human, where God and the human will act jointly as *co-effectors*.[129] In Oberman's words, "neither man alone — autonomy — nor God alone — heteronomy — finally decides the movement of the will."[130] Though Bradwardine was committed to a strong voluntarism, the deterministic consequences are offset by Bradwardine's Scotistic doctrine of *co-efficiency*.[131]

Rutherford's appropriation of the language of superior and subordinate causes ought to be understood both within a voluntaristic framework, as well as within the paradigm of co-causality, or *co-efficiency*, outlined above. Rutherford used his own example taken from antiquity, that being the king and the legate. This example neatly fits within the context of Bradwardine's remarks above concerning superior and inferior powers. The Roman *legatus* was a commander of a legion. The *legatus* had full command over all the affairs of his legion thus establishing the power of his dominion. And while maintaining full dominion over his legion, the dominion of the *legatus* was initially established by, and thus subordinate to that of the king.[132] Quoting Bradwardine, Rutherford noted that "the will has dominion of its own acts, but this does not exclude superior powers."[133] And while the will's dominion over its own acts does not exclude superior powers it is important to note that superior powers do not threaten the dominion of subordinate powers. The relationship between the two powers is not like the wife and her husband in Ruiz's example, where the guardian has power to bind, restrain, or compel the wife to do things she may not wish to do. In Rutherford's understanding of God's dominion and the dominion of the human free will, the similarity with the Scotist conception of essentially ordered co-causality safeguarded the dominion of the created human

---

128 Oberman, 77, fn 1.

129 "Ergo Deus est ibi necessarius coeffector, scilicet coeffector cum voluntate creata necessario requisitus." Bradwardine, *De Causa Dei*, Lib II.. Cap. XX, 540.

130 Oberman, 81.

131 The language of "co-effector" is Bradwardine's own. Nevertheless, Oberman is credited with naming it the "doctrine of coefficiency." Oberman, 77.

132 "The Tribunus," in *A Dictionary of Greek and Roman Antiquities*, ed. William Smith, William Wayte, and G.E. Marindin (Third, London: John Murray, 1901), 298.

133 "*Voluntas* (inquit) habet dominium sui actus, sed per hoc non excluditur superior potestas." Bradwardine quoted in: Rutherford, *Disputatio Scholastica*, 42. For the Bradwardine quote, see: Bradwardine, *De causa Dei*, Lib. 2, Q. 28.

will over its own acts while rendering an account of their co-causality.[134] Two causal powers, the independent and superior divine power, and the subordinate and dependent human power, each of a different nature, make contributions that jointly bring about an effect.[135] This account of dominion avoids the fatalistic implications that Ruiz sought to burden it with, while at the same time placing the freedom of the created will on the firm foundation of God's dominion as a superior cause.[136]

5.4 Summary

Rutherford's doctrine of God's power is set forward along lines that should be familiar by now. There is a natural, pre-volitional account of God's power that he calls omnipotence. There is also a free, post-volitional exercise of God's power that he terms sovereignty. As was discussed in this chapter, the distinction has strong resonances with the medieval distinction of God's *potentia absoluta* and God's *potentia ordinata*.

Rutherford employs God's omnipotence as a way to discuss the innumerable possibilities that exist by virtue of his being and power. These possibilities could be created entities such as animate or inanimate objects. Such entities could also be states of affairs that could be actualized by an influx of God's power, if God determined that such should be the case. Of critical importance to Rutherford's account of both divine and human freedom, is that the extreme terms that are combined to propositionally represent possible states of affairs are indeterminate prior to the act of divine willing. Because such are indeterminate, God's will is not conditioned by co-existing entities that could conceivably constrain God's

---

134 "At dominia subordinata, uti Regis, & legati, possunt esse penes duos; neque tale est voluntatis creatae dominium, quale est haeredum & uxorum, hi enim saepe aliter vellent disponere res suas, quam de facto disponunt, si liceret per tutores & maritum qui imperio ipsos cohibent: At praedeterminatio physica non ligat aut cohibet voluntatem, aut aliorsum impellit, quam ipsa vult, sed voluntatem, sese suo libero exercitio ligantem, & moventem, connaturali ductu movet in illud ipsum in quod ipsa sese agit & determinat." Rutherford, *Disputatio Scholastica*, 42.

135 Richard Baxter critiqued the position of Twisse and Rutherford, who he traced to Bradwardine, as making God the total and immediate cause of sin. In rejecting the position of these, Baxter found recourse in the language of *pars causae*, finding the language of "partial cause," an improper description. It seems that Baxter appears to have overlooked aspects of co-causality found in Bradwardine and Rutherford, and thus the power of his critiques are greatly reduced. See Richard Baxter, *Catholik Theologie: Plain Pure, Peaceable: For the Pacificatino of the Dogmatical Word-Warriors* (London: The Prince's Arms, 1675), 29, 89, 90.

136 The nature of this joint action is given thorough treatment in Chapter 7.4 of this study.

will or power. This is but one way God's absolute independence and freedom are emphasized in such discussions.

The divine independence and freedom is also emphasized in certain discussions pertaining to God's power as it relates to modalities of being. The necessary and the impossible are not so in and of themselves but are grounded in God's being. Modal properties such as possibility and contingency are established by God's omnipotence. Futurition and actuality are grounded in acts of God's knowledge, will, and power. Thus, the modal properties of all being are ultimately understood only with reference to God's own self. This underscores the independence and freedom of God, as well as the absolute dependence of the created order. This is particularly shown with reference to the future and actual created order, which depends upon God's sovereign decree and willing contribution of power for its real existence.

Certain Arminian and Jesuit theologians argued that the above accounting of God's power and possible beings raised problems associated with theological fatalism. They proposed an alternate understanding of God's dominion consistent with their account of God's knowledge in the *scientia media*. But as was shown, Rutherford demonstrated such new accounts of God's dominion subjected both God and the human agent to a new fatal necessity. Since certain states of affairs could not exist in any possible world, God's freedom is constrained as is the freedom of the human will.

Rutherford's own account of God's dominion rested upon an understanding of superior and subordinate powers, a concept that strongly resembled Scotus's doctrine of co-causality. According to this, the superior power and the subordinate power both retain dominion over their own acts. They jointly act to produce a common effect, preserving the freedom of each. Rutherford drew on an example from antiquity, this being the king and the legate. Rutherford's account of these two powers avoids the fatalistic problems associated with imposing certain states of affairs upon God's providence while rendering a sensible account of both the divine and human dominion over their own acts.

6. Creation and God's Providence

Providence maketh use of men and devils, for the refining of all the vessels of God's house, small and great: and for doing of two great works at once in you both for smoothing a stone, to make it take bond with Christ, in Jerusalem's wall; and for witnessing to the glory of this reproached and borne-down gospel, which cannot die, though hell were made a grave about it.[1]

Having treated God's being, knowledge, will, and power in the previous chapters, over the next two chapters we are prepared to enter an investigation of Rutherford's doctrine of divine providence. Rutherford defined divine providence as an "act or entelechy" of God's intellect, will, and power.[2] Thus the doctrines treated in the preceding chapters form the necessary foundation from which this analysis will proceed.

The object of God's providence is creation. Therefore this chapter will begin with a survey of Rutherford's doctrine of creation, with particular attention paid to creation as a dependent entity. From here Rutherford's scholastic definition of providence from his *Disputatio* will be outlined and analyzed. Having laid this foundation, two great controversies of the doctrine of providence will be examined. First, Rutherford's understanding of providence and the presence of evil will be analyzed. Following this section, providence and the problem of fatal necessity will be addressed. These discussions will set the stage for the final chapter, an in depth look at Rutherford's understanding of God's providence and human liberty.

6.1 Creation

6.1.1 An Overview of Rutherford's Doctrine

There is no dedicated scholastic treatment of the doctrine of creation in Rutherford's works.[3] He passes by the doctrine without treatment in his *Examen Arminianismi.*

---

1 Rutherford, *Joshua Redivivus*, 370.

2 "Providentia est actus sive εντελεχεια Dei…non est autem actus solius intellectus, sed & voluntatis & potentiae…" Rutherford, *Disputatio Scholastica*, 2.

3 The most extensive treatment thus far of Rutherford's doctrines of creation and providence may be found in the unpublished dissertation of Kim, "Time and Eternity," 208–86. Richard deals with the doctrine of creation tangentially to argue his case for Rutherford's moderate supralapsarianism couched in infralapsarian terminology. See: Guy Richard, "Samuel Rutherford's Supralapsarianism

The doctrine is a poor fit for the subject matter of the *Exercitationes*, thus also goes untreated. In the *Disputatio*, Rutherford briefly mentions creation as necessary to construct a scholastic definition of providence, but he offers no direct treatment comparable to what might be found in other works of scholastic theology.[4] Though there is no direct scholastic treatment of the doctrine of creation, there are indirect treatments to be found in the *Disquisitiones Metaphysicae*.[5]

Rather than being found in his works of scholastic theology, Rutherford's most focused comments on the doctrine of creation are found in his *Ane Catachisme*.[6] The comments are brief and straightforward, as would be expected from a catechetical treatment. Rutherford's comments on the creation of the world are Trinitarian, affirming creation by God the Father through the Son and Spirit.[7] In keeping with the biblical account and the traditional interpretation of the relevant texts, Rutherford states that creation was made "of nothing."[8] In a more scholastic setting, creation "ex nihilo" may target the Aristotelean concept of the necessary eternality of the world as well as pantheistic suggestions that would fail to maintain the Creator/creation distinction.[9] Rutherford exhibits a vested interest in guarding against both elsewhere in his writings but does not mention these in the *Ane Catachisme*.[10] Finally, Rutherford asserts that the purpose of creation is for God's "owne glorie."[11]

Revealed: A Key to The Lapsarian Position of the Westminster Confession of Faith?" *Scottish Journal of Theology* 59 (2006): 27–44. Fergusson draws attention to Rutherford's doctrine of creation, but again only tangentially. Fergusson's real target is Rutherford's doctrine of the divine decrees. See: Fergusson, "Predestination: A Scottish Perspective," 465–6.

4 See: Rutherford, *Disputatio Scholastica*, 2.

5 The *Disquisitiones Metaphysicae* deals indirectly with the doctrine of creation by examining such metaphysical questions as "Whether God is the ruling cause of all being and non-being" (QII), "Whether God is the Origin and Cause of all possible and impossible things" (Q III), among others. See Rutherford, *Disputatio Scholastica*, 532–38.

6 See: Rutherford, "Ane Catachisme," 164.

7 Rutherford, 164.

8 Rutherford, 164.

9 See T. Theo Pleizier and Maarten Wisse, "As the Philosopher Says" in *Introduction to Reformed Scholasticism*, ed. Willem J. Van Asselt et. al., Reformed Historical-Theological Studies (Grand Rapids, MI: Reformation Heritage Books, 2011), 36–8; Andreas J. Beck, "God, Creation and Providence in Post-Reformation Reformed Theology," in *The Oxford Handbook of Early Modern Theology, 1600–1800*, ed. Richard A. Muller and A.G. Roeber Ulrich L. Lehner (Oxford: Oxford University Press, 2016), 205–7; and Robert D. Preus, *The Theology of Post-Reformation Lutheranism: A Study of Theological Prolegomena* (St. Louis: Concordia Publishing House, 1972), 169–72.

10 See for example: Rutherford, *Disputatio Scholastica*, 557–9.

11 Rutherford, "Ane Catachisme," 164.

6.1.2 Creation and the Decrees

There are two aspects of Rutherford's doctrine of creation that deserve further comment. The first is his doctrine of creation as it relates to the order of the decrees. The second is the semantic content of the term "nothing" as it relates to God's act of creation. Concerning the first aspect, Rutherford wrote:

Q. How bringeth God his decrees to pass?
A. By three works — the creatione, the government of the world, and the redemption of mankynd.[12]

In the above, the specific doctrinal content of "decrees" is the double decree of salvation and reprobation. This is made plain in the previous section of the catechism, where Rutherford asked:

Q. Quhat decrees hes God concerning mankynd?
A. Two, the decrees of electione and reprobatione.[13]

Rutherford's ordering of the decrees, placing the decree of salvation and reprobation ahead of creation, place him firmly within the supralapsarian tradition.[14]

Objections to supralapsarianism are numerous, but there are two in particular worth noting regarding the doctrine of creation. The first objection is that a supralapsarian ordering of the decrees is opposed to the act of creation, inasmuch as the act of creation is assumed to be a communication of good to creatures. There are sixteenth and seventeenth century scholastic examples of this objection, as well as many modern examples.[15] The second objection is that a supralapsarian ordering of the decrees means that God's double decree of election and reprobation has, as its object, non-beings. Therefore it is non-sensical. God is effectively decreeing, as

---

12 Rutherford, 164.

13 Rutherford, "Ane Catachisme," 163.

14 Rutherford's supralapsarianism has been well documented. See Bell, *Calvin and Scottish Theology,* 70–84 and 465; Coffey, *Politics, Religion and the British Revolutions,* 127–8 and 205–7. More recently Richard has offered a reevaluation of Rutherford's supralapsarianism, rightly noting that "Rutherford has no dogmatic preoccupation with supralapsarianism or with decrees in general." Richard characterizes Rutherford's supralapsarianism as "surprisingly moderate," see: Richard, "Samuel Rutherford's Supralapsarianism Revealed," 28–29.

15 For sixteenth and seventeenth-century examples familiar to Rutherford, see: Arminius, "*Disputationes Privata*" in *Opera Theologica,* 364–366; Jackson, *A Treatise on the Divine Essence and Attributes,* 345. For a modern critique of supralapsarianism as being antithetical to the goodness of creation see: Fergusson, "Predestination: A Scottish Perspective," 465–66.

the objection goes, to save and damn nothing. Both objections were the subject of serious debates during Rutherford's lifetime.[16]

In regards to the first objection, that a supralapsarian ordering of the decrees is opposed to the act of creation, there are a few things that may be said. First, the objection depends upon the notion that the goal of creation is a communication of the good to creatures. This was certainly how it was described by Jacobus Arminius in his *Disputationes Privatae XXIV*. "That which is called the end (of creation)," wrote Arminius, "is goodness of the creatures themselves, and especially man, to which more so than the other creatures, are rendered to him (God) as useful, in accordance with the institution of divine creation."[17] Muller has argued that in the above, Arminius is demonstrating a theological tendency to circumscribe God's power. By defining the goal as the good of creatures (rather than the glory of God) as well as defining the goodness of creatures as their usefulness to God, Muller argues that Arminius creates space for a creature's independence. The point is further underscored by the notion that God is in some way dependent upon creatures because the good communicated to creatures is rendered back to God as useful.[18] It has been demonstrated in previous chapters that Rutherford exhibits the theological instinct to preserve the independence of God, and herein is no different. God's goal in creation is self-referential, being his own glory.[19] Furthermore, the supralapsarian nature of the ordering of the decrees solidifies his absolute independence, since he is not even dependent upon the object of the decree being an entity.[20]

Rutherford did not believe that God's independence exhibited in the supralapsarian scheme was opposed to a communication of some goodness to all creatures. In his *Ane Catachisme* Rutherford taught that though the reprobate are deprived of the

---

16 The object of the decree was a contentious issue in sixteenth and seventeenth-century theology born from philosophical objections sometimes described as "atheistical." Relevant objections include "ex nihilo tamen nihil fieri" as well as "omni potentiae activae respondere passivam." Some Jesuit and Arminian theologians resolved this dilemma by qualifying the term "nihil" in order to lend it a sense of objectivity in order to resolve both objections. For examples, see Simon Episcopius, *Opera theologica* (Amsterdam: Ioannis Blaen, 1650). Lib IV, Sectio III, 346; Jackson, *A Treatise on the Divine Essence and Attributes*, 31–41.

17 "Finis, qui cui dicitur, est bonum ipsarum creaturarum, & presertim hominis, ad quem plereque alia creaturae, velut ipsi utiles, referuntur, juxa institutionem creationis divinae." Arminius, "Disputationes Privata XXIV, ix," in *Opera Theologica*, 365.

18 Muller, *God, Creation, and Providence in the Thought of Jacob Arminius*, 230.

19 Rutherford, "Ane Catachisme," 164.

20 Rather than God being dependent upon an entity for creation, even the nothingness of non-being is dependent upon God for its ontological status as nothing. Rutherford argued that non-being was extrinsic in relation to the first being, God himself. The God of Rutherford's theology is radically independent, and even those things that are not are just as radically dependent upon him for their ontological status. See *Disputatio Scholastica*, 532–8.

particular goodness of efficacious grace, they are nevertheless given an abundant communication of goodness. In creation, God furnishes both elect and reprobate alike with created being as well as everything needed to sustain themselves.[21] In striking language, Rutherford compared the reprobate to "cursed children" in God's "verie arms" that "strike their mother's face evin as shee hes thim in hir armes."[22] According to Rutherford, God is continually communicating much goodness to all of creation, even to those that rebel against him. In a separate work, *Christ Dying, and Drawing Sinners to Himself*, Rutherford remarked that even those parts of creation who are condemned to perish because of sin continue to participate in a communication of divine goodness. This is a result of the "courtesy and freenes of mediatory grace, that the system and body of creation…should continue and subsist in being and beauty."[23]

Though Rutherford never stated it explicitly, this assertion, that even those creatures destined to perish still participate in the goodness of God, may further underscore God's independence and the radical dependence of his creatures. After all, it is the freeness of grace that works independently of the creature, which can ensure the ongoing revelation of divine beauty even in corrupted and rebellious creatures.

6.1.3 Creatio Ex Nihilo

One final aspect of Rutherford's doctrine of creation that deserves further comment is his understanding of the term "nothing" as it relates to creation *ex nihilo*. Rutherford's affirmation that God made all things "of nothing," is hardly exceptional. Nevertheless, his understanding of the term does distinguish him from some of his Arminian and Jesuit polemical opponents. In the *Examen*, Rutherford summarizes an objection found in Simon Episcopius's (1583–1643) *Apologia Pro Confessione Sive Declaratio*.[24] Rutherford's summary is as follows:

---

21 Rutherford, "Ane Catachisme," 164.
22 Rutherford, 168.
23 Samuel Rutherford, *Christ Dying, and Drawing Sinners to Himself*, vi.
24 Rutherford is referencing the following objection: "Hoc est quod volunt Remonstrantes; Calvinum et Doctores Orthodoxos, quos vocat, statuere, decretum absolutae praedestinationis, quod est decretum de Fine, id est, vita aut morte hominum aeterna, praecessisse non temporalem decreti illius executionem, id est creationem, uti inepte Censor Remonstrantium verba capit…sed decretum creandi homines: Eo ipso enim everti dicunt naturalem rerum ordinem. Ratio manifesta est. Sic enim statuitur Deus praedestinasse ad aeternam vitam & ad aeternam mortem, non dico id quod nondum erat, sed id quod a Deo ipso, non poterat considerari ut ens: Quicquid enim consideratur ut ens, sive existens, id supponit necessario decretum creationis, quia solius creationis terminus ad quem, est entitas, & decreti creandi terminus est conceptio entitatis." Episcopius, *Apologia pro confessione declaratione sententiae eorum, qui in foederato belgio vocantur remonstrantes, super praecipuis articulis religionis christianae. contra censuram quatuor professorum leidensium*, 67.

It is asked whether we don't invert the natural order of things, because we establish people who are to be created (and not yet created), as objects of predestination; who God thus establishes to glory as non-beings (non-ens)?[25]

The thinking behind Episcopius's objection, summarized above by Rutherford, is that God must first decree created being so that his decrees of salvation and reprobation respectively may have an object. According to this objection the supralapsarian order of decrees falls upon a non-object. Can God consider non-being as an object of his double decree? Episcopius's answer is a firm no. God is incapable of considering a non-being as an object of a decree. In order that the decree of salvation might have an object, God must first issue the decree of creation. But if God cannot issue a decree without an object, how then is he able to issue a decree of creation *ex nihilo*?

Episcopius navigated this difficulty by arguing that the decree of creation has the latent potency for being possessed by the *nihil* itself as its object. Under a section titled "Responses to the Objection of Creation *Ex Nihilo*," Episcopius raised two objections. "From nothing comes nothing, and all active potency must correspond to passive potency."[26] The first objection is easy enough to understand. To use a simple illustration, if a block of wood is potentially a statue, then the skill of the sculptor can produce the statue. But if there is no block of wood, there can be no statue.[27]

The second objection pertains to the relationship between active and passive potencies. For the purposes of this particular objection, it is enough to say that active potency refers to the capacity to bring about an effect and passive potency refers to the capacity to be effected.[28] In the *Metaphysics*, Aristotle held that there was a relation between active and passive potencies. He wrote, "That which is capable of heating [active potency] is related to that which is capable of being heated [passive potency], because it can heat it."[29] When this is applied to creation *ex nihilo*, the

---

25 "Quaeritur, An ideo naturalem ordinem non invertamus, quia statuimus objectum praedestinationi hominem creandum & nondum creatum; qui Deus sic statuit ad gloriam non-ens?" Rutherford, *Examen Arminianismi*, 271–2.

26 The first objection is principally attributed to Parmenides. See: Robin Waterfield, *The First Philosophers: The Presocratics and Sophists* (Oxford: Oxford University Press, 2000), 49–69; G. S. Kirk, J. E. Raven, and Malcolm Schofield, *The Presocratic Philosophers: A Critical History with a Selection of Texts*, 2nd ed. (Cambridge: Cambridge University Press, 1983), 247–50.

27 The sculptor and the sculpture is a simple illustration of a point made by Episcopius that finite beings are limited by their capacity. The *nihil* has no capacity and is thus ultimately limited. See: Episcopius, *Opera theologica, institutiones theolgica*, Lib IV, Sectio III, 346.

28 Feser, *Scholastic Metaphysics*, 39.

29 *Metaphysics* 1021a15–25. The translation is taken from "Metaphysics," in Aristotle, *The Complete Works of Aristotle: The Revised Oxford Translation*, ed. Jonathan Barnes, Bollingen Series (Princeton, NJ: Princeton University Press, 1984), 2:1612.

problem that arises is obvious. To return to the example above, it is easy to see how the sculptor is capable of sculpting and the block of wood capable of being sculpted. So too is it easy to see that God is capable of creating. But how can one say that the *nihil* is capable of creation? The statement is non-sensical. Therein lies the problem. With creation *ex nihilo*, there seems to be no relation between the active and passive potencies.[30]

Episcopius responded to this dilemma by arguing that in creation, active potency does not have to correspond to passive potency, but rather only to the objective potency established upon the *nihil's* non-contradiction to being. "It is not contradictory," he wrote, "that after nothing may be something, as it is not contradictory that after night, day comes about."[31] This last example gives the interpreter a clearer picture of how Episcopius conceives of the *nihil*. It is, as Muller has noted, "not a *nihil absolutum,* or *nihil negativum,* but rather a *nihil privativum* or latent potency for being."[32] Just as darkness was understood as a privation of light, so did Episcopius understand the *nihil* as a privation of being. This privation meant that the *nihil* does hold, as Episcopius suggested, an intrinsic objective potency.[33]

This is the theological and philosophical basis from which Episcopius argued that the decree of creation does not have non-being as its object. Its object is the latent potency of the *nihil*. This is also his resolution to the problem of the relation between active and passive potency. The active potency of the Creator has a relation to the passive potency of the dormant creatability of the *nihil*.[34] In the *Examen,* Rutherford's remarks are brief, though as will be seen he has extended comments on a similar issue in the *Disputatio*. In the *Examen,* Rutherford's two responses to

---

30 The objection is stated and resolved by: Thomas in the *Summa Theologiae* I, q 45, a 1. For useful comments on this section of the *Summa* see: Reginald Garrigou-Lagrange, *Reality: A Synthesis of Thomistic Thought* (Lexington: Ex Fontibus, 2012), 32–6.

31 "Non enim repugnant nihilo ut post aillud fiat aliquid, sicut non repugnant nocti ut post eam dies fiat." Episcopius, *Opera Theologica*, Lib IV, Sectio III, 346.

32 Muller, *God, Creation, and Providence in the Thought of Jacob Arminius,* 219–20.

33 "Hujusmodi potentiam objectivam in nihilo ponere nihil vetat." Episcopius, *Opera Theologica*, Lib IV, Sectio III, 346.

34 Garrigou-Lagrange describes the Suárezian approach to potency as "a force, a virtual act, merely impeded in its activity, as for example, the restrained force of a spring." Is the analogy of "the restrained force of a spring" appropriate for Episcopius's understanding of the passive potency of the *nihil*? Muller has argued, following Courtine, that Jacobus Arminius, Conrad Vorstius, and Simon Episcopius were heavily influenced by the metaphysics of Suárez. See Muller, *God, Creation, and Providence in the Thought of Jacobus Arminius,* 215–20; Jean-Francois Courtine, "Le Projet Suárezien De La Métaphysique," *Archives de Philosophie* 42, no. 2 (1979): 235–74. Nevertheless, the analogy may be too strong. Rather than potency waiting to be released, Episcopius's understanding of potency as it relates to the *nihil* is more of a vacuum with the capacity to be filled. Either way, there is a clear pre-existing objective, passive potency that the active potency of God can relate to. See Garrigou-Lagrange, *Reality: A Synthesis of Thomistic Thought,* 32.

this objection share similar logic. God decreed to give humankind being. Therefore the object of the decree to create humankind was non-being. God makes all things according to himself, the implication being he does not need an object, such as the latent potency of Episcopius's *nihil* in order to effect his will.[35] In the same vein, God's decree to create the world clearly has non-being as its object. That God is able to bring being out of non-being is to God's glory.[36] In these brief remarks, Rutherford asserts both God's absolute independence while also denying the independent nature of the latent potency of Episcopius's *nihil*. This is a familiar theme in the polemics seen thus far.

Rutherford has extended remarks on a similar issue in his *Disquisitiones Metaphysicae*, where he insisted that "God makes everything out of nothing, not out of a nothing of existence but of essence."[37] Here Rutherford explicitly denied the philosophical doctrine of essentialism, often attributed to Henry of Ghent (1217–1293), which held that though the existence of beings is contingent and brought about in time, the essence of beings are intrinsically necessary and eternal.[38] The similarities between Henry's position and the latent potency of Episcopius, outlined above, are tangible.[39]

Rutherford raised the doctrine of essentialism in order to critique the objectivity of potential being, which he saw a sophisticated portrayal of in both Episcopius as well as Suárez.[40] Rutherford's main target here is on Suárez's understanding of what

---

35 "Quia Deus omnia fecit propter seipsum. Ergo, decernit dare esse homini, ut ipse glorificetur." Rutherford, *Examen Arminianismi*, 272.

36 "Quia quaeritur, quo sine Deus decrevit creare mundum, ab aeterno? Nam mundus ab aeterno erat non-ens. Certe, ut ipse glorificaretur. Ergo, Deus decrevit non-entia ad gloriam suam." Rutherford, *Examen Arminianismi*, 272.

37 "Deus condidit omnia ex nihilo, non ex nihilo existentiae, sed essentiae." Rutherford, *Disputatio Scholastica*, 557.

38 Whether or not this doctrine is rightly attributed to Henry is subject to some debate. See: John F. Wippel, "The Reality of Nonexisting Possibilities According to Thomas Aquinas, Henry of Ghent, and Godfrey of Fontaines," *Review of Metaphysics* 33, no. 4 (1981): 729–58; Richard Cross, "Henry of Ghent on the Reality of Non-Existing Possibles: Revisited," *Archiv für Geschichte der Philosophie* 92, no. 2 (2010): 115–32.

39 Muller, *God, Creation, and Providence*, 219–20.

40 This may seem like a strange move. After all, Suárez repeatedly attacks Henry by name in Disp. XXXI of his *Metaphysicarum disputationum* and specifically repudiates essentialism. "Fatendum ergo necessario est, seclusa entitate existentiae, quae per effectionem aliquam communicatur creaturae, ipsam entitatem essentiae omnino nihil esse." Suárez, *Metaphysicarum Disputationum, In quibus et universa naturalis theologia ordinate traditur , et quaestiones ad omnes duodecim Aristotelis libros pertinentis accurate disputantur.* Disp. XXXI, Sec II.1 & Sec II.V. Recently, Embry has argued that Suárez was rejecting what he terms "Henrician essentialism." Embry argues that Suárez was nevertheless constructing his own version of essentialism. Rutherford might have agreed. See Brian Embry, "Francisco Suárez on Eternal Truths, Eternal Essences, and Extrinsic Beings," *Ergo: An Open*

constitutes a non-being. Suárez had argued for a difference between merely possible beings and fictitious beings (*ente ficto*). The difference between the two, as argued by Suárez, is that one is contradictory to actual being (i.e. the *hircocervus*) and the other is not, thus it is able to be made. This argument underscores Suárez's understanding of possible and impossible beings. Rutherford admitted the argument with a qualification that possibility and impossibility are not intrinsic to the proposed beings themselves, but extrinsic based upon a relation to God's omnipotence.[41]

Once Suárez established the difference between a possible being and a merely fictitious being, he then went a step further. Rutherford summarized the development of the argument as follows: "non-being (*non ens*) is not producible, but the possible is producible, therefore a possible being is not a non-being (*non ens*)."[42] If non-being lacks the capacity for creatability, then it cannot be the object of God's creative act *ex nihilo*. Rather, as seen above with Episcopius, there is a similar qualification of the *nihil* as latent, objective potency here with Suárez. Rutherford agreed with Suárez that a purely impossible being (that which involves a contradiction to being) is not producible by God. But Rutherford did not equate non-being with the purely impossible.[43] Rather, Rutherford equated non-being strictly with nothing. Nevertheless, the non-being of the *nihil* was still possible through an extrinsic denomination in relation to God's omnipotence. In this reading, the *nihil* has a dependent potency.[44]

Access Journal of Philosophy 4, no. 19 (2017), accessed April 10, 2020, http://dx.doi.org/10.3998/ergo. 12405314.0004.019.

41 "*Suárez dicit possibile differre ab ente ficto, puta, hircocervo, quod non repugnet possibile fieri, ut hircocervum esse repugnat.* Fateor differe possibile ab impossibili, sed non per differentias reales, sed per extrinsecam, ad Omnipotentiam, relationem. Licet impossibile complexum supponat possibile, & supponit sic suo modo possibile, ut antea dictum." Rutherford, *Disputatio Scholastica*, 559. Rutherford cites Suárez, *Metaphysicarum Disputationum, In quibus et universa naturalis theologia ordinate traditur , et quaestiones ad omnes duodecim Aristotelis libros pertinentis accurate disputantur*, 31, Sec. II, num 2.

42 "Suárez vero sic objicit, cum aliis, Non ens non est producible, sed possibile est producible, Ergo possibile non est non ens." Rutherford, *Disputatio Scholastica*, 559.

43 "Resp. Quod est non ens simpliciter, & neque potentia, neque actu est ens, sed simpliciter impossibile, & contradictionem fieri involvit, non est producibile, verum est: at possibile non est sic non ens, sed potest omnipotens ex non ente extrahere ens." Rutherford, *Disputatio Scholastica*, 559.

44 "Quia non entia possibilia ut sint possibilis, indigent omnipotentia Dei extra & citra quam sunt mere nihil, non ens, non possibile imo possibile licet improprie admodum, quia nullum est, hoc casu possibile ut statim demonstrabitur. Nec possibilis extra Deum dicuntur possibilis per aliquam potentiam realem, vel objective realiter inhaerentem in ipsis possibilibus, nam nulla realis forma est in non ente, neque non entis est accidens; nec est realis forma aliqua denominans antequam sit subjectum reale…Ergo possibile dicitur possibile per denominationem extrinsecam." Rutherford, *Disputatio Scholastica*, 534.

Rutherford argued that because of the extrinsic denomination that non-being held in relation to God's omnipotence, God is able to bring being out of non-being. His emphasis upon non-being as the object of God's creative act is intentional and well cultivated in the *Disquisitiones Metaphysicae*. Earlier in the *Disquisitiones* he explicitly linked the concept of *nihil* with non-being. He insisted upon God's authority and power to command being to come out of non-being. God speaks to "pure non-being," and being emerges (Gen. 1:32). In a moment of poetic flourish, rare for this work of scholastic theology, Rutherford wrote:

> The heavens therefore were not yet created, being at this point *non-beings*, as if by ears they heard the command of God *"come out and go forth from pure nothing!"* Therefore the word אָמַר is to command, to judge, to inscribe, *Gen 1.9, Lev 8.36, Deut 4.23, Isa 40.26*. "See *who created these, leading them out by number*, or who led out the host of them out of pure nothing, *Rom 4.17*. He calls those things that are not beings, as though they are beings. With a word and a nod of omnipotence he calls non-beings. Thus the word צָוָה means to call. Behold such dominion that non-being obeys God's calling.[45]

Here the object of God's decree is not the objective potency of the *nihil*, as per Suárez and Episcopius. Rather, the object of God's decree of creation is non-being, pure nothing. What is the significance of this? Underlying the concerns of some Jesuit and Arminian theologians is the philosophical objection to being arising from non-being, or something coming from nothing. The Jesuit and Arminian solution to this objection was to lend latent potency to the *nihil*. In doing so, it may be argued that they circumscribed God's power by arguing his dependence upon latent potency for the creative act. It could also be argued that they created a sphere that enjoys a limited independence from the Creator, a theme that Rutherford has identified in their writings before. Rutherford's denial of the latent potency of the *nihil*, insisting upon a more classically orthodox *nihil absolutum*, admits God's power extends even into non-being. It is not dependent upon latent potency. Furthermore, as the above quote makes clear, the *nihil* is not an independent space. But as Rutherford notes, even the *nihil* is radically obedient to the power and command of God. Because God's decree of creation is not dependent upon, nor conditioned by the latent potency of creation, neither is God's providence dependent upon nor conditioned

---

45 "Coeli ergo nondum creati, cum adhuc essent non entia, quasi auribus hauserunt illud mandatum *Dei, egredimini & exite e pure nihilo*. Id enim verbum אָמַר mandare, jubere, notat, Gen. 1.9. Lev. 8.36. Deut 4.23. Esai. 40.26. *Videte quis creaverit hac educens in numero*, vel qui educit e pure nihilo exercitum corum, *Rom 4.17*. Vocat τα μη οντα ώς οντα Verbo & nutu Omnipotentiae vocat non entia. Ita verbum צָוָה est vocare. Ecce tale dominium quo non entia obedient Deo vocanti." Rutherford, *Disputatio Scholastica*, 533.

by the same. The contours of the radical independence of God as well as the radical dependence of the created order are maintained.

6.2 *Quid sit providentia Dei?*

Providence follows God's work of creation inasmuch as without God's providential care, creation would cease to be. This further underscores the themes of radical independence and dependence outlined above. Rutherford described God's continual care of creation in the act of providence when he wrote that God "beareth up all things in his armes els they would turne to nothing (Acts 17:28; Col. 1:17; Heb. 1:3; Ps. 29)." [46] He began his discussion with an examination of the word *providere* before moving on to a careful, scholastic definition of the term.[47]

6.2.1 The Literal and Connotative Sense

The discussion on God's providence begins with an exposition of the *vox*, a term taken from Aristotle's *de Interpretatione* that defines both the literal sense of the word as well as its connotation.[48] The term *providentia* is taken from Gen. 22:8: "*dixit Abraham Deus providebit sibi victimam holocausti fili mi.*" The verse comes from the famous sacrifice of Isaac, wherein God commands Abraham to offer Isaac, his only son, as a sacrifice. When Isaac asks his father "where is the lamb for the burnt offering?" (Gen. 22:7), Abraham responds with "God himself *will provide* the sacrificial lamb for the burnt offering" (Gen. 22:8).

As Rutherford noted in the *Disputatio*, the matrix of words in the Latin (*providentia*), Greek (ὄψεται), and Hebrew (רָאָה), taken in the literal sense communicates vision and thus pertains to the activity of the divine mind. However, providence is more than a matter of vision and the mind. Following the French Huguenot theologian Andre Rivet (1572–1651), Rutherford noted that the connotation of the term is not strictly intellectual but also pertains to the divine will, inasmuch as providence implies God's compassion (*affectus*) and care (*cura*) for his creation.[49] Using a common sense example, Rutherford argued that neither parents with children nor captains with ships can properly be said to be exercising providence by merely

---

46 Rutherford, "Ane Catachisme," 168.

47 What follows comes largely from Chapter 1 of Rutherford, *Disputatio Scholastica*, 1–3.

48 See *De Interpretatione*, in Aristotle *The Complete Works of Aristotle: The Revised Oxford Translation*, ed. Jonathan Barnes (Princeton, N.J.: Princeton University Press, 1984), 29–31.

49 See Rutherford's comments in referencing *D. Rivetus* in *Disputatio*, 1. Rivet presided over the *Disputatio XI*, on divine providence. See: Johannem Poliandrum et al., *Synopsis purioris theologiae: Disputationibus quinquaginta duabus comprehensa* (Leiden: Elzeviriana, 1625), 107–16.

looking at their children or the captain merely looking at the ship. Rather, both parents and captains must earnestly take on concern and care for their respective responsibilities.[50]

Rutherford's exposition of the *vox* reveals that *providentia* is not merely looking at or even looking ahead. Rather, *providentia* is better reflected by the colloquial phrase "looking after", as the captain looks after the ship or parents look after their children. This looking after not only requires acts of God's intellect, will, and power but also requires acts of care, concern, compassion, and love towards creation.

6.2.2 Scholastic Definition

After Rutherford's brief exposition of the *vox*, he proceeded with a more comprehensive scholastic definition.

> Providence is an act or ἐντελέχεια, by which according to his most wise and free counsel, whereby each and every thing is seen as far as it is ordainable. To its own end, especially the ultimate end, namely the glory of God, he sees, upholds, and governs all things according to their nature, though sometimes, he irresistibly directs outside of nature.[51]

Providence is first and foremost an act of God, the foundation of which lies within the divine intellect and will. Its execution is a matter of divine power. As far as it pertains to the divine intellect, it has been shown in previous chapters that God knows every possible state of affairs by virtue of his knowledge of simple intelligence (*scientia simplicis intelligentiae*).[52] Out of this vast treasury of possibilities, he freely chooses to actualize some possibilities by virtue of his will of good pleasure (*voluntas beneplaciti*).[53] He knows the actual world as it is and as it will be by virtue of his free knowledge (*scientia libera*) or knowledge of vision (*scientia visionis*).[54] The

---

50 "Certe nec parens in liberos, nec Nauclerus in navem providentiam excercet, si hic tantum quid navi, ille vero quid gnatis eveniat, videat, oculisque intueatur, non vero etiam curam solicite gerat, hic navis ille gnatorum." Rutherford, *Disputatio Scholastica*, 2.

51 "Providentia est actus sive ἐντελέχεια Dei, qua secundum aeternum suum consilium sapientissimum & liberrimum, omnia & singula quatenus ordinabilia Deo visa sunt. Videt, tuetur, & gubernat, & ai suos fines praesertim vero ultimum, nempe Dei Gloriam, juxta omnium rerum naturas, interdum vero praeter, aut contra naturas irresistibiliter dirigit." Rutherford, *Disputatio Scholastica*, 2.

52 See Rutherford, *Disputatio Scholastica*, 559; Rutherford, *Examen Arminianismi*, 163.

53 See: Rutherford, *Exercitationes Apologeticae*, 200–19; Chapter 2 in Rutherford, *Disputatio Scholastica*, 3–12; and "Titulus Quintus: De Voluntate Dei" in Rutherford, *Examen Arminianismi*, 181–5.

54 See: Rutherford, *Disputatio Scholastica*, 559; Rutherford, *Exercitationes Apologeticae*, 158–99 and 559; Rutherford, *Examen Arminianismi*, 163.

actual world, chosen, known, and efficiently created by God is thus the object of the divine providence.[55]

Rutherford described the act of providence as an "ἐντελέχεια." The term ἐντελέχεια is a neologism coined by Aristotle, and as with some others of Aristotle's neologisms its interpretation is difficult.[56] The older and traditional interpretation, relying upon the supposed composition ἐντελής ἔχειν interpreted ἐντελέχεια as "having achieved completeness."[57] Recent interpretations of the term, such as that offered by A.P. Bos, have revealed a richer meaning that depends upon a twofold understanding of Aristotle's distinction. Such have argued that there is a first (and most basic) ἐντελέχεια and second ἐντελέχεια. The difference between first and second ἐντελέχεια is the difference between planning to take a ship to harbor and actually reaching harbor. First ἐντελέχεια represents the ship *en route* to its final destination, which requires intentionality, guidance, skill, etc. Second ἐντελέχεια applies to the goal or *telos*. The older interpretation placed an emphasis upon second ἐντελέχεια, and therefore overlooked or underemphasized those aspects of ἐντελέχεια that pertained to active involvement and guidance. But, as Bos has shown, once the distinction between first and second ἐντελέχεια is acknowledged, then ἐντελέχεια as an active, guiding, and orienting principle of the instrumental body (*organon*) can also be seen.[58]

Was Rutherford sensitive to such sophisticated readings of Aristotle and his neologism? It is almost a certainty that his scholastic training in the peripatetic tradition meant he understood ἐντελέχεια in a teleological sense within the broad context of hylomorphism. Here ἐντελέχεια is that which actualizes the potentiality (*potentia*) of prime matter (*materia prima*) into that of its substantial form (*forma*

---

55 Scripture proofs for Rutherford's definition are 1 Cor. 9:9; 1 Peter 5:7; Heb. 13:15; Deut. 32:10; Hos. 11:3; Ps. 91:1–2; Rom. 11:36; Ps. 104:35; Matt. 10:29; Eph. 1:11; Prov. 16:4; Heb. 1:2. See Rutherford, *Disputatio Scholastica*, 2.

56 For a survey of the contemporary discussion see: William. E. Ritter, "Why Aristotle Invented the Word Entelecheia," *The Quarterly Review of Biology* 7, no. 4 (1932): 377–404; Chen Chung-Hwan, "Different Meanings of the Term Energeia in the Philosophy of Aristotle," *Philosophy and Phenomenological Research* 17, no.1 (1956): 56–65; George A. Blair, "The Meaning of 'Energeia' and 'Entelecheia' in Aristotle," *International Philosophical Quarterly* 7, no. 1 (1967): 101–17; Daniel W. Graham, "The Etymology of Entelecheia," *American Journal of Philology* 110, no. 1 (1989): 73–80; George A. Blair, *Energeia and Entelecheia:"Act" in Aristotle* (Ottawa: University of Ottawa Press, 1992); A. P. Bos, *The Soul and its Instrumental Body: A Reinterpretation of Aristotle's Philosophy of Living Nature*, Brill's studies in intellectual history 112 (Leiden, Netherlands; Boston, MA: Brill, 2003); Jonathan B. Beere, *Doing and Being: An Interpretation of Aristotle's Metaphysics Theta*, Oxford Aristotle Studies (Oxford: Oxford University Press, 2009).

57 Graham, "The Etymology of Entelecheia," 74.

58 See: Bos, *The Soul and its Instrumental Body*, 132–5.

substantialis).[59] The public disputation from Rutherford's graduation in 1621 makes such an understanding explicit.[60] In the context of providence, the material in question is creation itself with its form being its purpose in relation to the glory of God. ἐντελέχεια in this regard is decidedly teleological, with an emphasis upon second ἐντελέχεια as God's direction of all things towards his own glory and appointed ends.[61]

While the teleological aspects are evident, this does not mean that Rutherford understood God merely sets the world on its course. Rather, providence as ἐντελέχεια also represents God's ongoing administration of the created order as well as his continual care over all of creation (*continuata rerum creatio*).[62] Thus, for Rutherford, the term also has connotations of an active, guiding, and orienting principle. Rather than a particularly sophisticated reading of Aristotle's neologism, it is most likely that Rutherford's commitment to the scriptural witness and Christian tradition required this dual emphasis upon ἐντελέχεια as final actualization as well as guiding principle. His abundant use of scriptural quotations in this section that emphasize God's guiding work, make this the most likely reason for this dual emphasis.

6.2.3 The Four Causes

Beyond this initial definition of God's providence, Rutherford also noted that providence may be distinguished according to the four causes. In the *Posterior Analytics*, Aristotle argued that proper knowledge of a thing consisted in an accurate knowledge of its cause or causes. In seeking the cause, one is seeking the answer to two closely related questions. The first is the "why?" question that seeks an explanation for why a thing is. The second question is a more intricate discussion

---

59 For an overview of the scholastic background of hylemorphism, as well as its resonances with early modern mechanical philosophy, see: Roger Ariew and Alan Gabbey, "Body and the Physical World: The Scholastic Background," in *The Cambridge History of Seventeenth-Century Philosophy*, ed. Daniel Garber and Michael Ayers (Cambridge: Cambridge University Press, 2003), 429–32.

60 See: Theses Physicae VII.i-vii. Andrea Junio, *Theses Quaedam: Ex Amplissimo Philosophiae camp decertae, pro quibus (auspice Deo) stabunt in publica adolescentes 42. hac vice Magisterio donandi* (Edinburgi: Andreas Hart, 1621). The disputation also places the faculty at Edinburgh as holding to a Thomist interpretation, which denied that prime matter could be brought into being without substantial form. The position outlined by Thomas would later be denied by Scotus and Ockham. See: Ariew and Gabbey, "Body and the Physical World: The Scholastic Background," 431.

61 Rutherford, *Disputatio Scholastica*, 2.

62 Rutherford, 2.

attempting to describe the process of change which in this case means the movement of a thing from a state of potentiality to actuality.[63]

Aristotle explained such phenomena in the *Physics* II.3 and *Metaphysics* V.2. He termed these causes the material, formal, efficient, and final cause. A brief explanation will be beneficial in understanding the nature of these causes and how they relate one to the other. Consider an artist sculpting a bronze statue. While intuitively, the artist is the cause of the statue, Aristotle understood that he was only one cause among four. First among the four is the material cause. In this case the material cause is the bronze metal that is the matter of which the statue is composed. Because the bronze contributes to a variety of the statue's ultimate features (look, feel, strength, etc.) it is considered a cause. Second is the formal cause. This is the form or shape that the bronze takes as it is sculpted. Third is the final cause. The bronze metal could be used for a variety of ends, but that the artist is sculpting a statue and not a paper weight is the final cause. The fourth cause is the efficient cause, this being the sculptor himself as the primary source of change.[64]

Rutherford began with the material cause, which he argued is twofold. The material cause is all being (*omnia entia*) taken in a general sense, as well as being considered under the divine care individually (*singula*).[65] Just as bronze gives a certain color, texture, and strength to a statue, created being considered generally and specifically lent God's providence its material aesthetics. Thus Rutherford describes a good providence as smooth or white, a bad providence as rough or black.[66]

The formal cause is all being, taken in its general and individual sense, inasmuch as being is ordainable to take on a form that brings glory to God. From this formal cause, Rutherford excluded consideration of God himself as an ultimate end. He is not entailed in the *omnia entia* to which the formal cause is applied. The second exclusion Rutherford made from the formal cause is that which is simply impossible (*simpliciter impossibilia*). Because God is already fully actualized and that which is simply impossible never will be, neither of these excluded objects are able to be directed towards their ultimate end.[67] But to those things ordainable by God, and

---

63 For an overview of the four causes and their relation to Reformed Orthodoxy see: Pleizier and Wisse, "'As the Philosopher Says': Aristotle," 39–42.

64 Pleizier and Wisse, 39–40.

65 "Materia seu objectum est duplex, materiale, *omnia entia*, quia Deus generaliter rerum omnium curam gerit, ut ait *Spiritus Sanctus*: & *singula*, nam singula etiam minutissima despectui Deus non habet." Rutherford, *Disputatio Scholastica*, 2.

66 Rutherford's letters are the best resource for seeing his colorful descriptions of the work of providence. See for example: Rutherford, *Joshua Redivivus*, 16, 88, and 127.

67 "Formale objectum est quatenus haec omnia & singula *sunt ordinabilia ad Dei Gloriam*: hinc duo ab hoc objecto excludo, 1. Deum ipsum ultimum finem. 2. Simpliciter impossibilia, nec enim haec nec ille ad finem ultimum dirigi possunt." Rutherford, *Disputatio Scholastica*, 2.

more so to those things that will be brought to actuality by the divine providence, they represent something of a history of God's glory. In his typically poetic language, he wrote to Lady Kenmure during a time of particular hardship the following:

> Madam, when you are come to the other side of the water, and have set down your foot on the shore of glorious eternity, and look back again to the waters and to your wearisome journey, and shall see in that clear glass of endless glory nearer to the bottom of God's wisdom, you shall then be forced to say, "If God had done otherwise with me than he hath done, I had never come to the enjoying of this crown of glory."[68]

Just as the sculptor has in mind the final form during his labors, so too does God have in mind his own glory as the final form of each and every created being. Rutherford's letter clearly stated that God's providence is mysterious, particularly in times of hardship. Nevertheless, the outcome is certain. The final form imprinted upon all created being reflects God's glory.[69]

God himself is the efficient cause according to his wisdom and works.[70] When placed on house arrest in Aberdeen, Rutherford could bluntly remark, "The Lord hath done it." He has, "the world on his wheels, and casteth it as a potter doth a vessel on the wheel."[71] God as the efficient cause does not mean that God is immediately involved in all that happens in the world, but rather that he is the primary cause of all that happens in the world.[72]

The fourth and final cause is the glory of God, for God makes everything for himself (Prov. 16:4). The difference at this point between the formal and final cause can be confusing since Rutherford links both to God's glory.[73] The final cause is best understood as the sake or reason for which a thing is done. For example, the final cause of Rutherford's *Disputatio* was educational. The formal cause of the *Disputatio* was also educational, but in this regard the emphasis is upon the form (i.e. written, Latin, scholastic style, etc.) that the lectures took in order to achieve the end. The final cause of divine providence is for God's glory. And though the formal cause is also for God's glory, the emphasis is upon the particular shape that the history of created being takes in order to accomplish this end. A further distinction between the formal and final cause is that the final cause is necessary. God always works

---

68 Rutherford, *Joshua Redivivus*, 327.

69 Rutherford, 327.

70 "*Efficiens* est Deus ipse secundum consilium suum omnia operans." Rutherford, *Disputatio Scholastica*, 2.

71 Rutherford, *Joshua Redivivus*, 279.

72 Rutherford, "Ane Catachisme," 169.

73 "Finis est Dei gloria, Nam Deus universi fecit propter seipsum, ut ait Sapiens." Rutherford, *Disputatio Scholastica*, 2.

for his own glory necessarily. However, how God achieves this end through this or that form is contingent, as Rutherford makes clear in his definition of the formal cause.[74]

6.2.4 Conservation, Cooperation, and Direction

Moving beyond the four causes, Rutherford concluded this section on the definition of providence with the three acts of God's providence. These are conservation (*conservationem*), cooperation with all secondary causes (*cooperationem*), and the direction of things towards their appointed ends (*directionem*).[75]

Rutherford began his discussion on the three acts with conservation, first distinguishing it from three acts that could easily be mistaken for conservation. Conservation is not "bare permission" (*nuda permissio*). Rutherford made the sense plain by an example from Exodus Ch. 1, where Pharaoh plans to kill the Hebrew male children. This was frustrated because the midwives "feared God and did not do as the King of Egypt commanded them, but let the male children live." (Exod. 1:17). As the example makes plain, conservation is not the mere permitting of creation to exist.[76]

Rutherford also denied that conservation is similar to the preservation of substance during an accidental change. In the *Physics,* Aristotle argued that there were two main types of change: accidental change and substantial change. Accidental changes are those changes whereby a subject is changed accidentally but not substantially, such as when a red ball is dipped in blue paint. The accidental property of color has changed, but the substance of the ball remains the same. Substantial changes are those changes whereby a substance comes into, or passes out of, existence.[77] Rutherford's example in this section of the *Disputatio* relates to the accidental change. Returning to the example of the red ball, the form of the red ball changes when it is dipped in blue paint. It is no longer red, but blue. Though the color is changed, the form of the ball is preserved. The conservation of the substantial property of the ball requires no action on the part of any agent. This

---

74 "Nam providentiae acceptum ferendum est, quod multa possibilia actu nunquam sint, quod non sint plures mundi, quam unus, quod arceantur Pestes, fames, bella, et sub hoc objectum cadunt res qua conservari, & qua annihilari a Deo possunt." Rutherford, *Disputatio Scholastica*, 2.

75 "Forma tres actus Dei Providentiae includit. I. Conservationem rerum. 2. Cooperationem cum omnibus causis secundis. 3. Deductionem irresistibilem rerum omnium ad suos fines." Rutherford, *Disputatio Scholastica*, 2.

76 "Conservatio autem Dei, non est nuda permissio, quo pacto, Obstetrics Haebreae masculos in vivis conservarunt..." Rutherford, *Disputatio Scholastica*, 2.

77 For a helpful overview see Thomas Ainsworth, "Form vs. Matter," *The Stanford Encyclopedia of Philosophy* (Spring 2016 Edition), Edward N. Zalta (ed.), URL = <https://plato.stanford.edu/archives/spr2016/entries/form-matter/> (accessed February 1, 2018).

purely passive form of conservation is not to be confused with God's providential act of conservation.[78]

Neither, said Rutherford, is conservation to be compared to a doctor who preserves the life of a sick patient. This is the only example given where the conserving agent is active rather than passive. In the first example, the Hebrew midwives merely allow the male children to live. In the second example, an outside agent is responsible for the change that the form undergoes but the agent is not needed to preserve the matter. In this final example, the doctor is an active agent. However, the doctor is only needed if the patient is sick. Otherwise, the patient would not need the doctor's conservation. This part-time conservation, active only when needed, is denied.[79]

Rutherford had something a bit more in mind both for God as well as the creature when he employs the word conservation. Based upon such biblical texts as Acts 17: 28, Col. 1:7, Heb. 1:3 and Ps. 29, the Christian metaphysical tradition generally presupposed the necessity of God's ongoing, active power of conservation to preserve created being from slipping back into the *nihil*. Rutherford cited Augustine, who argued that conservation is not like "that of a man who has built a house and has then gone away." Creation is, at every moment, entirely dependent upon God's sustaining power. "For, if God were to withdraw His rule from it," Augustine continued, "the world could not stand, even for the flick of an eye."[80] This tradition developed along with ever evolving polemical concerns. Rutherford also cited Thomas, Durandus, and others firmly rooting himself within the tradition, noting that God must bear "up all things in his armes else they would turne to nothing."[81]

The second work of God's providence is God's cooperation with all secondary causes. Cooperation with secondary causes is a theological necessity of divine conservation. After all, if each and every being is dependent upon God's ever-present sustaining power, it stands to reason that the divine conservation extends to causality. Speaking in the broadest of terms, divine cooperation applies to "all things that worketh and moveth to work." The divine cooperation is necessary for natural events such as the burning of fire or the falling of a stone. So too is the

---

78 "Nec Dei interna causatio, uti materia formam conservat recipiendo, & forma materiam actuando." Rutherford, *Disputatio Scholastica*, 2.

79 "Nec Deus res conservat per amicas qualitates fovendo, ut medicus aegrum conservat." Rutherford, *Disputatio Scholastica*, 2–3.

80 Augustine, *De Genesi ad litteram*, IV, 12 (PL, 34, col. 304). I have followed Bourke's translation in Thomas Aquinas, *Summa Contra Gentiles Book Three: Providence Part I*, trans. Vernon J. Bourke (Notre Dame: University of Notre Dame, 2001), 217. Rutherford also references Thomas Aquinas, *Summa Contra Gentiles* Lib 3.1.66; Durandus of Saint-Pourçain, *In sententias theologicas* Lib 2, Dist 44, Q. 1; Bonaventure, *Sententiarum*, Lib I. Dist. 37. Q. 1. For other references, see Rutherford, *Disputatio Scholastica*, 3.

81 Rutherford, "Ane Catachisme," 168.

divine cooperation necessary for contingent events brought about by the human will.[82]

There will be opportunity for extended remarks concerning God's relationship with secondary causes, especially regarding Rutherford's understanding of God's sovereignty and the freedom of the will. For now, a few general remarks will be sufficient. It has been argued that the scholastic language couched in terms of Aristotelean causality betrays a preference for pagan logic that comes at the expense of the biblical witness.[83] However, when Rutherford's comments are examined in context, it is more true to say that he is making sense of the biblical witness using Aristotelean logic and concepts as analytical aids. For Rutherford, Aristotle is in his proper place as a handmaid to theology by revealing and clearly articulating the depth of the biblical witness. Aristotelean causality was used to understand how God "works all things according to the counsel of his will" (Eph. 1:11) while at the same rendering some account of how his work does not eliminate the working of the secondary cause. In all cases, the biblical witness of scripture, such as Matt. 10:29, Job 39:5, and Job 38:35, leads the discussion.[84]

In addition to Rutherford's discussion being driven by the biblical witness, his concerns in the discussion are decidedly theological and pastoral. Rutherford's interest in defending God's active cooperation with secondary causes was to deny the fickle forces of fate and fortune. "Then nothing falls out by chance or fortune?", asks the questioner in the *Ane Catechisme*. "Noe, not a hair from our head (Matt. 10:29) nor a sparrow falleth to the ground but by Godis counsel, will and power (Luke 12:6)."[85] Beyond the terrors of fate and fortune, Rutherford also saw God's cooperation with secondary causes as being an essential aspect of Christian hope in prayer. Arguing against mere conservation, Rutherford wrote that "all our prayers to God that he wold move men to love and favour us, and bow our will to feare his name were in vaine if God did not suffer our will to begin to work, and then came in like a page to convoy it onlie."[86] In other words, Christians can pray with perseverance and hope in a variety of circumstances precisely because God does cooperate and direct secondary causes. The reader ought to be reminded Rutherford's points are not merely theoretical. He exhorted many to pray with such hope while he was

---

82 "De Cooperatione Dei cum causis secundis praesertim cum voluntate creata in actibus peccati, & de deductione rerum omnium ad suos fines serventiores & operosiores in hac materia extant disputationes." Rutherford, *Disputatio Scholastica*, 3.

83 See for example: Torrance, *Scottish Theology*, 105.

84 Rutherford, *Disputatio Scholastica*, 3.

85 Rutherford, "Ane Catechisme," 169.

86 Rutherford, 169.

suffering under house arrest in Aberdeen with the charge of treason hanging over his head.[87]

The third and final special work of God's providence is the direction of all things, "even sinne" to his own glory.[88] Just as conservation and cooperation are rooted in the doctrine of creation, so too did Rutherford link this work of providence to creation, citing Gen. 1:20 as his supporting scripture. "And God said, let the waters swarm with living creatures and the let birds fly above the earth across the expanse of the heavens." Not only are beings dependent upon God for their very existence, but they are also dependent upon God to direct them in the specific way they bring glory to God, as with the bird in flight or fish in the sea. "May not the creature be carried towards God's glorie of their own accord?", asks the questioner in the *Ane Catechisme*. "Nay, they cannot doe that more then ane shipp can saill to the right harbour without."[89] God's general direction of fish in the sea and birds in the air was hardly controversial. However, the questioner's next inquiry brings into focus the particular problem of God's direction of all being towards its appointed end.

> Q. Hes God any hand in sinn?
> A. He suffereth men to sinne, and punisheth sinne and directeth it to his owne glorie; bot he nether alloweth, loveth, nor commandeth sinne.[90]

Does God's direction of all things towards his own glory morally implicate him in the existence of evil in the world? Does the same impose a fatal necessity to sin upon beings which, absent God's providential direction, would otherwise be innocent? These questions will the subject of the remainder of this chapter.

6.2.5 Divine Permission and the Necessity of the Consequence

Rutherford argued that sin necessarily followed from the divine permission by using the distinction of the *necessity of the consequent* and the *necessity of the consequence*. Beck notes that the distinction between the necessity of the consequence (*necessitas consequentiae*) and the necessity of the consequent (*necessitas consequentis*) was a well-known distinction dating back to the arts faculties of the thirteenth century.[91] As Marenbon notes, this distinction was often put in Boethian terms of simple and

---

87 See for example: Rutherford, *Joshua Redivivus*, 87–9.

88 Rutherford, "Ane Catachisme," 170.

89 Rutherford, "Ane Catachisme," 169.

90 Rutherford, 170.

91 Beck, *Gisbertus Voetius*, 338–9; John Marenbon, "Boethius: From Antiquity to the Middle Ages," in *Medieval Philosophy*, ed. John Marenbon (London & New York: Routledge, 2003), 11–28; Vos et al, *John Duns Scotus*, 19–22.

conditional necessity.[92] Simple necessity is applied to that state of affairs that is universally true and therefore must be in each and every circumstance. Conditional necessity, on the other hand, is applied to that state of affairs that may be true under the condition of God's knowledge, will, and certain temporal circumstances.[93] When applied to the *necessitas consequentiae et consequentis* distinction, conditional necessity is the *necessitas consequentiae* and simple necessity is equivalent to the *necessitas consequentis*.[94]

Rutherford believed that the critique of the doctrine of divine permission rested upon a misunderstanding of this critical distinction. He argued that the following was falsely attributed to the Reformed:

> Permission and the thing permitted are related.
> If one of the two is posited.
> It is necessary to posit the other.[95]

The problem, as Rutherford and others saw it, rested in the conclusion. To argue that "to posit one, it is necessary to posit the other" is to attribute necessity to both the divine permission and the sin permitted. Not only is this not what Rutherford and other Reformed theologians held, but it represents an error in logic. Following Twisse, Rutherford demonstrated the faulty logic implied in the above by applying it to God's decree of creation:

> It is necessary: If God eternally decreed to create the world, then the world will be created.

If one were to argue that to "posit one" (God's decree) is to necessarily "posit the other" (the world will be created), then it follows that:

> It is necessary: That the world (from eternity) will be created.[96]

---

92 Marenbon, "Boethius: from antiquity to the Middle Ages," 22.

93 Simo Knuuttila, *Reforging the Great Chain of Being: Studies of the History of Modal Theories* (Dordrecht: D. Reidel Pub. Co., 1981), 140–1.

94 For a helpful overview of this distinction, with introductory comments in regards to the rules governing implications and relevant terms, see: Philip John Fisk, *Jonathan Edward's Turn from the Classic Reformed Tradition of Freedom of the Will*, New Directions in Jonathan Edwards Studies 2 (Göttingen: Vandenhoeck & Ruprecht GmbH & Co. KG, 2016), 325–7. See also: Vos et al, *John Duns Scotus*, 37–8.

95 "Censuram fert doctis. & claris. Vir D. Gul Twissus in Perkinsum & Piscatorum, eo quod docuerint illative sequi peccatum ex permissione, Sic arguebat Piscator. Permissio & res permissa sunt relata: at posito uno relatorum; necesse est poni alterum." Rutherford, *Disputatio Scholastica*, 80.

96 "Sic retorquet, D. claris. Twissus pari ratione, sequitur ab aeterno Deus voluit mundum (quippe ab aeterno mundum creare decrevit) sequitur ab aeterno mundus est volitus. At non sequitur. Ergo ab aeterno mundus est: ideoque non sequitur est permissio." Rutherford, *Disputatio Scholastica*, 80.

But as both Rutherford and Twisse noted, it does not follow. In Boethian terms, it is not a "simple necessity" that the world be created but rather a conditional necessity, based upon the divine will and its execution in time. The illustration goes to show that "to posit one" is not necessarily to "posit the other." Creation is not a simple necessity but a conditional one. "The world will (from eternity) be created," not by the necessity of the consequent but rather by the necessity of the consequence.[97]

For Rutherford, the doctrine of divine permission was conditioned by the doctrine of creation. After all, God cannot permit sin unless there is a creation within which sin may be permitted. Thus the construction above can be replicated with the decree to permit sin substituting for the decree to create the world.[98]

It is necessary: If God eternally decreed to permit sin S, then sin S occurs.

Again, if one were to "posit one" then one must necessarily "posit the other" then it follows that:

It is necessary: That sin S (eternally) occurs.

But, just as before it does not follow. Sin does not enter the world through the divine permission under the simple necessity of the *necessitas consequentis*. Rather, sin's entrance into the world, permitted by God, is conditional upon the divine will and the contribution of the secondary cause. Just as with the creation of the world, sin follows permission by necessity of the consequence. In this way, the divine permission does not impose simple necessity upon the sinner.[99] For example, Rutherford noted that when a sinner commits murder it is always or necessarily by the divine permission. However, just because God permits sinners to murder, this does not mean that sinners always murder. The divine permission clearly does not mean that evil must come about but that it may come about. Divine permission, when understood this way opens up an arena for human liberty and responsibility as far as it concerns sin and evil.[100]

---

97 In my summary representation of these comments above, I have followed Beck's representation of this distinction outlined in: Beck, *Gisbertus Voetius*, 339.

98 "Ergo ab aeterno mundus est: ideoque non sequitur est permissio. Ergo est peccatum permissum." Rutherford, *Disputatio Scholastica*, 80.

99 "Sic retorquet D. claris. Twissus pari ratione, sequitur ab aeterno Deus voluit mundum (quippe ab aeterno mundum creare decrevit) sequitur ab aeterno mundus est volitus. At non sequitur. Ergo ab aeterno mundus est: ideoque non sequitur est permisso. Ergo est peccatum permissum." Rutherford, *Disputatio Scholastica*, 80.

100 "Permittere est negare gratiam efficacem, qua vitaretur peccatum, Deus semper negat reprobis gratiam efficacem, qua dita, vitarent fornicationem, homicidium, & alia ia genus flagitia. At non

6.3   Providence, Evil, and Sin

The presence of evil and sin in a world under God's providential conservation, cooperation, and direction poses several serious theological and moral problems. If sin has entered God's good world apart from his providential care, then both God and humans are subject to the consequences of this evil. If such has entered the world under God's providential care, then his complicity in evil and sin opens the possibility of God's moral culpability. These thorny issues were traditionally handled under the broad heading of divine permission. Permission properly understood concerns the relationship between God's providence and the presence of evil in the world in general, specifically in regards to sin.[101] This entails a number of theologically and pastorally significant issues such as: (1) Is permission of sin morally just? (2) Is permission of sin opposed to God's will? (3) What is the mode or manner of permission?[102] Before these questions can be answered, the more basic question of "what is permission?" must first be explored.

6.3.1 Divine Permission Defined

Rutherford's basic definition of divine permission was a fulfillment of the will of good pleasure (*voluntas beneplaciti*) that directly effects nothing but permits something to be done.[103] To this very basic definition, he added two denials and one affirmation. The first denial is the denial of God's efficiency. "That which God permits, he does not effect as the author or as the one causing."[104] The second denial is more interesting and is worth quoting in full.

> What God permits, that he does not will as a moral cause, neither does he will it by any act of the approbative will and therefore by the will of the sign; but truly the permitting will includes an act of the will of decision in order that an act might exist or come about by some deviating or permitting to sin, and that it would include a positive act being pleasing to God will be explained.[105]

---

sequitur, Ergo reprobi semper fornicantur, semper occidunt." Rutherford, *Disputatio Scholastica*, 81.

101 "Permissio proprie circa peccatum versatur." Rutherford, *Disputatio Scholastica*, 67.

102 Rutherford, 67.

103 "Voluntas beneplaciti duplex est, alia efficiens...alia permittens vel permissiva qua Deus ipse nihil efficit, sed alium agere permittit." Rutherford, *Disputatio Scholastica*, 11.

104 "Negat efficientiam Dei: nam quod Deus permittit, id non efficit ut author, aut efficiens." Rutherford, *Disputatio Scholastica*, 11.

105 "Quod Deus permittit, id Deus non vult ut causa moralis, nec id vult ullo actu approbativae voluntatis, ideoque negat Dei voluntatem signi; at vero voluntas permittens includit actum voluntatis

There are a number of important features in the above, some of which will be given greater attention below. First, note that Rutherford denied that God is either the moral cause of sin or that he wills sin by his approbative or revealed will. By denying that God is the moral cause of sin, Rutherford is denying that the morality of the permitted act is to be imputed to God as the author. Denying that God wills the permitted sin via his revealed or approbative will, is to deny God's approval of the permitted act. Nevertheless, Rutherford affirmed that the permitted act is a positive willing according to the will of God's good pleasure. This may sound contradictory, that God could not approve of an act yet nevertheless will it according to his good pleasure (*voluntas beneplaciti*). It must be remembered, as was stated above, that the object of the will of good pleasure is not what is just or unjust, but rather what will come to be and what will not come to be. Thus, permission involves a positive act of willing that evil be permitted to come about. Such positive willing of evil is so that a greater good may come about. Even so, as can be seen in the above, God's approval from a moral perspective is never given to specific acts of evil.[106]

6.3.2 The Morality of Divine Permission

Rutherford's resolution to the problem of God's will and the presence of evil in the actual world is hardly unique. Nevertheless, the paths of divine permission are not smoothed over for the sake of being well trod. Problems abound, the first of which is the question of the morality of divine permission. "The first consideration is with respect to morality in regards to permission. Hence permission of sin is either just or unjust."[107] Citing commonly accepted juridical law, Rutherford argued that permission is morally just under two conditions. The first condition is that the evil outcome is an accidental effect (*effectus per accidens*) of the permitting agent.[108]

---

decernentis ut fiat vel existat actus ab alio deviante & peccare permisso, & quod actum positivum includat, Deo favente demonstrabitur." Rutherford, *Disputatio Scholastica*, 11.

106 Dekker's interpretation of Scotus's theory of divine permission may provide a useful paradigm for understanding Rutherford's definition of divine permission outlined above. Dekker posits that Scotus held a twofold understanding of divine permission, one deontic and one "factual" (Dekker's own term). Dekker describes deontic permission as an ineffective nolition of an evil act. Factual permission is described as a "willing to allow" sin through a second-order act of the will. The moral concerns of deontic permission, as well as the providential concerns of maintaining God's connection with factual states of affairs can be seen in the above. For more see: Eef Dekker, "The Theory of Divine Permission According to Scotus's Ordinatio I 47," *Vivarium* 38, no. 2 (2000): 231–42.

107 "Prima consideratio est respectu moralitatis in permissione. Hinc permissio peccati, vel est justa, vel injusta." Rutherford, *Disputatio Scholastica*, 67.

108 Applying the logic of causal series ordered *per se* or *per accidens* to the doctrine of divine permission has precedence in Thomas. See: Aquinas, *Summa theologiae*, I, q 49, a 3, 504–507.

The second condition is that the permitting agent is under no obligation to prevent the evil outcome.[109]

An example of the first condition, that the evil outcome is an accidental effect of the divine will, is that of a father who begets a son. The father is an effective, *per se* cause of the son. In other words he is directly involved in the action of begetting and lends efficiency towards the end of begetting. As the son grows however, he will gain agency of his own at which point he may use that agency to sin. The father is neither directly involved in the son's sin, nor does he lend efficiency towards his son's sinning. The son could not sin if he had not been begotten of his father, but the son's sinning is not essential to being begotten. It is incidental or accidental. Thus sin is a *per accidens* effect of being begotten. In a similar way, sin is a *per accidens* effect of free creatures. Therefore, God is just under the first condition.[110]

The second condition, that only those under obligation may be held liable under the law, is more difficult to explain. Rutherford raised the biblical example of Eli and his wicked sons (1 Sam. 3:13). Eli was the *per se* cause of his sons, giving them life and nourishment. As his sons grew and became sinners, Eli became the *per accidens* cause of their wickedness. Though Eli was the *per accidens* cause of his son's sin, he was nevertheless, as Rutherford pointed out, held responsible. He is not held responsible for his son's sin, but rather he is held responsible for not preventing it.[111] Rutherford argued that this standard cannot be applied to God, because God is not obligated under the law. "Truly," wrote Rutherford, "only the law gives rise to obligation, and he who is not under the law is not able to be marked imputable." God as the giver of the law may obligate his creatures to the law, but he is not obligated to the law. Thus his actions may not be judged by the law and therefore he is not culpable.[112]

6.3.3 The Manner of Divine Permission

Having answered the question of moral culpability, Rutherford moved the discussion forward to the mode or manner of permission. Here Rutherford has three comments. The first is the manner of permission as it refers to God. Permission

---

109 "Justa est interdum permissio, quia effectus per accidens (ut docent Jurisconsulti) sequutus ex actione vel omissione, non imputatur permittenti, nisi ei incumbat obligatio cavendi ne unum ex alio sequatur." Rutherford, *Disputatio Scholastica*, 67.

110 For a helpful overview of some of the issues involved, see R.G. Wengert, "The Logic of Essentially Ordered Causes," *Notre Dame Journal of Formal Logic* 12, no. 4 (1971): 406–21.

111 "Permissio est injusta, cum quis morali obligationi impediendi subest sic Eli culpabiliter filios suos praevaricari permisit, quia eos uti debuit, non repressit." Rutherford, *Disputatio Scholastica*, 68.

112 "Quia vero, sola lex obligationem inducit, nota imputabilitatis ei qui legi non subest, inuri minime potest." Rutherford, *Disputatio Scholastica*, 68.

is not opposed to God's will, vigilant care, prevention of sin, knowledge, or the determination of his counsel. Positively stated, divine permission is an expression of God's will, care, power, knowledge, and his deliberate intention.[113] This is opposed to the Jesuit understanding of divine permission, which is merely a matter of "non-violence, non-constriction, and non-predetermination of the freedom of the will."[114] Rutherford made the point that if permission is merely a matter of non-violence to the will, then there is nothing to distinguish permission of sin from positive acts of holiness and obedience. "It is absurd to say that God permits Christ to pray, to preach, etc."[115] Rather than bare non-violence, Rutherford argued that permission is a positive act of God's will to permit sin's existence in the world.[116]

Second is the manner of permission as it refers to the sin or evil permitted. Rutherford insisted upon two things. The first is that God concurs with the act. The divine *concursus* is still required for all secondary causes. The second is the denial that God is responsible for the evil intent of the act. Here it is necessary to distinguish between the act and the sinfulness of it. Rutherford relied upon the example of Adam eating from the tree of the knowledge of good and evil. Eating in and of itself is neither good nor evil. Thus God's *concursus* with the act can be said to be morally indifferent. However in this case, Adam intends disobedience and his act becomes evil.[117] Permission does not refer to the divine *concursus* in the act, but rather to the withdrawal of divine grace and rightness (*rectitudio*) of the act.[118] More specifically, permission refers to God allowing the joining of an act with the evil intention of a secondary cause.[119]

---

113 "Permissio consideratur modo, ut ad Deum refertur, sic vero permissio nec opponitur omnino Dei voluntati aut pervigili curae, quasi invitus, aut Epicurei more permitteret peccatum. Nec omnipotentiae contraria est permissio, quasi Deus impedire non valeret. Nec scientiae Dei. Nec denique determinato consilio aut intentioni est adversa. Quippe Deus, volens, curans, omnipotenter agens, sciens, & ex deliberata intentione res permittit." Rutherford, *Disputatio Scholastica*, 68.

114 Rutherford, 73.

115 "Et absurdum est dictu Deum permittere Christum orare, praedicare, aut Apostolos praedicare, credere, & omnia haec fieri permissione Dei." Rutherford, *Disputatio Scholastica*, 74.

116 "Permissio est actus positivus diviniae voluntatis, Deus enim sciens & volens permittit peccatum: at laxatio voluntatis Jesuitica est nuda non-actio, & actus mere negativus." Rutherford, *Disputatio Scholastica*, 75.

117 "Respondeo realiter forte separari non possunt, sed distinguantur necesse est. Quoniam Deus est Author & efficiens per se & causa actus entitativ in odio Dei, sicut est author actus entitativi manducandi fructum arboris scientiae; est enim causa & author omnis entis positivi & omnis actionis physicae. At vero Deus nec author nec causa est malitiae in odio Dei." Rutherford, *Disputatio Scholastica*, 335. Rutherford relies upon Bradwardine. See: Bradwardine, *De causa Dei*, lib 1 c. 26.

118 "Refertur ad malitiam actus, & videtur esse negatio gratiae & rectitudinis, quae si adesset, actum gratiose qualificaret, & sibi permittitur malitia." Rutherford, *Disputatio Scholastica*, 68.

119 "Refertur ad aggregatum ex actu & malitia. In hac relatione est proprie etiam permissio peccati." Rutherford, *Disputatio Scholastica*, 68.

The final consideration in regards to the mode or manner of permission is whether divine permission is moral or physical.[120] Moral permission may be considered in two ways. The first way is to release the rational creature from the obligations of the law, thus allowing him to sin. Rutherford argued that such an action would be impossible, since a rational creature's obligation under the law is an ontological fact.[121] The second way that moral permission is to be considered is when God freely allows people to enter into evil, or denies them knowledge of the Gospel or the gracious work of the Spirit.[122] This may be a disconcerting thought, but a thought that Rutherford nevertheless believed is found in scripture.[123]

Physical permission cannot entirely be disentangled from aspects of moral permission outlined above. Rutherford's first concern in defining the nature of physical permission is negative. Physical permission is opposed to efficient causality, in that God "always, not freely, but by necessity" permits sin and never effects sin.[124] "By necessity," here simply means that it is impossible for God to effect sin. Thus if sin comes about, it necessarily never comes about by efficiency but by permission. Physical permission is also opposed to impedition. God can freely hinder a rational creature from sinning.[125] From these two negative considerations a positive definition of physical permission can be constructed. Physical permission is non-efficient on God's behalf as well as a non-hinderance of sin. Positively stated, physical permission is when God chooses not to hinder sin, thus permitting the possibility of sin to actualize. Whereas the emphasis in moral permission is the permitting

---

120 "Permissio modo refertur ad Dei permittentis actionem vel moralem, vel physicam." Rutherford, *Disputatio Scholastica*, 69.

121 "Alia est quando voluntate revelata significat sic laxare creaturam rationalem a lege, quo possit licite peccare, & hoc est impossibile." Rutherford, *Disputatio Scholastica*, 69.

122 "Alia est moralis, quae physicam etiam permissionem includit, quando Deus suasoria argumenta peccati impediendi aliqualem vim habentia uti interdum Euangelium, interdum propter peccata, cognitionem salutarem substrahit, & sic hoc posteriore modo Deus libere permisit gentes in viis malis incedere, & permissione morali & physica, negando Euangelium & operationem gratiosam spiritus, quae Euangelium comitatur." Rutherford, *Disputatio Scholastica*, 69.

123 See for example: Acts 14:16; Acts 17:30.

124 "Permissione opposita effectioni, Deus non interdum, sed semper, non libere, sed necessario, permittit peccatum, quia nunquam efficit aut committit peccatum, & haec permissio necessario Deo convenit." Rutherford, *Disputatio Scholastica*, 69.

125 "at permissione opposita impeditioni, interdum tantum & libere, quoties ita visum fuerit, peccatum permittit, nam libere impedit, aut non impedit Angelos aut homines peccare, permittit Adamum peccare, poterat non permississe, hoc est, non impedire, vel impedire poterat." Rutherford, *Disputatio Scholastica*, 69.

of a morally evil act, the emphasis in physical permission is the removing of the hinderance between the rational creature and his potential sin.[126]

In summary of the above, it can be said that the mode of permission is a positive expression of God's knowledge, will, wisdom, care, and power. When God permits sin, he concurs with the secondary cause in bringing about the material act, but God is not the author of the evil intent, which gives the act its sinful nature. God permits rational creatures to "go their own way" and commit sinful acts, which is moral permission. When he does so, he intentionally wills to remove any obstacles between the creature and sin. This is the physical nature of permission. When taken together, Rutherford's doctrine of divine permission is best understood as a positive act of the will (a) to withdraw divine aid and (b) not impede sin. Therefore, to say that permission is a positive act of willing evil is misleading. Here a distinction between first and second order acts of the will, put forward by Voetius and noted by Beck, is useful in interpreting Rutherford's position. Though Rutherford describes God's will to permit as a positive act, it is not a positive first order act of the will, whereby God wills sin directly. Rather, divine permission is a second order act where God wills to permit. The object of the will is the permission of the act, not the act itself.[127]

6.4   Providence, Permission, and the Necessity of Sin

A critical question in regards to the nature of permission is whether or not sin necessarily follows from permission. The pastoral dilemma is easily spotted. If sin necessarily follows from the divine permission, then sinners necessarily sin by the will of God. As a consequence, such face the fatal doom of final judgment. The Arminians denied that sin necessarily follows from permission.[128] The Jesuits affirmed that sin necessarily follows from the divine permission but this is not by virtue of the divine will, rather it is by virtue of the divine vision in regards to the *scientia media*.[129]

---

126 "At quando Diabolus & homines malum suadent, Deus potest esse agens physicum, non impediens, quo minus suasiones Diaboli & hominum, eo directae sint, ut homines peccent." Rutherford, *Disputatio Scholastica*, 70.

127 Beck, *Gisbertus Voetius*, 334–43.

128 See for example: Episcopius, *Apologia pro confessione declaratione sententiae eorum*, C 6, Sec III, 63. See: Joanne Arnoldo Corvino, *Petri Molinaei novi anathomici mala encheiresis: Seu censura anotomes arminianismi* (Frankfurt: Erasmus Kempffer, 1622), C 6, Q 6, 236.

129 See for example: Pedro da Fonseca, *Commentariorum Petri Fonsecae Lusitani, doctoris theologi societatis iesu, in metaphysicorum aristotelis stagiritae libros, tomus tertius* (Cologne: Lazari Zetzneri, 1603), Lib VI, C. II, Q. V, sec. VII, 144. Also: Didaci Ruiz De Montoya, *Comentarii, ac disputationes ad quaestionem XXII & bonam partem quastionis XXIII, ex prima parte S. Thoma, De Providentia*

In agreement with the Jesuits, Rutherford argued that sin necessarily followed from the divine permission, however his position is distinguished from theirs in that he places an emphasis upon the divine will rather than the divine vision. In either case, to argue that sin necessarily follows from the divine permission introduces the pastoral difficulty noted above. How Rutherford navigated this dilemma is outlined below.[130]

6.4.1 Rules Pertaining to Sin and Permission

When God permits sin, humans sin by the necessity of the consequence.[131] Rutherford made clear that the relationship between the necessity of the consequence and the sinner's evil act is to be taken in a sense that God is not causally responsible for the sin nor is the sinner's agency denied.[132] He went on to offer five rules to better understand the logical bond (*nexu logicali*) between divine permission and the sin permitted.[133]

The first rule is that when a person is permitted to sin, concupiscence, which remains even in the regenerate, always overtakes the person leading them to sin.[134] The very first rule gives large scope to human freedom within the doctrine of divine permission, but critically, it is human freedom under the rule of sin. This freedom is underscored by an interesting passage from Rutherford's *Catechisme*, where he wrote the following:

Q. Can Sathan force us against our will to sinne?
A. No, he tempteth us and knocketh at the door without, bot our will and lust oppineth the doore. Sathan is midwife that helpeth forward the birth, bot our will and lust is father and mother to all our sins.

Temptations "knocketh at the door" but cannot open the door. Only the sinner, by his own lust and free will may open the door. The culpability of sin is placed

---

praedesiniente, ac praebente praedestinationis exordium (Lyon: Jacobi Andreae & Matthae Prost, 1631), Tract II, Disp 11, Sec II, fig III, 172.

130 The source for the following is Chapter 8 in: Rutherford, *Disputatio Scholastica*, 80–6.

131 "Hinc posita permissione, necessario sequitur peccatum necessite consquentiae." Rutherford, 83.

132 "At quando *David* est formaliter permissus, semper necessario necessitate consequentiae seu illativae, non consequentis & causali, moechatur." Rutherford, *Disputatio Scholastica*, 82.

133 Rutherford, 82.

134 "I. Regula. *Posita permissione in subjecto capace, semper valet consequentia ab ea ad peccatum habituale.* Ut Deus permittit, hoc est, non curat concupiscentiam in renatis. Ergo semper est concupiscentia in renatis." Rutherford, *Disputatio Scholastica*, 82.

squarely on the sinner, who when permitted will always pursue sin and rebellion against God as a free act of his own will and lust.[135]

The second rule assumes that in every good act, God's efficacious grace is required that the good act may be performed with the right intention.[136] Thus permission includes, but is not limited to, the denial of this efficacious grace. The third rule is that when sin is permitted for judgement, sin follows by virtue of a strong consequence. For example, Pharaoh is permitted to harden his heart as a judgment for detaining the people of God. As a result, his heart is hardened. That sin follows the divine permission, when that permission has judicial aspects, is an important feature of God's ability to carry out judgments.[137] If permission of sin is judicial, in that God punishes sinners by permitting them to sin, and they are able not to sin, then God is not able to punish. Rutherford bluntly noted that such a scenario is "absurd."[138]

The fourth rule states simply that "permission is opposed to efficiency," reminding us of the point made earlier from Twisse that "man is permitted to kill" but "therefore he kills" does not follow.[139] Rather, as the fifth and final rule states (as a partial summary of the preceding four) sin always follows when (1) an individual with the capacity to sin (2) is here and now (3) denied efficacious grace towards a specific act (4) and sins by his own free will as a necessity of the consequence.[140]

---

135 Rutherford, "Ane Catachisme," 172.

136 "2. Regula. Posita permissione in omni actu morali, hoc est, Deo negante gratiam efficacem requisitam ad serventiorem intentionem actas boni, necessario est culpabilis defectus in actu bone." Rutherford, *Disputatio Scholastica*, 82.

137 "3. Regula. *Si Deus puniat aliquem permissione judicali, tum valet consequentia. Pharaoh* judicaliter permissus est obdurare cor suum. Ergo, *Pharaoh* obdurat cor suum, tam firma est consequentia quam certum est peccatorem non posse poenam a supremo Judice infligendam evadere." Rutherford, *Disputatio Scholastica*, 82.

138 "Si qui permittitur peccare, potest non peccare: tum quia permissio est executio divini decreti de salvandis hominibus per Christum estque saepe poena peccati, fieri sic posset ut rescinderetur Dei decretum, & sic Deus aliquem puniret permissione judicali, & is qui permissus est, non peccaret, tum ictus judicii divini esset a creatura declinabilis, & Deus peccatorem puniret, & peccator non puniretur a Deo, quod absurdum." Rutherford, *Disputatio Scholastica*, 84.

139 "4. Regula. Posita permissione prout opponitur efficientiae, non valet consequentia ad illationem peccati. Ut recte probant D. Twisse rationes; homo permittitur occidere. Ergo occidit, non sequitur." Rutherford, *Disputatio Scholastica*, 82.

140 "5. Regula. Posita permissione proprie dicta, in subjecto capace, praecepto hic & nunc urgente, hoc est, Deo ad talem actum negante gratiosam suam influentiam ex speciali sua intentione dirigendi actum, actusve omissionem ad certum a se praeconstitutum finem, semper sequitur peccatum tanquam necessarium consequens ex suo antecedente." Rutherford, *Disputatio Scholastica*, 82.

6.5   Providence and Fatal Necessity

The Reformed emphasis upon the divine will, particularly in regard to its relation to the necessity of sin, prompted charges of fatalism. This is why immediately following his exposition of God's permissive will, Rutherford attempted to distinguish his own understanding of God's providence from pagan notions of fatal necessity. In this section of the *Disputatio* he also sought to discuss in what ways Christians might rightly comprehend fate as a theological concept.[141]

Rutherford surveyed whether or not Christians could rightly ascribe to God's providence the word fate. He admitted there was some conceptual truth to pagan notions of fate, in that the human experience of God's providence was interpreted as fatal. Nevertheless, Christians are to distance themselves from the word fate because it easily misrepresents providence by attributing power to fatal causes other than God. Since the term "fate" is to be judiciously avoided, Rutherford's task from here was to determine in what ways it might be conceptually admitted. In order to do this, Rutherford studiously distinguished Christian concepts of fate from pagan notions. Following Giovanni Pico della Mirandola (1463–1494), Rutherford identified three pagan understandings of fate from which he sought to distinguish the true Christian understanding of the word.[142]

6.5.1 Natural Fate

The first concept of fate that Rutherford sought to distinguish from the true, Christian understanding was what he called natural fate, which he introduced by means of a metaphor. In the metaphor, the cosmos is compared to a civil government with three critical parts: (1) The wise prince to govern the city, (2) the constitution of the law for government, and (3) the execution of the law. In the metaphor the wise prince is God. The law that God constitutes is nature itself. In terms of a law as it relates to nature, it might be said that it is a law of nature that rain is wet, that the wind blows, or that all living things die. The actual execution of these laws places the creation under the necessity of the laws of nature and in this sense can be understood as fatal.[143] Following the notable Jesuit scholar Francisco

---

141 "An admittendum sit fatum aliquod Christianum." In: Rutherford, *Disputatio Scholastica*, 99–118.

142 For an introduction to Giovanni Pico Della Mirandola, see: W. G. Craven, *Giovanni Pico Della Mirandola, Symbol of His Age: Modern Interpretations of a Renaissance Philosopher*, Travaux d'Humanisme et Renaissance 185 (Geneva: Librairie Droz, 1981).

143 "Fatum vero magis pra se fert ordinem ex aliquo principio pendentem quasi effatum, mandatum, & enunciatum; nam ut in civili imperio consideratur princeps, cui congruit sapientia & providentia, quam sequitur constitutio legum, promulgatio & executio, ita in universo princeps est omnium Deus cui congruit sapientia & providentia, tanquam constitutio legum universi. Providentiam

Suárez (1548–1617) and Discalced Carmelite friar Antonio de la Madre de Dios (1583–1637), Rutherford offers a critique of natural fate noting that while the laws of nature often appear to necessarily come about, they can nevertheless be impeded by supernatural interventions such as the ministry of angels.[144] Also cited are the death, resurrection, and ascension of Christ and the destruction of Sodom by fire from the sky. These are two examples that could not have come about if fate was of the necessity of nature. For this reason, Rutherford rejects the notion that there is a fatal necessity that follows the laws of nature since the laws of nature can be interrupted by miraculous events willed by God.[145]

6.5.2 Stoic Fate

Rutherford's second interpretation of the word fate was Stoic. It is this form of pagan fate that was most often associated with the Reformed doctrine of the decrees. Thomas Jackson, an Arminian in Laud's circle, argued that the Reformed doctrine made God "eternally subject to his own decrees."[146] Furthermore, God had "passed his omnipotent word…before it could be taken or accepted by any creature." Thus "irrevocable doom had passed upon some of his best creatures before their nonage [in their nonexistence]." Thus in the same sense that the Stoic poets believed that the pagan gods were subject to the fates, so too had God made both himself and his creatures subject to the decrees.[147]

Rutherford agreed that if the Stoics did indeed teach that all things, even God, was subject to fatal necessity, they are rightly condemned.[148] But Rutherford believed that the opinion above is falsely attributed to the Stoics.[149] He argued the Stoics un-

---

autem fatum tanquam promulgatio legum, fatum sequitur natura tanquam executio legum, adeo ut fatum praesertim servet naturam ad primum principium." Rutherford, *Disputatio Scholastica*, 100–1.

144 "Quia neque effectus naturales in hoc inferiore mundo, ut pluviae, venti, fati naturalis necessitate eveniunt, ut recte ait *Suárez*: quia saepe impediri possunt, & sepe interventu causae liberae, nempe Angelorum ministerio eveniunt." Rutherford, *Disputatio Scholastica*, 101.

145 "Multa vi plane extraordinariae & supernaturalis providentiae imperio contingunt, ut Mors, Resurrectio & Christi in Coelos Ascensio: *Sodome*, per ignem coelitus demissum, consumptio." Rutherford, *Disputatio Scholastica*, 101.

146 Jackson, *A Treatise on the Divine Essence and Attributes*, 342.

147 Jackson, 342.

148 "Secundum fatum est Stoicorum, estque talis series causarum quae absolute necessaria sit, alligans omnes causas inter se, ipsumque Deum fato necessitans, quae opinion Stoicis tribuitur...& hoc sensu sic sententiam *Stoicorum* hoc modo explicatam Patres & Doctores Ecclesiae jure optimo damnant." Rutherford, *Disputatio Scholastica*, 101.

149 "Verum enim vero haec opinio fortasse Stoicis immerito & gratis tribuitur." Rutherford, *Disputatio Scholastica*, 101.

derstood fate to be subject to the divine providence. To establish his case, he quoted a prayer attributed to Seneca cited also by Augustine and Thomas Bradwardine. The prayer reads:

> Lead me, Supreme Father, and ruler of the highest heavens,
> Whatever it pleases you, nothing will hinder obedience.
> I am energetically here. If you make unwilling, I will follow groaning,
> and suffer to do evil, which was permitted good.
> The fates lead the willing, and drag the unwilling.[150]

Rutherford used the prayer, as do Augustine and Bradwardine, as an example of how the Stoics believed the necessity of fate was dependent upon God (Jupiter) and that God himself was not subject to the chain of fates, but rather that the chain of fates was subject to him.[151] The experience of fatal necessity that the ancient pagans felt, and which the poets expressed, has less to do with the irresistible nature of fate in and of itself, but rather is a direct reflection of the immutability of God in relation to his eternal decrees. What the ancients sensed as immutable fate was really God's providence.[152]

The problem with the ancients was not that they discerned fatal necessity, but rather that they attributed this fatal necessity to a "perpetual chain of causes." God is the "governor or master of all," including the chain of causes the ancients attributed to fate.[153] What God has infallibly and unchangeably determined according to his will, he brings about by his power irresistibly. Thus all things determined by God's will have an aspect of inevitability to them, and in this sense are fatal. It is this aspect of inevitability that Rutherford believed to be one of the chief objections of his polemical opponents and one that they wrongly attribute to pagan notions of fate. "Such a fate as this is known by Scripture," argued Rutherford.[154]

---

150 The prayer can be found in Seneca, *Moral Letters to Lucilius*, trans. Richard Mott Gummere (Toronto: Aegitas, 2015), Epst. 107; Augustine, "City of God," in *Augustine. Vol 2. Nicene and Post-Nicene Fathers*, ed. Philip Schaff (Peabody, Mass: Hendrickson, 2004), Lib 5.8. See also: Thomas Bradwardine, *De causa Dei*, Lib I Cap. XXVIII.

151 "Quibus verbis veritas evincit, & Augustinus probat Stoicos, sentire Jovem fato superiorem & in fatum dominari." Rutherford, *Disputatio Scholastica*, 102.

152 "Unde Dei immutabilitas, (qua quod semel decrevit, retractare aut rescindere non magis potest, quam potest mentiri, mutari, aut sese abnegare) similis est fato, quod ferrea & adamantina lege nunquam, ne in aeternum, revocanda stat firmum & irrevocabile & haec causa erat cur Stoici Deum & fatum idem esse finxerunt." Rutherford, *Disputatio Scholastica*, 102–3.

153 Calvin (Inst I.XVI.8), quoted by Rutherford "Non enim cum Stoicis necessitatem comminiscimur ex perpetuo causarum nexa, &c. sed Deum constituimus Arbitrum ac Moderatorem omnium, &c." Rutherford, *Disputatio Scholastica*, 103.

154 "Sed tale fatum agnoscit Scriptura." Rutherford, *Disputatio Scholastica*, 103.

Therefore a thing is this or that, according to what is spoken, or the plan Jehovah began, although in and of itself it is most contingent, it will necessarily be, indeed if this thing is under the utterance (fato) and declaration, decree and plan of God, it is not able not to be. And this is everywhere in Holy Scripture. (Gen. 21:1; 24:51; 28:15; Exod. 32:13; Num. 10:29; 23:19 etc.)

What the ancients intuited as fatal necessity, was actually the authoritative speech act of God. Unlike the fatal necessity imagined by the ancients, the *fatum de deo* is contingent and free. As the scripture proofs at the end make clear, Rutherford's remarks are not driven by philosophical speculation or rational proof. The scriptural witness itself testifies to the above.[155]

6.5.3 Mathematical or Astrological Fate

The third and final type of pagan fate that Rutherford dealt with is what he called mathematical or astrological. Rutherford defined mathematical or astrological fate as fatal necessity that flows from the position of the stars, or certain seasons placing a fatal necessity upon all inferior causes, including the free will of man.[156] Just as Rutherford did not reject the notions of the Stoics outright, neither did he do so with mathematical and astrological fate. The ancients were right to intuit a certain association with fatal necessity and stars and seasons. After all, the star above Bethlehem announced what could be called the fated event of the birth of Christ in Bethlehem. However, it should be noted that the star does not determine the fate of the Christ child, but rather the Christ child determined the fate of the star. Hence, the ancients were right to intuit an association of fatal power with the stars, but they were wrong to think that the stars themselves held the source of this power.[157]

6.5.4 Christian "Fate"

Rutherford introduced Christian and divine fate and distinguished it from these three pagan concepts of fate. He began with reference to Thomas Bradwardine:

---

155 "Ergo res haec vel illa, de qua fatus est, vel de qua Jehova consilium inivit, licet in se contingentissima necessario futura est, Vel haec res prout subest Dei fato & enunciato, decreto & consilio non potest non esse. Ita ubique sacrae Scripturae." Rutherford, *Disputatio Scholastica*, 111.

156 "At vero fatum imponens, ex astrorum influxu, in omnes causas inferiores, etiam voluntates liberas hominum." Rutherford, *Disputatio Scholastica*, 104.

157 "Ideo Gregorious Nissenus, Chrysostom, Augustin, Isidorus, Ambrosius, Hyrenimus, Fulgentius dicunt stellam non fuisse fatum pueri, sed puerum fuisse fatum stellae." Rutherford, *Disputatio Scholastica*, 110.

Divine fate is without doubt conceded, is it not written in the beginning of creation, God said (*fatus est*)? And this is the divine fate, and it is the greatest [part] of the divine will which is the effective cause of things.[158]

In the above, Rutherford followed an Augustinian tradition carried on by Bradwardine in regards to Christian discussions on fate. Here fate is considered less in terms of destiny, oracle, doom, or calamity. Rather here, *fatum* is seen as an authoritative speech act on behalf of God whereby he decrees all that was, is, and will be. The effect of the quote is to cement the creator/creature distinction, whereby God the Divine King speaks authoritatively and creation is (fatally) the product of this authoritative speaking. Thus there is a sense whereby every created thing is under the *fatum de Deo*, or the utterance of God. Two important features of Rutherford's doctrine of divine providence are established here. First, creation is conceptually subject to a certain kind of Christian fate, whereby what God freely decrees necessarily comes about. Second, because creation is subject to the *fatum de Deo*, it is free from the pagan concepts of fatalism outlined above. Later in the *Disputatio*, Rutherford wrote:

The created will is in fact made to be embraced, with his own internal moving, and thus the free act under the decree is more free because it is placed under the decree, because the decree stands by an agreement (*concursus*) of God whereby in a natural and most agreeable way it assists the free will of the creature.[159]

Unlike natural, Stoic, and mathematical fate, where impersonal forces impose fatal necessity upon the human will, God is able to exercise his providence in such a way that the human will is embraced rather than overthrown. God is able to do so, precisely because he is free from fatal necessity. Here, Rutherford's previous critiques against the Jesuits, Arminians, and Remonstrants come into sharp focus. The ontological presupposition upon which they relied upon to establish the *scientia media*, such as the determinate truth value of a proposition antecedent to God's will, imposes necessity upon both God and the human agent. In Rutherford's

---

158 Bradwardine, *De Causa Dei, Contra Pelagium, Et de virtute causarum, ad suos Mertonenses*, I.28 quoted in Rutherford's *Disputatio*: "Fatum divinum (inquit Bradwardin) est proculdubio concedendum, nonne scriptum est in principio creaturae, dixit (fatus est) Deus, istud autem est fatum divinum, estque maxime voluntatis divinae, quae est efficax rerum." Rutherford, *Disputatio Scholastica*, 110–1.

159 "Sed decretum conspirat in id quod creata voluntas de facto amplexabitur, idque motu suo interno, & sic actus liber subditus decreto est liberior quod subdita sit decreto, quia decretum statuit de concursu Dei qui connaturaliter & suavissime obstetricatur voluntati liberae creaturae." Rutherford, *Disputatio Scholastica*, 588–9.

accounting, this deprives God of the very freedom needed in order to guarantee the freedom of the human agent and, as a result, is as fatal as the pagan fates outlined above.[160] However, because God is free from fatal necessity, God is free to work in unison with secondary causes, including the human will, with all of its aspirations, intentions, and desires. The *fatum de Deo* comes to the human will not as an enemy to overthrow it but as a friend to help the will actualize the possibilities God has already decreed.[161] God's providence, even in regards to sin and evil, is not a thing to be feared. It poses no threat to the freedom and moral responsibility of the human will. How Rutherford understood this to work is the subject of the following, and final chapter.

6.6 Summary

Rutherford's doctrine of divine providence followed his doctrine of creation. Tendencies of Rutherford's polemical opponents to achieve independence for created entities were again identified here. The Remonstrant, Simon Episcopius, and the Jesuit, Francisco Suárez, both posited a latent, independent potency prior to creation. This was firmly denied by Rutherford, who argued that the scriptural witness testifies that God's power is able to call being out of non-being. Thus the created order, which is the object of the divine providence, is absolutely dependent upon God for its existence and continued care.

Rutherford's scholastic definition of divine providence was surveyed. It was shown that he relied upon certain distinctions from philosophy and the catholic tradition to elucidate the biblical witness. Providence is an act of God, whereby he applies his wisdom, power, and will to each and every ordainable thing, guiding all created being toward the goal of his own glory. God's providence conserves creation, lest it slip back into non-being. God directs all of creation towards his own glory and he cooperates with, rather than destroys secondary causes.

Controversial features pertaining to the doctrine of divine providence were also surveyed, specifically the relationship between God's providence and evil, as well as fatal necessity. Rutherford held that God never positively, directly, nor fatally effects sin in human agents. Rather, he permits them to sin. When permitted to sin, the human agent always sins, but this is by necessity of the consequence rather than by necessity of the consequent. The distinction is important, because it denies a

---

160 Hence Rutherford's many associations with the *scientia media* and pagan fate. For notable examples see Rutherford, *Disputatio Scholastica*, 17, 20, and 431.

161 "Non neganda est haec amicissima consotiatio creaturae, ejusque modi vel libere vel necessario agendi cum invicta Creatoris efficacissima voluntate, etsi non homunciones minime mente capere, vel intellectu comprehendere possemus tale mysterium." Rutherford, *Disputatio Scholastica*, 113.

causal relationship between God's permission and the sinner's sin. The sinner is the moral cause of the sin, as Rutherford made clear in a series of rules that outlined the relationship between permission and sin.

Finally, Rutherford discussed associations between the Christian concept of providence and the pagan concept of fate. In a nuanced discussion, Rutherford acknowledged certain associations. He also drew some fine distinctions. Unlike fatal necessity, God's providence is free and contingent. It is precisely because of the free and contingent nature of God's providence that God's creatures can enjoy freedom as well. Here the threat of certain logical apparatus that support the *scientia media*, which precede the divine will, is made apparent. If God is subject to something such as the pre-volitional determinate truth value of a proposition, then he is not free to ensure the freedom of his creatures. Such an accounting is therefore fatal. Rutherford on the other hand, held that God is free from such fatal necessity and is therefore free to ensure the freedom of his creatures. The manner of this relationship is outlined in the final chapter.

7. Providence, *Concursus*, and Human Freedom

> For we know that all things work together for the good of them that love God: hence I
> infer, that losses, dissapointments, ill tongues, loss of friends, houses or country, are God's
> workmen, set on work to work out good to you, out of every thing that befalleth you.[1]

In the previous chapter Rutherford's scholastic definition of God's providence
was outlined, followed by a summary of typical problems associated with God's
providence such as the presence of evil in the world and theological fatalism. This
chapter aims to explain and analyze Rutherford's theology of providence at the
more detailed level of the interaction between God's providence and specific acts of
being. We begin with two sections on the divine *concursus*. The first section will be a
survey of the Jesuit and Arminian doctrine of general and indeterminate *concursus*
along with Rutherford's critiques. This will be followed by Rutherford's presentation
of the Reformed doctrine of specific and determinate *concursus*. From here, his
understanding of the integrity of created free will under God's predetermination
will be outlined. Finally, this chapter will conclude with Rutherford's understanding
of how God and human determinations act jointly to produce specific acts of being.

7.1 Jesuit and Arminian Divine *Concursus*

7.1.1 Preliminary Considerations

Divine *concursus* falls under the heading of God's cooperation with all secondary
causes.[2] There are a variety of concerns regarding God's cooperation with secondary
causes. One concern is simply a matter of definition. What do the sixteenth and
seventeenth century theologians mean by the word "cause"? Beyond the matter of
definition, one must also be careful to consider how primary and secondary causes
relate to one another. Early modern theologians inherited a rich selection of models
from their medieval forbears. Given this, interpreters must avoid reductionistic

---

1 Rutherford, *Joshua Redivivus*, 88.

2 It may be remembered from the previous chapter that divine providence consists of three distinct
acts. These are (a) the conservation of all things, (b) cooperation with all secondary causes, and
(c) the direction of all things towards their appointed end. Concursus falls under the heading of
"cooperation." Rutherford, *Disputatio Scholastica*, 3; Muller, "Conservatio," in *Dictionary of Latin and
Greek Theological Terms*, 76.

readings of causality. Simplistic readings of causal relationships have not assisted in an accurate portrayal of Rutherford.[3]

The specific manner of God's cooperation with secondary causes, especially the created human will, was subject to fierce debate in the sixteenth and seventeenth centuries. The debate caused significant turmoil in the Roman Catholic Church with the Controversy *de Auxiliis*.[4] Within the Protestant world, the focal point of the debate centered upon Jacobus Arminius and the Remonstrants. As with many doctrines treated in the *Disputatio*, Rutherford did not begin with a positive explanation of his own doctrine, but rather with a critique of his opponent's. By beginning with the Jesuit and Arminian position, we follow Rutherford's own organizational principle.

7.1.2 General and Indeterminate *Concursus*

Rutherford made important distinctions between Jesuit and Arminian theologians regarding the divine *concursus*.[5] Though he could draw distinctions, he understood that the two shared important similarities. Broadly speaking, both the Jesuit and Arminian theologians understood the divine *concursus* to be both general as well as indeterminate.[6] These two features of the Jesuit and Arminian *concursus* will be outlined below along with Rutherford's critiques.[7]

To describe God's *concursus* as general first means that God's *concursus* is required as a necessary prerequisite for any secondary cause to produce an effect. Here there is no difference between Rutherford and his so-called adversaries. The critical difference is not that God's *concursus* is required to produce the effect, but that the general *concursus* of the Jesuits and Arminians does not concur immediately

---

3 For example, consider T. F. Torrance's description of Rutherford's doctrine of election and predestination as "interpreted in necessary, causal, and forensic terms" that "forced his thinking into line with the teaching of Beza and the Synod of Dort." See Torrance, *Scottish Theology*, 105.

4 The controversy is said to have begun at a public debate at the University of Salamanca in 1582 and ended unresolved in 1607. The controversy concerns the nature of efficacious grace and free will, with the Dominicans emphasizing God's sovereign grace in election along with their doctrine of physical premotion, and the Jesuits denying physical premotion and relying upon the *scientia media* to account for God's knowledge of future salvation. For a good historical overview, see Robert Joseph Matava, *Divine Causality and Human Free Choice: Domingo Báñez, Physical Premotion and the Controversy de auxiliis revisited*, Brill's Studies in Intellectual History 252 (Leiden: Brill, 2016), 16–36.

5 See for example: Rutherford, *Exercitationes Apologeticae*, 400.

6 See: Rutherford, *Disputatio Scholastica*, Chapter 25, 371–83.

7 A notable exception to Rutherford's focus on Jesuit and Arminian theologians is the Franciscan Capuchin Ludovicus a Dola. For Rutherford's reference, see Rutherford, *Disputatio Scholastica*, 373. The reference may be found in: Ludovico a Dola, *Disputatio quadripartita de modo coniunctionis concursuum dei et creaturae ad actus liberos ordinis naturalis* (Leiden: Iacobi & Petri Prost fratr, 1634), 222.

with the secondary cause to determine it to one effect. How does this work? In Molina's account cited by Rutherford, God's general *concursus* is not an influx of power in the secondary cause, pre-moving the created will. Rather it is an influx of power to produce the effect concurrently with the secondary cause.[8] The created will acts. Through this action of the created will, an effect is determined to which God obligingly concurs. Though the created will determines the effect, it cannot produce the effect on its own. The created will depends upon the divine *concursus*, which acts with the created will to produce the effect. This is the general nature of this *concursus*.[9]

The key to understanding the indifferent nature of the Jesuit and Arminian accounts of *concursus* is to note that God does not determine the secondary cause to one effect. Rutherford cited the Jesuit theologian and philosopher Roderico de Arriaga (1592–1667) as an example. Arriaga grounded the indifferent nature of the general *concursus* both in the attribute of God's omnipotence as well as in God's conditional will. Following Aristotle's famous example of voluntariness and involuntariness, Arriaga compared God to a merchant who wishes to convey his goods by sea. In doing so, the merchant wills two things. He wills to sell his goods and preserve life on the ship. He recognizes however, that these two wills may be at odds with one another. In good weather, both ship and the merchant's wares arrive safely in harbor and are congratulated. But, in the unfortunate instance of a storm, the merchant's goods may have to be abandoned to save the life of the crew. The merchant has power to send the ship on its way, but he does not have power to determine the outcome of the journey. Rather, the condition of the storm determines the outcome.[10] Like the example of the merchant and the ship, God wills

---

8 "Concursus nanq; Dei generalis cum causa secunda, not est influxus Dei in causam, sed in effectum una cum causa secunda, ut explicatum est: quare causa secunda non prius mota a Deo concursu generali producit effectum, sed influere simul Deo cum ipsa in effectum per concursum generalem, ut cum igne in calore inducendum in aquam, producit effectum..." Molina, *Concordia Liberi Arbitrii*, Q 14, Art.13, Dispt. 34, 217.

9 Molina's comments here are a clarification of Cajetan's, where Molina wants to distance Cajetan's understanding of concursus from Scotus. The primary cause does not pre-move the secondary cause, as per Scotus. Rather, the primary cause works with the secondary cause *in the effect*. "Quamvis enim videatur concedere Scoto, a causa prima moveri causam secundam per concursum generalem, ait tamen, motionem illam non esse propriam, quasi causa secunda motionem aliquam praeviam, accipit a prima: sed esse causam primam intime cooperari cum secunda in effectum, quod non videtur esse aliud, quam intime, una cum illa, influere per concursum generalem immediate in effectum absque actione aliqua in causam." Molina, *Concordia Liberi Arbitrii*, Quest 14. Art 13. Disp 34, 217. For Molina's reception of Scotus see Jean-Pascal Anfray, "Molina and John Duns Scotus," in *A Companion to Luis de Molina*, ed. Matthias Kaufmann and Alexander Aichele, Brill's Companion to the Christian Tradition 50 (Leiden, Boston: Brill, 2014), 325–64.

10 "Exemplo res haec pulchre declaratur. Mercator conscendens navim habet duas voluntates, & conservandi merces in navi, si fuerit prospera navigatio, & simul proiiciendi easdem in mare,

to apply his omnipotence to human action, but this willing is ineffectual regarding the outcome. The outcome, as Arriaga notes, is determined by the human will, not by God.[11]

7.1.3 Rutherford's Critique of the General *Concursus*

Rutherford offered a series of arguments against the general *concursus*, some of which are reviewed below. His first argument is that the general *concursus* introduces an imperfection in God's will.[12] According to this *concursus*, God generally concurs with the created will, but does not determine the specific acts until the created will is considered. Thus God must investigate the created will in order to determine whether or not to concur with acts of willing or not willing, or acts of love or hatred toward God.[13] The problem here is that God's perfect uncreated will is determined by the acts of an imperfect created will.[14] As Paul teaches in Romans (Rom. 11:34),

---

si ad tutandum vitam necessum fuerit: est tamen magnum discrimen inter has duas voluntates; nam conservare merces, si non sit tempestas, est illi voluntarium simpliciter, hoc appetit, hoc desiderat, in hoc complacet: at proiicere merces nullo modo illi placet, seu quasi necessitate coactus id appetit, quia aliter vitam tutari nequit: unde rursus provenit, ut conditionem illam, id est, serenitatem, ex qua pendet retentio mercium, ex se simpliciter optet, in ea presenti sibi congratuletur: e contrario vero tempestatem, quae est altera opposita conditio, a qua pendet mercium in mare proiectio, nec appetat, nec velit, nec de ea praesenti laetetur, sed tristetur, sed omnibus modis eam, si posset, sedaret. Ita suo modo Deus vult inefficaciter & actionem bonam, item & malam, diverso tamen valde modo." Roderico de Arriaga, *Cursus Philosophicus* (Paris: Franciscum Piot, 1647), 346. Thomas uses the same example in his *Summa Contra Gentiles*, Book 3, Part 1, Chapter 6. Unlike Arriaga, in this instance Thomas does not apply the example to the divine concursus. See: Thomas Aquinas, *Summa Contra Gentiles Book Three: Providence Part I*, trans. Vernon J. Bourke (Notre Dame: University of Notre Dame, 2001), 47. For the original example as found in Aristotle, see: Aristotle, *Nichomachean Ethics*, III, 1 (1110a 8–29); *The Complete Works of Aristotle*, 2, 1752. Rutherford's citation may be found in Rutherford, *Disputatio Scholastica*, 440.

11 "Si Deus se ipsum libere deberet determinare ad operandum, tunc futurum necessarium actum efficacem, quo omnipotentiam applicaret: at quia in eo concursu determinatur a creatura, sufficit illa voluntas inefficax quod ut intelligas, aduerte, Dei omnipotentiam ex natura rei esse indifferentem, ut subiiciatur quasi potestati voluntatis creatae, ad modum quo habitus voluntatis cum illa concurrens subiicitur ipsi voluntati, & sicut sol subiicitur causis particularibus, eumque determinantibus." Arriaga, *Cursus Philosophicus*, 347.

12 "Concursus ille in Deo non est fingendus qui imperfectionem ponit in Dei voluntate. Sed talis est hic concursus. Ergo, in Deo non est fingendus talis concursus." Rutherford, *Disputatio Scholastica*, 375.

13 "Nam opportet Deus dicat. Decerno generalem concursum praebere creaturis, sed nondum determinavi qualis in specie futurus sit, donec consulam voluntatem creatam. 2. Dicit Deus necesse est explorem voluntatem creatam, ut sciam nam identificandus sit concursus meus cum volitione, an cum nolitione, cum actu amori Dei, an cum actu odii Dei." Rutherford, *Disputatio Scholastica*, 375.

14 "Deus non in sese, sed in creaturis videt futuritionem actuum liberorum." Rutherford, *Disputatio Scholastica*, 375.

and as the Prophet Isaiah testifies (Isa. 40:13), God has no need to consult with the created will.[15]

The second objection, in which Rutherford followed the Dutch Reformed minister Antonius Walaeus (1573–1639), is that the general *concursus* renders prayer meaningless.[16] Because the general *concursus* is determined by acts of the created will, when Jacob prays that the patriarchs would find favor with Joseph (Gen. 43:14), or when Esther solicits prayers that she would find favor with King Ahasuerus (Esther 4:16), whether the prayers are answered or not is not determined by God but rather determined by the created will of Joseph and King Ahasuerus, respectively.[17] Thus answered prayers are either a matter of fortune or rest in the power of the created will. God is obliged to concur with either fortune or the human will to produce the effect, being helpless to actually determine the outcome himself. If this is true, the prayers of the saints are ultimately fruitless.[18] A third and fourth argument are closely related to the second; the former being that the general *concursus* makes God's promises empty and the latter being that Christian prayers of thanksgiving are made in vain.[19]

Another objection concerns the uncertain nature of the effects of the general *concursus*. If the effects are determined by the general *concursus*, meaning those things that will be or will not be, the effects themselves as well as the number of those effects is not dependent upon God but rather upon the secondary cause of the created will.[20] It follows, argues Rutherford, that the promise of God to bless

---

15 Rutherford, *Disputatio Scholastica*, 375.

16 See: Antonius Walaeus, *Responsio ad censuram Joannis Arnoldi Corvini, in cl. viri d. Petri Molinaei Anatomen arminianismi, et adscripta Remonstrantium qui ad Synodum Dordracenam citati sunt: pro defensione doctrina in eadem Synodo explicatae et stabilitate* (Leiden: Arnoldi Hoogenackeri, 1625), 89–90; Rutherford, *Disputatio Scholastica*, 376.

17 "Frustra oratur ut Deus Patriarchis *Josephi* favorem, & *Estherae* Deus conciliaret gratiam Assueri; non enim a Deo movente cor concursu determinabili & indifferente ad vel favoris vel odii actus, est quod *Josephus* potius odio aestuet, quam gratia viris arrideat, sed a voluntate *Josephi & Ahasueri* determinante concursum Dei ad actum gratiae potius quam ad actum odii." Rutherford, *Disputatio Scholastica*, 376.

18 "Preces ergo vel concipiendae sunt fortunae, vel hominibus ipsis, in quorum potestate absolute est, quod nos habeant in deliciis; nullo vero modo, Deo qui nec odium hominum constare, nec gratiam conciliare potest, nisi prout attribuerit hominibus *Dei* motionem determinantibus. Imo hic Sancti orarent influxum generalem Dei, Nihil enim talibus precibus jejunius." Rutherford, *Disputatio Scholastica*, 377.

19 These may both be found in Rutherford, *Disputatio Scholastica*, 377.

20 "Si effectus omnes fiant per Dei talem concursum indifferentem, per quem tam nono fiant, quam fiant, & per quem tam contrarii effectus fiant, quam hi; tum sequitur copiam aut inopiam frugum, ovium, leonum, piscium, item auri & argenti & divitarum, quae obediunt hominibus, actibus liberis mercandi, non esse a Deo." Rutherford, *Disputatio Scholastica*, 377.

the nation of Israel with abundance (Deut. 15:6) is false because God does not have power to effectually determine either abundance or poverty.[21]

Rutherford offered another interesting critique: what does the general *concursus* do to the traditional Christian understanding of fortune?[22] The Christian tradition maintained a place for fortune, but critically fortune was understood to be subject to fate, which was ultimately subject to God's providence.[23] In Thomas's account, which Rutherford seems to follow, fortune exists at the level of particular causes but not at the level of the universal cause. An example employed by Thomas is of two servants who meet along the road seemingly by chance. This chance encounter was arranged by their master, who intended all along that the two should meet. In the example, the servants represent particular causes and the master represents the universal cause. Fortune or chance is a real experience from the perspective of the particular causes but ultimately all things are attributed to God as the ultimate cause.[24]

Rutherford's criticism of the general *concursus* is that it inverts this sequence. Whereas Thomas placed the experience of fortune at the particular cause and attributed the effect to the universal cause, Rutherford noted that the Jesuits and Arminians placed the experience of fortune at the universal cause and attribute the effects to particular causes. Citing the Italian Jesuit Cardinal Roberto Bellarmine (1542–1621), Rutherford noted that under the general *concursus* the created will

---

21 "Hinc sequitur falsum esse, quod ait Scriptura epulentiam & pauperiem esse a Deo." Rutherford, *Disputatio Scholastica*, 377.

22 "Si concursus Dei sit indifferens omnino, multis modis evertitur particularis Dei providentia. Nam I. *Dispositio fortium non est a Deo.* Quia a Dei concursu, ad hanc vel illam fortem plane indifferente, non est egressus hujus potius quam illius fortis, sed vel a fortuna, vel a manu fortem apprehendente." Rutherford, *Disputatio Scholastica*, 377–378. To properly understand Rutherford's criticism, one must carefully distinguish between the concepts of fate and fortune as well as how the Christian tradition appropriated the concept of fortune. As was seen in the previous chapter, pagan fate is the imposition of necessity upon beings, even God himself. Christian "fate," is God's providential control over all things. The emphasis on the discussions surrounding "fate," in either the pagan or Christian sense is ultimate causes. Fortune (*fortuitum*) also translated as "chance" has more to do with unintended effects which are attributed to concepts of hazard or luck. See for example: Thomas, *Summa theologiae*, I, q. 22, a.2. For an excellent overview of the concepts as understood in the early modern era, see: Antonio Poppi, "Fate, Fortune, Providence, and Human Freedom," in *The Cambridge History of Renaissance Philosophy*, edited by Charles B. Schmitt, Quentin Skinner, Eckhard Kessler, and Jill Kraye (Cambridge: Cambridge University Press, 1988), 641–667. For an overview of the Christian appropriation of the concepts from the patristic to medieval period, see: Jerold C. Frakes, *The Fate of Fortune in the Early Middle Ages: The Boethian Tradition* (Leiden, New York: E. J. Brill, 1988); Vincent Cioffari, *Fortune and Fate From Democritus to St. Thomas Aquinas* (Whitefish, Montana: Literary Licensing LLC. 2011).

23 Frakes, *The Fate of Fortune in the Early Middle Ages*, 161.

24 Thomas, *Summa Theologiae*, I, q 22, a 2, 245–247.

determines effects to which God generally concurs.[25] However, placing the effects at the level of particular causes effectively establishes fortune as a determining cause. Thus, for Rutherford, once it is admitted that effects are determined at the level of particular causes, a great many consequences follow. No longer is the death of a sparrow, the judgements of a judge, or the accidental killing of a man by a faulty axe handle under the care of divine providence. Each is now caused by chance.[26] Rutherford argued that the result is that the Christian understanding of divine providence is rendered in terms of Epicurean providence.[27]

Rutherford also argued that the general *concursus* releases free acts of the will from God's dominion. The general *concursus* requires God to concur with secondary causes and makes it impossible for him not to concur.[28] Rutherford supplied two arguments for this assertion. The first is that the general *concursus*, being indifferent, has no more power to produce an act than not to produce an act. Such denies God's authority to administer the acts of his own creation, thus overthrowing his dominion.[29] The second objection argues that the general *concursus* inverts the natural sequence of primary and secondary causes posing significant logical

---

25 "Respondet Bellarminus. Actionem humanam plane totam esse a Deo, & ab ipso habere non solum esse genericum, sed etiam specificum & singulare: caeterum id habere per concursum Dei determinatum ad actionem talem a voluntate humana (seu a creatura) ac proinde non habere esse specificum ex modo agendi Dei, sed ex modo agendi voluntatis humanae (seu creaturae). Rutherford, *Disputatio Scholastica*, 378. Rutherford cites from: Robert Bellarmine, *De controversiis Christianae Fidei, adversus huius temporis hereticos* (Leiden: Joannem Pillehotte, 1610), Lib II. Cap. XVIII.

26 "Nec est a Deo, quod passer decidas in terram, quia volatus potius, quam non volatus a Deo non determinatur. Quando *unusquisque faciem judicis expetit, non est tamen a Domino uniuscujusque sententia:* quia Deus concurrens cum judice sententiam juridice dicente, indifferenter se habet ad aequam & iniquam sententiam. 4. Nec est a Deo quod homo occidatur a securi hominis ligna cedentis, & nihil tale intendentis: quia concursus Dei cum cadentis manu, & securis motione, est tam indifferens ad non occisionem viatoris, quam ad occisionem." Rutherford, *Disputatio Scholastica*, 378.

27 "Hi omnes sunt effectus determinati: at Deo non possunt tribui, stante hac sententia Epicurea." Rutherford, *Disputatio Scholastica*, 378. The Epicureans denied that the gods had any involvement in the affairs of humans. Both Christians as well as Stoics understood this as a denial of providence. In the Epicurean system, the affairs of humans were left to fortune and chance. See: Howard Jones, *The Epicurean Tradition* (London: Routledge, 1992), 97–106; and also Charles Partee, *The Theology of John Calvin* (Louisville: Westminster John Knox Press, 2008), 109–11.

28 "Non est talis in Deo concursus fingendus, qui actus liberos Dei dominio exsolvit, qui Deum ad agendum necessitat, & ad non agendum impossibilitat. Sed concursus Dei indifferens est talis. Ergo talis concursus non est fingendus." Rutherford, *Disputatio Scholastica*, 379.

29 "Si Deus concursu suo non magis actum quam non actum producit, non habet per suum concursum, ac proinde nullo alio causandi actu, in sua potestate actum potius, quam non actum." Rutherford, 379.

and theological problems.[30] For example, if God's *concursus* is determined by the secondary cause, then God's will is determined by the created will. If this is the case, a temporal cause will be the cause of something eternal.[31]

Following along similar lines, Rutherford stated a commonly held principle that determining causes, by nature of the determination, are both more actual and more perfect than the secondary causes upon which they act. But if God's *concursus* is determined by the secondary cause, as with the general and indefinite *concursus*, then God's concurring act would be less perfect than the secondary cause.[32] He supported his claim with an uncharacteristic appeal to the medieval Franciscan theologian and philosopher Bonaventure (1221–1274), as well as a citation from the Spanish Dominican Domingo Báñez (1528–1604).[33]

His final objection heightens the critique along the lines of causality. The general *concursus* places an influx of God's power posterior to the secondary cause. Rutherford argued that if this is so, then God could not be the cause of the action (*causa actionis*) of the secondary cause, since causes do not follow from effects. [34] Though unacknowledged, Rutherford's objection is most likely influenced by comments from Thomas's *De potentia*, q. 3, a. 7, where Thomas argued for four ways that a cause can be considered a cause of another's action. First, when a primary cause grants power to a secondary cause to act, the primary cause is said to be a cause

---

30 Rutherford follows Bradwardine here but wrongly cites *De Causa Dei*, lib. 2. Chapter 9. The actual quotation comes from *De Causa Dei*, lib. 2, Chapter 30. See: Bradwardine, *De causa dei*, 579–80.

31 "Si est in mea potestate concursus Dei, est etiam in mea voluntate, Dei voluntas aeterna concurrendi, & sic aliquid temporale causabitur aeternum." Rutherford, *Disputatio Scholastica*, 380.

32 "Causa omnis determinans, quia actualior est determinabili, est etiam perfectior. Ergo si Dei concursus a causa secunda determinatur, Deus erit causa minus perfecta quam causa secunda." Rutherford, *Disputatio Scholastica*, 380.

33 Bonaventure is not a common source for Rutherford. In this instance he appeals to Bonaventure but does not give the citation. For Báñez, see: Domingo *Báñez, Scholastica commentaria in primam partem angelici Doctoris D. Thomae usque ad sexagesimamquartam quaestionem* (Salamanca: S. Stephanum, 1585). Prima Pars, Q. 19, Ar. 8, ad. 2. Regarding Bonaventure's contribution to providence and causality, Schmutz has a generally negative appreciation of Bonaventure's role, arguing that Bonaventure's doctrine of general and special concursus is a doorway to semi-pelagianism. See J. Schmutz, "*La doctrine médiévale des causes* et la *théologie* de la *nature pure*," *Revue Thomiste* 102 (2001): 229–32. Cullin presents a more positive view of Bonaventure that emphasizes creaturely dependence and the need for grace, as well as God's freedom and the contingency of the created world. See Christopher M. Cullen, *Bonaventure*, Great Medieval Thinkers (Oxford: Oxford University Press 2006), 70–71. For more on Báñez and his understanding of causality, especially as it relates to concursus, see: Matava, *Divine Causality and Human Free Choice*, 37–99.

34 "Si concursus hic est posterior influentia causae secundae, tum non potest esse causa actionis causae secundae: quod absurdum. Nam causa non est effectu posterior. Si est prior, non potest ab influentia causa secundae determinari: quia omne determinans est prius non posterius determinato." Rutherford, *Disputatio Scholastica*, 382.

of the action. Second, when a primary cause is said to preserve the powers of the secondary cause, it is said to be a cause of the action. Third, when a primary cause moves the secondary cause to act, it is said to be a cause of the action. Fourth, when a principal agent causes the action of an instrument, it is said to be the cause of the action. In each of these ways, the primary cause of the action must be prior to the secondary cause, otherwise it would not be a cause of the act. But the general *concursus* places God as the cause of the action posterior to the effect. Furthermore, Thomas denied the possibility that a secondary cause can act without the power of God being the primary cause of the act. Thus, the general *concursus*, within the framework set out by Thomas, would render the action of secondary causes an impossibility.

Rutherford's critiques of the general *concursus* are a mix of theological, biblical, and metaphysical objections accompanied by a sensitivity to its negative effects on Christian piety. From these objections one can gain a sense of the difficulties of the general *concursus* from Rutherford's perspective. A key theme in the above, which has been identified in previous chapters, is that the general *concursus* of the Jesuits and Arminians deprives God of his own freedom, thus subjecting not only God, but the creation, to the impersonal forces of fate and fortune. If God is deprived of his freedom, not only are his own promises difficult to fulfill, but he is unable to guarantee created freedom. What is needed is an account of God's freedom whereby God's freedom is exercised in such a way as to ensure created freedom. Such an account is supplied by Rutherford. To this we now turn.

7.2 Rutherford's Doctrine of General *Concursus* and Physical Predetermination

7.2.1 Rutherford's Doctrine of the General *Concursus*

Before treating his own understanding of God's special and determined *concursus*, Rutherford offered a few interesting remarks on the general *concursus* and whether the term could be admitted by the Reformed. He understood the term may be admitted in two ways. In the first way, general *concursus* is applied to acts within the sphere of nature. This is contrasted with God's special *concursus*, which is applied to supernatural acts pertaining to the sphere of grace.[35]

---

35 "Uti generalis contradistinguitur a speciali: & sic generalis est Dei concursus in agentibus in sphaera naturae, specialis in sphaera gratiae. Et sic concedo concursum Dei generalem dari." Rutherford, *Disputatio Scholastica*, 383.

What might Rutherford have meant by acts of *concursus* in the "sphere of nature" and in the "sphere of grace"? A clue may come from the development of a similar distinction in Bonaventure, whom Rutherford employed earlier in a critique against the Arminian and Jesuit understandings of the general *concursus*. This may also help explain Rutherford's unusual reference to the same mentioned above.[36] Keeping with the general consensus of catholic teaching, Bonaventure held God's immediate *concursus* with all secondary causes to be a necessity of creation. No secondary cause could act without God's cooperation; thus God exercised a general influence upon the whole of creation.[37] It was also understood however, that God exercised a special influence upon creatures when it was necessary for the creature to perform an action above and beyond its natural capabilities. For example, the true knowledge of God gained through the study of scripture is not gained through the ordinary means of human investigation but through divine revelation. Through the special influence of the "blessed Trinity," the Holy Spirit divides and distributes the spiritual gift of faith, that Christ might dwell in the heart.[38] This Bonaventurian understanding of the general and special *concursus* aligns well with Rutherford's own use.[39]

There is another sense in which Rutherford was willing to admit the general *concursus*. This has less to do with the terms (i.e. general and special) and more to do with the way that primary causes and secondary causes interact. As was seen above, in the general *concursus* of the Jesuits and Arminians, the secondary cause determines the act to which the primary cause must concur to achieve the effect. While Rutherford was not willing to admit that the primary cause is subject to the secondary cause in regards to determination, he was willing to admit that the secondary cause limits the manner in which the primary cause acts.[40] He

---

36 See: 184, fn. 33 above.

37 "Quia enim Deus est causa primordialissima, ideo est influentiae maximae in causas secundas; et adeo magnae influentiae, ut nec modicum; seu quantumcumque parum, dum tamen aliquo modo sit ens procedat ab aliqua causa creata, nisi cooperante divina potentia." Bonaventure, "Sententiarum Lib. II," in *Opera omnia Tomus Tertius*, ed. A.C. Peltier (Paris: Ludovicus Vives, 1864–1871). Dist. XXXVII. Art. I. Q. 1. Conclusio, 491–2.

38 "Ortus namque non est per humanam investigationem, sed per divinam revelationem, quae fluit *a Patre luminum, ex quo omnis paternitas in coelo et in terra nominatur*, a quo per filium ejus Jesum Christum manat in nos Spiritus sanctus; et per Spiritum sanctum *dividentem*, et distribuentem dona *singulis, sicut vult*, datur fides; et *per fidem habitat Christus in cordibus nostris*." The language of the particular influence of the "blessed Trinity" is found in the paragraph immediately above this section. Bonaventure, "Breviloquium," in *Opera omnia Tomus Septimus*, ed. A. C. Peltier (Paris: Ludovicus Vives, 1864–1871), 240.

39 Rutherford applies the same distinction of natural and supernatural means of learning. See: Rutherford, *A Survey of the Spiritual Antichrist*, 47.

40 "Concedere possumus etiam concursum Dei generalem, qui determinetur a causa secunda in genere causae materialis, *a qua modificatur quatenus* (inquit *Cumel*) *concursus Dei recipitur a causa secunda juxta naturam, modum & exigentiam natura recipientis*." Rutherford, *Disputatio Scholastica*, 383.

cited the Spanish Mercedarian philosopher and anti-Molinist Francisco Zumel (1540–1607), Thomas Aquinas, and John Duns Scotus in support of his position. Thomas's remarks are the most helpful in plainly setting forth the idea Rutherford was advancing.[41]

In the *Summa Contra Gentiles*, Thomas stated that secondary agents were "particulizers and determinants of the primary agent's action."[42] Rutherford noted that the Jesuits seized upon these comments from Thomas to support their own understanding of the secondary cause's power to determine the primary cause to concur to one effect.[43] But according to Rutherford, this does not seem to be the sense of Thomas's remarks. Rather, what Thomas was saying is that when a primary agent concurs with a secondary agent, the primary agent's power is limited to act within the proper effect of the secondary agent. For example, the proper effect of fire is to burn. If God concurs with the secondary cause of a fire, God's power will be expressed through the proper effect of the fire thus concurring with a burning effect.[44] This achieves at least two things regarding God's providence. First, it ensures that the divine *concursus* preserves the natural order of secondary causes rather than destroying them. Second, it is an important feature in building towards a robust account of human freedom under God's sovereignty. If God does not destroy the proper effect of secondary causes but works within them, then God will not destroy free choice, which is a proper effect of the will. As will be seen later in this chapter, God's concurrence with the human will works within the bounds of the proper effect of the secondary cause.[45]

---

41 Rutherford cites: Francisci Zumel, *Variarum Disputationum* (Lyons: Ioannis Pillehotte, 1609), Par 3, 216; Thomas, *Summa Contra Gentiles Book Three: Providence Part I*, Chapter 66.6–8; John Duns Scotus, *In VIII. libros Physicorum Aristotelis Quaestiones, cum Annotationibus R .P. F. Francisci Pitigiani Arretini* (Lyons: Laurentii Durand, 1639), L.2, C.4.

42 "Secundum autem agentia, quae sunt quasi particulantes et determinantes actionem primi agentis, agunt sicut proprios effectus alias perfectiones, quae determinant esse." I have followed the translation in Thomas Aquinas, *Summa Contra Gentiles Book Three: Providence Part I*, trans. Vernon J. Bourke (Notre Dame: University of Notre Dame, 2001), 66.6, 219–220.

43 "Hoc sensu Thomas (licet Jesuitae mentem ejus depravent in alium sensum) dicit causas secundas esse quasi particularizantes actionem causae primae." Rutherford, *Disputatio Scholastica*, 383.

44 "Quod est per essentiam tale, est propria causa eius quod est per participationem tale: sicut ignis est causa omnium ignitorum." Thomas, *Summa Contra Gentiles Book Three: Providence Part I*, 66.6, 219–220.

45 God's concurrence does not destroy nature but rather perfects it. "Nam Deus, *cujus providentia* (ut ait *Dyonisius) est salvativa natura*, causas omnes etiam naturales non violentat; nam concurrendo cum sole illuminante, igne calefaciente, lupo ovem devorante, non vim infert, sed tales causas modo connaturalissimo agere finit." Rutherford, *Disputatio Scholastica*, 74.

7.2.2 Physical Predetermination

Unlike the Jesuit and Arminian *concursus,* which was general and indeterminate, Rutherford understood the divine *concursus* to be both specific as well as determined, even predetermined. The word predetermined, if not properly understood, is misleading in that it could convey a sense of fatal doom that deprives human freedom and implicates God in sin. As will be seen, such an understanding is far removed from what was intended by Rutherford.[46]

Rutherford began his discussion on predetermination by asking whether predetermination makes God the author of sin.[47] The question is a summary of objections posed by various interlocutors, though Rutherford chiefly engaged the Spanish Jesuit Diego Ruiz de Montoya (1562–1632).[48] Ruiz concluded that physical predetermination did make God the author of sin. This conclusion was largely based upon Ruiz's understanding of predetermination as causal in the sense that the effect of sin could be traced back to God's predetermination as the root cause.[49] But this is not how Rutherford understood the causal relationship between predetermination and sin. In fact, he believed such a relationship to be a metaphysical impossibility.[50]

Though the concept is introduced earlier in Rutherford's *Disputatio,* the first time that physical premotion appears in a chapter heading to receive dedicated treatment is in Chapter XXVI under the *Quaestio* heading: "Whether physical predetermination, by which God premoves the will to entitative acts of sin, makes God the author of sin?"[51] The question highlights Rutherford's preference for the term *physical predetermination (praedeterminatio physica)* over the term *physical*

---

46 The relevant sections of the *Disputatio* are Chapters 26–29. See Rutherford, *Disputatio Scholastica,* beginning on 383. See also Rutherford, *Exercitationes Apologeticae,* 396.

47 "An praedeterminatio physica, qua Deus praemovet voluntates ad actum entitativum peccati, faciat Deum authorem peccati?" Rutherford, *Disputatio Scholastica,* 383.

48 Rutherford interacts with: Ruiz, *In primam partem D. Thomae de voluntate Dei, disputatio XXVII*; Ludovico a Dola, *Disputatio quadripartita de modo coniunctionis concursuum dei et creaturae ad actus liberos ordinis naturalis* (Leiden: Iacobi & Petri Prost fratr, 1634); and Arriaga, *Cursus philosophicus.*

49 "Actio materialis individua includit bonitatem moralem secundum rationem genericam, specificam & numericam; moralitas itaque debet reduci in Deum, ut in primum agens morale. Ergo si Deus praedetterminat ad hanc actionem materialem odii Dei claudentem in se malitiam, potest esse causa moralis peccati." Ruiz quoted in: Rutherford, *Disputatio Scholastica,* 385. See also: Ruiz, *In primam partem D Thomae de voluntate Dei.* Disp. XXVII, Sect. 2.

50 It is important to remember that Ruiz is not interacting with Rutherford, but rather is participating in the *De Auxiliis* controversy. It is possible that some of Ruiz's critiques, aimed at Spanish Dominicans such as Domingo Báñez (1528–1604), whose theology could be described as "Thomistic," are not as effective against Rutherford, who resourced his understanding of predetermination from what he terms "Scotistic" theologians. See: Rutherford, *Disputatio Scholastica,* 386.

51 "An praedeterminatio physica, qua Deus praemovet voluntates ad actum entitativum peccati, faciat Deum authorem peccati?" Rutherford, *Disputatio Scholastica,* 383.

premotion (*praemotio physica*), though the question clearly shows that Rutherford understood there was a relation between the two terms. Beck states that the terms emerged in the scholastic literature of the sixteenth century prompted by the controversy surrounding middle knowledge (*scientia media*) and were likely coined by the Spanish Dominican Domingo Báñez (1528–1604) and the Spanish Mercedarian and anti-Molinist philosopher Francisco Zumel (1540–1607).[52] Though the term was never used by Thomas Aquinas, it nevertheless gained Thomistic associations because it became one of the distinctive marks of the neo-Thomistic, anti-Molinist doctrine of grace, especially within the Dominican school.[53]

There are three important elements to these two terms. The first is the adjective "physical." The second element is the prefix "pre." The third and final element is the root word of the compound, being *motio* in physical premotion (*praemotio physica*) and *determinatio* in physical predetermination (*praedeterminatio physica*). Each element will receive brief comments.

The first important element to the term is the adjective "physical," which is contrasted with "moral" in the scholastic literature. There will be opportunity for further comment on the differences between these two. For now, it is sufficient to say that a physical cause produces a physical effect. Examples of physical causes in Rutherford's writing include fairly straightforward examples such as the taking of the apple from the Tree of Knowledge, as well as the eating of the same apple. Also included in physical causes is the determination of the human intellect towards a physical act. Therefore, physical causes also include the intangible operations of the mind and the will whereas moral causes produce moral effects. Rutherford held that God predetermined the physical act only.[54] This is in keeping with other Reformed scholastics, who as Muller notes, denied a *praemotio moralis*, or moral premotion. Such would imply divine interference in human moral choices.[55]

The second important element is the prefix "pre," which serves as an indication that God's motion in the case of physical premotion, or determination in the case of physical predetermination, is prior to the action of the secondary cause. As Rutherford notes, the prefix is the controversy. The Jesuits preferred the prefix "con," indicating a temporally simultaneous event occurring between the divine and human wills.[56] It is important to note however, that Rutherford's emphasis here is not that this motion or determination is prior in time, rather prior in causality.

---

52 Beck, "The Will as Master of Its Own Act," 165.

53 Beck, 165.

54 "Physice determinare intellectum est actus Physicus: at consilium dare est actio ethica." Rutherford, *Disputatio Scholastica*, 384.

55 "Praemotio physica," in: Muller, *Dictionary of Latin and Greek Theological Terms*, 279.

56 "Quaestio tantum est de modo concursus; an condeterminando, seu an praedeterminando concurrat, uterque concursus utrinque agnoscitur ut causativus. Scilicet pauperes hae duae praepositiones *con,*

Like the Jesuits, Rutherford held that God's concurrence is temporally simultaneous with a creature's actions. God's *premotion* and *predetermination* on the other hand are structurally prior to creaturely action.[57]

The third and final important feature of the term is the root word *motio* in *praemotio physica* and *determinatio* in *physica praedeterminatio*. Regarding the first, *motio* is not understood as a collision between bodies in motion, such as a tennis racket sending a ball across the court. Rather, "motion" should be understood as the cause behind a created potency moving from a state of non-operation to operation.[58] The Aristotelean physics of the day assumes rest unless motion is introduced. Since all movers are themselves moved because they would otherwise be at rest, there must be a first, unmoved mover. This further underscores the point made by the prefix "pre."[59]

Finally, the root word "determinatio," in *physica praedeterminatio,* was most often employed by Rutherford to explain God's divine determination with respect to future contingent events. For example, consider Jesus's certain knowledge of the future contingent event of Peter's denial of Christ recorded in Matt. 26:34. This event, as well as Jesus's knowledge of it, was often represented in the literature of the day, including in Rutherford, as a pair of contradictory conditional propositions.

(a) If Peter is tempted, he will sin.
(b) If Peter is tempted, he will not sin.

Jesus's prophesy at the last supper, as well as the events later in the evening, demonstrate that (a) is a determinately true proposition and that Jesus had certain knowledge of its determinate truth. On this point, all agreed. The point of disagreement was how the proposition could be known to be determinately true. The Jesuits and Arminians relied upon some version of the *scientia media*, whereby God infallibly sees which proposition was determinately true. This explanation depended upon the assumption that in a pair of contradictory conditional propositions, one part of the pair must be determinately true and the other determinately false before a determination of the divine will.[60] As was shown earlier in this study, Rutherford held that neither (a) nor (b) must be determinately true before the divine

---

& *prae,* Deum vel peccati condemnant, vel crimine absolvunt." Rutherford, *Disputatio Scholastica,* 384.

57 Matava, *Divine Causality and Human Free Choice,* 44.

58 Matava, *Divine Causality and Human Free Choice,* 43–44.

59 "Motus," in: Muller, *Dictionary of Latin and Greek Theological Terms,* 223–24.

60 "Replicant, Pet. De. Arrubal, & Ariaga, non esse parem rationem, quia in disparatis nulla est connexio omnino, quia posita conditione, nempe si Petrus tentabitur, repugnat ut Petrus nec determinate peccet, nec determinate non peccet, alera ergo pars est determinate vera, altera falsa, & qui hoc

decree. Rather, the propositions are neutral in regard to their truth value.[61] The propositions gain truth value because God freely wills for one part of the pair to be determinately true, thus making a divine determination. It is a "pre" determination, because God's determination of (a) is antecedent to Peter's temptation and subsequent determination to sin.[62]

Physical premotion may therefore be said to be an act of God, which is antecedent to the action of a secondary cause, awakening the powers of the secondary cause to produce a physical rather than moral effect. Physical predetermination emphasizes the role of God's will to make a divine determination, this is prior to the free determination of the human will. Though Muller correctly notes Rutherford's use of *praemotio physica*, it is important to note that between the pair of terms, Rutherford shows a clear preference for the term *physica praedeterminatio*, using it almost exclusively. His clear preference for this term is consistent with his overall emphasis upon the critical role of the divine will in his theological system. Both *praemotio physica* as well as *physica praedeterminatio* can be represented schematically as follows:

---

praedicit re ita se habente, veram pracdicit. Ergo erat verum ante praedictionem." Rutherford, *Disputatio Scholastica*, 16.

61 "Uti in simplice & prima operatione intellectus, quae compositione & divisione careat, nihil veritatis, nihil falsitatis est, quia omnis veritas est in affirmatione & negatione, *prout ita res sese habet vel non habet*, in objectiva connexione rerum quae subjecti & attributi locum tenent." Rutherford, *Disputatio Scholastica*, 541; There is a similar remark in the *Exercitationes* that is polemically focused upon Suárez's notion of intuition. Nevertheless, the point is very much the same. "De ente vere futuro, neutra pars ante Dei Decretum, est vel ver, vel falsa proprie, quia extrema propositionis nempe (*Petrus*) (constitutio in tali-ordine) & (peccatum) sunt non entia, ideoque non vera, non scibilia, ac proinde eorum connexio est non ens and non verum, sed indifferens ad veritatem & falsitatem." Rutherford, *Exercitationes Apologeticae*, 191. For more on Scotus's theory of neutral propositions see: Beck, "'Divine Psychology and Modalities."

62 The joining of the extreme terms and the determination of the divine will is explained as follows: "Quoties ergo sacra Scriptura hujusmodi consequentiis utitur, toties valet consequentia non ex connexione terminorum simpliciter, sed ex libera constitutione & predeterminatione Dei: Haec enim consequentia plane ridicula & vana foret. (*Tyrii videbunt signa, Ergo Tyrii resipiscent*) Si per impossibile ponamus nullum esse decretum, nullamve in Deo providentiam quae connectat inter se haec extrema, nam ex se, & ex rei natura, nullo modo indeclinabiliter inter se cohaerent, Tyriorum resipiscentia & signorum visio." Rutherford, *Disputatio Scholastica*, 22.

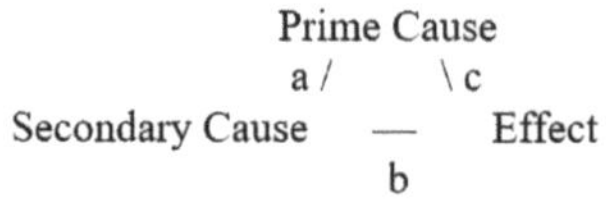

Prime Cause
a /   \ c
Secondary Cause   —   Effect
b

Fig. 5 Physical Predetermination

In the above, (a) represents the physical predetermination or physical premotion that awakens the powers of the secondary cause to act, (b) represents the action of the will towards an effect, and (c) represents God's concurrence with the secondary cause to produce the effect.[63]

There is a way to interpret the above in a determinist sense. Jesuits such as Diego Ruiz de Montoya (1562–1632), who Rutherford engaged throughout this chapter, argued that God's predetermination imposes a necessity upon the human will by effectively determining the secondary cause to only one effect. Schematically, this critique may be presented as follows:

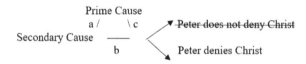

Prime Cause
a /   \ c   ⬉ ~~Peter does not deny Christ~~
Secondary Cause   ——   <
b   ⬊ Peter denies Christ

Fig. 6 Jesuit Critique of Physical Predetermination With Freedom of Indifference Removed

---

63 I have used van Ruler's schematic from J. A. van Ruler, "New Philosophy to Old Standards: Voetius's Vindication of Divine Concurrence and Secondary Causality," *Nederlands archief voor kerkgeschiedenis / Dutch Review of Church History* 71, no. 1 (1991): 58–91.

Just as before, (a) represents God's premotion or predetermination awakening the powers of the secondary cause and (b) represents the action of the human will towards an effect. However, as can be seen above, Ruiz argued that God's predetermination effectively rules out one of the objects of choice, thus determining the secondary cause to only one effect. Thus, (c) represents God's concurrence to this pre-determined effect. The Jesuits with whom Rutherford interacts concluded that not only did physical predetermination" make God the author of sin, but the same also deprived the human agent of its freedom of indifference, since one object of choice was effectively removed through the divine determination.[64]

7.2.3 Physical Predetermination and Co-Efficiency

Rutherford denied the characterization immediately above. His position is based upon a distinction between the physical nature of the act and the moral nature of the act.[65] Consider the act of Adam eating from the Tree of the Knowledge of Good and Evil (Gen. 3.6). The act has two causes and two effects.[66] Regarding the present discussion, the physical cause accounts for a variety of natural phenomena. Such physical causes have physical effects. For example, the physical cause of chewing has the physical effect of food grinding between the teeth. Critical to this discussion is to note that physical causes are morally indifferent. There is nothing morally good nor bad about eating fruit from a tree.[67]

---

64 "Actio materialis individua includit bonitatem moralem secundum rationem genericam, specificam & numericam; moralitas itaque debet reduci in Deum, ut in primum agens morale. Ergo si Deus praedetterminat ad hanc actionem materialem odii Dei claudentem in se malitiam, potest esse causa moralis peccati." Ruiz quoted in Rutherford, *Disputatio Scholastica*, 385. See also Ruiz, *In primam partem D Thomae de voluntate Dei*, Disp. XXVII, Sect. 2.

65 The following discussion retreads some previously covered ground. See this study: Ch. 4.4 and Chapter 6.3.

66 The two causes and two effects cannot be separated, but they must be distinguished. "Aliud est rectitudo moralis simplex quae adhaeret actui entitativo: aliud vero rectitudo moralis complexa resultans ex compositione vel divisione. Nam aequitas adhaerens actui entitativo diligendi Deum est simplex aequitas. Uti iniquitas adhaerens actui entitativo odio habendi Deum est simplex anomia & illegalitas. Dices non distingui, actum odii Dei entitativum, & ανομια vel malitiam actus. Respondeo realiter forte separari non possunt, sed distinguantur necesse est. Quoniam Deus est Author & efficiens per se & causa actus entitativi in odio Dei, sicut est author actus entitativi manducandi fructum arboris scientiae; est enim causa & author omnis entis positivi & omnis actionis physicae. At vero Deus nec author nec causa est malitiae in odio Dei." Rutherford, *Disputatio Scholastica*. 335.

67 Rutherford leans on Bradwardine to establish the point. "Amplius autem videtur, quod nullus interior actus per se malus sit, quia nec blasphemia nec odium Dei quod potest ostendi, sicut & de actibus exterioribus est ostensum in Morionibus & etiam furiosis: & quia quilibet talis actus est quaedam naturalis perfectio talis potentia naturalis." Bradwardine, quoted in: Rutherford, *Disputatio Scholastica*, 335. See also: Bradwardine, *De causa dei*, Lib. I, c. 26.

Distinct from physical causes are moral causes. In order to be a moral cause, the agent must have the capacity to be morally culpable for the act. This can only be the case when the moral agent is under the law.[68] Returning to the case of Adam and the Tree of Knowledge, Adam was a moral agent because he was subject to the divine prohibition of eating from the tree. While the physical act of eating is indifferent from a moral perspective, the malicious intentions of breaking the divine command are not morally indifferent. These intentions are what lend moral status to the physical act.[69]

Rutherford held that God predetermined the physical cause only.[70] In what amounts to a remarkable affirmation of the bedrock goodness of creation, he argued that God not only predetermined the physical acts but that such predetermination was an act of divine love. He loves the material acts he predetermined from eternity and concurs with in time. Malice can only be joined to such acts by moral agents under the law. It is not the act, but the malice joined to the act that God hates.[71]

As was shown in the last chapter, only those held under the law can be morally culpable. Since God is not under the law, he cannot be held morally culpable. Because he cannot be held morally culpable, he cannot be a moral cause.[72] This is how Rutherford understood it to be a metaphysical impossibility that God could be the author and cause of sin. God merely predetermines the physical act, providing the sufficient condition or necessary substructure for the existence of the moral act.

---

68 "Quia vero, sola lex obligationem inducit, nota imputabilitatis ei qui legi non subest, inuri minime potest." Rutherford, *Disputatio Scholastica*, 68.

69 Rutherford appeals to Thomas's *de Malo*, both to draw distinctions between physical and moral acts as well as to explain how the evil intention of the act, and not the physical nature, gives it the quality of sin. "Ad secundum dicendum quod deformitas peccati non consequitur speciem actus secundum quod est in genere natura: sic autem a Deo causatur; set consequitur speciem actus secundum quod est moralis, prout causatur ex libero arbitrio, sicut in alia quaestione dictum est." Thomas Aquinas, *De Malo*, trans. Richard Regan, ed. Brian Davies (Oxford: Oxford University Press, 2001), Q 3, Art 2., 238. See also Rutherford, *Disputatio Scholastica*, 401.

70 "Nemo nostrum sic loquitur, Deum esse causam physicam peccati, nam peccatum qua tale & essentialiter est effectus moralis, nec habet causam physicam proprie loquendo." Rutherford, *Disputatio Scholastica*, 386. Similar arguments are repeated in numerous places and are a key feature of Rutherford's overall argument. The significance is not merely to absolve God from moral culpability, but it also functions to deny God's causal role in sin.

71 "Amari potest actus materialis complacentia physica, non morali, quando non amatur malitia nisi complacentia morali. Et Deus physica complacentia primae causae propria ama actum materialem, & tamen respectu complacentiae moralis Legislatoris propriae, moraliter odit malitiam ei annexam." Rutherford, *Disputatio Scholastica*, 401.

72 See this study Ch. 6.3.2.

It is the moral agent, such as Adam, who joins malice to what would otherwise be a morally indifferent endeavor, thus lending it the moral status of sin.[73]

Rutherford described God's predetermination as the *conditio causandi*, that is the condition or ground of causing.[74] This is distinct from the *formalis ratio causandi*, or formal reason of causing. Muller defines the *ratio formalis* as the "reason or basis in a thing or act for it being what it is."[75] In regard to sin, the reason or basis in an act for it being a sinful act is the malicious intent of the moral agent.

In the scholastic discourse of the day, the *conditio causandi* was not as often distinguished from the *formalis ratio causandi* as Rutherford did above, rather it was distinguished from the *virtus causandi*, or the power of causing. This more traditional distinction helps the interpreter better understand Rutherford's point. The distinction between the *virtus causandi* and the *conditio causandi* is helpfully explained by the Carmelite priest Raphael Aversa (1588–1657) in his explanation of causes.[76] Consider a man warmed by a fire. The power to cause (*virtus causandi*) the warming is held in the fire itself. In this regard, the fire could be said to be the formal reason for the warming of the man, but the fire itself is not sufficient to warm the man. The man must be near the fire. Unless he is near the fire, he will not be warmed. His nearness to fire constitutes the necessary condition (*conditio causandi*) for his being warmed, but his proximity to the fire does not have the power in and of itself to warm him.[77]

---

73 "Sol igitur non est causa effectuum sublunarium quod absurdum; sol enim est in se causa indeterminata, & ad generationem & ad corruptionem, ad molliendum & indurandum, ut ab his inferioribus determinatur: Deo autem concursus de se inclinat ad actum; quia omnis causa per se in effectum inclinat, non dicimus concursum Dei inclinare in peccatum, sed in actum, hunc vel illum, prout Deo libitum est, uti habitus inclinat in actum hunc vel illum, prout determinatur ab eo qui habitu praeditus est, & sic eo modo concursus Dei est causa actu substrati malitiae, uti habitus est causa actus. Nec Dei praedeterminatio est causa inclinans ad malitiam de se: sed praedeterminatione abutitur mala voluntas." Rutherford, *Disputatio Scholastica*, 434–5.

74 "Determinatio est tantum conditio causandi, non formalis ratio causandi." Rutherford, *Disputatio Scholastica*, 394.

75 Muller, "ratio formalis," in *Dictionary of Latin and Greek Theological Terms*, 305.

76 Rutherford does not appeal to Aversa here, nevertheless Aversa's more detailed remarks provide a useful opportunity to understand how this term was applied in the scholastic discourse of the day.

77 "Ad causandum concurrere solent quaedam conditiones: quae vel possunt se habere tanquam adjuvantes causam ad facilius seu celerius operandum: vel possunt esse simpliciter necessaria & requisita ad causandum, huiusmodi conditio appellatur sine qua non, idest sine qua causa non causaret, ut se habet propinquitas ignis ad calefaciendum, & aliae plurimae. Differt autem conditio a virtute causandi; quia haec virtus per se & directe exercet actum causandi, conditio autem tantum comitanter requiritur, ad hoc ut ipsa causa per suam virtute exerceat actu causandi: calefactio v.g. per se exercetur a potentia calefactiva ignis, no vero a propinquitate, sed propinquitas est tantum conditio requisita." Raphaele Aversa, *Philosophia metaphysicam physicamove complectens quaestionibus contexta in duos tomos distributa* (Bologna: H. H. Euangeliste Ducciae, 1650), 378.

What Rutherford has been asserting is that God's predetermination merely provides the necessary condition (*conditio causandi*) for the will's power to act to produce a certain effect. Regarding a decision by the human will, just as the man's proximity to the fire does not affect the burning of the fire, Rutherford argued that God's predetermination does not cause the human will to act any differently than it would have otherwise. God freely determines to provide the physical cause, while the human agent freely determines to act physically and with moral intent.[78] Thus, God and the human agent provide two partial causes, each of a different nature, one physical, the other moral, which act jointly to produce a total effect. Schematically it can be represented as follows:

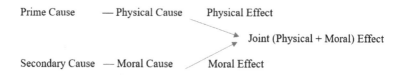

Prime Cause   — Physical Cause   Physical Effect

Joint (Physical + Moral) Effect

Secondary Cause   — Moral Cause   Moral Effect

Fig. 7 Dual Causality

Predetermination therefore is the determination (by God) to provide the sufficient physical condition to which a moral intent may be joined (by man).[79]

Muller has described Rutherford's doctrine of predetermination as drawing from the Thomist *praemotio physica*.[80] Though Rutherford uses the Thomist term, he credits the Franciscan theologian Theodorus Smising (1580–1626), who Rutherford identified as a Scotist, as having been his resource in exegeting this doctrine.[81] As was seen earlier with Rutherford's use of the *scientia simplicis intelligentiae et*

---

78 "Non sunt aliud in ratione causandi, *Deum effective concurrere ad actionem peccandi materialem, Et. Deum proprie & per se eandem actionem operari.* Quia utrumque sit salva libertate: quia praedeterminatio non ponit aliquid in voluntate ipsam fortius necessitans, quam actio Dei non determinans in ea ponit." Rutherford, *Disputatio Scholastica*, 393. Rutherford is challenging remarks made in: Ruiz, *In primam partem D Thomae de voluntate Dei*, Disp. 32, Sec. 7.

79 See fn. 66 above.

80 Muller, *Divine Will And Human Choice*, 319.

81 Rutherford, *Disputatio Scholastica*, 386.

visionis distinction, Rutherford appears to be using terms traditionally understood as Thomist but building upon them with Scotist solutions. What is portrayed in the above are two partial causes, one physical and one moral, which act jointly to produce one effect. This is reminiscent of Bradwardine's doctrine of co-efficiency, covered earlier in this study, and also resonates with the Scotistic conception of co-causality.[82]

There is an important point to be made above in terms of God's moral culpability and association with sin. In Rutherford's construction, God predetermines the physical act to which malice is annexed by a moral agent in time. Though questions could rightly be posed as to whether God is implicated in the moral act by providing the physical substructure, the moral culpabilities are clearly delineated. God is the physical cause. The human is the moral cause. In the Jesuit and Arminian scheme, as Rutherford points out, the matter of moral culpability is not as clear. Whereas in Rutherford's scheme God predetermines the physical act antecedent to the annexation of malice by the moral agent, in the Jesuit and Arminian scheme God determines to concur consequent to the determination of the moral agent.[83]

Rutherford identified problems with this construction insofar as it pertains to moral culpability. Jesuits, such as Ruiz, argued that God does not will sin directly and expressly, but rather God wills it in another. But as Rutherford pointed out in his critique of Ruiz, if God does not will sin directly and expressly, he wills it indirectly and virtually. This is, admitted Rutherford, very close to the Reformed position outlined above. The difference however, is that since in the Jesuit account God's will to concur follows an act of the human will, then God is obligated to concur with a sinful act. This both deprives God of his freedom as well as forces him to serve the cause of sin.[84] Though it could be said God acts unwillingly, he nevertheless is

---

82 For more on co-causality, see: Frank, "Duns Scotus on Autonomous Freedom and Divine Co-Causality"; Bac, *Perfect Will Theology*, 443–53. Also see this study Ch. 5.3.3.

83 See Ch. 6.3.3.

84 "Et mysterium latet in hic adverbiis, *directe & expresse*. Nempe igitur *indirecte & virtualiter*, & quasi coactus & contra voluntatem optativam quae in bonum inclinat, vult Deus ut fiat peccatum, & id qua tale produci desiderat at certe hoc est in sententiam fere nostram ire, sed si concurrero physice ad actum faciat Deum causam peccati, tum deterior est hic *Jesuitarum & Arminianorum* sententia, quam nostra, quia cogitur Deus munere causae universalissime velle peccatum & peccatum causari, at servilius est cogi ad causandum peccatum, quam libero id causari." The adverbs "directly and expressly" are taken from Ruiz, who argued that God did not will sin directly and expressly. It is Rutherford who draws the conclusion from Ruiz, that if God does not will sin directly and expressly then he wills it indirectly and virtually, which it is worth noting that he believes this to be very close to the Reformed position. However, Rutherford believed that the actual Jesuit and Arminian position, as can be seen above, makes God serve the cause of sin since his determination to concur follows the human will. See Rutherford, *Disputatio Scholastica De Divina Providentia*, 390; also Ruiz, *In primam partem D Thomae de voluntate Dei*, Disp. 51, sec. 3.

obliged to concur, thus associating him with the sinful act. Rutherford's insistence that God's predetermination precedes human willing and is merely physical, while not alleviating all concerns regarding God's moral culpability in sin, nevertheless avoids the thorny implications he perceived in the general *concursus*.[85]

The above remarks were prompted by the question as to whether physical predetermination implicates God as the author of sin. For Rutherford, the distinction between physical and moral causes was enough to say "no." Though the above is in response to the question of predetermination and sin, this does not mean that there is nothing to say in relation to physical predetermination and acts of righteousness. When the human being is suffering under the condition of sin, the wounded will is disordered and always intends malice towards God.[86] God's physical predetermination provides the sufficient physical conditions to which the human joins malicious intent. Under the aid and restorative powers of divine grace however, the healed will supplies different moral intentions. In his *Tryal and Triumph of Faith*, Rutherford wrote:

> There is no goodnesse in our will now, but what it hath from Grace, and to turn the will from ill to good, is no more natures work, then we can turn the wind from the East to the West: when the wheels of the clock are broken and ruined, it cannot go. When the birds wing is broken, it cannot flye: When there is a stone in the sprent and the work of the lock, the key cannot open the door. Christ must oyle the wheels of misordered will, and heal them, and remove the stone, and infuse Grace (which is wings to the bird), if not the motions of the will are all hell-ward.[87]

God's grace restores the ruined wheels of the clock, mends the broken wing of the bird, and repairs the lock on the jammed door. Having done so, God's physical predetermination works with a properly functioning will, which intends the good.[88]

---

85 For a summary of a similar argument developed by Báñez during the controversy *de Auxiliis*, see Matava, *Divine Causality and Human Free Choice*, 95–101. A strong critique of Báñez, and perhaps by default some of Rutherford's points, may be found in David Bentley Hart, "Providence and Causality: On Divine Innocence," in *The Providence of God*, ed. Francesca Aran Murphy and Philip G. Ziegler (New York: T&T Clark, 2009), 34–56. Hart's critique is weakened by overlooking certain key distinctions and elements, most importantly that the *praemotio physica* is not an efficient cause of sin, but merely the sufficient physical cause for which a moral act may be annexed.

86 See Ch. 6.4.

87 Rutherford, *The Tryal and Triumph of Faith*, 7–8.

88 For Rutherford, the human will's new inclinations to acts of obedience to God are a sure sign of efficacious grace. In response to how one may know that God has made him a new creature, Rutherford answers: "If he be willing to obey God in all things, and for the love of God renounce all sinnes (Acts ix.6; ii.37; Psxl. 8, 9; cxix; James ii. 10)., Rutherford, *Ane Catechisme*, 201.

Whether suffering under sin, or restored by divine grace, physical predetermination does not jeopardize the freedom of the will.

7.3   The Human Will and Its Determination

Having outlined Rutherford's understanding of God's role in physical predetermination, we now turn to understanding the role of the human will in supplying its own determination. In order to do this, we need to understand Rutherford's definition of the human will as a free cause, its objects and operations, and its determination. From here we will be better prepared to appreciate Rutherford's understanding of how God's will and the human will act together in a joint determination.

7.3.1 The Human Will as Free Cause

The human will is first and foremost a free cause. Just as was seen earlier, "cause" is a deceptive word for the concept being conveyed here. Rutherford's understanding of the will as a "free cause" has less to do with causal laws, and more to do with the capacity and activity of the will as causal agent.[89] The key difference between the natural cause and the free cause is that the free cause is not determined to one effect. It is free to function as a cause or not. Natural causes on the other hand, such as fire, are determined to one effect (i.e. fire burns). Presupposing all necessary conditions (i.e. air, fuel, etc.), the fire is not free not to burn. The human will, according to Rutherford, is a free cause which acts from its own internal principle. To the degree that it is a free cause, it is free from any external causes that might deprive the will from making its own determination. Thus, the will is free from violence (*violentum*), fortune (*fortuitum*), and the supernatural (*supernaturale*).[90]

Rutherford did not define what he meant by "violence," perhaps because he thought it was unnecessary to do so. The term had been used by previous Reformed scholastics to describe when a "type of action in which the movement by an external

---

89 Osborne's comments in regard to Medieval thinkers and causation rings true in Rutherford. "Medieval thinkers generally understand causation in terms of capacities and activities of agents, and they are not preoccupied with causal laws." See Thomas M. Osborne Jr, *Human Action in Thomas Aquinas, John Duns Scotus, and William of Ockham* (Washington, DC: The Catholic University of America Press, 2014), 1–2.

90 "Causa ex communi sententia, alia est naturalis, quae ὸν ωρὰς ὸν τάτεσεεσαι, ut habet philosoph. & agit necessario, ut ignis; alia libera, quae potest vel operari, vel non; sic, vel alio modo ut libertas humana, quae quamvis naturaliter, ex interno principio, hoc est opposite ad violentum & fortuitum, vel etiam ad supernaturale, agat, ideoque hoc sensu causa naturalis dici debeat, tamen non determinatur ad unum effectum producendum, & sic jure, non naturalis, sed libera causa censetur,…" Rutherford, *Exercitationes Apologeticae*, 1.

principle does not correspond with or rather is contrary to the internal principle of the object."[91] An example, given by the Reformed scholastic Girolamo Zanchi (1516–1590) is when a stone is thrown upward. This is termed violent, because the upward motion of the throw is contrary to the natural inclination of the stone to fall. The will is free from such violent external causes.[92]

So too is a free cause opposed to an external cause that is fortuitous (*fortuitum*). In the *Disputatio Scholastica de Divina Providentia*, Rutherford set forward a fairly standard definition of fortune as stated by Aristotle, noting his agreement with the Jesuits in Coimbra who defined fortune as an "accidental cause, because it is contrary to intention."[93] Not only is it a cause contrary to intention but it is also contrary to a decision born by deliberation (*consilio*). As a cause "contrary to intention," it is opposed to a truly free cause because it is contrary to the internal principle of the will.[94]

The last external cause mentioned by Rutherford was that of the supernatural. This does not mean that supernatural causes such as God, angels, or the devil cannot influence the will. They could bring the will under an ineffectual moral suasion, but they cannot impose a necessary determination upon the will thus depriving it of its freedom.[95] The point here is that these supernatural causes do not necessarily determine the will to one effect.[96] When viewed with the previous external causes (i.e. violence and fortune), it is clear that Rutherford was attempting to rule out the possibility that an external cause could rob a free cause of its ability to act or not act, or to force it into one effect. The point in ruling out external causes was to underscore the integrity of the human will as a free cause.

7.3.2 The Objects and Acts of the Will

The freedom of the will may be applied to two spheres, its objects and actions. Object is understood as an object of choice. For example, Rutherford may choose to eat an apple or a pear, the fruits being presented by the senses and intellect to his will as objects of choice. Acts are understood to be acts of the will that can be

---

91 Dolf te Velde, "Always Free, But Not Always Good: Girolamo Zanchi (1516–1590) on Free Will," in *Reformed Thought on Freedom: The Concept of Free Choice in Early Modern Reformed Theology*, ed. Willem J. van Asselt, J. Martin Bac, and Dolf T. te Velde, Texts and Studies in Reformation and Post-Reformation Thought (Grand Rapids, MI: Baker Academic, 2010), 85.

92 te Velde, "Always Free, but Not Always Good: Girolamo Zanchi (1516–1590) on Free Will," 85.

93 "Sic Doctores Conymbricenses Franciscus Murcia de llana. Fortuna (inquit) appelatur causa per accidens quia est praeter intentionem." Rutherford, *Disputatio Scholastica*, 363.

94 "*Fortuna* formaliter opponitur intentioni & consilio..." Rutherford, *Disputatio Scholastica*, 364.

95 Rutherford, 70.

96 There is precedence for this in other Reformed scholastics. See: te Velde, "Always Free, but Not Always Good," 59.

applied to the objects of choice. There are three such acts: willing, not willing, and suspending action.[97] When applied to two different objects, for example the apple and the pear, Rutherford may will one object (the apple) and not the other (the pear). It is possible that Rutherford has already had breakfast, and thus refrains from willing either the pear or the apple, thus suspending any action of the will.[98]

Regarding the objects of the will, they may be understood according to their material or formal aspects. The material aspects of the objects of the will are either good, bad, or indifferent. The formal aspects of the objects of the will are every electable thing able to be joined to a good end.[99] Rutherford's two-fold distinction of the objects of the will into their material and formal aspects shares similarities with another common distinction dating back to Aristotle's *Ethics*, which classifies actions of the will as the desire for self-evident ends on one hand (θελησις) and the pursuit of means acceptable to pursue good ends on the other (προαιρεσις). There is however, a clear difference. In Aristotle's scheme there are certain self-evident goods that are absolutely desirable that the will pursues naturally without any hesitation or need for deliberation.[100] Rutherford held that the will had a natural predisposition or inclination towards pursuing the good.[101] There will be more to say on this later, but for now it is enough to note that Rutherford held that this natural disposition did not determine the will to one effect, even in the case of such self-evident goods referenced above. Rutherford understood that the mind may apprehend such goods, such as eternal blessedness, but that the will could divert the mind to lesser goods

---

97 Rutherford calls these operations "fonts" or "acts" of the will. "Ponamus enim, rei enuncleandae gratia, esse in voluntate libera tres numero distinctos fontes e quibus featuriunt tres rivuli vel tres actus nolendi, volendi, & actum suspendendi, voluntatemque pro sua libertate interna posse exhaurire quemvis rivulum, vel ex primo vel ex secundo vel ex tertio fonte, non autem potest ex omnibus tribus fontibus simul elicere & velle, & nolle & suspendere actum copulative, sed unum tantum disjunctive ex natura rei necessario eliciet." Rutherford, *Disputatio Scholastica*, 408.

98 Beck links the freedom to do or refrain from doing to both the freedom to exercise (*libertas exercitii*) as well as the freedom of contradiction (*libertas contradictionis*). See Beck, *Gisbertus Voetius*, 404–5.

99 "Objectum liberi arbitrii est duplex, vel materiale vel formale. Materiale est bonum, malum, αδια-φορον. Formale est totum hoc eligibile qua bonum ad finem conducens." Rutherford, *Exercitationes Apologeticae*, 2.

100 See: te Velde, "Always Free, but Not Always Good," 80–81.

101 "Itaque voluntas qua libera agit, in seipsam quatenus est voluntas per naturam ad bonum volendum determinata, & libertas haec in actu primo nec radicaliter, nec formaliter est in intellectu, quippe facultas haec appetens immediate inhaeret animæ, absque ullo mentis ratiocinio intermedio, & non parum miror, qui potentia libera conveniat voluntati, mediante potentia intellectiva, quia voluntas tam immediate & per se est libera, quam mens est cognoscitiva." Rutherford, *Exercitationes Apologeticae*, 2.

in order to please the flesh.[102] This final point roots the power of election firmly in the will, since the will could reject the practical judgment of the intellect.

7.3.3 The Nature of the Will

Having established the above, Rutherford advanced the discussion to consider the nature of the will and the formal principle of its liberty. He noted that the will may be considered according to:

(I)   Its nature, and this it has in common with other agents, in that it seeks the good.

(II)   As it is such a nature, and thus it is drawn to blessedness by an essential inclination antecedent to freedom, as Thomas says, not by a deliberation of the mind or freely.

(III) As it is free.

(IV) As it is good or bad.[103]

The first point simply states that just as a plant strives for sunshine, or an animal strives for food and water, the will strives for its own good. The human will has this in common with other agents. The will is distinguished from these other agents in two ways. First, non-sensory agents such as plants, or even sensory gifted agents such as animals, pursue goods necessarily and unreflectively. The human will on the other hand, as point (III) above makes plain, pursues its goods rationally and freely. Goods are presented to the will via the senses, judged to be good or bad by the intellect, and freely elected by the will.[104] The second difference between such agents and the human will is that the ultimate good that the human will desires is

---

102 "At vero stante ultimo in se & formaliter, videtur quod possit voluntas intellectum avocare a cogitando de illo objecto ita ultimate proposito, ad alia quae quamvis minus efficaciter moveant & suadeant voluntatem, quam illud ultimum, attamen, quia voluntas potest duo hic praestare. I. avocare mentem a consideratione illius ultimi objecti ad aliud contemplandum, & 2. Avocare mentem ab actuali collatione hujus posterioris boni terreni, cum illo coelesti, quod in se efficacious movebat voluntatem, ideo non necessario determinat libertatem." Rutherford, *Exercitationes Apologeticae*, 398.

103 "Voluntas consideratur I. ut natura, & hoc ei commune est cum aliis agentibus, ut in bonum feratur. 2. ut est talis natura, & sic feratur in beatitudinem, inclinatione essentiali libertatem antecedente, ut innuit *Thomas*, non mentis deliberatione, aut libere. 3. ut est libera. 4. ut est bona vel mala." Rutherford, *Exercitationes Apologeticae*, 3.

104 This distinction is addressed in Thomas, upon whom Rutherford is relying upon to develop this argument. Thomas argued that the different parts of creation function together in order to achieve a common end. The common end being the glory of God. Thomas draws a distinction between how non-rational beings and human beings pursue this common end when he writes: "Ulterius autem, singulae creaturae sunt propter perfectionem totius universi. Ulterius autem, totum universum, cum singulis suis partibus, ordinatur in Deum sicut in finem, inquantum in eis per quandam imitationem divina bonitas repraesentatur ad gloriam Dei, quamvis creaturae rationales speciali quodam modo

blessedness (*beatitudo*).[105] Rutherford called this desire for spiritual blessedness an inclination of the will, antecedent to the judgment of the mind and prior to the freedom of the will.[106]

The will's inclination to the good means that though the will may be indifferent, it is not neutral. The will is by nature inclined to willing good in this life and most of all, eternal blessedness in the life to come.[107] Rutherford followed Thomas to briefly establish the prior inclination of the will to the good, as well as to establish how such an inclination is not contrary to freedom.[108] Put simply, the will is an appetitive faculty. It desires and can even be said to be hungry for the good. If the senses present an object to the intellect, and the intellect judges the object to be good, then it will be desired by the will. Though the inclination is not subject to free will, acting upon that inclination is dependent upon an action of the will. The will may elect to pursue that particular good. Contrarily, the will may call the intellect away from the contemplation of that good in order to pursue a greater or lesser good.[109] A vivid example of this in Rutherford comes from his remarks on Abraham's sacrifice of Isaac in *Christ Dying and Drawing Sinners to Himself.* Rutherford noted that Abraham had a "naturall inclination and love" for his son as well as a "desire that hee may live." He also noted that God did not command Abraham to "root out of thine heart all desire and inclination naturall in a father to preserve the life of the child." Rather, the command to sacrifice Isaac presupposes that the natural inclination remains, but that the will is able to set this inclination aside to choose something contrary to the inclination. In this instance, the contrary inclination is the sacrifice of Isaac. In Rutherford's understanding, inclinations residing in the will in no way jeopardize its freedom.[110]

Rutherford's position concerning the will's relation to the intellect is an interesting feature of his overall position on human freedom. As can be seen from the above, the will is subject to certain natural inclinations as well as the judgement of the intellect.

---

supra hoc habeant finem Deum, quem attingere possunt sua operatione, cognoscendo et amando." Aquinas, *Summa theologiae*, I, q 65, a. 2, 140.

105 Rutherford understands blessedness as a moral condition where one has a "holy walk" before God, empowered by the Holy Spirit. Blessedness also entails a state of communion with God. See Rutherford, *Influences of the Life of Grace*, 156, 223, 321.

106 See Ch. 7, 198–199, fn 102. See also Rutherford, *Exercitationes Apologeticae*, 2.

107 Poetically expressed in Rutherford's "Ane Catechisme" as follows: "He (man) was made with his face to look to heaven to teach him to follow his look, and condemn those whose face looks up to heaven and their soull down to clay." Rutherford, "Ane Catachisme," 167.

108 For Rutherford's citation see Rutherford, *Exercitationes Apologeticae Pro Divina Gratia*, 3. See also: Aquinas, *Summa theologiae*, I, q.83 a.1, 317–18.

109 For a useful and straightforward account of how this functions in Thomas see Eleonore Stump, "Aquinas's Account of Freedom: Intellect and Will," *The Monist* 80, no. 4 (1997): 577–83.

110 Rutherford, *Christ Dying and Drawing Sinners to Himselfe*, 140.

Nevertheless, according to Rutherford, the will is not necessarily obligated to either. Natural inclinations may be set aside by the will, and the practical judgment of the intellect can be redirected by the will. This sets Rutherford apart from other Reformed Orthodox theologians such as Francis Turretin (1623–1687), who held that the will necessarily follows the last practical judgement of the intellect, a position Muller has described as "more Thomistic than a broadly Franciscan" or Scotist approach.[111] Rutherford's position on the other hand, which denied that the will must necessarily follow the judgment of the intellect, not only roots human liberty in the will but it also associates him with a position regarded by many to be distinctly Scotist. Here again, Rutherford may be seen initiating a discussion with a nod to Thomas while concluding it in an implicitly Scotist manner.[112]

Rutherford's final point above (IV) states that the will may be considered good or bad. Before the fall, the will was inclined to good.[113] However, the power to do evil nevertheless existed. When Adam sinned against God, he was exercising a natural power of the will.[114] Though the act of eating the fruit from the Tree of the Knowledge of Good and Evil considered in and of itself is morally indifferent, when this act is considered under the law it is sin.[115] Since any act of the human will is never considered simply, but always under the law, the acts of the will are moral in nature. This is a key feature of Rutherford's overall argument of divine *concursus*. As was shown earlier, God contributes a physical determination to human actions. Here, the basis for the human contribution of a moral action is made plain.

---

111 "Quarta *necessitas rationalis determinationis ad unum ab* intellectus practici judicio, cui refragari non potest voluntas." Francis Turretin, *Institutio Theologiae Elencticae* (Fredericum Haring & Ernestum Voskuyl: Leiden, 1696), 729. See Muller's remarks in Muller, *Divine Will and Human Choice*, 253.

112 "Potest enim voluntas intellectum avertere ad consentiendum uni conclusioni et non alteri." Scotus, *Lectura II, dist. 7–44*, in *Opera Omnia*, vol. 19, edt. Commissio Scotistica (Città del Vaticano: Typis Polyglottis Vaticanis,1993), *Lect II.*, d. 25.29. Anfray has argued this is a distinct feature of Scotism and has argued for its presence in the Scottish Universities in the early modern era. See Jean-Pascal Anfray, "Scottish Scotism? The Philosophical Theses in the Scottish Universities, 1610–1630," *History of the Universities*, vol XXIX/2, ed. Alexander Broadie (Oxford: Oxford University Press, 2017), 100.

113 "At vero in *Adamo* ante lapsum, non erat inclinatio ad malum, nam voluntas ipsius sancta inclinabatur ad Dei legem praestandam." Rutherford, *Exercitationes Apologeticae*, 4.

114 "Erat in eo potentia naturalis ad τὸ comedere, & ad τὸ non comedere fructus, qui erant actus natura mere indifferentes, & accedit iis actibus ut quid extrinsecum, quod essent legi cohibiti aut determinati, *Adamus* autem tantum actuabat potentiam naturalem." Rutherford, *Exercitationes Apologeticae*, 4.

115 "In eo vel *Adamus* o peccabat, non quod simpliciter actuaret potentiam naturalem, sed quod actuabat potentiam legi subditam & restrictam per Dei interdictum, ex non consideratione libera objecti interdicti." Rutherford, *Exercitationes Apologeticae*, 4.

When Adam exercises this power towards a bad end, the will was deformed.[116] The will still seeks its own good and could even be said to be inclined to good. The problem is that the deformed will no longer perceives good as good. Rather, the will perceives evil as good. Like a compass that no longer points to true north, the fallen will is inclined towards objects that appear to it to be good but are not truly good. Thus, Rutherford can argue that when demons do evil it appears good to them because their "misshapen desires" make it so.[117] What is true of the demonic will is true of the human will. The will believes itself to be hungering for and electing the good but is now inclined to evil and incapable of choosing good.[118] These capabilities are restored under grace.[119]

Rutherford noted that following the fall, the will no longer enjoys freedom to the same extent it did before the fall. As was seen above, the will no longer enjoys the freedom to pursue the highest good.[120] Following Calvin, Rutherford noted that the will now lacks "the natural ability to mount up unto the clear and pure knowledge of God."[121] He also looked to Thomas, who notes in the *Summa Theologiae* that man has lost freedom from fault and from unhappiness. And though freedom of the will has demonstrably changed after the fall, there is a sense in which freedom of the will is said to remain. Again, looking to Thomas, Rutherford notes that freedom from coercion remains after the fall.[122] And to Lombard, he noted that the will retains the freedom to move willingly and spontaneously.[123] Looking to Bonaventure, he

---

116 "Potentia enim peccandi vel respicit actum entitativum peccati, & hæc ex se non erat potentia moralis indifferens, vel ἀνομίαν ipsam, & hæc non suit propriè potentia, sed naturalis ipsa potentia quatenus legi subdita, quæ quidem potentia nulla suisset, si Deus legem, (uti potuit, libere enim suæ creaturæ leges ponit) non præscripsisset homini; servitus quidem & vitiosa ad peccandum inclinatio inest homini post lapsum, ea vero non tam potentia est, quam curvitas potentiæ, nec magis est de natura liberi arbitrii, quam potentia claudicandi, est de formali ratione facultatis locomotivæ." Rutherford, *Exercitationes Apologeticae*, 4.

117 "*Demon* tentando non intendit malum qua malum ipsi Daemoni, hoc verum est, quia quo inhonestius est illud ad quod Diabolus solicitat, eo Diaboli pravae voluntati melius & jucundius apparet, ideoque est illi bonum." Rutherford, *Disputatio Scholastica*, 413.

118 Rutherford, "Ane Catachisme," 172.

119 See Ch. 7, 196, fn. 87.

120 "Forma liberi arbitrii, non est spontaneitas, aut non coactio, haec intellectui & voluntati in relatione ad summum bonum convenit." Rutherford, *Exercitationes Apologeticae*, 5.

121 John Calvin, *Institutes of the Christian Religion*, trans. Ford Lewis Battles, vol. I, ed. John T. McNeill (Louisville: Westminster John Knox Press, 1960), Lib 1, Chapter 5, Sect. 14–15; Rutherford, *Exercitationes Apologeticae*, 5.

122 "Ita *Aquinas*: homo no quoad libertatem naturalem, quae est a coactione, sed quantum ad libertatem, quae est a culpa lib. ar. perdidit." Rutherford, *Exercitationes Apologeticae*, 5. See also Thomas, *Summa Theologiae*, 1–2. q. 83. a. 2, 131–133.

123 "Ita *Lombard*. libere moveri est voluntarie & spontaneo motu moveri." Rutherford, *Exercitationes Apologeticae Pro Divina Gratia*. 5. See also Peter Lombard, *The Sentences*, trans. Giulio Silano, vol.

asserts that the fallen will is free from the necessity of coercion.[124] Rutherford's point here was to demonstrate that the Reformed (via Calvin) and the *Pontificii* share broad agreement in regards to their understanding of freedom after the fall. The human will, both before and after the fall is a free cause, not determined to one effect. It is free from violence, from supernatural determination, fortune, and coercion. Nevertheless, since the will is no longer free for the good, it is bad in the sense of point (IV) above.[125] Only under the power of God's efficacious grace is the deformed will restored to a measure of goodness.[126]

7.3.4 The Freedom of the Will

Having developed his understanding of what the will is free from, both before and after the fall as well as under grace, Rutherford proceeded to a more succinct definition of what freedom of the will means. He begins with a definition of freedom provided by the Jesuits and embraced by the Remonstrants. The definition stated, "Free will is the power to act or not act, all things requisite for the action being posited."[127]

2, ed. Joseph Goering and Giulio Silano (Toronto: Pontifical Institute of Medieval Studies, 2008), Lib 2. d. 25, 116–122.

124 "Necessitas coactionis (inquit *Bonaventura*) repugnat libero arbitrio, non necessitas immutabilitatis." Rutherford, *Exercitationes Apologeticae*, 5.

125 Rutherford is well within the Reformed Orthodox tradition in his understanding both in the loss of certain freedoms as well as the freedoms retained after the fall. For examples see: te Velde, "Always Free, but Not Always Good," 63–9; B. J. D. van Vresswijk, "An Image of Its Maker: Theses on Freedom of Franciscus Junius (1545–1602)," in *Reformed Thought on Freedom*, ed. Willem J. van Asselt, J. Martin Bac, and Dolf T. te Velde, Texts and Studies in Reformation and Post-Reformation Thought (Grand Rapids: Baker Academic, 2010), 104–5; and E. Dekker and M. A. Schouten, "Undisputed Freedom: A Disputation of Franciscus Gomarus (1563–1641)," in *Reformed Thought on Freedom*, ed. Willem J. van Asselt, J. Martin Bac, and Dolf T. te Velde, Texts and Studies in Reformation and Post-Reformation Thought (Grand Rapids: 2010), 130–1.

126 See: Rutherford, *Tryal and Triumph of Faith*, 7–8.

127 "Jesuite Zuarez, Vasquez, Fonseca, Lod. Molina, Becanus, & Jac. Armin. Remonsr. In script. Synodorum, Corvinus, volunt naturam ipsius esse potentiam ad agendum vel non agendum, etiam positis requisitis ad operationem omnibus, quod an sacrilego in Dei providentiam, & gratiam ausu fiat, cum bono Deo videbimus." Rutherford, *Exercitationes Apologeticae*, 6. Rutherford's rhetorical and polemical question at the end may imply that he does not accept the definition. As will be seen, this is not so. He embraces the definition but does not believe it to render a sufficient account of the freedom of the will. His definition draws from Pedro da Fonseca, *Commentariorum Petri Fonsecae Lusitani, Doctoris Theologi Societatis Iesu, In Metaphysicorum Aristotelis Stagiritae Libros, Tomus Tertius* (Cologne: Lazari Zetzneri, 1603), lib 6. Cap. 2. Q. 5. sect. 8; Molina, *Concordia Liberi Arbitrii: Cum Gratiae Donis Divina Praescientia, Providentia, Praedestinatione, Et Reprobatione*, q. 14, a. 13, disp. 2, sec. 3; Simon Episcopius, *Apologia Pro Confessione Declaratione Sententiae eorum*,

There are a few features in the above worth pointing out. First, it is worth noting how similar the first portion of the definition is to Rutherford's own definition of a free cause.[128] As Rutherford did earlier, here the Jesuits and Arminians set forward the so-called freedom of contradiction, since acting and not acting are contradictory actions. Second, the definition presupposes that the will is indifferent to acting or not acting. Again, there was significant agreement between Rutherford and the position being outlined. Finally, the power to act or not act is dependent upon "all things requisite for the action being posited." Here again, there was near universal agreement between Rutherford and his Jesuit and Arminian polemical opponents. As Beck notes, all agreed that certain prerequisites, such as the divine decree, the divine *concursus*, and the practical judgment of the intellect needed to be in place for the will to act. Despite these points of agreement, there was a significant point of controversy. The point of disagreement lay in whether these prerequisites (i.e. the divine decree, the divine *concursus*, etc.) had power to determine the will to one effect by implying a specific act.[129]

Rutherford addressed this point of controversy shortly after introducing the Jesuit and Arminian definition of free will. He stated the power of free will (*potentia libera*) may be considered in two ways. First, the power of free will may be considered simply in and of itself, apart from the decree and the act of God's providence. When considered in such a way, the Jesuit and Arminian definition is sufficient.[130] But as Rutherford noted, the created will does not exist independently apart from God's decree and providence, rather it is subject to both. God's will, being eternally decisive, has determined all things. This raises questions about the freedom of indifference as outlined above. Consider again the following disjunctive conditional propositions:

(a) If Peter is tempted, he will sin.
(b) If Peter is tempted, he will not sin.

Qui in Foederato Belgio vocantur Remonstrantes, super praecipuis Articulis Religionis Christianae. Contra Censuram Quatuor Professorum Leidensium. (1630)., among others.

128 Rutherford's definition of a free cause was an agent that is able to work or not work (*potest vel operari, vel non*). The summary definition that Rutherford takes to be the Jesuit position states that the nature of free will is a power that is able to act or not act (*potentiam ad agendum vel non agendum*).

129 Beck, "The Will as Master of Its Own Act," 155.

130 "Not. potentia libera spectatur dupliciter. I. ut res individualis, & terminus individualis divinae creationis, uti creatio distinguitur ab actu providentiae, & sic est simpliciter indifferens ad nolle & velle, quia secundum naturalem agendi modum, non magis τό velle, quam τό non velle spectat ad essentiam libertas." Rutherford, *Exercitationes Apologeticae*, 6.

The Jesuit and Arminian understanding of free will considers Peter's will as free to act or not act. Thus, Peter's will could act in such a way that (a) obtains in time by willing sin. Or, Peter's will could act in such a contradictory way that (b) obtains in time if Peter elects not to sin. The problem Rutherford raised is that God has already determined that one part of the disjunctive proposition will obtain in time. If God has determined that (a) will obtain in time, can Peter's will still be said to be indifferent and thus free regarding the two possibilities set before him? Jesuits and Arminians erred in limiting the question to whether the will is indifferent. The question, according to Rutherford, is whether the will maintains its power of indifference and liberty under a decree that determines all things.[131]

Rutherford's argument was that the will does maintain its power of indifference, and thus its liberty, even under God's decree. Using the famous example of Shadrach, Meshach, and Abednego in the fiery furnace (Daniel Chapter 3), Rutherford noted that the relationship between God's determination and human liberty does not function in the same way as God's miraculous power in the story of the three friends. In the story, the fire burned but did not produce heat, thus God's miraculous power suspended the natural laws of fire. Rutherford argued that God's determination does not suspend the natural powers of the will. Rather the will retains its freedom even as it is subject to God's determination and providence.[132]

---

131 "Ut eadem potentia providentiae subjicibilis est, & sic disjunctiva potentia determinatur ad unam partem (salva potentiae natura) non ad aliam: Deo enim sive scientia ipsius spectemus, quippe omnia scit, sive voluntatem, quae ad nihil creatum vel creabile est suspensa, sed ab æterno determinata, nulla est potentia disjunctiva; considerari quidem potest potentia creata, non considerato divino decreto, & in signo rationis decretum Dei antecedente, sed in tali chymerica consideratione, adversarii nobis litem vitiosa nuce haut emptitanda, frustra serunt; at vero non est ulla potentia creata, nisi quae subest aeterno Dei decreto, nisi quis cum ἀθέως divinae providentiae renuntiare velit, priore consideratione potentia quidem est actu ens determinatum, at actus potentiae sunt tantum possibiles & esse habent tantum in relatione ad omnipotentiam, non ad Dei decretum: at vero posito decreto, praesertim conditionato, tum quaestio an potentia libera sit indifferens ad agendum vel non agendum, vana est; nam potentia tum sub eo casu est determinata, & idem est ac si quaestio esset, an potentia non indifferens sed determinata, sit indifferens, & indeterminata, & posito decreto absoluto de rebus omnibus, insulsè quaeritur an potentia libera sub eo decreto sit indifferens, nam decretum absolutum ponit futuritionem determinationis, & ablationem futura fore indifferentiae, ideoq; sensu Jesuitico-arminiano, nempe prout illi sumunt vocem indifferentiae, inanis & vana est quaestio, at vero vox indifferentiae si referatur ad objectu, nempe pro indifferetia objectiva judicii proponentis objectu, quod nempe voluntas velle vel nolle potest, pro sua natura, quippe quia non magis laederetur essentia libertatis, si libertas hoc potius qua illud amplecteretur, tum facile solveretur quaestio: sed quia difficile est cum protervis adversariis limites quaestionis figere, quo fata disputationis nos ducant, sequi & persequi hostes oportet." Rutherford, *Exercitationes Apologeticae*, 6–7.

132 "At contra hanc indifferentiam objicient, talem indifferentiam competere causae naturali, nam non calefactio non magis laedit essentiam & actum primum ignis, quam calefactio. Sed respondeo, quamvis in casu miraculi salvetur essentia ignis sub non calefactione, non tamen salvatur naturalis

Rutherford argued that the integrity of the free will is maintained by a twofold freedom of indifference.[133] One he calls "objective" and the other "internal, vital, and elective." The objective indifference is the freedom of indifference that most closely aligns with the Jesuit and Arminian indifference. Objective indifference is the freedom of the will in regards to objects proposed by the mind as a means to attaining what is thought to be the highest good. Since the free will is indifferent to these objects, the will is free to choose the object or not. This freedom is also known as the freedom of contrariety. This is freedom to choose this object or that object.[134]

The other indifference identified by Rutherford was the "internal, vital, and elective" indifference by which the free will out of its own self (*ex se*) is able to will or not will according to its own most natural way of acting.[135] The significance of this definition is explained when Rutherford noted that the formal reason of free choice (*ratio formalis electionis*) is not that the object proposed by the intellect imposes necessity upon the will, but rather that the will elects the object out of its own internal and vital power.[136] Employing an example from the Old Testament, Rutherford argued that when Cyrus released the people of God from captivity in Babylon, permitting them to return to Jerusalem (2 Chron. 36:22–23), God supplied the *esse effectivum* because he "stirred up the spirit of Cyrus King of Persia" (Ezra 1:1).

---

modus agendi in igne, At nec actus primus, nec actus secundus potentiae libere laeditur, sive voluntas hoc velit, sive non." Rutherford, *Exercitationes Apologeticae*, 7–8.

133 Rutherford's insistence on this twofold indifference as essential to rendering a proper account of freedom distinguishes him not only from the Jesuit and Arminian theologians of the early modern era, but also from contemporary determinists such as Thomas Hobbes (1588–1679) and later determinists such as Jonathan Edwards (1703–1758). Such argued that freedom from coercion and a fundamental spontaneity of the will was sufficient to account for the freedom of the will. See: Richard Muller, "Jonathan Edwards and the Absence of Free Choice: A Parting of Ways in the Reformed Tradition," *Jonathan Edwards Studies* 1, no. 1 (2011): 3–22. For a critical view see: Paul Helm, "Jonathan Edwards and the Parting of Ways?" For a detailed analysis of Edwards's determinism and departure from the classic Reformed tradition on the freedom of the will see: Philip Fisk, *Jonathan Edward's Turn from the Classic Reformed Tradition*.

134 For more on the freedom of contradiction and contrariety respectively, see "libertas a coactione," "libertas contradictionis," and "libertas contrarietatis," in: Muller, *Dictionary of Latin and Greek Theological Terms*, 198–9.

135 "Dabimus itaque duplicem indifferentia in potentia libera, aliam objectivam, nempe quando intellectus proponit eligibile libertati ut medium summo bono absolute intento non necessarium, aliam internam, vitalem, electivam, qua voluntas libera ex se potest tam hoc velle, quam nolle, salva tum essentia libertatis, tum salvo naturalissimo agendi modo suo." Rutherford, *Exercitationes Apologeticae*, 8.

136 "Ratio formalis electionis, est unio objectiva boni non ut necessarii fini intento propositi ab intellectu, atqui ipsa libertas est causa intrinseca & vitalis, & quidem sola hujus unionis." Rutherford, *Exercitationes Apologeticae*, 8.

Nevertheless, Rutherford noted that in doing so, God contributed nothing formal or vital to Cyrus's willing. God cannot be said to be a cause of Cyrus's willing, nor even a co-cause of Cyrus's willing. In fact, it would not be Cyrus's will but God's willing in Cyrus, which would be an absurd contradiction.[137] Thus God could not be the cause of uniting the object proposed to Cyrus with the act of election. Only Cyrus's will is capable of doing so. Because this internal, vital, and elective indifference is maintained, Rutherford asserted that no external force could overturn free will in its natural way of acting. It is conceivable that God could, but he does not.[138] The will, according to Rutherford, retains dominion over its own acts. This is true even under the pre-determination and providence of God.

7.4   Joint Action, a Friendly Union

What then is the relationship between the created free will and the uncreated sovereign will of God? In this section we turn towards this special relationship, which Rutherford termed a "friendly union." The core concept is that God's will and the created human will both act freely and jointly to determine the same effect.

---

137 "Quod hypothesi sic declaro, Vult ex sua libertate Cyrus populi Dei liberationem, Deus quidem adhanc Cyri volitionem contribuit esse effectivum, Quippe excitavit Jehovah spiritum Cyri, at vero nullum esse vitale aut formale contribuit Deus in illam volitionem, tum quoniam causa efficens utpote externa non potest τὸ esse formale aut internum effectui contribuere, nisi efficiens causa evaserit, causa vel concausa formalis: Atqui Deus non fuit causa vel concausa formalis volitionis Cyri. Sic enim non voluntas Cyri, sed Deus in Cyro formaliter & vitaliter eam liberationem voluisset, quod plane αθεόλογον: & rationi repugnans; tum etiam quoniam Deus non majorem unionem objectivam, inter Cyri. libertatem & populi liberationem facit quam ut effective approximet objectum illud indifferens vitali suae causae, excitando rationes efficaces illius volitionis, & physice predeterminando libertatem Cyri, ut illud velit, & tamen Cyrus eam liberationem ut medium tantum suæ fælicitatis cognovit, & ipsius libertas, & in actu primo, & in naturali agendi modo permansisset illaesa, sive eam liberationem voluisset, sive non." Rutherford, *Exercitationes Apologeticae*, 9. Beck has observed a nearly identical passage in Voetius. See Beck's helpful comments in Beck, *Gisbertus Voetius*, 410–1. Also see Beck's translation of Voetius in Beck, "The Will as Master of Its Own Act," 149–50.

138 "Quia positis his indifferentiis, nullum agens externum, ne quidem Deus, potest evertere libertatem in naturali agendi modo. Ergo semper relinquetur voluntati dominium sui actus." Rutherford, *Exercitationes Apologeticae*, 8.

7.4.1 A Structural and Logical Analysis of Joint Action

A structural and logical analysis of joint action may be found in both the *Exercitationes Apologeticae* as well as the *Disputatio Scholastica*.[139] Beck has offered an analysis of a similar point in Voetius and his analysis is useful in understanding Rutherford on these points.[140] Rutherford's analysis proceeded by outlining the structure of a determination from both the divine as well as the human perspective. Rutherford did so by putting forward four possible objects of election represented symbolically as *A, B, C,* and *D*. God's eternal determination is represented as follows:

---

139 Rutherford makes use of the same argument in various locations of his writings. See Rutherford, *Disputatio Scholastica*, 391 and 588; Rutherford, *Exercitationes Apologeticae*, 108–109. Rutherford's example is made more accessible through a rare use of a visual aid outlining possible choices and structural moments involved in divine and human determinations found in Rutherford, *Disputatio Scholastica*, 588. This is reproduced above. I have added a "structural moment 1" to represent a moment of genuine indifference, which is more clearly indicated in the readings from Rutherford, *Disputatio Scholastica*, 391 and Rutherford, *Exercitationes Apologeticae*, 108–9.

140 See: Beck, "The Will as Master of Its Own Act," 162–5. Beck has also noticed a resonance here with Scotus's theory of neutral propositions. See: Beck, "'Divine Psychology' and Modalities: Scotus's Theory of the Neutral Proposition." I have followed Beck in describing these as "structural moments." Helm has criticized the use of the term "structural moments," on two fronts. First, he argues that the terms symbolize a logical sequence where no such sequence exists. Second, he argues that the Reformed Scholastics had no such term as "structural moments," thus an interpretive tool is being introduced into the analysis that might unhelpfully color the interpretation. See Paul Helm, "*Reformed Thought on Freedom*: Some Further Thoughts," *Journal of Reformed Theology* 4 (2010)., 201. I have followed Beck in describing these as "structural" moments for two reasons. First, the description of the structural moments as they pertain to God avoids the implication that these are temporally sequential moments. Second, though in regards to the human will they are temporally sequential moments, the modal operators that Rutherford applies to the objects of choice implies he is making a broader point about the enduring possibility of each object. Though Rutherford does not use the term "structural moment," it is nevertheless an adequate description of his point.

Structure of the Divine Determination

Structural Moment 1	Structural Moment 2	Structural Moment 3
A: Able to choose	A: Actual Choice	A: Future
B: Able to choose	B: Able to choose	B: Not future, but possible
C: Able to choose	C: Able to choose	C: Not future, but possible
D: Able to choose	D: Able to choose	D: Not future, but possible

Fig. 8 Structure of Divine Determination

Structural moment one represents a moment of genuine objective indifference towards the possible choices open to the divine determination. Such a moment of genuine indifference is represented elsewhere in Rutherford's writings, most notably in his discussion of the indeterminate truth value of future conditional propositions.[141] Structural moment two represents the moment of divine determination. As can be seen, *A* has moved from being a potential choice to an actual choice (*actu eligere*). And though *A* has become an actual choice, *B*, *C*, and *D*, remain possible objects of choice (*potens eligere*). The final structural moment represents that what God elects in structural moment two will obtain in the future as an actual event. Here *A* is simply described as a future event (*futurum*). Just as the election of *A* does not rule out *B*, *C*, and *D*, as possible objects of choice, neither does *A* obtaining as a determinately future event diminish the modal properties of *B*, *C*, and *D*. Though not future, they remain possible (*non futurum sed possibile*).[142]

An interesting feature of the above is the enduring capability of choice in structural moment two and the enduring modal property of "possible" in structural

---

141 See: Rutherford, *Disputatio Scholastica*, 541; Rutherford, *Exercitationes Apologeticae*, 191.

142

	Potens eligere	— A. non futurum, sed possibile.
Decretum Dei	Actu eligens	— B. futurum.
	Potens eligere	— C. non futurum, sed possibile

	Potens eligere	— A. non futurum, sed possibile.
Libertas Humana	Actu eligens	— B. futurum
	Potens eligere	— C. non futurum, sed possibile

Rutherford, *Disputatio Scholastica*, 588.

moment three. This deserves further comment. One thing that Rutherford could be demonstrating is God's simultaneity of potency to more than one effect (*simultas potentiae*). When applied to the above, this means God simultaneously has the power to choose *A*, *B*, *C*, or *D*. It does not mean that, having chosen *A* God has the power to bring about the contrary effect *B* at the same time (*potentia simultatis*).[143] Though the power to bring about contrary effects at the same time (*potentia simultatis*) is denied, there was nevertheless a way of logically analyzing the choices above in such a way as to maintain their property as possible objects of choice. One way this could be done is by applying the scholastic distinction of the composite sense (*sensus compositus*) and divided sense (*sensus divisus*). The sources Rutherford engaged on this distinction trace its use in scholastic theology to Anselm of Canterbury (1033–1109).[144] The distinction served two uses. One is logical. The other is theological.[145]

First, the distinction serves a logical purpose in that it provides clarity to sentences containing a modal term that admit some form of structural ambiguity. The ambiguity is created by the sentence itself, which can be read in two senses. In the composite sense, the subject is understood to have a necessary connection with its predicates or attributes. The divided sense reads the same sentence as a compound sentence composed of two separate yet somehow connected elements.[146]

This logical purpose was put to theological use to lend clarity to statements pertaining to God's will and God's certain knowledge of future contingent events.[147] Consider the following statement that could be formed from the above chart: God who chooses A, can not choose A. The statement, being ambiguous, can be rendered in two senses, each with very different meanings. In the compound sense, the statement may be formed as follows:

---

143 For more on these distinctions, see Muller, "Sensus Divisus," in *Dictionary of Latin and Greek Theological Terms*, 330–1; Muller, *Divine Will and Human Choice*, 49.

144 Rutherford references the Jesuit Francisco Suárez and the Franciscan Theodore Smising, both of whom trace the distinction to Anselm. See: Suárez, *De divina gratia*, 21–22; Smising, *Disputationum theologicarum de Deo Uno et Trinio*, 515–6.

145 For a helpful summary introductions to this distinction see *Basic Issues in Medieval Philosophy*, 2nd ed, Richard N. Bosley and Martin M. Tweedale, eds. (Ontario: Broadview Press, 2006), 812; Simo Knuuttila, "Modality," in: John Marenbon, ed., *The Oxford Handbook of Medieval Philosophy* (Oxford: Oxford University Press, 2012), 111–31. See also Beck's analysis of this distinction in Voetius, with whom Rutherford enjoyed a mutual admiration and dependence. Beck, *Gisbertus Voetius*, 348–51.

146 See: Richard N. Bosley and Martin M. Tweedale, eds., *Basic Issues in Medieval Philosophy* (Ontario: Broadview Press, 2006), 812.

147 In constructing some of the following statements concerning the divine choice, I have applied Rutherford's chart to the analysis provided by Beck in: Beck, *Gisbertus Voetius*, 348–51.

It is possible that God chooses A and does not choose A.

Read in the compound sense, the modal operator (possible) applies to everything that follows it. However, when read this way, the sentence contains a contradiction and is therefore false. The same sentence, when read according to the divided sense, may be formed as follows:

God chooses A, and it is possible that at the same he could not have chosen A.

The divided sense takes the sentence as two separate elements. Read as separate elements, there is no contradiction. God's choice of *A* does not exclude the possibility that he could have chosen *B*, *C*, or *D*. Thus, as Beck notes, when the chart is read in the divided sense, *B*, *C*, and *D* remain synchronically viable alternatives.[148]

Not only does this distinction help us understand the enduring capability of choice in structural moment 2 and the enduring possibilities of counterfactuals in structural moment 3, this distinction also has far reaching implications for human freedom under the divine decree. Rutherford argued that the will under the divine decree retained the power of the proximate cause to act or not act in the divided sense.[149] A sentence signifying the relation between the divine decree and the human agent could be rendered in the divided sense as follows:

God chooses A and Rutherford chooses A, but it is possible that Rutherford could not have chosen A.

As was mentioned above, a sentence read in the divided sense is read as a compound sentence with two separate, yet related elements. The two elements may be separated as follows:

(God chooses A and Rutherford chooses A) (it is possible that Rutherford could not have chosen A.)

When the elements are read separately it can be seen that God's determination of *A* in the first element does not diminish Rutherford's ability to choose an alternative object in the second element. In the divided sense, the divine decree neither adds to nor takes away the fundamental powers of the human will to choose another object.

---

148 Beck, "The Will as Master of Its Own Act," 163.

149 "Voluntas habitu gratiae instructa sub Dei decreto est in potentia proxima ad non agendum in sensu diviso, si nempe removeatur decretum Dei, & ponatur contrarium." Rutherford, *Exercitationes Apologeticae*, 115.

Using a practical example to emphasize the point, Rutherford drew a comparison between the above and the human eye. An eye plunged in darkness still retains the proximate power to see. Likewise, the same eye is not given new powers when in the light of day. The eye retains the power to see whether in daylight or the dark. Similarly, argued Rutherford, the will neither gains nor loses its fundamental power of freedom under the divine decree.[150] Though the human will only chooses what has been freely determined by God, the will retains the power to will the opposite.[151]

After outlining the decisive moment from the divine perspective, Rutherford considered the decisive moment from the human perspective. He did so assuming the absence of the divine decree and *concursus* and was able to do so precisely because, as was shown above, the decree did not change the modal properties of the objects of choice as they present to the human. Neither does the decree diminish the power of the will towards opposite objects. Thus, the decree does not threaten the will either in regard to its objective indifference or its internal, vital, or elective indifference. The purpose of supposing a human act absent the divine decree and *concursus* is to establish how the human would act (if possible) under such conditions.[152] Rutherford illustrated the structure of the decision as follows:

---

150 "Nam neq; decretum, tempus, aut locus, aut ejusmodi ponunt in voluntate, novam potentie aut dispositionis accessione. Nam oculus in tenebris, hoc modo, est in potentia proxima ad videndu, quonia accessio luminis non addit novam potentiam visivam oculo, quam non habuit in tenebris." Rutherford, *Exercitationes Apologeticae*, 115.

151 "Hinc recte infero, quamvis homo actu libere velit id solum ad quod decretum libertatem determinat, mediante, potentia, tamen, sive Deus tale decretum habuerit, sive non, potest voluntas contrarium velle." Rutherford, *Exercitationes Apologeticae*, 114. Rutherford is following the Spanish Dominican Diego Álvarez. See: Didaco Álvarez, *De auxiliis divinae gratiae et humani arbitrii* (Rome: Stephanum Paulinum, 1610), 167.

152 "Et de facto ex sese erupturam tantum in A, non in B, non in C, non in D, (etiam si supponamus voluntatem acturam sine omni decreto, & concursu Dei) ut de facto in actum." Rutherford, *Disputatio Scholastica*, 392.

Structure of the Human Determination (posited absent divine decree)

Structural Moment 1	Structural Moment 2	Structural Moment 3
A: Able to choose	A: Actual Choice	A: Future
B: Able to choose	B: Able to choose	B: Not future, but possible
C: Able to choose	C: Able to choose	C: Not future, but possible
D: Able to choose	D: Able to choose	D: Not future, but possible

Fig. 9 Structure of Human Determination

The first thing worth noticing is that the human freedom is effectively a mirror image of the divine freedom. Just as before, the capability of choice endures in structural moment two for *B*, *C*, and *D*. So too does the modal property of possibility endure for *B*, *C*, and *D* in structural moment three. The same observations noted above about the simultaneity of potencies, as well as modal properties of the objects of choice still hold here. Finally, it is important to notice that Rutherford's model presupposed that both the divine and human agents choose the same object.[153]

Though the similarities are apparent, there are nevertheless notable differences. Unlike the divine determination, which is independent and precedes any act of the human will, the human determination is dependent and follows the divine determination. The problem posed by the above is that God has already determined *A*, and thus *A* is a determinately future event. If such is the case, then it could be understood that God's determination imposes an absolute power on the human will both bending it towards *A* while also impeding the will's ability to alternative objects. Rutherford understood this to be the characterization of the Reformed position by his opponents. Nevertheless, he rejected this characterization.[154]

While true that the divine determination precedes the determination of the human will, this does not mean that the divine determination of *A* is the cause of the human determination of *A*. Rather, as was seen above, Rutherford argued that once God determines *A*, the human will retains the ability to will *A*, *B*, *C*, or *D* from itself (*ex se*). The divine determination does not irresistibly bend the will towards one or the other, neither does the divine determination impede or

---

153 Concerning Voetius's argument, Beck notes that the "basic structure of both involvements" in the determination is "exactly the same." See: Beck, "The Will as Master of Its Own Act," 162.

154 Rutherford is summarizing an objection offered by Jacobus Arminius. His summary may be found in Rutherford, *Exercitationes Apologeticae*, 108–9.

constrain the human will in any way.[155] The will acts in the same way under the divine determination as it would if (though impossible) there were never any divine determination. Rutherford's assertion, that the human will would not act any differently under the divine decree, in the divided sense, than it would outside of the divine decree, rests upon two assertions. The first pertains to the freedom of indifference. The second pertains to the kind of necessity, hypothetical, that the divine determination places upon the human will.[156]

In regard to the freedom of indifference, Rutherford held that the divine determination has no greater effect upon the human will than its own determination does. The point is taken up against the Remonstrants. Rutherford noted that the Remonstrants argued in their confession that the will must retain its freedom of indifference both in itself as well as in its use.[157] Rutherford did not disagree with the Remonstrants on the first point. A free determination is indifferent to opposites and this is an essential component to the freedom of the will. But he did disagree with the Remonstrants that the freedom of indifference is retained in its use. To establish this point, Rutherford made a distinction between the power of indifference and the use of this power. As *Figure 9* shows, the will has power to will *A, B, C,* or

---

155 "Arminius dicit auferri usum libertatis cum opus est, & forte hoc est actum impedire, sed falso & absurde, bone Deus, quia hoc innuunt voluntatem inclinare ad volendum A. B. C. D. & decretum absolutu vi torquere inclinationem a volitione τὸ A. B. D. & efficere, ut impedita & constricta velit C, non A, non B, non D, hoc somnium est ipsorum non doctrina nostra, imo volumus voluntatem ex se posse velle, A, B, C, D, & quoad aeternam futuritionem volituram esse liberrime C, non A, non B, non D, etiam posito per impossibile, quod non esset in Deo decretum, at vero Dei decretum superveniens & antecedens volitionem τὸ C, non constringit voluntatem; de voluntatem in eo vitali situ locat, in quo electione liberrima, admiranda conspiratione, id est, volitura, & non aliud, quod Deus absoluto decreto definivit volendum, & rursus Deus absoluto decreto illud praedefinit, & non aliud, quod libertas humana actu eliget: jam quaerant hi Davi impeditionem suam commentiam." Rutherford, *Exercitationes Apologeticae*, 108–9.

156 "An decretum Dei conspiret in eundem numero actum quem voluntas ipsa eliceret, si poneremus per impossibile nullum esse in Deo decretum? Respondeo affirmative, quia necessitas decreti, & necessitas actualis exercitii libertatis, eandem removent libertatis indifferentias. Neque Dei decretum alio torquet voluntatem invitam, quam in illud punctum, in quod de facto est inclinare." Rutherford, *Disputatio Scholastica*, 588. A similar point is made in Rutherford, *Exercitationes Apologeticae*, 108–9.

157 The section of the *Confessio* that Rutherford cites pertains to the divine permission. "Permissio enim vera requirit, ut non tantum potentia voluntatis in se; sed usus etiam potentiae liber sit, atque ad opposita indifferens: sive ut ab omni, interna simul & externa, necessitat maneat immunis." *Confessio, sive Declaratio, Sententiae Pastorum, qui in Foederato Belgio Remonstrantes vocantur, Super praecipuis articulis Religionis Christianae*, Chap 6.3, 20–1. The citation may be found in Rutherford, *Exercitationes Apologeticae*, 109–10.

D. However, once the will uses this power to elect *A*, the same power to elect *B*, *C*, or *D* is removed by the will's own determination.[158]

When this is applied to the relationship between the divine and human determinations, Rutherford argued that both the divine and human will share the power to will opposites. He also argued that this power is removed in its use. These are separate processes pertaining to the two distinct wills occurring at two distinct structural moments. The divine will uses its own power to elect *A*, and by this determination outside of time the freedom to elect *B*, *C*, or *D* is removed in the composite, but not divided sense. In a mirror image of the above, the human will uses its power of indifference to elect *A*, and by its own determination, the freedom to elect *B*, *C*, or *D* is removed in the compound sense, not the divided sense, insofar as it pertains to the human will. Though the two wills act jointly to elect the same object, they each act distinctly. The divine freedom of indifference is removed by the divine decree, but the divine decree does not remove indifference from the human agent. The human freedom of indifference is removed by the actual exercise of its own liberty.[159] Returning to the original objection of the Remonstrants, that the divine decree removes freedom of indifference from the human will, it has been shown that Rutherford categorically rejected this characterization of the Reformed position. The freedom of indifference is removed by the human agent only in its own exercise of freedom.[160]

In regard to the problem of the necessity imposed upon the human will, Rutherford wrote, "It is undeniable that there is not able to be certain degrees of necessity for it is more necessary that God is just than that the sun will rise tomorrow."[161] Just as the sun rising represents a lesser degree of necessity, so does God's predetermination represent a lesser degree of necessity upon the human will. This weaker version of necessity is effectively harmless in terms of its effect on the human will. Rutherford stated plainly that it imposes no stronger necessity upon the will than

---

158 "Usum indifferentem ad opposita, est repugnans in adjecto, ita tamen loquuntur *Remonstrantes*: nam usus liber est actus libertatis, actus libertatis est actualis determinatio voluntatis, at vero determinationem libertatis esse indifferentem ad opposita, est determinationem esse determinabilem, & non determinationem & album esse nigrum, deinde potentia dicitur indifferens ad opposita, non actus, vel usus libertatis: nam quando adest usus, tollitur indifferentia ad actus oppositos." Rutherford, *Exercitationes Apologeticae*, 109.

159 "Respondeo affirmative, quia necessitas decreti, & necessitas actualis exercitii libertatis, easdem removent libertatis indifferentias." Rutherford, *Disputatio Scholastica*, 588.

160 See also Beck's analysis of Voetius: "The structural indifference that holds for both in the structural moment prior to choice of one option rather than another is removed for both by nothing but the choice itself." See Beck, "The Will as Master of Its Own Act," 164.

161 "Negari enim non potest esse quosdam gradus necessitatis: nam majore necessitate Deus est justus, quam sol orietur cras." Rutherford, *Disputatio Scholastica*, 392.

the will imposes upon itself when the freedom of indifference is removed by a moment of election.[162]

What Rutherford concluded in his examination of the human determination, is that the human agent would not act any differently under the divine predetermination than it would act if it were not under the divine predetermination. Predetermination, at least insofar as Rutherford understands it, is no threat to the freedom of the will.[163] According to Rutherford, both God and man are free causes which concur, albeit in different ways, to bring about the same contingent effect. The significance of this, as Beck has noted, is that "inasmuch as they both freely bring about the same effect, there is no competition, rivalry, or manipulation involved." God's predetermination does not endanger human freedom in any way.[164]

7.4.2 Joint Determination and the Friendly Union

In the *Exercitationes* Rutherford argued that some understand God's predetermination of the will to be a power that penetrates to the deep parts of the will, its vital inclinations and its forcefulness of choice (*impetuositatis electivae*), inclining the will to whatever direction that God, the predetermining agent wills. This is the classic determinist position. Rutherford noted that this sense is "falsely attributed to us by our adversaries."[165] This is significant, because it represents an explicit repudiation of determinism.

Contrasting with this position, Rutherford argued that God's predetermination is not a power that penetrates the will, but rather it "settles into the impulsive nature," indeclinably bending the will in such a way that both God and the will choose together the same object, in the same time and place. The will under God's direction

---

162 "Hinc si necessitas ex praedeterminatione sit necessitas ut 6. necessitas exercitii, qua necesse est voluntas agat, ex hypothesi, quod agat, sit etiam necessitas ut 6. Quod necessario dicendum puto, praedeterminatio tum non fortiore vinculo necessitatis voluntatem adigit in A, non in B, non in C, non in D, quam ipsa voluntas se adigit in A, non in B, C, D. Et sic praedeterminatio nullo modo laedit libertatem." Rutherford, *Disputatio Scholastica*, 392.

163 "Non est tamen causa peccati: quia ita est hic primaria causa ut voluntati in actum constet sua libertas illibata: quia Deus voluntatem gravidam & parturientem quasi in quatuor actus ita praedeterminat; ut Deus voluntatem erupturam in actum A, B, C, D. Et de facto ex sese erupturam tantum in A, non in B, non in C, non in D, (etiam si supponamus voluntatem acturam sine omni decreto, & concursu Dei) in actum. A. tantum flectat, non in B, non in C, non in D." Rutherford, *Disputatio Scholastica*, 391.

164 Beck, "The Will as Master of Its Own Act," 162.

165 "Sensus hic est, quod gratia praedeterminans vi sua intrinseca penetret quasi ad profunditatem vitalis inclinationis & impetuositatis electivae, atque ita primam ὁρμήν & impetum naturæ in libertate cohibeat, & voluntatem inclinantem ad angulum, (ut sic loquar) borealem talis volitionis, & Dei praedeterminatio torqueat ad angulum australem: hunc sensum falsissime nobis assingunt adversarii." Rutherford, *Exercitationes Apologeticae*, 436.

does not reach towards another object than the one and the same that the will freely inclines towards itself. The will subordinately and dependently, from its own internal power, vital and commanding, and out of a free decision, aims for the same object that God also intends. "This," wrote Rutherford, "is the true sense."[166]

When God's freedom is exercised in a determination of the will, thus predetermining future contingent events, this does not remove the same freedom in the human agent. The freedom of both God and the human agent is maintained in that they both have a pre-volitional power of indifference and exercise this freedom in the choosing of the same object. The only difference is that God's decisive moment happens in an eternal moment outside of time, the human's decisive moment happens in time, at a specific place, and towards a specific object. These two free, willing agents act in unison towards the same object. Even if God's own indifference is removed through the divine decree, this does not remove the indifference of the human will, because God doesn't incline freedom principally to any other angle than to the same that the created will subordinately and freely inclines itself.[167]

The language of "principally" as well as "subordinately" is significant. Rutherford's denial that God is a "principal cause" in determining the will rules out an understanding of God's sovereignty as an inwardly determined final causality, thus calling into question whether a compatibilist reading is the best interpretation of the Reformed Orthodox view as it concerns Rutherford.[168] Absent of an inward bias or inclination, the will acts subordinately and dependently upon God's predetermination in such a way that a genuine moment of indifference remains, and freedom is established through a genuine and meaningful choice.[169]

---

166 "Quod Dei gratia praedeterminans non vi ita penetrans, sed insidens impetuositati naturae, ita indeclinabiliter flectat voluntatem, ut modo admirando gratia fortiter & voluntas vitaliter & elective conspirent in idem objectum numero, eodem tempore, loco, & intensione, & voluntas sub illa Dei motione non in aliud tenderet objectum, quam in illud idem in quod liberè se inclinasset, hoc dato quod per impossibile, nulla fuisset in Deo praedeterminatio, ita tamen ut gratia primo & principaliter id objectum non aliud praedeterminet, & voluntas subordinate & dependenter, ex vi interna, vitali, & imperiali, & electiva libertatis in illud idem objectum tenderet. Hic etiam est verus sensus." Rutherford, *Exercitationes Apologeticae*, 436–7.

167 "Nam quando ipsa libertas vitaliter suam indifferentiam removet, eodem modo praedeterminans gratia illam eandem indifferentiam externe & non vitaliter removet, quoniam Deus non ad alium angulum flectit libertatem principaliter, quam ad illum, ad quem se flectit libertas subordinate." Rutherford, *Exercitationes Apologeticae*, 510–11.

168 For similar conclusions applied to the Reformed Orthodox in general, see: Muller, *Divine Will and Human Choice*, 295.

169 For the application of "dependent" or "created" freedom to describe similar ideas in other Reformed Orthodox theologians, see van Asselt, Bac, and te Velde, Schouten, "Introduction," in *Reformed Thought on Freedom*, 15; Bac, *Perfect Will Theology*, 429–40.

These two willing agents act jointly, one superior and outside of time, the other subordinately and in time, to achieve an effect.[170] There is an example of superior and subordinate powers in Rutherford's writing that was contemporary to his own political situation. This example comes from Rutherford's theory on the origins of government as presented in his enduring work of political theology, *Lex Rex*. Rutherford presents God's activity as the superior cause, determining a government. Nevertheless, God's determination is not sufficient for such a government to exist. The subordinate cause, the "free consent of the people," must be joined to the superior cause of God's determination in order to achieve the effect of a particular kind of government. Having made a determination, both the superior and subordinate causes apply powers to achieve an affect. Rutherford described it as follows:

> The Creator of all Beings did both *immediately* without freedome of election in the creature, create the being of all creatures, and their essential degrees of superiority and inferiority, but *God* created not *Saul* by nature *King* over *Israel*; nor is *David* by the act of creation, by which he is made a man, created also a *King* over *Israel*; for then *David* should from the wombe and by nature be a *King*, and not by *Gods* free gift. Here both the free gift of *God*, and the free consent of the people interveene: indeed *God* made the office and royaltie of a *King* above the dignitie of the people; but *God* by the intervening consent of the people maketh *David* a *King*.[171]

Rutherford notes that the *Jurisconsulti* denied that dominion could be shared between two powers. One agent might will and apply his power towards an object that the other agent does not will.[172] However, through the language of superior and subordinate powers, Rutherford was able to conceive of a scenario where God and the human will, each maintaining dominion over their own acts, both will and apply their power jointly to achieve the same effect.

In the *Disputatio Scholastica*, Rutherford described this joint determination as a "friendly union" that existed between creature and creator. Neither word is inconsequential. The relationship between the two determinations of the divine and human will is *friendly*, because the divine predetermination does not come as a tyrant seeking to overthrow or manipulate the freedom of the human agent. It is a *union*, because the two willing agents must act jointly to achieve the common effect. This is a great mystery and defies even the detailed logical analysis of one

---

170 Superior and subordinate powers were introduced and analyzed in this study: Chapter 5.3.3.

171 Rutherford, *Lex Rex*, 67.

172 "Juris consulti negant dominium ejusdem rei posse esse in solidum penes duos; quia voluntas utendi eadem re, in uno, potest repugnare voluntati utendi eadim, in alio." Rutherford, *Disputatio Scholastica*, 42.

of the seventeenth centuries greatest scholastic theologians. Nevertheless, it is a mystery that Rutherford confessed.[173]

7.5   Irresistible Grace and Human Liberty

There is one final feature of Rutherford's understanding of God's providence and human liberty that has mostly gone unexplored: the relationship between God's providence, human liberty, and grace. The problem is posed by a Reformed perspective on grace, sometimes described as "irresistible," particularly as it relates to conversion. Put simply, how can a predetermining grace, that is both irresistible and invincible, not be a threat to human freedom?[174] Rutherford's polemical context was dictated on one side by Arminians and Jesuits, who to various degrees emphasized the role of the human will in consenting to converting grace. On the other side, Rutherford had to contend with Familists and Antinomians, who in caustic terms denied any contribution of the free will to converting grace.[175]

7.5.1 The Resistibility of Grace

In the *Examen,* Rutherford began his discussion on irresistible grace and human liberty by asking the question whether grace irresistibly works in conversion or not.[176] Rutherford appealed to the Italian philosopher Giacomo Zabarella (1533–1589) to briefly define the concept of resistance.[177] According to Zabarella, resistance is an act of obstruction, the repulsing of an action, or a non-admission of an action. Resistance is carried out by *the patient,* who is subject to the action of *the agent.*

---

173 "Non neganda est haec amicissima consociatio creaturae, ejusque modi vel libere vel necessario agendi cum invicta Creatoris efficacissima voluntate, etsi non homunciones minime mente capere, vel intellectu comprehendere possemus tale mysterium." Rutherford, *Disputatio Scholastica*, 113.

174 According to Rutherford, "influences of grace" are both invincible and irresistible. See Rutherford, *Influences of the Life of Grace*, 426.

175 See Rutherford, *Exercitationes Apologeticae,* Exercitatio 3; *Examen Arminianismi,* Ch. 11. For Rutherford's engagement with the Familists and Antinomians, respectively, see Rutherford, *A Survey of the Spiritual Antichrist.*

176 "Quaeritur, *An gratia operetur conversionem irresistibiliter, an non?*" Rutherford, *Examen Arminianismi,* 453.

177 Rutherford cites Giacomo Zabarella, *De Rebus Naturalibus Libri XXX* (Venice: Pau Meier 1590), 303–306. For Rutherford's citation see Rutherford, *Examen Arminianismi,* 303–307. For more on Zabarella, see José Manuel García Valverde, "Introduction", in *De Rebus Naturalibus, Vol. 1,* ed. José Manuel García Valverde, Brill Texts and Sources in Intellectual History 17/1–2, (Leiden and Boston: Brill 2016), 1–50; Heikki Mikkeli, "Giacomo Zabarella", *The Stanford Encyclopedia of Philosophy* (Spring 2018 Edition), Edward N. Zalta (ed.), URL = <https://plato.stanford.edu/archives/spr2018/entries/zabarella/> (accessed July 13, 2020).

Resistance is not successful when the agent is more powerful than the patient, or when the agent and patient are equal in strength. When the agent and patient are not equal, more specifically, when the patient is stronger than the applied power of the agent, then the patient can successfully resist the agent.[178] In relation to the question, if a human patient could somehow obstruct, repulse, or refuse to allow efficacious grace to bring about conversion, then the human would be said to have successfully resisted God's grace.

According to Rutherford, there are indeed instances where the human patient has the ability to resist God's grace. Citing Jer. 7:13 as well as Ps. 81:14, Rutherford noted that God's persuasive and inviting grace, which he associates with external calling, is resistible.[179] In the *Tryal and Triumph of Faith,* Rutherford wrote: "God's will standeth in the people's way, bidding them return. They answer, 'There is no hope, but we will walk in our own devices."[180] God may indeed graciously invite sinners to come to him, but they may refuse. Furthermore, the illumination of the mind through the preaching of God's word may also be resisted.[181]

7.5.2 Dominican, Jesuit, Arminian, and Antinomian Perspectives on Converting Grace

Rutherford believed the above positions on the resistibility of certain graces to be non-controversial. The specific point of disagreement, according to Rutherford, was whether the created will is able to fully and finally resist the special grace of regeneration, which flows from God's eternal decree concerning election.[182] In the *Examen,* he presented three different perspectives on this question: the Dominican, Jesuit, and Arminian. Outside of the *Examen,* a fourth perspective that Rutherford described as "antinomian" may drawn from his *A Survey of the Spiritual Antichrist.* These will be briefly surveyed below.[183]

---

178 "Deinde agentium & patientium vires, vel sunt aequales, unde resistentia *aegra* & *incomplectae;* vel inaequales, unde resistentia *ad victoriam & completa.*" Rutherford, *Examen Arminianismi,* 454.

179 "Fatemur, respectu I. Gratiae suadentis & invitantis, quae quibusdam dicitur *praeveniens excitans & vocans externe,* gratiam minime esse irresistibilem, sed ei plurumque a nobis resisti. Jer 7.13, *Loquutus sum & non audivistis. Psal. 81.14 Utinam populus mens obediisset!*" Rutherford, 454.

180 Rutherford, *The Tryal and Triumph of Faith,* 7.

181 "Concedunt Adversarii illuminationem fieri irresistibiliter." Rutherford, 454.

182 "*An Deus ita nova gratia afficiat Voluntatem,* nempe, *gratia speciali Regenerationis, quae ab aeterna Electione Dei manat; ut penes sit Voluntatem, eam gratiam complecte & finaliter repudiare, ejusque actioni validissimae ita finaliter obstare, ut plane repugnet Deo vocanti, ostiumque aperire ei pulsanti, renuere possit?*" Rutherford, 456.

183 See Rutherford, *Examen Arminianismi,* 457; and Rutherford, *A Survey of the Spiritual Antichrist,* Part II, 55.

The first position Rutherford offered, and the one that most closely aligns with his own, is the Dominican. Theologians that Rutherford associated with this position were *Diego Álvarez (1555–1632), John Matthew Rispoli (1582–1639),* Domingo *Báñez* (1528–1604), as well as the Spanish Mercedarian, Francisco Zumel (1540–1607), who worked closely with the Spanish Dominicans while at the University of Salamanca.[184] Also associated with this position are the Salamancan doctors and the *Collegium Complutense Philosophicum.*[185] According to Rutherford, the Dominicans held to the insuperability of converting grace, while nevertheless also maintaining that those who are unconverted are not converted because they do not wish to be.[186] Though Rutherford presented this position as distinct from his own, it is difficult to find in which way the Dominican position characterized here departs from his own position presented elsewhere.[187]

Rutherford associated *congruism*, the second position, with the Jesuits.[188] Though he associated this position with the Jesuits in the *Examen,* it is important to note that not all Jesuits with whom Rutherford interacted with held to this position. *Congruism,* associated with the Jesuit Francisco Suárez, marks a development that can be distinguished from that of Molina and Fonseca in the understanding of conversion as it relates to the *scientia media.*[189] According to this position, on the basis of middle knowledge, God knows how a particular person would respond to the illumination and inspiration of grace under certain circumstances. God's grace is accommodated to the person and circumstances in such a way that it is efficacious, touching and softening the heart and eliciting consent from the created will. Through the totality of this process, including the consent of the free will,

---

184 For Zumel's role in opposing the *scientia media,* see Freddoso's note in Molina, *Concordia,* 89, fn. 11.

185 Rutherford's positive relationship with theses theologians and schools, except for Rispoli, has been demonstrated in this study. See Ch. 3.3.1; 184.

186 "*Prima* est *Dominicanorum,* agnoscentium gratiae vim insuperabilem; sed docentium, ideo hominem non converti, quia non vult. Ita *Álvarez,* Gumel, Rispolis, Doctores Salmanticenses, & Comlutenses, *Báñez.*" Rutherford, *Examen Arminianismi,* 457.

187 If the rules of sin and divine permission are applied to rejecting the Gospel call to convert, then it seems Rutherford's position would be that the sinner willfully and freely denies the grace of conversion. See this study, 6.4.2.

188 "*Secunda est* Iesuitarum, vocationem congruam astruentium in I. Suasione, 2. Contemperatione suasionis tali dispositioni; ut forte resolvatur efficacia conversionis in pomeridianam compotationem." Rutherford, *Examen Arminianismi,* 457.

189 There is a distinction to be made between Jesuits such as Molina and Fonseca and *congruism.* See Craig, *The Problem of Divine Foreknowledge from Aristotle to Suárez,* 228. Elsewhere, in the *Exercitationes,* Rutherford does draw a distinction between Jesuits such as Fonseca and Suárez, demonstrating he does note a difference in the two positions. See Rutherford, *Exercitationes Apologeticae,* 426–427.

conversion takes place.[190] Like the Dominican position outlined above, congruent grace is efficacious. Unlike the Dominican position, the efficacy of congruent grace depends upon the fulfilling of all requisite circumstances as well as the cooperation and consent of the created will. Though God knows with certainty, via his *scientia media,* that such cooperation and consent will infallibly be forthcoming, the dependence upon the consent of the will appears to be Rutherford's major problem with this doctrine.[191] It can also be observed that *congruism* runs into other problems outlined in earlier chapters of this study. In an attempt to grant independence to the will, the efficacy of God's grace is made subject to circumstances, severely limiting God's freedom.

Interestingly, Rutherford distinguished *congruism* outlined above, from a position he simply describes as "*Scientiae Mediae.*" In the *Examen,* Rutherford associated this position with the Arminians, Socinians, and "Pseudo-Lutherans." It is only this third position that Rutherford argued is outright Pelagianism and only this third position did he understand to posit resistible grace.[192] Here God gives sufficient grace to all, and according to his *scientia media,* knows who will respond to sufficient grace and offer the consent of the will, thus bringing about conversion. Rutherford saw this position in some Jesuits such as Fonseca and Molina. He typically understood this to be the position of all Arminians.[193]

---

190 In the *Exercitationes Apologeticae,* Rutherford cites Suárez: "Sed in quo consistit haec congruitas? Quidam censent consistere, in quadam proportione, quae est inter talem illuminationem, vel inspirationem tali modo a Deo effectam in homine talis complexionis naturae & conditionis: Deus enim haec omnia exactissime comprehendens in quocunque homine, novit etiam, quis modus vocationis sit illa accommodatus, ut, si ita cor eius tangatur, emolliatur, & consentiat." Francisco Suárez, *Varia Opuscula Theologica* (Mainz: Balthasarum Lippium, 1622), 269. For Rutherford's citation of Suárez, see Rutherford, *Exercitationes Apologeticae,* 423. For more on congruent grace, see Craig, *The Problem of Divine Foreknowledge from Aristotle to Suárez,* 228.

191 "Huic vero cooperanti gratiae adjungendum dicimus cooperationem liberam nostrae voluntatis in cujus potestate est impedire effectum gratia (hoc est ut sit inefficax, praestat voluntas) & illum efficere, (hoc est ut sic efficax, facit) *si voluntas resistat gratie, digna est poena: si vero illi cooperatur, digna est laude & gloria.*" Suárez, quoted in Rutherford, *Exercitationes Apologeticae,* 426.

192 "*Scientia mediae fulcro;* quod est ingeniorum maleferiatorum cerebrosum figmentum. *Tertia sententia est Pelagianorum, Arminanorum Socinianorum, Pseudo-Lutheranorum,* ponentium gratiam resistibilem." Rutherford, *Examen Arminianismi,* 457.

193 Rutherford quotes the Jesuit Fonseca regarding the consent of the will to sufficient grace: "Deinde cum agitur de liberis actibus, ut agi solet semper actio Dei ad flectendas voluntes intelligenda est moraliter, hoc est, suadendo rationibus, alliciendo commodis, terrendo periculis, erigendo spe consequutionis, comprimendis pravis affectibus, & aliis huiusmodi auxiliis, quibus ipse scit certo, ut summus omnium bonorum autor, summae; sapientiae rector, voluntate praemovendam: non autem pure efficienter, hoc est, sola efficientia interna, quam physicam appellat: quod ea efficientia, si determinativa sit absoluti consensus volutatis, & no motiva tantum per modum affectus, cuique; actui libere eliciendo repugnet." Fonseca, *Commentariorum Petri Fonsecae Lusitani, doctoris theologi societatis iesu, in metaphysicorum aristotelis stagiritae libros, tomus tertius,* 169.

Apart from these three positions outlined in the *Examen,* there is a fourth position on converting grace and free will found in Rutherford's *A Survey of the Spiritual Antichrist.* Whereas the Jesuit position and that of the *scientia media* outlined above, afford a critical role to the consent of the created will in the work of conversion, this position ascribed to the "radical" Puritan Tobias Crisp (1600–1643), left no room whatsoever for a role for the created will in the work of conversion.[194] In Crisp's *Christ Alone Exalted,* a work cited by Rutherford, Crisp wrote:

> This is to be understood of the state and condition, in which a man is, when God comes first to work upon him, in which he is passive; and the simile made use of, of a physician forcing a man's mouth open, and pouring physic against his will, is intended to illustrate and does illustrate, the enmity and rebellion of the heart of man against Christ and his grace; and shews how disagreeable, to the carnal mind, are the methods which God takes when he first works upon it, either by afflictive providences, or by letting the law into the conscience, which works rather there.[195]

Crisp's language above exalts God's work of efficacious grace in conversion. This may be why, as Pederson notes, Rutherford's criticism of Crisp is moderate.[196] At one point, Rutherford even described Crisp as a "godly man."[197] Nevertheless, Rutherford sought to distinguish himself from this position. In Crisp's evaluation, converting grace irresistibly overwhelms and even acts contrary to the will. Inasmuch as Rutherford disapproved of the Jesuit and Arminian instincts to provide independence to the created will in the work of conversion, he nevertheless sought to maintain a subordinate role for the will, contra Crisp, as will be seen.[198]

Rutherford's citation can be found in Rutherford, *Exercitationes Apologeticae,* 424. He also quotes the Remonstrant Nicolaas Grevinckhoven: "Totius autem hujus complexi (quare scilicet in Paulo, & in Petro, potius quam in Iuda gratia sit efficax) causa communis alia dari non potest, quam libertas voluntatis." Grevinckhoven, quoted in Rutherford, *Exercitationes Apologeticae,* 326. See also Nicolaas Grevinckhoven, *Dissertatio Theologica De Duabus Quastionibus Hoc Tempore Controversis* (Rotterdam: Mathias Sebastiani 1615), 214.

194 Rutherford characterizes Crisp as an "antinomian." See Rutherford, *A Survey of the Spiritual Antichrist,* Part II., 55. For more on Crisp, see Randall J. Pederson, *Unity in Diversity: English Puritans and the Puritan Reformation, 1603–1689* (Brill: Leiden, 2014), 237–259. Pederson covers Rutherford's engagement with Crisp. See Pederson, 226–227.

195 Tobias Crisp, *Christ Alone Exalted in the Perfection and Encouragements of the Saints, Notwithstanding Sins and Trials,* in *The Complete Works of Tobias Crisp, D.D.,* Vol I., 4th Edition, edited by John Gill (London: R. Noble for J. Murgatroyd, 1791), 168.

196 Pederson, *Unity in Diversity,* 227.

197 Rutherford, *A Survey of the Spiritual Antichrist,* 193.

198 Rutherford, Part II, 55.

7.5.3 Rutherford and Converting Grace

Rutherford's understanding of converting grace was that it is efficacious, meaning that once it is applied it infallibly achieves the effect of conversion. Citing Eph. 1.18–20, Rutherford noted that God must efficaciously give us faith, since the same power at work in us is what raised Christ from the dead.[199] Appealing to John Ch. 6.44–45, he notes that the Father draws the elect to Christ, and that all those who hear and are taught by the Father come to Christ. Adding an interesting gloss to the text, Rutherford observed that "no one resists" the drawing and teaching of the Father, neither do they resist the application of God's incomparably great power in the work of conversion.[200] This gloss is significant. Rather than saying that the converted are not able to resist, he simply noted that they do not resist.[201]

Broadly speaking, God ordinarily contributes two causes to the work of conversion, one moral and one physical. These are outlined in the *Examen,* shortly after Rutherford asked whether God's work of conversion is only moral, consisting merely in persuasion, invitation, promises and commands, or whether God's work also consists in a real and physical predetermination of the will.[202] Moral influences such as those outlined above are given by grace alone, in that the sinner does not deserve to be persuaded and invited by God, nor does the sinner have a right to hear the Gospel. In addition to this, Rutherford considered such graces to be ineffectual without a physical predetermination of the will. "It is hard to affirm," he wrote in the *Tryal and Triumph of Faith,* "that all who are prepared with these preparations of order are infallibly converted."[203] Nevertheless, such moral influences are part of God's ordinary way of effecting the work of conversion, where moral influences are

---

199 "Quia Deus efficit in nobis fidem, ea vi & potentia sua, qua suscitarit Christum a mortuis. Eph 1.18–19." Rutherford, *Examen Arminianismi*, 458.

200 "Quia tractui *Patris, Joan. 6.44* nemo resistit; & *omnes qui audiverunt & didicerunt a* Patre *ad* Christum *veniunt. v. 45.*" Rutherford, *Examen Arminianismi*, 458.

201 Compare with John Owen. Commenting on the same text, he writes concerning irresistible grace: "As also, it [Irresistible grace] may be used on the part of the will itself, which will not resist it: "All that the Father giveth unto Christ shall comme to him, John vi. 37." See John Owen, "A Display of Arminianism," in *The Works of John Owen,* vol. 10, edt. William H. Gould (Edinburgh: Johnstone & Hunter 1850–53), 134.

202 "Quaeritur, *An tota Dei gratiosa operatio, qua* Spiritus Sanctus *utitur in conversione hominis, sit* moralis *tantum, ita ut* Deus *hic agat invitando tantum, rationibus suadendo, & alliciende tum minis, tum promissis & mandatis; an vero* Deus *agat per gratiae efficientiam* realem & physicam, & *habitum gratiae infundendo,* & *voluntatem* physice & realiter praedeterminando." Rutherford, *Examen Arminianismi,* 473.

203 Rutherford, *Tryal and Triumph of Faith,* 10.

understood to act upon the mind and the will prior to God's physical determination of the will.[204]

Whereas God's moral influences are ineffectual and subjective, God's physical acts regarding conversion are effectual and objective. The physical nature of converting grace may be understood in two ways. First, God's converting grace is said to be physical, objective, and real, in that a new heart is actually given to the converted sinner and new powers are really granted to the will.[205] Second, the physical nature of efficacious grace is emphasized by God physically predetermining certain acts associated with walking in obedience to God's commands (Deut 8.6). Earlier in this chapter it was said that God's physical predetermination provided the sufficient condition or the necessary substructure to which moral intent could be joined. God's efficacious grace, which predetermines physical acts of assent, belief, and will, provide the sufficient condition to which the good intentions of a converted saint may be joined.[206]

Though God could conceivably convert the sinner in one immediate act of physical predetermination, Rutherford described God's "ordinary" work of conversion as "successive." In a rich passage from his *The Tryal and Triumph of Faith*, Rutherford outlined this successive, and at times seemingly cotemporaneous work of God's moral and physical influences as follows:

> Because conversion is a rationall work, and the *Gospel* is a morall instrument of conversion therefore *Christ* here openeth a veine ere he give Physick; he first cutteth and then cureth, for though in the moment of formal conversion, men be patients, and can neither prevent *Christ,* nor co-operate with *Christ,* yet the whole work about conversion is not done in a moment; for men are not converted as the *Lillies grow, which do not labour nor spin;* there be somme pangs in the new birth; nor are men converted as *Simon* carried *Christs Crosse,* altogether against their will, they do hear and read the word freely; nor are men converted beside their knowledge, as *Caiaphas* prophesied; nor are we to think with *Enthusiasts,* that *God* doth all with one immediate rapt, as the sun in its rise inlightneth the aire.[207]

---

204 Rutherford, 10–11.

205 "Quia Deus *infundit Spiritum supplicationis Zach 12.10. cor novum dat, & faxeum amovet. Ezech 36.26. vivificat nos* Eph. 2.4,5. Ergo, non sola actione morali; quia vita nunquam infunditur morali tantum actione." And also, "Quia si haec infusio luminis sit objectiva, & a sola litera suasionis, est tantum suasio externa, ut vocant; si vero haec infusio sit realis novae potentiae Libero Arbitrio collatio, tum non est suasio, sed actio physica & plusquam suasio: nulla enim suasio infundit nobis novas vires." Rutherford, *Examen Arminianismi,* 474, 476.

206 "Arbitrium immediate influere active in actum credendi; sed motum, flexum, & determinatum a gratia interna, quae efficit velle & operari." Rutherford, *Examen Arminianismi,* 472. See this study, Ch. 7.2.3.

207 Rutherford, *The Tryal and Triumph of Faith,* 10–11.

The above quote should disabuse the notion that God's gracious moral influences are unnecessary simply because they are not efficacious. Furthermore, though the physical nature of predetermining grace is the sole efficacious cause in conversion, it is not the only cause. Rutherford's emphasis of the role of God's gracious moral influences in conversion introduced the role of the sinner in hearing and understanding the Gospel, as well as assenting to the Gospel through an act of the will. The role of God's moral influences in the work of conversion invites us to as what role Rutherford allowed for the free will in the work of conversion. To this we now turn.

7.5.4 Converting Grace, Human Liberty, and the Centrality of Love

In addition to the two causes outlined above, Rutherford surprisingly allowed for a third to be added, and this is the contribution of the created will. Rutherford insisted that God's grace is the only efficacious cause that can actually bring sinners to Christ, teach them, and predetermine them to works of righteousness.[208] Nevertheless, he does allow that the created will is a passive cause in the work of conversion. Though passive, free will (*liberum arbitrium*) is a vital cause that shares an association with God's work in efficacious grace. Furthermore, in language reminiscent of earlier discussions, Rutherford also described it as subordinate.[209]

Rutherford's description of the human will as contributing a "vital" cause, implies that the human will, posterior to the work of conversion, supplies a causal contribution from its own internal powers.[210] Granted, the human free will cannot render acts of righteousness to God without the regeneration of the heart and a real influx of God's grace: nevertheless, once such has been given, the will is able to believe, consent, and respond to God's gracious work from its own vital operations. If such acts cannot be attributed to the created will, even though it is assisted by

---

208 "*Gratia* est causa realiter trahens, intus docens, predeterminans, sola & adaequata." Rutherford, *Examen Armininismi,* 465.

209 "*Liberum Arbitrium* sic tractum & motum, est causa *socia vitalis,* sed subordinata gratiae praevenienti." Rutherford, *Examen Arminianismi,* 465. For the significance of the language of "subordinate," see this study Ch. 5.3.3.

210 In the *Summa Theologiae,* Thomas defines vital operations as those operations "whose principles are within the operator, and in virtue of which the operator produces such operations of itself." "Ad secundum dicendum quod opera vitae dicuntur, quorum principia sunt in operantibus, ut seipsos inducant in tales operationes." Rutherford's use of vital cause, understood as those contributions of belief and consent, as flowing from the regenerate will, fits well with Thomas's understanding of vital operations quoted above. In the above quote from the *Summa Theologiae,* I have followed the translation in Thomas Aquinas, *Summa Theologiae,* trans. O. P. Fr. Laurence Shapcote, ed. John Mortensen and Enrique Alarcon (Lander: The Aquinas Institute for the Study of Sacred Doctrine, 2012), I, q. 18. A 2, 202.

divine grace, it makes little sense for Christ to praise the faith of the Canaanite woman (Matt 15:21–28), the Roman centurion (Matt 8:5–13), or for Paul to praise the faith of the Patriarch Abraham (Rom 4:3–25).[211]

Though such acts belong to the will, they are nevertheless predetermined by God and dependent upon an influx of God's grace. Just as before, when discussing predetermination and sin, God's predetermination does not threaten the integrity of the created will. If God's predetermination in acts of grace were to "over-drive and over-act the free inclination [of the will], contrary to reason, light, and the judgment of the mind, and to the moral and free elective inclination of the will, [God] should constrain and force free-will."[212] However, this is not how Rutherford understood God's predetermination as it relates to the operations of the free will. God certainly can overwhelm nature, as he does in miraculous operations converting water into wine or turning the staff of Moses into a serpent, but regeneration is not a miraculous change of substance, as in the miracles just mentioned.[213] Rather, God's converting grace pre-moves the will, that it might move itself "most freely" towards the same thing God intends.[214] Thus, God's physical influence of converting grace is "contempered and sweetly accommodated" to human nature and the elective power of the free will.[215]

For Rutherford, the consummation of conversion was consent freely offered by the regenerate will. Though the grace of conversion is irresistible in the sense that it effectually achieves what God intends, and it is unilateral in the sense that God does not seek the consent of the individual to be converted, God does nevertheless, according to Rutherford, seek an assent to the work after the fact. "God seeks not our consent to our first conversion," he wrote in *Influences on the Life of Grace*, but God does seek our "after consent."[216] God wins this "after consent" by liberally pouring divine love upon the regenerate heart. Rutherford wrote:

---

211 "Nec negamus actum credendi nostrum esse, & proprietatem aliquam moralem, etiam Arbitrio ascribendam; quippe *Christus* laudat *Chananea* mulieres, *Centurionis*, *Abrahami*, & aliorum fidem, & eam remuneratur." Rutherford, *Examen Arminianismi*, 472.

212 Rutherford, *Influences of the Life of Grace*, 432.

213 "Quia Deus infinite sapiens & omnipotens, non evertis naturam causarum secundarum, nisi in casu miraculosae transmutationis substantiarum; ut cum aquam in vinum convertit & baculum *Mosis* in serpentem. At conversio non est miraculosa ejusmodi transmutatio substantiarum; Sed qualitatum ejusdem substantiae in natura sua permanentis." Rutherford, *Examen Arminianismi*, 486.

214 "Quia Deus ita movet liberam voluntatem, ut ipsa sese ad illud idem moveat liberrime, ad quod a Deo praemovetur." Rutherford, *Examen Arminianismi*, 486.

215 Rutherford, *Influences of the Life of Grace*, 431.

216 Rutherford, 428.

The Lord by casting an ague of love-sickness in the soul, moves the free-will of the Spouse, and of the Martyrs to die for Christ, rather then deny him, because love of it self considered as separated from the Lord's physical motions on the soul, works upon the will more strongly and insuperably, than many floods upon a fire, and is hard *as hell,* or the place of the dead, and marriage-love is cruel as the grave, *Cant. 8.6.* yet love infers no violence to the will.[217]

That Rutherford distinguished this pouring out of divine love from the "physical motions on the soul," strongly implies that this outpouring of divine love is a moral influence, and thus subject to the created will. Though subject to the created will, it still works "more strongly and insuperably" than natural causes such as floods upon a fire. Nevertheless, the insuperable nature of divine grace does not deny the freedom of the created will. Rather, created will is freely won by divine love and freely gives itself back to the divine love.[218]

An interesting observation can be made in light of Rutherford's compelling statement concerning the "love sickness of the soul." This is the similarity between the divine and human free wills as each relates to love. As was shown earlier in this chapter, human liberty considered in its choices, is a mirror image of divine liberty.[219] Given that both the divine will and created will are free causes, how can the actions of each be explained? When one considers the befuddling questions of why a just God would save sinners, or why an innocent God would elect to redeem sinners through the suffering of Christ, especially in light of Rutherford's voluntaristic assumptions that God did not need to do either, the question as to why God freely did both becomes all the more pertinent. In his *Covenant of Life Opened*, Rutherford wrote: "There was a sad and bloudy warre between divine justice and sinners: *Love, Love,* pressed Christ to warre, to come and serve the great *King,* and the State of lost Mankind, and to do it freely."[220] It appears that the love that inclines the created will to freely render acts of love to God is a mirror image of that divine love that first moved the Holy Trinity to acts of love towards humankind. For the elect, the mystery of the "friendly union," is elevated by God's "freest love," where the saint not only contemplates the mysteries of God's sovereignty and human liberty, but also the "infinite turnings and foldings of this mysterious love" that freely moved God to pour out divine love upon the world.[221]

---

217 Rutherford, 431.
218 Rutherford, 431.
219 See Ch. 7.4.
220 Rutherford, *Christ Dying and Drawing Sinners to Himself,* 14.
221 Rutherford, 15.

7.6 Summary

This chapter covered the most controversial element of the doctrine of divine providence, namely the relationship between God's sovereign determination and the determination of the created will. Keeping with Rutherford's own manner in addressing points of controversy, this chapter began with an examination of the position of his polemical opponents, the Jesuits and Arminians. The Jesuit and Arminian approach to the specific problem of God's providence and created free will was termed the general *concursus* (*concursus generalis*). Though there are points of difference among different representatives from these theological traditions, there is broad agreement. God's *concursus* is said to be general because his power is necessary for any secondary cause to act. God's *concursus* is said to be indeterminate because God's power does not determine a free cause to one effect.

Rutherford's acerbic tone might cause the interpreter to overlook significant points of agreement. It was shown that all parties believe God's power was necessary for secondary causes to act. Thus God's "general" supply of power to all secondary causes is taken for granted. In addition to God's power, there was also broad agreement between all parties as to other required prerequisites (i.e. God's decree, *concursus*) for the acting of secondary causes. The point of disagreement lay in the indeterminate nature of God's *concursus*. The Jesuits and Arminians argued that God's power was given to the secondary cause in such a way as not to determine it to one effect. The determination lay in the hands of the created will and God's determination was obliged to follow.

Of the many objections by Rutherford presented above, the most critical was that the general *concursus* as outlined by the Jesuits and Arminians, obligating God to follow the determination of a created will, deprived God of his own freedom. As some of his other objections illustrated, if God is not responsible for determining future contingent events then such events are left in the hands of fate or fortune. Such an outcome would ultimately deprive the human will of its freedom leaving it in the hands of a deterministic fatalism.

Rutherford's solution was to insist upon God's absolute sovereignty over all things. Unlike the Jesuit and Arminian position, Rutherford has given priority to God's freedom to determine future contingent events. But as was shown, this was not done in order to deprive the created will of its freedom, subjecting it to God's determination. Rutherford relied upon the distinction of the composite and divided sense (*sensus compositus et divisus*) to demonstrate that God's divine determination does not impose any more necessity on the created will than the created will imposes on itself in the moment of decision. This was demonstrated by a structural and logical analysis of joint action, presented from Rutherford's *Disputatio Scholastica* and *Exercitationes Apologeticae*. God's determination was outlined as a series of structural moments, beginning with a moment of genuine indifference. This moment of indifference is followed by a moment of choice. What God chooses will obtain in the future as an actual event. God's determination, in the divided sense, neither imposes necessity upon nor removes indifference from the created will. According to Rutherford, the created will's determination is a mirror image of God's own determination, retaining all three essential features. The only difference between the two is that God's determination is eternal. The human determination is made in time.

Given that the divine will does not impose fatal necessity upon the human will, the two are free to act jointly, albeit mysteriously, in a "friendly union." The relationship between the divine and human will is described as *friendly* because there is no need for the created will to fear the divine will overthrowing or manipulating its freedom. It is described as a *union*, because the two willing agents act jointly to achieve a common effect. This friendly union is not made vulnerable by the irresistibility of God's grace, but rather God's grace greatly enhances and elevates the friendly union. God's grace is not irresistible because the will cannot resist it, but rather because the renewed will moved by love would not resist it. Rutherford's account of God's freedom from fatalism, beginning at the foundational level of God's being and carrying through to his account of God's providence, ensures that God is free to guarantee the freedom his creatures.

Conclusions

This study provided an analysis of Rutherford's doctrine of divine providence, set against the background of early modern and medieval scholasticism. Having provided this analysis, this section aims to offer brief conclusions in light of the overall study. Following these conclusions, some areas of further enquiry are suggested.

1.   Rutherford and Scholasticism

This study presupposed that Rutherford's doctrine of divine providence could not be properly understood outside of its scholastic context. The reasons for this were outlined in section five of the Introduction. Many of the biographers who have made Rutherford their subject, as well as scholars who have studied him recently, have exhibited an aversion to scholasticism. This was seen in Murray who was Rutherford's earliest biographer. The trend continues all the way through to Richard, who contributed the most recent book length study. The recent shorter studies of Burton and Goudriaan demonstrate both expertise and patience with Rutherford's scholasticism, yielding fresh perspectives on their subject.

Rutherford's scholastic context begins in his own educational setting which was surveyed in Chapter One. The scholastic nature of his education provided Rutherford with a vocabulary and method of argumentation, as well as a repository of traditional authorities that he shared with the European academic tradition dating back to the thirteenth century. Scholasticism is primarily a method of argumentation and disputation that was employed by Rutherford rather than a system with its own doctrinal and philosophical content. Two conclusions can be drawn from this.

First, it was shown in section one of the Introduction that scholasticism has been viewed by previous scholars as a cause of a variety of undesirable results in Rutherford's theology. Scholasticism was seen as evidence of a departure from the Reformation tradition. It was also thought that those who used it were predisposed towards necessitarian thinking. Finally, it was thought to be the reason that theologians such as Rutherford exposited a theology of providence that was starkly necessitarian and even akin to pagan fatalism. However, it was seen throughout this study that though Rutherford employed the scholastic method, he viewed himself as very much within the developing Reformation tradition. Recent scholarship on Reformed Orthodoxy surveyed in this study has shown that scholasticism was employed by the Reformers themselves and is no clear indication of a departure from the Reformation tradition. Furthermore, it was shown that Rutherford employed scholastic methodology to set forth a radically contingent understanding of the created order as well as a robust understanding of human freedom. Far from predisposing him to necessitarianism, Rutherford used the tools of scholasticism to arrive at a theology of providence where a high view of God's sovereignty ensures a wide arena for the practice of human liberty.

Second, in some of the secondary literature, the polemical nature of scholasticism has given cause to characterize Rutherford as intolerant or even bigoted. If intolerance is meant to convey Rutherford's attitude towards those ecclesial bodies that were not in uniformity with the Covenant, then Rutherford was clearly not in favor of toleration. However, if intolerance is meant to describe Rutherford's attitude towards people and ideas outside of his own tradition of Reformed Orthodoxy, then Rutherford was clearly not intolerant. Rutherford's commitment to scholasticism, which included a shared method, vocabulary, sources, and language, meant he was a participant in an international and ecumenical theological conversation. The *quaestio* method meant Rutherford was well acquainted with his theological adversaries, often quoting them fairly and citing them correctly. At times, as was seen in this study, Rutherford even cited his co-called Roman Catholic, Jesuit, and Arminian adversaries positively, signaling agreement between himself and them.

Here, a simple point may be made regarding the study of Reformed Orthodoxy in general, and Rutherford in particular. That Rutherford is a Reformed Scottish scholastic should not be taken to mean he is anti-Catholic, or anti-Arminian on all issues. Assuming this to be the case has hindered some of the previous scholarship on Rutherford. With Rutherford, there are points of discerning agreement as well as points of major disagreement. This is so not only with typical polemical opponents, but even within his own tradition of Reformed Orthodoxy. Care must be taken to acknowledge points of agreement to better understand the significant areas of disagreement.

2.   God's Providence and Freedom from Fatalism

Rutherford's scholastic definition of divine providence was presented in Chapter Six. There it was seen that providence is first and foremost an act of God, the foundation of which lies within God's being and the divine attributes of intellect, will, and power. For this reason, after introducing Rutherford's life and works, this study proceeded with an analysis of God's being (Chapter Two), knowledge (Chapter Three), will (Chapter Four) and power (Chapter Five). This follows a presupposed structure of organizing doctrine common to scholasticism. The purpose is not merely for the ordering of doctrine, but the doctrines are structurally dependent upon one another. What is said of God's being in Chapter Two has direct implications for what can be said of God's knowledge in Chapter Three, God's will in Chapter Four, and God's power in Chapter Five. Likewise, the doctrine of God's providence and human liberty in Chapter Six and Chapter Seven directly depend upon all that was previously said.

Considering the above, Rutherford shows a certain sensitivity throughout to themes of independence and dependence that begin at the foundational level of God's being, treated in Chapter Two. This was seen particularly in two features of his doctrine of God. The first feature is Rutherford's essentialist reading of the divine name (Chapter 2.2.1). Essentialist readings of the divine name were hardly uncommon, but how Rutherford put his essentialist reading of the divine name to use is interesting. As was shown, certain Jesuits had argued that there were rock bottom principles of demonstration, such as the law of non-contradiction, which they argued enjoyed an existence and logical coherence independent of God. However, as was seen, Rutherford argued that the law of non-contradiction was not an independent truth, but rather a dependent truth that had its source in God's being expressed through the divine name. Here the contours of God's radical independence, as well as the radical dependence of entities outside of God, are being clearly delineated.

The same can be seen in discussions concerning God's presence in imaginary spaces (Chapter 2.2.3). Rutherford argued that God is present not only in heaven and the actual world, but God is also present in an infinite number of merely possible worlds. Just as with the law of non-contradiction, Rutherford's polemical opponents argued that possibility, and thus possible worlds, held a logical integrity independent of God. Rutherford's insistence that God is essentially present even in merely possible worlds, as well as his insistence that their possibility is a modal property dependent upon God, further reinforces the contours of God's independence and creaturely dependence outlined above.

These themes carry over into Rutherford's understanding of God's knowledge, treated in Chapter Three. Here attention is briefly drawn to Rutherford's understanding of indeterminate and determinate knowledge as a useful demonstration of the concept (3.3.1). The *scientia media*, employed by Jesuits and Arminians of the period, held that God knew what a person would do under certain circumstances. The object of such knowledge was the truth-value of propositions concerning future contingent states of affairs. According to the Jesuits surveyed in this chapter, God arrived at such knowledge pre-volitionally, basing the determinate truth-value of the proposition on the connection between antecedent and consequent terms. For Rutherford, this meant future contingent states of affairs were fatally imposed upon God, leaving him with no free decision in regards to such events. His solution was to deny that the truth-value of such propositions could be determined antecedent to the divine will. Rutherford argued that God initially knew propositions as having an indeterminate truth value. God only knows a proposition as determinately true after freely willing it to be so. Furthermore, he insisted there was no necessary connection between the extreme parts of a proposition, but these were freely joined by God's will as well. Rutherford is not merely asserting God's sovereignty and independence. He understands God's sovereignty and independence to be the only logical means of accounting for the contingency of the actual world over and against necessitarian outcomes.

Rutherford's doctrine of God's will, treated in Chapter Four, is another subject that strongly features God's independence as a safeguard against theological fatalism. As with God's knowledge and being, this is a running theme of the chapter. Rutherford identifies several attempts by Arminians, Jesuits, and even some of the Scottish Reformed, such as John Cameron, to necessarily obligate God to created beings. Some argued that God was necessarily obligated to actualize a maximally good created order. Others argued that God was necessarily obligated to reward righteousness and punish evil. In Cameron's sophisticated account, God contingently rooted his image in creation and henceforth was necessarily obligated to love what he freely constituted as good. Again, in the loss of God's absolute independence, Rutherford saw the specter of theological fatalism. This was particularly evident in Thomas Jackson's account of strong and weak fates, where through a series of sins, a human might become irretrievably and necessarily damned. As was seen in the earlier chapters, Rutherford reasserted God's absolute independence, which safeguards contingency in the created order. God is under no necessary obligation to create this world, nor is he under any necessary obligation to reward the just or punish the wicked. He does both freely, though as was seen, God's freedom is ultimately informed by his being and character. This last feature is a measure to safeguard against a capricious and arbitrary God. God's freedom, according to Rutherford, is conditioned by his holiness. Though God wills freely, his will is not a law unto itself. God's will is free, but it is also good and holy.

Rutherford's doctrine of God's power, set out in Chapter Five, brings many of the aforementioned themes together. God's knowledge of every possibility is a knowledge of what is made possible by his own omnipotence. From this treasury of omnipotence, God wills some possibilities to be actualized. The actualization of these possibilities by the divine power is what constitutes created reality. As was shown in Chapter Five, Rutherford argued that every logically possible state of affairs was available to God as an object of his knowledge, will, and power. However, he pointed out that this was not a belief shared by his Jesuit adversaries. As was shown, the Jesuits argued that there was a necessary connection between two extreme parts of a conditional proposition, such as *If Peter is tempted, then he will sin*. Though it is logically possible that Peter could be tempted and not sin, the Jesuits argued that because of the connection between Peter's temptation and sin, there was no possible world known to God by his *scientia media* where Peter was tempted and did not sin. Rutherford argued that such imposed fatal necessity not only upon Peter, but also upon God, who was not free to apply his power to actualize a world where Peter was tempted and did not sin. Rutherford avoided the same deterministic implications by arguing every logically possible state of affairs was open to God as objects of his knowledge, will, and power. God's freedom from every kind of necessity allows him to ensure the freedom of his creatures, which Rutherford explained through his use of superior and subordinate powers, a concept built upon Bradwardine's doctrine of co-efficiency, which also strongly resembled Scotus's doctrine of co-causality. Here, God's superior power and the human will's subordinate power each retain dominion over their own acts, while acting jointly to achieve a common effect. This explanation of the relation between God's power and human power prepared the reader for Rutherford's doctrine of providence and human freedom in the final two chapters.

Having established God's absolute independence at the foundational level of God's being, intellect, will, and power, the implications of this for human liberty are seen in the final two chapters concerning God's providence (Chapters Six and Seven). God's providence is an act of God by which according to his wisdom, knowledge, will and power each and every ordainable thing is directed towards an end appointed by God. In Chapter 6, Rutherford was shown to be sensitive to critiques of theological fatalism. This is particularly evident in his understanding of sin and evil, as well as pagan associations of fate. His doctrine of divine permission, which skillfully employed a range of scholastic distinctions and logical tools, is an important first step in establishing a robust account of human liberty (sections 6.3–6.4). God's will to permit sin, according to Rutherford, places the human under no necessary obligation to sin. Rather, the human wills to sin freely. This is the first explicit picture presented of God's will and the human will both willing freely. How such a thing is possible is seen when Rutherford addresses the problem of providence and fatal necessity (section 6.5). Rutherford argued that God's absolute freedom from fatal necessity is how God is able to ensure the freedom of his rational creatures. Though perhaps well intentioned, previous attempts to provide the created order with some level of independence inevitably subjected God himself to necessary obligations. In doing so, God was denied the freedom to ensure freedom to his creatures. Rutherford's insistence on God's sovereignty and independence throughout is not merely zeal for God's glory, but it is the centerpiece of his accounting of human liberty.

As was seen in Chapter 7, Rutherford had a robust accounting of human liberty. The human will is first and foremost a free cause, meaning it is free to act or not. The will is free from violence, fortune, or supernatural coercion. Most importantly, the will enjoys a fundamental indifference towards the objects presented to it. This indifference is only removed by the act of the will itself, by choosing one object it necessarily rules out the other. Though the will may be influenced externally by circumstances or persuasion, and internally by the intellect, the will is ultimately the "master of its own acts." The human will enjoys a fundamental liberty that not even the divine will can deprive it of. This remains true whether the will is under sin or under grace (section 7.4.3).

Rutherford's understanding of how the divine will interacts with the human will is not one whereby the divine will fatally determines the will to one effect, rather it is one where the divine will freely chooses one object outside of time and the human will freely chooses the same object in created time (section 7.5). This is an improvement over the Jesuit and Arminian position, where God's will is obligated to follow the human will. As was demonstrated earlier, if God does not enjoy freedom antecedent to human willing, he is not free to ensure the consequent freedom of the human will. In Rutherford's account however, God's antecedent and independent freedom secures the consequent and dependent human freedom. This begins at the foundational level of God's being and is carried forward into Rutherford's doctrines of God's knowledge, will, and power. It is applied here in the doctrine of providence and its relevance to human liberty.

The relationship between God's will and human liberty can be represented logically, as was done in Chapter 7.5.1. There it was shown that God and the human freely and jointly will the same object. The same was shown in Chapter 7.5, where even under God's "irresistible" grace, the fundamental freedoms of the will remain intact. Nevertheless, even the great Reformed scholastic must admit the limitations of logic here. How God freely determines the future, while preserving creaturely freedom, is ultimately a divine mystery that transcends logic. Nevertheless, it is a mystery that must be confessed.

Rutherford's sensitivity to the issues of divine independence and creaturely dependence are integral to his overall account of divine providence. God's freedom from fatal necessity is what allows God to guarantee the freedom of creatures. Far from scholasticism driving necessitarian conclusions, Rutherford employs it to present a radically contingent created order and a robust account of human liberty under God's sovereignty.

3. Rutherford and the Freedom of the Will

Here is not the place to retrace or summarize Rutherford's accounting of human liberty put forward in Chapter Seven. Rather, the aim is to draw some specific conclusions about the best description for Rutherford's understanding of the subject. Muller has challenged the helpfulness of modern terms such as "determinism," "indeterminism," "compatibilism," and "libertarianism." He offers an analysis of these terms, demonstrating the difficulty in their applicability to the Reformed Orthodox. A summary is offered below:

- If libertarianism is taken to mean that human free choice is absolutely independent, brought about solely by the human agent, or in relation to soteriological matters that human beings have the power to choose or refuse the gift of grace, then Reformed Orthodox theology is not libertarian.
- If indeterminism is taken to mean that the final result of an action, or a series of actions is random, unpredictable, and unknowable then the Reformed Orthodox were not indeterminist.
- If determinism is taken to mean that there is no contingency in the created world, to include human acts and effects of the will, implying that things could not have been otherwise, then the Reformed Orthodox were not determinist.
- If compatibilism is taken to mean that the determination of human acts by God is epistemically compatible, and furthermore that this determination which rules out freedom of contradiction and freedom of contrariety is also compatible with human freedom, then the Reformed Orthodox were not compatibilist.
- If compatibilism is taken to mean the ontic compatibility of the divine determination with freedom of the will, but that this determination rules out freedom of contradiction and freedom of contrariety, then the Reformed Orthodox were not compatibilist.
- If, however, compatibilism was taken to mean that the divine determination is ontically and epistemically compatible with freedom of contradiction and contrariety, then the Reformed Orthodox were compatibilist.[1]

Regarding the final point, Muller notes that such an account of compatibilism would set the older position of the Reformed Orthodox apart from classical and modern philosophical understandings, which renders the term questionable in its ability to adequately describe the Reformed position.[2]

If the above is applied to Rutherford, as Muller has done with Reformed Orthodoxy in general, similar conclusions may be drawn with Rutherford specifically. Understood in the ways outlined above, Rutherford is neither libertarian, indeterminist, nor determinist. Neither is he a compatibilist, at least when understood in the classical sense. The suggestion of "dependent freedom," put forward by the authors of *Reformed Thought on Freedom* and endorsed by Muller, is an adequate description.[3] There are a few additional remarks, pertaining to Rutherford, that further fill out the concept of dependent freedom.

Considering the above, "dependent" is not accidental. In Rutherford's account, creaturely independence is detrimental to a robust account of human liberty. In

---

1 Muller, *Divine Will and Human Choice*, 322–3.
2 Muller, 323.
3 van Asselt, Bac, and te Velde, *Reformed Thought on Freedom*, 32–3; Bac, *Perfect Will Theology*, 429; Muller, *Divine Will and Human Choice*, 323.

order to be free, creaturely freedom must be a dependent freedom. Furthermore, this dependent freedom is understood in a genuine sense. Rutherford argued that the human will (a) was a free cause, (b) free from violence, fortune, and supernatural coercion, (c) which enjoyed a freedom of indifference in regards to its objects, and (d) was not determined by any causes external or internal, but was a "master of its own acts." God's determination does not rule out the second point, but rather guarantees it. God, being free from fatal necessity, is free to guarantee the freedom of his creatures. This freedom, though dependent, is nevertheless real.

Rutherford's phrase *amicissima consotiatio*, or a most friendly union, is helpful in understanding the concept of dependent freedom. The human will having freedom that is subordinate to God, or dependent upon God, does not represent a threat to human liberty. God's will does not come to overthrow or coerce the human will. Rather, God's will comes to the human will as a friend. The two causes act jointly, determining the same object, at the same time, and at the same place, in such a way that the freedom of both is preserved. Rutherford's poetic term further reinforces that dependent freedom is no mirage or trick but is genuine freedom, guaranteed by an absolutely independent God.

4. Rutherford, "Scotism," and Synchronic Contingency

The historical thesis regarding synchronic contingency is far reaching. It argues for a determinist reading of Aristotle, which is then traced to Thomas Aquinas. An epistemological breakthrough is seen with John Duns Scotus, marking a transition from diachronic contingency to synchronic contingency. For the authors of *Reformed Thought on Freedom*, synchronic contingency is seen as critical for establishing the genuine, dependent freedom articulated by the sixteenth and seventeenth century Reformed Orthodox.[4]

Recently, Muller critiqued this thesis arguing that determinist readings of Aristotle and the Christian tradition leading up to John Duns Scotus are unwarranted.[5] Furthermore, he argues that the Reformed Orthodox were not dependent upon developments and understandings of contingency and freedom that can be traced to Scotus, but rather they were eclectic in their use of traditional sources. Muller argues that discussions pertaining to contingency and freedom are part of a broad tradition of Christian Aristotelianism that include both Thomistic and Scotistic approaches to the problem. He employs Rutherford in support of the above when he

---

4 van Asselt, Bac, and te Velde, *Reformed Thought on Freedom*, 40–1; Andreas J. Beck and Antonie Vos, "Conceptual Patterns Related to Reformed Scholasticism," *Nederlands Theologische Tijdschrift* 57 (juli 2003): 223–33; Beck, *Gisbertus Voetius*, 403–25.

5 For a summary see: Muller, *Divine Will and Human Choice*, 317–22.

notes that Rutherford used the Thomistic concept of *praemotio physica* as a distinct alternative to Scotist co-causality.[6]

When the above is applied to Rutherford, it is clear that he operates within the broad tradition of Christian Aristotelianism. Furthermore, it is clear that he employs both Thomistic and Scotistic approaches to the problem of contingency and free will. This does not necessarily mean that "eclectic" is the best description of his use of traditional sources. Neither does it mean that there is not a certain debt to Scotus owed in the development of his arguments.

It should be clear from numerous references in this study that Rutherford heavily relied upon Thomas. Often, Rutherford's use of Thomas requires little qualification. There are times however when Rutherford will use terms commonly identified with Thomas and the intellectualist tradition but employ them in a manner more consistent with the voluntarist tradition. For example, Rutherford often uses the *scientia simplicis intelligentiae et visionis* distinction, a distinction that Muller notes has intellectualist implications. Nevertheless, as was shown in Chapter 3.2.2, Rutherford employs this within an overtly voluntarist framework. Rather than beholding the objects themselves through God's infinite vision, Rutherford notes that God infallibly sees future objects only in light of his decree. Rutherford gives these intellectualist terms a noticeably voluntarist reinterpretation.

What about Muller's example of Rutherford's use of the Thomist concept of the *praemotio physica*? Chapter 6.2.1 shows that Rutherford clearly employed an understanding of God's physical predetermination, which was partially indebted to Thomas. As was also shown in the same chapter and section, it was not Thomas that Rutherford credits with resourcing his understanding of physical predetermination but rather the erudite Scotist, Theodore Smising. Furthermore, once Rutherford's understanding of physical predetermination is set within the larger context of Bradwardine's doctrine of co-efficiency, as well as Rutherford's understanding of the joint willing of God and the rational creature, it strongly resonates with the Scotist concept of co-causality (Chapter 6.5).

Just as with the *scientia simplicis intelligentiae et visionis* distinction, here is another example of certain terms being built upon using the resources from a later tradition. This example is most useful because Rutherford is explicit about his use of the Scotist tradition. In this critical account of God's sovereignty and human liberty, Thomist terms are used within an explicitly Scotistic framework. It would appear that Rutherford found a structural and modal account of contingency in Scotus, as well as in others within the voluntarist tradition, that supported his aims to provide an account for how God's sovereignty could be reconciled with creaturely freedom. In Rutherford there is confirmation of the initial thesis that

---

6 Muller, *Divine Will And Human Choice*, 319.

was generally applied to the Reformed Orthodox, which was set forward by the authors of *Reformed Thought on Freedom*, that Scotus was an important influence on Reformed Orthodox thought concerning human liberty.

More can be said concerning the above. Muller has commented that the language of synchronic contingency is philosophically "quite uninteresting." He also questions the value of arguing the case for freedom by lodging a contrary effect in a synchronically possible, yet unactualized world in which the agent must be identified as a different being.[7] The arguments that Muller finds quite uninteresting and even philosophically useless gain intrigue when placed within the larger framework of early modern polemics on God's sovereignty and human liberty. As was shown in Chapter 5.3, the *scientia media* accounts for God's knowledge of Peter's sin upon the condition of his temptation. The *scientia media* also accounts for God's knowledge of a world where Peter is not tempted and does not sin. However, it does not account for God's knowledge of an actual world where Peter is tempted in such and such a way and does not sin, thus raising serious questions about Peter's freedom under the condition of his temptation.

Placed within the polemical context of sixteenth and seventeenth century Reformed Orthodoxy, the concept of synchronic contingency suddenly becomes quite interesting as does lodging a contrary effect in a synchronically possible world. In the face of the polemical context with the Jesuits, this concept gives a foundational account for how Peter could have done otherwise. Peter's temptation in such a way, time, and place is not fatally determined to lead to sin precisely because a synchronically possible alternative remains.

The relevant conclusion here is that both Scotist influences as well as the value of synchronic contingency for an accounting of freedom in Reformed Orthodoxy continue to demand close attention. Muller's book advances the discussion greatly, but it by no means concludes the discussion. There are many avenues left to be explored.

5. Potential Areas of Further Research

In closing, three areas of further research are proposed. The first involves Rutherford studies in particular. The second applies to the development of understandings of human liberty in Enlightenment Scotland. The third pertains to Scotist influences on Reformed Orthodoxy.

---

7 Muller, *Divine Will and Human Choice*, 314–5.

5.1 Rutherford, Human Liberty, and Early Modern Political Thought

Rutherford's political thought has been a fruitful avenue of exploration. Rarely has his political thought been viewed through the lens of his scholastic theology. An exception to this has been John Coffey, whose excellent intellectual biography skillfully incorporated Rutherford's theology with his political thought. Nevertheless, Coffey is primarily a historian, not a theologian and thus some of the more technical matters of Rutherford's theology are left unapplied. An intriguing area of exploration would be to apply Rutherford's understanding of God's sovereignty and human liberty outlined in Chapter Seven of this study to his political thought. There are several tantalizing statements in his famous political treatise Lex Rex that invite such an exploration. Consider the following passage, where Rutherford details how God and human beings freely and jointly elect their government:

> God is the first Agent in all acts of the Creature, where a people maketh choise of a man to be their King, the States doe no other thing under God but create this man, rather then another; and we cannot here find two actions, one of God, another of the people; but in one, and the same action; God by the peoples free suffrages & voices createth such a man King, passing by many thousands, and the people are not patientes in the action, because by the authoritative choise of the States, the man is made of a private man, and no King, a publick person, and a crowned King.[8]

The above is one of many intriguing examples of how Rutherford's sophisticated account of joint action appears in the Lex Rex. There is opportunity here to explore how Rutherford's understanding of God's sovereignty, providence, and human liberty informed and undergirded his political thought.

5.2 Understandings of Human Liberty in Enlightenment Scotland

Rutherford's interaction with Enlightenment figures is non-existent. This does not mean that there is not work to be done concerning Rutherford and the emergence of Enlightenment thought in Scotland. Within a generation of Rutherford's death, David Hume (1711–1776) would set forth his compatibilist theory on human liberty in A Treatise of Human Nature. In his The Case for the Enlightenment, John Robertson has traced the development of Enlightenment ideas from Hume back through the Scottish universities arguing that an Epicurean and Augustinian synthesis began to emerge sometime in the 1660's, shortly after Rutherford's death.[9]

---

8 Rutherford, Lex Rex, 11.
9 Robertson, The Case for the Enlightenment, 134–46.

It would be beneficial not only to the emergence of Enlightenment ideas in early modern Scotland, as well as to further outline the differences between compatibilism and the classic Reformed position on freedom, to examine a transitional figure between the older Reformed teaching on human liberty and that which was emerging. Two such figures are Sir George Mackenzie (1636–1691) and James Dalrymple, Viscount Stair (1619–1695). Robertson notes Stair relied upon the Protestant natural law theorist Hugo Grotius (1583–1645) in the development of his own political theory. Rutherford offers a critique of Grotius, thus providing a point of contact in the development of ideas concerning human liberty and political thought in early modern Scotland. Furthermore, Robertson notes Rutherford was Stair's "closest Scottish intellectual predecessor."[10] How much continuity and discontinuity existed between these two could be applied to Rutherford and the emergence of Enlightenment in Scotland, as well as to how much of a division exists between Rutherford's own conception of human liberty and what would emerge by the time of David Hume.

5.3   "Scotist" Influences on Reformed Orthodoxy

As was seen above, the thesis pertaining to Scotist influences on Reformed Orthodoxy is far from settled. Muller's depiction of the Reformed Orthodox appropriation of traditional sources as "eclectic" does not sufficiently describe the role that Scotist influences had upon Rutherford. There may be opportunities to continue to explore such influences. One such opportunity is the Franciscan theologian Theodorus Smising (1580–1626).

Smising appears in Rutherford's *Disputatio Scholastica de Divina Providentia*, where he is described throughout as a Scotist. Bac has also noted that the Dutch Reformed theologian Melchior Leydecker (1642–1721) displayed "profound acquaintance with the Scotist Theodor Smising."[11] Beck also identifies Smising's influence upon the Dutch Reformed theologian Gisbertus Voetius (1589–1676), who also described Smising as a Scotist.[12] The close relationship between Voetius and Rutherford has been shown in Beck's work, as well as this study. In addition to this, Bac notes that Leydecker used Rutherford's *Disputatio* to resource his own dissertation on divine providence.[13] The tight network of relationships and influence that existed between Rutherford, Voetius, and later Leydecker, would provide a clearly defined area of research to explore the Scotist Smising's influence upon these significant voices within Reformed Orthodoxy.

---

10 Robertson, 136.
11 Bac, *Perfect Will Theology*, 232.
12 Beck, *Gisbertus Voetius*, 241 and 296.
13 Bac, *Perfect Will Theology*, 232.

6.   Final Thoughts

Samuel Rutherford, Scotland's premier theologian of the seventeenth century, remains a fruitful subject for study and research. His mysticism, poeticism, and pastoral sensitivity seem unusual traits to be matched with that of a scholastic theologian in the era of high orthodoxy. His high view of God's sovereignty belies a startlingly robust account of human liberty. For all his insistence on Covenant orthodoxy in Scotland, he demonstrates familiarity and even appreciation for theologians outside of his own tradition. His catholic and ecumenical interests and obsessive citations make Rutherford a doorway to a theological conversation that goes well beyond the boundaries of Scotland, and even far outside the confines of the seventeenth century. These aspects of Rutherford will no doubt continue to intrigue and reward those who take the time to immerse themselves in his work and seek to understand him on his own terms.

Bibliography

Primary Sources

Τα Των Μουσων Εισοδια: The Muses Welcome to the High and Mightie Prince Iames by the Grace of God King of Great Britain France and Ireland, Defender of the Faith &c. At his Majesties Happy Returne to his Olde and Naiue Kingdome of Scotland, After 14 Yeeres absence, IN ANNO 1617. Edinburgh, 1618.

A DOLA, LUDOVICO (1634), Disputatio quadripartita de modo coniunctionis concursuum dei et creaturae ad actus liberos ordinis naturalis, Leiden: Iacobi & Petri Prost fratr.

ALTENSTAIG, JOHANNES (1576), Theologicum complectens vocabulorum descriptiones, omnibus sacrae Theologiae studiosis ac Divini verbi Concionatoribus magno usui futurum, summo studio & labore concinnatum a Joanne Altenstaig Mindelhaimensi, sacrae Theologiae Doctore, Antwerp: Petri Belleri.

_____."Causae", Theologicum complectens vocabulorum descriptiones, diffinitiones & interepretationes, 21–22.

_____. "Ens", Theologicum complectens vocabulorum descriptiones, diffinitiones & interepretationes, 98.

_____."Omnipotens", Theologicum complectens vocabulorum descriptiones, diffinitiones & interepretationes, 218.

_____."Prior", Theologicum complectens vocabulorum descriptiones, diffinitiones & interepretationes, 262.

ÁLVARES, DIEGO (1610), De auxiliis divinae gratiae et humani arbitrii, Rome: Stephanum Paulinum.

AMES, WILLIAM (1658), Amesii rescriptio scholastica et brevis ad nic. grevinchovii responsum illud prolixum, quod opposuit dissertationi de redemptione generali, & electione ex fide praevisa. Amsterdam: Joannem Janssonium.

_____.The Marrow of Theology (1997), John D. Eusden (ed.), John Dykstra Eusden (tran), Grand Rapids, MI: Baker Books.

ANTONIO DE LA MADRE DIO (1629), Collegium Complutense Philosophicum. Frankfurt: Erasmi Kempfferi.

AQUINAS, THOMAS. *De malo* (2001), Brian Davies (ed.), Richard Regan (tran), Oxford: Oxford University Press.

_____. *Quaestiones disputate de potentia dei* (1952), Westminster, Maryland: Newman Press.

_____. *Summa Contra Gentiles Book Three: Providence Part I.* (2001), Vernon J. Bourke (tran). Notre Dame, IN: University of Notre Dame.

_____. *Summa Theologiae* (2012), O.P. Fr. Laurence Shapcote (tran), John Mortensen and Enrique Alarcon (eds), Lander: The Aquinas Institute for the Study of Sacred Doctrine.

ARISTOTLE. (1984), De Interpretatione, in The Complete Works of Aristotle, 2 vols. Vol 1, Jonathan Barnes (ed.), Princeton, NJ: Princeton University Press.

_____. (1984) The Complete Works of Aristotle: The Revised Oxford Translation, 2 vols. Vol. 2 Jonathan Barnes (ed.), Princeton, NJ: Princeton University Press.

ARMINIUS, JACOBUS (1629), Apologia D. Jacobi Arminii adversus articulos xxxi, in Opera Theologica, Leiden: Godefridum Basson, 134–183

_____. "Articuli nonnulli perpendendi." In *Opera Theologica*, 948–66. Leiden: Goderfridum Basson, 1629.

ARRIAGA, RODERICO DE, *Cursus philosophicus*. Paris: Franciscum Piot. 1647.

ARRUBAL, PETRO DE, *Commentariorum ac disputationum in primam partem divi thomae*. Madrid: Thomam Iuntam, 1619.

AUGUSTINE. "City of God." In *Augustine*. Vol. 2, *Nicene and Post-Nicene Fathers*, edited by Philip Schaff, 1–511. Peabody, MA: Hendrickson. 2004.

_____. "On the Holy Trinity." In *Augustine*. Vol. 3, *Nicene and Post-Nicene Fathers*, edited by Philip Schaff, 1–228. Peabody, MA: Hendrickson, 2004b.

An Abridgment of the Acts of the General Assembly of the Church of Scotland from 1560–1830. Edinburgh: Robert Buchanan, 1831.

AVERSA, RAPHAELE, *Philosophia metaphysicam physicamove complectens quaestionibus contexta in duos tomos distributa*. Bologna: H. H. Euangeliste Ducciae, 1650.

BAILLIE, ROBERT. *The Letters and Journals of Robert Baillie, A.M. Principal of the University of Glasgow. M.DC.XXXVII.—M.DC.LXII.* Edited by David and Lang. Edinburgh: Robert Ogle, 1842.

BÁÑEZ, DOMINGO. *Scholastica commentaria in primam partem angelici doctoris D. Thomae usque ad sexagesimamquartam quaestionem*. Salamanca: S. Stephanum, 1585.

BELLARMINE, ROBERT. *De controversiis christianae fidei, adversus huius temporis hereticos*. Leiden: Joannem Pillehotte, 1610.

BONAVENTURE. "Breviloquium." In *Opera omnia tomus septimus*, edited by A.C. Peltier. Paris: Ludovicus Vives, 1864–1871.

_____. "Sententiarum Lib. II." In *Opera omnia tomus tertius*, edited by A.C. Peltier. Paris: Ludovicus Vives, 1864–1871.

BRADWARDINE, THOMAS. *De causa dei, contra pelagium, et de virtute causarum, ad suos mertonenses*. London: Joannem Billium, 1618.

BRUTUS, STEPHANIUS JUNIUS. *Vindiciae contra tyrannos: sive, de principis in populum, poplique in principem, legitima potestam*. Frankfurt: Lazari Zetzneri, 1608.

BUCHANAN, GEORGE. *De jure regni apud scotos, dialogus, authore Georgio Buchanano Scoto*. Edinburgh: Johannem Rosseum pro Henrico Charteris, 1579.

CAJETAN, THOMAS. *Summa sacrae theologiae in tres partes divisa, et quattuor distincta tomis, d. thoma aquinate angelico doctore authore*. Bergamo: Comini Venturae, 1590.

CALVIN, JOHN. *Institutes of the Christian Religion*. Translated by Ford Lewis Battles. Edited by John T. McNeill. Louisville: Westminster John Knox Press, 1960.

CAMERON, JOHN. *Praelectionum, in selectiora quaedam N. Test. loca, Salmurij habitarum*. Saumur: Girardum & Dan Lerpinerium, 1628.

COLLEGII SALMANTICENSIS. *Cursus Theologicus et Moralis*. Lyon: Joannis Antonii Huguetan, & Soc, 1679.

CORVINUS, JOANNES ARNOLDI. *Petri Molinaei novi anathomici mala encheiresis: seu censura anotomes arminianismi*. Frankfurt: Erasmus Kempffer, 1622.

CRISP, TOBIAS. *Christ Alone Exalted in the Perfection and Encouragements of the Saints, Notwithstanding Sins and Trials*. In *The Complete Works of Tobias Crisp, D.D.*, Vol I., 4th Edition, edited by John Gill. London: R. Noble for J. Murgatroyd, 1791.

A Declaration and Brotherly Exhortation of the General Assembly of the Church of Scotland, met at Edinburgh August 20. 1647. To Their Brethren of England. (1647), Edinburgh: Evan Tyler.

DURANDUS OF SAINT-POURÇAIN. *In sententias theologicas Petri Lombardi commentariorum*. Venice: Gulielmum Rovillium, 1563.

EPISCOPIUS, SIMON. *Opera theologica*. Amsterdam: Ioannis Blaen, 1650.

————. *Apologia pro confessione declaratione sententiae eorum, qui in foederato belgio vocantur remonstrantes, super praecipuis articulis religionis christianae. Contra Censuram Quatuor Professorum* Leidensium. 1630.

England and Scotland's Covenant with Their God. London: Edward Husbands, 1645.

FONSECA, PEDRO DE. *Commentariorum Petri Fonsecae Lusitani, Doctoris Theologi Societatis Iesu, In Metaphysicorum Aristotelis Stagiritae Libros, Tomus Tertius*. Cologne: Lazari Zetzneri, 1603.

FASOLUS, HIERONYMUS. *In Primum partem summae D. Thomae commentariorum tomus secundus: cum tribus indicisum locupletissimis*. Lyon: Andreae, Jacobi, & Matthaei, 1629.

GREVINCHOVIUM, NICOLAAS. *Dissertatio theologica de duabus quaestionibus hoc tempore controversis, quarum prima est de reconciliatione per mortem christi impetrata omnibus ac singulis hominibus: altera, de electione ex fide praevisa*. Rotterdam: Matthias Sebastiani, 1615.

HENRY OF GHENT. *Quodlibeta Tomus Primus*. Venice: Jacobum de Franciscis, 1613.

JACKSON, THOMAS. *The Works of Thomas Jackson, D.D. Sometime President of Corpus Christi College, Oxford and Dean of Peterborough*. Vol 5, *A Treatise on the Divine Essence and Attributes*. Oxford: Oxford University Press, 1844.

JUNIO, ANDREA. *Theses quaedam: Examplissimo philosophiae camp decertae, pro quibus (auspice deo) stabunt in publica adolescentes 42 hac vice magisterio donandi*. Edinburgh: Andreas Hart, 1621.

KNOX, JOHN. *The Historie of the Reformation of the Church of Scotland; Containing Five Books: Together with Some Treatises Conducing to the History*. Vol. 1. London: John Raworth for George Thomason and Octavian Pullen, 1644.

_____. *The Historie of the Reformation of the Church of Scotland; Containing Five Books: Together with Some Treatises Conducing to the History*. Vol. 2. London: John Raworth for George Thomason and Octavian Pullen, 1644.

LESSIUS, LEONARDUS. *De Gratia Efficaci Decretis Divinis: Libertate Arbitrii Et Praescientia Dei Conditionata. Disputatio apologetica*. Barcelona: Sebastiani Matheuad & Laurentij Deu, 1610.

LIGHTFOOT, JOHN. *The Whole Words of the Rev. John Lightfoot D. D.* Vol. 13. Edited by J. R. Pitman. London: J. F. Dove, 1824.

LIPSIUS, JUSTUS. *De Constantia*. Antwerp: Christophorum Plantinum, 1583.

LOMBARD, PETER. *The Sentences Book 2: On Creation*. Translated by Giulio Silano. Vol. 2. Edited by Joseph Goering and Giulio Silano. Toronto: Pontifical Institute of Medieval Studies, 2008.

MACCOVIUS, JOHANNIS. *Metaphysica, ad usum quaestionum in philosophia ac theologia*. Leiden: Francisci Hackil, 1650.

MAXWELL, JOHN. *Sacro-Sancta Regum Majestas: or the Sacred and Royal Prerogative of Christian Kings*. London: Thomas Dring, 1680.

MENCHACA, FERNANDO VASQUEZ DE. *Illustrium controversiarum*. Frankfurt: Joannis Baptistae Schonwetteri, 1668.

Minute Book Kept by the War Committee of the Covenanters in the Stewartry of Kirkcudbright, in the years 1640 and 1641. Kirkcudbright: J. Nicholson, 1855.

Mitchell, Rev. Alex F. and Rev. John Struthers, eds. *Minutes of the Sessions of the Westminster Assembly of Divines*. Edinburgh: William Blackwood and Sons, 1874.

Mitchell, Rev. Alex. and J. Christie, eds. *The Records of the Commissions of the General Assemblies of the Church of Scotland Holden in Edinburgh in the Years 1646–1647*. Edinburgh: Edinburgh University Press, 1892.

MOLINA, LUIS DE. *Concordia liberi arbitrii: Cum gratiae donis divina praescientia, providentia, praedestinatione, et reprobatione*. Lisbon: Antonium Riberium, 1588.

_____. *On Divine Foreknowledge: Part IV of the Concordia*. Translated by Alfred J. Freddoso. Ithaca: Cornell University Press, 1988.

OVIEDO, FRANCISCO. *Cursus philosophicus*. Leiden: Phillippie Borde, Lavrentii Arnaud, Petri Borde, & Guilielmi Barbier, 1663.

OWEN, JOHN. "A Dissertation on Divine Justice." In Vol X of *The Works of John Owen*, edited by William H. Goold, 482–618. Edinburgh: Johnstone & Hunter, 1850–53.

PISCATORE, JOHANNE. "Ad disputationem de praedestinatione contra Schaafmannum." In *Thesium theologicarum in illustri schola nassovica, partim herbornae, partim sigenae disputatarum: Praeside Johanne Piscatore*. Herborn: Christophori Corvini, 1607.

POLYANDER, JOHANNES, ANDRE RIVET, ANTONIUS WALAEUS, and ANTOINE THYSIUS. *Synopsis purioris theologiae: Disputationibus quinquaginta duabus comprehensa*. Leiden: Elzeviriana, 1625.

RAMSAY, A. *A Warning to Come Out of Babylon, in a Sermon Preached by Master Andrew Ramsay, Minister at Edinburgh; at the Receiving of Thomas Abernathie, Sometime Jesuite, into the Society of the Truly Reformed Church of Scotland*. Edinburgh: George Anderson, 1638.

RAYNAUD, THEOPHILE. *Theologica naturalis, sive entis increati et creati*. Leiden: Horatius Boisat & Georgii Remeus, 1665.

RIPALDA, JUAN MARTINEZ DE. *De ente supernaturali*. Lyon: Horatii Boissat & Georgii Remeus, 1663.

ROLLOCK, ROBERT. *Tractatus de vocatione efficaci, quae inter locos theologiae communissimos recensetur, deque locis specialioribus, qui sub vocatione comprehenduntur. Ut doctrina de Vocatione illustrior evaderet, adjecta sunt quaestiones alisquot de modis illis, quibus Deo visum est jam inde a principio, homini verbum utrius que federis sui, revelare*. Christopher Corvinus, 1600.

RUIZ, DIDACI. *Commentarii ac disputationes de scientia de ideis, de veritate ac de vita dei: Ad primam partem Sancti Thomae, a questione 14 usque ad 18*. Paris: Sebatiani Cramoisy, 1629.

_____.*In primam partem d thomae de voluntate dei*. Lyons: Jacobi, Andreae, ac Matthaei Prost, 1630.

RUTHERFORD, SAMUEL. "Ane Catachisme: Conteining The Soume of Christian Religion." In *Catechisms of the Second Reformation*, edited by Alexander F. Mitchell, 161–242. London: James Nisbet & Co., 1886.

_____. *A Free Disputation Against Pretended Liberty of Conscience*. London: Andrew Crook, 1649.

_____. *A Survey of the Spiritual Antichrist*. London: Andrew Crooke, 1648.

_____. *A Survey of the Survey of That Summe of Church Discipline*. London: Andrew Crook, 1658.

_____. *Christ Dying and Drawing Sinners to Himselfe or a Survey of our Saviour in His Soule Suffering, His Lovelyness in His Death, and the Efficacie Thereof*. London: J. D. for Andrew Crooke, 1647.

_____. *Disputatio Scholastica de Divina Providentia*. Edinburgh: Georgii Andersoni, 1649.

_____. *Examen Arminianismi*. Edited by Matthia Netheno. Utrecht: Antoninii Smitegelt, 1668.

_____. *Exercitationes apologeticae pro divina gratia*. Amsterdam: Henricum Laurentii, 1636.

_____. *Fourteen Communion Sermons*. 2nd Edition. Edited by Andrew A. Bonar. Glasgow: Charles Glass & Co., 1878.

_____. *Influences of the Life of Grace*. London: Andrew Cook, 1659.

_____. *Joshua Redivivus: Or, Three Hundred and Fifty-Two Religious Letters, by the late Eminently Pious Mr. Samuel Rutherford, Professor of Divinity, at St Andrews*. Edited by Robert McWard. 9th Edition. Glasgow: John Bryce, 1765.

_____. *Lex Rex: The Law and the Prince*. London: John Field, 1644.

_____. *Quaint Sermons of Samuel Rutherford Hitherto Unpublished.* London: Hodder and Stoughton, 1885.

_____. *The Covenant of Life Opened.* Edinburgh: Robert Brown, 1655.

_____. *The Divine Right of Church Government and Excommunication: Or a Peaceable Dispute for the Perfection of the Holy Scripture in Point of Ceremonies and Church Government.* London: John Field for Christopher Meredith, 1646.

_____. *The Due Right of Presbyteries or, A Peaceable Plea, for the Government of the Church of Scotland.* London: E. Griffin for Richard Whittaker and Andrew Crook, 1644.

_____. *The Tryal and Triumph of Faith: Or an Exposition of the History of Christs Dispossessing of the Daughter of the Woman of Canaan.* London: John field, 1645.

SCOTUS, JOHN DUNS. *Lectura II, dist. 7–44.* In *Opera Omnia*, Vol. 19. Edited by Commissio Scotistica. Città del Vaticano: Typis Polyglottis Vaticanis, 1993.

_____. *In VIII. libros physicorum Aristotelis quaestiones, cum annotationibus R.P.F. Francisci Pitigiani Arretini.* Lyons: Laurentii Durand, 1639.

_____. *Quaestiones in lib I. sententiarum.* Lyon: Lavrentii Durand, 1639.

SENECA. *Moral Letters to Lucilius.* Translated by Richard Mott Gummere. Toronto: Aegitas, 2015.

SMALCIO, VALENTINO. *Responsio ad librum.* Racovia: Sternacianis, 1613.

SMISING, THEODORE. *Disputationum theologicarum de Deo Uno et Trinio.* Antwerp: Gulielmum Lesteenium, 1627.

SOARES, FRANCISCO. *Cursus Philosophicus in Quatuor Tomos Distributus.* Coimbra: Pauli Craesbeeck, 1651.

SUÁREZ, FRANCISCO. *De Divina Gratia.* Mainz: Hermanni Mylii Birckmanni, 1620.

_____. *Metaphysicarum Disputationum, In quibus et universa naturalis theologia ordinate traditur , et quaestiones ad omnes duodecim Aristotelis libros pertinentis accurate disputantur.* Mainz: Balthasarus Lippius, 1614.

_____. *Disputationes in Primam Partem Divi Thomae, De Deo uno & trino.* Mainz: Balthasarus Lippius, 1608.

_____. "Tractatus de gratia dei seu de deo salvatore, justificare, et liberi arbitrii adjutore per gratiam suam." In *Opera omnia. tomus septimus complectens. commentaria ac disputationes in primam secundae D. Thomae de gratia. Operis de gratia divina tripartiti partem primam hic reperies, continentem prolegomena sex, duosque priores de necessitate gratiae ad honesta opera libros.* Paris, 1857.

_____. *Varia Opuscula Theologica.* Mainz: Balthasarum Lippium, 1622.

TWISSE, WILLIAM. *Vindiciae gratiae, potestatis, ac providentiae dei: hoc est, ad examen libellil perkinsiani, de praedestinationis modo & ordine, institutum a iacobo arminino, responsio scholastica, III libris absoluta.* Amsterdam: Guilielmum Blaen, 1632.

USHER, JAMES. *A Body of Divinitie, or the Summe and Substance of Christian Religion, Catechistically Propounded, and Explained, by way of Question and Answer: Methodically and Familiarly Handled.* London: The Downes, 1653.

VALENCIA, GREGORY DE. *Commentariorum theologicorum tomi IIII*. Leiden: Horatii Cardon, 1609.

VOETIUS, GISBERTUS. *Selectarum disputationem theologicarum*. Utrecht: Joannem Waesberge, 1648.

VORSTIUS, CONRAD. *Apologetica exegesis sive plenior declaratio*. Lugdunum Batavorum: Joannis Patij, 1611.

_____. *Amica duplicatio ad johannis piscatoris, theologi herbonensis, apologeticam responsionem & notas eiusdem amicae collationi oppositas*. Gouda: Andream Burier, 1617.

_____. *Apologetica responsio ad ea omnia*, 1618.

_____. *Tractatus theologicus de deo, sive natura & attributis dei, omnia fere ad hanc materiam pertinentia (saltem de quibus utiliter & religiose disputari potest) decem disputationibus, antehac in illustri schola steinfurtensi, diverso tempore, publice habitis, breviter & methodice comprehendens*. Steinfurt: Theophilus Caesar, 1606.

WALAEUS, ANTONIUS. *Responsio ad censuram Joannis Arnoldi Corvini, in cl. viri d. Petri Molinaei anatomen arminianismi, et adscripta Remonstrantium qui ad Synodum Dordracenam citati sunt: pro defensione doctrina in eadem Synodo explicatae et stabilitate*. Leiden: Arnoldi Hoogenackeri, 1625.

ZABARELLA, GIACOMO. *De Rebus Naturalibus Libri XXX*. Venice: Pau Meier 1590.

ZUMEL, FRANCISCI. *Variarum Disputationum*. Lyons: Ioannis Pillehotte, 1609.

Secondary Sources

A Topographical Dictionary of Scotland, Comprising the Several Counties, Islands, Cities, Burgh and Market Towns, Parishes, and Principle Villages, with Historical and Statistical Descriptions Embellished with a Large Map of Scotland and Engravings of the Seals and Arms of the Different Burghs and Universities. London: Lewis and Co, 1846.

ADAMS, MARILYN MCCORD, and ALLAN B. WOLTER. "Memory and Intuition: A Focal Debate in Fourteenth Century Cognitive Psychology." *Franciscan Studies* 53, no. 1 (1993): 175–92.

AHN, SANG HYUCK. "Covenant in Conflict: The Controversy Over the Church Covenant Between Sameul Rutherford and Thomas Hooker." PhD diss., Calvin Theological Seminary, 2011.

AINSWORTH, THOMAS. "Form vs. Matter." In *The Stanford Encyclopedia of Philosophy*, (Spring 2016 Edition), edited by Edward N. Zalta, https://plato.stanford.edu/archives/spr2016/entries/form-matter.

ANFRAY, JEAN-PASCAL. "Molina and John Duns Scotus." In *A Companion to Luis de Molina*, edited by Matthias Kaufmann and Alexander Aichele, 325–64. Brill's Companion to the Christian Tradition 50. Leiden and Boston: Brill, 2014.

_____. "Scottish Scotism? The Philosophical Theses in the Scottish Universities, 1610–1630,." In *History of the Universities,* vol XXIX/2. Edited by Alexander Broadie, 96–120. Oxford: Oxford University Press, 2017.

ARIEW, ROGER, and ALAN GABBEY. "Body and the Physical World: The Scholastic Background." In *The Cambridge History of Seventeenth-Century Philosophy*, edited by Daniel Garber and Michael Ayers, 425–53. Cambridge: Cambridge University Press, 2003.

ARMSTRONG, BRIAN G. *Calvinism and the Amyraut Heresy; Protestant Scholasticism and Humanism in Seventeenth-Century France*. Madison, WI: University of Wisconsin Press, 1969.

ASHTON, ROBERT. *Counter-Revolution: The Second Civil War and Its Origins, 1646–8*. New Haven, CT: Yale University Press, 1994.

ASHWORTH, E. J. *Language and Logic in the Post-Medieval Period*. Syntheses Historical Library 12. Dordrecht: D. Reidel Publishing Company, 1974.

AUGUSTIJN, CORNELIS. "Wittenberga contra Scholasticos." In *Reformation and Scholasticism: An Ecumenical Enterprise*. Edited by Willem J. van Asselt and Eef Dekker, Text & Studies in Reformation & Post-Reformation Thought, 65–77 (Grand Rapids: Baker Academic, 2001).

BAC, J. MARTIN. *Perfect Will Theology: Divine Agency in Reformed Scholasticism as against Suárez, Episcopius, Descartes, and Spinoza*. Brill Series in Church History 42. Leiden: Brill, 2010.

BADDELEY, MOUNTFORD and JOHN BYRDE. *Scotland*. Edited by M.J.B. Baddeley and C.S. Ward. London: Dulau and Co., 1901.

BAGCHI, D.V.N. "Sic et Non: Luther and Scholasticism." In *Protestant Scholasticism: Essays in Reassessment*. Edited by Carl R. Trueman and R. Scott Clark, 1–15. Studies in Christian History and Thought. Eugene, Or: Wipf and Stock, 2005.

BARKER, E. "The Authorship of the Vindiciae Contra Tyrannos." *Cambridge Historical Journal* 3, no. 2 (1930): 164–81.

BARTH, KARL, *Church Dogmatics I.1. Study Edition*. Edited by G.W. Bromily and T.F. Torrance. New York: T & T Clark, 2009.

BAVINCK, HERMAN, and WILLIAM HENDRIKSEN. *The Doctrine of God*. Edinburgh; Carlisle, PA: Banner of Truth Trust, 1977.

BEALE, J. M. "History of the Burgh and Parochial Schools of Fife from the Reformation to 1872." PhD diss., University of Edinburgh, 1953.

BECK, ANDREAS J. "'Divine Psychology' and Modalities: Scotus's Theory of the Neutral Proposition." In *John Duns Scotus (1265/6–1308): Renewal of Philosophy*, edited by Egbert P. Boss, 123–138. Elementa 72. Amsterdam: Rodopi, 1998.

_____. "God, Creation and Providence in Post-Reformation Reformed Theology." In *The Oxford Handbook of Early Modern Theology, 1600–1800*, edited by Richard A. Muller, A.G. Roeber, and Ulrich L. Lehner, 195–212. Oxford: Oxford University Press, 2016.

_____. "The Will as Master of Its Own Act: A Disputation Rediscovered of Gisbertus Voetius (1589–1676) on Freedom of the Will." In *Reformed Thought on Freedom: The*

Concept of Free Choice in Early Modern Reformed Theology, edited by Willem J. van Asselt, J. Martin Bac and Roelf T. te velde, 145–170. Texts and Studies in Reformation and Post-Reformation Thought. Grand Rapids, MI: Baker Academic 2010.

_____. *Gisbertus Voetius (1589–1676). Sein Theologieverständnis und seine Gotteslehre.* Forschungen zur Kirchen- und Dogmengeschichte 92. Göttingen: Vandenhoeck & Ruprecht, 2007.

BEERE, JONATHAN B. *Doing and Being: An Interpretation of Aristotle's Metaphysics Theta.* Oxford Aristotle Studies. Oxford: Oxford University Press, 2009.

BELL, M. CHARLES. *Calvin and Scottish Theology: The Doctrine of Assurance.* Edinburgh: Handsel Press, 1985.

BENEDICT, P. "The Saint Bartholomew's Massacres in the Provinces." *Historical Journal* 21, no. 2 (1978): 205–25.

Biographia Scoticana. or, a Brief Historical Account of the Lives, Characters, and Memorable Transactions of the Most Eminent Scots Worthies, Noblemen, Gentlemen, Ministers, and Others. Glasgow: Khull, Blackie, & Co. and by A. Fullerton & Co. Edinburgh, 1824.

BLAIR, GEORGE. A. "The Meaning of 'Energeia' and 'Entelecheia' in Aristotle." *International Philosophical Quarterly* 7, no. 1 (1967): 101–17.

_____. *Energeia and Entelecheia: "Act" in Aristotle.* Ottawa: University of Ottawa Press, 1992.

BLAKEWAY, A. *Regency in Sixteenth-Century Scotland.* St Andrews Studies in Scottish History. Woodbridge: The Boydell Press, 2015.

BOH, IVAN. "Consequences." In *The Cambridge History of Later Medieval Philosophy*, edited by Norman Kretzmann, Anthony Kenny and Jan Pinborg, 300–14. Cambridge: Cambridge University Press, 1982.

BONAR, ANDREW. "Sketch of Samuel Rutherford" in *Letters of Samuel Rutherford With a Sketch of his Life and Biographical Notices of His Correspondents*, 1–32. Edinburgh and London: Oliphant Anderson and Ferrier, 1891.

BONNER, E. "Scotland's 'auld Alliance' with France, 1295–1560." *History* 84, no. 273 (1999): 5–30.

BOS, A. P. *The Soul and Its Instrumental Body: A Reinterpretation of Aristotle's Philosophy of Living Nature.* Brill's Studies in Intellectual History 112. Leiden, Netherlands; Boston, MA: Brill, 2003.

BOSLEY, RICHARD N. and MARTIN M. Tweedale, eds. *Basic Issues in Medieval Philosophy.* 2nd ed. Ontario: Broadview Press, 2006.

BOWMAN, LEONARD J. "The Cosmic Exemplarism of Bonaventure." *The Journal of Religion* 55, no. 2 (1975): 181–98.

BRETT, ANNABEL S. *Liberty, Right, and Nature: Individual Rights in Later Scholastic Thought.* Ideas in Context 44. Cambridge: Cambridge University Press, 1997.

BRETZKE, JAMES T. "Potentia Obedientialis," in *Consecrated Phrases: A Latin Theological Dictionary,* 2nd ed. Collegeville, Minn: The Liturgical Press, 2003.

BROWER, JEFFREY. "Medieval Theories of Relations." In *The Stanford Encyclopedia of Philosophy*, edited by Edward N. Zalta, https://plato.stanford.edu/archives/win2018/entries/relations-medieval.

BRUNNER, E. *Dogmatics I: The Christian Doctrine of God*. Cambridge: James Clark & Co., 2002.

BURGESS, J.P. "The Problem of Scripture and Political Affairs as Reflected in the Puritan Revolution: Samuel Rutherford, Thomas Goodwin, John Goodwin and Gerrard Winstantley." PhD diss., University of Chicago, 1986.

BURNETT, A. M. "The Educational Roots of Reformed Scholasticism: Dialectic and Scriptural Exegesis in the Sixteenth Century." *Nederlands archief voor kerkgeschiedenis* 84, (2004): 299–317.

BURNS, ROBERT M. "The Divine Simplicity in St. Thomas." *Religious Studies* 25, no. 3 (1989): 271–93.

BURREL, S. A. 1964. "The Apocalyptic Vision of the Early Covenanters." *The Scottish Historical Review* 43, no. 135 (1964): 1–24.

BURTON, SIMON J. G. "Disputing Providence in Seventeenth-Century Scottish Universities: The Conflict between Samuel Rutherford and the Aberdeen Doctors and its Repercussions." In *History of the Universities*, vol XXIX/2, edited by Alexander Broadie, 121–142. Oxford: Oxford University Press, 2017.

_____."Samuel Rutherford's Euthyphro Dilemma: A Reformed Perspective on the Scholastic Natural Law Tradition." In *Reformed Orthodoxy in Scotland: Essays on Scottish Theology 1560–1775*, edited by Aaron Clay Denlinger, 123–140. London: Bloomsbury Academic, 2014.

_____."The Scholastic and Conciliar Roots of Samuel Rutherford's Political Philosophy: The Influence of Jean Gerson, Jacques Almain, and John Mair" in *Scottish Philosophy in the Seventeenth Century*, edited by Alexander Broadie, 208–225. A History of Scottish Philosophy. Oxford: Oxford University Press, 2020.

_____. *The Hallowing of Logic: The Trinitarian Method of Richard Baxter's Methodus Theologiae*. Brill's Series in Church History 57. Leiden: Brill, 2012.

BUTTON, C.N. "Scottish mysticism in the seventeenth century, with special reference to Samuel Rutherford." PhD diss., University of Edinburgh, 1927.

CAMPBELL, W. "Samuel Rutherford, propagandist and exponent of Scottish Presbyterianism: an exposition of his position and influence in the doctrine and politics of the Scottish Church." PhD diss., University of Edinburgh, 1937.

CESALLI, LAURENT. "Propositions: Their Meaning and Truth" in *The Cambridge Companion to Medieval Logic*, 245–264, edited by Catarina Dutilh Novaes and Stephen Read. Cambridge Companions to Philosophy. Cambridge: Cambridge University Press, 2016.

CHUNG-HWAN, CHEN. 1956. "Different Meanings of the Term Energeia in the Philosophy of Aristotle." *Philosophy and Phenomenological Research* 17, no.1 (1956): 56–65.

CIOFFARI, VINCENT. *Fortune and Fate from Democritus to St. Thomas Aquinas*. Whitefish, Montana: Literary Licensing LLC. 2011.

COFFEY, JOHN. "Letters by Samuel Rutherford (1600–1661)." In *The Devoted Life: An Invitation to the Puritan Classics*, edited by Kelly M. Kapic and Randall C. Gleason, 92–107. Downers Grove: InterVarsity Press, 2004.

————. *Politics, Religion and the British Revolutions: The Mind of Samuel Rutherford.* Cambridge Studies in Early Modern History. Cambridge: Cambridge University Press, 1997.

COLLINS, GEORGE NORMAN MACLEOD. *Samuel Rutherford, Saint and Statesman.* S.l.: The Evangelical Library, 1961.

CONGAR, YVES. *Tradition and Traditions: The Biblical, Historical, and Theological Evidence for Catholic Teaching on Tradition.* New York, NY: Macmillan, 1967.

COURTINE, JEAN-FRANCOIS. "Le Projet Suárezien De La Metaphysique." *Archives de Philosophie* 42, no. 2 (1979): 235–74.

COWAN, I. B. 1968. "The Covenanters: A Revision Article." *The Scottish Historical Review* 47 (143): 35–52.

COWARD, BARRY. *The Stuart Age: England, 1603–1714.* 4th edition. Harlow: Longman, 2012.

CRAIG, WILLIAM LANE. *The Problem of Divine Foreknowledge from Aristotle to Suárez.* Brill: Leiden, 1988.

CRAIGIE, J. *A Bibliography of Scottish Education Before 1872.* London: University of London Press, 1970.

CRAUFURD, THOMAS. *History of the University of Edinburgh: From 1580–1646.* Edinburgh: A. Neill & Co., 1808

CRAVEN, W.G. *Giovanni Pico Della Mirandola, Symbol of His Age: Modern Interpretations of a Renaissance Philosopher.* Travaux d'Humanisme et Renaissance 185. Geneva: Librairie Droz, 1981.

CRISP, OLIVER. *Deviant Calvinism: Broadening Reformed Theology.* Minneapolis: Fortress Press, 2014.

CRONIN, TIMOTHY J. *Objective Being in Descartes and in Suárez.* Analecta Gregoriana 154. Rome: Gregorian University Press, 1966.

CROSS, RICHARD. *Duns Scotus.* Great Medieval Thinkers. New York and Oxford: Oxford University Press, 1999.

————. "Henry of Ghent on the Reality of Non-Existing Possibles Revisited." *Archiv für Geschichte der Philosophie* 92, no. 2 (2010): 115–32.

CULLEN, CHRISTOPHER M. *Bonaventure,* Great Medieval Thinkers (Oxford: Oxford University Press 2006)

DALZEL, A. *History of the University of Edinburgh From Its Foundation.* Vol. 2. Edinburgh: Edmonston and Douglas, 1862.

DAWSON, JANE E. A. *John Knox.* New Haven and London: Yale University Press, 2015.

————. "Bonding, Religious Allegiance and Covenanting" in *Kings, Lords and Men in Scotland and Britain, 1300–1625: Essays in Honor of Jenny Wormald,* 155–172, edited by Julian Goodare and Steve Boardman. Edinburgh: Edinburgh University Press, 2014.

_____. *The Politics of Religion in the Age of Mary, Queen of Scots: The Earl of Argyll and the Struggle for Britain and Ireland.* Cambridge Studies in Early Modern British History. Cambridge: Cambridge University Press, 2002.

DE LUBAC, H. *Augustinianism and Modern Theology.* Translated by Lancelot Capel Sheppard. Milestones in Catholic Theology. Chestnut Ridge, NY: Crossroad Publishing Company, 2000.

DE RIJK, L. M. *Aristotle Semantics and Ontology.* Vol. I, *General Introduction, The Works on Logic.* Philosophia Antiqua 91. Leiden: Brill, 2002.

DE WITT, JOHN R. *Jus divinum: The Westminster Assembly and the divine right of church government.* Kampen: J.H. Kok, 1969.

DEKKER, EEF. "The Theory of Divine Permission According to Scotus' Ordinatio I 47." *Vivarium* 38, no. 2 (2000): 231–42.

DEKKER, EEF, and M. A. SCHOUTEN. "Undisputed Freedom: A Disputation of Franciscus Gomarus (1563–1641)." In *Reformed Thought on Freedom*, edited by Willem J. van Asselt, J. Martin Bac, and Dolf T. te Velde, 127–44. Texts and Studies in Reformation and Post-Reformation Thought. Grand Rapids: Baker Academic, 2010.

DENLINGER, AARON CLAY. "The Aberdeen Doctors and Henry Scougal." In *The History of Scottish Theology*, vol. 1., *Celtic Origins to Reformed Orthodoxy.* Edited by David Fergusson and Mark W. Elliott, 279–295. Oxford: Oxford University Press 2019.

_____. Editor. *Reformed Orthodoxy in Scotland: Essays on Scottish Theology 1560–1775.* London: Bloomsbury, 2015.

DIEFENDORF, B. B. *Beneath the Cross: Catholics and Huguenots in Sixteenth-Century Paris.* Oxford: Oxford University Press, 1991.

DOLEZAL, JAMES E. *God Without Parts: Divine Simplicity and the Metaphysics of God's Absoluteness.* Eugene, OR: Wipf and Stock, 2011.

DONALD, PETER. *An Uncounselled King: Charles I and the Scottish Troubles 1637–1641.* Cambridge Studies in Early Modern British History. Cambridge: Cambridge University Press, 2004.

DONALDSON, G., and R.S. MORPETH. *Who's Who in Scottish History.* Cardiff: Welsh Academic Press, 1973.

DORAN, S. "The Politics of Renaissance Europe." In *Shakespeare and Renaissance Europe*, edited by Andrew Hadfield and Paul Hammond, 21–52. Arden Critical Companions. London and New York: Bloomsbury Methuen Drama, 2004.

DOYLE, JOHN P. "Another God: Chimerae, Goat-Stags, and Man-Lions: A Seventeenth-Century Debate about Impossible Objects." *The Review of Metaphysics* 48, no. 4 (1995): 771–808.

DUBY, STEVEN J. *Divine Simplicity: A Dogmatic Account.* T&T Clark Studies in Systematic Theology. London: Bloomsbury Publishing, 2015.

DUHAMEL, P. A. "The Logic and Rhetoric of Peter Ramus." *Modern Philology* 46, no. 3 (1949): 163–171.

DUMONT, STEPHEN D. "Theology as Science and Duns Scotus's Distinction between Intuitive and Abstractive Cognition." *Speculum* 64, no. 3 (1989): 579–99.

_____."John Duns Scotus" in *A Companion to Philosophy in the Middle Ages*, edited by Jorge J.E. Gracia and Timothy B. Noone, 353–369. Oxford: Blackwell, 2002.

ELAZAR, DANIEL. J. *Covenant and Commonwealth: From Christian Separation through the Protestant Reformation + The Covenant Tradition in Politics* Vol. 2. New Brunswick and London: Transaction Publishers, 1996.

EMBRY, BRIAN. "Francisco Suárez on Eternal Truths, Eternal Essences, and Extrinsic Beings." *Ergo: An Open Access Journal of Philosophy* 4, no. 19 (2017).

Extracts from the Records of the Burgh of Edinburgh, 1604–1626. Edited by M. Wood. Edinburgh, 1931.

FEINGOLD, MORDECHAI. "English Ramism: A Reinterpretation." In *The Influence of Petrus Ramus: Studies in Sixteenth and Seventeenth Century Philosophy and Sciences*, edited by Wolfgang Rother, Mordechai Feingold and Joseph S. Freedman, 127–76. Schwabe philosophica 1. Basel: Schwabe, 2001.

FEREJOHN, MICHAEL T. "Aristotle on Necessary Truth and Logical Priority." *American Philosophical Quarterly* 18, no. 4 (1981): 285–293.

FERGUSSON, DAVID. "Divine Providence." In *The Oxford Handbook of Theology and Modern European Thought*, edited by Nicholas Adams, George Pattison and Graham Ward, 655–74. Oxford: Oxford University Press, 2013.

_____. "Predestination: A Scottish Perspective." *Scottish Journal of Theology* 46, no. 4 (1993): 457–478.

FESER, EDWARD. *Scholastic Metaphysics: A Contemporary Introduction.* Piscataway, N.J.: Transaction Books, 2014.

FESKO, J.V. *The Theology of the Westminster Standards: Historical Context and Theological Insights.* Wheaton, IL: Crossway, 2014.

FIERING, S. "Will and Intellect in the New England Mind." *The William and Mary Quarterly* 29, (1972): 515–58.

FISK, PHILIP JOHN. *Jonathan Edward's Turn from the Classic Reformed Tradition of Freedom of the Will. New Directions in Jonathan Edwards Studies* 2. Gottingen: Vandenhoeck & Ruprecht, 2016.

FISSEL, MARK CHARLES. *The Bishop's Wars: Charles I's campaigns against Scotland 1638–1640.* 1994.

FORD, JOHN D. "Lex, rex iusto posita: Samuel Rutherford on the origins of government." In *Scots and Britons: Scottish political thought and the union of 1603*, edited by Robert A. Mason, 262–92. Cambridge: Cambridge University Press, 1994.

_____. "The Lawful Bonds of Scottish Society: The Five Articles of Perth, the Negative Confession and the National Covenant." *The Historical Journal* 37, no. 1 (1994b): 45–64.

FRAKES, JEROLD C. *The Fate of Fortune in the Early Middle Ages: The Boethian Tradition.* Leiden, New York: E.J. Brill, 1988.

FRANK, WILLIAM. "Duns Scotus on Autonomous Freedom and Divine Co-Causality." *Medieval Philosophy and Theology* 2, (1992): 142–64.

FREDDOSO, ALFRED J. "Introduction." In *On Divine Foreknowledge: Part IV of the Concordia*, 1–81, Ithaca, New York: Cornell University Press, 1988.

FROST, GLORIA RUTH. "Thomas Bradwardine on God and the Foundations of Modality." *British Journal for the History of Philosophy* 21, no. 2 (2013): 368–80.

GARRIGOU-LAGRANGE, REGINALD. *Reality: A Synthesis of Thomistic Thought*. Lexington: Ex Fontibus, 2012.

GARSON, JAMES. "Modal Logic." In *The Standford Encyclopedia of Philosophy*, (Fall 2018 Edition), edited by Edward N. Zalta, https://plato.stanford.edu/archives/fall2018/entries/logic-modal.

GASKIN, RICHARD. "Molina on Divine Foreknowledge and the Principle of Bivalence." *Journal of the History of Philosophy 32*, no. 4 (October 1994): 551–571.

GELLERA, GIOVANNI. "Philosophy and Theology After John Mair," in *The History of Scottish Theology*, vol. 1, *Celtic Origins to Reformed Orthodoxy*. Edited by David Fergusson and Mark W. Elliot, 109–123. Oxford: Oxford University Press, 2019.

GENEST, JEAN-FRANÇOIS. *Prédétermination et Liberté créée à Oxford au XIVe Siècle: Buckingham contre Bradwardine*. With an Edition of Thomas Buckingham *Determinatio de contingentia futurorum*. Etudes de Philosphie Medievale, 70. Paris: J. Vrin, 1992.

GOODARE, JULIAN. "The Scottish Parliament of 1621." *The Historical Journal* 38, no. 1 (1995): 29–51.

GOOTJES, ALBERT. *Claude Pajon (1626–1685) and the Academy of Saumur: The First Controversy Over Grace*. Leiden: Brill, 2014.

GORONCY, JASON. "'Tha mi a' toirt fainear dur gearan:' J. McLeod Campbell and P.T. Forsyth on the Extent of Christ's Vicarious Ministry." In *Evangelical Calvinism: Essays Resourcing the Continuing Reformation of the Church*, edited by Myk Habets and Bobby Grow, 253–86. Eugene, OR: Pickwick Publications, 2012.

GOUDRIAAN, AZA. "Samuel Rutherford on the Divine Origin of Possibility." In *Reformed Orthodoxy in Scotland: Essays on Scottish Theology 1560–1775*, edited by Aaron Clay Denlinger, 141–156. London: Bloomsbury, 2014.

_____. "The Synod of Dordt on Arminian Anthropology." In *Revisiting the Synod of Dordt*, edited by Aza Goudriaan and Fred van Lieburg, 81–106. Brill's Series in Church History 49. Leiden: Brill, 2011.

GRACIA, JORGE J.E. "English-Latin Index." In *Suárez on Individuation. Metaphysical Disputation V: Individual Unity and Its Principle*, 289–96. Milwaukee: Marquette University Press, 1982.

GRAHAM, DANIEL W. 1989. "The Etymology of Entelecheia." *American Journal of Philology* 110, no. 1 (1989): 73–80.

GRANT, EDWARD. "The Effect of the Condemnation of 1277." In *The Cambridge History of Later Medieval Philosophy*, edited by Norman Kretzmann, Anthony Kenny and Jan Pinborg. Cambridge: Cambridge University Press, 1982.

_____. *Much Ado About Nothing: Theories of Space and Vacuum from the Middle Ages to the Scientific Revolution*. Cambridge: Cambridge University Press, 1981.

GRAVES, F. P. *Peter Ramus and the Educational Reformation of the Sixteenth Century*. New York, NY: The Macmillan Company, 1912.

GREAVES, R. L. "John Knox and the Covenant Tradition." *Journal of Ecclesiastical History* 24, no.1 (1973): 23–32.

HAMPTON, STEPHEN. *Anti-Arminians: The Anglican Reformed Tradition from Charles II to George I*. Oxford: Oxford University Press, 2008.

HARRISON, P. *The Bible, Protestantism, and The Rise of Natural Science*. Cambridge: Cambridge University Press, 1998.

HARRISON, ROBERT. *The Brownists in Norwich and Norfolk about 1580*. New York, NY: The MacMillan Co., 1920.

HART, DAVID BENTLEY. "Providence and Causality: On Divine Innocence." In *The Providence of God*, edited by Francesa Aran Murphy and Philip G. Ziegler, 34–56. New York, NY: T&T Clark, 2009.

HELM, PAUL. "Jonathan Edwards and the Parting of Ways?" *Jonathan Edwards Studies* 4, no.1 (2014): 42–60.

_____. "Reformed Thought on Freedom: Some Further Thoughts." *Journal of Reformed Theology* 4, (2010): 185–207.

_____. "Review of Perfect Will Theology." *Themelios* 36, no. 2 (2011): 321–23.

_____. "Structural Indifference." *Journal of Reformed Theology* 5, (2011): 184–205.

_____. "Synchronic Contingency in Reformed Scholasticism: A Note of Caution." *Nederlands Theologisch Tijdschrift* 57, 3 (2003): 207–22.

HENDERSON, G.D. *Religious Life in Seventeenth-Century Scotland*. Cambridge: Cambridge University Press, 1937.

HERON, ALASDAIR. "Foreword." In *Evangelical Calvinism*, edited by Myk Habets and Bobby Grow. Eugene: Pickwick Publications, 2012.

HEWISON, JAMES KING. *The Covenanters: A History of the Church in Scotland From the Reformation to the Revolution*. Vol. 2. Glasgow: John Smith and Son, 1913.

HILL, BENJAMIN, and HENRIK LAGERLUND. *The Philosophy of Francisco Suárez*. Oxford; New York: Oxford University Press, 2012.

HOFFMANN, TOBIAS. "Intellectualism and Voluntarism." In *The Cambridge History of Medieval Philosophy*, edited by Robert Pasnau and Christina Van Dyke, 414–27. Cambridge: Cambridge University Press, 2017.

HOLLOWAY, E. R. *Andrew Melville and Humanism in Renaissance Scotland 1545-1622*. Studies in the History of Christian Traditions 154. Leiden: Brill, 2011.

HOLT, M. P. *The French Wars of Religion, 1562-1629*. New Approaches to European History 36. Cambridge and New York: Cambridge University Press, 1995.

HORNER, W. B. *Nineteenth Century Scottish Rhetoric: The American Connection*. Carbondale; Edwardsville: Southern Illinois University Press, 1993.

HORTON, MICHAEL S. "Participation and Covenant." In *Radical Orthodoxy and the Reformed Tradition*, edited by James K. A. Smith and James H. Olthuis, 107–34. Grand Rapids, MI: Baker Academic, 2005.

HOUSTON, R. A. "Literacy Campaigns in Scotland, 1560–1803." In *National Literacy Campaigns: Historical and Comparative Perspectives*, edited by Robert F. Arnove, and Harvey J. Graff, 49–64. New York: Plenum Press, 1987.

————. "The Literacy Myth?: Illiteracy in Scotland 1630–1760." *Past and Present* 96, (1982): 81–102.

————. *Scotland: A Very Short Introduction*. Oxford: Oxford University Press, 2008.

————. *Scottish Literacy and the Scottish Identity: Illiteracy and Society in Scotland and Northern England 1600–1800*. Cambridge Studies in Population, Economy and Society in Past Time 4. Cambridge: Cambridge University Press, 1985.

HOWIE, JOHN. *The Scots Worthies: Containing a Brief Historical Account of the Most Eminent Noblemen, Gentlemen, Ministers, and Others, Who Testified or Suffered For the Cause of Reformation in Scotland From the Beginning of the Sixteenth Century to the Year 1688*. New York: Robert Carter and Brothers, 1853.

HUDSON, WINTHROP S. "The Scottish Effort to Presbyterianize the Church of England during the Early Months of the Long Parliament." *Church History* 8, no. 3 (1939): 255–82.

HUTTON, RONALD. *Charles the Second, King of England, Scotland, and Ireland*. Oxford: Oxford University Press, 1999.

HUTTON, SARAH. "Thomas Jackson, Oxford Platonist, and William Twisse, Aristotelian." *Journal of the History of Ideas* 39, no. 4 (1978): 635–52.

IRWIN, TERRENCE. *The Development of Ethics: A Historical and Critical Study*. Vol. 2, *From Suárez to Rousseau*. Oxford: Oxford University Press, 2007.

————. *Aristotle's First Principles*. Oxford: Oxford University Press, 1990.

JACKSON, CLARE. *Restoration Scotland, 1660–1690: Royalist Politics, Religion and Ideas*. Studies in Early Modern Cultural, Political, and Social History. Suffolk: The Boydell Press, 1972.

JARDINE, L. "Humanism and the teaching of logic." In *The Cambridge History of Later Medieval Philosophy*, 797–807. Cambridge: Cambridge University Press, 1992.

JONES, HOWARD. *The Epicurean Tradition*. London: Routledge, 1992.

KENDALL, ROBERT TILLMAN. *Calvin and English Calvinism to 1649*. Studies in Christian History and Thought. Eugene, OR: Wipf and Stock, 2011.

KENNY, ANTHONY. *A New History of Western Philosophy*. Oxford: Clarendon Press, 2012.

————. *The God of the Philosophers*. Oxford: Oxford University Press, 1986.

KIM, SAN-DEOG. "Time and Eternity: A Study in Samuel Rutherford's Theology, with Reference to His Scholastic Method." PhD diss., University of Aberdeen, 2002.

KING, PETER. "Scotus on Metaphysics." In *The Cambridge Companion to Duns Scotus*, edited by Thomas Williams, 15–68. Cambridge Companions to Philosophy. Cambridge: Cambridge University Press, 2003.

KING, STEPHEN. "'Your Best and Maist Faithfull Subjects: Andrew and James Melville as James VI and I's 'loyal opposition.'" *Renaissance and Reformation / Renaissance et Reforme* 24, no. 3 (2000): 17–30.

KIRK, G. S., J. E. RAVEN, and MALCOLM SCHOFIELD. *The Presocratic Philosophers: A Critical History with a Selection of Texts*. 2nd ed. Cambridge: Cambridge University Press, 1983.

KNEALE, W. C., and MARTHA KNEALE. *The Development of Logic*. New York: Oxford University Press, 2008.

KNUDSON, CHRISTIAN. "Intentions and Impositions." In *The Cambridge History of Later Medieval Philosophy*, edited by Norman Kretzmann, Anthony Kenny and Jan Pinborg, 479–95. Cambridge: Cambridge University Press, 1982.

KNUUTILA, SIMO. "Anselm on Modality." In *The Cambridge Companion to Anselm*, edited by Brian Davies and Brian Leftow, 111–31. Cambridge Companions to Philosophy. Cambridge: Cambridge University Press, 2004.

————. "Future Contingents." In *Encyclopedia of Medieval Philosophy: Philosophy Between 500 and 1500*, edited by Henrik Lagerlund, 371–73. Dordrecht: Springer Science and Business Media, 2010.

————. "Modality." In *The Oxford Handbook of Medieval Philosophy*, edited by John Marenbon, 312–41. Oxford: Oxford University Press, 2012.

————. "Time and Modality in Scholasticism." In *Reforging the Great Chain of Being*, edited by Simo Knuuttila, 163–258. Dordrecht: D. Reidel Publishing Company, 1981b.

————. *Reforging the Great Chain of Being: Studies of the History of Modal Theories*. Vol. 20, *Synthese Historical Library*. Dordrecht: D. Reidel Pub. Co.,1981a.

KONYNDYK, KENNETH. *Introductory Modal Logic*. Notre Dame, IN: University of Notre Dame Press, 1986.

KOROLEC, J. B. "Free Will and Free Choice." In *The Cambridge History of Later Medieval Philosophy*, edited by Norman Kretzmann, Anthony Kenny and Jan Pinborg, 629–41. Cambridge: Cambridge University Press, 1992.

KRAYE, JILL, "Introduction." In *Moral Philosophy on the Threshold of Modernity*, edited by Jill Kraye and Risto Saarinen, 1–6. New Synthese Historical Library 57. Dordrect: Springer, 2005.

KRISTELLER, P. O. *Renaissance Thought and its Sources*. New York, NY: Columbia University Press, 1979.

LEFF, GORDON. *William of Ockham: The Metamorphosis of Scholastic Discourse*. Manchester: Manchester University Press, 1975.

LEFTOW, BRIAN. "Aquinas, Divine Simplicity and Divine Freedom." In *Metaphysics and God: Essays in Honor of Eleonore Stump*, edited by Kevin Tempe, 21–38. Routledge Studies in the Philosophy of Religion. New York, NY: Routledge, 2009.

LETHAM, ROBERT. "The Foedus Operum: Some Factors Accounting for Its Development." *The Sixteenth Century Journal* 14, no. 4 (1983): 457–67.

_____. *The Westminster Assembly: Reading its Theology in Historical Context*. Phillipsburg: P&R Publishing, 2009.

LEWIS, SAMUEL. "Anwoth." In *A Topographical Dictionary of Scotland, Comprising the Several Counties, Islands, Cities, Burgh and Market Towns, Parishes, and Principle Villages, with Historical and Statistical Descriptions Embellished with a Large Map of Scotland and Engravings of the Seals and Arms of the Different Burghs and Universities*. London: Lewis and Co., 1846.

LLOYD, A. C. "The Later Neoplatonists." In *The Cambridge History of Later Greek and Early Medieval Philosophy*, 272–330. Cambridge: Cambridge University Press, 1980.

LONG, A. A. "Stoicism in the Philosophical Tradition: Spinoza, Lipsius, Butler." In *The Cambridge Companion to the Stoics*, edited by Brad Inwood, 365–92. Cambridge Companions to Philosophy. Cambridge: Cambridge University Press, 2003.

LONGEWAY, JOHN. "Medieval Theories of Demonstration." in *The Stanford Encyclopedia of Philosophy* (Spring 2009 Edition), edited by Edward N. Zalta, https://plato.stanford.edu/archives/spr2009/entries/demonstration-medieval.

LUSCOMBE, D. E. "Natural Morality and Natural Law." In *The Cambridge History of Later Medieval Philosophy*, edited by Norman Kretzmann, Anthony Kenny and Jan Pinborg, 705–20. Cambridge: Cambridge University Press, 1992.

MACDONALD, ALAN R. "David Calderwood: The Not So Hidden Years,1590–1604." *The Scottish Historical Review* 74, no. 197 (1995): 69–74.

_____. *The Jacobean Kirk, 1567–1625: Sovereignty, Polity, and Liturgy*. Aldershot: Ashgate, 1998.

MACGREGOR, G. *Scotland: An Intimate Portrait*. New York, NY: Dodd & Mead, 1985.

MACINNES, A. I. *Charles I and the Making of the Covenanting Movement 1625–1641*. Edinburgh: John Donald Publishers, 2003.

MACINTOSH, GILLIAN H. *The Scottish Parliament under Charles II, 1660–1685*. Edinburgh: Edinburgh University Press, 2007.

MACLEAR, J. F. "Samuel Rutherford: The Law and the King." In *Calvinism and the Political Order: Essays Prepared for the Woodrow Wilson Lectureship of the National Presbyterian Center Washington, D.C.*, edited by George L. Hunt, 65–87. Philadelphia, PA: The Westminster Press, 1965.

MACLEOD, JOHN. *Scottish Theology in Relation to Church History Since the Reformation*. 3rd ed. Edinburgh: Banner of Truth Trust, 1974.

MAKEY, WALTER. *The Church of the Covenant 1637–1651: Revolution and Social Change in Scotland*. Edinburgh: John Donald Publishers Ltd., 1979.

MARC, COHEN. S. "Aristotle's Metaphysics." In *The Stanford Encyclopedia of Philosophy* (Winter 2016 Edition), edited by Edward N. Zalta, https://plato.stanford.edu/archives/win2016/entries/aristotle-metaphysics.

MARCUS, RALPH. "The Tree of Life in Proverbs." *Journal of Biblical Literature* 62, no. 2 (1943): 117–20.

MARENBON, JOHN. "Boethius: from antiquity to the Middle Ages." In *Medieval Philosophy*, edited by John Marenbon, 11–28. London & New York: Routledge, 2003.

MARRONE, STEVEN P. "Duns Scotus on Metaphysical Potency and Possibility." *Franciscan Studies* 56 (1998): 265–89.

MARSHALL, J.L. "Natural Law and The Covenant: The Place of Natural Law in the Covenantal Framework of Samuel Rutherford's *Lex Rex*." PhD diss., Westminster Theological Seminary, 1995.

MARSHALL, ROSALIND K. *John Knox*. Edinburgh: Birlinn Limited, 2013.

MARTIN, CATHERINE GIMELLI. *Milton Among the Puritans: The Case for Historical Revisionism*. Burlington: Ashgate, 2010.

MASON, R. "George Buchanan, James VI and the Presbyterians." In *Kingship and Commonweal: Political Thought in Renaissance and Reformation Scotland*. Eastwell: Tuckwell Press, 1998.

MATAVA, ROBERT JOSEPH. *Divine Causality and Human Free Choice: Domingo Báñez, Physical Premotion and the Controversy de auxiliis Revisited*. Brill's Studies in Intellectual History 252. Leiden: Brill, 2016.

MAURER, ARMAND. *The Philosophy of William Ockham: In the Light of its Principles*. Studies and Texts 133. Toronto: Pontifical Institute of Mediaeval Studies, 1999.

_____. *Being and Knowing: Studies in Thomas Aquinas and Later Medieval Philosophers*. Papers in Mediaeval Studies 10. Toronto: Pontifical Institute of Mediaeval Studies, 1990.

MAURY, GASTON BONET. "John Cameron: A Scottish Protestant Theologian in France (1579–1625)." *The Scottish Historical Review* 7, no. 28 (1910): 325–45.

MAYRL, DAMON, AND FREEDEN OEUR. "Religion and Higher Education: Current Knowledge and Directions for Future Research." *Journal for the Scientific Study of Religion* 48, no. 2 (2009): 260–75.

MCCRIE, THOMAS. *The Life of Andrew Melville Containing Illustrations of the Ecclesiastical and Literary History of Scotland, During the Latter Part of the Sixteenth Century and Beginning of the Seventeenth Century with an Appendix Consisting of Original Papers*. Edinburgh: William Blackwood, 1819.

_____. *The Life of Andrew Melville, the Scottish Reformer; Abridged for the Board, From McCrie's Life of Melville*. Philadelphia: Presbyterian Board of Publication, 1840.

_____. *The Life of Andrew Melville: Containing Illustrations of the Ecclesiastical and Literary History of Scotland, during the Latter Part of the Sixteenth and Beginning of the Seventeenth Century*. 2nd ed., 2 vols. Edinburgh: William Blackwood, 1824.

_____. *The Life of John Knox: Containing Illustrations of the History of The Reformation in Scotland with Biographical Notices of the Principal Reformers, and Sketches of the Progress of Literature in Scotland, During a Great Part of the Sixteenth Century*. Vol 1. Edinburgh: William Blackwood, 1818.

MCGRATH, ALISTER. *Reformation Thought: An Introduction*. 3rd ed. Oxford: Blackwell, 2001.

MCGREGOR, P. *A System of Logic, Comprising a Discussion of the Various Means of Acquiring and Retaining Knowledge, and Avoiding Error*. New York: Harper & Brothers, 1862.

MCKIM, D. K. "The Functions of Ramism in William Perkins' Theology." *The Sixteenth Century Journal* 16, no. 4 (1985): 503–517.

MIKKELI, HEIKKI. "Giacomo Zabarella." In *The Stanford Encyclopedia of Philosophy*. Spring 2018 Edition. Edited by Edward N. Zalta. https://plato.stanford.edu/archives/spr2018/entries/zabarella/.

MILBANK, JOHN, CATHERINE PICKSTOCK and GRAHAM WARD, eds. *Radical Orthodoxy*. London: Routledge, 1999.

MILBANK, JOHN. "Alternative Protestantism: Radical Orthodoxy and the Reformed Tradition." In *Radical Orthodoxy and the Reformed Tradition*, edited by James K.A. Smith and James H. Olthuis, 25–42. Grand Rapids: Baker Academic, 2005.

_____. *Theology and Social Theory: Beyond Secular Reason*. Oxford: Blackwell, 1990.

MILLER, P. *The New England Mind: The Seventeenth Century*. Cambridge, MA: Harvard University Press, 1954.

MORTIMOR, SARAH. *Reason and Religion in the English Revolution: The Challenge of Socinianism*. Cambridge Studies in Early Modern British History. Cambridge: Cambridge University Press, 2010.

MUHLING, ANDREAS. "Arminius und die Herborner Theologen: am Beispiel von Johannes Piscator." In *Arminius, Arminianism, and Europe*, edited by Th. Marius van Leeuwen, Keith D. Stanglin and Marijke Tolsma, 115–34. Brill's Series in Church History 39. Leiden: Brill, 2009.

MULLAN, DAVID GEORGE. *Narratives of the Religious Self in Early-Modern Scotland*. St Andrews Studies in Reformation History. Farnham: Ashgate, 2010.

_____. *Scottish Puritanism 1590–1638*. Oxford: Oxford University Press, 2000.

MULLER, RICHARD. *After Calvin: Studies in the Development of a Theological Tradition*. Oxford Studies in Historical Theology. Oxford: Oxford University Press, 2003.

_____. "Concursus." In *Dictionary of Latin and Greek Theological Terms: Drawn Principally from Protestant Scholastic Theology*, 2nd Ed., 73–74. Grand Rapids, MI: Baker Academic, 2017.

_____. "Distinctio." In *Dictionary of Latin and Greek Theological Terms: Drawn Principally from Protestant Scholastic Theology*. 2nd Ed., 95. Grand Rapids, MI: Baker Academic, 2017.

_____. "Libertas a coactione." In *Dictionary of Latin and Greek Theological Terms: Drawn Principally from Protestant Scholastic Theology*. 2nd Ed., 198. Grand Rapids, MI: Baker Academic, 2017.

_____. "Libertas contradictionis." In *Dictionary of Latin and Greek Theological Terms: Drawn Principally from Protestant Scholastic Theology*. 2nd Ed., 199. Grand Rapids, MI: Baker Academic, 2017.

_____. "Motus." In *Dictionary of Latin and Greek Theological Terms: Drawn Principally from the Protestant Scholastic Theology*. 2nd Ed., 223–4. Grand Rapids, MI: Baker Academic, 2017.

_____. "Praemotio physica." In *Dictionary of Latin and Greek Theological Terms: Drawn Principally from Scholastic Theology*. 2nd Ed., 279. Grand Rapids, MI: Baker Academic, 2017.

_____ "Divine Covenants, Absolute and Conditional: John Cameron and the Early Orthodox Development of Reformed Covenant Theology." *Mid-America Journal of Theology*, no. 17 (2006): 11–56.

_____. *Divine Will and Human Choice: Freedom, Contingency, and Necessity in Early Modern Reformed Thought*. Grand Rapids, MI: Baker Academic, 2017.

_____. "Jonathan Edwards and the Absence of Free Choice: A Parting of Ways in the Reformed Tradition." *Jonathan Edwards Studies* 1, no. 1 (2011): 3–22.

_____. *God, Creation, and Providence in the Thought of Jacob Arminius: Sources and Directions of Scholastic Protestantism in the Era of Early Orthodoxy*. Grand Rapids, MI: Baker Book House, 1991.

_____. *Post-Reformation Reformed Dogmatics*. Vol 1, *Prologomena to Theology*. Grand Rapids, MI: Baker Academic, 2003.

_____. *Post-Reformation Reformed Dogmatics*. Vol. 3, *The Divine Essence and Attributes*. Grand Rapids, MI: Baker Academic, 2003.

_____. "Scholasticism in Calvin: A Question of Relation and Disjunction," in *The Unaccommodated Calvin: Studies in the Foundation of a Theological Tradition*, Oxford Studies in Historical Theology (Oxford: Oxford University Press, 2000), 39–61.

MULLINGER, J. BASS. *A History of the University of Cambridge*. London: Longmans, Green, and Co., 1888.

MURRAY, THOMAS. *The Life of Samuel Rutherford, One of the Ministers of St Andrews, and Principal of the College of St. Mary's With an Appendix*. Edinburgh: William Oliphant, 1828.

NORMORE, CALVIN G. "Duns Scotus' Modal Theory." In *The Cambridge Companion to Duns Scotus*, edited by Thomas Williams, 129–160. Cambridge Companions to Philosophy. Cambridge: Cambridge University Press, 2003.

NOVIKOFF, ALEX. J. *The Medieval Culture of Disputation, Pedagogy, Practice and Performance*. Philadelphia, PA: University of Philadelphia Press, 2013.

NOVOTNY, DANIEL. *Ens rationis from Suarez to Caramuel: A Study in Scholasticism of the Baroque Era*. Medieval Philosophy Text and Studies. New York, NY: Fordham University Press, 2013.

OAKLEY, FRANCIS. "The Absolute and Ordained Power of God in Sixteenth and Seventeenth Century Theology." *Journal of the History of Ideas* 59, no. 3 (1998): 437–61.

OBERMAN, HEIKO A. "Some Notes on the Theology of Nominalism: With Attention to Its Relation to the Renaissance." *The Harvard Theological Review* 53, no. 1 (1960): 47–76.

ONG, W. J. "Ramist Method and the Commercial Mind." In *Studies in the Renaissance* 8 (1961): 155–72.

————. *Ramus, Method, and the Decay of Dialogue: From the Art of Discourse to the Art of Reason*. Chicago: The University of Chicago Press, 2004.

OSBORNE JR., THOMAS M. *Human Action in Thomas Aquinas, John Duns Scotus, and William of Ockham*. Washington, DC: The Catholic University of America Press, 2014.

PARTEE, CHARLES. *The Theology of John Calvin*. Louisville, KY: Westminster John Knox Press, 2008.

PEDERSON, RANDALL J. *Unity in Diversity: English Puritans and the Puritan Reformation, 1603–1689*. Brill: Leiden, 2014.

PHILLIPS, J. E. "George Buchanan and the Sidney Circle." *Huntington Library Quarterly* 12, no. 1 (1948): 23–55.

PLEIZIER, T. THEO, and MAARTEN WISSE. "'As the Philosopher Says': Aristotle." In *Introduction to Reformed Scholasticism*, edited by Willem J. Van Asselt et. al, 26–44. Reformed Historical-Theological Studies. Grand Rapids, MI: Reformation Heritage Books, 2011.

POLLOCK, DARREN M. "Early Stuart Polemical Hermeneutics: Andrew Willet's 1611 Hexapla on Romans." PhD diss., Calvin Theological Seminary, 2016.

POPPI, ANTONINO. "Fate, Fortune, Providence, and Human Freedom." In *The Cambridge History of Renaissance Philosophy*, edited by Charles B. Schmitt, Quentin Skinner, Eckhard Kessler, and Jill Kraye, 641–67. Cambridge: Cambridge University Press, 1988.

PREUS, ROBERT D. *The Theology of Post-Reformation Lutheranism: A Study of Theological Prolegomena*. Vol. 1. St. Louis, MO: Concordia Publishing House, 1970.

RAIT, ROBERT S. "Andrew Melville and the Revolt Against Aristotle in Scotland." *The English Historical Review* 14, no. 54 (1899): 250–60.

REALE, GIOVANNI. *Plato and Aristotle: A History of Ancient Philosophy*. New York, NY: State University of New York Press, 1990.

REHNMAN, SEBASTIAN. "Theistic Metaphysics and Biblical Exegesis: Francis Turretin on the Concept of God." *Religious Studies* 38, no. 2 (2002): 167–86.

————. "The Doctrine of God in Reformed Orthodoxy." In *A Companion to Reformed Orthodoxy*, edited by Christopher M. Bellitto, 353–402. Brill's Companions to the Christian Tradition 40. Leiden: Brill, 2013.

REID, JAMES. *Memoirs of the Lives and Writings of Those Eminent Divines, Who Convened the Famous Assembly at Westminster in the Seventeenth Century*. Vol. I. High Street: Stephen and Andrew Young, 1811.

REID, S. J. "Andrew Melville and Scottish Ramism." In *Ramus, Pedagogy, and the Liberal Arts: Ramism in Britain and the Wider World*, edited by Stephen J. Reid and Emma Annette Wilson, 25–46. Surrey: Ashgate, 2011a.

————. "Andrew Melville and the Law of Kingship." In *Andrew Melville (1545–1622): Writings, Reception, and Reputation*, edited by R. Mason, 47–74. St Andrews Studies in Reformation History. Surrey: Ashgate, 2014.

_____. "Early Polemic by Andrew Melville: The 'carmen Mosis' (1574) and the St. Bartholomew's Day Massacres." *Renaissance and Reformation / Renaissance et Réforme* 30, no. 4 (2007): 63–81.

_____. *Humanism and Calvinism: Andrew Melville and the Universities of Scotland, 1560–1625.* St Andrews Studies in Reformation History. Surrey: Ashgate, 2011b.

RENDELL, KINGSLEY G. *Samuel Rutherford: A New Biography of the Man & His Ministry.* Fearn: Christian Focus, 2003.

RICHARD, GUY M. "Samuel Rutherford's Supralapsarianism Revealed: A Key to the Lapsarian Position of the Westminster Confession of Faith?" *Scottish Journal of Theology* 59 (2006): 27–44.

_____. *The Supremacy of God in the Theology of Samuel Rutherford.* Studies in Christian History and Thought. Eugene, OR: Wipf and Stock, 2008.

RITTER, WILLIAM. E. "Why Aristotle Invented the Word Entelecheia." *The Quarterly Review of Biology* 7, no. 4 (1932): 377–404.

ROBERTSON, JOHN. *The Case for the Enlightenment: Scotland and Naples 1680–1760.* Ideas in Context. Cambridge: Cambridge University Press, 2005.

RODDA, J. *Public Religious Disputation in England, 1558–1626.* St Andrews Studies in Reformation History. Surrey: Ashgate, 2014.

ROHLS, JAN. "Calvinism, Arminianism, and Socinianism in the Netherlands Until the Synod of Dordt." In *Socinianism and Arminianism: Antitrinitarians, Calvinists, and Cultural Exchange in Seventeenth-Century Europe*, edited by Martin Mulsow and Jan Rohls, 3–48. Brill's Studies in Intellectual History 134. Leiden: Brill, 2005.

ROUWENDAL, PIETER L. "The Method of the Schools: Medieval Scholasticism." In *Introduction to Reformed Scholasticism*, edited by Willem J. Van Asselt, T. Theo J. Pleizier, Pieter L. Rouwendal and Maarten Wisse, 56–72. Grand Rapids, MI: Reformation Heritage Books, 2011.

RYKEN, P.G. "Scottish Reformed Scholasticism." In *Protestant Scholasticism: Essays in Reassessment*, edited by Carl R. Trueman and R. Scott Clark, 196–210. Studies in Christian History and Thought. Eugene, OR: Wipf & Stock, 2005.

SCHAEFFER, FRANCIS A. *A Christian Manifesto.* Westchester, IL: Crossway Books, 1981.

SCHMIDT, LEIGH ERIC. *Holy Fairs: Scotland and the Making of American Revivalism.* 2nd Edition. Grand Rapids, MI: W. B. Eerdmans., 2001.

SCHMUTZ, J. "La *doctrine médiévale* des *causes* et la *théologie* de la *nature pure.*" *Revue Thomiste* 102 (2001): 217–64.

SCHUTTE, ANNE JACOBSON. "An Early Stuart Critique of Machiavelli as Historiographer: Thomas Jackson and the 'Discourse.'" *Albion: A Quarterly Journal Concerned with British Studies* 15, no. 1 (1938): 1–18.

SCOTLAND, J. *The History of Scottish Education.* London: University of London, 1969.

SCOTT, DAVID. *Politics and War in the Three Stuart Kingdoms, 1637–49.* British History in Perspective. New York, NY: Palgrave Macmillan, 2004.

SERENE, EILEEN. "Demonstrative Science." In *The Cambridge History of Later Medieval Philosophy*, edited by Norman Kretzmann, Anthony Kenny, and Jan Pinborg, 496–518. Cambridge: Cambridge University Press, 1982.

SHIMP, ROBERT E. "A Catholic Marriage for an Anglican Prince." *Historical Magazine of the Protestant Episcopal Church* 50, no. 1 (1981): 3–18.

SHRIVER, FREDERICK. "Orthodoxy and Diplomacy: James I and the Vorstius Affair." *The English Historical Review* 85, no. 336 (1970): 449–74.

SKINNER, QUENTIN. "Meaning and Understanding in the History of Ideas." In *Visions of Politics*. Vol 1. *Regarding Method, 57–89.* Cambridge: Cambridge University Press, 2002.

SMITH, ROBIN. "Aristotle's Logic." In *The Stanford Encyclopedia of Philosophy.* Summer 2019 Edition. Edited by Edward N. Zalta. https://plato.stanford.edu/archives/sum2019/entries/aristotle-logic.

SOUTH, JAMES B. 2002. "Scotus and the Knowledge of the Singular Revisited." *History of Philosophy Quarterly* 19, no. 2 (2002): 125–47.

SPRUNGER, K. L. "John Yates of Norfolk: The Radical Puritan Preacher as Ramist Philosopher." *Journal of the History of Ideas* 37, no. 4 (1976): 697–706.

STANGLIN, KEITH D., and Thomas H. McCall. *Jacobus Arminius: Theologian of Grace.* Oxford: Oxford University Press, 2012.

STEINMETZ, DAVID C. "The Scholastic Calvin." In *Protestant Scholasticism: Essays in Reassessment.* Edited by Carl R. Trueman and R. Scott Clark, 16–30. Studies in Christian History and Thought. Eugene, Or: Wipf and Stock, 2005.

STEVENSON, DAVID. *The Scottish Revolution 1637–1644: The Triumph of the Covenanters.* Edinburgh: John Donald Publishers, 2003.

STEWART, LAURA A. M. "The Political Repercussions of the Five Articles of Perth: A Reassessment of James VI and I's Religious Policies in Scotland." *The Sixteenth Century Journal* 38, no. 4 (2007): 1013–36.

————. *Rethinking the Scottish Revolution: Covenanted Scotland, 1637–1651.* Oxford: Oxford University Press, 2016.

STREVELER, PAUL A. "Ockham and His Critics on Intuitive Cognition." *Franciscan Studies* 35, no. 223–236 (1975): 223–36.

STRICKLAND, DAVID. "Union With Christ in The Theology of Samuel Rutherford." PhD diss., University of Edinburgh, 1972.

STUMP, ELEONORE. "Aquinas's Account of Freedom: Intellect and Will." *The Monist* 80, no. 4 (1997): 576–597.

TE VELDE, DOLF. *The Doctrine of God in Reformed Orthodoxy, Karl Barth, and the Utrecht School: A Study in Method and Content.* Studies in Reformed Theology 25. Leiden: Brill, 2013.

————. "Always Free, but Not Always Good: Girolamo Zanchi (1516–1590) on Free Will." In *Reformed Thought on Freedom: The Concept of Free Choice in Early Modern Reformed Theology*, edited by Willem J. van Asselt, J. Martin Bac, and Dolf T. te Velde, 51–94. Texts and Studies in Reformation and Post-Reformation Thought. Grand Rapids, MI: Baker Academic, 2010.

TE VELDE, R. A. "Intuïtieve Kennis En Contingentie Bij Duns Scotus." *Tijdschrift voor Filosofie* 47, no. 2 (1985): 276–96.

THOMSON, ANDREW. *Samuel Rutherford.* 4th ed. London: Hodder and Stoughton, 1889.

TORRANCE, J. B. "Covenant or Contract?: A Study of Theological Background of Worship in Seventeenth-Century Scotland." *Scottish Journal of Theology* 34, no. 3 (1981): 225–43.

TORRANCE, THOMAS F. "The Distinctive Character of the Reformed Tradition." *Reformed Review* 54, no. 1 (2000): 5–16.

_____. *Scottish Theology: From John Knox to John McLeod Campbell.* Edinburgh: T&T Clark, 1996.

TRENTMAN, J. A. "Scholasticism in the seventeenth century." In *Cambridge History of Later Medieval Philosophy*, edited by Norman Kretzmann, Anthony Kenny, and Jan Pinborg, 818–37. Cambridge: Cambridge University Press, 1992.

TREVOR-ROPER, HUGH. *Archbishop Laud 1573–1645.* 2nd ed. London: Macmillan and Co. Ltd., 1962.

_____. "The Scottish Enlightenment." In *Studies on Voltaire and the Eighteenth Century*, edited by Theodore Besterman, 1635–58. Geneva: Institut et Musee Voltaire, 1967.

TRUEMAN, CARL R. *John Owen: Reformed, Catholic, Renaissance Man.* Great Theologians. Burlington, VT: Ashgate, 2007.

_____. *The Claims of Truth: John Owen's Trinitarian Theology.* Carlisle: Paternoster Press, 1989.

TUTINO, STEFANIA. "Huguenots, Jesuits and Tyrants: Notes on the Vindiciae contra Tyrannous in Early Modern England." *Journal of Early Modern History* 11, no. 3 (2007): 175–196.

TYACKE, NICHOLAS. "Puritanism, Arminianism, and Counter-Revolution." In *Origins of the English Civil Wars*, edited by Russel, 119–43. London: MacMillan.

_____. *Aspects of English Protestantism c. 1530–1700.* Politics, Culture, and Society in Early Modern Britain. Manchester: Manchester University Press, 2001.

VALLANCE, EDWARD. *Revolutionary England and the National Covenant: State Oaths, Protestantism and the Political Nation, 1553–1682.* Woodbridge, NJ: The Boydell Press, 2005.

VAN ASSELT, WILLEM J., AND EEF DEKKER. "Introduction." In *Reformation and Scholasticism: An Ecumenical Enterprise*, edited by Willem J. van Asselt and Eef Dekker, 11–44. Text and Studies in Reformation and Post-Reformation Thought. Grand Rapids, MI: Baker Academic, 2001.

VAN ASSELT, WILLEM J., THEO J. PLEIZIER, PICTER L. ROUWENDAL, MAARTEEN WISSE. *Introduction to Reformed Scholasticism.* Translated by Albert Gootjes. Reformed Historical-Theological Studies. Grand Rapids, MI.: Reformation Heritage Books, 2011.

_____.van Asselt, William J. "Open Hand and Fist: Humanism and Scholasticism in the Reformation." In *Introduction to Reformed Scholasticism*, Translated by Albert Gootjes,

73–85. Reformed Historical-Theological Studies. Grand Rapids, MI: Reformation Heritage Books, 2011.

_____.van Asselt, Willem J., and Pieter L. Rouwendal. "Introduction: What Is Reformed Scholasticism?" In *Introduction to Reformed Scholasticism*, Translated by Albert Gootjes, 1–9. Reformed Historical-Theological Studies. Grand Rapids: Reformation Heritage Books. 2011.

_____. "The State of Scholarship: From Discontinuity to Continuity." In *Introduction to Reformed Scholasticism*, Translated by Albert Gootjes, 10–25. Reformed Historical-Theological Studies. Grand Rapids, MI: Reformation Heritage Books, 2011.

VAN ASSELT, WILLEM J., J. MARTIN BAC, and DOLF T. TE VELDE, eds. *Reformed Thought on Freedom: The Concept of Free Choice in Early Modern Reformed Theology.* Texts and Studies in Reformation and Post-Reformation Thought. Grand Rapids, MI: Baker, 2010.

VAN DIXHOORN, CHAD B. "Unity and Disunity at the Westminster Assembly (1643–1649): A Commemorative Essay." *The Journal of Presbyterian History* 79, no. 2 (2001): 103–17.

VAN RULER, J. A. "New Philosophy to Old Standards: Voetius' Vindication of Divine Concurrence and Secondary Causality." *Nederlands archief voor kerkgeschiedenis / Dutch Review of Church History* 71, no. 1 (1991): 58–91.

VAN VREESWIJK, B. J. D. "An Image of Its Maker: Theses on Freedom of Franciscus Junius (1545–1602)." In *Reformed Thought on Freedom*, edited by Willem J. van Asselt, J. Martin Bac and Dolf T. te Velde, 95–126. Texts and Studies in Reformation and Post-Reformation Thought. Grand Rapids, MI: Baker Academic, 2010.

VALVERDE, JOSÉ MANUEL GARCÍA. "Introduction." In *De Rebus Naturalibus, Vol. 1.* Edited by José Manuel García Valverde. 1–50. Brill Texts and Sources in Intellectual History 17/1–2. Leiden and Boston: Brill 2016.

VOS, ANTONIE., H. VELDHUIS, A. H. LOOMAN-GRASSKAMP, EEF. DEKKER, and NICO. W. DEN BOK. *John Duns Scotus: Contingency and Freedom.* The New Synthese Historical Library 42. Dordrecht: Kluwer Academic Publisher, 1994.

VOS, ANTONIE. "Ab uno disce omnes." *Bijdragen* 60, (1999): 173–204.

_____. "Knowledge, Certainty and Contingency." In *John Duns Scotus (1265/6–1308): Renewal of Philosophy*, edited by Egbert P. Boss, 75–88. Elementa 72. Amsterdam: Rodopi, 1998.

_____. "Reformed Orthodoxy in the Netherlands." In *A Companion to Reformed Orthodoxy*, edited by Herman Selderhuis, 121–76. Brill's Companions to the Christian Tradition 40. Leiden: Brill, 2013.

_____. "Scotus' Significance for Western Philosophy and Theology." In *Lo scotismo nel Mezzogiorno d'Italia: atti del Congresso Internazionale* (Bitonto 25–28, marzo 2008), *in occasione del VII Centenario della morte di Giovanni Duns Scoto*, edited by Francesco Fiorentino, 173–209. Textes et études du moyen âge 52. Porto: Brepols, 2010.

_____. *The Philosophy of John Duns Scotus.* Edinburgh: Edinburgh University Press, 2006.

WADDINGTON, A. "L'Auteur Des 'Vindiciae Contra Tyrannos." *Revue Historique* 51, no. 1 (1893): 65–69.

WAINWRIGHT, WILLIAM J. "Theological Determinism and the Problem of Evil: Are Arminians any Better Off?" In *Issues in Contemporary Philosophy of Religion*, edited by Eugene Thomas Long, 81–96. Studies in Philosophy and Religion 23. Dordrecht: Springer Science and Business Media, 2001.

WALKER, JAMES. *The Theology and Theologians of Scotland: Chiefly of the Seventeenth and Eighteenth Centuries.* Edinburgh: T&T Clark, 1888.

WEBB, O.K, JR. "The Political Thought of Samuel Rutherford." PhD diss., Duke University, 1964.

WEBSTER, B. "Anglo-Scottish Relations, 1296–1389: Some Recent Essays." *The Scottish Historical Review* 74, no. 197 (1995): 99–108.

WENGERT, R. G. "The Logic of Essentially Ordered Causes." *Notre Dame Journal of Formal Logic* 12, no. 4 (1971): 406–421.

WESLEY, JOHN. "Extracts from the Letters of Mr. Samuel Rutherford." In *Christian Library: Consisting of Extracts from and Abridgements of the Choicest Pieces of Practical Divinity Which Have Been Published in the English Tongue.* Bristol: Felix Farley, 1753.

WHYTE, ALEXANDER. *Samuel Rutherford and Some of His Correspondents. In Lectures Delivered in St. George's Free Church Edinburgh.* Edinburgh and London: Oliphant Anderson and Ferrier, 1894.

WHYTOCK, JACK C. "An Educated Clergy." In *Scottish Theological Education and Training in the Kirk and Secession, 1560–1850.* Studies in Christian History and Thought. Eugene, OR: Wipf and Stock, 2008.

WILLIAMSON, A. H. *Scottish National Consciousness in the Age of James VI: The Apocalypse, the Union and the Shaping of Scotland's Public Culture.* Edinburgh: John Donaldson, 1979.

WIPPEL, JOHN F. "The Reality of Nonexisting Possibilities According to Thomas Aquinas, Henry of Ghent, and Godfrey of Fontaines." *Review of Metaphysics* 33, no. 4 (1981): 729–58.

WOLTERSTORFF, NICHOLAS. "Divine Simplicity." *Philosophical Perspectives* 5, (1991): 531–52.

WOODROW, ROBERT. *Analecta: Or Materials for a History of Remarkable Providences; Mostly Relating to Scotch Ministers and Christians.* Edinburgh, 1842.

WOOLRYCH, AUSTIN. *Britain in Revolution 1625–1660.* Oxford: Oxford University Press, 2002.

Index of Names

Index of Subjects